D1234772

THE STORY OF
POETRY

By the same author

Criticism

Fifty Modern British Poets: an introduction
Fifty English Poets 1300–1900: an introduction
Reading Modern Poetry
Lives of the Poets
The Story of Poetry: Volume One

Anthologies

Eleven British Poets
New Poetries I, II, III
Poets on Poets (with Nick Rennison)
The Harvill Book of Twentieth-Century Poetry in English

Poetry

Choosing a Guest
The Love of Strangers
Selected Poems

Fiction

The Colonist
The Dresden Gate

Translations

Flower & Song: Aztec Poetry (with Edward Kissam)
On Poets & Others, Octavio Paz

THE STORY OF
POETRY

VOLUME TWO

*English Poets and Poetry
from Skelton to Dryden*

Michael Schmidt

Weidenfeld & Nicolson

LONDON

For Eavan Boland

First published in Great Britain in 2002
by Weidenfeld & Nicolson

© 2002 Michael Schmidt
The moral right of Michael Schmidt to be identified as the author
of this work has been asserted in accordance with the
Copyright Designs and Patents Act of 1988.

All rights reserved. No part of this publication may be reproduced,
stored in a retrieval system, or transmitted in any form or by any means,
electronic, mechanical, photocopying, recording, or by any means
without the prior permission of both the copyright owner
and the above publisher of this book.

A CIP catalogue record for this book
is available from the British Library.

ISBN 0 297 82938 6

Typeset by Selwood Systems, Midsomer Norton
Set in Minion

Printed in Great Britain by
Butler & Tanner Ltd, Frome and London

Weidenfeld & Nicolson

The Orion Publishing Group Ltd
Orion House
5 Upper St Martin's Lane
London WC2H 9EA

CONTENTS

An Informal History

Anthology

An Informal History

A MIRROR FOR MAGISTRATES

Who builds stronger than a mason, a shipwright, or a carpenter? ... And when you are asked this question next, say 'a gravemaker'. The houses he makes lasts till doomsday. Go, get thee in, and fetch me a stoup of liquor.

> In youth when I did love, did love
> Methought it was very sweet ...

Clown Gravedigger (Hamlet, V, i, 1600–1601)

In November 1558 Mary Tudor was dying. Calais and the infidelities of her Spanish husband were etched upon her miserable heart. One poet of her reign, the first woman poet in the English tradition, was at Hatfield House, seat of the Cecil family, quietly studying the classics in a seclusion shaded – we must imagine – by English oaks. Earlier in Mary's reign this poet, who was also the Queen's half-sister Elizabeth (**39–45**), daughter of Anne Boleyn, had been detained at Woodstock where, with a diamond, she had scratched a tiny verse into a window pane:

> Much suspected by me,
> Nothing proved can be;
>   Quoth Elizabeth prisoner.

She may have wanted for paper, because she also wrote a longer poem on a shutter:

> Oh, Fortune, thy wresting, wavering state
> Hath fraught with cares my troubled wit,
> Whose witness this present prison late
> Could bear, where once was joy's loan quit.
> Thou caused'st the guilty to be loosed
> From bands where innocents were enclosed,
> And caused the guiltless to be reserved,
> And freed these that death had well deserved.
> But all herein can be nothing wrought,
> So God send to my foes all they have taught.

Elizabeth's vengeful prayer was answered: Mary's life was an intense punishment, for herself and her country, and her death was sorrowful.

In his *History of England* Keith Feiling gathers the reigns of Edward VI and Mary Tudor into a single chapter entitled 'Anarchy', where he recounts how Edward, who was crowned as a boy, died just as he was coming into his own. During his seven-year reign the Reformation hurried forward, partly because Archbishop Thomas Cranmer was no longer braked by the conservative instincts of Henry VIII. When Edward died of consumption, the succession to the Roman Catholic Mary was briefly contested, but nevertheless she had five years on the throne.

In his play *Queen Mary* (1875), Alfred, Lord Tennyson drives the fictionalised queen to the brink of madness and, perhaps, comes close to the truth of her bizarre tragedy. In the text, after Mary discovers the treachery of her beloved young husband, Philip of Spain ('My star, my son!'), after all her supports are gone and she is dying, and Elizabeth is come triumphantly to see her, she says to a maid in waiting in a moment of lucidity, 'What is the strange thing happiness? Sit down here. / Tell me thine happiest hour.' Happiness was something Tennyson's Mary experienced only briefly, more as promise than on the pulse itself, at the beginning of her political marriage.

Set between Henry VIII's reign, during which English lyric poetry was re-born, and Elizabeth's, which saw the great flowering of English literature in all its kinds, Mary's five years are lean in verse. There is a Henrician period – Skelton, Wyatt, Surrey and others – and an Elizabethan age. But there is not a Marian interlude or, indeed, a single major poet who stands out in her reign. Later poets regard her, if they regard her at all, as a bigot, a dumpy, self-deluded caricature of a queen, and as a monster, the author of 300 *autos da fe* – the burnings of Protestants. Ted Hughes evokes her in an early poem, 'The Martyrdom of Bishop Farrar' as 'Bloody Mary'. He quotes Farrar's words: 'If I flinch from the pain of the burning, believe not the doctrine that I have preached.' The poem begins:

> Bloody Mary's venomous flames can curl:
> They can shrivel sinew and char bone
> Of foot, ankle, knee and thigh, and boil
> Bowels, and drop his heart a cinder down;
> And her soldiers can cry, as they hurl
> Logs in the red rush: 'This is her sermon.'

Whether Mary's flames were venomous or fearful, their consequences were the same. She came to the throne tentatively; there was time for a number of the leading Protestants and reformers to emigrate, but as fear and zeal overtook the Queen, those who stayed behind found retreat cut off. Cranmer, in Tennyson's play, reflects:

To Strasburg, Antwerp, Frankfurt, Zurich, Worms,
Geneva, Basle – our bishops from their sees
Or fled, they say, or flying – Poinet, Barlow,
Bale, Scory, Coverdale; besides the deans
Of Christchurch, Durham, Exeter and Wells –
Ailmer and Bullingham, and hundreds more;
So they report. I shall be left alone.
No; Hooper, Ridley, Latimer, will not fly.

Later, Tennyson's Cranmer foresees his death:

Last night I dreamed the faggots were alight,
And that myself was fasten'd to the stake
And found it all a visionary flame,
Cool as the light of old decaying wood;
And then King Harry look'd from out a cloud,
And bade me have good courage; and I heard
An angel cry, 'There is more joy in Heaven' –
And after that the trumpet of the dead.

Cranmer's difficulties were political *and* theological. He couldn't credit the doctrine of transubstantiation in the Mass. 'No man can make his Maker,' he said.

The great writing of Mary's reign was ecclesiastical and political. It consisted of mighty sermons, homilies, tracts and pamphlets from the Protestant and Catholic sides, as well as from the conflicting sides of protestantism, and of speeches either actually delivered at the stake or invented later as propaganda. The Word was a force in the land, censors were busy, and books, like men, women and children, were burned. In 1554 many Protestant ears were, in Feiling's phrase, literally 'nailed to the pillory'. In 1555, the burnings began in earnest. Thomas Cranmer, whose turn was to come, saw the flames that consumed Latimer and Ridley from the window of his cell at Oxford. At the stake, Latimer declared to Ridley that in the conflagration, Mary had lit a candle that would not be put out.

I begin this history with Mary not because her five years mark a distinct period in themselves, but because during them the energies of a new poetry were gathering and two key anthologies were assembled. The first of these, *Tottel's Miscellany*, brought together in summary form many of the great lyric poems from her father's fruitful reign and defined the Silver Age of English poetry. The other, *A Mirror for Magistrates*, was a long-term project begun by George Ferrers when he was Henry VIII's Master of Pastimes. The book was licensed in the first year of Mary's reign, partly printed by John Elder, and brought to fruition by William Baldwin of

Oxford in Mary's last year. It was first published in full in 1559, a few months after her death, not under the imprint of the Roman Catholic John Wayland, who had taken it on but was no longer in business, but of Thomas Marsh. Marsh later invited John Higgins and later still, Thomas Blenerhasset, to extend the book with their own and others' work, but although the publishing history of A Mirror in its various different extensions is complex, the work itself is of limited poetic interest today. It did, however, shape the reading tastes of three generations and fed strongly into the development of the drama, as well as into verse and prose narrative. Michael Drayton, Samuel Daniel, the Shakespeare of The Rape of Lucrece and many others either imitated or were inspired by it.

A Mirror grew and grew until it occupied 1,400 tightly-printed pages. The 1610 edition was left to Richard Niccols who, following a suggestion of Thomas Sackville, omitted the prose passages between the poems and handed the whole book over to a single Muse. Though in the first printing the stories begin with Richard II, in subsequent editions they have a much wider base; they constitute a world history in verse told through the sorrowful lives and in the sorrowful voices of great men. The anthology first led and then followed public taste, helping to redefine and popularise the genre of historical narrative. It renews the debt to Boccaccio (Bochas) whose Fall of Princes was cherished in Lydgate's version and with which, initially, the Mirror was to be bound up in a single volume. It also diluted some, at least, of the systematically allegorical features which had deadened the English fifteenth century. The title may allude respectfully to Gower's huge poems, the French Mirour de l'Homme (Speculum Meditantis). Baldwin's contributors, with differing degrees of competence, tell not only how princes fall, but how they respond to their fates. The rudimentary psychology of the better tales foreshadows the greater penetration of the dramatists of Elizabeth's reign. The handling of verse at its best shows, if not inspiration, at least a growing competence in extended forms. Like Tottel's Miscellany, A Mirror was reprinted and expanded time after time. One novel element is the way in which the tragic figures retell their tragedies in their 'own voices'. These narrators are monarchs and great men (and even women) whose fates are cautionary; this is an age when even rulers such as Mary and Philip require instruction: 'our queen because she is a woman, and our king because he is a stranger'. Those who read the entire Mirror in its various editions find not a single spark of deliberate humour in it: the tone is doggedly and often tritely moralistic. All the same, it affected and reflected its age and passed into bibliographical history.

The poets of Mary's reign were understandably much concerned with reversals of fortune, such as those displayed in A Mirror, as well as with death. They had lived through Henry's reign, and Mary herself had toppled some substantial personages. The most powerful poetic voice in her Court was that of Thomas, Lord Vaux, who died in the middle of her reign.[1] Notably, one of his poems – 'The Image of Death' (25) – is dramatically misremembered by the Clown digging Ophelia's grave in *Hamlet*, proof of how popular Tottel's book remained half a century after its first publication.

Lord Vaux may strum too insistently on a single note, but it was the note that everyone heard and harkened to, and his vivid emblematic images and clear expression are exemplary. They extend the lyric tradition that had come into focus under Henry VIII, a time in which wise men kept their counsel. 'Companion none is like unto the mind alone.' Contentment came not from secular preferment and success but from thought and reflection in solitude. Here is a stanza from another poem by Lord Vaux (26):

> Our wealth leaves us at death, our kinsmen at the grave;
> But virtues of the mind unto the heavens with us we have:
> Wherefore, for Virtue's sake, I can be well content
> The sweetest time of all my life, to deem in thinking spent.

'Our wealth leaves us at death, our kinsmen at the grave.' That and the lines 'And tract of time begins to weave / Grey hairs upon my head' and 'For age with stealing steps / Hath clawed me with his crutch' are a keynote to the elegiac mood of the time. Lord Vaux's poems are quiet, strong and complete.

Another contemporary was Nicholas Grimald, who survived, like Tottel, well into Elizabeth's reign. His inventive dialogue poem, often entitled 'A Description of Virtue', is 'true' in the way that Lord Vaux's poems are. If the language is conventional, the precisions are not.

> What one art thou, thus in torn weed yclad?
> Virtue, in price whom ancient sages had.
> Why, poorly 'rayd?° For fading goods past care.   *arrayed*
> Why double-faced? I mark each fortune's fare.
> This bridle, what? Mind's rages to restrain.
> Tools why bear you? I love to take great pain.
> Why, winges? I teach above the stars to fly.
> Why tread you death? I only cannot die.

Grimald wasn't always lugubrious. He wrote of his garden (37) in ways Andrew Marvell might relish, evoking 'Bees, humming with soft sound

---

[1] There is disagreement on the date of his death: 1556 or 1562?

(the murmur is so small)'. And he says, 'The garden, it allures, it feeds, it glads the sprite; / From heavy hearts all doleful dumps the garden chaseth quite.' He concludes, 'O, what delights to us the garden ground doth bring; / Seed, leaf, flower, fruit, herb, bee, and tree, and more than I may sing.' The abundance breaks the bounds of metre and can't be contained. Some sense in Grimald's verse the first tremor of metaphysical wit, but if this is the case, it is very faint.

Less exuberant, more dogged and thorough in detail, is Thomas Tusser. Kipling loved his long aphoristic poem, *Five Hundred Points of Good Husbandry* (38), which was written largely during Mary's reign. It is a kind of almanac, describing, at a time of tribulation, the arts of peace, and Tusser's advice is very English and sound. C.H. Sisson quotes some charming passages:

> Where stones be too many, annoying the land,
>   Make servant come home with a stone in his hand.
> By daily so doing, have plenty ye shall,
>   Both handsome for paving and good for a wall.

It is not exactly good verse, but it is sufficient for what it sets out to do. Don't overwater new plants, he says:

> Now sets do ask watering, with pot or with dish,
>   New sown do not so, if ye do as I wish:
> Through cunning with dibble, rake, mattock, and spade,
>   By line, and by level, trim garden is made.
>
> Who soweth too lateward, hath seldom good seed,
>   Who soweth too soon, little better shall speed...

The most famous poet to write would-be major work under Mary and to collaborate with Thomas Norton on the tragedy *Gorboduc* under Elizabeth was Thomas Sackville, Earl of Dorset, who survived Mary and Elizabeth and died under King James. A man of law, he wrote the 'Induction' (46) to *A Mirror for Magistrates.* He also contributed, later on, the melancholy voice of Buckingham, though the tradition that he actually assembled the book no longer holds. Sackville is verbose. The sound of his language and its flow blur and dissipate sense. Alexander Pope praised him for 'a propriety in sentiments, a dignity in the sentences, an unaffected perspicuity of style, and an easy flow of numbers'. He was certainly fluent, and there are moments of beautiful writing in the Induction, for instance, where nature is evoked and comes alive in a way that takes us beyond allegory.

The soil, that erst so seemly was to seen,
 Was all despoilèd of her beauty's hue;
And soot° fresh flowers (wherewith the summer's queen   *sweet*
 Had clad the earth) now Boreas' blasts down blew.
  And small fowls flocking in their song did rue
   The winter's wrath, wherewith each thing defaced
   In woeful wise bewailed the summer past.

There is more of the alliterative tradition alive and well – or at least alive – in Sackville than one might expect after the Petrarchan broom had swept out the cobwebs in English poetry during Henry's reign. His work is further evidence of the atavism that led to the reprinting of *Piers Plowman.*

Thus musing on this worldly wealth in thought,
 Which comes and goes more faster than we see
The flickering flame that with the fire is wrought,
 My busy mind presented unto me
 Such fall of peers as in this realm had be:
  That oft I wished some would their woes descrive,
  To warn the rest whom fortune left alive.

In Sackville, a wonderful lyric poet may have been struggling to escape from the treacle of conventionalised poetic language. But when Edmund Spenser invokes him for protection and approval, and Pope summarises his qualities as 'chaste', we sense how far our age is from his, and indeed from Pope's. My favourite stanza of Sackville's Induction is excessive, even silly, but also moving in unexpected ways:

Not worthy Hector, worthiest of them all,
 Her hope, her joy; his force is now for nought.
O Troy, Troy, Troy, there is no boot but bale;
 The hugy horse within thy walls is brought;
 Thy turrets fall, thy knights, that whilom fought
  In arms amid the field, are slain in bed,
  Thy gods defiled, and all thy honour dead.

That is as good as Sackville gets. He is verbose, mechanical in unpacking the nuances of conventional metaphor: what's Hecuba to him? Yet the closing couplet is not remote in cadence or impact from Alexander Pope's 'Eloise and Abelard'. It is a moment of prosodic definition, drawn from a rather rumbustious mess of language.

Mary presided over a dark kingdom: even the weather during her reign was unusually English. Spiritually and politically, she stopped the clocks but could not turn them back. The Roman Catholic faith she tried to restore was too unpopular, the lands that had been confiscated too valuable to return. The intelligentsia – apart from the great Catholic musicians who returned under her promising protection – was dead or exiled. Her death was lamented mainly by Catholic factions. There is a telling elegy by George Cavendish, the apologist-biographer of Cardinal Wolsey, written in a broken form where the caesura is expressed by a gap, as it was in Old English. It is sympathetic and genuinely grieves: it seems Mary could inspire such emotions. Indeed, Cavendish risks conflating the unhappy monarch with the Holy Virgin. In part, the poet says:

> Descend from heaven   O muse Melpomene,
>> Thou mournful goddess   with thy sisters all.
>> Pass in your plaints   the woeful Niobe;
>> Turn music to moan   with tears eternal.
>> Black be your habits,   dim and funeral,
>> For death hath bereft,   to our great dolour,
>> Mary our mistress,   our queen of honour.
>
> Our Queen of honour,   compared aptly
>> To *veritas victrix*,   daughter of time,
> By God assisted,   amassed an army,
>> When she a virgin clear,   without crime,
>> By right, without might,   did happily climb
>> To the stage royal,   just inheritor,
>> Proclaimed Mary   our queen of honour …
>
> And as a *victrix*   valorous endued
>> With justice, prudence,   high mercy and force,
> Dreadless of danger   with sword subdued
>> Her vassals rebellious,   yet having remorse
>> With loss of few   she saved the corse:°   *body politic*
>> Such was thy mercy   surmounting rigour,
>> O Mary mistress,   O queen of honour!
>
> To a virgin's life   which liked thee best
>> Professed was thine heart,   when moved with zeal
> And tears of subjects   expressing request,
>> For no lust but love   for the common weal,
>> Virginity's vow   thou diddest repeal,
>> Knit with a king   co-equal in valour,
>> Thine estate to conserve   as queen of honour.

The Rose and Pomegranate   joined in one,
   England and Spain   by spousal allied.
Yet of these branches   blossoms came none
   Whereby their kingdoms might be supplied;
   For this conjunction   a comet envied,
   Influence casting   of mortal vapour
   On Mary the Rose,   our queen of honour.

Then faded the flower   that whilom was fresh …

… High Priest of Rome,   O Paul Apostolic,
   And College Conscript of Cardinals all,
And ye that confess   the faith Catholic
   Of Christ's Church   in earth universal,
   O clerks religious,   to you I call:
   Pray for your patron,   your friend and founder,
   Mary our mistress,   our queen of honour.

Which late restored   the right religion
   And faith of our fathers observed of old,
Subdued sects   and all division,
   Reducing the flock   to the former fold;
   A pillar most firm   the Church to uphold …

When sacred altars   were all defaced,
   Images of saints   with outrage burned;
Instead of priests   apostates placed;
   Holy sacraments   with spite down spurned;
   When spoil and ravin   had all overturned,
   This chaos confuse,   this heap of horror
   Dissolveth Mary,   as queen of honour …

Elizabeth excellent   of God elect,
   With sceptre to sit   in seat imperial,
In throne triumphant   where thou art erect,
   Have death alway   in thy memorial.
   Death is th'end   of flesh universal.
   The world is but vain: make for your mirror
   Mary thy sister,   late queen of honour …

Mary will be a mirror for Elizabeth: Cavendish alludes to that most popular book of the day and obliquely contributes to it. Elizabeth certainly read *A Mirror* and took it to heart, but no doubt she also took to heart the experience of her half-sister; the religious choice she made, and the dreadful political marriage that resulted from it.

TOTTEL'S *MISCELLANY*

I had rather than forty shillings I had my Book of Songs and Sonnets here.
How now, Simple! Where have you been? I must wait on myself, must I?
You have not the Book of Riddles about you, have you?

Slender (Merry Wives of Windsor, *I, i, 1597–1601*)

In 1555, two years into Queen Mary's reign, Richard Tottel, who hitherto
had printed mainly law books, brought out Stephen Hawes's *History of
Graunde Amoure and la Bel Pucell.* It was already an old poem, written
probably in 1505 or 1506. In bringing it back into circulation Tottel sig-
nalled his own commercial interest in publishing poetry – albeit by a
writer safely dead and, in that violent time, uncontroversial. He also put
down a marker for Edmund Spenser, because Hawes's *History* is a poor
great-uncle, although not a grandparent, of *The Faerie Queen* (**67**). There
are numerous parallels between the two poems, some of which may reflect
direct debts. But there are two crucial differences: the English language
has settled down by the time Spenser is writing; and he is a far greater poet
than Hawes. Spenser's poem lives because for him there was a literal,
living point of focus for allegory. His *Bel Pucell* is not a flimsy idealisation,
but it finds a body in Elizabeth I, Queen of England, which means that
everything acquires a specific political as well as a chivalric-poetical
meaning. Spenser wrote with an *actual* occasion, even when his allegory
seems to build away from it. Cavendish aside, no poet thought to set the
pathetic, ill-starred Queen Mary on such a pedestal; and though Hawes
was patronised by Henry VII, he did not think to praise and flatter him in
quite the systematic manner of Spenser's poem.

The poetry Tottel published is out of key with the age in which he lived.
In February 1555 John Rogers, Queen Mary's first Protestant martyr, was
burned at Smithfield, not far from 'flete strete, within Temple barre, at the
sygne of the hand and starre', where Tottel conducted his business. In
October, Bishops Latimer and Ridley were burned in Oxford. It cannot
have been an easy time for a printer. Words were carefully scrutinised in
the light of the Word – and the Word in the ascendant, after all Henry
VIII's efforts, was once again Roman Catholic. At Winchester the year
before, the Queen had married Philip of Spain; and at Dover Cardinal

Pole, the Pope's legate and exiled great-nephew of Edward IV, arrived, signalling formally the reconciliation between England and the papacy. Parliament obligingly revived the laws for punishing heresy. Meanwhile, inflation ran out of control and the price of basic commodities doubled in twelve months.

Stephen Hawes (1475?–1523/1530?) was temperamentally an elegist, thinking the great tradition of 'true poetry' which began with Chaucer and reached (he believed) a mighty climax in the longueurs, deserts and steppes, of the interminable poetry of Lydgate, was destined to die with him, the last 'faithful votary' of the sacred art. His work is more amply considered in *The Story of Poetry I: from Caedmon to Caxton,* the first volume in this series. He stands at the start of something new even as he ruefully shuts down the bleak English fifteenth century. Here is how he commends his great predecessors, 1,310 lines into the enormous poem:

> O pensive hartè in the stormy pery°   *sphere*
> Mercury northwest thou mayest see appear
> After tempest to glad thine hemispery°   *hemisphere*
> Hoist up thy sail for thou must drawè near
> Toward the end of thy purpose so clear
> Rememberè thee of the trace° and dance   *paths*
> Of poets old with all thy purveyance

> As moral Gower whose sententious° dew   *morally uplifting*
> Adown reflaireth with fair golden beams
> And after Chaucer's all abroad doth show
> Our vices to cleanse his deparèd streams
> Kindling our hartès with the fiery leams°   *rays of light*
> Of moral virtue as is probable
> In all his books so sweet and profitable ...

> ... And after him my master Lydgate
> The Monk of Bury did him well apply
> Both to contrive and eke to translate
> And of virtue ever in especially
> For he did compile than full nially
> Of our Blessed Lady the conversation°   *dealings of*
> Saint Edmundès lifè martyrèd with treason

> Of the Fall of Princes so right woefully
> He did endite in all piteous wyse°   *ways*
> Following his author Bocas ruefully
> A right great book he did truely comprise

A good ensample° for us to despise   *model*
This world so full of mutability
In which no man can have a certainty...

... O Master Lydgate the most dulcet° springè   *sweetest*
Of famous rhetoric with ballad ryall
The chief original of my learningè
What vaileth° it on you for to call   *avails*
Me for to aidè now in especial
Sythen° your body is now wrapt in chest*   *Since; coffin*
I prayè God to give your soul good rest

In his brittle allegorical mode, the social and literary world that Hawes laments is, of course, idealised. It is rendered with a finish it never possessed, acquiring a clarity of purpose and fulfilment that belong to the completions of literature rather than the rough ends of life.

This idealisation itself appealed to Tottel's customers. It appealed to Sir Philip Sidney when he composed *Arcadia,* and to Spenser in all his writing. In Chaucer – especially the *Canterbury Tales* – a recognisable England lived, breathed and *spoke*, but it was then almost silent until the Elizabethan drama came of age. Poetry was a place for sugared instruction; the order, the colour, voices and movements of verse were themselves idealised. It was a kind of escapism: not *from* moral and theological seriousness, but rather *into* it, leaving behind the world's harsh contingencies. Good was good and bad was clearly bad; the moral and perceptual shading of Chaucer, the Gawain poet, even upright John Gower, and notably the great Scottish poets of the fifteenth century, has no place in Hawes.

The year after his edition of Hawes, Tottel published another book which, although not in verse, characterises what were to be key themes for poets and gentlemen as Queen Elizabeth I succeeded to the throne in 1559 and verse began to find new energies on paper and on the stage. This was *De Officiis,* the sombre final work of the Roman orator and statesman Cicero, a treatise concerning *Duties.* It was translated by Tottel's close collaborator (one might even regard him as Tottel's commissioning editor) Nicholas Grimald, an early and complex manifestation of a new type of writer, the man of letters. *De Officiis* was a favourite book of Petrarch, himself a recent presence in English verse, and of Erasmus, purveyor of the humanism in which John Skelton first excelled and against which he eloquently rebelled.

De Officiis is in the form of a three-part epistle to Cicero's son. In the first part he sets out the key civic virtues: wisdom, justice, fortitude and temperance; and then, with abundant examples from history, he illustrates their application and demonstrates that what is virtuous and what is expedient coincide when looked at dispassionately. It is the examples from history as much as the moral order he proposes for the making of gentlemen, that recommended the book to poets, for here was another template for the long, instructive wheel of fortune sequence, *A Mirror for Magistrates*.

Tottel got the 'privilege' to print law books in 1553, lived a very long commercial life – until 1595 – and obtained a law book monopoly for a time under Elizabeth. In 1585 he unsuccessfully petitioned for a further monopoly to produce paper. He was a shrewd and vigorous entrepreneur. His name survives in English poetry thanks to one original book. That book, which Shakespeare's Slender calls out for almost half a century later in *The Merry Wives of Windsor*, is *Songes and Sonnettes*, better known as *Tottel's Miscellany*.

It was published on 5 June 1557, at the time when England, allied to Spain, declared war on France in the campaign which led to English defeat two years later. Only one copy of the first edition survives; it is currently in the Bodleian Library, Oxford. The *Miscellany* was one of those books so popular that it was thumbed to bits, and on 31 July Tottel published an enlarged edition. It was a labour-intensive job which took fifty-seven days, including Sundays, to complete. He was busy with poetry that year, also publishing Henry Howard, Earl of Surrey's translation of Virgil's *Aeneid* Books II (27) and IV. The *Miscellany* kept selling and further editions were published in 1559, 1565, 1567, 1574, 1585 and 1587. Thereafter the book fell from fashion and it was 130 years before another edition appeared.

The book is so important because it was the first real English anthology. True, the huge edition of Chaucer's *Works* which Thomas Godfray printed in 1532 packed in, alongside Chaucer, poetry by Lydgate, Hoccleve, Scoggin, Gower and others, but all of it was under Chaucer's name. Tottel had his star, the Earl of Surrey, but he did not pretend that the work in his anthology was *all* by Surrey. Nevertheless, the book's title pages did reflect the fact that most poets of any social standing did not wish to be identified *as* poets. What happened after their deaths was another matter, but for the living the fact of writing poetry was shared only with close friends and perhaps lovers. The desire to remain anonymous led to false attributions; it meant, for example, that Thomas Nashe's prose work (some call it the first English novel) *The Unfortunate Traveller*, was attributed to Michael Drayton; a canny writer could pretend that a work by some self-effacing aristocrat was his, and receive credit where it wasn't due.

The arrival of printing was principally to blame for the shyness of the Court poets. If you were a courtier and penned a compelling poem about the King's mistress, the last thing you wanted was for the King to trace you through the voice-print of your words. 'They flee from me, that sometime did me seek,' said Sir Thomas Wyatt in one of the most beautiful and corrupt (thanks to Tottel) of English lyric poems. Though a Court poet wished to excel in composition and be recognised among his friends, he recoiled from the idea of his ditties spilling out into the streets, or even into the homes of merchants and professionals. It was less a matter of class nicety than of privacy and propriety; a courtly lady who played an instrument with accomplishment would, similarly, not wish to appear at the Wigmore Hall of the day. To circulate poems in manuscript was one thing; in printed form it was quite another. The published poet was, therefore, one of three things: anonymous, dead, or a moralist imparting precept in verse. Some of the precept poets were noble like Thomas Sackville, but they only released precept poetry – work for a book like *A Mirror for Magistrates* – and it was this type of poetry that the emerging class of professional men of letters detached from the Court, writers like Grimald, released into print. The moral muse belonged principally to the middling classes, while the lyric muse detained nobler folk, for the most part men, of course, until the Elizabethan age was under way.

Sir Thomas Wyatt had been dead fourteen years when *Tottel's Miscellany* was published, and the potential wrath of Henry VIII at the idea that one of his chief courtiers was tampering with one of his eventual wives had died along with the Queen. Henry Howard, Earl of Surrey, had been dead a full decade when the *Miscellany* appeared. Sir Francis Bryan, perhaps one of the authors of the verses of uncertain origin, had been dead eight; and if the 'uncertains' include George Bullen, Earl of Rochford, he had been executed on Tower Hill twenty-one years before. Among the living authors was the forty-six year old Lord Vaux; the not aristocratic but nonetheless accomplished Grimald, who was thirty-nine; Heywood who was fifty; and Churchyard who was thirty-seven. Apart from his lordship, the other living poets in the book were closer to the Church and the bourgeoisie than to the Court.

At this time Grimald's patron was the benign Roman Catholic Bishop of Ely, Thomas Thirleby, who may also have been a patron of the *Miscellany*, supporting it even as Mary cooked Protestant bishops on bonfires around the country. Grimald is named in the first printing, but his poems vanish from the second, where his name is replaced with the initials N.G. Was this simply a further move towards anonymity? Or did Tottel decide that Grimald's acknowledged presence in the book worked against it? For Grimald is reputed to have been a chaplain to Bishop Ridley; he had gone to prison and recanted his Protestantism, and was suspected by some to be a Marian spy amongst his erstwhile friends. Politics were never far away, and Tottel had a publishing business to run.

All the poems in *Tottel's Miscellany* were written between 1527 and 1557.

George[2] Puttenham in his *Arte of English Poesie* (1589) draws many examples from Tottel. It was, one might say, the *Palgrave's Golden Treasury* of its day. It was here that the reticence of the noble English poets began to be eroded, and here too that a wider public first developed an appetite for lyric poems in a new manner.

To satisfy that appetite, more anthologies appeared, first *The Paradyse of Daynty Devises*, which was printed in 1576 but compiled and circulated much earlier, and which contained the powerful bulk of Lord Vaux's surviving verse. It is more instructive in purpose than Tottel. There was the dreadful *A Gorgious Gallery of Gallant Inventions* (1578), gargling with alliterations, perhaps in an atavistic response to the recent re-publication of that 'native' poem *Piers Plowman*. The book, the editor declares, was 'joyned together and builded up' but certainly shows no signs of having been edited. Only two copies survive and only one edition seems to have been printed. Then came *A Handefull of Pleasant Delites* (1584), published by a printer better known for ballad work and carrying indications of tunes for each poem's accompaniment. There was *The Phoenix Nest* (1593) and, at the very end of the century, the magnificent *England's Helicon* (1600). The anthology had come of age. As early as 1586 William Webbe, in *A Discourse of English Poetrie*, had declared: 'Among the innumerable sorts of English Books, and infinite fardles of printed pamphlets, wherewith this Country is pestered, all shops stuffed, and every study furnished: the greatest part I think in any one kind, are such as are either mere Poetical, or which tend in some respect (as either in matter or form) to Poetry.' Already the commodity existed in excess. *Plus ça change.*

[2] Sometimes called Richard

CAXTON'S CLOWN

...the Price of Writing of Manuscripts, before the use of Printing, was xxx shillings per quire.

John Aubrey, Brief Lives, *p. c*

Behind the Tottels and Waylands and Marshes, men involved as stationers and in the manufacture of books for profit, stands William Caxton, the father of English printing. It was he who introduced the sea change in our culture, revolutionising the dissemination of literature and literacy, but unlike his successors, printing mainly what he wanted people to read rather than responding to perceived demand. He contributed no theories to the intellectual world; his writings are largely forgotten, and he invented nothing, but his legacy has proved more radical than that of Wycliffe, Latimer, Cromwell, or any other Englishman. He was not a democrat, and yet what he started in England made its democracy possible. His taste was medieval and reactionary, yet he built a turnpike for the new.

Caxton, whose ambivalent attitude towards the new classical humanism of the Continent is discussed in *The Story of Poetry I*, is a great and serious figure, gothic-featured, monumental. Beside him stands his brilliant sometime editor-collaborator or – some declare – his clown, the renegade humanist, the butt of Gavin Douglas's scholarly scorn, and the first major poet of the sixteenth century, John Skelton. Skelton was the natural radical, the inventor of a new poetic language. In his outspoken impatience with authority and his love for the common folk (especially women, it would seem), he is if not a proto-democrat at least an early anarchist. After sombre Hawes, his laughter, now Rabelaisian and hysterical, now playful, now learned, now charged with eroticism, is a welcome sound in what had become the sombre halls of English poetry (only the occasional Scottish irruption reminded readers that Chaucer, the greatest of jesters and tragedians, headed the still relatively new literature).

Skelton looks forward, at and then through Humanism, while the Scottish poet William Dunbar remains decidedly medieval, despite their similarity of temperament, vocation and their range of angers and loves. Dunbar wrote on into the sixteenth century but, like Hawes, something ends with him. He is rooted in a Scotland whose defeat he witnesses; he laments the death of poetry. He too seems to draw a line under the fifteenth century. The centre of gravity, after the decisive Scottish poetic flowering and subsequent military defeat, shifts back to the South. Ford Madox Ford calls the Tudor and Stuart years the Spacious Age. How much our writers owe to the Mediterranean, especially to Boccaccio and Petrarch! He adds: 'With the sixteenth century the art of letters had become essentially a matter of movements rather than one of solitary literary figures.' English begins to acquire a coherent *literature.* Classical humanism was in part responsible; so was the development of the popular theatre, and also the growth of printing. With printing the author has an editor, the text is subjected to various forms of scrutiny, some technical, some creative and critical, some commercial. The act of writing for publication becomes collaborative. Dunbar had little truck with the new; Skelton did, but as he grew older became necessarily a 'solitary literary figure' in an exemplary way.

At the beginning of the sixteenth century, the constant in English poetry was rhyme, metre being uncertain and irregular because the language had not stabilised. (The status of the final '-e' remained unresolved right through the reign of Henry VIII.) John Skelton depends on rhyme to an unusual extent: his 'Skeltonics' are based on little else. It was not just because of his apparent formal crudeness that Alexander Barclay, the monkish Scot, calls him a 'rascolde poet': he was indeed something of a rascal. But he was an unusual one: classically educated, Skelton could – Robert Graves reminds us in the first of his *Oxford Addresses on Poetry* (1961) – 'forget his Classics when looking at the countryside and not see Margery Milke-Ducke as Phyllis and Jolly Jacke as Corydon, or find "behind every bush a thrumming Apollo" (John Clare's criticism of Keats)'. He stands like Janus at the threshold of the English Renaissance, facing both ways. He teases the tired old courtly traditions and discharges satire without mercy. He writes astonishing religious poetry, but his poems of celebration, social comment, parody and praise, and those headlong 'Skeltonics', are what make him alive. His is the first modern English: we read him without constant recourse to a glossary.

No Englishman more relished the Scottish defeat at Flodden than Skelton. He gloated in his indecently chauvinistic poem 'Against the Scots'. He played for a time in the Tudor Court a role comparable to Dunbar's in the Court of James IV. Like Dunbar he was a man of the cloth and a courtier with royal duties. He tutored the Duke of York, later Henry VIII. He commented wryly on the pleasures and vices of the royal milieu. With Dunbar he shared a certain public heartlessness; but he was never a convincing courtier, and kept getting into trouble. He wasn't convincing as a priest, either, though he was rector of Diss, Norfolk, a thriving living at that time of wool and trade, where his diocesan Bishop punished him for 'having been guilty of *certain crimes* AS MOST POETS ARE'.

Milton agreed with the Bishop: 'I name him not for posterity sake, whom Henry the 8th named in merriment his vicar of hell.' Milton declines to understand the King's jest: the rector of Diss, the rector of *Dis* (Latin for Hell). Milton calls him: 'One of the worst of men, who are both most able and most diligent to instil the poison they suck into the courts of princes, acquainting them with the choicest delights and criticisms of sin.' The poet of *Paradise Lost* and the author of the classic tract against censorship, *Areopagitica*, would gladly have censored the anarchic, joyous laureate, as though he single-handedly had derailed the future king. Alexander Pope dismissed him as 'beastly Skelton'. This had nothing to do with the fact that Skelton was a kind of editor, assisting Caxton with his Virgil; had Pope known this, he might have disparaged him – as Gavin Douglas did – even more vehemently.

Skelton isn't formally competent in the way Dunbar is. Instead of a diverse skill he possesses a distinctive style, with certain affectations such as those insistent and surprising rhymes, and a refusal to stay still before his subject. His poetry is in touch with the spoken language of the day. He is not, of course, a reporter of Court or gutter speech, but his language includes what he heard from highly-placed and humble people alike. His pastoral work took him among wool-merchants, farmers and clerics, all with different accents and ways of talking; and new religious notions flowed in at the port.

He is capable like Dunbar of savage flytings; he spares no foe. But his best work is compassionate and moral – despite what Milton says – in a new manner. In his time allegory was no longer an entirely viable mode. The new humanism found it crudely scholastic. Skelton drew upon it to exaggerate and satirise, driving it to the extreme by individual idiosyncrasy.

Born probably in 1460, possibly in Cumberland, he was first known to the world as a classical humanist. He studied at Cambridge, went to 'Oxforth' where he was made Poet Laureate and took a further degree in 1488, a degree which 'implied a diligent study of medieval grammar and rhetoric', Graves tells us, 'though the *Poeta Laureatus* need not have written any poems – except perhaps a hundred Virgilian hexameters, and a Latin comedy, both eulogising Oxford, to prove that he had mastered Latin prosody and the Aristotelian unities'. He translated Diodorus Siculus's *History of the World* (*c.* 1485) and the *Epistles* of Tully (Marcus Tullius Ciceronis, a.k.a. Cicero). In 1489 he was laureate of Oxford and Louvain, a scholar of international repute. Erasmus called him *Britannicarum literarum decus et lumen.*[3] He compiled *A New English Grammar*, now lost with much of his other work. In 1489 he was also

---

[3] *Of British writers the finest and brightest*

admitted laureate of Cambridge. In 1498 he took religious orders and wrote a bitter satire, *The Bowge of Court*. The next year he was tutoring the future King: 'I gave him drink of the sugared well / Of Helicon's waters crystaline.'

His Latin verses were praised even by Thomas Warton, who finds little to admire in the rest of his work. The verses on refusing to return a borrowed palfrey are in character; other verses express his doubt about the real presence in the sacrament. There is a frailty in his theological poems which contrasts with the imaginative force of his devotional writing ('Woefully arrayed', for example). It makes sense to distinguish between theological poems, which examine tenets of faith, and devotional poems which respond to Christian verities, especially the Crucifixion.

Skelton was first rewarded for his labours as tutor to Prince Henry by the future king's mother: she gave him a curacy 'to reward his conscientious tutorship and good influence on the unruly boy'. *Good* influence: Milton take note. His praise for her father, Edward, is undoubtedly sincere. It was 1504 when he removed to Diss, where his vernacular poetry came into its own. No record survives of the shock his fresh and extremely 'low' verses provoked in humanist erstwhile colleagues. *Philip Sparrow* (7), which includes the first mention in English poetry of some seventy species of bird, *The Tunning of Elinour Rumming*, celebrating a seriously unlicensed publican, and other pieces did his reputation as a serious scholar no good. His conduct as rector did him no credit either. He was said to keep 'a fair wench in his house'. When the Bishop instructed him to expel her through the door, Skelton obeyed, only to receive her back again – legend has it – through the window. But his faith was almost orthodox, however unorthodox his character as rector.

By 1509 he was back at Court. The King pardoned him for an unrecorded offence. Advanced in years in 1512, after being created *Orator Regius*, a sort of Latin Secretary, by his former pupil, he made, says Graves, 'a startling public avowal of devotion to the Muse-goddess, when he appeared wearing a white and green Court dress embroidered with the golden name CALLIOPE. He chose Calliope ("lovely face") rather than any of the Goddess's eight other names because, as he writes in an *amplificatio* of Diodorus Siculus's *History*, Calliope combines "incomparable riches of eloquence with profound sadness".' In 1516 he wrote *Magnificence*, his one surviving interlude and a not negligible contribution to the development of secular drama. Some of the passages call Blake to mind: 'To live under law it is captivity: / Where dread leadeth the dance there is no joy nor pride.'

By 1519, living in a house within the sanctuary of Westminster, Skelton expressed his freedom by launching a campaign, with bleak and comic consequences, against Cardinal Wolsey as traitor to King, Church and people in *Colin Clout* and other work. He was a 'cur and butcher's dog'. The next year, *Why Come Ye Not to Court* brought the conflict to a head. The King could no longer protect his Orator. Skelton was abandoned to the Cardinal, who sent him to prison. He earned his liberty by a penance and a jest. Kneeling before Wolsey, he suffered a long lecture, and at last said, 'I pray your grace to let me lye doune and wallow, for I can kneele no longer.'

Speak Parrot (2) was composed in 1521. He enjoyed the patronage of the Howards in Yorkshire, wrote his self-staged apotheosis in *The Garland of Laurel*, and returned to London, where he now flattered Wolsey in the hope of receiving a prebend. It was not granted. In old age he called himself the 'British Catullus'. He died in 1529, the year before Wolsey fell, leaving several children by a marriage he confessed to upon his deathbed. He was buried at St Margaret's, Westminster, and his stone reads *Joannes Skelton, vates Pierius, hic situs est.*[4]

There is a strong case against Skelton. In *The Arte of English Poesie* George Puttenham called him 'but a rude railing rhymer, and all his doings ridiculous; he used both short distances and short measures, pleasing only the popular care'. Francis Meres in his invaluable *Palladis Tamia, Wit's Treasury* (1598) branded him 'buffoon'. Warton states the case most fully: 'Skelton would have been a writer without decorum at any period', his humour 'capricious and grotesque'. Not only his subjects but his manner Warton finds objectionable: 'He sometimes debases his matter by his versification.' But Caxton claimed that Skelton improved the language. How could this be so, asks Warton (forgetting that Caxton died in 1491, before Skelton had begun to give offence), for Skelton 'sometimes adopts the most familiar phraseology of the common people'. About the style he is emphatic. It is an 'anomalous and motley form of versification'. 'Motley': Skelton as jester once again.

Warton describes fairly, but we reach a different verdict. Our prejudice, the flip-side of his, favours 'the most familiar phraseology of the common people', the spoken language. Not that anyone ever *spoke* Skeltonics, but his diction draws on the demotic of various classes. Warton does not mention the large number of invented and obscure words that are also found in the poems, a literariness which derives from his master Lydgate and from Chaucer. Sufficient evidence of artistry exists to make us trust even his most apparently off-the-cuff verses. Graves and W.H. Auden find in him the crucial English poet of the transition between the Middle Ages and the Renaissance. Graves insists that 'a study of the *Oxford English Dictionary* will show that Skelton enriched our vocabulary more than any other poet before or since, even Chaucer'.

---

[4] *John Skelton, priest of the Muses, is placed here*

The taproots of his English work go deep into the fourteenth century and beyond. The rhyming Goliardic tradition of medieval Latin verse attracted him. He called his poems 'trifles of honest mirth', which aligns him with the Goliardic, though he preferred accentual to syllabic prosody. If his Latin elegiacs were free of monastic phraseology, as Warton says, his English verses sometimes incorporate monastic Latin tags, developing a macaronic style of mixing English and Latin and sometimes French, which had been practised in English for centuries, although more often in carols, hymns and religious compositions, than in so light-hearted and witty a fashion. Skelton is a renegade humanist who recognised – having contributed to the movement – the spiritual and linguistic impoverishment that doctrinaire humanism entailed. He came to relish elements in language that humanism tried to extirpate in its frenzy to purify Latin and, in a different sense, English.

His first English poem is an elegy on Edward IV. It is less elegy than meditative monologue, spoken by the King reflecting on ephemerality, fortune (with 'sugared lips'), and 'mutability'. The complex verse form includes Latin refrains and an effective use of the *ubi sunt* ('where have they gone') motif, celebrating deeds even as it acknowledges their passing. The poem is not all wooden; it suggests what is to come. The accentual verse, with a marked caesura, falls into two short, phrased lines, with a truncated Anglo-Saxon feel. Though not systematically alliterative, it has the pondered emphases of alliterative verse, with short syntactic phrases.

In his next poem, also an elegy, he asks Clio to help him 'expel' his 'homely rudeness and dryness'. 'My words unpolished be, naked and plain, / Of aureat poems they want illumining.' But nakedness and an individual plainness were to be his hallmarks, until the exuberance of the late poems. With *The Bowge of Court* he came of age. 'Bowge' (bouche) means 'rewards'. In this secular allegory a dreamer takes ship and experiences the comradeship of courtly Disdain, Riot, Dissimulation and other perilous personifications. Boarding in innocence, he is reduced to paranoid dread. Chaucer is Skelton's master: the stanza form is that of *Troilus and Criseyde*, and when the language is most achieved, we feel Chaucer in the very movement of the verse. Riot is described in these terms:

His cote was checkerd with patches rede and blewe,
Of Kirkbye Kendall° was his short demye;*   *Kendal cloth; gown*
And aye he sang *in fayth decon thou crewe:*
His elbowe bare, he ware his gere so nye:°   *his clothes were so threadbare*
His nose droppings, his lippes were full drye:
And by his syde his whynarde,° and his pouche,   *short sword*
The devyll myght dance therin for any crouche.

Entering his forties (an older age then than it is today), living in the provinces, perhaps intellectually uncompanioned and driven upon himself, Skelton changed his style of life and writing. The eccentric poet hinted at in earlier poems came into his own in *Philip Sparrow*. He used Goliardic verse, parodying the sacred rituals of the Church, to celebrate Jane Scroop's sparrow eaten by the convent cat. The first line reads '*Pla ce bo*', the first word of the Office of the Dead, divided into three mock-solemn syllables which set the rhythmic pattern: short-lined, three-stressed. The first part of the poem is spoken by Jane, lamenting the bird. The elegy develops to ranging parody and satire. The famous catalogue of birds is not just a list: it evokes some of Philip's cousins, 'The lark with his long toe', 'And also the mad coot, / With balde face to toot' and more. An erotic sub-text gives the poem its force; Jane laments her sparrow as a lover:

It had a velvet cap,
And would sit upon my lap,
And seek after small worms,
And sometime white bread-crumbs;
And many times and oft
Between my breastès soft
It would lie and rest;
It was proper and prest.
   Sometimes he would gasp
When he saw a wasp;
A fly or a gnat,
He would fly at that;
And prettily he would pant
When he saw an ant. (7)

Jane pleads her simplicity and ignorance, then proceeds to entertain with a show of erudition and an enormous reading list. Finally Skelton's voice takes over and praises her. She loved the bird, the poet loves her. It is a Catullan syndrome and a very English poem.

The Tunning of Elinour Rumming is certainly not charming: a poem in seven 'fits', it is indebted to *Sir Gawain and the Green Knight*. Elinour's obnoxious 'tunning' or alcoholic brew, luridly described in its vat, attracts fallen women of all sorts. Elinour herself, based on an actual publican who practised near Leatherhead, Surrey, is Skelton's most repulsive creation. Her face, 'Like a roast pig's ear, / Bristled with hair'. The poem is the quintessence of his 'motley' verse, which he describes in *Colin Clout*:

For though my rhyme be ragged,
Tattered and jagged,
Rudely rain-beaten,
Rusty and moth-eaten,
If ye take well therewith,
It hath in it some pith.

The 'pith' is that of satirical moralist. In the poems against Wolsey he satirises with equal verve ecclesiastical corruption and the faithless laity. He is an establishment man opposed to those who use rather than serve it. Skeltonics, a helter-skelter measure bordering on doggerel, suit the helter-skelter social world he mocks.

When, late in his career, he chose to use a long line, a more relaxed syntax and greater depth followed. *Speak Parrot* is – even in the corrupt texts we have – his masterpiece. The years of learnedness laugh at themselves in obscure references and allusions. He shifts attention from immediate effects to a more integrated poetic language that reflects a mind which, to begin with, seems abandoned to eloquent mania. The parrot who speaks is a Polly-glot, stuffed with knowledge, all of it – given the situation of the bird, a pet and a captive, caged – garbled and useless.

My lady mistress, Dame Philology,
Gave me a gift in my nest when I lay,
To learn all language ...   (2)

Speak Parrot celebrates language and, in the same breath, acknowledges its impotence in the world of action. The poem slides away from mock allegory, rhetorical and linguistic jollity, until we are left with a bold, unmasked indictment of the state of learning, morality, the Church and the judiciary.

In Skelton's later work there is a constant pull towards dramatic form. The poems employ dialogue and idiomatic speech and develop character. In this as in other ways Skelton is a poet of transition, still dignified with the authority of the Middle Ages, yet expert in the new learning and the new forms. In *The Garland of Laurel* occur those lyrics – 'With marjoram gentle', 'By Saint Mary, my lady', 'Merry Margaret' and others – which crown the medieval lyric tradition and are at the same time, on a small scale, among the finest celebratory lyrics of the early Renaissance. Unlike the lyrics that follow, his do not invite musical setting: they are poems wholly in and for language, containing all the music that they need.

PETRARCH COMES TO ENGLAND

Think you, if Laura had been Petrarch's wife,
He would have written sonnets all his life?

Byron

Great lyrics are not to be found in Skelton. We have to look beyond him to someone conventionally greater, a man who belongs entirely to the Renaissance and whose blood has been warmed by the Mediterranean. Sir Thomas Wyatt (1503–1542) is the first great English lyric poet. 'But here I am in Kent and Christendom, / Among the Muses where I read and rhyme.'

Almost all of his lyrics are dramatic. The reader plunges *in medias res*, usually into a complaint against an unregarding or unattainable lady. The poems can be located on a map of passion. They are thrifty, with little but telling detail and a minimum of physical evocation. Like other poems in the song tradition, their imagery is conventional.

Wyatt (8–20) used over seventy different stanza forms, many of which he invented. At times he taxes himself beyond his technical skills. Critics disagree about his metres and until the middle of the twentieth century it was fashionable to regularise them by actually changing his words and word order. Are the irregularities poetic flaws, manifestations of peculiar genius, or proof that his language is still in a state of accentual transition? Metre apart, one cannot argue against the *rhythm* of the best poems, the variations – less numerous than is normally thought – on a metrical norm. They ensure his poetic superiority over Surrey and even Sidney, whose smoothness can be cloying. Violations of metrical decorum answer – or seem to answer – to modulations of emotions.

Sir Thomas involved himself in his King's affairs (in every sense) more deeply than Skelton did. A courtier, soldier and gentleman, not a priest, he was born at Allington Castle, beside the Medway in Kent, in 1503. His father, who was devoted to the Tudors, presented his son at Court when he was thirteen. Wyatt then attended St John's College, Cambridge. At seventeen, he married Lord Cobham's daughter, who bore him a son and a daughter, then proved unfaithful. Wyatt refused to have her under his roof.

At twenty-three he began actively serving Henry VIII. He accompanied an embassy to France, and the next year another to the Pope. Captured by

Spanish troops, he managed to escape. In 1528 he became Marshal of Calais, a post he held for four years. When he returned to England he held prominent posts in Essex and was Chief Ewer (in his father's place) at the coronation of Anne Boleyn.

Legend has it that he was in love with Anne. It is likely both that this was the case, and that his confession to the King before the royal marriage on 1 June 1533 saved him his head when she lost hers on 19 May 1536. He was imprisoned in the Tower that year – but that was as a result of a quarrel with the Duke of Suffolk, and the situation had none of the sinister overtones that Roman Catholic propagandists and romantic critics suggest. Wyatt was soon back in favour. He became Sheriff of Kent and, in 1537, Ambassador to Spain. He returned from Spain in 1539, on his father's death. He bade the post farewell with noble exuberance:

> Tagus, farewell, that westward with thy streams
>   Turns up the grains of gold already tried:
> With spur and sail for I go seek the Thames
>   Gainward the sun that sheweth her wealthy pride
> And to the town which Brutus sought by dreams
>   Like bended moon doth lend her lusty side.
> My King, my Country alone for whom I live,
> Of mighty love the wings for this me give.

The lines speak with honest zeal on the King's behalf. Wyatt had detractors at home, and a trial at which he was acquitted of charges of treason and immorality. He returned to his post at Calais, later served as MP for Kent, then as Vice-Admiral of a new fleet under construction. He died suddenly in Sherborne in 1542, of a fever while on his way to accompany a Spanish envoy from Falmouth to London.

Wyatt's poems were first published in *Tottel's Miscellany* and Tottel was the first to regularise Sir Thomas's metre by altering his language. The poems were thus misprinted from the outset, but with the best intentions: Tottel, and his collaborator Nicholas Grimald, knew that the poems would not please readers if they were irregular. Wyatt's work presents serious textual difficulties even now. What we read today was collected largely by G.F. Nott in 1816 and revised and improved by A.K. Foxwell in 1913, with some later adjustments. Our Wyatt is not the Wyatt that the sixteenth century read.

Some verse forms Wyatt invented, others he imported. From Italy he brought *terza rima, ottava rima* and the sonnet. Though he was the first great English sonneteer, the sonnets he translated and composed had little effect on his smooth-mannered successors, who went to the fountainhead in Petrarch rather than to Wyatt's efforts. He failed to domesticate *terza rima*, which he used with mixed effects in his three satires. They tend towards blank verse, with enjambements so frequent that the rhymes appear accidental rather than elements of form, except in a few passages. One is the opening of the first satire, on Court life:

> Mine own John Poyntz, since ye delight to know
>> The cause why that homeward I me draw,
>> And flee the press of courts whereso they go,
> Rather than to live thrall, under the awe
>> Of lordly looks, wrapped within my cloak,
>> To will and lust learning to set a law... (17)

The theme is familiar from Skelton; but the added note of personal seriousness in line six is an important development. The tone is intimate, not public, the image 'wrapped within my cloak' quick, vivid, part of the subject, not decorative. And the syntax is supple and expansive.

If Wyatt sometimes failed to acclimatise his imported forms, he did add to the resources of English poetry. His immediate legacy to his successors was 'poulter's measure', an alexandrine followed by a rhyming fourteener. C.S. Lewis finds it hard to forgive him this invention, though Surrey, Turberville, Gascoigne, Golding and others, used it with a kind of authority.

Wyatt and Henry Howard, Earl of Surrey, are bracketed together as the fathers of English Petrarchism. Puttenham saw them as 'the two chief lanterns of light to all others that have since employed their pens upon English poesy: their conceits were lofty, their styles stately, their conveyance clear, their terms proper, their metre sweet and well-proportioned, in all imitating very naturally and studiously their master Francis Petrarcha'. This is more true of Surrey than Wyatt who Puttenham read in Tottel's polished text. Certainly Wyatt's imitations of Petrarch are neither studious nor merely Petrarchan.

The introduction of Petrarch into England was not an unalloyed good. He taught two lessons, one of form and one of subject. The formal lesson provided dangers for native syntax and diction, requiring adjustments and mannerisms against the grain of the language. The thematic lesson imperilled lesser talents. Petrarchan love conventions recast courtly conventions in a new age, and their chief novelty for an English poet depended on his disregarding elements latent in the native tradition. Petrarch required not so much translation as transposition into English. This Wyatt did. Those who followed were less successful.

Wyatt found the refined, spiritual love of Petrarch uncongenial, even incredible. He was a man of flesh and fiery blood and his best poems are decidedly un-Platonic, arising out of carnal passion. He indulges only sparingly in the aureate style which later Petrarchans developed. In Petrarch's sonnets the octave normally establishes a specific occasion – a thing perceived, an emotion felt. The sestet generalises from that occasion. Wyatt saw Petrarch's skill in structuring an idea, a structuring more allusive and concise than the mechanical procedure of allegory, but not unrelated to it. His own poems structure emotions: the generalisations that emerge relate to physical passion and hardly seek to transcend it. He is forthright, clear in outline, colloquial, undecorated. Shakespeare was able to use Wyatt's poems familiarly in, for example, *Hamlet* and *Twelfth Night*. Surrey and Sidney bring orthodox Petrarchism to England but in Wyatt the energy of an old tradition, mediated through imported models, remains alive.

The best illustration of Wyatt's freedom with Petrarch is his imitation of '*Una candida cerva*' (*Canzoniere* cxc), which he renders in 'Whoso list to hunt'. In Petrarch's sonnet the speaker sees a doe and follows her, coveting her as a miser covets gold. Around her neck he notices a diamond and topaz collar which says, '*Nessun mi tocchi*'. She is Caesar's. He follows half a day and falls exhausted. She disappears. Wyatt takes the poem and rearranges the halves of the sestet. '*Nessun mi tocchi*' he translates with superb blasphemy into Christ's words, '*Noli me tangere*'. He does away with the miser image and from the outset presents the lover as a tired hunter. He heightens the hunting image – not in Petrarch at all – with the words, 'Yet may I by no means my wearied mind / Draw from the deer' – suggesting an arrow (a Cupid's arrow, too) that has hit its mark without slaying it. Wyatt imparts dramatic unity, with a fitting climax in the last three lines. The poem lacks Petrarch's intellectual clarity, but it has been transmuted into Wyatt's manly, less reflective idiom. The doe may be Anne Boleyn.

Most of his poems develop a single theme. Statements of feeling are tight-lipped and masculine, not overstated or ironised. At his best he uses rhetorical devices with restraint: means of expression, not ends in themselves. An older native tradition survives in him, despite Petrarch, and it helps to explain his prosody. He combines metre with the older accentual verse. Unless we read him with a metronomic ear, we must expect to hear at times a regular iambic pentameter line followed by a line indebted to the accentual tradition, with a marked caesura and probably two strong stresses (and perhaps a secondary stress) in each half line. His best-known poem, which uses verbs and adjectives suggesting animal passion, reflects this:

> They flee from me that sometime did me seek
> With naked foot stalking in my chamber.
> I have seen them gentle, tame and meek

That now are wild and do not remember
That sometime they put themself in danger
To take bread at my hand ...   (11)

It includes the most prosodically contested of Wyatt's lines, 'But all is turnèd thorough my gentilness / Into a straunge fashion of forsaking', which Tottel amended for regularity, as he did the first passage. It is futile to force Wyatt to scan, as, for example, by voicing the 'e' in 'straunge'. The two accented syllables, followed by three unaccented, 'stránge fáshion of forsáking', force a brief pause and then an acceleration not substantiated by syntax or metre, an irregularity with dramatic aural rightness if we listen with both ears.

The persona of the unhappy lover, like a glum Hilliard miniature, becomes repetitive and tiresome. He has little to celebrate. Occasionally he risks a female voice, but the effect is not striking. The poems vary greatly in quality, from the twenty or so masterpieces – among the best lyrics in English – to conventional works in which word-play, so cherished by sixteenth-century poets, displaces thought and experience, or where a poem develops by accretion rather than progression.

Much ill is spoken of Wyatt's *Penitential Psalms*: one critic even declares that the real penance is to read them at all. Yet they are among the first and certainly among the better of the modern metrical versions. A comparison between Wyatt's uneven efforts and those of Sternhold and Hopkins, or Archbishop Parker, proves that, though they do not crown his achievement, they do him no discredit. He is the first of a *type* – the noblest type – of poet in English literature: a man of action, servant of his King, his God and of his muse, like Surrey, Ralegh, Sidney, Fulke Greville, Lovelace and others. Surrey defines the type in his elegies to Wyatt. They fall short of Wyatt's achievement but have the merit of sincerity.

Henry Howard, Earl of Surrey, having outshone Wyatt until this century, has now been eclipsed. He is still a magnificent poet, a great inventor, not least of a modern English Virgil and of blank verse.

I call to mind the navy great
That the Greeks brought to Troyè town,
And how the boisterous winds did beat
Their ships, and rent their sails adown,
Till Agamemnon's daughter's blood
Appeased the gods that them withstood.

His virtues tell against him: prosodic skill, formal competence. He contributes more to the development of poetry in his century than Wyatt does. He develops the unrhymed iambic pentameter (blank verse), and his sonnets are influential, while Wyatt's are only admired. He is a thoroughgoing Petrarchan. He may be essentially only a stepping-stone from Wyatt to Sidney, but that is not an unworthy fate.

He was born in Kenninghall Palace, Norfolk, in 1517. From the outset he had advantages. His father was the third Duke of Norfolk. The learned, widely-travelled tutor John Clerke took his education in hand and made him an exemplary linguist. He mastered Latin, Italian, French and Spanish. As a boy he was close to the young Duke of Richmond, illegitimate son of Henry VIII, and stayed with him at Windsor. He recalled this happy period later in life, after Richmond's death and during his own detention in the castle,

> Where each sweet place returns a taste full sour,
> The large green courts, where we were wont to hove,°   *linger*
> With eyes cast up unto the maiden's tower,
> And easy sighs, such as folk draw in love ...   (31)

He recalls the ladies, the dances, the tales, games, tournaments and confidences:

> The secret thoughts imparted with such trust,
> The wanton talk, the diverse change of play,
> The friendship sworn, each promise kept so just,
> Wherewith we passed the winter nights away ...   (31)

In a sonnet he remembers those years with unusual physical particularity, more like Gascoigne than conventional Surrey in its realisation: 'When Windsor walls sustain'd my wearied arm, / My hand my chin, to ease my restless head' (32).

In 1532 he married the Earl of Oxford's daughter, enhancing his position. He progressed as courtier and warrior, fighting on land and at sea. In 1545 he was given command of Boulogne, but the next year he was arrested and charged with high treason for conspiring against the succession of Edward VI. Henry resented the popularity of his knight – a man who was ostentatious and also ambitious, though not for the crown. He was a blood relation of Catherine Howard, and this too the King held against him: in January 1547, Surrey was beheaded at the Tower.

He passed into legend on a slightly lower plain than Sidney was to do. Thomas Nashe fictionalised him, enhancing his qualities and simplifying his deeds, in *The Unfortunate Traveller*. One speech Nashe attributes to Surrey is certainly in character: 'Upon a time I was determined to travel, the fame of Italy, and an especial affection I had unto poetry my second mistress' (the first being Elizabeth Fitzgerald, the Geraldine of the sonnets, who had doubtful Italian origins) 'for which it was so famous, had wholly ravished me unto it.' Geraldine was to Surrey what Laura was to Petrarch, an incarnate Muse, a pretext for poems, an ideal. Warton calls her 'a mistress perhaps as beautiful as Laura', and describes Surrey's achievement in Petrarchan terms: 'At least with Petrarch's passion if not his taste, Surrey led a way to great improvements in English poetry, by a happy imitation of Petrarch and other Italian poets.' He was more imitative, even in love, than Wyatt, and most of his poems concentrate on love's anxieties. He returned from his first journey to Italy, Warton tells us, 'the most elegant traveller, the most polite lover, the most learned nobleman, and the most accomplished gentleman, of his age'. He would have seemed a bit out of place at Hampton Court. Excess of accomplishment contributed to his undoing. It was rumoured that he had designs to wed Princess Mary.

A not altogether native grace characterises his lyrics. There is little of the suggestive awkwardness of Wyatt but instead a studied facility in which the pressure of feeling and thought is less intense than the requirements of a prescribed form. The poems please rather than move us. Warton approved: 'Surrey, for justness of thought, correctness of style, and purity of expression, may justly be pronounced the first English classical poet. He unquestionably is the first polite writer of love-verses in our language.' Correct, pure, classical, polite: also, a little dull. The poems can have a metronomic regularity, though the syntax is extended and complex. From Wyatt he learned poulter's measure and could write well in it:

I know to seek the track of my desirèd foe,
And fear to find that I do seek. But chiefly this I know:
That lovers must transform into the thing beloved,
And live (alas, who could believe?) with sprite from life removed.

Poulter's measure is best used for serious statements or for burlesque. It can undermine the tone of a sober poem: 'And when I felt the air so pleasant round about, / Lord, to myself how glad I was that I had gotten out!' The lighter tone mars with human warmth an otherwise chilly poem. His best-known poem in poulter's measure, 'In winter's just return', succeeds despite rather than because of the verse form he has chosen.

Surrey developed what came to be known as the Shakespearean sonnet and – most importantly – the blank verse of his translations of Books II and IV of Virgil's *Aeneid*. Grudging respect has been paid to this work, yet it is subtly conceived and executed with exemplary plainness, a verse direct and transparent, displaying its matter rather than its manner. Roger Ascham approved Surrey's attempt to write without what Warton called the 'gothic ornament' of rhyme. It was part of a humanist strategy. In the

hands of Surrey's successors, in the drama and in narrative and philosophical verse, it proved to be much more. A passage from his version of
Book II illustrates the virtues of his form. The Greek fleet withdraws
behind Tenedos.

> There stands in sight an isle, hight° Tenedon,   *called*
> Rich, and of fame, while Priam's kingdom stood;
> Now but a bay, and road unsure for ship,
> Hither them secretly the Greeks withdrew,
> Shrouding themselves under the desert shore.
> And, weening° we they had been fled and gone   *thinking*
> And with that wind had fet° the land of Greece,   *reached*
> Troyè discharged° her long continued dole.*   *abandoned grief*
> The gates cast up, we issued out to play,
> The Greekish camp desirous to behold,
> The places void, and the forsaken coasts ...

Though rhyme has gone, the sound structure within each line, and
between consecutive lines, is tight; assonance and alliteration, inner
rhyme and half-rhyme, keep the verse taut. It lacks the verve of Gavin
Douglas's translation, but it is direct and faithful to the original. It moves
at a pace at once dignified and speakable. Surrey attempts to approximate
Virgil's means as well as his meaning, and in this he reveals himself to be
the first English poet thoroughly in the humanist tradition promoted in
England by scholars such as Roger Ascham and Sir John Cheke. By following rather than dragging Virgil into English, Surrey extends English verse
technique. Douglas, who was after the meat of his original, served it up
according to a medieval and a very personal recipe.

Forty of Surrey's poems appeared, alongside Wyatt's, in *Tottel's
Miscellany* – their first publication. A decade had passed since his death,
but his reputation was still fresh. He was the only poet singled out by
name on Tottel's title-page. It is hard to summon up much enthusiasm
for the lyrics. 'The soote season, that bud and bloom forth brings' (34)
recalls Langland in phrase and alliteration, and in the not entirely
conventional particularity of its images:

> The hart hath hung his old head on the pale;°   *fence*
> The buck in break his winter coat he flings;
> The fishes flete° with new repairèd scale;   *float*
> The adder all her slough away she slings ...

But in a poem with preponderantly end-stopped lines and only two
rhymes, the effect is of accretion, not progression, a common vice in

Surrey; his poems draw on conventional tropes but do not integrate them into statement. 'Brittle beauty' and even 'Set me whereas the sun', each poem in its way memorable, are assortments of image and allusion, not coherent structures.

'Alas, so all things now do hold their peace', 'When raging love', 'O happy dancer', 'Laid in my quiet bed', 'Epitaph on Thomas Clere' and 'Sardanapalus' possess as poems some of the virtues of his blank verse, but in rhymed forms, where thought and image develop together. They are among the best poems of the time. Those that record personal experience are often the most memorable. And Surrey can be memorable. Thomas Hardy echoed lines of Surrey such as 'Now he comes, will he come? alas, no, no!', and who can deny that the poet who wrote 'I Look into My Glass' did not have deep in memory Surrey's lines, 'Thus thoughtful as I lay, I saw my wither'd skin, / How it doth show my dinted jaws, the flesh was worn so thin'?

Surrey's debt to Wyatt is occasionally apparent in style and image. 'Wrapt in my careless cloak' recalls Wyatt's first satire; a poem with an extended chess conceit has a Wyatt-like lightness of touch; there are poems of mere word play, too; and verses spoken by women. But Surrey's four elegies for Wyatt bear witness to the fact that the older poet was for him an inspiration rather than a model. Surrey was more ambitious and sophisticated than Wyatt, and though a fine poet, a lesser one.

THE GREEN KNIGHT

Signor Edouardo, since promise is debt, and you (by the law of friendship) do burden me with a promise that I should lend you instructions towards the making of English verse or rhyme, I will essay to discharge the same...

George Gascoigne, *from* Certain Notes of Instruction
concerning the making of verse or rhyme in English *(1575)*

In the sixteenth century the native tradition of lyric poems builds on and away from medieval traditions of grammar and rhetoric. A line can be drawn from Skelton to Sir Thomas More, author of *Utopia*, polemicist, beheaded in 1535; to Wyatt, Lord Vaux, George Gascoigne, and then Barnabe Googe, first writer of English pastorals in his *Eclogues, Epitaphs and Sonnets* (1563); to George Turberville and Sir Walter Ralegh. Theirs is, generally, a poetry both austere and rich, true without sentiment, wise with the real wisdom of lives lived in the world.

These poets explore broad, generic themes of permanent significance and moral importance. Personal experience, stripped of contingency and universalised, is one ingredient. Reasonable men address reasonable readers with wit, with passion. Their structures are argumentative or cumulative, the purpose didactic, cautionary. Metaphors revive the force of allegorical figuration: they affect us as *meaning* on several levels. But they need not be 'construed' according to an interpretative code in the way that allegorical figures do. A fashion for the Petrarchan made native poetry appear old-fashioned, hackneyed; it resurfaced at the end of the century in another form.

Bad native poetry is immediately recognisable as bad. It has nothing to hide behind. The most obvious is the 'useful' or 'instrumental' poem. Thomas Tusser's *Five Hundred Points of Good Husbandry* (1557) is full of instruction on farming, housekeeping and gardening. We may think it charming at first, but after a time it becomes tedious and flat. Rudyard Kipling made an edition of this 'serviceable' verse and contemporary poets like C.H. Sisson enjoy it because the age's customs and habits are unfolded before our eyes from the irregular little pleats of Tusser's couplets. Bad in another way is the Queen's cousin Thomas Sackville, Earl of Dorset. His 'Induction' for *The Mirror for Magistrates* we have already encountered, and he was also responsible for 'The Complaint of Buckingham'. Like Edward de Vere, Earl of Oxford, he wrote verse early and fell silent in later life. Wyatt, Surrey and Sidney died young: lyric poetry was a young man's art. Here is the simple, figurative, logical, wonderful voice of the young Edward de Vere (52–57):

> Were I a king, I could command content;
>   Were I obscure, hidden should be my cares;
> Or were I dead, no cares should me torment,
>   Nor hopes, nor hates, nor loves, nor griefs, nor fears.
>   A doubtful choice, of these three which to crave,
>   A kingdom, or a cottage, or a grave.

Plain diction, general equivalence between metrical and syntactical units: the poem examines the tentativeness of feelings in a verse of bold subtlety, choosing characteristic detail, universal images, and avoiding nuanced concreteness and specificity of image. The native style at its best beguiles because it is clear in intention and lucid in execution.

Isabella Whitney, the first woman to publish a volume of her verses, *A Sweet Nosegay or Pleasant Posy, Containing a Hundred and Ten Philosophical Flowers* (1573), flourished in the decade after 1565. She adopted the plain style with prosaic confidence and a kind of tripping energy that tends to fall over its feet in its eagerness to close a rhyme. Her fictional 'The Manner of her Will, and what she left to London: and to all those in it: at her departing' (159) is less predictable and derivative than her aphoristic, Senecan *Philosophical Flowers*: it is a rapid doggerel, almost rising to satire. Death was – figuratively – not unlike going into the country for a long stay. Her poem gives the sense of a busy voice of her day, of the world she walked in, and there is a very nice sense of irony in the way she bequeaths the world itself unto itself. The teeming world of Isabella Whitney's poem was visited with merciless regularity by the plague, which also became a potent muse for her contemporaries. No one apprehended life's end as memorably as Thomas Nashe in 'Adieu, farewell earth's bliss', for example, and that neglected poet Anon had a lot to say about the plague.

George Gascoigne exemplifies the plain style as no one else does, and because he is 'transitional' (falling between the stools of 'silver' and 'golden' poets, between Wyatt and Spenser, between the first and second halves of the century) he is often forgotten.

> My worthy Lord, I pray you wonder not
> To see your woodman shoot so oft awry,
> Nor that he stands amazèd like a sot
> And lets the harmless deer, unhurt, go by.   (50)

His neglect is one of the not uncommon outrages in English poetry: Donne and Herbert were overlooked and misvalued for centuries; Smart and Cowper are only now being restored. Gascoigne for centuries has been more a footnote than part of the living text. He deserves as much celebrity at least as Surrey, as Ralegh – maybe even as much as Sidney.

The American poet Yvor Winters considers Gascoigne to be 'one of the great masters of the short poem in the century'. Winters loves 'sentence' in poetry: the concise, sometimes aphoristic expression of general truths (taken to excess 'sentence' becomes 'sententious'). Gascoigne's best poems are extraordinarily good. No wonder he was among Ralegh's favourites. Ben Jonson admired him, and Shakespeare was touched by him; there are echoes in the language of his plays. Gascoigne takes up the original qualities of Wyatt – and Wyatt's vices, especially facile word-play and poulter's measure, which he puts to good use. He advances the native tradition, occasionally dusted but ungilded by Italian influences. He advances it because he understands it, in the way that Skelton, recoiling from humanism, understood the medieval in a new light.

Born in 1530 in Cardington, Bedfordshire, George was descended from Sir William Gascoigne, Henry IV's chief justice. His father, Sir John, was a man of substance. George studied at Trinity College, Cambridge, and in 1555 entered Gray's Inn, London, and represented Bedfordshire in Parliament. At Gray's Inn he produced two plays. One, *Supposes*, out of Ariosto's *Suppositi*, is probably our first English prose comedy. It provided Shakespeare with the sub-plot of *The Taming of the Shrew*. The other was a translation of an Italian version of Euripides, the first classical Greek play to appear on the English stage.

A prodigal, Gascoigne was disinherited. To mend his finances, and perhaps even for love, he married, in 1562, Elizabeth Breton, a widow and the mother of the poet Nicholas Breton. Debt continued to dog him. He fled from his creditors to Holland, where he served the Prince of Orange (1572–4), was imprisoned by the Spanish and released. On his return to England he discovered that some of his poems had been issued in unauthorised versions; piracy of work by living authors was not unusual. He contacted another printer and together they published authorised versions in the laboriously entitled *An Hundred Sundrie Floures bound up in one Poesie*. This included the first linked sonnet sequence in English (an example of the form is 'Gascoigne's Memories IV') and the prose narrative *The Adventures of Master F.J.* which, if not translated from an Italian original, has claims to being the first English 'novel' or *roman à clef*. In 1575 he issued *The Posies*, in which he scored another first by including 'Certain Notes of Instruction', a treatise on the writing of English verse derived from Ronsard's 1565 treatise. James I later based his *Reulis and Cautelis of Scottish Poesie* on it.

The next year Gascoigne produced *The Glass of Government* (a 'prodigal son' play, perhaps rooted in his own life) and *The Steele Glass*, the first use of blank verse for non-dramatic original composition. His *Complaint of Philomene*, also in 1576, set the pattern of Ovidian narrative verse that Shakespeare follows in *Venus and Adonis* and *The Rape of Lucrece*. When he died in 1577, he had been an MP, courtier, soldier, farmer, writer and friend of writers, including Spenser. He has as many 'firsts' to his credit in poetry as Christopher Columbus does in geography. Yet by his own account, especially in 'Gascoigne's Woodmanship' (50) and 'The Green Knight's Farewell to Fancy' (51), he had failed in all he attempted.

In his time he was not regarded as a failure. Indeed, he was the best-known writer of his day. *The Steele Glass*, a satire on the debasing effect of Italian manners in England, provoked Ralegh's first surviving poem. His plain-speaking style appealed widely. Yvor Winters calls it 'almost an affectation of plainness, even of brusqueness'. His 'I' talks in the diction of the day ('like a sot'); it is not refined and artificial like the constructed 'I' of polite writers. Gascoigne makes no secret of his circumstances, or of his incompetence and failure; he plays them up and jokingly exaggerates them. There is candour in his confessions, without the self-pity and self-regard of Thomas Hoccleve's heart-on-sleevery in the previous century or the poised disappointment, moaning and bellyaching of Wyatt and Surrey.

An advantage of a plain style is that good poems stand out from bad; no figured veil obscures the faults. And from the weak poems good passages float free with the force of aphorism:

> If so thy wife be too, too fair of face,
> It draws one guest too many to thine inn;
> If she be foul, and foilèd with disgrace,
> In other pillows prickst thou many a pin.

If she is pretty, she will deceive you; if ugly, you will deceive her. The thought is commonplace; but tone, diction, conciseness bring the commonplace to life. What is good in Gascoigne – and there is considerable and varied good – has an abrupt clarity and a positive verbal impact.

Elegy – serious and satirical – is his natural mode. He memorialises failure and loss in a tone without resignation. An almost physical sense of the material reality and the desirability of what he has lost or failed in is captured in the accentual and alliterative lines of his 'native' poems. His most delicate achievement is his humour: it is bitter-sweet without burlesque and without loss of poetic seriousness.

In 'Certain Notes of Instruction' Gascoigne emphasises poetic 'invention': find the right word or phrase to illustrate and amplify; avoid '*trita et obvia*', the merely conventional and familiar. Verbal discovery, surprise: he revives convention in new structures, new metaphors. The alliteration that binds many poems together produces, not the archaic effect we might expect, but a colloquial tone, a sense of unrefinement. In writing about failure his mastery is clearest. 'The Lullaby of a Lover' (48), who puts his youth, his eyes, his will, his sex, to sleep, is in metrical verse, heightened by alliteration and assonance. Here he sings his youth to sleep:

> First lullaby my youthful years,
> It is now time to go to bed,
> For crooked age and hoary hairs
> Have won the haven within my head:
> With lullaby, then, youth be still,
> With lullaby content thy will,
> Since courage quails and comes behind,
> Go sleep, and so beguile thy mind.

He advances naturally, from image to image. Other poems, for instance the religious 'Gascoigne's Good Morrow' (49), are less alive, accumulating imagery, repeating a theme, but not developing a poetic argument.

In 'Gascoigne's Memories III' he celebrates spiritual and material failure:

> The common speech is, spend and God will send;
> But what sends he? A bottle and a bag,° *a beggar's possessions*
> A staff, a wallet, and a woeful end
> For such as list in bravery° to brag. *fine clothes*

Is this Thomas Tusser at Court, proffering the hackneyed advice he could not follow himself? It is similar in kind, yet different in effect. One begins to hear, not fancifully I think, the tones of the Ben Jonson of *Timber*, and even suggestions of the colloquial Shakespeare.

In 'Gascoigne's Woodmanship' (50) the poet confesses to his lord that he has failed in hunting, philosophy, everything. He is luckless, ill-starred. A quiet, persistent line of satire accompanies his confession: he is not the sole object of his irony. 'The Green Knight's Farewell to Fancy' (51) shows him at his most accomplished. Another account of failures, it is his most original and witty production. Here he gardens:

> To plant strange country fruits, to sow such seeds likewise,
> To dig and delve for new found roots, where old might well suffice;
> To prune the water-boughs, to pick the mossy trees
> (Oh, how it pleased my fancy once!) to kneel upon my knees,

To graft a pippin stock, when sap begins to swell;
But since the gains scarce quite° the cost, *Fancy* (quoth he) *farewell.*   requite

The greenness of this 'Green Knight' is not medieval or magical: Sir Gawain would have made short shrift of him. Gascoigne's is green with inexperience and unsuccess. He is a version of the poet himself and the visor does not hide him. His one hope is divine grace, for on earth he is doomed to fail in each vocation. Coming to Gascoigne after reading Surrey is like stepping out of a library into the wide open air: a thoroughly English air. Only he could have written off his own Muse so disarmingly, and only a dull reader would believe him:

A fancy fed me once, to write in verse and rhyme,
To wray my grief, to crave reward, to cover still my crime:
To frame a long discourse, on stirring of a straw,
To rumble rhyme in raff and ruff, yet all not worth a haw:
To hear it said *There goeth the man that writes so well,*
But since I see what poets be, *Fancy* (quoth he) *farewell.*

'A LITTLE MAN WITH LITTLE BANDS
AND LITTLE CUFFS'

Golden Apollo, that thro' heaven wide
  Scatter'st the rays of light and truth's beams!
In lucent words my darkling verses dight,
  And wash my earthy mind in thy clear streams,
  That wisdom may descend in fairy dreams...

William Blake, 'An Imitation of Spenser' (written between 1769–77)

If ever there was a poet reared in a library, it is Edmund Spenser. There is something a bit monstrous about him. Queen Elizabeth valued, though she could not like, this 'little man with little hands and little cuffs', her most complex and accomplished flatterer and apologist. The fussy, disorganised antiquary and irresistible gossip John Aubrey (1626–97), who knew everything (not all of it true) about everybody who was anybody in his own generation and the two preceding it, confirms at second hand that Spenser was 'a little man, wore short haire, little band and little cuffs'. His allegorical epic *The Faerie Queene* (67) celebrates Elizabeth; she features, always idealised, elsewhere – everywhere – in his work. He was an eager poet of the established order: monarchy, Court, the English Church, powers that sustained and rewarded him. His was not a critical but a celebratory commitment. He never got quite enough thanks for his labours: portraits show, beneath his domed brow and emphatic nose, lips a little petulant, and eyes which gaze coldly back. Tetchy. And he could speak with forked tongue: his shepherds unburden themselves, allegorically, of some harsh truths about Spenser's world.

His books sold steadily until the latter half of the twentieth century. Poets especially warmed to him. Keats pays him the tribute of imitation in his apprentice work and draws nourishment from him throughout. He calls him the 'elfin poet'. Coleridge said: 'In Spenser...we trace a mind constitutionally tender, delicate and...I had almost said effeminate.' He might well have used the term: there are in *The Shepheardes Calender* (58) and at other points in the poetry moments of sexual and erotic ambiguity. Over a century earlier than Coleridge, Milton (who would not have permitted himself to perceive such irregularities) regarded Spenser as a great poet and a moral teacher: his own work is full of direct debts to Spenser's poems. Blake, Wordsworth and Thomas Hardy imitated him at the outset of their careers. His formal influence is felt in the early poems of Byron and, pre-eminently, in James Thomson's *The Castle of Indolence*. Well into the twentieth century, poets pay him tribute. Walter Savage Landor sounds a lonely dissenting note a century before. He wrote to Wordsworth, 'Thee gentle Spenser fondly led, / But me he mostly sent to bed.' The present age agrees with Landor, and yet without Spenser English poetry would have had quite a different trajectory.

Spenser says he is Chaucer's heir, a claim it is hard to take seriously unless we consider an archaising style to be Chaucerian. The differences between Chaucer and Spenser are more striking than the similarities. Chaucer 'makes it new'; Spenser deliberately antiquates, not least in reverting to systematic allegory, whereas Chaucer had rumbled, in his middle years, the bankruptcy of that mode. Chaucer's poetry evolves from allegory towards a world of real people rather than personifications. Spenser moves back, deserting the ground Chaucer helped to prepare, in which Marlowe, Shakespeare and other writers of the time took root. Chaucer reached into the literal world, Spenser back into the figurative and ideal. The fourteenth and sixteenth century poets do share a sensuous imagination. Chaucer makes the world visible and tangible. Spenser at his best exploits the senses to make ideas imaginable.

Yet when Spenser calls himself Chaucerian, it is more than a gesture. By the latter half of the sixteenth century Chaucer's music was muted. His language could hardly be heard. Edmund Waller judged that he could only boast of 'sense', 'The glory of his numbers lost'. We are back to the voiced final '-e' which linguistic transformations silenced. Poets who could not hear saw Chaucer as awkward and faulty, a man whose numbers did not add up. Spenser read him somehow, perhaps inspired by Gascoigne's cogent enthusiasm, and sensed the equal length of lines, perhaps even allowing himself to voice that treacherous '-e'. He wrote a conclusion to Chaucer's unfinished *Squire's Tale* which found its place in *The Faerie Queene*. Certainly the example of Chaucer was monitory to the classical humanists. If language could change so radically over a century and a half, it needed to be stabilised, to be given an Augustan fixity, and from the labour to 'stabilise' it emerged strict laws, and rules of decorum.

Many a radical poet – Milton, Pope and Eliot spring to mind – have a strategy in the markers they put down in their critical writings. The purpose is to be a great poet and to be received as a great poet, and their prose work clears a space for them, showing how and what they read and how they might be read. In Spenser the art, scholarship or dedication are not lacking; nor is the politicking. Chaucer and Virgil give an equal light. Spenser wanted to be read by the same eyes that read the *Eclogues*, *Georgics* and *Aeneid, Troilus and Criseyde* and *The Canterbury Tales.* He wanted the transition from the classical poems to his own poems to be smooth and clearly understood.

In his age political and social ideas had a peculiarly potent embodiment. Elizabeth would preside over a recovery of classical learning and discipline, the re-establishment of true religion, the growth of power. The virgin Queen embodied a new start, she was the just Astraea, the English Augustus, 'fair vestal, thronèd by the West', bringing back (as Sir John Davies declares in one of his 'Hymns' to her) 'the golden days, / And all the world amended.' Such optimism survived the first decade of her reign. *Semper eadem* ('Immutable') was her motto, the Phoenix her symbol, suggesting her red hair and England's recrudescence. Surrounding her was unprecedented pomp and ceremony, at Court or when she went on her spectacular progresses to the castles, palaces and new 'prodigy houses' of her noble subjects (Wollaton, Burghley, Holdenby, Theobalds, etc.), and that pomp spread through the institutions of her rule: Church, the law, the universities all developed formality and ceremony. Portraits and tomb effigies from her period display a new magnificence. The fronts of houses become heraldic statements and define the character and status of the master and his family, even if behind them the amenities are poor. Poems, too, share in this 'refacing'. New decorum, rhetorical propriety, generic correctness are practised, rule books written. The Queen, even as she grows old, is never portrayed as ageing, ill, or bald: she always embodies splendour and a vigorous England.

Born in London around 1552, Spenser was the son of a gentleman, but one who also worked as a journeyman in cloth making. Later in life, the poet claimed a not impossible kinship with the noble Spencers of Northampton. He spent some of his childhood in Burnley, Lancashire, where he may actually have experienced the unrequited love that 'Colin' laments in *The Shepheardes Calender.* He was educated at the Merchant Taylors' School under the headmastership of Richard Mulcaster, a humanist deeply interested in singing and instrumental music and in the English language. Memorably, he declared: 'It is our accident which restrains our tongue, and not the tongue itself.' Spenser was already writing verse, translating from the French sonnets of Joaquim Du Bellay (1522–60) – 'Bellay, first garland of free poesy' – and probably studying the Platonists who were to direct his philosophical imagination.

He went up to Pembroke Hall, Cambridge, in 1569. It was the year in which Archbishop Parker oversaw the publication of the Bishops' Bible, an attempt to counterbalance the Calvinist versions. Lancelot Andrewes, who was to become one of the most eloquent churchmen of his age, was a contemporary, but Spenser took up instead with Gabriel Harvey, an opinionated young college fellow senior to him, who advocated the modish humanist and Puritan prejudices of the day, and a man so close to his bookseller (his publisher) that he was sometimes subsidised by him as an early species of paid editor and adviser. *The Shepheardes Calender* Spenser entrusted for printing to Hugh Singleton, who a year before had published a tendentious Puritan tract called *The Discovery of a Gaping Gulf* that resulted in the author, John Stubbs, having his right hand chopped off. The printer was still in prison but his printing works functioned in his absence. There is more Puritan sentiment and argument latent in the poem than we see today. Like the young Milton, young Spenser was bold, cheered on by Harvey, who held him in thrall for some time.

Harvey's dogmatic revulsion from the medieval made him hostile to Spenser's eventual plans for *The Faerie Queene*. He wanted his protégé to write English in classical metres, and they debated the adaptability of Latin and Greek prosodies to English. Spenser obligingly experimented, but Harvey's arguments were to have a stronger, though not a radical, effect on Sir Philip Sidney's work.

In *The Shepheardes Calender* Spenser tried to make pastoral a more serious mode than it had traditionally been. He mingled the pastoral of *Colin Clout* (from Skelton) and *Piers Plowman* (from Langland) with Arcadian and English flora and fauna. Formal 'pastoral' diction he laced with rustic terms and archaisms. His first notable poem, it consists of twelve eclogues that exploit thirteen different metres and forms. Colin Clout, Spenser's bucolic self, speaks the first and last eclogues – lamenting frustrated pastoral love. The other ten poems are dialogues with recognisable characters. Hobbinol, for example, is Harvey. One poem celebrates Eliza, the Queen. Four are about love, four are religious and moral allegory in pastoral disguise, one is an elegiac lament, and one, 'October' (58), is devoted to a perennial theme: the low regard and reward for the art (and artist) of poetry. The swain called Cuddie exclaims:

> They han the pleasure, I a slender price;
> I beat the bush, the birds to them do fly:
> What good thereof to Cuddie can arise?

His friend Piers consoles him: 'Cuddie, the praise is better than the price.' But it never feels that way (and the publisher is usually blamed).

Spenser's art takes shape here in an archaic diction and characteristic, generic – rather than specific – images and metaphors. Though in a 'low style', the eclogues do not sound *spoken*. The rusticity is posed, the aphoristic truths rehearsed:

> To kirk the nar,° from God more far,   *the nearer to church*
>   Has been an old-said saw,

And he, that strives to touch a star
   Oft stumbles at a straw.

Such commonplaces he may have gleaned from his days in Burnley, and rendered them polite in verse. He has glimpsed an actual, natural world through the veil of literary pastoral, and the verse sometimes sees with amazing clarity: 'Keeping your beasts in the budded broom' is a line Keats must have valued, as is:

See'st how brag° yond bullock bears,   *boastfully*
So smirk,° so smooth, his prickèd ears?   *neat*
His horns bene as broad as rainbow bent,
His dewlap as lithe as lass of Kent.

We will not respond to the poem with the surprise, delight and pride of its first readers. Here they discovered the new poetry in English, unprecedented and fully fledged. E.K. (whoever he was) provided notes which drew attention to every detail of rhetoric exploited with a deliberate intent. E.K. reveals not only what Spenser wants him to say but how a particularly alert Elizabethan might have read, construed, or even deconstructed, the poem, by means of an understanding of its rhetorical elements, so judiciously deployed.

Harvey secured Spenser a place in the Earl of Leicester's household. He was there when *The Shepheardes Calender* was published in 1579, a momentous year for English literature not least because the new poetry is established. The poem appeared anonymously, but Spenser was generally known to be the author. He met Sir Edward Dyer (author of 'My mind to me a kingdom is') and befriended Sir Philip Sidney, to whom the *Calender* is dedicated. Indeed the poem exemplifies the rules and qualities that Sidney and his circle had been advocating. Spenser was original and brave. He drew from every source, yet copied hardly at all. From the classics he sought legitimacy, transposing their terms to his own setting and situation rather than merely translating them.

Aubrey gives an amusing, if not dependable, account of Spenser paying court to the noblest of the knight poets. He was at work on *The Faerie Queene* and brought Sir Philip Sidney a copy. Sidney was busy and did not peruse it immediately. Spenser departed tetchily, but when Sidney did begin to read, he was impressed and called the poet back, 'mightily caressed him, and ordered his servant to give him so many pounds in gold...'

With Gabriel Harvey, Fulke Greville and Sidney, Spenser formed a literary club called the Areopagus, devoted to Harvey's pet project of naturalising classical metres in English. Was this the first English poetry society, devoted to promoting a movement? It chose an aloof name: the Areopagus is the hill of Ares in Athens, near the Acropolis, where the 'Upper Council', the city's supreme judiciary, convened.

In 1580 Spenser was appointed secretary to Lord Grey of Wilton, new Lord Deputy of Ireland, and left his friends for Ireland, where he made new ones, including Sir Walter Ralegh. He may have seen action during the Desmond Rebellion (though it is hard to imagine him as a soldier) and in 1586 was awarded as one of the 'undertakers' an estate including the ruined castle of Kilcolman in County Cork, with 3,000 acres of land. The first poem he wrote there was prompted by Sir Philip Sidney's death: his fine elegy 'Astrophel' (1586), with its circular rhetoric and repetitions. And there he prepared the first books of *The Faerie Queene* for press. Ralegh encouraged him to return to England and publish the first three books of his epic.

In Ireland he saw some brutal sights, including 'the execution of a notable traitor at Limerick, called Morrogh O'Brien. I saw an old woman which was his foster-mother take up his head whilst he was quartered, and sucked up all the blood running thereout, saying that the earth was not worthy to drink it; and therewith also steeped her face and breast and torn hair, crying and shrieking out most terribly.' His matter-of-factness implies, not so much that he was unmoved, as that this extreme scene was one among many that he witnessed.

In 1589 Spenser was in London to entrust the text to the printer. Ralegh, in favour with the Queen, presented him at Court and she gave him a £50 pension. By the time the first part of the epic appeared in 1590, the Earl of Essex had succeeded the late Earl of Leicester as Spenser's patron. The poet reluctantly returned to Kilcolman in 1591. He wrote *Colin Clout's Come Home Againe* and dedicated it to Ralegh (1591, published 1595). In 1594, to lessen his solitude, he married Elizabeth Boyle. His great *Epithalamion* (1595) followed, and the eighty-eight sonnets in the *Amoretti* may be attributable to the same sacrament. In 1596 he completed the next chunk of *The Fairie Queene* and it was published in 1597. The following year his castle at Kilcolman was burned in the insurrection. His youngest child perished in the fire and his work-in-progress on *The Faerie Queene* burned too. 'It is possible that Spenser had completed, or nearly completed, the last six books of his poem.' He returned to London and died destitute in 1599. He was buried at the Earl of Essex's expense and lies near Chaucer in Westminster Abbey.

Beside the sonnets of Sidney and Shakespeare, Spenser's *Amoretti* (59–65) appear, for all their accomplishment, uninspired. The best is sonnet LXXV, 'One day I wrote her name upon the strand'. But his praise of marriage and the courtly sentiment – lacking the ambivalent vigour of *The Shepheardes Calender* – seldom rises above convention. Courtly sentiment is best expressed in *The Faerie Queene* itself. One sonnet admits a personal note, referring to the epic and to his exhaustion:

> After so long a race as I have run
> Through Faeryland, which those six books compile,
> Give leave to rest me being half foredone,°   *finished*
> And gather to myself new breath awhile.

The *Epithalamion* is superior in conception and execution. Following in the tradition of classical marriage odes, it displays in pure form that idealised sensuality which animates parts of *The Faerie Queene* and, like the epic, is meticulous in organisation, structured around the twenty-four hours of the wedding day. A stanza of introduction is followed by ten stanzas in which the procession gathers and leads the bride in to the ceremony. The two central stanzas tell of the ceremony itself, then a group of ten more stanzas brings home the bride and beds her, and a final stanza rounds out the whole. Within this horological architecture are other symmetries: the words 'day' and 'night' are repeatedly counter-balanced as part of the device. It might seem to us a cold thing, to structure a love and marriage poem so deliberately; yet part of the passion of an Elizabethan poem is a passion of intelligence: deep feeling elicits the deepest art of which the poet is capable. Much of the pleasure he seeks to impart to a reader is of an intellectual kind. Whether or not we are aware of structural features, we cannot but respond to the declared feeling. Eager for the bridal night, the poet exclaims:

> How slowly does sad Time his feathers move!
> Haste thee, O fairest planet, to thy home,
> Within the western foam.

When in Book IV of his epic he came to adapt Lucretius's invocation to Venus from *De Rerum Natura*, it was with this refined passion that his chorus of lovers is made to exclaim:

> Great God of men and women, queen of the air,
> Mother of laughter, and wellspring of bliss,
> O grant that of my love at last I may not miss!

The *Prothalamion* (1596) (**66**), written for the marriage of others, is less intense. But its refrain which echoes strongly in Eliot's *The Waste Land* – 'Sweet Thames! run softly, till I end my song' – and the control of rhythm over long sentences in a complex stanza form, demonstrate the poet's baroque virtuosity. Coleridge enjoins us to 'mark the swan-like movement of his exquisite Prothalamion. His attention to metre and rhythm is sometimes so extremely minute as to be painful even to my ear, and you know how highly I prize good versification.'

Spenser follows, as Milton was to do, the Virgilian pattern for becoming a Great Poet. You must prove yourself in each of the principle genres. First you write your Eclogues, then your Georgics, then your Epic. In his patriotic and moral epic *The Faerie Queene* he translates qualities of *The Shepheardes Calender* into a 'high style' where they acquire an enhanced allegorical dimension. He retains sensuous directness, for instance in the catalogue of trees in the first canto of Book I, especially:

> The yew, obedient to the bender's will;
> The birch for shafts,° the sallow* for the mill;   *arrows; shrub willow*
> The myrrh sweet-bleeding in the bitter wound.

The first three books of *The Faerie Queene* are prefaced with an explanatory letter to Ralegh. Of the projected twelve books, the first six and fragments of the seventh, the 'Mutability Cantos' from the Legend of Constance, survive. Spenser declares that his purpose is moral: 'To fashion a gentleman or noble person in virtuous and noble discipline.' Milton took Spenser at his word, presenting him as a moral teacher in the *Areopagitica*. Nineteenth-century admirers lost sight of the moral teaching, disregarded the system of allegory and appreciated the poem's 'beauty'. Coleridge wrote: 'The whole of the *Faerie Queene* is an almost continued instance of beauty.' This is true, although incomplete, but it became the general view, and the poem was emancipated from its moral and historical purpose. The morality was archaic, the allegory obscure; the poem survived – like *Paradise Lost* (273–276) – by virtue of prosody, images, techniques and incidents, rather than of its intentions: in short, by virtue of its poetry, not its declared purpose.

Borrowing from Tasso's discourses on epic poetry and from Ariosto, in his prefatory letter Spenser distinguishes between the historian's and the poet's perspectives: 'an historiographer discourseth of affairs orderly as they were done ... but a poet thrusteth into the midst, even where it most concerneth him, and there recoursing to the things forepast, and divining the things to come, maketh a pleasing analysis of all ... The beginning therefore of my history, if it were to be told by an historiographer should be by the twelfth book, which is the last; where I devise that the Faery Queene kept her annual feast twelve days; upon which twelve several days, the occasions of the twelve several adventures happened, which, being undertaken by the twelve several knights, are in these twelve books severally handled and discovered.' There follows a description of how the completed poem would have worked, but the description does not fit the poem we have, and of course the twelfth, key book was burned.

'A gentle Knight was pricking on the plain,' the poem starts. Book I (67) belongs to the Red Cross Knight who defends Una from Archimago and Duessa or, in the allegory, Anglicanism defends truth. Sir Guyon (Temperance) destroys the Bower of Bliss in Book II. Book III is dominated by Britomart and Belphoebe (Chastity); in Book IV Triamond and Cambell exemplify Friendship, and we encounter Scudamour and Amoret. Artegall, Knight of Justice, appears in Book V, and Spenser devotes much of his allegory to events in recent English history. Sir Calidore, in Book VI, embodies Courtesy.

The projected twelve books would have contained twelve cantos each, presenting twelve virtues and twelve exemplary knights. Prince Arthur, who symbolises Magnificence, the perfection of all the virtues, sets out after a vision to seek the Faerie Queene (Elizabeth, variously figured by Belphoebe, Gloriana, Mercilla and others). Arthur is to seek her for twelve days, encountering each day one of her knights and assisting each to triumph. The poem was to end in Arthur's marriage to Gloriana (Glory). Spenser hoped by the device of Arthur to give the poem unity, without forfeiting the freedom to develop each romantic book as a largely self-contained unit.

So mechanical a conception of form and allegory, arbitrarily conceived, not rising out of an integrating action, accounts for most of the difficulties which confront a modern reader. In part the allegory derives from legend and convention, in part it is devised to shadow Spenser's ideas. It works like a code, while traditional allegory functions at best as an accessible common language based on accepted 'readings' of accepted figures. Spenser, with a humanist education, returned to the Middle Ages for his form, but he took only part of what he found there, leaving behind necessary substance. And he only partly archaised his language, giving it an antique patina. His allegory is overcharged with moral and conventional elements. Britomart is not only Chastity: she stands for aspects of the Queen, and for the religious figure of St Catherine and, to some extent, Camilla. Artegall recalls Achilles in action and dress, if not temperament. Arthur contains some of Aeneas, Guyon some of Odysseus. These literary dimensions are apposite up to a point, but they complicate figures who lose rather than gain expressive value when they come to act.

Spenser 'characterises' allegorical figures in varying degrees. Some are cardboard, only just two-dimensional, such as 'Despair'. More particularised, often with emblematic names – 'Sansfoy' and his brothers, for example – are those who act, but in a limited area. Amoret belongs to a more differentiated category, type more than figure; recognisable flesh on stylised bones. Central to the poem are the vital actors representing virtues: developed as characters, their virtues are vulnerable. When such almost-real representations move among static figures of allegory, dramatic interest is low. The moments of tension in the poem are not when a dragon appears or a battle is fought, but the seductions in which human motive and action are recognisable. A special moment is when Paridell woos the miser's wife with his eyes, speaking not a word.

Spenser's condensed history of the British kings in Book II is expository verse of a high order. He moralises the story of King Leyr (Lear) even as he tells it:

> But true it is that, when the oil is spent,
> The light goes out, the wick is thrown away:
> So, when he had resigned his regiment,
> His daughter gan despise his drooping day,
> And weary wax of his continual stay.

This is psychology on a par with Gower's, if not Chaucer's; and the verse moves with transparent ease.

For this poem Spenser invented his own 'Spenserian Stanza', comprising eight iambic pentameter lines and a final hexameter, rhyming a-b-a-b-b-c-b-c-c. It is slow-moving, the hexameter giving a finality to each stanza. Compared with the natural expressive flow of Chaucer's stanza in *Troilus and Criseyde*, with its central climax, Spenser's dignified, ceremonial measure at worst retards, at best paces, the narrative. It is most effective in description or where the poet expresses motion rather than action. A rich passage occurs in the fourth canto of Book III, where Cymoënt speeds over the sea to the side of wounded Marinell:

> Great Neptune stood amazèd at their sight,
> Whiles on his broad round back they softly slid,
> And eke° himself mourned at their mournful plight,   *even*
> Yet wist° not what their wailing meant; yet did,   *knew*
> For great compassion of their sorrow, bid
> His mighty waters to them buxom be:
> Eftesoons the roaring billows still abid,
> And all the grisly monsters of the Sea
> Stood gaping at their gate, and wondered them to see.

> A team of Dolphins raungèd in array
> Drew the smooth chariot of sad Cymoënt:
> They were all taught by Triton to obey
> To the long reins at her commandèment:
> As swift as swallows on the waves they went,
> That their broad flaggy fins no foam did rear,
> No bubbling roundel they behind them sent.

The rest, of other fishes drawen were,
Which with their finny oars the swelling sea did sheare.

By contrast, *action* is magnified and slowed down; the procession is impressive rather than exciting.

We miss 'human interest' in Spenser's mature work. And the poetry works by extension rather than concentration, a medieval feature he gets from Gower, Lydgate and Hoccleve. One must take *The Faerie Queene* in large doses: the impact is cumulative. The best effects are so much a part of the overall verbal context that they do not detach as aphorism or vivid image. Yet Spenser's manner is at present anathema to habits of modern reading and new addictions to this once most addictive poet are rare.

The Spenserian tradition includes Milton, Keats, Byron, Tennyson, Hardy and others, but his creative spell is now broken. He has been called a poet's poet. In the latter half of the twentieth century he became an academic's and a theorist's poet. Numerologists find him especially satisfying (one need only note how often the word 'twelve' has appeared above to see why). His work does not merit so reductive a fate. For ease and lucidity of language over long stretches of narrative he has no superior but Chaucer. Ignorance of Spenser is ignorance of a fountainhead of English poetry.

Aubrey adds to his account of Spenser that, 'Lately, at the college,' – Pembroke Hall – 'taking down the Wainscot of his chamber, they found an abundance of cards, with stanzas of the *Faerie Queen* written on them.' This sounds like another shard of Aubrey's fascinating misinformation. Or is it possible that the last books of *The Faerie Queene* may one day be discovered?

'OF LOVE, AND LOVE, AND LOVE'

A neutral tone is nowadays preferred.
And yet it may be better, if we must,
To praise a stance impressive and absurd
Than not to see the hero for the dust.

Donald Davie, 'Remembering the 'Thirties'

It is chiefly Sir Walter Ralegh, whose year of birth (like Spenser's) is supposedly 1552, who tempts us to hope that great poems may be rediscovered centuries after they vanish. Of all the sixteenth-century poets' lives, his is the most intriguing in its adventures and mishaps. If anyone understood the wheel of fortune, it was this Edmund Hillary of social and political climbing, this indomitable adventurer, lover and explorer.

'He was a tall, handsome and bold man; but his *naeve* [...] was that he was damnable proud,' Aubrey tells us. Later he embellishes 'handsome' in ways which make us wonder at Queen Elizabeth's taste: 'He had a most remarkeable aspect, an exceeding high forehead, long-faced and sour eie-lidded, a kind of pigge-eie. His beard turned up naturally.' He kept his Devonshire burr and had a small voice. In his age the effortlessly aristocratic Sidney was loved and revered; Ralegh was feared and despised by all but his close circle. Both were legends alive – and dead. Sidney was born with the silver spoon, but Ralegh's spoon was merely plated. He had to make his way by talent, wit, chicanery and strength.

Born in East Budleigh, Devon, Ralegh was the son of a not particularly distinguished gentleman. In his mid-teens he went up to Oriel College, Oxford, and then to the Middle Temple. Anthony à Wood reports that he was 'worthily esteemed' there, and we know that Francis Bacon, his friend, walked arm in arm with him around the gardens of Gray's Inn. By 1576 he was writing verse.

His life as a soldier included service with the Huguenots in the French Wars of Religion. He was active in Ireland and his name is associated particularly with Smerwick and Youghal and the suppression of Irish resistance. In 1582, an army officer aged thirty, he came home from Ireland. Already known at Court, he instantly climbed the north face of royal favour. Sir John Harrington recalls Elizabeth in a letter: 'When she smiled, it was pure sunshine, that every one did choose to bask in, if they could; but anon came a storm from a sudden gathering of clouds, and the thunder fell in wondrous manner on all alike.' Ralegh experienced both weathers. Did he spread a cloak over a puddle for her? He became her favourite because he exceeded all the other courtiers in the inventiveness and extravagance of his courtesies. He understood the codes of sentiment to which she responded and sported her favours in all the right ways. It cannot have been easy. Spenser in *Colin Clout's Come Home Againe* reflects on the hollowness of court love, so different from the courtly love of Chaucer:

> For all the walls and windows there are writ,
> All full of love, and love, and love my dear,
> And all their talk and study is of it.
> Ne any there doth brave or valiant seem,
> Unless that some gay mistress' badge he bears:
> Ne any one himself doth aught esteem,
> Unless he swim in love up to the ears.

Ralegh enjoyed such play, having the parts for it more than Spenser did. He became a Knight in 1584, was appointed Captain of the Guard in 1587, and received other preferments. The Queen granted him a monopoly in connection with wine trading and a patent to conquer and colonise in her name. For a decade he was generally in favour. Ralegh re-sealed her affection when he gave her *Oceanus to Cynthia*, and when he presented to her little Edmund Spenser, carrying under his arm (as it were) the first three books of *The Faerie Queene*. Ralegh wore Elizabeth's favours ostentatiously and did not prepare for (though he paved the way to) his fall.

He fell because he got Elizabeth Throckmorton, the Queen's maid of honour, pregnant. He married her secretly in 1592 and that was that, although after a spell in the Tower he was released to live in Sherborne, Dorset. Aubrey, who knew the places Ralegh lived, evokes the splendours both of his London residence, Durham House on the Thames, and of Sherborne Castle. His provincial exile was not long. He served the Queen again in naval action against Spain and later in his apparently unsuccessful voyage of exploration to Guiana. It did have some long-term consequences: the potato returned with him, and, Aubrey says, 'Sir Walter was the first that brought Tobacco into England and into fashion.' This is another of Aubrey's embroideries: it was John Hawkins (initiator of the slave trade between Sierra Leone and Hispaniola) who introduced tobacco into England in 1565, though Ralegh may have made it fashionable. As early as 6 December 1492 Europeans were raking their lungs with New World smoke: Columbus landed in Hispaniola (Quisqueya) and Luis de

Torres y Rodrigo first records smoking tobacco (describing natives who 'drink smoke'). Rodrigo de Jerez was the first European to take up the habit. More credible is Aubrey's statement that Ralegh took a trunk of books on his travels to study, and that he was a 'Chymist' (an Alchemist). 'He was no Slug; without doubt he had a wonderfull waking spirit, and a great judgment to guide it.'

The Queen – 'a Lady whom Time had surprised' – died in 1603. The accession of James VI of Scotland, James I of England, did not enhance Ralegh's fortunes. The poet made James 'laugh so that he was ready to beshitt his Briggs' at some coarse verses, but the suspicious new monarch was not long beguiled. He worked quickly: Ralegh was tried for treason, condemned to death, reprieved and detained in the Tower for thirteen years. In 1615 the King released him unpardoned to pursue the royal interest in further exploration of Guiana, where Ralegh claimed to have discovered a gold mine. He went under impossible conditions and lost his son on the expedition. He returned broken and dying to a pitiless King who – urged on by his relative the Spanish monarch, who 'proved' the gold mine was a fabrication – had him beheaded in 1618 (ostensibly still on grounds of treason) for what he had done long before in the struggle against Spain. On the scaffold Ralegh revealed his true colours. Aubrey is surely a dependable witness here: 'He was an a-christ, not an atheist.' He spoke there of and to God, never mentioning Jesus. Even within the supposed geometrical symmetries of the Trinity he detected, and directly addressed, the angle at the top.

Ralegh did not entirely die. Izaak Walton in *The Compleat Angler* recalls a wonderful moment some years after his death. In a field (like Wordsworth two centuries later) he beholds 'a handsome milk-maid that had not yet attained so much age and wisdom as to load her mind with any fears of many things that will never be, as too many men too often do: but she cast away all care, and sung like a nightingale: her voice was good, and the ditty fitted for it: it was that smooth song which was made by Kit Marlowe, now at least fifty years ago: and the milk-maid's mother sung an answer to it, which was made by Sir Walter Ralegh in his younger days.' Thus Marlowe's 'The Passionate Shepherd' ('Come live with me and be my love') (109) receives a timeless rebuff, the commonplace wisdom of the flesh speaking, in 'If all the world and love were young'. Ralegh's lines 'But Time drives flocks from field to fold, / When rivers rage and rocks grow cold…' release literal weather on Marlowe's ideal landscape and show the authentic cast of Ralegh's imagination. He writes not out of habit but necessity. Satire, parody, elegy, lament and lyric are the product of occasions or experiences which demand expression. He speaks for and as himself. At his trial in 1603 he declared he was 'wholly gentleman, wholly soldier'. This man wrote the poems.

Gascoigne was his first poetic mentor. His tribute 'In Commendation of George Gascoigne's *Steel Glass*' reveals Ralegh's preference for plain style and brusque, masculine utterance. Two sententious lines may have come back to him during his trials and imprisonment: 'For whoso reaps renown above the rest, / With heaps of hate shall surely be opprest.' Gascoigne literalises convention, planting Petrarchan flowers in English soil. Ralegh, first by logic and later in a passion of disappointment, reduced the conventional to the absurd, as in the reply to Marlowe, or distorted and personalised it. His verse, though fragmentary and formally flawed, bears the impress of an imagination more agitated and powerful than Gascoigne's. Gascoigne took failure with wry grace. Ralegh had to swallow disappointment after success and endure the punishments of very different monarchs. He has no distinctive style: now he resembles Surrey, now Gascoigne, Sidney or Spenser. He succeeds on their terms, with no poetic terms of his own. But he has a distinctive voice.

'Epitaph on Sir Philip Sidney' is his first reckonable work. The poem follows roughly the chronology of Sidney's life; it informs, celebrates and laments all at once. It is superior to Surrey's elegies to Wyatt which, equally sincere, lack the courage to particularise.

Ralegh's sonnet 'Farewell to Court' prefigures in its three quatrains the verse form and tone of *Oceanus to Cynthia* (75). It must have been important to him since in the later 'Conceit Begotten of the Eyes' he alludes back to it, and quotes it outright in *Oceanus*. The original passage is among his best.

> As in a country strange without companion,
> I only wail the wrong of death's delays,
> Whose sweet spring spent, whose summer well nigh done;
> Of all which past, the sorrow only stays.

In *Oceanus* he recalls:

> Twelve years entire I wasted in this war;
>   Twelve years of my most happy younger days;
> But I in them, and they, now wasted are:
>   'Of all which past, the sorrow only stays' –
>
> So wrote I once, and my mishap foretold,
>   My mind still feeling sorrowful success;
> Even as before a storm the marble cold
>   Doth by moist tears tempestuous times express.

The presence of transcending, spiritual love even in the frustration of worldly love raises some complaints to the level of devotional poetry. 'True love' is not 'white nor brown'; she is a form, angel and nymph. 'As you came from the holy land / Of Walsinghame', about the Queen of England, includes the Queen of Heaven. The human queen 'likes not the falling fruit / From the withered tree'. The pilgrim has seen her, the ageing poet's true love:

Such an one did I meet, good Sir,
    Such an angelic face,
Who like a queen, like a nymph, did appear
    By her gait, by her grace.

The poise of the last line, a semantic surprise anticipated by the repetitive construction Ralegh favours, places him not where C.S. Lewis does, in an archaic school, but in the company of his metaphysical successors. In another poem he writes, 'She is gone, she is lost, she is found, she is ever fair'. The extra four syllables in his line are inevitable: pressure of experience overrides prescriptions of form.

But the pressure is not always high, and Ralegh can sometimes bind a poem together by a specious logic, using 'or' and 'but' to pretend connection. The underlying principle is contrast or juxtaposition. Discontinuity is only intellectual, since images develop consistently over gaps in argument. By sequential discontinuity and subversion – deliberate or inadvertent? – he sometimes defeats his great foe, time, and gains freedom within memory. But memory itself embitters the present, history offers frail consolation: 'On Sestus' shore, Leander's late resort, / Hero hath left no lamp to guide her love.' Marlowe was a friend, and Marlowe's *Hero and Leander* was deep in his memory.

Among Ralegh's poems are tributes to Spenser's epic (he was dedicatee of the first three books). The sonnet appended to the first part of *The Faerie Queene* out-Spensers Spenser and strikes a beautifully Petrarchan note new to Ralegh, even as it sets Spenser as a 'celestial thief' above Petrarch (and Homer).

Methought I saw the grave, where Laura lay,
    Within that temple, where the vestal flame
Was wont to burn, and passing by that way,
    To see that buried dust of living fame,
Whose tomb fair Love and fairer Virtue kept,
    All suddenly I saw the Faerie Queene;
At whose approach the soul of Petrarch wept,
    And from thenceforth those Graces were not seen,
For they this Queen attended, in whose stead

Oblivion laid him down on Laura's hearse.
Hereat the hardest stones were seen to bleed,
   And groans of buried ghosts the heavens did pierce;
      Where Homer's spright did tremble all for grief
      And cursed th' access of that celestial thief

Spenser compliments Ralegh more modestly as 'the summer's Nightingale'; and in *Colin Clout's Come Home Againe* evokes Ralegh fallen from royal grace:

His song was all a lamentable lay,
Of great unkindness, and of usage hard,
Of Cynthia the lady of the sea,
Which from her presence faultless him debarr'd.

'A lamentable lay' describes those poems reflecting on fortune, ephemerality, fate. Resigned at last, he meditates on the pilgrimage through death towards judgement. 'Give me my scallop-shell of quiet', said (doubtfully) to have been written by Ralegh while awaiting execution in the Tower, is penitence in a man so wedded to this world, finding religious hope. 'Go, Soul, the body's guest', is less resigned. From the point of death it turns and regards the world. A cumulative, incantatory indictment follows: not argument but an envenomed series of specific condemnations, with a modulated refrain. This is a poem after experience, not after thought.

Say to the court, it glows
   And shines like rotten wood;
Say to the church, it shows
   What's good, and doth no good.
If church and court reply
Then give them both the lie.

Tell potentates, they live
   Acting by others' action,
Not loved unless they give,
   Not strong but by a faction.
If potentates reply
Give potentates the lie.

Shakespeare's Antony and Ralegh have much in common: both have great gifts, passionate disposition, impulsiveness, influence, great friends and foes. Each is undone in service of a queen.

Poetry was a small part of Ralegh's activity. He took few precautions to preserve his poems. His principal literary undertaking was to write while in the Tower, with what books to hand we do not know, his vast digressive *History of the World*. Ironically, the prose he is remembered for today is letters and miscellaneous works. Even in his own day he found it hard to interest people in his *History*, though it lived after him and touched later writers, most decisively Milton. Aubrey recalls the author's frustration with his readership and his publisher: 'His Booke sold very slowly at first, and the Booke-seller complayned of it, and told him that he should be a loser by it, which put Sir W. into a passion, and sayd that since the world did not understand it, they should not have his second part, which he tooke and threw into the fire, and burnt before his face.' Volume I ends with the death of Prince Henry, who would have been Ralegh's patron had he survived.

Also in the Tower, that gloomy incubator of poetry, he composed – or recomposed – his longest and most ambitious surviving poem, of which 'The 21st (and last) Book of the Ocean to Cynthia' survives, a fragment of what may have been an essentially autobiographical epic romance. The manuscript was lost until 1860, when it turned up among the Cecil Papers at Hatfield House, an appropriate location, for it was here that Princess Elizabeth studied, walked and waited for the crown. The poem was first published in 1870. Apart from this large fragment, fifty-odd other poems survive, about a dozen more doubtfully attributed, and some sixty metrical translations of passages from Latin and Greek authors scattered through the *History*. Ralegh's work, like Wyatt's, was in no useful sense available until the later nineteenth century.

Ocean to Cynthia (75) is not the poem Ralegh presented to his Queen: that went missing. Did the Queen see through Ralegh's attempt to curry favour, after the 'betrayal' of his marriage to her lady-in-waiting, and destroy it? She released him from prison at the end of 1592 less because of a poem than because his expedition returned to England with a rich prize ship – the *Madre de Dios*, which with £800,000 of treasure made it one of the most bullioned of those brought into English ports, and he bought himself out. His restoration to favour was late and partial. Did James discard the poem when he swept out the palace on taking up residence in London? Our *Ocean* is a sequel of sorts.

Addressed by a lover to his mistress in the figure of the Ocean addressing the Moon, there can be no doubt of the relationship or its occasions. The Moon is the Queen, the Court, England, whose service commanded Ralegh's entire commitment. Reason says his struggle isn't worth the candle, but it is powerless against his fixed will to serve and 'her' cyclic, irresistible influence.

> To seek new worlds for gold, for praise, for glory,
> 　To try desire, to try love severed far,
> When I was gone, she sent her memory,
> 　More strong than were ten thousand ships of war,
>
> To call me back...

The poem is fragmentary and can be read as 'modernist' *avant la lettre*; we are tempted to suppose the discontinuities and gaps are deliberate, but the manuscript suggests it was a draft, or – what seems more likely to me – an attempt at recollection or reconstruction, made in prison, to reclaim from memory a text which, with no copy taken, had been given to the Queen and lost.

Something odd is at work, beyond the problematic nature of the manuscript. It is the sounds the poem makes. Ralegh has moved beyond the aphoristic style, pithy and spare, to an elaboration brushed by the wings of Spenser and Petrarch, rich in verbal texture and in metaphor extended sometimes to 'metaphysical' lengths. Like other longer poems, it mixes styles and, like some of his short poems, lacks progression. But the trajectory of this poem, and of the work as a whole, traces English poetry's transition from plain to aureate style. When the axe was to fall on his nape, however, the plain style asserted itself in the most amazing confrontation with death in English verse:

> And this is my eternal plea
> To Him that made heaven, earth, and sea:
> That since my flesh must die so soon
> And want a head to dine next noon,
> Just at the stroke, when my veins start and spread,
> Set on my soul an everlasting head.
> Then am I ready, like a palmer fit,
> To tread those blest paths which before I writ.

Ralegh was flesh and blood, no doubt about it.

But Sir Philip Sidney, to judge from the purity of his diction, the conventionality of his writing and the elevation of his sentiment, was pure spirit. 'Reason, look to thyself! I serve a goddess.' He is the first major English poet-critic, a model of correctness, clarity and measure. A man with enviable social advantages, he put them to full use and excelled in all he did. He has been portrayed as the most unambiguously attractive English writer, a renaissance *uomo universale* without Surrey's ambition or Ralegh's hubris. He was all of a piece, a bit brittle, with a carefully acquired polish, but noble and consistent in thought and action. Fulke

Greville – a lifelong friend, editor of the 1590 *Arcadia*, and his first biographer – called him 'the wonder of our age' in his 'Epitaph' (**91**), which concludes:

Now rhyme, the son of rage, which art no kin to skill,
And endless grief, which deads my life, yet knows not how to kill,
Go, seek that hapless tomb, which if ye hap to find,
Salute the stones, that keep the limbs, that held so good a mind.

Sidney, the hope and the patron of English poetry, died at the age of thirty-two, in 1586, of wounds received at Zutphen in the Netherlands campaign.

Most of his contemporaries elegised him. Ralegh's contribution retells the life:

A king gave thee thy name; a kingly mind,
That God thee gave, who found it now too dear
For this base world, and hath resumed it near,
To sit in skies, and sort with powers divine.

Kent thy birth-days, Oxford held thy youth;
The heavens made haste, and stay'd nor years nor time,
The fruits of age grew ripe in thy first prime;
Thy will, thy words; thy words the seals of truth.

Great gifts and wisdom rare employ'd thee thence,
To treat from kings with those more great than kings...

Ralegh's final stanza calls Sidney 'Scipio, Cicero, and Petrarch of our time'. On the tombstone of Fulke Greville appear the words 'Servant to Queen Elizabeth, Counceller to King James, Frend to Sir Philip Sidney, Trophaeum Peccati'. Such friendship was equivalent to royal service, an appropriate distinction for the eternal record.

Sidney was born in 1554 at Penshurst Place, Kent, the estate Ben Jonson celebrated in 'To Penshurst' (**214**). The king who gave him a name was Philip of Spain, his godfather. He entered Shrewsbury School, Shropshire, on the same day as Fulke Greville. From there he went up to Christ Church, Oxford, but left on account of the plague. He spent time at Elizabeth's Court, writing a masque in her honour in 1578 to mark her visit to Wanstead – with modest music, recorders and cornets; and going on missions to the Continent. He spent time as well with his beloved sister Mary, later Countess of Pembroke, in Wiltshire. He seems to have lived up, in every page of his life, to the prescriptions and advice of Castiglione's influential textbook *The Courtier*, even down to the matter of writing verse – not in the expectation of becoming a great writer but because 'at the least wise he shall receive so much profit, that by that exercise he shall be able to give his judgment on other men's doings'. So too he should know music and painting.

His travels began early. At the age of eighteen he was in Paris during the St Bartholomew's Day Massacre. He travelled on to Germany and to Italy, where at Padua his portrait was painted by Veronese. He also visited Ireland and Wales with his father, Deputy of Ireland and President of Wales, and ably defended his conduct of Irish policy. He received from Spenser the dedication of *The Shepheardes Calender*, and from Richard Hakluyt the dedication of the *Voyages*. In 1580 he briefly forfeited the Queen's favour by opposing her proposed marriage to the Duke of Anjou. That cloud past, he served as an MP, was knighted in 1582, and in 1583 married the daughter of Sir Francis Walsingham. He made preparations to accompany Ralegh and Drake to the West Indies in 1585, but he was sent instead to the Netherlands where in 1586 he died. As he lay wounded he called for music, 'especially that song which himself had entitled *La cuisse rompue*'. His was a musical family.

Another book dedicated to Sidney was Stephen Gosson's famous attack on writers, *The School of Abuse, Containing a Pleasant Invective against Poets, Pipers, Players, Jesters, and such like Caterpillers of a Commonwealth* (1579). The young poet did not find it 'pleasant' and in reply composed his *Apology for* (later *Defence of*) *Poesy* (probably 1581, published 1595). Sidney does not refute Gosson with invective but writes an urbane, reasoned argument. Without originality of thought but with clarity he distils the literary criticism of the Italian Renaissance. In the words of J.E. Spingarn, 'so thoroughly is it imbued with this spirit, that no other work, Italian, French, or English, can be said to give so complete and so noble a conception of the temper and principles of Renaissance criticism.' Sidney's original sources were the critical treatises of Minturno and Scaliger. What his essay lacks in novelty it makes up for in conviction, unity of feeling, and elegance of style.

For Sidney poetry is the first art, the light-bearer. Following Aristotle (as mediated through his disciples) he defines art as imitation, mimesis: poetry is 'a speaking picture' whose end is 'to teach and delight'. Sidney's aesthetic is inseparable from his general view of life. The idea of imitation was crucial. The artist is a second creator producing a second nature. He imitates the ideal, showing what may or should be rather than merely copying what is. This moral art frees the will from the trammels of nature and the contingent world and draws it to virtue. The astronomer looks for stars and sees only stars, the geometer and arithmetician look for shapes and numbers and find shapes and numbers. Musicians, too, are constrained by their discipline and inclination. The natural philosopher and the moral philosopher teach according to their subjects, the lawyer follows his books and precedents and the historian is bound by what men have done. The grammarian 'speaketh only of the rules of speech', and the rhetorician and logician are similarly trammelled. The metaphysician, too, must 'build upon the depth of nature'. Only the poet is free to marry precept and example, 'disdaining to be tied to any such subjection, lifted up with the vigour of his own invention'. He 'doth grow in effect another nature, as the Heroes, Demigods, Cyclopes, Chimeras, Furies, and such like: so as he goeth hand in hand with nature, not enclosed within the narrow warrant of her gifts, but freely, ranging only within the zodiac of his own wit'. Where philosopher, historian and the others address the learned, the poet addresses all men.

The liberality of Sidney's sense of poetry emerges in passage after passage, but chiefly when he reflects on the purpose of the art: 'This purifying of wit – this enriching of memory, enabling of judgment, and enlarging of conceit – which commonly we call learning … the final end is to draw us to as high a perfection as our degenerate souls, made worse by their clayey lodgings, can be capable of.' The poet is 'the least liar' among writers: 'He nothing affirms, and therefore never lieth. For, as I take it, to lie is to affirm that to be true which is false.' The poet has thus a boundless freedom to invent and the sanction of inspiration.

The *Defence* remains a living text. It makes a case now seldom heard, and the more interesting for that reason. Sidney knows that the poetic art is unique, enfranchising, and at the same time limited if not limiting. Nature's 'world is brazen, the poet only delivers a golden'. So in *Astrophel and Stella* (77–87), when the Muse – echoing Petrarch – says, 'Look in thy heart and write', or when Sidney criticises in other poets 'a want of inward touch', he is not after vulnerable candour or breaches of convention, but a creative power that animates an imaginative world, different from this world but consistent with it and, in that specialised Platonic sense, 'real'. Why, one is tempted to ask, this insistence on a wholly autonomous world for poetry, a world parallel to the real world, with its own laws, patterns – and values? The reply to Gosson is more than a justification of poetry. It is a justification of the freedom of language, exploration and concern that poetry might enable. The strategy Sidney adopts, which is not to answer the attack but to advocate 'in parallel', is a rhetorical approach rarely used. In recent years a writer like Eavan Boland, trying within Irish poetry to clear a female space, employs the same kind of unaggressive, reasonable and reasoned strategy. It is hard to answer because it adjusts the counters of argument in an unexpected way.

A century after Sidney's death Aubrey apostrophises him thus: 'Sir Philip Sydney, Knight, whose Fame shall never dye, whilest Poetrie lives, was the most accomplished Cavalier of his time. He was not only an excellent witt, but extremely beautiful: he much resembled his sister, but his Haire was not red, but a little inclining, viz. a darke ambor colour. If I were to find a fault in it, methinkes 'tis not masculine enough; yett he was a person of great courage.' There is a hint of ambivalence in 'not masculine enough'. In his brief life of Sir Philip's sister Mary, later Countess of Pembroke, the incomparable translator of the Psalms and (after Queen Elizabeth, who mastered four languages, translated Boethius, and passed her time in prison and in Court with making verses) the first reckonable English woman poet, he lets certain real or tittle-tattle cats out of the bag. As John Lyly said in quite another context, 'Appion, raising Homer from Hell, demanded only who was his father; we, calling Alexander from his grave, seek only who was his love ...'

Today Sidney attracts interest not for what his poetry and fictional prose say, but for what they do not quite say, for what they imply and withhold even as they twitch the curtain over it. And for what his too-celebrated life does not disclose. We might do worse than start with his sister, whose saintly reputation as a translator of the Psalms is perhaps as partial as her brother's knightly fame. Mary Herbert, Countess of Pembroke (1561–1621) was raised at Ludlow Castle, where Milton's *Comus* was first performed a century later. Her father, Sir Henry Sidney, was President of Wales. She was well educated (Latin, Greek, Hebrew) and loved learning and learned people. Philip was her constant companion in her early years. Queen Elizabeth made her a member of the royal household in 1575 and she accompanied the sovereign on progresses. That same year she became the third wife of Henry, Earl of Pembroke. The Earl of Leicester (then in favour) advanced part of her dowry since her father was not well heeled at the time. It was she who proposed *The Old Arcadia* to Philip, who then revised and added to it as the never completed *Arcadia*, instructing on his death – as Virgil did with the *Aeneid* – that his friends should destroy it. (His friends were no more obedient than Virgil's.) In dedicating the first text to Mary he recalls how he wrote it at her house in Wilton, 'in loose sheets of paper, most of it in your presence, and the rest by sheets sent unto you as fast as they were done'. Not a collaboration, but a creative intimacy as close as that between Dorothy and William Wordsworth. 1586 was Mary's *annus horribilis*: her mother, father and brother died. Piously, she followed up Philip's projects (including the Psalter and *Arcadia*) and became, as he had been, patron of various poets including Spenser, Samuel Daniel, Nicholas Breton, Thomas Nashe, Donne and Jonson. Her version of Psalm 57 begins:

> Thy mercy, Lord, Lord now thy mercy show,
> On thee I lie°   *rely*

> To thee I fly,
> Hide me, hive me as thine own,
> Till these blasts be overblown,
> Which now do fiercely blow. (102)

The very movement of her Psalms can be heard in the mature work of George Herbert.

There is no reason to *believe* Aubrey, but it is hard to resist listening to him. When Mary was engaged to Pembroke, we are told, the Earl's father feared she would 'horne his sonne' and urged the Earl to keep her in the country. Aubrey goes the full length of slander; it may be that Philip and Mary were closer than brother and sister ought to be and that 'Philip Earle of Pembroke' was *their* issue. 'She was a beautifull Ladie and had an excellent witt, and she had the best breeding that that age could afford. Shee had a pritty sharpe-ovall face. Her haire was of a reddish yellowe.' She liked in spring to watch the stallions mounting the mares ('She was very salacious'). Having watched the horses she would horse about herself. 'One of her great Gallants was Crooke-back't Cecill, Earl of Salisbury.'

'In her time, Wilton House was like a College, there were so many learned and ingeniose persons. She was the greatest Patronesse of witt and learning of any Lady in her time.' Alchemy was one of her enthusiasms; her resident adviser was Adrian Gilbert, Sir Walter Ralegh's half-brother. It was a kind of proto-Bloomsbury.

In place of a saintly, noble brother and sister we have an image of individuals of talent in love with life and with one another; people who under the excessive clothing of the day had bodies with the cravings and needs that all but saintly bodies cannot avoid. It is not hard to believe this of Skelton, or Wyatt, or Gascoigne, or Ralegh. But *Sidney*? Like Surrey before him, he seems above all that. The seeming comes from the hagiography – as patron and friend he was revered – and from the poems which are fictions, in contrast with Ralegh's, which wear historical occasions on their sleeves even when most conventional. The sentiments are not real, or are not necessarily those expressed. Something is missing in Sidney's poems. Is this absence what the poems are about? Or are they politenesses, accomplishments like horsemanship or fencing or singing or playing the spinet? Or have they, if not attestable occasions, then personal motives? *The Old Arcadia* exists, we suppose, to entertain: Mary proposed it and he wrote it. But what did he write? A complicated tale of strange ambivalences, sexual and emotional confusions, 'happily' resolved but still puzzling. In the twentieth century, they caught the eye of Thom Gunn. Early in his career, fascinated by Elizabethan and Jacobean poets and not yet able to inscribe his homosexuality openly in his poetry, he begins to pick at the idyllic tapestry in 'A Mirror for Poets', its title echoing *A Mirror for*

Magistrates. Here, against the sordid, violent reality of Elizabethan England he evokes 'Arcadia, a fruitful permanent land':

> The faint and stumbling crowds were dim to sight
> Who had no time for pity or for terror:
> Here moved the Forms, flooding like moonlight,
> In which the act or thought perceived its error.
> The hustling details, calmed and relevant.
> Here mankind might behold its whole extent.
>
> Here in a cave the Paphlagonian King
> Crouched, waiting for his greater counterpart
> Who one remove from likelihood may seem,
> But several closer to the human heart.
> In exile from dimension, change by storm,
> Here his huge magnanimity was born.

It is only within the stabilities of a fiction, set apart from a world of political, religious and moral custom, that characters, themselves fictional, are free to enact instinctive relationships and desires. But even there constraints are beamed in from the social world. In Elizabethan times – how different the Jacobean age, before the theatres were closed! – fiction, whatever the complications of sexual desire and impulse, had to end by affirming the norm. If a man desires a youth, that youth must be a girl disguised or have a twin sister who elicits the same response from the man when she is produced in the nick of time. We are given real complications but they culminate in fictional resolutions.

It would be foolish to suggest that Sidney was homosexual: the category is only defined in the latter half of the nineteenth century. In Sidney's time, specific sexual acts, principally sodomy, were proscribed and effeminacy was satirised, but close relations between men were commonplace, and it was not considered disreputable for a man to praise the physical charm of another or of a youth. A social stigma might attach to effeminacy and a moral and legal stigma to 'disclosure', and in the seventeenth century the stigmas became more acute. But Marlowe in his translations of Ovid, in *Hero and Leander* and the plays, Shakespeare in the *Sonnets* and some of the plays, Donne in the *Holy Sonnets* and other writers seem to accept (without in-your-face emphasis) elements in their nature or in the nature of their characters which were to become attenuated or inexpressible later on. They find ways of saying that are not confessional or penitential or hortatory. They weave the subject in among others, and they resolve it into an unexceptionable dominant narrative.

The love that dared not speak its name could only not speak it once it had been named. Unnamed it was ambiguously privileged. 'The one salient fact about homosexuality in early modern England, as in early modern Europe generally,' writes Bruce R. Smith in *Homosexual Desire in Shakespeare's England*, 'is the disparity that separates the extreme punishments prescribed by law and the apparent tolerance, even positive valuation, of homoerotic desire in the visual arts, in literature, and ... in the political power structure. What are we to make of a culture that could consume popular prints of Apollo embracing Hyacinth and yet could order hanging for men who acted on the very feelings that inspire that embrace?'

Weaving a subject in was perhaps a less compromising task for writers of the 'newer' writing classes than for those who breathed the scented air of the Court. A knight, still habituated to courtly convention and aspiring within its confines, would be less keen, one suspects, to write 'Was it the proud full sail of his great verse' or others of Shakespeare's vulnerable sonnets, assuming his desire inclined that way, than one of Sidney's plaintive, almost bodiless poems of desire or rejection. The very position of Sidney in the public scheme of things checked his pen. No matter how private or how personal, a poem written or recited, circulated among friends or printed, is a public act. He could read the work of friends and protégés, talk and carouse, but his own written record was prepared with caution. However cautious he was, he was a man of integrity: his concerns emerge in prose as part of larger concerns, and can be sensed elsewhere in his writing.

If, in Ford's Spacious Age, 'The art of letters had become essentially a matter of movements rather than one of solitary literary figures,' excepting of course Shakespeare (though he too is a collaborator and some of his own works are technically collaborations), poets didn't earn a living *as* poets, unless they had a patron. 'There was as yet no publishing system to make this possible,' – booksellers were working at it but needed a sufficient market before they could remunerate poets – 'and when finally the stationer (a publisher-cum-bookseller) set up shop, no copyright law at first protected the author. A poem was not a physical object of agreed value, liable to be stolen in the usual sense. Unless the author could prove theft of a manuscript book of poems (an obvious felony, because vellum had value, and copyists' fees were high), he had no cause for complaint if someone memorised and printed his poems.' Part of the importance of Elizabethan and Jacobean dedications to noble and powerful people resided in this: they were symbols of security, demonstrating endorsement and connection, proving the writer was not a hack and suggesting the possibility of protection.

Tottel set a fashion for anthologies. He was canny: he knew that the printer and bookseller, not the poet, *could* profit; after the Charter of 1566 to the Stationers' Company (granted as a means for effecting censorship as dissent was spread by print) the bookseller, not the poet, held the copyright. When Thomas Thorpe got hold of Shakespeare's sonnets from the mysterious Mr W.H., and recorded them at Stationers' Hall, Shakespeare could neither legally prevent their publication nor profit from their success. Nor indeed had he a right to correct the proofs, guard against deliberate corruption, or assert his moral right. It was fortunate that in Thomas Thorpe he had a responsible printer.

A few fine lyrics did not entitle a man to be called a poet. Nor did plays. Sonnet clusters and sequences, or epyllia, epistles and epics were necessary. Many men wrote several excellent poems and did not have the effrontery to regard themselves as poets. Many wrote bad long sequences, epyllions and epics, and did. Sidney could regard himself as a poet. *Astrophel and Stella* (published first in 1591, six years after his death), the first major sonnet sequence in English and the model for later sequences; the poems from the *Old Arcadia*; and a few additional pieces, constitute his oeuvre. Within a small body of work he proves himself as inventive in form and metre as Spenser. The sonnets have a linguistic and intellectual thrift and an emotional control that place them in a class of their own. Petrarchan in manner, but with an overall unity of theme and image and, though without plot, a progression of feeling, *Astrophel and Stella*, written between 1581 and 1582, the period of his courtship but not about his wife, is his masterpiece. Astrophel is lover, Stella the beloved. The names ('lover of stars' and 'star') correspond nicely to the theme, like Ralegh's Ocean and Cynthia. Astrophel both is and is not Philip, and Stella both is and is not Lady Penelope Rich, whom he met when she was a girl of fourteen and he a successful soldier of twenty-one. If only, he reflects, his heart had shown more foresight! There is no hint that the two ever had anything beyond social dalliance. Possibly later poems in the sequence are addressed to his wife-to-be, who as his widow married the legendary Earl of Essex, that other worshipped knight of his age.

When Sidney sets a sonnet in time, it is usually night. Images of light and dark insistently remind us of the relationship. In the sequence the poet first labours to express his love, then to win its object. He gets her at last, then circumstances part them. There are 108 sonnets and eleven 'songs' in the sequence. The tone changes from poem to poem: the reader must continually adjust expectation. We are not directly involved. We witness rather than participate in the emotion.

Many individual sonnets are dramatic in structure. 'What, have I thus betray'd my liberty?', deriving from Catullus's '*Miser Catulle, desinas ineptire*' (viii), declares his liberty from Stella – and his thralldom:

I may, I must, I can, I will, I do
Leave following that which it is gain to miss.
Let her go! Soft, but here she comes ...

Another sort of drama develops in 'Be your words made, good Sir, of Indian ware', in which he demands of his interlocutor 'whether she did sit or walk; / How cloth'd; how waited on; sigh'd she or smil'd'. We are put in mind of Cleopatra demanding news of Octavia in Shakespeare's play. Sidney addresses his heart, desire, absence as if they were persons. He debates with a sage whose wisdom is powerless against love. Poems develop logically, but often a last line or couplet trips logic by declaring emotional fact. In more than one sonnet he debates with himself:

Come, let me write. And to what end? To ease
A burthened heart. How can words ease, which are
The glasses of thy daily vexing care?
Oft cruel fights well pictured-forth do please.
Art not ashamed to publish thy disease?
Nay ...

Passion can reduce the poet to a flow of sounds as near a cry as sense allows: 'I. I. O I, may say that she is mine' is a line of astounding vocalic values, as is: 'No, no, no, no, my dear, let be.'

'Come, Sleep, oh Sleep, the certain knot of peace' made its impact on Shakespeare; 'As good to write, as for to lie and groan. / O Stella dear'; 'I am not I: pity the tale of me'; and Herbert's line, 'Let me not love thee if I love thee not', has a source in Sidney's 'That I love not without I leave to love'. Herbert may have been touched by the line, 'But ah, Desire still cries: "Give me some food!"' The spell is often achieved by simple repetition: 'Do thou then – for thou canst – do thou complain / For my poor soul.' The non-sonnets that punctuate *Astrophel and Stella* advance the narrative, relieve the tension, and have merit beyond smoothness. The first printer altered the interspersing of sonnets and songs, and in arranging a continuous sequence solely of sonnets, with the songs at the end, ruined the progression and set the trend for 'pure' sonnet sequences which was never Sidney's intention. His aim was to invent a tale of love, clean of allegory; as Nashe said: 'The argument cruel chastity, the Prologue hope, the Epilogue despair'. These are love poems in lieu of love. Giles Fletcher says in *Licia* – and we must agree with him if we are to read the Elizabethans at all – 'A man may write of Love and not be in love; as well as of husbandry and not go to the plough; or of witches and be none; or of holiness and be flat profane.'

Sidney wrote his *Old Arcadia* between 1578 and 1580. The first version was an 'idle work' for Mary at eighteen, a young wife expecting her first child. He revised the first part radically and sent it to Greville. This became the basis of the first edition (1590), which Greville broke into shorter chapters within the larger books and provided with part titles. Incomplete as it was, readers and piety demanded that the revised part be wedded with the unrevised first version (the *Old Arcadia*) in 1593. This too proved unsatisfactory; as usual, the printer was blamed, and a more cogent third version was published in 1613. It became the most popular English prose narrative of its period and for a long time after, until it was finally displaced by Samuel Richardson's *Pamela* a century and a half later. *Arcadia*, after its two false beginnings, substantially profited publishers. It also influenced poets and prose writers in Britain and on the Continent. Shakespeare and Milton made it a resource for their work. Lady Mary Wroth, the poet's niece, wrote a romance inspired by it and Anne Weamys composed a sequel. The Queen of France, Marie de Médicis, sent Jean Baudoin to England to translate it for her. Its fame comes down to our century in which Virginia Woolf made use of it ('as in some luminous globe, all the seeds of English fiction lie latent') in *Orlando*. Now it is less read even than *The Faerie Queene*, yet anyone wishing to get a handle on the poetic milieu of the time cannot afford to ignore it.

The first version was novelistic, while in revised form it is more in the spirit of Spenser, or Ovid's *Metamorphoses*, a romance to be sure but always tending towards allegory. Sannazaro instructed Sidney in romance: from him he learned to alternate prose and verse. Prose supplies a context – plot and setting – for the verse. Despite pastoral trappings, *Arcadia* is an heroic romance.

Much of the metrical verse in *Arcadia* is smooth, over-smooth, the impulse diffuse, the content thin. There are lapses of taste. 'The lively clusters of her breasts' recalls the sonnet where Sidney promises in future to kiss, rather than bite, Stella's nipples. But there are triumphs: 'Reason tell me thy mind, if there be reason', 'Phoebus, farewell ...', 'My true love hath my heart', and the long and inventive 'The lad Philisedes'. There are a few fine lyrics on age and love, including 'My sheep are thoughts, which I both guide and serve'. One senses here and in the sonnets a religious spirit which given time might have written more than the one great religious poem 'Leave me, O love, which reachest but to dust', a resolution of carnal in metaphysical desire, of human in divine love.

Sidney's brand of integrity is not fashionable. Nor does his verse appeal as widely as it did in the past. 'So good a mind,' Greville said, and so it is. Sidney's verse, like his prose, like his official life, is exemplary, statue-like: it is handsome and evocative of an age, an intelligence, even if the stone is cold. Yet it is not so cold, or so white, as it has come to seem. There is more of Ralegh, and perhaps of Marlowe, in Sidney than the record has admitted; and perhaps in Ralegh more of Sidney than his blustery history leads us at first to acknowledge. Yet on Elizabeth's poems – she was after all an accomplished writer – his imprint is firm. Her poem 'On Monsieur's Departure' (43) has some of her fallen knight's nice delicacy:

> Some gentler passion slide into my mind,
> For I am soft and made of melting snow;
> Or be more cruel, love, and so be kind.
> Let me float or sink, be high or low
>   Or let me live with some more sweet content,
>   Or die and so forget what love e'er meant.

SUBSTANCE WITH AND
WITHOUT RITES

… And as the contemplative life is most worthily and divinely preferred by Plato to the active, as much as the head to the foot, the eye to the hand, reason to sense, the soul to the body, the end itself to all things directed to the end, quiet to motion and Eternity to Time, so much prefer I divine Poesie to all worldly wisdom …

George Chapman, from 'The Preface to the Reader', Homer's Iliads

George Chapman in his early work confuses obscurity with profundity. It is in his translations of Homer and in the four sestiads he wrote to complete Marlowe's *Hero and Leander* that his gifts are seen to full advantage, following as it were in the wake of preceding clarities. T.S. Eliot tried to put his finger on a specifically Elizabethan-Jacobean quality, a quality he associates more with Donne than Chapman: 'In common with the greatest – Marlowe, Webster, Tourner, and Shakespeare – they had a quality of sensuous thought, or of thinking through the senses, or of the senses thinking, of which the exact formula remains to be defined.' When the poet-critic Edgell Rickword praises Chapman and draws attention to the end of the third sestiad of *Hero and Leander* (97) as prefiguring Donne, he has something similar in mind. He singles out the lines 'Graceful Aedone that sweet pleasure loves, / And ruff-foot Chreste with the tufted crown', revealing Chapman's skill and proving it equal, at least some of the time, to Marlowe's. He might have looked at Chapman's syntax, too. Chapman unfolds a sentence further than almost any other poet in English, and does it without obscurity or effort, like a singer with amazing lungs, who never needs to draw breath, yet keeps the flow of words, the flow of sense and of feeling, unbroken. *De Guiana* is a classic instance. Rickword, writing in 1924 of *Hero and Leander*, declares: 'What an example for our distracted poetry, which so often now strikes at the absolute and achieves the commonplace! These poets [Chapman and Marlowe] lived life from the ground upwards.'

Chapman is capable of some of the strangest writing of his age as well, as though the nineteenth century's most eccentric curiosity, Thomas Lovell Beddoes, had an ancestor in the sixteenth:

Kneel then with me, fall worm-like on the ground,
And from th' infectious dung hill of this round,
From men's brass wits and golden foolery,
Weep, weep your souls, into felicity.   (97)

In the dedicatory letter to *Ovid's Banquet* (1595) (96) he writes, after Horace, 'The profane multitude I hate.' He consecrates his 'strange poems to those searching spirits, whom learning hath made noble and nobility sacred'. If he wrote plainly it would 'make the ass run proud of his ears'. After Sidney's classical, aristocratic clarity, we meet another class of intelligence, a self-indulging mind at work. Ideas become unstable, vapoury. *Ovid's Banquet*, at moments vivid, is mechanical in progression. It does not add up. Decoration passes for development of thought. The poem is intellectually complicated, not poetically complex. Chapman's thought processes, Rickword says, 'are nearer the surface [than Marlowe's], and interfere with [the poetry's] crystallisation, first into imagery and then into formal expression.'

The fault is not peculiar to Chapman. As the dedicatory letter suggests, he is a man who stands apart, 'positions' himself: he thinks things out, and the act of thinking is involved in the act of making. A colourful theory, no longer generally credited, suggests that there existed, centred on Ralegh, a 'School of Atheism' (as its detractors called it) or a 'School of Night', perhaps the butt of the chaste college in Shakespeare's *Love's Labours Lost*. It was said to include Marlowe as well as other notable thinkers and scientists. This improbable School might have taken as its anthem Chapman's lines:

Sweet Peace's richest crown is made of stars,
Most certain guides of honoured mariners;
No pen can anything eternal write
That is not steeped in humour of the Night.

Chapman was born of gentleman-farmer stock in or near Hitchin, Hertfordshire, around 1559. Little is known of his early life. He may have attended Oxford, though by his own account he was self-taught. He may have seen service in the Netherlands: there is lived vigour in his Homeric battle scenes. His first published poems were 'The Shadow of Night' and a companion piece (1594). In both he developed a theory of false and true dreams. The poems mix eloquence, obscurity, and dull comprehensibility. The matter was not so deep as he thought. He grew away from but never outgrew his clouding aesthetic.

In 1595 his first play was produced. He was admired by Spenser, Samuel Daniel, Shakespeare and others. Some associate him with the 'rival poet' in Shakespeare's *Sonnets*, the one who lures away the beloved. 'Was it the proud full sail of his great verse, / Bound for the prize of all too precious you.' If so, there are no answering poems. Chapman became a sonneteer with the elegant 'Coronet for his Mistress' appended to *Ovid's Banquet*. In 1596 he wrote *De Guiana*, supporting Ralegh in his troubles with the Queen. The poem did not influence Elizabeth but includes a fine evocation of Chapman's figure of the hero, a figure often encountered in his plays, a man of intellect and passion:

> But you patrician spirits that refine
> Your flesh to fire, and issue like a flame
> On brave endeavours, knowing that in them
> The tract of heaven in morn-like glory opens;
> That know you cannot be the kings of earth,
> Claiming the rights of your creation,
> And let the mines of earth be kings of you;
> That are so far from doubting likely drifts,
> That in things hardest y' are most confident;
> You know that death lives, where power lives unus'd,
> Joying to shine in waves that bury you,
> And so make way for life e'en through your graves ...

This is a portion of an immensely spacious sentence, a whole verse paragraph. *De Guiana*, his one poem in blank verse, is a *carmen epicum* (epic song) without narrative plot, an oration addressed to the Queen, dramatic in rhetoric.

His hero, like many of Shakespeare's, has some affinities with the heroes evoked in one of the great translations of his age, Sir Thomas North's rendering of Plutarch's *Lives of the Noble Grecians and Romans* (which replaced the *Lives of the Saints* and was in turn replaced, a couple of generations later, by John Fox's *Book of Martyrs* as inspirational reading). This was the period in which the indomitable Bess of Hardwick cut the faces of saints out of the copes from Lilleshall Abbey which she acquired to hang at Chatsworth, and stitched in classical faces, embroidering their names above them. Plutarch taught action, civic responsibility and devotion to the larger order now embodied in the Queen. North says as much.

In 1598 he completed *Hero and Leander* (97) and began his translations of Homer. In 1609 *Euthymiae Raptus*, a philosophical poem subtitled 'The Tears of Peace', was published. In it Homer as guide reveals to the poet the figure of Peace in tears. The poem is dedicated to James I's son Prince Henry, a patron of Chapman's translation work and an ally of Ralegh who died two years later. Chapman composed the 'Epicede on Prince Henry'.

The loss of his noble patron was a disaster to him and his purse. Chapman was impecunious: he was first arrested for debt in 1599, and the last ten years of his life were plagued by creditors.

He saw prison, too, after the accession of James I. With his then friends Ben Jonson and John Marston he was locked up for staging the comedy *Eastward Ho*, which included ill-timed jests at the expense of the Scots. Chapman turned hostile to Jonson, resenting his arrogance and success. In 1634 he died in poverty and probably bitterness. He was buried in St Giles-in-the-Fields, London, and Inigo Jones (who also fell out with Jonson) provided a monument.

It is *de rigueur* to criticise Chapman's four sestiads of *Hero and Leander*. Warton long ago commented on the 'striking inequality' between Marlowe's and Chapman's parts of the poem. Edward Thomas said: 'Marlowe died, and Chapman knew not the incantation.' If there is justice, the tide against Chapman should begin to turn. Edgell Rickword pointed to the crucial line in the transition to the third sestiad. 'Love's edge is taken off' – the moral must follow. Marlowe enacted the consummation; Chapman, temperamentally suited to the task, had to enact the consequences. Chapman is a thinker. Some of his best writing is expository – and so is some of his worst.

He understands from the outset his task in *Hero and Leander*. 'New light gives new direction, fortunes new.' Dawn breaks upon two lovers who have transgressed the moral law. The poem finds an altered register, and intensity. There are moments of Marlovian physicality. Of Leander he says: 'Now (with warm baths and odours comforted) / When he lay down he kindly kiss'd his bed.' Hero treats her bed with similar sexual piety. Chapman's sestiads abound in small transformations, preparing for the culminating metamorphosis of the lovers into birds. He has a sense of the whole poem, his *and* Marlowe's parts. The parallelisms are not mechanical but poetically and dramatically right, the characters develop; there is nothing static in how they recognise the consequences of their actions.

The lovers have sinned against Ceremony, furtively committing an act for which they should have sought religious sanction. Leander is visited by Thesme, goddess of Ceremony. She appears

> ... with a crown
> Of all the stars, and heaven with her descended,
> Her flaming hair and her bright feet extended,
> By which hung all the bench of deities;
> And in a chain, compact of ears and eyes,
> She led Religion; all her body was
> Clear and transparent as the purest glass:
> For she was all presented to the sense;

Devotion, Order, State and Reverence
Her shadows were; Society, Memory;
All which her sight made live; her absence die.

For C.S. Lewis this is the classic evocation of the Elizabethan world order. Chapman's Ceremony is what Concord is to Spenser and Degree to Shakespeare: it is that ordained, hierarchical proportion that provides institutions with legitimacy and authority. Ceremony draws a human and divine meaning from mere nature. To offend against her is to offend against her shadows, Devotion, Order, and State and Reverence; it is to deny society's custom, ignore the past, usurp authority. Ceremony admonishes Leander. She

Told him how poor was substance without rites,
Like bills unsign'd, desires without delights;
Like meats unseasoned; like rank corn that grows
On cottages, that none or reaps or sows ...

That final humble metaphor, suggesting an abandoned village, has the rustic precision of Homeric simile. The drama of two lovers broadens out into an interpretation of all human experience. Hero is compared with a city surprised and pillaged: thoughts are invading troops. So broad a simile would seem absurd in another context. Chapman makes it work. The development of their reactions – Leander's decision to act, Hero's to accept – is realised with a psychological aptness that recalls *Troilus and Criseyde*.

There is the other Chapman. His name is best remembered because of Keats's sonnet 'On First Looking into Chapman's Homer':

Much have I travelled in the realms of gold,
   And many goodly states and kingdoms seen;
   Round many western islands have I been
Which bards in fealty to Apollo hold.
Oft of one wide expanse had I been told
   That deep-brow'd Homer ruled as his demesne;
   Yet did I never breathe its pure serene
Till I heard Chapman speak out loud and bold:
Then felt I like some watcher of the skies
   When a new planet swims into his ken;
Or like stout Cortez when with eagle eyes
   He star'd at the Pacific – and all his men
Look'd at each other with a wild surmise –
   Silent, upon a peak in Darien.

Keats – ridiculed by his educated contemporaries for being unable to read Homer in the original and for confusing Balboa with Cortez – was right: Chapman 'speak[s] out loud and bold'. If his boldness is different in complexity from Marlowe's, there is similar vigour and a livelier intelligence. He made Homer integral to English literature. His *Iliad* and his *Odyssey* are – alongside Golding's translation of Ovid's *Metamorphoses* – neglected masterpieces, like most translations.

Chapman's notion of the 'great man' hardly squared with the Homeric hero, and he distorts to some extent. For him Homer is 'learning's sire'. He makes him didactic, seeks a deep sense in each phrase and action, interpolates, moralises. Prefacing the *Iliad*, Chapman writes, 'It is the part of every knowing and judicious interpreter, not to follow the number and order of words, but the material things themselves, and sentences to weigh diligently.' Sentences are 'meanings'. The prescription is thoroughly Horatian. It accounts for the virtues and flaws of his versions. Warton is harsh: Chapman forfeits dignity and simplicity, writes redundantly, impoverishes where he cannot 'feel and express'. Warton calls the fourteeners used in the *Iliad* 'awkward, inharmonious, and unheroic'. Pope, himself a notable translator of Homer, was less dismissive. Chapman, Pope noted, covers his defects 'by a daring fiery spirit that animates his translation, which is something like what one might imagine Homer himself to have writ before he arrived at years of discretion'. Pope had arrived at years of discretion, and perfected the precise couplet that clicks shut like a latch.

Homer was Chapman's destiny – 'angel to me, star and fate'. He completed the *Iliad* (**99**) in 1611, the *Odyssey* in 1616, and the *Hymns* in 1624. 'The work that I was born to do, is done,' he says. Whatever its flaws, it is a triumph. It can be properly appreciated only *in extenso*. I offer a sample, the death of Hector from the *Iliad*:

> ... Then all the Greeks ran to him,
> To see his person; and admired his terror-stirring limb:
> Yet none stood by, that gave no wound, to his so goodly form;
> When each to other said: O Jove, he is not in the storm
> He came to fleet in, with his fire; he handles now more soft ...

The verse is plain, the syntax loose but clear and dramatically phrased to the climax, and the choice of words as right as it is unexpected.

Chapman was prolific. He did not suffer academic critics gladly, especially when they attacked his Homer. His purpose was 'with poesy, to open poesy'. In translating Homer he became a form of his own notion of the hero. There are four hundred pages of his poetry and about a thousand of his translations. More than many neglected Elizabethan and

Jacobean poets, Chapman is worth persisting with. There are always rewards – seldom a whole poem, but passages so fine that they outshine, however dull their context, some of the classic lyrics of the age. Yet he will never be forgiven for daring to complete Marlowe's *Hero and Leander*.

That is why it is best to praise Chapman before cueing Marlowe on stage. Marlowe's first two sestiads of *Hero and Leander* are uniquely wonderful in English: they are witty, easily erotic in a dozen ways and the language is unaffected and riveting. No wonder ten editions of the poem appeared in the forty years after its first publication: after Sidney's *Arcadia* it was the best-seller of its time. Few copies survive: it was so popular that it was 'read to rags'. Linley's 1598 edition was the second, the first to contain Chapman's 'completion'. (There are other 'completions', the first by Henry Petowe who prefaces his with a panegyric on Marlowe: 'I being but a slender Atlas to uphold so large a burden'. His happy ending turned the lovers into pine trees.) The irony is that Marlowe stops at the point beyond which he would have lost interest: fulfilment. In lighter mood, the great tragedian leaves it to the stage hands to deal with the consequences and clean up the psychological, moral and metaphysical mess he created.

In his plays as here, Marlowe's characters exist at the perilous brink of caricature. In *Hero and Leander* his 'over-reaching' sweetens with a hint of comedy. Michael Drayton – author among much else of the great topographical poem *Polyolbion* and of memorable sonnets (including 'Since there's no help, come let us kiss and part' (**107**)), heroic verse and the 'Ballad of Agincourt' (**108**) ('Fair stood the wind for France') – loved Marlowe's verse and in his 'Elegy of Poets and Poesie' Marlowe appears 'bathed in the Thespian springs'. He

> ... had in him those brave translunary things,
> That the first poets had: his raptures were
> All air, and fire, which made his verses clear:
> For that fine madness still he did retain
> Which rightly should possess a poet's brain.

Like all his contemporaries, Marlowe is a borrower. Eliot demonstrates how he borrows from that very different poet, Spenser. The evidence is in *Tamburlaine*, and less nakedly elsewhere: Spenser showed him a way of being lyrical, importing into his vigorous verse strange and complementary tones. Marlowe, like Spenser, repeats lines and passages, recycling, sometimes improving as he goes.

His first important borrowing is from Ovid, the undervalued *Amores*, wonderfully simple, the language transparent.

In summer's heat, and mid-time of the day
To rest my limbs upon a bed I lay.
One window shut, the other open stood,
Which gave such light as twinkles in a wood,
Like twilight glimpse at setting of the sun,
Or night being past, and yet not day begun. (111)

Christopher Marlowe the poet achieves quite different effects from Kit Marlowe the playwright. The playwright evokes ambition and power, but the poet is a younger man, creating a world of balance and proportion. The poems lack the exaggerated action, the grandiloquence of the 'mighty line'. Puttenham dispraised Marlowe's hyperbolic dramatic style – 'the over reacher, otherwise called the loud liar' – and Nashe commented on 'the specious volubility of a drumming decasillabon'. The poems aren't vulnerable to these strictures. They neither over-reach nor drum. None of his 'monstrous opinions' (unless you consider sexual frankness monstrous) disfigures them. They are thrifty of language and serious in content, though the tone is light.

Marlowe, born in Canterbury in 1564, was the son of a shoemaker. He became a scholar at the King's School, Canterbury, and afterwards at Corpus Christi College, Cambridge. He took his BA in 1584, his MA three years later, by which time he had probably completed *Tamburlaine*. He was the first of the University wits to employ blank verse. It is generally thought that most if not all of his small surviving body of non-dramatic verse – *Hero and Leander*, 'The Passionate Shepherd', and the Ovid and Lucan translations – were written in his University years, the fruit of youth and relative leisure. The six years that elapsed between his taking his MA and his shadowy death – possibly as a result of drink or low political intrigue or a romantic entanglement with a rough character 'fitter to be a pimp, than an ingenious *amoretto*', or perhaps a tussle over the bill ('le recknynge') – at the hand of Ingram Frisar in a Deptford tavern on 30 May 1593 were busy ones. He wrote plays, was attacked for atheism, was associated (whether or not actively, if it existed) with Ralegh's 'School of Night', and lodged with Thomas Kyd (author of *The Spanish Tragedy*) who later brought charges of blasphemy against him. These he had to answer before the Privy Council in 1593, the very council which secretly employed him to spy on English Catholics on the Continent. He cast more shadows than most men do, even in so short a life.

Had Chapman not brought it to a competent end, Marlowe's *Hero and Leander* (110) might almost be taken as a whole poem. Completion, or moral conclusion, was not necessary. If Marlowe wrote it at Cambridge, he could have moralised it himself had he felt the need to do so. The absence of a moral is moral statement enough, and characteristic of this poet. The poem is an epyllion or miniature epic, a form common in the sixteenth century, that derives from Theocritus, Catullus and Ovid. Marlowe knew his Ovid, and his poem is Ovidian mythological-erotic verse of a high order.

It provides a contrast with Shakespeare's efforts in the same genre, *Venus and Adonis* and *The Rape of Lucrece* (116). Shakespeare begins in action. In his earlier poem, 'rose cheek'd Adonis' is at chase by line three, laughing love to scorn in line four, and being loved in line five. *The Rape of Lucrece* begins with the lustful Tarquin off hotfoot, 'Borne by the trustless wings of hot desire'. Conventionally dramatic, both poems awkwardly accommodate the reflective laments which, excellent in themselves, interrupt like static arias the dramatic pace.

We cannot judge Marlowe as a tragic poet in *Hero and Leander*. He portrays consummation: *desunt nonnulla* ['the rest is missing'] leads into Chapman. But it is not absence of tragedy that makes his poem superior to Shakespeare's: it is a difference of procedure and tone. Shakespeare's six-line pentameter stanzas rein in his natural pace and hobble narrative continuity, much as the sonnet form can distort thought and weaken emphasis in his great sequence. The stanzas are conclusive, with the resolving couplet at the end, a tonal sententiousness or closure just when fluid movement is required. Marlowe chose the more versatile pentameter couplets, which move swiftly when they must, and can be used for reflection as well as description. They carry a voice, its passions and ironies, lightly modulating from register to register.

Marlowe avoids, or deflates, the heroic exaggeration that vitiates other epyllia, humanising his protagonists in the process. They are, in the end, girl and boy. The mission of the poem is to get them to this natural end. When Hero first appears in the temple, she wears a gaudy veil of artificial flowers and is covered from head to foot in leaves. She looks rather like a pot of ivy. In seeming to praise her, Marlowe defines the unnatural conventions that overlie the natural girl. He praises her chastity but does not condemn her for letting drop her fan. Only her eyes and hands are plainly visible. He thwarts idealisation by ironising ideality and by simple satire. The truth he presents boldly: 'Love is not full of pity, as men say, / But deaf and cruel where he means to prey.' The word 'prey' is at one with the animal images running through the poem: animal desire, not courtly refinement, drives the action. The animal images are natural, not censuring. Love is stripped of mystique. Hero is finally naked. Leander's argument against chastity does not convince; his desire does. He speaks 'like a bold sharp sophister' with borrowed arguments, for he is (like Hero, but in a different sense) 'a novice'. 'My words shall be as spotless as my youth, / Full of simplicity and naked truth.'

The core of his argument is charming: I shall be faithful to you as you are more beautiful than Venus. With such logic Satan prevailed upon Eve. The indictment of virginity, 'Of that which hath no being do not boast, / Things that are not at all are never lost', can indict all metaphysical belief. The poem is wedded to the physical world. The images undergo metamorphosis, making the poem more sensually vivid. Hero has 'swallowed Cupid's golden hook / The more she striv'd, the deeper was she strook'. Neptune fondles Leander's swimming body, making it exquisitely real. Gods too are lusty.

The love of Hero and Leander is not consummated in the Temple. Hero will not let Leander so much as touch her sacred garments. She bids him 'Come thither' to her turret set squarely in the natural world:

> Upon a rock, and underneath a hill,
> Far from the town, where all is whist and still
> Save that the sea, playing on yellow sand,
> Sends forth a rattling murmur to the land,
> Whose sound allures the golden Morpheus
> In silence of the night to visit us,
> My turret stands ...

The deferred subject and verb and the dramatic unpleating of the syntax demonstrate the flexibility of Marlowe's handling. The drama is in language and character, not action.

Metamorphosis is the heart of the poem: Hero's change is richly Ovidian. She is the first and last character we see, her transformation complete. At the start she is Leander's opposite. Her wreath and veil 'shrub her in', her costume and scent are hyperbolically described, she exists only as a figure. Leander, by contrast, is 'beautiful and young'. 'His body was as straight as Circe's wand.' It was with her wand that Circe transformed men into beasts.

Their first encounter is in Venus's temple, among portrayals of 'heady riots, incests, rapes', the loves of the gods, especially those in which they became animals – bulls or swans. In this place Hero sacrificed turtledoves. The mythological pictures amuse and affect us; their significance is ironic. Hero's change is complete at last:

> Thus near the bed she blushing stood upright
> And from her countenance behold ye might
> A kind of twilight break, which through her hair,
> As from an orient cloud, glims here and there.

In the very completeness of his two sestiads, Marlowe suggests that no lessons can be drawn from love, only about it.

His versions of Ovid's *Amores*, the *Elegies* – the first translated into

English – deserve more attention than they receive. For his contemporaries his translation of Lucan may have been more important. For us that labour has lost its force, but the Ovid remains fresh, with an expressive range almost as wide as that of *Hero and Leander*. Jonson, Donne and other poets owe him a debt for the *Elegies*. 'Elegy' was originally the generic term used for a song of mourning in alternate hexameters and pentameters. The elegiac metre was later adopted for the expression of personal feelings. For Ovid, as for Jonson, Donne, Marvell, Carew, it was a language of reflection, exhortation, tribute, varied in subject-matter and tone, and often amorous.

Marlowe condensed Ovid's *Amores* from five into three books. This exercise sharpened his prosodic skill with the couplet and the Ovidian manner. There are direct echoes of *Hero and Leander* or, if the *Elegies* came first, there is in *Hero and Leander* a similar variety of emotion and allusion. We find the same arguments against chastity, the same quest for pleasure as an end, and the same 'atheism' ('God is a name, no substance, fear'd in vain') in both.

'The Passionate Shepherd', Marlowe's best-known poem, which has been attributed to a range of poets including Shakespeare, is the more memorable for the number of replies it inspired, among them Ralegh's and perhaps, indirectly, Marvell's 'To his Coy Mistress'. Marlowe's poems and translations make a small body of work. He may have given up writing poems at the age of twenty-three, but it is this Marlowe who is lamented in *As You Like It* as the dead shepherd: the author of *Hero and Leander*, 'The Passionate Shepherd' and the *Elegies*.

BAD FEELINGS

Imprinted by Richard Field, and are to be sold at
the signe of the white Greyhound in
Paules Church-yard.
1593.

Colophon from Venus and Adonis, *Shakespeare's first published work*

When drama began to be printed, blank verse was an ugly medium. Printers did their best to set it out prettily but got little enough thanks for their labours. For reasons not wholly unconnected with this, some early publishers harboured bad feelings about William Shakespeare, about his work and the way in which it broke upon the world. Their resentment had little to do with the man himself, who was born in the same year as Marlowe yet somehow seemed his junior and his apprentice.

The great painter William Turner once said of Thomas Girtin who died at twenty-seven, 'Had Tommy Girtin lived, I should have starved.' But Girtin died, Marlowe died; and Turner and Shakespeare survived. Laurels are awarded accordingly. When the First Folio of the complete plays was planned, Richard Field, who had printed the bard's *Venus and Adonis* in 1593 and *The Rape of Lucrece* (116) in 1594, stood aside because he did not like the theatre (the audiences were unruly and the weather at times inclement); besides, he reflected, the texts of the plays proposed were so corrupted that it would have been dishonest to serve them up, they were not Shakespeare's. So much for the wages of integrity: the plays *were* served up, and Richard Field was not at table to savour a portion of the profits. When you see the text of a Shakespeare play – *Lear*, for instance, which in one edition in 1979 sold 112,000 copies – think of Richard Field, getting by on pamphlets and jobbing printing, while a series of corruptions in the name of his friend the poet spun out in unstoppable circulation, to benefit his competitors unto the twentieth and thirtieth generation.

The First Folio of Shakespeare's plays was published by a temporary syndicate in 1623. Two printers produced it, William and Isaac Jaggard. Three publishers were responsible, Smethwicke, Aspley and Blount, working with the acting company which owned Shakespeare's manuscripts and copies of the plays. The price was high at 20s. (one pound), but the book consisted of nearly 1,000 pages, and prices were rising at the time. Shakespeare had been dead seven years. His widow and family did not benefit from what was to be (after the Bible) the greatest book ever published in English. The publishers did a peremptory job with the editing, providing future scholars with an endless source of research and controversy.

The greatest poet of the age – the greatest poet of all time, for all his corruptions – inspires in publishers and in other writers a kind of vertigo. For Donald Davie Shakespeare represented 'a vast area of the English language and the English imagination which is as it were "charged", radio-active: a territory where we dare not travel at all often or at all extensively, for fear of being mortally infected, in the sense of being *overborne*, so that we cease to speak with our own voices and produce only puny echoes of the great voice which long ago took over that whole terrain for its own.' This is undeniably true of the plays. But had Shakespeare produced only the epyllia, *Sonnets* and the occasional poems, we would have a more pro-portioned view of him. He would appear smaller in scale than Jonson, Donne, Spenser and Marlowe.

The poems are excellent, but it is the language and vision of the plays that dazzles. The slightly absurd scenario of *Venus and Adonis*, the excess-es of *Lucrece* and the uneven brilliance of the *Sonnets* would not by them-selves have changed the world. *Venus and Adonis* was, it is true, Shakespeare's commercially most successful poem. By the time he died, ten editions had been published, and six followed in the two decades after his death. There was money in that large, bossy, blousy goddess almost eating alive the pretty lad. Nowadays it is read – if it is read at all – because it is by Shakespeare, not because it is regarded as 'major'. And *Lucrece* with its cruel eloquence, its harsh tracing of one of the most brutal tales of rape in the classical repertory, while better-balanced and constructed, touches unreflectingly on matters which require a less restrained psychol-ogy than the poet can provide. The movement from sublime to ridiculous is swift, as in the stanza where Lucrece's father and husband vie with one another in hating Tarquin the ravager:

> Yet sometime 'Tarquin' was pronouncéd plain,
> But through his teeth, as if the name he tore,
> This windy tempest, till it blow up rain,
> Held back his sorrow's tide, to make it more.
> At last it rains, and busy winds give o'er;
>   Then son and father weep with equal strife
>   Who should weep most for daughter or for wife.   (116)

In Ted Hughes the epyllia had a passionate modern advocate and expositor, who reads them as a key to Shakespeare's work. In the more than 500 pages of his wildly wayward and suggestive *Shakespeare and the Goddess of Complete Being* (1992), about which Peter Levi said, 'The man has gone mad, quite mad,' Hughes asserts: 'The basic physiology of the schema within which [Shakespeare's] heart worked then simply stepped out, "wrapp'd in a player's hide", as a combination of the myths behind the two long narrative poems, *Venus and Adonis* and *Lucrece*, which, as I was already aware, secreted the two fundamental myths of Christianity.' And, hey presto, 'That gave me the essential equation – Shakespeare's "myth".'

But there are problems in the poetry which no amount of explication can resolve, such as the closing couplets in the different stanza forms of *Venus* and *Lucrece*, where each stanza rises to epithetic closure. Concluding couplets, like the refrain or tag phrase in a ballad, are an *automatic* 'release'; such formally predictable 'releases' can cease to be effective precisely because they are expected. In narrative poems they can seriously impede the progress of the story.

Shakespeare's epyllia, like those by his contemporaries, are poetry made out of poetry. His sonnets, however, though they employ many literary conventions, are poetry apparently made out of life, much as the plays are written out of the life of England and London at the time. Aubrey takes us to the heart of Shakespeare's London. 'Near [the Bear Garden] was a Theatre, known by the name of the GLOBE Play-House, to which Beaumont, Fletcher, and Philip Massinger belonged and wrote for; and though the most eminent Place for Tragedies, Comedies and Interludes, was, because of its Situation, only used in the hot Summer Months.' He takes us by the arm and steers us on: 'Not far from this Place were the Asparagus-Gardens, and Pimblico-Path, where were fine walks, cool Arbours, &c. much used by the Citizens of London and their Families, and both mentioned by the Comedians at the Beginning of 1600; "To walk to Pimblico" became Proverbial for a Man handsomely drest; as these walks were frequented by none else.' Much nearer the playhouse another form of entertainment was available. 'Next the Bear-Garden on this Bank was formerly the Bordello, or Stewes, so called from the severall licensed Houses for the Entertainment of lewd Persons, in which were Women prepared for all Comers. The Knights Templars were notable wenchers...' The 'stewes' had various privileges confirmed by the Court and numerous regulations honoured more in the breach than the observance. They were occasionally closed down. In 1506 there were eighteen houses; Henry VII closed them and reopened twelve. In 1546 they were shut again 'by Sound of Trumpet' – 'by King Henry VIII, whose tender Conscience startled at such scandalous and open Lewdness'. Henry, tutored by John Skelton, may have overcome his aversion. 'These Houses were distinguished by several Signs painted on their Fronts, as, a Boar's Head, The Crane, the Cardinal's Hat, the Swan, the Bell, the Crosse-Keys, the Popes Head, and the Gun.' In Shakespeare's day the neighbourhood was not Mayfair, that is clear. The stewes were owned by the Church, purveyor of vice and virtue.

This book is an account of poetry, not drama; plays concern us less than poems. In the case of Shakespeare, what is relevant is not what made him great but 'the rest', the handful of works that the poet himself took most seriously and saw in print: the epyllia Richard Field published, the 154 *Sonnets*, and 'The Phoenix and the Turtle'. We could add songs from the plays, but once one dips into drama where does one stop? A monologue is like an aria, a description can be like a whole pastoral or satire. And which songs are Shakespeare's, which did he pull out of Anon's bran tub? *Two Gentlemen of Verona, Love's Labour's Lost, A Midsummer Night's Dream, The Merchant of Venice, Much Ado, As You Like It, Twelfth Night, Hamlet, Measure for Measure, Cymbeline, The Winter's Tale* and *The Tempest* all include detachable songs, but the plays snared them and that is where they properly belong.

Shakespeare is so much at the heart – is the heart – of this story that even by skirting round him we take his measure. Apart from his genius, Shakespeare had some real advantages. The world for him was new, as it had been for Chaucer. There were the navigators' discoveries, there was the rising power of the monarch, new industry, new learning. The daily world was fuller, too: Aubrey tells us how cherries came to England under Henry VIII (from Flanders); but not until Elizabeth's time did hops arrive in Kent. Beer of a sort came in under Henry VIII, along with turkeys: 'Greeke, Heresie, Turkey-cocks, and Beer, / Came into England all in a year.' No fishmongers existed inland; most estates had fishponds or kept fish in the moat for fasting days. Carrots 'were first sown at Beckington, in Somersetshire', and turnips in the early seventeenth century came from Wales; early on, all cabbages were imported from Holland. The catalogues of flora and fauna that occur not only in Shakespeare but in the works of other writers are records as much of novelty as heritage. And new things kept coming in the seventeenth century: 'clovergrass' was brought in out of Brabant and Flanders; pines and fir trees were first planted in England in the 1640s, and the first canals were built. Tabby cats came in and replaced 'the common English Catt' which 'was white with some blewish piedness: sc. A gallipot blew. The race or breed of them are now almost lost.' Also the modern brown rat supplanted the black rat, which had carried the plague. Under Charles II gardens bloomed in England. Jasmine and laurel were added to the shrubberies.

To the advantages of a new world, Shakespeare could add the advantages of a singularly complicated personal libido. 'The Phoenix and the

Turtle' (115), a lament and metamorphosis first published in Robert Chester's *Love's Martyr* in 1601, sounds a little like the incantations of *A Midsummer Night's Dream*. A charm is cast: nothing should mar the melancholy requiem of turtle-dove and phoenix, perfect but ill-assorted in their love:

> So they loved, as love in twain
>   Had the essence but in one;
>   Two distinct, division none;
> Number there in love was slain.

It is as if Shakespeare was toying with a mystery like the Trinity, in which three are one and one is three.

> Hearts remote, yet not asunder;
>   Distance, and no space was seen
>   'Twixt the turtle and his queen;
> But in them it were a wonder.

> So between them love did shine,
>   That the turtle saw his right
>   Flaming in the phoenix's sight;
> Either was the other's mine.

> Property was thus appalled,
>   That the self was not the same;
>   Single nature's double name
> Neither two nor one was called.

The love is immortalised, but without issue, as between two whose different natures are overwhelmed by an *almost* metaphysical affection. The poem, like Marvell's 'My love is of a birth', does not develop: it grows by accretion and assertion. So strange is the subject, so strange the affection, that it can only be affirmed. Language is uneasy with it: 'Either was the other's mine.'

This passionate disparity is at the heart of all Shakespeare's poems and of some of the plays. The *Sonnets* (117–157) have attracted a critical literature second in vastness only to that on *Hamlet*, and so various that at times it seems the critics are discussing works entirely unrelated. They contain a mystery and the critic-as-sleuth is much in evidence. Unlike sonnets by Shakespeare's contemporaries, none of these poems has a traced 'source' in Italian or elsewhere; most seem to emerge from an actual occasion, an occasion not concealed, yet sufficiently clouded to make it impossible to say *for sure* what or who it refers to. Setting these veiled occasions side by side can yield a diversity of plots: a Dark Lady, a Young Man, now noble, now common, now chaste, now desired, possessed and lost. All we can say for sure is that desire waxes and wanes, time passes. Here certainly, the critic says, are 'hidden meanings'; and where meanings are hidden, a key is hidden too. Only, Shakespeare is a subtle twister. Each sleuth-critic finds a key, and each finds a different and partial treasure. A.L. Rowse found his key, affirming that Shakespeare's mistress was the poet Emilia Lanyer (1569–1645) (**186**), illegitimate daughter of an Italian royal musician and also an intimate of the astrologer Simon Forman, who gives a brief picture of a brave, cunning operator. Her 1611 volume of poems includes ten dedications and cleverly celebrates the Dowager Countess of Cumberland, the aspiring poet's particular quarry, in company with Christ and Biblical heroines. The words she attributes to Eve are the first clear glimmer of English feminism in verse. Eve may – almost innocently – have handed Adam the apple; but Adam's sons crucified, in the bright light of day and reason, Jesus Christ. 'This sin of yours hath no excuse, or end.'

In Shakespeare there is a further mystery: who is 'the only begetter of these ensuing sonnets Mr. W.H.' to whom the poet (or the publisher?) wishes 'all happiness and that eternity promised by our ever-living poet'? The T.T. who signs the dedication is Thomas Thorpe, publisher-printer in 1609 of the poems: W.H. may have been a friend, who procured the manuscript, or Shakespeare's lover, or a common acquaintance: William Herbert, Earl of Pembroke? Henry Wriothesley, Earl of Southampton (dedicatee of the two epyllia)? William Hervey, Southampton's stepfather, who may have asked the poet to encourage his stepson to marry? Much passionate energy is expended on the riddle but there is no definitive answer. Thomas Thorpe was a mischievous printer, who may well have known what he was doing: no title page in history has been more vigorously and vainly pored over.

In 1598 Francis Meres compiled a catalogue of English writers of the day and lists Shakespeare's 'sugred sonnets among his private friends' – kept private, perhaps, because of their subject-matter. Two of the *Sonnets*, 138 and 144, were printed by William Jaggard in 1599 in *The Passionate Pilgrim*, a miscellany erroneously attributed to Shakespeare. After three editions the error was corrected. The whole sequence was published by one G. Eld for Thomas Thorpe in 1609. Only thirteen copies of this remarkably reliable quarto survive. Did Shakespeare see it through press? Was it withdrawn from circulation? We can assert no more than what survives on paper. Are the poems written early or late? W.H. Auden believes them early; it seems more likely, given that so many refer to the youth of the young man and the age of the courting poet, and given the theme of time and competition for the beloved between established writers, that they are in large part the product of the poet who was edging his way through *The Merchant of Venice, Julius Caesar* and *Twelfth Night* (1596–1600) to *Hamlet* (1601).

There is not a linear plot to the sequence of the sonnets. There are 'runs', but they break off and other 'runs' begin. Is it a series of sequences, or a miscellany of them? Some editors reorder the poems without success. Sonnets 1–126 are addressed to a young man or men; the remainder to a Dark (-haired) Lady. There may be a triangle (or two): the beloveds perhaps have a relationship as well. The poems are charged with passionate ambiguities.

Those who read the poems as a sonnet sequence were for a long while baffled. As late as 1774 it was the received opinion (here delivered anonymously in an edition of the plays) that, 'If Shakespeare's merit as a poet, a philosopher, or a man was to be estimated from his Poems, though they possess many instances of powerful genius, he would, in every point of view, sink beneath himself in these characters.' And why? Because 'Many of his subjects are trifling, his versification mostly laboured and quibbling, with too great a degree of licentiousness.' The *Sonnets* were neglected, or virtually so, until 1780 when they were dusted down and re-edited by Edmond Malone in a volume supplementing Doctor Johnson's and George Steevens's edition of the *Plays*. They did not immediately appeal; indeed Steevens, in 1793, praising Malone, dispraises his judgement of the poems; his 'implements of criticism, like the ivory rake and golden spade in Prudentius, are on this occasion disgraced by the objects of their culture.'

But gradually, during the nineteenth century, the *Sonnets* caught fire – fitfully at first, like wet kindling. Wordsworth, Keats, Hazlitt and Landor failed to appreciate them. Those who love them properly are fewer than those who enjoy arguing about them. W.H. Auden asserts (credibly) that 'he wrote them … as one writes a diary, for himself alone, with no thought of a public'. T.S Eliot suggests that like *Hamlet* they are 'full of some stuff that the writer could not drag to light, contemplate, or manipulate into art. And when we search for this feeling, we find it, as in the sonnets, very difficult to localise.' Now the public clambers over them, prurient, with several dozen authoritative guides.

Shakespeare's life is so nearly erased that it provides no assistance in elucidating the verse. Aubrey, writing only a couple of generations after his death, misinforms us that Shakespeare's 'father was a Butcher, and I have been told heretofore by some of the neighbours, that when he was a boy he exercised his father's Trade, but when he kill'd a Calfe he would doe it in a high style, and make a Speech.' He contrasts the excellence of Shakespeare as an actor with Jonson, who 'was never a good Actor, but an excellent Instructor'.

Drama could be profitable: this discovery coincided with 'the coming into the field of the first pupils of the new grammar schools of Edward VI', men who did not resent or distrust commerce and entrepreneurship. A new class of 'mental adventurers', the classically educated sons of merchants, made the running. Marlowe was the son of a cobbler, Shakespeare of a prosperous glove maker of Stratford-upon-Avon, where the poet was born in 1564. Both were provincials, one educated at the Grammar School in Stratford, the other at King's, Canterbury. They were harbingers of the social change that would culminate in the Commonwealth.

One of Shakespeare's advantages was an apparent disadvantage. He did not attend university. 'When Shakespeare attempts to be learned like Marlowe, he is not very clever', Ford Madox Ford said. That is part of the problem with his epyllia. But Ford reminds us that he had 'another world to which he could retire; because of that he was a greater poet than either Jonson or Marlowe, whose minds were limited by their university-training to find illustrations, *telles quelles*, from illustrations already used in Greek or Latin classics. It was the difference between founding a drawing on a lay figure and drawing or painting from a keen and delighting memory.' Sidney advises: 'Look in thy heart and write.' In the *Sonnets*, Shakespeare takes Sidney's counsel without the platonising that the great courtier intended. The heart he looks in is complex and troubled, and the poems he writes from this impure 'I' are full of a different life from that of the plays, but it is one as intense and in some respects more vulnerable. Conventionality can heighten candour.

A reader discriminates in Shakespeare's sonnets between the poem written of necessity and that written as an act of will or duty. He begs his lover to declare himself, in Sonnet 32, after the poet's imagined death:

> Oh then vouchsafe me but this loving thought,
> *Had my friend's Muse grown with this growing age,*
> *A dearer birth than this his love had brought*
> *To march in ranks of better equipage:*
> > *But since he died and poets better prove,*
> > *Theirs for their style I'll read, his for his love.*

The range of what seems to be true feeling, from admiration to passion, anger, jealousy, resentment, self-pity, from heterosexual to homosexual (the Austrian poet Stefan George in 1909 called it 'supersexual') love, is astonishing. These 154 uneven, oblique and inexhaustible lyric poems provoked some of the key critical clarifications of the twentieth century: Laura Riding's and Robert Graves's *A Survey of Modernist Poetry* demonstrated how textual scholarship and critical reading could illuminate or distort a poem, depending on interpretative rigour. They declared:

'Making poetry easy for the reader should mean showing clearly how difficult it really is...' These considerations were developed by William Empson, who contributed to the thinking of John Crowe Ransom and other fathers of the New Criticism which not discreditably held the ascendancy for years in anglophone schools and universities.

WORDS STRUNG ON AIR

And yet [limning] excelleth all other painting whatsoever in sundry points, in giving the true lustre to pearl and precious stone, and worketh the metals gold or silver with themselves, which so enricheth and ennobleth the work that it seemeth to be the thing itself, even the work of God and not of man...

Nicholas Hilliard, Treatise Concerning the Arte of Limning, *1598/9*

Shakespeare happened; he towers so high that most who shared the world with him are dwarfed by his sheer scale. The poets that suffer least are the most specialised. Beside the Giant, I set one of the smallest perfections in the tradition.

'The world,' wrote Thomas Campion, doctor, poet, and musician, 'is made by symmetry and proportion, and is in that respect compared to music, and music to poetry.' Campion's poetry was liked at Court and circulated beyond its confines. In the middle of the seventeenth century it dropped out of sight and was not recovered until 1887 when A.H. Bullen issued the first collected edition. Campion hadn't played his immortality cards very cleverly. A disciple of Sidney and fascinated by classical metres, he published his *Observations in the Art of English Poesie*, in which he attacked rhyme and experimented in classical forms, in 1602, a decade after the controversy had blown over, the cause defeated. He wrote masques, the most transient of literary forms. (Apart from Milton's *Comus*, how many masques are remembered?) His art does not *require* music, but it seems to: the poems were originally songs. He set many of them himself, but as musical styles changed, the settings disappeared.

One is put in mind of the miniature art of Nicholas Hilliard, the Elizabethan goldsmith turned painter, whose tiny, brilliant images bring his subjects to life in intimate detail. Hilliard evolved his art of 'limning' out of the residual medieval art of manuscript illumination, one source of our tradition of portrait art. His is not art for common men, it is not useful – you cannot hang his pictures or integrate them into tapestries. It is an art to be valued in aesthetic terms alone. One must hold it near to the eye, or wear it about the neck: it is art as token. Campion's best songs are more 'public' than that: they are not made exclusively for intimate occasions. But they are *useless*: they do not satirise, render thanks, flatter or praise. The love they invoke is unattributable, their seasons archetypal.

> See how the morning smiles
> On her bright eastern hill
> And with soft steps beguiles
> Them that lie slumbering still.
> The music-loving birds are come
> From cliffs and rocks unknown,
> To see the trees and briars bloom
> That late were overflown.   (178)

He was very nearly anonymous, though people sang his songs and knew the best of them by heart. Little information survives about Campion's life. He was born probably in London (possibly in Essex) in 1567. His father, a clerk of the County of Chancery, died when the boy was nine. His mother remarried but died when he was thirteen. His stepfather sent him to Peterhouse, Cambridge, but he left at the age of seventeen without taking a degree. He entered Gray's Inn, London, in 1586. There is no evidence that he ever practised law, and in verse he expresses a mild distaste for the profession. How he earned a living before 1605 is unknown. In that year he qualified in medicine at the University of Caen and thereafter probably practised as a physician in London. With several other writers patronised by the Howards or their retainers, he was implicated in the notorious case of the slow murder by poison of Sir Thomas Overbury in the Tower. Overbury had opposed the marriage of his patron, Francis Howard, with the divorced countess of Essex. Campion remained faithful to Thomas Monson, who took the rap on the Howards' behalf, attending him during his imprisonment and dedicating a book to him on his release. Campion died in 1620, leaving all he had to his close friend the lutenist Philip Rosseter, with whom he composed many of his songs and ayres and collaborated on books. His estate was valued at £22.

Campion first appeared in public as the figure of 'Melancholy' in a masque in 1588. But 'Content' was the pseudonym under which his first poems were published in Thomas Newman's careless 1591 edition of Sidney's *Astrophel and Stella*. His early work is 'out of' Sidney. The first volume of poems under his own name was *Thomae Campiani Poemata* (1595), which included a minor epic about the defeat of the Armada as well as elegies, epigrams and Ovidian fragments, all of which were written in Latin. In 1601, with Rosseter, he published in English *A Book of Ayres*, those 'superfluous blossoms' of his 'deeper studies'. He spent the concluding two decades of his life writing ayres, lyrics, masques and prose treatises, one against rhyme, which elicited Samuel Daniel's spirited defence, and one on counterpoint which was often reprinted, down to Charles II's reign.

'What Epigrams are in Poetry, the same are Ayres in Music, then in their chief perfection when they are short and well seasoned.' This peremptory definition is fitting: an 'ayre' is a poem sung by solo voice with, in Campion's case, a harmonised accompaniment, 'Skilfully framed, and naturally expressed'. Unlike other writers of ayres, Campion often composed words *and* music, achieving correspondences between the mediums. The ayre conventions were as strict as those for madrigals. The poems, taken apart from the music, appeal most to what Campion's editor W.R. Davis calls the 'auditory imagination'. There is little vital imagery, but no English poet – not even Herrick – had a nicer sense of vowel values or of the force of monosyllables.

As a Latin epigrammatist second only to Sir Thomas More, Campion turned his attention to classical metres and their use in English. He believed them more 'ayreable' than accentual metres. Sidney inspired his *Observations* and experiments in classical metres. The *Observations* are elliptical, sometimes obscure, and cover ground explored by Roger Ascham and Thomas Watson in the previous century, and by Drant, who influenced Spenser and Harvey. The argument against rhyme and for an alien prosody was exhausted. He revived it as argument, practising it only in a few illustrations. His dimeters have authority:

Yet not all the glebe
His tough hands manured
Now one turf affords
His poor funeral.
Thus still needy lives,
Thus still needy dies
Th' unknown multitude.

His contribution to the debate was to identify quantity with accent, at the same time positioning the accent according to classical rules. He sought a rationale for his system in English itself. 'We must esteem our syllables as we speak, not as we write, for the sound of them in verse is to be valued, and not their letters.'

Samuel Daniel's *Defense of Rhyme* (1603) answers Campion on patriotic grounds, but makes the valid point that Campion frequently dresses up the iambic, so natural to English, in new names and pretends it is something rich and strange. The virtue of *Observations* is local. There are points of perfect clarity. A caesura is 'the natural breathing place' in the line. Campion hears rather than reads poetry. His case against rhyme is worth attending to. Rhyme *distorts* the work of many poets: 'It enforceth a man oftentimes to abjure his matter, and extend a short conceit beyond all bounds of art.' In Shakespeare's *Sonnets*, for example, the final couplet forces conclusion, and a sense of conclusiveness, even upon the most tentative or unresolved matter.

The publication in 1613 of Campion's 'Songs of Mourning' for the death of Prince Henry (of whom every poet seems to have had high hopes) was preceded by *Two Books of Ayres*, the first of *Divine and Moral Songs*, the second of *Light Conceits of Lovers*. In 1614 his treatise on music, *A New Way of Making Fowre Parts in Counterpoint*, appeared. He expended much effort on masques, and the images in his verse have some of the brittle sharpness of masque properties. The poems are sparse in physical particularity: their effect depends on prosodic virtuosity. Few poets used a greater variety of stanza forms to such effect, within a narrow range of diction, allusion and theme.

Campion requires close attention, his work vanishes if you stand at a distance from it. Anyone reading him should try to hear sung at least some of the ayres and consider the precision of his musical structures; in performance he organises the musicians like syllables in an elaborate stanza. The masque he wrote for Lord Hay's wedding in 1607, presented before the King in Whitehall, used all the resources of the King's Music. He arranged the musicians carefully in groups: 'On the right hand were consorted ten musicians, with bass and mean lutes, a bandora, a double sackbut, and an harpsichord, with two treble violins; on the other side ... were placed nine violins and three lutes; and to answer both the consorts (as it were in a triangle) six cornets and six chapel voices were seated almost right against them, in a place higher in respect of the piercing sound of those instruments.' He marshals syllables with similar consideration and precision.

In his Latin poems he acknowledges a debt to Chaucer. More tangible debts are to Wyatt, Surrey and Sidney; and to the Latin poets. The poems fall into four general categories: amorous laments (and rare celebrations of love); (not very) wanton and witty fancies; devotional poems; and frank declarations of love. His natural world is not the world of nature: it is Arcadia, a masque setting with nymphs and shepherds. We must accept this convention: if we do, we hear a clear personal note and sometimes glimpse a solid reality. Invention in sound, balanced syllables, manipulation of rhythm and rhyme, attempts to give vowels 'convenient liberty', juxtaposition of stanzas with similar syntax and rhythmic progression but contrasting emotional content – such techniques create the effects. Many lines have an odd number of syllables and begin with a stress, an effect required by the music.

The enjambement serves the meticulous craftsman well. Yvor Winters singles out one example to illustrate a general point:

Now winter nights enlarge
   The number of their hours,
And clouds their storms discharge
   Upon the airy towers ...
                                                        (179)

The suspension of syntax at the end of the first and third lines suggests two possible directions for the meaning. The following lines take up one meaning, but the second remains active in our mind – and in the poet's. He takes it up later. 'Enlarge' can mean increase in number or increase in space. It is number the poet means, but space is suggested and developed in the last stanza. Such effects give the poem aural and intellectual point. It is on a small scale, but is carried out with the assurance of one of the most brilliant craftsmen in the language.

At the opening of the *Fourth Book of Ayres* (1617), Campion describes his lyric art: 'The apothecaries have books of gold, whose leaves being opened are so light as that they are subject to be shaken with the least breath and yet rightly handled, they serve both for ornament and use; such are light ayres.' It would be hard to find poems more perfect in form than 'When to her lute Corinna sings', 'Follow thy fair sun', 'The man of life upright', 'To music bent is my retired mind', 'Fire, fire, fire, fire!', 'There is a garden in her face' – with or without music. Even in his day Campion must have seemed a bit archaic and refined. Marlowe, Jonson and Donne were contemporaries. Their world was beyond his grasp – or his interest. In his field, however, Campion is nearly incomparable.

SINGING SCHOOL

What a deal of cold business doth a man mis-spend the better part of life in! in scattering compliments, tendering visits, gathering and venting news, following feasts and plays, making a little winter-love in a dark corner.

Ben Jonson, 'Jactura Vitae', Timber *or* Discoveries, *1620/1*

Campion is only *nearly* incomparable. Ben Jonson – another man described as 'the first poet laureate' – compares with any poet of his age and the next. He is the most versatile writer in the history of English poetry. In the area of ayres, he can almost out-Campion Campion and he fathers Robert Herrick's lyrics and those of other 'Sons of Ben', Jonson's followers, who climb near to Campion's heights:

Drink to me, only, with thine eyes,
    And I will pledge with mine;
Or leave a kiss but in the cup,
    And I'll not look for wine.
The thirst, that from the soul doth rise,
    Doth ask a drink divine:
But might I of Jove's Nectar sup,
    I would not change for thine.
I sent thee late a rosy wreath,
    Not so much honouring thee,
As giving it a hope, that there
    It could not withered be.
But thou thereon did'st only breathe,
    And sent'st it back to me;
Since when it grows, and smells, I swear,
    Not of itself, but thee.

He can set himself on a par with the satirists of the generations that fol-lowed his own, with a greater fluidity in his use of the couplet:

At court I met it, in clothes brave enough,
    To be a courtier; and looks grave enough,
To seem a statesman: as I near it came,

It made me a great face, I ask'd its name,
A lord, it cried, buried in flesh, and blood,
    And such from whom let no man hope least good,
For I will do none: and as little ill,
    For I will dare none. Good Lord, walk dead still.

Or he writes 'On English Monsieur':

Would you believe, when you this Monsieur see,
    That his whole body should speak French, not he?
That so much scarf of France, and hat, and feather,
    And shoe, and tie, and garter should come hither,
And land on one, whose face durst never be
    Toward the sea, farther then half-way tree?
That he, untravell'd, should be French so much,
    As French-men in his company, should seem Dutch?
Or had his father, when he did him get,
    The French disease, with which he labours yet?
Or hung some monsieur's picture on the wall,
    By which his dam conceiv'd him clothes and all? ...

The common elements in these poems and the epistles, elegies and plays, are balance, construction and proportion (except in flattery). Even at his most intemperate, his art brings disparate elements into tight control. The fireworks hang suspended in the air, a promise, a pleasure even at their harshest.

And since our dainty age
    Cannot endure reproof,
    Make not thyself a Page,
To that strumpet the Stage,
    But sing high and aloof
Safe from the wolf's black jaw, and the dull
    Ass's hoof.

His epitaph in Westminster Abbey reads: 'O RARE BENN JOHNSON'. Cutting the stone, Aubrey tells us, cost 18d. paid by Jack Young, later Sir Jack. He also tells us that the living poet had a certain peculiarity of face: 'Ben Jonson had one eie lower than t'other, and bigger, like Clun the Player; perhaps he begott Clun.' If there is dirt to be dished, and even if there isn't, we can trust Aubrey to do it.

Jonson suffers one irremediable disability: Shakespeare. Alexander Pope underlines the point in his *Preface to the Works of Shakespeare* (1725):

'It is ever the nature of parties to be in extremes; and nothing is so proba-
ble, as that because Ben Jonson had much the more learning, it was said
on the one hand that Shakespeare had none at all; and because
Shakespeare had much the most wit and fancy, it was retorted on the
other, that Jonson wanted both. Because Shakespeare borrowed nothing,
it was said that Ben Jonson borrowed everything.' In the plays the proxim-
ity of Shakespeare does Jonson most harm, though he writes plays so different from his friend's that they seem distinct in kind and period. Part of
that difference is Jonson's poetic balance, deliberate artistry: he knows
what he wants to say and has the means of saying it, no more or less. He
reaches a conclusion and stops: no discovery leads him beyond his destination. He speaks for his age, while Shakespeare speaks for himself.
Jonson's art is normative, Shakespeare's radical and exploratory. In
Jonson there is structure and gauged variegation, in Shakespeare movement and warmth. Coleridge disliked the 'rankness' of Jonson's realism
and found there no 'goodness of heart'. He condemned the 'absurd rant
and ventriloquism' in the tragedy *Sejanus*, staged by Shakespeare's
company at the Globe. At times Jonson's words, unlike Shakespeare's,
tend to separate out and stand single, rather than coalesce, as though he
had attended to each individual word. His mind is busy near the surface.
He is thirsty at the lip, not in the throat.

All this is true, but it is not the whole truth. Jonson's attitude to the
very sound of language can seem casual. Except in songs from the plays
('Queen, and huntress, chaste and fair', for instance) and the lyrics that
rival Campion's, he chooses words first for their sense and accent, second
for their sound value: *meaning* is what he is about: not nuance but sense.
So there are clumps of consonants and a sometimes indiscriminate collo-
cation of vowels. Swinburne called him 'one of the singers who could not
sing'. Dryden pilloried him as 'not only a professed imitator of Horace,
but a learned plagiary of all others; you track him everywhere in their
snow.' It is the kind of poetry Jonson writes that irritates his critics: they
disapprove of what he is *doing*. When he isn't singing, he speaks, an art
Swinburne never learned. If his poetry is 'of the surface', he has made his
surfaces with a special kind of care, and to effect. If he borrowed from
classical literature, he was no different from his contemporaries, except
that he had a deeper knowledge of what he was quarrying than many did
(he did not always acknowledge a debt). He translated Horace's *Ars
Poetica*. Many poets borrow lines but Jonson integrates them into his
verse. He is of a stature with Martial and Juvenal: collaboration, not pla-
giarism, is the term for what he does. Eliot concedes that Jonson and
Chapman 'incorporated their erudition into their sensibility'. So, too, did
Eliot.

Dryden's criticism is telling at one point: Jonson 'weaved' the language 'too closely and laboriously' and he 'did a little too much Romanise our tongue, leaving the words he translated almost as much Latin as he found them'. Dryden ends with the inevitable verdict: 'I admire him, but I love Shakespeare.' Yet Jonson, not Shakespeare, paves the way to Dryden and Pope.

Shakespeare – who, as Pope insists, 'lived on amicable terms' with Jonson, and 'was introduced upon the stage,' and encouraged by him – does not overshadow Jonson's non-dramatic verse, which stands as a model to two generations of writers and includes poems so distinctively his own in kind that we could confuse them with the work of no one else. Most notable among these are the 'country house' poems, elegies and epigrams. A line begins in earnest with him (and with Emilia Lanier's 'The Description of Cookeham'), is practised by Ben's sons Carew and Herrick, by Edmund Waller and most memorably by Marvell, and is still practised in the era of Dryden, Anne Finch and Alexander Pope.

In Classical times an 'epigram' was the inscription on a tombstone, usually in elegiac verse. But like the term 'elegy' itself, 'epigram' outgrew its original sense. For Jonson it named the short and not so short occasional poem with a single mood or idea: satirical, amatory, dedicatory or elegiac. He and the 'Sons of Ben' developed it to high perfection. His long poems tend to 'epigram' in the newer sense of 'pithy brief statement': couplets and other passages detach themselves and catch like burrs in the mind.

If not a consistent master of mere 'music' in verse, Jonson is a master of stress. His poems are regular, with the authority of speech, even in his most intricate forms, an intricacy at times of alternation between a constant and a variable line length, as in 'Her Triumph':

> Have you seen but a bright lilly grow,
>   Before rude hands have touched it?
> Ha' you marked but the fall o' the snow
>   Before the soil hath smutched it?
> Ha' you felt the wool o' the beaver?
>   Or swan's down ever?
> Or have smelt o' the bud o' the briar?
>   Or the nard in the fire?
> Or have tasted the bag of the bee?
> O so white! O so soft! O so sweet is she!

These lines spoke to Ezra Pound: the more we read Jonson the more we see him as an enabling figure comparable to Pound. Clarity of expression is matched by intellectual and perceptual rigour. His aesthetic is expressed in an aphorism: 'Language most shows a man. Speak that I may see thee.'

In the poems we hear and see the man. He addresses a variety of subjects with equal variety of feeling. He does not save poetry for moments of crisis or climax; it is a natural language that answers any occasion. Edmund Bolton, writing in his *Hypercritica* in 1722, comments, 'I never tasted English more to my liking, nor more smart, and put to the height of use in poetry, than in the vital, judicious, and most practicable language of Benjamin Jonson's poems.' Smart, vital, judicious, practicable: Jonson wrote with feeling, tempered thought and wit. His was a language close to speech: comprehensive and colloquial.

His ability to catch the tone of each situation, class and calling, was due in part to his background. He was born in London in 1572, probably a month after his father's death. His mother married again, a bricklayer, and he spent his boyhood working with his stepfather, Aubrey tells us, 'particularly on the Garden-wall of Lincoln's Inne next to Chancery Lane' where a passing nobleman, hearing him reciting Greek as he worked and discovering his wit, had him given an Exhibition to Trinity College, Cambridge. This pretty story may be untrue; but we know he was educated at Westminster School under William Camden ('Camden, most reverend head, to whom I owe / All that I am in arts, all that I know ... '). Like Marlowe and Shakespeare he was the new kind of writer, from the new classes. In 1588 he left school and began bricklaying, a fact which his enemies later used against him. After military service in Flanders, he married in 1594. Two children were born, both died and were lamented in elegies: 'Here lies to each her parents ruth' (211), and the harrowing, resigned 'On My First Son', Benjamin:

> Farewell, thou child of my right hand, and joy;
> My sin was too much hope of thee, loved boy.
> Seven years thou wert lent to me, and I thee pay,
> Exacted by thy fate, on the just day.
> O, could I lose all father, now. For why?
> Will man lament the state he should envy?
> To have so soon 'scaped world's, and flesh's rage,
> And, if no other misery, yet age?
> Rest in soft peace, and, asked, say here doth lie
> Ben Jonson his best piece of poetry.
> For whose sake henceforth all his vows be such,
> As what he loves may never like too much. (212)

In 1597 he was acting and writing for the Admiral's Company of Players. His first work for the stage may have been additional scenes for Kyd's *Spanish Tragedy*. In that year he was imprisoned for his part in *The Isle of Dogs*, a seditious play of which he was probably part author. During his spell in prison he became a Roman Catholic, a faith he held for twelve years. In 1598 he killed a fellow actor with a rapier and narrowly escaped hanging. (Aubrey reports with wild implausibility that he killed Marlowe, 'the poet, on Bunhill, comeing from the Green-curtain play-house' – 'a kind of Nursery or obscure Play-house'.) He was branded on the thumb. *Every Man in His Humour*, in which Shakespeare played a part, was staged at the Globe in 1598. Jonson made progress as a playwright and was soon established as a leading tragic and comic dramatist. He was a heavy drinker. 'Canarie was his beloved liquor', Aubrey assures us. He would carouse, go home to bed, and after a good sweat get up to study: 'I have seen his studyeing chaire, which was of strawe, such as olde woemen used ... '

In 1612–13 he completed the first book of *Epigrams*. The next year he travelled abroad with Ralegh's son and wrote a fine commendatory poem for Ralegh's *History*. In 1616, the year of Shakespeare's death, Jonson's 'First Folio' was published – the only first folio to be seen through the press by its author. It was a crucial book, its success paving the way for Shakespeare's First Folio seven years later, in which Jonson had a financial stake and for which he composed his famous elegy 'To the Memory of my Beloved, the Author, Mr William Shakespeare: and what he hath left us', one of the most eloquent blurbs ever written.

After 1616 begin what Dryden calls Jonson's 'dotages', a string of unsuccessful plays. But Jonson was far from doddery. He made his legendary journey on foot to Scotland to visit William Drummond of Hawthornden, with whom he stayed for three weeks until Drummond's wine-cellar was drunk dry. Drummond gave an account of his conversations with Jonson and, since he as a *poeta doctus* was vain of his achievements, took pleasure in commenting on Jonson's ignorance. In effect, he says that Jonson had little French and less Italian. Certainly Jonson was not in the contemporary European swim. He took his bearings from the Classics.

In later years he may have been a deputy professor of rhetoric at Gresham College, London. Such an appointment would explain the pedagogic relations he had with the 'Sons of Ben'. He earned respect as a technical master, as Pound was to do. He was venerated by younger poets, those who knew him and those who knew only his work, notably Herrick, Carew, Lovelace and Suckling: the Cavaliers. Jonson was and perhaps still is *the* poet to emulate: he serves the language, he does not inscribe it with his 'own character' or weave it in accordance with personal myth. The most classical of poets, he nourished himself on the Classics and imparted classical virtues. His 'school', 'tribe' and 'sons' affirm something as salutary as it is strange to our age in which poets are required to have 'a voice'. He and his followers were masters of an art, with meanings to convey. In their art is an element little valued now: self-effacement before the rigours of form and the challenge of subject. They do not lack 'subjectivity', yet what interests us is not subjectivity, eccentricity or individuality, but their centredness, a sense of sanctioned authority, the legitimacy of the Classics.

Rejecting the false, fatuous excesses of the stage in its decline, Jonson says in 'Ode to Himself' (218):

> Leave things so prostitute,
>   And take the Alcaic lute;
> Or thine own Horace, or Anacreon's lyre;
>   Warm thee by Pindar's fire:
> And though thy nerves be shrunk, and blood be cold,
>   Ere years have made thee old,
>   Strike that disdainful heat
>   Throughout, to their defeat:
> As curious fools, and envious of thy strain,
> May blushing swear, no palsy's in thy brain.

The poem ends conventionally, flattering the King, but before that (how reluctant we are to accept praise of kings, though we admire the cult of Elizabeth) he ventures successfully as near to the complexity and purity of Pindarics as any English poet could do. He received an MA from Christ Church, Oxford, in 1619.

He worked like Campion in the ephemeral mode of masques and drew images from masque conventions, for instance in the elegies that end in staged apotheoses. He collaborated with the architect and designer Inigo Jones, but as Jones grew more self-important, they fell out. Jonson resented the superior success of friends and juniors, and they rounded on him. Jones certainly did, and Jonson's satires on his one-time friend are brutal and distasteful. His later years, in which he suffered from palsy and paralysis, were especially bitter. He was neglected by King Charles upon his accession (James had paid him attention). Six petitions of debt were filed against him. Charles eventually realised his value and the poet found new aristocratic patronage. He did not die, as Chapman did, in want. He was buried in 1637 in Westminster Abbey, with Chaucer and Spenser his only peers in that poetic afterworld.

Two modern poets, Yvor Winters and Thom Gunn, insist that Jonson is the man from whom we learn most not only about his age, but about our art. Winters places Jonson at the heart of what he calls the 'native tradition', heard in the plain-spoken poems of Wyatt, Gascoigne, Greville and others. From Marlowe he learned that the best verse integrates images rather than using them decoratively. He could control rhetoric for complex tone. Expository rather than persuasive, he has, Winters says, a *specific* morality, and the poems apply it to a social world: relations between people and between people and God.

Gunn suggests that Jonson chose classical models to balance a personal tendency towards extremes – a credible reading, given what we know of Jonson's life and what we sense in the controlled vehemence of the satires, as in the dark world of the comedies. Gunn senses a problem of 'willed feeling' which modern readers dislike, especially in poems of flattery that protest they are not flattering. Those to King James, King Charles and noblemen of various stations are fulsome and repetitive – for instance, 'How, best of Kings, do'st thou a sceptre bear!' (Rochester found a distinctly disrespectful way of depicting that sceptre.) Jonson's flattery only works when it is indirect, as in 'To Penshurst' (214) and 'To Sir Robert Wroth' (215), where he praises patrons by celebrating their estates and style of life. The sincere tributes to Camden, Shakespeare, Donne, Drayton and others, are in a different league of seriousness.

All poetry, Gunn reminds us, is occasional, and a good poem remains true to its occasion, its subject. It can be the death of a prince or a boy actor ('Weep with me all ye that read'); it can be a moment of anger at social affectation; a thank-you letter or an impulse to translate a classical poem ('Drink to me only', 'Come, my Celia', 'Follow a shadow'). It can be a large-scale social indictment ('On the Famous Voyage'), the publication of a book, a sickness, or a journey. It can be a weekend at a country house. Such poems are 'works of a diverse nature', united by a sensibility to some extent typical of the best of its age. The religious verse has its occasions, too: 'A Hymn to God the Father' (217) is utterly chaste and precise:

> Who more can crave
>   Than thou hast done:
>   That gav'st a Son
> To free a slave?
>   First made of nought;
>   Withal since bought.

Only in the love poetry does Jonson descend to the commonplace, but even there with a command which makes the verse readable. Aubrey reports: ''Twas an ingeniose remarque of my Lady Hoskins, that B.J. never writes of Love, or if he does, does it not naturally.' Best are the elegies in which an old man addresses a young mistress:

> Alas, I ha' lost my heat, my blood, my prime,
> Winter is come a quarter ere his time,
> My health will leave me; and when you depart,
> How shall I do, sweet mistress, for my heart?

In the elegy 'Let me be what I am' there is less resignation. We see one face of the speaker in such work. The poems that moralise give a certain solidity to their moral categories by their setting. They take off from a specific point. In 'To John Donne' he writes:

> ... Those that for claps do write
> Let pui'ness',° porters', players' praise delight,   *novices*
> And, till they burst, their backs, like asses, load:
> A man should seek great glory, and not broad.

In another poem, 'He that departs with his own honesty / For vulgar praise, doth it too dearly buy.'

Jonson is a moral critic of writing and of society. Even personal poems, the elegies for his children, the 'Execration upon Vulcan' (after a fire destroyed his manuscripts and library), the 'Ode to Himself', have general point and reference, they do not exist for themselves. Poetry is occasional and *applied* writing. Development in Jonson is moral, not formal; we follow from poem to poem a mind which sometimes runs deep. The work should be read *in extenso*, taking the *Epigrams*, *The Forest*, *The Underwood* and *Miscellany* whole, prose aphorisms along with verse. The best poems have a tone of just approval or censure, this justice a product of formal control, balance and conclusion, and of an equitable wisdom. It is important to remember that poetry feigns; the tone and texture can say one thing while the poet is keen for us to infer something else. 'Rare poems ask rare friends', 'A good poet's made, as well as born', 'In small proportions, we just beauties see; / And in short measures, life may perfect be'. Pithy rightness is his hallmark. He is our greatest epigrammatist.

'To Penshurst' (214) and 'To Sir Robert Wroth' (215) are original in ways we have to remind ourselves how to appreciate. Notions of 'landscape' took shape rather late. Among the first painted landscapes were Inigo Jones's idealised scenarios for Jonson's masques. 'Such are the distinguished beginnings of the kind of painting in which Englishmen have excelled.' Such too were the beginnings of a literary tradition which takes pastoral convention into the actual countryside and finds in the harmony between nature and nurture a civilising theme. The 'country house' poems are occasional, responding to external events. 'To Penshurst' in pentameter couplets and 'To Sir Robert Wroth', in pentameter/tetrameter couplets, progress with tidy conclusiveness, each detail moralised and added to the tally, developing broader themes of order, proportion, and natural hierarchy. 'To Penshurst' is the finest 'country house' poem, celebrating a place associated with Sir Philip Sidney. Jonson first praises its lack of affectation and deliberate grandeur, and its healthy naturalness. In classical terms he evokes the park and generalises its qualities by subtle use of the definite article and the possessive pronoun with collective and plural nouns, much in the manner that Pope was to perfect:

> The lower land, that to the river bends,
> Thy sheep, thy bullocks, kine, and calves do feed:
> The middle grounds thy mares, and horses breed.
> Each bank doth yield thee coneys; and the tops,
> Fertile of wood, Ashore, and Sidney's copse,
> To crown thy open table, doth provide
> The purpled pheasant, with the speckled side:
> The painted partridge lies in every field
> And, for thy mess, is willing to be killed.   (214)

This is more alive than Pope's 'Windsor Forest' because the *kind* of pastoral language is new. The past participles 'painted' and 'purpled' suggest the hand of nurture. The word 'open' unostentatiously marks the host's hospitality as much as nature's. Jonson presents less an artificial than a cultivated and compliant landscape, a refiguring of Eden. It is a distinction worth bearing in mind. It is Pope, in 'Windsor Forest', who artificialises. 'To Penshurst' celebrates responsible hierarchy, natural proportion: it is praise justly and gratefully rendered, not flattery. In the end the order of such a place is Edenic, a fact the poet allows us to infer: 'To Penshurst' may be Jonson's greatest religious poem.

'To Sir Robert Wroth' with its diminishing couplets sounds a similar note of just praise. Sir Robert is the natural squire, hunter and farmer, with fields, livestock and fruit-trees. The natural cycle is contained in the simple couplet: 'The trees cut out in log; and those boughs made / A fire now, that lent a shade!' Jonson evokes a golden age, cultivating landscape with classical tools, avoiding pastoral idealisation. 'Strive, Wroth, to live long innocent,' he urges. Others can be soldiers, merchants, usurers profiting from their victims' distress, or sycophantic courtiers. Wroth leads a life of service: he serves God, his country and his neighbours. And he earns the friendship, gratitude and service of one of the great poets of his age.

It is worth remembering that from Jonson he also earned a degree of obloquy. Wroth's wife was Lady Mary, Sidney's grandniece (or granddaughter, if we credit Aubrey), a poet of merit 'unworthily married to a jealous husband' (the words are Jonson's, and Jonson, who did not like sonnets, liked hers) to whom she dedicated *A Treatise on Madde Dogges*. She wrote the first English sonnet sequence by a woman ('Pamphilia to Amphilanthus') and built on her great-uncle's prose romance one of her own, scandalously publishing it under her own name. Wroth died in 1614 leaving her with a baby and numerous debts, and she fell into a relationship with her cousin William Herbert, Earl of Pembroke, bearing him two bastards. Jonson's praise of her husband in his great poem, qualified by dispraise in his prose, underlines a paradox at the heart of his enterprise. He is a poet not quite in the Court and thus not secure in patronage, though not yet wedded to Grub Street, its disciplines and treacheries. The world of such a man is unstable, and part of his greatness is to have survived in it and to have made it survive in his verse.

Jonson makes us guests at great houses and lets us hear the age's mannerly speech and savour its hospitality. We hear his songs, too; and we meet, through his eyes, friends and foes as real as any in poetry. We also smell the poorer neighbourhoods and hear their musty clatter. He was among the first great poets to take an active interest in publishing, to seek fortune and solace from the printing of his work in book form. He is the grandfather, or godfather, of Grub Street.

'THE WORLD'S A BUBBLE'

In Donne's best work we 'find again' a real author saying something he means and not simply 'hunting for sentiments that will fit his vocabulary'.

Ezra Pound, ABC of Reading, *1934*

In 1608 John Donne wrote to Sir Henry Goodyer regretting that he had allowed his *Anniversaries* to be printed: 'The fault that I acknowledge in myself is to have descended to print anything in verse, which, though it have excuse, even in our times, by example of men which one would think should as little have done it as I; yet I confess I wonder how I declined to it, and do not pardon myself.' Not only were the poems ill-received (by Ben Jonson among others); he felt exposed and ridiculous. He had fallen to Grub Street level. Unlike Sidney, he *acquiesced* in publication; no piracy was involved. A contemporary described him: 'Mr John Donne, who leaving Oxford, liv'd at the Inns of Court, not dissolute but very neat; a great Visitor of Ladies, a great Frequenter of Plays, a great Writer of conceited Verses.' Such a summary Donne found displeasing, the more so because anyone might have access to his verses.

In his age privacy and 'nicety' were finding language and an art: the portrait and portrait miniature, like Hilliard's; easel paintings for private appreciation, for sharing in a gallery with select friends, or for secret appreciation – like the composer's chamber-sized ayres, or the courtier's lyrics and elegies, each encoding a specific occasion – are examples. Privacy implied that a picture or poem had meaning only, or only in full, to the recipient, the dedicatee, and those in the know. A great violator of such privilege and privacy was the often inaccurate Aubrey, poison-pen portraitist, whose prurience evokes a century of large and little lives. In Donne's Court years the age of vast allegorical tapestries and historical canvases was giving way to human scale. There were inadequate antecedents for such an art. No wonder that in a poem to Goodyer Donne writes:

Who makes the Past, a pattern for next year,
  Turns no new leaf, but still the same things reads,
Seen things, he sees again, heard things doth hear,
  And makes his life, but like a pair of beads.

The subject is spiritual: the fortifying of the soul. But the religious and secular, soul and body, are so intertwined in Donne, and his thinking and feeling are so of a piece, that what he says of one sphere remains true of another. That is why his religious and devotional poems affect with force even readers who disbelieve or detest the vexed Anglican faith they rise from. C.H. Sisson invokes him in 'A Letter to John Donne':

> I understand you well enough, John Donne
> First, that you were a man of ability
> Eaten by lust and by the love of God ...

Sisson goes on to contrast Donne with modern men of ability:

> That you should have spent your time in the corruption of courts
> As these in that of cities, gives you no place among us:
> Ability is not even the game of a fool
> But the click of a computer operating in a waste
> Your cleverness is dismissed from this suit
> Bring out your genitals and your theology.
>
> What makes you familiar is this dual obsession;
> Lust is not what the rutting stag knows
> It is to take Eve's apple and to lose
> The stag's paradisal look:
> The love of God comes readily
> To those who have most need.

Donne intended to speak to a few, but in the complex clarity of his speaking he engaged, three centuries later, a far wider readership than most of his public-voiced contemporaries.

He allowed his poems to circulate in manuscript among special friends. One of them might copy out a piece for private pleasure, another make a secret record, but the public that knew Donne at Court or later heard his sermons in St Paul's was generally ignorant of his poetry. He, like George Herbert, Andrew Marvell, Henry Vaughan, Richard Crashaw, Thomas Traherne and others, did not welcome the sobriquet 'poet'. Did Doctor Johnson misvalue him and his fellow 'Metaphysicals' because they did not *say* they took themselves seriously as poets? It is not that they insisted on amateur status, only that they did not see writing poems as imparting a status or constituting a recognisable identity. They lived off their wit, but in a wider world.

Struggling with his vocation in 1608, Donne wrote to Goodyer in depression and indecision; at no point did he consider becoming a *writer*:

'...I would fain do something, but that I cannot tell what is no wonder. For to choose is to do. But to be no part of anybody is to be nothing. At most, the greatest persons are but great wens and excrescences, men of wit and delightful conversation but as moles for ornament, except they be so incorporated into the body of the world that they contribute something to the sustentation of the whole.' Here, in the intimacy of a letter, we hear in subtle voice the man who would one day deliver the great 'No man is an Island' sermon. He had yet to act, but he knew he could not contribute – or not sufficiently – to 'the sustentation of the whole' by being a poet. Besides, he had only a limited appetite for reading the stuff: 'His library contained little poetry, and he confessed that he was "no great voyager in other men's works".'

One man whose works he did voyage in was Francis Bacon. Among the papers he kept by him until he died was a copy of Bacon's then famous poem 'The World'.

> The world's a bubble, and the life of man
> > Less than a span,
> In his conception wretched, from the womb,
> > So to the tomb;
> Cursed from the cradle, and brought up to years
> > With cares and fears.
> Who then to frail mortality shall trust,
> But limns on water, or but writes in dust...

The poem led to a debate in 1597 that harked back to the ancient debate preserved in the Classic Greek Anthology: which life is best, the Court, the country or the city? The Church is not offered as an option. Bacon's poem is more than a philosopher's curious reflection. Formally accomplished, it uses metaphor suggestively, enough indeed to have affected the twenty-year-old Donne whose 'Satires' date from around the time 'The World' was circulated among friends, 1592.

Bacon's poem affirms the vanity of life, the fact of death and the need to prepare for it. These were urgent themes for Donne in later years. Nowhere is the Jacobean way of death better illustrated than in Donne's preparations. Most men, even though they might have made suggestions, allowed their survivors to bury them as they thought appropriate. Donne, however, took his death into his own hands. The rehearsals as much as the memorial tell us more about him than we could learn from the rooms he lived in. His single aim was to die and remember death appropriately, leaving an adequate monument to commemorate the spiritual struggle and teach others to consider their fate: a sermon in deeds leading to a sermon in monumental stone. Izaak Walton in his wonderful *Life of Donne* tells the story. 'Dr

Donne sent for a carver to make for him in wood the figure of an urn, giving him directions for the compass and height of it; and to bring with it a board of the just height of his body. These being got, then without delay a choice painter was got to be in readiness to draw his picture, which was taken as followeth. – Several charcoal fires being first made in his large study, he brought with him into that place his winding sheet in his hand, and, having put off all his clothes, had this sheet put on him, and so tied with knots at his head and feet, and his hands so placed, as dead bodies are usually fitted to be shrouded and put into their coffin, or grave. Upon this urn he thus stood with his eyes shut, and with so much of the sheet turned aside as might show his lean, pale and deathlike face.' He kept the picture by his bed 'where it continued, and became his hourly object till his death'. Before he prepared for death, however, he lived life to the full, first outside, and then inside the Church.

Only a little over a decade separates Marlowe's *Elegies* (111–114) and Donne's love poems, yet the differences are startling. Set Marlowe's thirteenth elegy from Book One beside Donne's 'The Sun Rising'. Both are in the same genre and draw on similar conventions. This is Marlowe:

> Now o'er the sea from her old love comes she
> That draws the day from heaven's cold axle-tree.
> Aurora, whither slid'st thou? down again,
> And birds for Memnon yearly shall be slain.
> Now in her tender arms I sweetly bide,
> If ever, now well lies she by my side.
> The air is cold, and sleep is sweetest now,
> And birds send forth shrill notes from every bough:
> Whither runn'st thou, that men and women love not?
> Hold in thy rosy horses that they move not.

Donne, by contrast, must have seemed to his friends rawly impassioned and possessed of new energies:

> Busy old fool, unruly Sun,
> Why dost thou thus,
> Through windows and through curtains call on us?
> Must to thy motions lovers' seasons run?
> Saucy pedantic wretch, go chide
> Late schoolboys, and sour 'prentices,
> Go tell court huntsmen, that the King will ride,
> Call country ants to harvest offices;
> Love, all alike, no season knows, nor clime,
> No hours, days, months, which are the rags of time.   (189)

Between the cadenced couplets of Marlowe and the harsh, spoken lines of Donne there are obvious formal differences and, consequently, stark contrasts. Marlowe's language of convention (no less expressive for its conventionality) has been replaced by an 'unpoetic', dramatic handling of the conventions themselves. The main difference is conceptual. Marlowe's elegy, with the tenderness of lines five to seven, creates with each image a specific scene of love. Donne, by line four, is dealing with generalities. His attention has been distracted from his beloved onto the image of the sun, and thence to the street and the world. We lose sight of the ostensible subject in a poetry of extension, until the third stanza when the poet's mind returns to bed, and his relationship, a microcosm, swells superbly to the proportions of a macrocosm: 'She is all states, and all princes, I, / Nothing else is.' Donne's attitude to the sun changes from rancour to charitable pity. Yet the reader remains enlightened about the relationship which occasions such superb arrogance. Donne's poem has wit, but one is undecided whether it has an actual subject or is simply a pretext for developing poetic conceit.

Robert Graves notes how Donne's opening inspirations wear out after two or three lines, and mere wit propels him forward. There is fitfulness, a counterpoint between imagination and artifice. This is a virtue for a casual reader whose delight is continuously rekindled; but if the poems are re-read, delight diminishes. Graves remarks: 'Donne is adept at keeping the ball in the air, but he deceives us here by changing the ball.'

A juggler who, unperceived, changes the balls as he juggles was bound to appeal to the Modernists. After centuries of relative neglect, Donne found in T.S. Eliot an advocate. But even as he celebrates Donne, Eliot suggests that the work will speak to the first half of the twentieth century more eloquently than to the second. The case – or cases – against Donne and the Metaphysicals are of long standing, and it is worth remembering the terms in which they were made and – Eliot suggests – would be made again.

Jonson, after initial reservations, admired Donne above most of his contemporaries, but added that 'for not keeping number' he deserved hanging. Donne incorporates the energy of speech in his metres and his phrased verse is effective, though we have to agree with Yvor Winters that there are examples 'more of rhythmic violence than subtlety'. He lacks Marvell's metrical agility. 'It was as if, impatient as he was of women, love, fools and God, he was impatient too of the close steps of metre.' His satire consciously roughens the surface and defies scansion. Take a passage from the second satire: having pilloried different kinds of writer he lights on plagiarists:

But he is worst, who (beggarly) doth chaw
Others' wits' fruits, and in his ravenous maw

Rankly digested, doth those things out-spew,
As his own things; and they are his own, 'tis true,
For if one eat my meat, though it be known
The meat was mine, th' excrement is his own:
But these do me no harm, nor they which use
To out-do Dildoes, and out-usure Jews.

In this coarse manner he speaks after Juvenal, harshly departing from metre without quite abandoning the norm. Yet the first half of the second line is very nearly unsayable and the last unspeakable.

Dryden's case against him goes beyond prosody. Even in the amorous poems Donne is, he says, 'metaphysical', he 'perplexes the minds of the fair sex with nice speculations of philosophy, when he should engage their hearts'. For Dryden, he is a great wit, not a great poet. The force of this case is felt by those who, in the brilliance of Donne's word-play, his spinning out of startling analogies and conceits, find at work deliberate intelligence, not imagination: a talent of the surface rather than the depths, for which dalliance with language is more erotic than dalliance with the beloved. He moves us by surprise rather than by truth. Marvell and Herbert deliver a kernel of experience, while Donne might seem to deliver the husk that held it. We're aware of a person delivering the poems in various voices. 'The vividness of the descriptions or declamations in Donne, or Dryden,' says Coleridge, 'is as much and as often derived from the forced fervour of the describer as from the reflections, forms or incidents which constitute their subject and materials. The wheels take fire from the mere rapidity of their motion.' Having hoisted Dryden on the same petard, Coleridge offers an epigram on Donne:

With Donne, whose muse on dromedary trots,
Wreathes iron pokers into true-love knots;
Rhyme's sturdy cripple, fancy's maze and clue,
Wit's forge and fire-blast, meaning's press and screw.

'Self-impassioned': that is Coleridge's verdict and 'Valediction Forbidding Mourning' justifies it. Metaphor and conceit develop by association of idea or semantic nuance, not appropriateness of physical form. The image of the dying man suggests the lovers' separation. Stoically, the poet prays that it be without tempests (tears); tempests suggest sky and moving earth, an image detailed without reference to preceding images. Astronomy follows naturally and is developed until, on the word 'refined', Donne's mind turns to metals and alchemy: gold is the next image. The expansion of hammered gold suggests attachment in separation, and in come the famous compasses. Double meaning or intellectual (but not logical) association lead from stanza to stanza. A powerful pseudo-argument develops, convincing because of the *sense* of logic, and the spell holds for the duration of the poem. As Winters says, the 'rational structure' is used to 'irrational ends'. Donne elaborates and decorates at the expense of theme, sometimes so far that he displaces it altogether.

Doctor Johnson's is the most concise case against Donne. In his *Life of Cowley*, Johnson says that Abraham Cowley specialised in what he calls 'enormous and disgusting hyperboles', a bad habit contracted from Donne. 'Who but Donne,' he asks, 'would have thought a good man was a telescope?' Applying Dryden's term 'metaphysical' to Donne and other poets of his time, he calls them 'men of learning' whose 'whole endeavour' was 'to show their learning'. They wrote verse rather than poetry, 'and very often such verses as stood the trial of the finger better than the ear'. Dryden, Johnson says, ranks below Donne in wit but surpasses him in poetry. For Johnson wit is what is 'at once natural and new', not obvious but 'upon its first production, acknowledged to be just', so we wonder how we ever missed it. In Donne the thought is new, but seldom natural; it is not obvious, but neither is it just.

Yet if we define wit as *discordia concors*, sensed similarity in things dissimilar, then Donne and the Metaphysicals have that – at a certain cost: 'Their courtship is void of fondness, and their lamentation of sorrow.' They are neither sublime nor pathetic, they evince none of 'that comprehension and expanse of thought which at once fills the whole mind'. They replace the sublime with hyperbole, 'combinations of confused magnificence, that not only could not be credited, but could not be imagined'. An example from 'Twickenham Garden' (196):

> Blasted with sighs and surrounded with tears,
>   Hither I come to seek the spring,
>   And at mine eyes and at my ears
> Receive such balms, as else cure every thing.
>   But O, self traitor, I do bring
> The spider love, which transubstantiates all,
>   And can convert Manna to gall;
> And that this place may thoroughly be thought
>   True Paradise, I have the serpent brought.

What have we here? A storm-tossed wandering lover – a self-traitor, an alchemist, a god and an Adam. We have a serpent and a spider. We have various levels of experience and metaphor woven in a resonant, affective, but meaningless stanza – or meaningful only to the exegete, who patiently teases out sacramental themes and recognises the dramatic inversion of religious images in service of carnal passion.

Johnson does not set out to dismiss the Metaphysicals but to characterise them. Herbert and Marvell he overlooks. For Johnson, the best poems are true from any angle of approach, and Donne's are true from only one angle. Each word is restricted by context to a single significance. Joan Bennett makes this into a virtue in her account of Donne, explaining how he impresses words and images into service in a specific way, so that they appear clean of conventional association, without nuance or ambiguity.

Johnson's most telling criticism is that Donne's allusive strategy always points away from the poem's occasion; it does not refer back and concentrate. Readers must bring various bits of information to their reading, where ideally 'every piece ought to contain in itself whatever is necessary to make it intelligible'. Again it is clear why Eliot and the Modernists fell for Donne.

The thematic concerns and radical procedures of Donne's poetry reveal a personality as complex and controversial as the verse itself. Born in London in 1572, he was a city creature. When he had to reside outside London for a time he complained bitterly. He retained in his heart no place for the pastoral. His father was an ironmonger who prospered and died when the poet was four years old. Images of metallurgy and alchemy had a special resonance for him. His mother was the daughter of John Heywood, poet, playwright, and a descendant of Sir Thomas More: it was a Roman Catholic family which, in his great uncle Thomas Heywood, included a Catholic martyr. Two uncles were Jesuit priests. Donne received a Roman Catholic education and was reared a firm recusant. For a decade, from the age of twelve, he studied at Hart Hall, Oxford, with his brother Henry; then both proceeded to the Inns of Court, referred to at the time as the 'third university'. Henry gave refuge to a seminary priest and both brothers were arrested. Henry died of the plague in Newgate Prison before he came to trial. The priest was hanged, taken down and disembowelled before an appreciative crowd.

Though he harboured a dislike for the Jesuits, Donne found the transition to Anglicanism hard. To achieve preferment, he had to abandon a faith which blocked his progress. But the struggle between faith and loyalty on the one hand, and burning ambition on the other, made him a writer who had more in common with the poets of the Continent than with his British contemporaries. As Ford says, 'The greatest of all these great ones have invariably about them a note of otherworldliness: they have seen Hell, they have wrestled with God, they have sounded horrors superhuman and inconceivable.' In Dante, Villon, Isaiah, St Augustine, we find this 'greatest'. And sometimes in Donne. *Amour* is bleached out of him, his very gender changed, by the blast of faith and the hunger and doubts it brought him. Other Metaphysicals are more or less comfortable in conscience and in their material circumstances. Donne was virtually compelled against a recusant conscience to turn Anglican and, in order to put food in his family's mouth, to live a kind of partial truth, to take orders from the King in a church he regarded as in a sense heretical, and to preach sermons on themes and occasions where political interests claimed the right to use him.

Following his heart, he made certain crucial miscalculations. After military service with Essex at Cadiz, and an expedition to the Azores, as well as diplomatic missions, he was secretary to the shrewd and influential Sir Thomas Egerton, Lord Keeper. It was a good job, which gave him insights into the devious workings of court and the state machine. At twenty-nine he fell in love with Anne More, daughter of a rich Surrey landowner whose sister was Egerton's new wife. By the time of their clandestine marriage Donne had composed the *Satires* (1593–8), the majority of the *Elegies* and many of the *Songs and Sonnets*. He had completed *The Progress of the Soul* and had become a Member of Parliament. Egerton drove him out when the marriage was uncovered, and they were never reconciled. For fifteen years Donne struggled to support a growing family. 'John Donne, Anne Donne, Un-done,' he wrote when he was dismissed. And for a long time it seemed he was right.

He was briefly imprisoned. Forced to live off the generosity of friends, he pursued his study of canon and civil law to provide himself with a livelihood. His depressions were acute: he contemplated suicide. He wrote *Biathanatos*, a partial justification of suicide, in 1606. In that year he removed with his growing family to Mitcham, where living was cheaper than in London, retaining for himself lodgings in the Strand. He made a number of valuable friends, among them Mrs Magdalen Herbert, mother of the poet George and of Lord Herbert of Cherbury; the Countess of Pembroke; and the Countess of Huntingdon. Several of them received tributes of verse.

By 1609, drawn by Dean Thomas Morton's anti-Jesuit pamphleteering, he contributed to the debate his *Pseudo-Martyr*, an incitement to papists to take the oath of loyalty to the Crown. This and other pamphlets attracted the King's attention. In the next two years the King urged him – some say, ordered him – against his secular ambition into the Church. During the period of his resistance to the King he wrote the *Holy Sonnets* (1609–11) (**199–206**), an expression of faith and of his doubt of vocation. He continued to resist through 1614, when he was able briefly to return to Parliament. In 1615, after a final attempt at secular preferment, he took orders and completed his *Epicede and Obsequies*, probably begun in 1601. They are Donne at his most fantastic and 'public'. The bulk of his religious verse was by then completed as well.

Having taken orders, he was made a royal chaplain, preaching to King and court, and his talent for sermons was such that some are still read today. He dealt too with diplomatic correspondence (a form of secular work more to his taste). He travelled. In 1617 at Paul's Cross, outside the old St Paul's which was destroyed in the Great Fire of 1666 and replaced by Wren's defiant thimble, he ascended to the outdoor pulpit to deliver a Sunday forenoon sermon, the commendatory sermon on the anniversary of the death of Queen Elizabeth (who had reigned for the first thirty-two, largely recusant, years of his life). His audience that day included Sir Francis Bacon (the Lord Keeper), the Earls of Arundel and Southampton, the Archbishop of Canterbury, and a throng of Londoners, from merchants to tramps, and from great ladies to whores. He was a catch for the English Church. Four years later he was appointed Dean of St Paul's. Between 1619 and 1623 he wrote his three *Hymns*, almost the last of his verse; and in 1623, as a result of serious illness (he expected death), he composed the *Devotions*. But he survived another eight years. In 1630 he began to weaken and in 1631 he preached the sermon he knew would be his last, now entitled 'Death's Duel', and died in just the way he had rehearsed.

During his life, his verse circulated – it is impossible to determine how widely – in manuscript. Two years after his death the poems were published. The publisher may have felt a slight indecency in handling the work: 'So difficult and opaque it is, I am not certain what it is I print.' But the book sold rather well, running through six editions before 1670. Here the Dean – celebrity, monster of eloquence, performer, eccentric – is discovered as a man with a body that felt lust, pain and love, and a mind whose attunement to circumstance was not always easy. The American poet Allen Tate has the effrontery to speak of him as 'a contemporary', perhaps because of his lusts and religious uncertainties, and proceeds to misread him in his light. With Donne, if one misunderstands the man one misreads the poems. T.S. Eliot wanted to draw him back into the mainstream of English verse and his attempt involved a little critical distortion. But Eliot did not misread the man. Donne's scepticism is unlike our own. His religious struggle was due to an uncertainty about the terms, not the fundamentals, of faith. His problem was not in believing, but in believing rightly, and having accepted right belief, to behave accordingly. We do Donne no justice by loading on him our doubts; nor does he (as Herbert does) offer us help with the kinds of doubt that beset us. His struggle in the secular poems was to determine and resist the finitude of man's nature; in the religious poems it was to establish finite man's relations with an infinite God manifested in the Incarnation and celebrated in the Mass.

The poems seem logical but work by association. Mario Praz reflects on the baroque quality of the verse. Donne's 'sole preoccupation is with the whole effect': not so much a quest for truth as for effectiveness. The poems *enact*, rather than argue or explore. Imagery is imported into rather than implicit in the situation. Analogies with modern techniques can be drawn, but poets who claim kinship with him do not pursue his formal ends or share the philosophical and theological verities that underpin his work. 'A thought to Donne was an experience; it modified his sensibility,' wrote Eliot. True, but Donne had a consistent sensibility secured by a consistent faith which provided him with an *identity*, however tormented. The difference between his sensibility and those of modern poets who learn from him (Eliot and Edgell Rickword excepted) is the difference between a poet turning an idea into poetry and a poet ruminating poetically on an idea. Donne's poems generate ideas. They are concentrated, dramatic and realised.

He is inevitably the dramatic centre of his poems, as actor or acted upon. He detaches himself from experience in order to set that self in the dramatic frame. Even in the religious poems he presents a self struggling. But at times we doubt the actual – if not the dramatic – intensity of the struggle. Rickword calls it Donne's 'intense preoccupation with the individual at the extreme tension of consciousness'; we might regard it, less charitably, as a form of posturing. Technique favours the ungenerous reading, given Donne's unwillingness to focus long on an actual subject. His wit hops off at a tangent, he cannot resist a grandiloquent phrase or its suggestions, peripheral drama or sub-plot. Often the tangents are memorable.

It is worth making the case against Donne because his actual achievement has been obscured by those who praise his eccentricities, paint him as a contemporary, and deprive him of his authority as a rich, even an alien, *other*. Donne, lover and divine, apprehends ambivalence in himself and fastens it to objects outside himself, keeping his love but forfeiting the object of his love until he finds the greater object, and in it finds self doubt.

In the physical world he experiences now ecstasy, now disgust; the ecstasy is as intense as the disgust. A love of timeless pleasure in one poem becomes in another a bitterness at the ephemeral nature of all attachments. On the spiritual plane he knows both exalted joy and a deep sense of unworthiness. Idealism is checked by realism and spiritual pessimism. The city, love affairs, longing for secular preferment and later for religious grace produce a profoundly ambiguous poetry. Such perplexity occasions that 'forcing of congruities' which is responsible for the best and worst in his work. Where the Augustan solves the perplexity in one way and the Romantic in another, Donne, like Crashaw, Vaughan and Herbert, leaves it unresolved, laying it with a reluctant trust on the altar of a living faith. He wrestles with idea and reality at once, and cannot lie in a single rapture in bed with his beloved the way that Marlowe can in his 'Elegy'.

Songs and Sonnets and *Divine Poems* contrast principally in dramatic form. The persistent wooer becomes the penitent object of divine wooing. As a lover Donne can be passionate and sometimes cruel, but he is seldom tender. In 'The Jeat Ring' he writes, 'Circle this finger top, which didst her thomb', revealing how small her hand is in relation to his own, and exposing an imbalance of power in the relationship. In the *Divine Poems* the tables are turned; he experiences such treatment from God. He is amazed that God should look his way, is 'drawn to God by the mystery of his condescension' in the Incarnation. In the first of the *Holy Sonnets* he writes,

> Despair behind, and death before doth cast
> Such terror, and my feeble flesh doth waste
> By sin in it, which it towards hell doth weigh ... **(199)**

giving us the sense of a man hemmed in before and behind, and like Faustus weighed downward by his own guilt. God is a magnet drawing him to heaven. As in the love poems, emotion – in this case fear born of a sense of unworthiness – stimulates thought; it is not a drug pleasing to the senses. Emotion accentuates his egotism: there is no broad typicality about his struggle, as about Herbert's. It is too extreme.

This is its dramatic virtue and its poetic bound, but it is a bound he can transcend, as he does in the meditative ninth Elegy, 'The Autumnal', which is so infused with affection and regard that it is rapt, adjusting in a tone of appreciative banter its bizarre elements into a series of aphoristically precise statements. It is also transcended in the best religious sonnets and poems, especially in 'Thou hast made me', 'I am a little world', 'This is my play's last scene' (with the 'I' acquiring a sort of typicality), and in the Hymns. It is found more rarely in the *Songs and Sonnets*. 'Donne's muse ranged through almost every mood save Herbert's and Crashaw's serene belief in the Saviour who saves ... or Marvell's serene, almost cavalier indifference.' Yet who before Donne so weds piety and wit? The witty preacher, 'He punned even with God, and inserted wit among the attributes of divinity.' And he lay prostrate before Him like a bride.

PASTORAL CARE

The bed is ready, and the maze of love
Looks for the treaders; everywhere is wove
Wit and new mystery; read, and
Put in practice, to understand
And know each wile,
Each hieroglyphic of a kiss or smile,
And do it to the full; reach
High in your own conceit, and some way teach
Nature and art one more
Play than they ever knew before.

*Robert Herrick, 'The Epithalamy on
Sir Clipsby Crew and his Lady'*

Donne celebrates his own love, Robert Herrick (222–231) the love of others. His poetic antecedents can be traced to 'rare arch-poet Jonson', but his poems have a complete polish only seldom found in the arch-poet's. He concentrates less on argument than elaboration. Swinburne was hard on Jonson, but he calls Herrick the 'greatest songwriter ever born of English race'. Coming from the deliriously melodious Swinburne, this alerts us to certain verbal qualities: a concentration on sound, even at the expense of sense.

Figurative language, delightful conceit, revived conventions: these are part of Herrick's small, intimate poetic arsenal, developed far from the urban commotion that surrounded Jonson's verse. Even his epigrams seem leisurely. He expects us, after hearing a poem, not to judge or act, but to reflect and savour. His is a generally benign universe, with some of the charm of Marvell's, though only a little of its latent violence and lacking its intellectual qualities. For Herrick, the natural order is rural. He gave up seeking the aristocratic patrons who drew writers such as Marvell into the turbulent politics of the day. History broke in on Herrick's life with the English Civil War, and like other Cavaliers (those loyal to Charles I) he was cut to the quick by the execution of his King, but as a poet he was remote from affairs: pastoral in every sense.

Herrick was born in London in 1591. His father was a goldsmith and banker from Leicestershire, his mother a mercer's daughter. The year after his birth, his father fell out of an attic window and died, leaving a sizeable estate of £5,068 which was initially attached by the Crown because the dead man was presumed a suicide, which meant the estate was forfeit. After an anxious time Juliana, the widow, saved the estate. Robert, his three brothers and two sisters were raised in Hampton, Middlesex, far enough from London for him to enjoy the river eyots, meadows and chalk hills, and Hampton Court with its stately toing and froing.

It is uncertain where he was educated, but he certainly mastered the Latin classics. In 1607 he was apprenticed goldsmith to his rich uncle. After six years he had had enough of his overbearing relation, though his head was filled with the intricacies of his craft and feelings about the fine ladies for whom his handiwork was destined. He went up to St John's College, and later Trinity Hall, Cambridge, to study law and there – despite a continual duel with his uncle to get funds from his inheritance – he secured a BA in 1617 and an MA in 1620. Three years later he was ordained along with his college friend John Weekes, to whom (under the name of Posthumus) he dedicated 'His Age', a long poem grounded in Horace. His formal mastery is nowhere clearer than in the fourth stanza, on his favourite theme of ephemerality. The fifth and sixth lines contain the essential quality of Herrick's art:

> But on we must, and thither tend,
> Where Anchus and rich Tellus blend
>   Their sacred seed;
> Thus has infernal Jove decreed;
>   We must be made,
> Ere long, a song, ere long, a shade.
> Why then, since life to us is short,
> Let's make it full up, by our sport.

The last couplet offers feeble consolation.

There is a biographical blank for a time: probably the young poet lived in London, earned the patronage of Endymion Porter, a friend of the Duke of Buckingham, and joined the Sons of Ben at the Apollo Chamber of the Devil and St Dunstan in Temple Bar. His first (brief) recognition as a poet came in 1625 with verses on the death of James I. He must have started writing earlier, two or three years before he went to Cambridge. He was a perfectionist, a goldsmith even in his verse, and revised, compressed and rendered smooth with great dedication. Some of his epigrams are in poor taste, but few are flawed in execution.

In 1627 Porter secured him a place as chaplain to the Duke of Buckingham during the ill-starred expedition to the Isle of Rhé in the Bay of Biscay to support the French Huguenots. Weekes went with him. The next year the Duke was murdered. Herrick's mother died and he inherited far less than he had hoped. After the treble set-back – loss of patron, parent and expectations – he was given the living of Dean Prior, Devon.

Situated on the road between Exeter and Plymouth, on the edge of Dartmoor, it was a small and manageable parish and in some weathers and some frames of mind it seemed idyllic. The larger landscape finds no place in his poems, but the detail of blossom, river and meadows is there in full. The parishioners were rural folk – small land owners and farm workers, and maybe a handful of weavers – a far cry from the Devil and St Dunstan. He was not in a hurry to become a parish priest: he did not settle there until 1630, maybe reluctantly. He expresses a dislike:

> More discontents I never had
>   Since I was born than here,
> Where I have been and still am sad,
>   In this dull Devonshire.

It may be mere imitation of classical dissatisfaction: he wrote contented poems as well. Notable among them is 'A Country Life: To his Brother', which in form and moral resembles Jonson's 'To Sir Robert Wroth'. The difference is of class. Wroth was an aristocrat, Herrick's brother a less exalted being. Herrick calls him to a life of paternity and good husbandry. 'A Panegyric to Sir Lewis Pemberton' follows Jonson's poem more closely, to good effect.

Herrick was ejected from his living in 1647 by the Parliamentarians. After some years in London, where in 1649 he published his *Hesperides* and *Noble Numbers*, without success for himself or his printer, he was reinstated at the Restoration in 1662 and remained there until his death in 1674. He had his devoted servant Prudence Baldwin and many friends. Most of his surviving poetry – over a thousand poems – was written before 1649.

He was a Cavalier. Loyalists said they liked his book, but few others did. A hundred and fifty years went by before it was reprinted. Abraham Cowley and Edmund Waller found readers, but Herrick, whose work is not unlike theirs in some respects, did not appeal and he was not asked to contribute with other Sons of Ben to the memorial volume of 1638. He may have stopped writing because no one read him. It is possible that a growing fashion for Donne's poems which hindered the reception of the work of Michael Drayton and others, had the effect of making Herrick seem anachronistic.

For Herrick the execution of Charles I ended a natural social order; he never adjusted to the new world. His best poem on the subject, 'The bad season makes the poet sad', speaks through convention with a profound personal conviction:

Dull to myself, and almost dead to these
My many fresh and fragrant mistresses;
Lost to all music now; since every thing
Puts on the semblance here of sorrowing.
Sick is the land to th' heart; and doth endure
More dangerous faintings by her desperate cure.
But if that golden Age would come again,
And Charles here rule, as he before did reign;
If smooth and unperplexed the seasons were,
As when the sweet Maria livéd here:
I should delight to have my curls half drowned
In Tyrian dews, and head with roses crowned;
And once more yet (ere I am laid out dead)
Knock at a star with my exalted head.

The note is Horatian: intense feeling is contained and heightened by technical skill. Herrick does not judge. Perhaps the state was sick, but the 'cure' was 'desperate' and destroyed as much as it cured. Little work survives from the years after the death of the 'brave Prince of Cavaliers'. Herrick, losing his England, lost his voice as well.

Like other Cavaliers, he is an 'agreeable' writer, 'consciously urbane, mature, and civilised' as F.R. Leavis notes. He owed debts to Donne as well as Jonson, but his real masters were the Latin Classics. Leavis overstates the 'close relation to the spoken language' of the Caroline lyric. Herrick's language is remote from the English spoken in his Devonshire parish, or the language of the merchant class from which he came. His is the language of the wits, old fashioned even for the times. It is *clear*, but that is not to say it is close to speech. On the contrary, had it been idiomatic it would have dated as much as the language of Jonson's coarser comedies.

The poems abound in transitive verbs, suggesting movement if not action, and Herrick rejects the Spenserian manner *tout court*. He rejects too the refined Arcadian landscape. Literal experience underlies his pastoral. One might regard it more properly as rural, for nymphs and shepherds are replaced with figures very like his parishioners. It is England and Devon he writes of. At the opening of *Hesperides* he lists his subjects:

I sing of brooks, of blossoms, birds, and bowers:
Of April, May, of June, and July-flowers.
I sing of Maypoles, hock-carts, wassails, wakes,
Of bride-grooms, brides, and of their bridal-cakes.
I write of youth, of love, and have access
By these, to sing of cleanly-wantonness.

Youth, love, and that wonderful phrase 'cleanly-wantonness'; weather, luxuries, ephemerality, myth, fairyland, dreamland, heaven and hell: the 'Argument of his Book' accurately advertises its contents. Generally the poems address a single or imagined hearer. Sometimes he talks with himself, or with 'Prew' (Prudence, his housekeeper). His words emerge from a shared solitude, as though to answer a rural silence. There is no public authority about them. His lived pastoral, enhanced with classical allusion, includes a good deal of practical wisdom and close observation. The earthy influence of Thomas Tusser's verse advice to farmers is felt, but Herrick keeps his hands clean, his prosody under control.

Although he was a clergyman, it is striking that his poetry is almost totally innocent of the Fall. He is classical to such a degree that most of his poems are pagan in attitude. His 'many fresh and fragrant mistresses', pre-eminently Julia, but also Anthea, Perila, Sappho, Electra, Lucia, Corinna, Amarillis and others, are not virginal, are not Dante's Beatrice or Petrarch's Laura. They are courtable girls without metaphysical preten- sion. The poems can be erotically frank and joyful. When he celebrates a wedding, it is to enjoin the couple (notably his dear college friend Sir Clipsby Crew) to enjoy lawful bliss. The bed itself he animates enthusiastically:

> And to your more bewitching, see, the proud
> Plump bed bear up, and swelling like a cloud,
> > Tempting the two too modest; can
> > Ye see it brustle like a swan,
> > > And you be cold
> To meet it, when it woos and seems to fold
> > The arms to hug it? Throw, throw
> Yourselves into the mighty over-flow
> > > Of that white pride, and drown
> > The night, with you, in floods of down.

He urges consummation in those amazing pillows, his theme: *carpe noctem*. Frankness within a refined, conventional style gives it authority. He is seldom solemn, always a wooer or a sad (though not bitter) elegist of happiness. In his 'Farewell' and 'Welcome' to sack he speaks with a whole voice, as if to a wife or mistress.

He suggests, with a few paradoxical adjectives, actual passion or disrup- tion underlying a formal statement. The poems are perfect but celebrate the conscious or unconscious imperfections or relaxations of rule that beguile the heart. 'A sweet disorder in the dress', 'an erring lace', 'bewitch' him more than 'when art / Is too precise in every part' (225). He is delight- ed with the way Julia's petticoat transgresses. A phrase such as 'harmless folly' in 'Corinna Going a Maying' provides a key. Or in 'Upon Julia's Clothes' (226) – his most famous poem – the unstated, underlying image of fish and hook livens a brittle conceit. And in 'To Music', 'the civil wilderness' – a phrase met with elsewhere in his poetry – is one of those illuminating expressions bordering on oxymoron. Some of the elegies – for example the one on the death of Endymion Porter's brother, or his own dying brother – and poems such as 'To Live Merrily, and to Trust to Good Verses' (223), address the dark realm of passion and ephemerality. But usually the bright surface is unclouded. There are hints, sufficient to recommend present pleasure. 'Gather ye rosebuds while ye may', 'Fair daffodils, we weep to see' – such poems are suasive and in no sense morbid.

This generous, pagan poet, living at Dean Prior, with his cure of souls, made little impression on the poetry of the time. He was the last Cavalier, the man in whom the Elizabethan tradition of song-writing reaches – too late – its perfection. In the nineteenth century his verse was revived. In the twentieth, his work and that of other Cavaliers was overshadowed by the Metaphysicals. Herrick is as charming as Marvell, though he lacks his intelligence; technically he is a peer of Donne, though without his scope. He speaks in many tones of a range of human experience. He does not get lost in Arcadia and he is free too of the extremes of attitude, the posturing, which mar much metaphysical verse. He does not display his learning: he uses it. His work is not, in Doctor Johnson's phrase, 'singular' but general in application and normative in effect – it is a 'moral' art, like Jonson's, only gentler, more temperate, more pagan, and as durable.

Herrick made a poem – not a particularly good one – in the shape of a cross. George Herbert gave poems shapes too: one looks like an altar on the page, another is made to resemble Easter wings. This ingenious form of poetic devotion had to be appropriate and decorous. It traced its ancestry to the *technopaegnia* of the Alexandrians, who insisted that shape must be relevant to content. The 'corona' or linked sonnet sequence, the acrostic poem which embedded the name of the Queen, the beloved, or a religious figure (for example Sir John Davies's *Hymns of Astraea*, which build around the acrostic ELISABETHA REGINA), are part of the classically sanctioned spiritual and secular play of poets who give themselves an additional formal challenge, on top of metre and rhyme, to try their skills. Such experiments prefigure the more arbitrary experimentation of Auden in suppressing the use of articles in certain poems, or the OuLiPo writers, or John Ashbery, who in *The Tennis Court Oath* sets himself challenges which baffle, then enhance, sense. Only poets in love with their language and their virtuosity set themselves such tasks.

There are analogies with music, the ways in which composers develop a 'lettered' theme, or restrict themselves to a narrow range of notes and combinations in order to 'say' something. George Herbert, like his brother Lord Herbert of Cherbury, was a musician, and when he was Rector at Bemerton used to walk into Salisbury to make music with friends. In the slight poem 'Church Music' (238) there is a wonderful movement of gratitude, expressed with natural, unforced synaesthesia:

> Sweetest of sweets, I thank you: when displeasure
>   Did through my body wound my mind,
> You took me thence, and in your house of pleasure
>   A dainty lodging me assigned.
>
> Now I in you without a body move,
>   Rising and falling with your wings;
> We both together sweetly live and love,
>   Yet say sometimes, *God help poor Kings*.
>
> Comfort, I'll die; for if you post from me,
>   Sure shall I do so, and much more;
> But if I travel in your company,
>   You know the way to heaven's door.

God help poor Kings. When Charles I awaited execution, he read Herbert's *The Temple* for consolation.

Born in 1593 in Montgomeryshire, Wales, George was the fifth son of Richard Herbert, scion of a distinguished Anglo-Welsh family, and Magdalen, a woman of parts and friend of Donne, who – in her widowhood – dedicated his celebrated 'Autumnal' to her: 'No spring, nor summer beauty hath such grace / As I have seen in one autumnal face…' Richard Herbert died in 1596 leaving ten children. After three years the family removed to Oxford, and two years later to London. From twelve to sixteen, Herbert attended Westminster School. Lancelot Andrewes, then Dean of Westminster, taught there during his first year, introducing the boys to a style of elaborate and trenchant expression. At the age of twelve he was writing satiric Latin verses against the Presbyterian polemicist Andrew Melville. He started his music studies and became proficient, especially (like Campion) as a lutenist.

After a decade of widowhood Magdalen married Sir John Danvers, a man twenty years her junior, in 1609, the year George went up to Trinity College, Cambridge. She continued to influence her son until her death in 1627. To her, when he was sixteen, he wrote from college a New Year letter reproving 'the vanity of those many love-poems, that are daily writ and consecrated to Venus', and lamenting 'that so few are writ, that look towards God and Heaven'. He enclosed two sonnets (quoted by Walton in his moving *Life of Herbert*), one of them good, foreshadowing the Metaphysical aesthetic of 'Jordan (I)' (244), and resolves, 'that my poor abilities in poetry, shall be all, and ever consecrated to God's glory'.

> My God, where is that ancient heat towards Thee
>   Wherewith whole shoals of martyrs once did burn,
> Besides their other flames? Doth Poetry
>   Wear Venus' livery? only serve her turn?
> Why are not sonnets made of Thee, and lays
>   Upon Thine altar burnt? Cannot Thy love
> Heighten a spirit to sound out Thy praise
>   As well as any she? Cannot Thy Dove
> Outstrip their Cupid easily in flight?

Milton is gently prefigured here, as is Herbert's mature verse. His eldest brother, Lord Herbert of Cherbury, poet, diplomat and Platonist, was urbane and worldly; he abandoned religion. George began on a similar path but took a different turning, from secular to divine vocation, particularising his language as he went. He wrote these lines as much to please his mother as God. Yet all his surviving English poems are devotional, despite his early secular ambitions and his reluctance – like Donne's – to enter religious orders.

From this beginning he is a figurative writer: flame (faith), livery (the secular Court), altar, song, dove. These are not counters to decorate an idea. Through development and contrast they extend meaning. Paraphrase cannot displace them. Ornamental metaphor merely glosses meaning which is essentially unpoetic, conceit tends to displace meaning altogether. (For a vivid chain of conceits, one need look no further than Donne's 'Autumnal'.) Herbert's figures – adapting familiar religious matter – *are* the argument, which moves with inherent logic.

In 1613 he took his BA, became a minor fellow of Trinity College and wrote two Latin elegies on the death of that most elegised of men, Prince Henry. Despite delicacy of health, he took his MA and a fellowship in 1615–16. He was required to take orders within seven years, which he failed to do. At this time he was friendly with Donne, who had just taken orders himself.

He took the first step towards a secular career in 1618 when he became Reader (Praelector) in Rhetoric at Cambridge. The next was in 1620 when he was elected Public Orator of the University. His friendships with Bacon (who let him read his works before submitting them for publication and whose *Advancement of Learning* he helped translate into Latin), Donne and Lancelot Andrewes, flourished. Lord Herbert, appointed Ambassador to France in 1619, dedicated his treatise *De Veritate* to George, and to

William Boswell. In 1623–4 he served as MP for Montgomeryshire; a fellow MP was his Cambridge contemporary Nicholas Ferrar, who plays a crucial part in his immortality. In 1624 he was at last ordained deacon. Thus he debarred himself from further secular preferment.

The deaths of friends and patrons – including James I in 1625, Bacon and Andrewes in 1626, and his mother in 1627 (Donne preached her funeral sermon) – and the influence of Donne and Nicholas Ferrar, sobered him. He was installed a canon of Lincoln Cathedral and received the living of Leighton Bromswold in 1626. Many poems of discontent and uncertainty date from this period. In 1628 he resigned his Oratorship. He married (happily) Jane Danvers, a relation of his stepfather's, after a three day courtship and in 1630 received the living of Fugglestone with Bemerton, near Salisbury. In September of that year he was ordained priest at Salisbury Cathedral. Aubrey reports that the Earl of Pembroke 'gave him a Benefice at Bemmarton (between Wilton and Salisbury) a pittifull little chappell of Ease at Foughelston. The old house was very ruinous. Here he built a very handsome howse for the Minister, of Brick, and made a good garden and walkes.' Donne died in 1631 and Herbert's last firm link with London was severed.

His last three years were marked by devotion and unostentatious charity. In 1633 he died of consumption. At Bemerton, Aubrey tells us, 'He lyes in the Chancell, under no large, nor yet very good, marble grave-stone, without an Inscription.' Shortly before his death he sent a manuscript of his poems, *The Temple*, to Ferrar at his religious community of Little Gidding, urging him to publish or burn the book as he saw fit. Ferrar published it, and before the year was out a further edition had appeared.

Ferrar is a key figure. Herbert was his friend and they must have discussed, at Cambridge and later, issues of faith. Ferrar was more assertive than Herbert. At Little Gidding – it is not surprising that T.S. Eliot chose to name the last of his *Four Quartets* after the place – Ferrar maintained among his family a strict devotion to the Book of Common Prayer, to the forms of worship, and especially, in an age when Communion occurred in many parishes at most twice a year, a devotion to the central sacrament of the Anglican Church which was celebrated at least every month (as it now is every Sunday). Prayers voiced aloud, drawn from the prayerbook, and a thorough knowledge of the Psalms were keys of Ferrar's simple discipline. (As Eliot says, 'You are here to kneel / Where prayer has been valid.') It is possible that Herbert, whose poems are, for all their freshness, a tissue of allusion to and expansion on scripture, shared Ferrar's view – his vision – though within a parish, not a specialised community. Both men steered a perilous course between Puritanism and Papism. What Herbert shares with Ferrar is a sense of the joy of faith when grace is present: as Maycock says in his *Chronicles of Little Gidding*, 'It was a note that had not been heard in English devotional writing, a quality that had not been displayed in English religious life, for something like a hundred years.' Ferrar was not attempting to re-establish monasticism: his was a private venture, an attempt to live truly, according to scripture, with his family, and to bear witness through his and through their life. Hebert's approach to his vocation and family, if less rigorously structured, was not unlike Ferrar's.

In his short time at Bemerton Herbert revised poems and composed more than half of *The Temple*. The collection begins with 'The Church Porch', an extended moral and stylistic preparation for what follows.

> Harken unto a Verser, who may chance
> Rhyme thee to good, and make a bait of pleasure.
>   A verse may find him, who a sermon flies,
>   And turn delight into a sacrifice.

The short poems he described as 'a picture of the many spiritual conflicts that have passed betwixt God and my soul'. There is throughout the book a continuity of tone, yet each poem represents a single experience.

His tone and phrasing affected Henry Vaughan. Indeed Vaughan echoes lines and forms, not as an imitator but as one whose poetic and spiritual imagination Herbert helped to constitute. Less directly, Richard Crashaw is Herbert's debtor. Herbert had a number of near contemporary imitators and his book went through several profitable editions. Then, late in the seventeenth century, it went out of fashion. Addison, the most mechanical versifier of his age and a maker of fashion, pilloried him as a 'false wit'. The error of Herbert's early champions – men of faith – was to sell the poet on the strength of his piety, not his poetry (as Wilfred Owen's advocates sold him, taking him at his word, on the strength of his pity, not his poetry). Even Ferrar's advertisement for the first edition attests to this. Herbert's form of piety became unfashionable even before the Enlightenment was in full swing.

Yet piety contributed to his re-emergence. John Wesley, in the eighteenth century, adapted several poems as hymns, adjusting their prosody to suit the form, and published a selection without alteration. It remained for Coleridge, in his *Biographia Literaria*, to revalue Herbert's poetry. In a letter he confessed that at one time he had read Herbert to chuckle over quaint, obscure passages with indecorous diction. The mature Coleridge saw the matter differently: he praises the 'style where the scholar and the poet supplies the material, but the perfect well-bred gentleman the expression and arrangements'. He perceives complex and fantastic thought expressed in a clear, plain language. With this he contrasts those later poets whose elaborate and stylised language conveys trivial thoughts. 'The latter is a riddle of words; the former an enigma of thoughts.'

Edgell Rickword says: 'A writer survives in each generation, otherwise

than as a figure in literary text-books, precisely to the extent that he interests us as a contemporary; one of the qualities of the classics is a perennial
modernity.' This is wrong. A 'Classic' can emerge into different moderni-
ties and be eclipsed between times, as Jonson, Langland, or Blake demonstrate. The same is true of Donne, or Spenser, who are now obscured, and
of George Herbert.

It is in his development of syntax that Herbert resembles Donne.
Otherwise, they have less in common than is normally supposed. Donne
fills the canvas with himself and his drama; Herbert keeps proportion,
retaining in his poems a sense of the context of his experience. A context
can be natural, temporal or spiritual. He looks through or beyond manifest nature towards God. His eye never stops on mere detail. In this way he
is the most *transitive* of the Metaphysical poets, passing from the finite
and particular to the eternal, or recording a longing – or failure – to do so.
He had what Charles Cotton described in 1675 as 'a soul composed of harmonies'. Images are at times far-fetched, but generally suitable. Such qualities – the transitive nature of prayer, the surprising appositeness of image
and diction – appealed to the imprisoned Charles I, and to William
Cowper in his depression. The poems travel to extremes of experience but
are shot through with consolation.

Herbert's spiritual struggle puts our different struggles into form; this
is part of the universality of his poems. Another part is the pleasure they
give, the surprise at each reading of finding not the same poem but something slightly different, as some new semantic nuance takes us into an area
of the verse we had not felt before, or a metrical effect surprises us, or an
image suddenly comes clear. Like Donne, he gives his poems a dramatic
cast. Many begin *in medias res*, addressing, cajoling, lamenting. But he
shies away from Donne's attitudinising. His poetic develops correctly: it is
not Donne's pseudo-logic, but the strict logic of Sidney. A medieval
quality, different from Donne's new scholasticism, survives in the work.
His allusions, his direct use of scripture and traditional imagery, his
natural reversion to parable and allegory, imply that the Anglican devotional poet cannot but return to time-proven processes of spiritual imagination and response. A dependence on scripture takes the brittleness out
of his erudition. He finds his bearings in a common source of wisdom.
The esoteric he introduces either to make it familiar or to debunk it.
Critics can attend too closely to the personal nature of his spiritual struggle, undervaluing the universal and didactic elements of poems spoken
out of faith by a priest, albeit a priest who is not above direct, sermony
didacticism from time to time.

Herbert is a formal genius. Stanza shapes visually corroborate meaning
or process. There are the picture-stanzas, the *technopaegnia*. In a more
subtle sense, in a poem such as 'Mortification' (**249**), the stanza contracts

and expands, a process that depends on syllabic length and indentation and imitates breathing:

> When man grows staid and wise,
> Getting a house and home, where he may move
> Within the circle of his breath,
> Schooling his eyes;
> That dumb enclosure maketh love
> Unto the coffin, that attends his death.

Each stanza enacts an identical rhythmic and visual process, as the baby grows into an old man bound for death. Life in all its ages is a rehearsal for the final verity. The shape is an emblem of mortification and finally of grace. The poem has an appropriate dwelling, an architecture, in this case heightened by the repeated 'breath' and 'death' rhymes in each stanza. 'Denial', 'The Star' and 'Frailty' are among the poems in which form itself is an object of meditation.

In 'Love bade me welcome', as Christopher Ricks points out, we sense an unstated, underlying pun on the word 'host'. It is the structural occasion of the poem: God is the soul's host at the table; he is also the consecrated host of which the sinner partakes at the holy table. Similarly, in 'The Temper (I)' (242), the word 'temper' takes on a complement of meanings, including the tempering of steel.

The colloquial tone of the best poems is sustained by an undecorated diction. 'Jordan (I)' advocates plainness, though in itself it is so complex that it is at odds with its statement. In general Herbert rejects verses that 'burnish, sprout and swell, / Curling with metaphors'. His imagery includes stars, trees, food, wine – each with symbolic value but a firm literal sense. Objects begin as themselves, then cast a shadow beyond themselves, tracing a pattern of grace. Herbert works from small clauses and word-clusters, advancing an idea or emotion by stages, controlling nuance to achieve a consistent metaphorical and literal meaning. 'Prayer (II)' begins:

> Of what an easy quick access,
> My blessed Lord, art thou! How suddenly
> May our requests thine ear invade!

The simple words are simply arranged. Yet 'quick' means 'speedy' and 'vital'; 'access' and 'invade' carry military overtones. These suggestions corroborate literal meaning without distorting or displacing it. 'Thou can'st no more not hear, than thou can'st die.' God is all-powerful, yet constrained by his own nature to be accessible and eternal. The paradox is contained:

> Of what supreme almighty power
> Is thy great arm, which spans the east and west,
>   And tacks the centre to the sphere!

Even at the height of cadence, Herbert contrives to bring divine action to simple comprehensibility by the verb 'tack', which makes solid the vast motion of God. A minimal verb, it magnifies the agent and the action. Often, when he develops a rhetorical description, Herbert magnifies the effect by reducing the terms of action.

He can be as personal as Donne, but we focus less on his voice than on the experience he tells of. 'Affliction (I)' (240) is directly autobiographical but presents a general type, despite allusions to university, illness, incumbency, private frustrations: it is a type for the development of faith. Grief instructs him: 'Grief did tell me roundly, that I lived.' Learning is of little use:

> Now I am here, what thou wilt do with me
>   None of my books will show:
> I read, and sigh, and wish I were a tree,
>   For sure then I should grow
> To fruit or shade: at least some bird would trust
> Her household to me, and I should be just.

The man afflicted longs for purpose, a tree's purpose to give fruit and shade, a tree's foundation, its roots. If he were a tree, he would stand in the same relation to a bird as God stands to him; only (by implication) unlike God he would be just to his tenant. This oblique blasphemy heightens a contrast in the following stanza and highlights the poet's longing for a *sign*, even a negative proof. Colloquial diction builds to a metaphysical paradox suggested by Sidney's love poems, used with an urgency beyond Sidney's scope. Each monosyllable calls for a stress: 'Let me not love thee, if I love thee not.'

> Yet, though thou troublest me, I must be meek;
>   In weakness must be stout.
> Well, I will change the service, and go seek
>   Some other master out.
> Ah my dear God! Though I am clean forgot,
> Let me not love thee, if I love thee not.

When the poet dares to speak in the voice of Christ, it is with reversed affliction: he shows a Christ unable to comprehend the conduct of man, just as man is perplexed by God's conduct, both His grace and His with-holding of it. Herbert's Christ is always in the night garden or on the Cross.

His verbs like Herrick's are usually transitive. A catalogue of verbs in any of the better poems proves him to be a poet of moral action rather than gesture. There is movement even when thought is static. This quality we relish the more when we come up against the assured, elegant verse of Dryden and the brittle century for which his refinements paved the way. The simple drama of Herbert's sonnet 'Redemption' is unequalled in English poetry before or since. A new parable, worthy of the old:

> Having been tenant long to a rich Lord,
> Not thriving, I resolvèd to be bold,
> And make a suit unto him, to afford
> A new small-rented lease, and cancel th' old.
> In heaven at his manor I him sought:
> They told me there, that he was lately gone
> About some land, which he had dearly bought
> Long since on earth, to take possession.
> I straight return'd, and knowing his great birth,
> Sought him accordingly in great resorts;
> In cities, theatres, gardens, parks and courts:
> At length I heard a ragged noise and mirth
> Of thieves and murderers: there I him espied,
> Who straight, *Your suit is granted*, said, and died.

The Temple, or Sacred Poems and Private Ejaculations appeared with Nicholas Ferrar's authority in 1634, *The Country Parson* (1652) and *Jacula Prudentium* followed. Walton says that 20,000 copies of *The Temple* were sold in only a few years.

THE ECCENTRIC

Milton is the worst sort of poison. He is a thorough-going decadent in the worst sense of the term. If he had stopped after writing the short poems one might respect him.

Ezra Pound, 'The Renaissance', Poetry *(Chicago), 1914*

'Milton, with the possible exception of Spenser, is the first eccentric English poet, the first to make a myth out of his personal experience, and to invent a language of his own remote from the spoken word.' Thus wrote W.H. Auden, forgetting Chaucer who 'invents' the language Milton was to use, the self-involved excess of Hoccleve, the wild candour of Skelton stepping across the threshold into modern English, the plain-speaking of Gascoigne, and the erotic and spiritual adventures of Donne. No: Milton is not the first or even the second eccentric poet. It is in the nature of a poetic vocation – if we contrast it with a vocation for verse – to be eccentric, to work at a slight or sheer tangent to prevailing conventions, to invent a language which speaks or sings in ways that 'the spoken word' does not aspire to. The spoken word, in Auden's sense, is generally instrumental, conveying instructions, information, feelings. The words that poems speak may do those things, but they have another dynamic, which is to honour one another, to exist together as a whole entity which, while it has an occasion, *becomes* an occasion, autonomous at once of the events that give rise to it and of the poet who utters it.

Yet Auden's *view* of Milton is not eccentric. Milton was revered through two and a half centuries. Before Eliot and Pound tried to knock the bust off its plinth, only Doctor Johnson had expressed damaging misgivings, and he tempered criticism with grudging respect. Milton became a spiritual and literary duty, a task and test, a measuring stick, and a rod for every poet's back. Shakespeare was also monumentalised, but while he remained engaging, inspiring and inimitable, Milton furrowed the brow of most readers. Landor looked up and saw:

Milton, even Milton, ranked with living men!
Over the highest Alps of mind he marches,
And far below him spring the baseless arches
Of Iris, colouring dimly lake and fen.

The 'fen' recalls Cambridge where Milton, a beautiful youth with long locks, studied. 'His harmonicall and ingeniose Soul,' writes Aubrey, 'did lodge in a beautifull and well-proportioned body. He was a spare man... He had abroun hayre. His complexion exceeding faire – he was so faire they called him *the Lady of Christ's College*. Ovall face. His eie a darke gray.' For Landor, Milton's poetry and prose constitute a huge stone arch, compared with the ephemeral rainbows of other poets. For Wordsworth, in one of his great sonnets, it is Milton the radical who demands attention. There is that fen again:

> Milton! thou should'st be living at this hour:
> England hath need of thee: she is a fen
> Of stagnant waters: altar, sword, and pen,
> Fireside, the heroic wealth of hall and bower,
> Have forfeited their ancient English dower
> Of inward happiness. We are selfish men;
> Oh! raise us up, return to us again;
> And give us manners, virtue, freedom, power.
> Thy soul was like a Star, and dwelt apart;
> Thou had'st a voice whose sound was like the sea:
> Pure as the naked heavens, majestic, free,
> So did'st thou travel on life's common way,
> In cheerful godliness; and yet thy heart
> The lowliest duties on itself did lay.

Yet Wordsworth was one of the few English poets of his time to struggle out from under the burden of Milton and write back into English. Milton leaves his mark less on the diction and more on the syntax and cadence of his verse and the wonderful way he handles line endings.

Though often at loggerheads, Robert Graves and T.S. Eliot agree on one thing. They do not like Milton. Graves dislikes him as a man, and finds in his verse the very faults his life displays. His book *Wife to Mr Milton* is savagely judicious. In an essay he cast aspersions on the moral integrity of this most high-minded of authors, on the Milton Wordsworth invokes. 'By the time he had been made Secretary of State for the Foreign Tongues to the Council of State (a proto-Fascist institution) and incidentally Assistant Press Censor – why is this fact kept out of the text-books when so much stress is laid on the *Areopagitica*? – he had smudged his moral copybook so badly that he had even become a "crony" of Marchmont Needham, the disreputable turncoat journalist.'

This says much about Milton, and about Graves. Eliot is less *ad hominem*, though as an Anglican and latter-day Royalist he cannot have felt comfortable with so vehement a man. 'In Milton the world of Spenser was reconfigured and almost unrecognisable ... What had been reasonable and courteous, a belief in the *fact* that men of culture and intellect will be able to engage in rational discussion and agree to disagree, had been displaced by faction and sometimes violent intolerance. The moderate had stood down and the fanatic had taken his place, in the pulpit, in Parliament, and on the very peaks of Parnassus.' Eliot focuses on the impact of such changes on prosody. During the Elizabethan and Jacobean periods, blank verse was a fully expressive medium; 'After the erection of the Chinese Wall of Milton, blank verse has suffered not only arrest but retrogression.'

The Lady of Christ's College is Protean and no critic has held him satisfactorily for long. If you grapple with his complex language, you lose sight of its place within his elaborate, allusive forms; if you try to characterise his politics, you find the texture of the verse often running against the structure, as though his imagination was correcting what his partisan mind wanted to say. Can we believe even the simple sentiment of the Panglossian lines that close *Samson Agonistes*?

> All is best, though we oft doubt
> What th' unsearchable dispose
> Of Highest Wisdom brings about,
> And ever best found in the close.

Can *he* believe them, or is that possible only within the context of his artifact?

John Milton was born on 9 December 1608, 'half an hour after 6 in the morning', Aubrey says, 'in Bread Street, in London, at the Spread Eagle, which was his [father's] house (he had also in that street another howse, the Rose; and other houses in other places)'. Milton *père* was a well-to-do scrivener and money-lender who had attended Oxford, rebelled against his own father's Roman Catholicism, and been disinherited when an English Bible was found in his chamber. He was, Aubrey says, 'an ingeniose man; delighted in musique; composed many Songs now in print, especially that of *Oriana*'. He died in 1647 and was buried in Cripplegate Church.

He instilled in his son a taste for music and encouraged his ambition to be a writer. If Milton as a boy of nine or ten wanted to read late, his father made sure that a maid sat up with him until midnight and after. According to Aubrey, by the age of ten Milton was already a poet. 'His school-master then was a Puritan, in Essex, who cutt his haire short.' By the time he went to St Paul's School, it had begun to grow back. There he studied under the excellent Alexander Gill. Gill used English verse in his lessons, and Milton may have had his first exposure to Spenser there. He learned Latin, Greek and Hebrew and wrote what are regarded as exemplary Latin verses. In his last year at St Paul's, at fifteen, he wrote a poem with which any church-goer is familiar from the Hymnal, a paraphrase of Psalm 136:

> Let us with a gladsome mind
> Praise the Lord, for he is kind,
>   For his mercies aye endure,
>   Ever faithful, ever sure.

Less successful but still dazzling is his paraphrase of Psalm 114, in couplets, which includes the beguiling lines:

> The high, huge-bellied mountains skip like rams
> Amongst their ewes, the little hills like lambs.

Metaphor here, and later in his work, has a different function from the one we recognise: the awkward juxtaposition of 'huge-bellied' and 'skipped', the strange figuring of the mountains and hills, creates a tension of unlikeness remote from 'all the clouds like sheep / On the mountains of sleep' that Edward Thomas gives us. Milton's imagination incorporates the suggestive Hebrew usage into his largely classical culture. If we deplore mixed metaphor we will find much to cavil at in Milton. For him metaphor is not exclusively, and sometimes not even primarily, visual.

When he went up to Christ's College, Cambridge, in 1625 he found the place disappointing and the curriculum dry and narrow. He craved a broader, more liberal education than was offered. He composed Latin poems in the manner of Ovid and Horace, as well as epigrams, a Latin mock-epic on the Gunpowder Plot, Italian sonnets, more English paraphrases of the Psalms, and the eleven stanzas 'On the Death of a Fair Infant Dying of a Cough'. His Latin elegies are in some ways his most personal utterances, including details of his life and thought not recorded elsewhere. He was at this time as much at home in Latin as in English verse.

'On the Death of an Infant' is a remarkable production for a nineteen-year-old poet. It is Elizabethan in manner and full of conceits which attest to his mastery of convention. It is notable for its finish rather than for its feeling. In the seventh stanza there is a hint of things to come:

> Wert thou some star which from the ruined roof
> Of shaked Olympus by mischance did'st fall;
> Which careful Jove in nature's true behoof

Took up, and in fit place did reinstall?
Or did of late Earth's sons besiege the wall
   Of sheeny heav'n, and thou some goddess fled
Amongst us here below to hide thy nectared head?

Images of falling, rebellion, and the pagan gods are here with the delicacy (marred by archness) of the poet of *Comus*: we see accomplishment awaiting a subject.

After taking his BA in 1629, Milton stayed on at Cambridge. It was the period of his three religious poems, 'On the Morning of Christ's Nativity', the incomplete 'The Passion' and 'Upon the Circumcision'. The Nativity ode is his first important English poem, celebrating the birth as an event without losing sight of its theological and cultural consequences. The central paradox is crucial to all his verse: human child and Son of God. The poet, like one of the Magi, arrives at the manger. Four introductory stanzas are followed by a hymn. He evokes the cold weather, not Mary or Joseph. Nature, humbled and bared before the swaddled infant, almost displaces the Virgin in the poem. Those who expect an imperious Messiah stand in awe before the helpless infant who becomes a focus for the whole natural world. The image of musical harmony acquires force. It is not, however, the Millennium:

But wisest Fate says no,
This must not yet be so;
   The Babe lies yet in smiling infancy,
That on the bitter cross
Must redeem our loss,
   So both himself and us to glorify;
Yet first, to those ychained in sleep,
The wakeful trump of doom must thunder through the deep.

These lines are so powerfully elliptical that the image is of the *babe* crucified. Into a hymn of joy flows the future, the sombre truth that the dragon is not dead. The pagan gods depart, and we lament them: this babe is a swaddled Puritan. In the last stanza babe and Virgin are left together, one asleep, the other watching, protected by angels.

Milton took his MA in 1632. By then his career was well begun. Not only the great sonnet 'On Shakespeare' (1630) but 'L'Allegro' (270) and 'Il Penseroso' (271) had been completed (1631). The latter two, delicate and clear, use the tetrameter couplet with complete assurance and achieve, in prosody and syntax as well as diction, a distinction of *tone* between the voices of the happy and the melancholy man. The thoughtful man lingers in our company (176 lines) longer than the happy man (152). Both poems refer to the same conventionally visualised world, rather as William Blake's 'Innocence' and 'Experience' offer two perspectives upon the same material. Milton evokes distinct temperaments or humours, 'L'Allegro' pastoral, 'Il Penseroso' elegiac. 'Il Penseroso', which displays Milton's passion to know the secrets of the dark and his concern with death, is a little silly. An echo of Chaucer's gentle self-mockery is just audible – an unusual note in Milton. Chaucer is directly referred to in lines 109–120 and echoed in lines 8–9. 'Il Penseroso' is scholastic; meanwhile 'L'Allegro' is less reflective, a renaissance sort of fellow, patronising 'sweetest Shakespeare, Fancy's child', who will 'Warble his native woodnotes wild'. He mentions *en passant* Jonson's 'learned sock'. Milton was young enough to encompass both moods. History had yet to instruct him in the sombre facts of political life, and his religious faith, though firm, was not yet hard.

After Cambridge, he retired for six years to his father's Buckinghamshire estate – having written one of his ambitious and certainly his most respectful and flattering Latin poems to him, 'Ad Patrem' – in order to complete his poetic training. 'I take it to be my portion in this life, joined with a strong propensity of nature, to leave something so written to aftertimes, as they should not willingly let it die.' He prepared himself more systematically than any other English writer has ever done: he wanted to know *all* that a man could know. He wrote three significant works at this time. *Arcades*, a diminutive masque for the Dowager Countess of Derby, was the fruit of his musical interests and brought him into contact with his father's friend the composer Henry Lawes. *Comus* (1634), his great masque, was produced by Lawes. And there is his elegy 'Lycidas'. Other work included a sonnet on the flight of youth ('How soon hath time, the subtle thief of youth' (265)) marking his twenty-fourth birthday, and three poems based on Italian madrigals.

Arcades shows Milton's command of Elizabethan idiom and his skill in addressing an aristocratic audience. Lawes was confident to commission *Comus*, to celebrate the inauguration of the Earl of Bridgewater as Lord President of Wales. It was performed at Ludlow Castle, Shropshire. Milton, it is conjectured, played the part of Comus, a seductive prototype for Satan.

Comus is not dramatic but ceremonial. The theme of chastity brings both elements into play. Here Milton again fuses Platonic and Christian thought. The Lady rejects Comus's very specific advances and is freed into a universal love of the good. The allegory is simple: the Lady, lost in a wild wood, is tested, and in the end is found, and found virtuous. The Earl of Bridgewater's three children were shown off to advantage and received instruction from the masque: on the first night they played the Lady and her two brothers.

A *mélange* of styles is tried in *Comus*, a transitional work, the fruit of retired studies in philosophy, theology and poetry. Little of the contemporary world finds its way in. Some of the writing is richly Elizabethan; some can't but remind us of Dryden. Spenser and Shakespeare are nearby. Matthew Arnold speaks of Milton as being at the 'close' of Elizabethan poetry. If this is so, *Comus* must be the last Elizabethan poem, already an anachronism when performed. It resists the excess of metaphysical wit, yet opens out, beyond that, to the drier regions of the late seventeenth and early eighteenth centuries, when language began to hover above its subject and to regard itself; when, as Arnold puts it, expression took precedence over action.

The character of Comus is a triumph. He not only tempts but embodies the temptation he promotes, a corrupt corrupter who exclaims of her vocal ravishments, when he hears the Lady sing:

> How sweetly did they float upon the wings
> Of silence, through the empty-vaulted night,
> At every fall smoothing the raven down
> Of darkness till it smiled.

The word 'wings' belongs to silence, but prepares the way for 'down'; silence and darkness are smooth-feathered birds. These overlaid images establish expectations of texture and movement which Comus bears out in verbs of flight and in specific phrases: 'the winged air darked with plumes'; 'smooth-haired silk' which 'spinning worms' weave 'in their green workshops'. It is almost the voice of his friend Marvell, only it is *not* a voice; it shrinks away from the coarseness of common speech.

The tone of the poet of *Paradise Lost* is audible too:

> But he that hides a dark soul and foul thoughts
> Benighted walks under the mid-day sun;
> Himself his own dungeon.

These lines belong to the Elder Brother, a priggish character, who echoes (to refute) an earlier speech by Comus. Milton was unsuccessful with protagonists. Christ, God and Samson repel us in different ways; what they represent they do not recommend. His antagonists can be admirable. They are given much of the best verse. Comus and Satan are attractive villains. Blake could claim Milton as 'of the Devil's party' and John Middleton Murry branded him a 'bad man' on these grounds. Robert Burns declared, 'I have bought a pocket Milton, which I carry perpetually about with me, in order to study the sentiments – the dauntless magnanimity, the intrepid, unyielding independence, the desperate daring, the noble defiance of hardship, in that great personage, SATAN.' Milton's unequal skill in moral characterisation is inevitable. Goodness and virtue cannot be particularised without limiting or containing them. Virtues are flimsy, tend towards abstraction when they aspire to be comprehensive. Evil, however, *has* to be particularised. Fallen men fall in different ways. Evil acts in a world of characters we recognise. The devil has the best, because the most diverse and seductive, tunes. A marriage between virtue and character, between pure qualities and mundane objects, is beyond most art, even his. Or is it beyond our comprehension? Is there a modern prejudice which finds the individual invariably more real, more attractive, than the universal?

'Lycidas' (272) was composed for a collection of elegies dedicated to Edward King, a fellow undergraduate of Milton's at Cambridge, who was drowned. King was not intimate with Milton, but the poet knew him as a Latin versifier and a candidate for holy orders. A pastoral-elegiac mode, lamenting a fellow 'shepherd-poet', was appropriate. King's intended vocation, pastoral in another sense, provided a pretext for introducing the religious strain; and the manner of his death, by water, supplied a wealth of classical references suitable to the idiom.

Although there are verbal echoes and borrowed motifs from Spenser's *Shepheardes Calender*, 'Lycidas' is a very different kind of poem. Johnson condemned it for its diction, rhymes and prosody, but he disliked pastoral and found distasteful the introduction of criticism of the Church in such a context. He also comments that 'Where there is leisure for fiction there is little grief.' The grief in the poem is no more or less real than that of other pastoral elegies. The poem is not lament but elegy in a wider sense, like Milton's Latin elegies. King's death provoked in the no-longer-so-young Milton (he was twenty-nine) reflections on his own mortality, his limited achievement, and on the Church for which he himself had been destined. Bitter at the loss of so promising a life, he asks why the just and good should be squandered.

Each element in the poem belongs to a baptised tradition of pastoral elegy. The procession of mourners, the catalogue of flowers, the lament to nature, were off-the-peg. How he combines conventions, what he puts into them, is what matters. They are part of a classically sanctioned frame-work. Something else, specifically Protestant and highly developed, is there too.

We should be surprised that Doctor Johnson was deaf to the kinds of feeling that inform and unify the poem, which moves from apprehension of death, through regret, to passionate questioning, rage, sorrow and acceptance. The poem begins in a minor key but progresses to a larger music, of divine justice and human accountability. The poem's climax is a harsh attack on the clergy: 'shepherds' corrupted by self-interest. Beside this indictment is set the catalogue of flowers, a superb tonal contrast. Lycidas has drowned: there is no hearse on which to place the flowers, so Milton evokes the body afloat in the sea. Beside this emblem of nature's impersonal force he places the affirmation of resurrection. Order returns to the pastoral world ('Tomorrow to fresh woods, and pastures new'). 'Lycidas', more than *Paradise Lost* (273–276), justifies God's ways to man. It has claims to being the finest elegy in the language, though not all readers agree. Graves, for instance, complains that 'the sound of the poem is magnificent; only the sense is deficient.' The sense is deficient only to those who wish to limit the kind of sense poetry can make. Graves cannot forgive Milton for having been the man he was; he cannot forgive the poem for not being lyrical. Most misreadings of 'Lycidas' proceed from a lyric expectation. From a lyric we tend to expect a single, stable perspective on a specific area of experience; we expect integration and singleness of effect. 'Lycidas' is a chain of effects: argument, lament, doubt, celebration. Single passages are 'lyric' but the poem as a whole is in another mode. It is the most complex poem of Milton's youth. It is also the last.

In 1638 he travelled to Italy. He was away from England for fifteen months, recalled only at the outbreak of the Civil War. On his return he memorialised in his best Latin elegy, the 'Epitaphium Damonis', his only intimate friend, Charles Diodati, whom he met in Geneva. Sir Henry Wotton, ambassador at Venice, had also delighted in his company. In England he became a private tutor and began to plan an epic. It was to be Arthurian, celebrating the English nation. He describes it in the 'Epitaphium'.

The Civil War drew him into political life; he began pamphleteering. If, as he says, he wrote prose with his left hand and poetry with his right, the left hand produced four fifths of the surviving opus. His whole endeavour was to see the Reformation through. For him the true reformers were, in England, 'the divine and admirable spirit of Wyclif', the Lollards, Marian martyrs and suppressed sectaries who followed him. Wycliffe was a necessary martyr, one to be revered both for what he did and wrote, and for what he represents in English and European radical and reformist history.

In 1642 Milton, the learned and formidably accomplished poet, married a sixteen-year-old Roman Catholic girl. It was a disaster. Aubrey is kind about the first Mrs Milton, and Graves wrote a book giving her side of the miserable story. So troubled was Milton by the whole affair that after the marriage broke down, he wrote his pamphlet on divorce, which was censored. This experience provoked his best-known prose work, the *Areopagitica* (1644), an attack on official censorship. The strength of feeling in this is obviously genuine, though Milton would have been inclined to censor poems he found obnoxious and, indeed, became a censor under Cromwell. When we consider the calculated adjustments –

his detractors call them hypocrisies – in Dryden's spiritual and political career, we should remember Milton who embodies the same kinds of compromise with circumstance, though he ended up on the Anglican, Dryden on the Roman, side of the spiritual fence. The sonnets of 1642–58 are very different from the seven Italianising sonnets of his youth. Written in the gaps between his substantial prose writings, they divide between the polite and the public. It is the trumpet call of the public sonnets that astonished Wordsworth, in 'Cromwell, our chief of men' (his only Shakespearean sonnet, where he asks the Leader to 'save free conscience from the paw' of Cromwell's extremist followers, 'hireling wolves whose gospel is their maw'); and, especially, in 'Avenge, O Lord, thy slaughtered saints', the great English poem of rage and revenge. Others might have been alerted by his vehement little translation from Seneca's *Hercules Furens*, for *The Tenure of Kings and Magistrates:*

> There can be slain
> No sacrifice to God more acceptable
> Than an unjust and wicked king.

It was published in 1649, the year of Charles I's execution.

In 1646 Milton's first volume of *Poems* appeared. It included Latin, Greek, Italian and English work. In 1649 he waded deep into politics, defending the regicides in print. He was appointed Secretary for Foreign Tongues to Cromwell's Council of State, a post he held for ten years. He had no say in policy but was required to compose official propaganda. This he did with skill and conviction. Blindness overtook him in 1652. He wrote his famous sonnet, 'When I consider how my light is spent'; but he did not stint in his secretarial labours. During this period he suffered another loss. In 1656 (his first wife having left him long before) he married Katharin Woodcock. This marriage was happy, but Katharin died in 1658. For her he wrote his last sonnet, one of the most moving in English:

> Methought I saw my late espousèd saint
>   Brought to me like Alcestis from the grave,
>   Whom Jove's great son to her glad husband gave,
>   Rescued from death by force, though pale and faint.
> Mine, as whom washed from spot of child-bed taint
>   Purification in the old Law did save,
>   And such, as yet once more I trust to have
>   Full sight of her in Heaven without restraint,
> Came vested all in white, pure as her mind:
>   Her face was veiled, yet to my fancied sight,
>   Love, sweetness, goodness, in her person shined

> So clear, as in no face with more delight.
> > But O as to embrace me she inclined,
> > I waked, she fled, and day brought back my night.　　　　　**(268)**

Robert Graves has nothing to say about this poem, but it would have been hard for him to dismiss: it conforms to the rules of the lyric and, oddly, even more than 'Lycidas', to the expectations of elegy. Milton was to marry once again in 1662. His third wife, Elizabeth Minshull, survived him. He married her 'the year before the Sicknesse' – 'a gent. person, a peaceful and agreable humour'.

We think of the poet, going blind, his cause (the Commonwealth) coming undone, as being of melancholy disposition, but Aubrey, a contrary witness, makes him out to have been a congenial chap. 'He would be chearfull even in his Gowte-fitts, and sing.' He adds, 'He pronounced the letter R (*littera canina*) very hard – a certaine signe of a Satyricall Witt – *from John Dryden.'* And reflecting how after the Restoration he was visited by foreign admirers, 'He was much more admired abrode then at home.'

The Restoration put an end to Milton's pamphleteering and it seemed that he might be punished. But, though he was briefly imprisoned, several of his friends, among them Andrew Marvell and Cavalier poets whose corner he had fought behind the scenes under Cromwell, secured his safety. The Commonwealth extracted from him, beyond the sonnets, little verse. In his remaining years he made up for lost time, completing three major works upon which he had been engaged before: *Paradise Lost* (published in 1667 in ten books, revised 1674 in twelve). *Paradise Regained* (1671) and *Samson Agonistes* (1671). His revised *Poems* appeared in 1673. Internationally known, he was invited abroad but stayed at home. He died in 1674.

'My mind,' wrote Coleridge of the later Milton, 'is not capable of forming a more august conception than arises from the contemplation of this greatest man in his latter days: poor, sick, old, blind, slandered, persecuted: "Darkness before and danger's voice behind", in an age in which he was as little understood by the party for whom, as by that against whom, he had contended, and among men before whom he strode so far as to dwarf himself by the distance; yet still listening to the music of his own thoughts, or, if additionally cheered, yet cheered only by the prophetic faith of two or three solitary individuals, he did nevertheless,

> …argue not
> Against Heaven's hand or will, nor bate a jot
> Of heart or hope; but still bore up and steered
> Right onward.

Does Coleridge overstate the case? Milton had the slave labour of his daughters who read to him and scribed for him (the first women scribes thus recorded, who earned as meagre a keep as the apprentice scribes in the old scriptoria); he had his agreeable plague of visitors who brought gifts; and it is doubtful that he was so weak as to find 'slander' and 'persecution' more than the buzz of gnats. He was busy, he became the Oliver Cromwell of his little world.

It was long assumed that the sequence of publication of the three last great works reflected the sequence of their composition. But a different chronology has been proposed. W.R. Parker suggests that *Samson Agonistes* was begun in the late 1640s and pursued in the 1650s. By 1655 Milton had probably written the dialogues of *Paradise Regained* – about three quarters of the poem. This places *Paradise Lost* at the end rather than the beginning of the last period. Poetically, this makes sense. *Samson Agonistes* is the thinnest-textured of the three, not because it is a drama but because Milton's mature style was still in formation while he was writing it. Images are switched on, as it were, and then switched off when they have done their illumination: they do not inter-qualify and build, they exist for their moment. Intellectual and moral aridity; the uncompromising and obnoxious coldness in the words of Samson's father on hearing of the destruction of the theatre, the foe (and his son), 'Come, come; no time for lamentation now'; undigested debts to Shakespeare; the intensity of Samson's lament on blindness which implies that the poet had contracted the disability recently (later he accepts it calmly enough): these things suggest not a culmination of his work but a transition towards the largely dialogue-form of *Paradise Regained*. *Samson Agonistes'* magnificent passages are well known: the description of Delilah, the lament on his blindness, arias in a Puritan opera. But the tragedy as a whole is intolerable. It is a political, not a moral poem.

Paradise Regained refers *back* to *Paradise Lost* in its opening lines, but this does not confirm a chronology of composition. In conception it is much more modest than *Paradise Lost*: the poetry lacks the style and lushness of the epic. Spenser, after the model of Virgil, proceeded from pastoral eclogue to epic. Did Milton follow the same prescribed route? E.M.W. Tillyard noted the similarities between *Paradise Regained* and Virgil's *Georgics*. If one prefers to argue for *Paradise Regained* as a dramatic poem, one must apologise for its shortcomings in every aspect, from characterisation to dialogue and action: a conflict in the mind of Christ, it deals exclusively with his temptations in the wilderness. We observe not the mind's processes, but stylised temptations. There is a continuous parallel between Old Testament history and Christ's New Testament development. The poem is epic neither in style nor manner: it sings inaction, not action – refusals of temptation which are action only on a moral plane. Read as a Puritan georgic it makes formal sense, converting 'the modes of classical poetry into the service of Christianity'. A georgic is a poem about the cultivation of the spirit, not the soil. Simple phrasing, lack of decoration, a general plainness, set it apart from *Paradise Lost.* The diction and style of the closing passages of each poem register their radical difference. In *Paradise Regained* 'characters' exist solely as clauses in Christ's self-discovery.

Paradise Lost (273–276) deals with the Fall, from which Christ redeems us. By the middle of the Commonwealth Milton's social optimism and desire to celebrate England in Arthurian epic had faded. Christian epic was the highest form to which a poet could aspire. Its scope was cosmic, timeless, its moral purpose clear. Other forms of poetry were trivial by comparison. He began writing it in 1658 and finished around 1663. He defended his choice of blank verse on aesthetic and political grounds: his authorities were Homer and Virgil. He advanced the usual arguments against 'trivial' rhyme: 'True musical delight,' he says, 'consists only in apt numbers, fit quantity of syllables, and the sense variously drawn out from one verse to another.' The key implement is supple and clear syntax, mimetic in some passages, analytic in others. Milton is expert at this drawing out, spreading his meanings, as Spenser does, sometimes over more than a dozen lines. Each sentence, every image, every word, has a number of functions to perform on literal and moral levels. Latinate syntax and diction allow flexibility and through echo or etymology create complex harmonies inaccessible in a simpler style. In using blank verse Milton claimed he was recovering an 'ancient liberty' for English, long confined to the bondage of rhyme. Arnold praised Milton above all for this style, the poet's 'perfect sureness of hand': nothing could be changed without violence to the prosodic or intellectual content.

Along with Latinate syntax and diction comes a panoply of classical and Biblical allusions. The use of particular geographical names gives the poem enormous scope in space. The forward narration of the angels makes it possible for him to include all historical time, and in portraying the godhead he incorporates eternity. *Paradise Lost* positively bristles with learning. It is deliberate in plan, development and decoration. Despite the design, the poetry transcends its formal conception, characters are real, stand up and speak with some independence. They have distinct idioms: each fallen angel who joins in the great debate in Hell speaks with a different inflection. Satan has as many voices as forms. The poet, who intrudes in the first person at several junctures, establishes a voice and orientation of his own: we can attribute the narrative. Autobiographical matter adds authority. There are, too, the perspectives. Scenes are presented through the eyes of particular characters, so that we see not only what but *as* they see. Satan's vision of Paradise is more vivid than an 'objective' vision could be. He sees with the eyes of resentment and revenge.

Milton integrates the levels of meaning. There is literal story, moral drama, political argument. Images of natural process substantiate the action or figure the movement of the poem, most poignantly in Book IX, when nightfall and the human Fall are expressed side by side. 'Earth felt the wound' of the Fall: the act changed not only the human condition but nature itself.

The twelve books move from the defeat of the rebel angels, their expulsion and fall, to the Fall of man and his expulsion from the Garden. There is 'architecture' in the parallelism of scenes, and in the development of clusters of imagery connected with the several themes. But is there too *much* design? Has Milton done more than revive the medieval mode of allegory? Johnson was not alone in objecting to the 'want of human interest' in the poem. Adam and Eve – apart from the Archangel Michael's prophecies – are the only *people* we meet, and they are remote first in their innocence and then in their earth-shattering guilt. We observe, standing apart. Coleridge distinguishes between the epic and the dramatic imagination. Both discover unity in variety, but the epic discovers unity by throwing its subject into the past, regarding it from a distance, while the dramatic brings it up close. A useful distinction, it illuminates both the failure of *Samson Agonistes* and the success of *Paradise Lost*. Our human access to *Paradise Lost* is, initially, through the realised character of Satan. Milton progressively diminishes him, through animal imagery and transformations, until he is a mere serpent. Thereafter we follow a sensuous argument, a symbolic enactment of our fall. The longueurs of a poem whose action is so simple and whose telling so majestic and gradual come especially in the long conversations of Adam with Raphael and Michael. Expression exceeds occasion. We may agree occasionally with Yvor Winters's criticism of the 'pompous redundancy' of the verse, the rhetoric working as it were in spite of and away from the subject, 'a dependence on literary stereotypes'. But whole books of the poem, notably the first, second, fourth and ninth, survive such criticism, and none of the books is wholly unastonishing.

For *Paradise Lost* Milton received an initial payment – generous in a way, given the length of the poem, Milton's fall from grace, and the uncertainty of its success – of £5 and a further £5 when the first edition of 1,300 copies was sold through. The edition of 1674 broke Books Seven and Ten in two, bringing the epic to the appropriate twelve books. That was the year of Milton's death. Six years later his widow sold out the rights for £8. That particular arrangement was shrewd on the publisher's part.

The case against Milton is largely a case against his effect on the eighteenth and nineteenth centuries. It was universal in Britain, and not confined to these islands. Milton is strictly inimitable: a radical and an anachronism. T.S. Eliot delivered telling blows, some of them against the moral content. The poem's moral purpose, like that of *The Faerie Queene*, has become muted and remote. We read it for reasons other than edification. It fell to F.R. Leavis to square his shoulders before the master and try to knock him down. Leavis attacks first *Paradise Lost* and the grand style. He finds it predictable: 'routine gesture', 'heavy fall', 'monotony'. He speaks of Milton's 'sensuous poverty' – the language is self-regarding, not turned to 'perceptions, sensations, or things'. Elevation and remoteness impoverish rather than enrich our experience. Milton is 'cut off from speech ... that belongs to the emotional and sensory texture of actual living'. His style is 'an impoverishment of sensibility'. Milton 'renounced the English language'. Having finished with *Paradise Lost*, Leavis turns to the other poems and makes short work of them.

Many of his charges are in part true. There is monotony; the grand style does compel an attitude in the reader (it has designs on us), the language is cut off from speech – except when it is speaking. But such facts need not be incriminating. The poem answers the more serious case. It is far from 'sensuous poverty': only a reader deaf to Milton's complex forms of integration could level such a charge. It is richly imagined and in part richly realised, *imaginable*. There is subtle and delicate life in the verse, and a variety of subtleties and delicacies. Very few lines are 'regular': our attention is kept in part by the cunning patterns of variation Milton achieves. In dismissing Milton, Leavis assaults the wide area of English poetry Milton influenced; and his effect is still felt. The prejudice of our age, as much an unwritten rule as the rules of decorum were in the eighteenth century, is contained in Leavis's declaration that Milton's language is 'cut off from speech'. His sin is his language.

Yet for two and a half centuries – even for a 'speaker' like Wordsworth – Milton's virtue was this language, which engaged and developed subjects difficult to combine, moral verities and the created world. The language of speech is not the only, or first, language of poetry. To criticise work in terms strictly irrelevant to it is of little value: a critical act of 'brute assertive will', or a prejudice so ingrained as to be indistinguishable, for uncritical readers, from truth itself. With the decline of literary culture Milton, like Spenser, becomes a more difficult mountain to scale, more remote from the 'common reader'. Yet Chaucer and Shakespeare, the only poets in the tradition who are Milton's superiors, both grow and recede in the same way and are not dismissed. They *seem* more accessible. In the end Leavis's hostility, like Empson's and Richards's in other areas, is to the emphatic Christian content of the poems, which in Milton *is* obtrusive. We read Herbert's and Donne's divine poems even if we are unbelievers: there is their doubt to engage with, and the framed drama of specific situations. But Milton will not allow disbelief to go unchallenged: his structures and narratives are not rooted in individual faith but in universal belief. The question of revealed *truth* raises its head as in no other poet in the language. Readers who resist have to make do with Satan and Comus.

Difficult, too, is the first poet of America, Anne Bradstreet, a woman who shared the rigours of Milton's faith, and who stands at the threshold of a new tradition but is too reticent to force her foot in the door. Her verse for the most part looks back to her native England for form and diction and tells an English story even as it speaks from a new continent. She was born in Northamptonshire around 1612 into the highly-placed Dudley family. She was a great reader in the well-stocked library of her Puritan father. At eighteen she married a Cambridge graduate nine years her elder and – under Governor Winthrop, crossing in the *Arbella* – they joined the Puritan emigrants in Salem, Massachusetts, becoming pioneers and moving out to Ipswich and North Andover. She bore eight children there ('I had eight birds hatcht in one nest, / Four cocks there were, and hens the rest…' (**283**)), wrote verse on myriad themes – including long works on English history and on Biblical subjects – 'the fruit of some few hours, curtailed from her sleep and other refreshments'. She is remembered for her more domestic pieces, as though – she being a woman – this were her proper sphere. Yet there is energy and spiritual force in her large-scale work. In 1652 *The Tenth Muse lately sprung up in America* was published in England. She died in 1672 and her book appeared in revised form in Boston in 1678 – the first volume of verse to be published there and 'most vendible'. Her widower became governor of Salem during the witch-hunt trials.

There was little encouragement for her writing in the Puritan severity of the New World where women had a specifically secondary role, which her poems acknowledge even as they make their anxiously modest claims. Governor Winthrop wrote ruefully of 'a godly young woman' who had given herself up to a kind of madness: to reading and writing 'many books'. She kept her writing to herself and her circle, but her brother-in-law had it published without her knowledge in London.

She had absorbed Ralegh, Sidney and Francis Quarles, and she was passionately drawn to the French Calvinist Guillaume du Bartas's compendious poem that Joshua Sylvester translated as *The Divine Weeks and Works*. Du Bartas is her problematic Muse. She was writing, but she was also writing against, no matter how readily she accepted, her situation and circumstances. Her literary culture was arrested in 1630 when she set sail. One of her most celebrated poems is an encomium for Elizabeth I, long deceased. Milton's Puritan wing never brushed her; in a culture of denial she was giving, humane, and even ambitious. Out of the extreme exigencies of motherhood she wrote – as Adrienne Rich says – 'the first good poems in America'. The best of these are poems to her husband, her father, and a poem on the burning of her house in 1666, which includes the brutally self-punishing Puritan lines:

Then, coming out, beheld a space,
The flame consume my dwelling place.

And, when I could no longer look,
I blessed His name that gave and took,
That laid my goods now in the dust:
Yea, so it was, and so 'twas just.

Milton would applaud the sentiment but find the crude end-stopping of lines and the awkward rhyming rebarbative.

John Berryman's first major poem, *Homage to Mistress Bradstreet*, gives her a more flexible voice. His imaginative advocacy turned attention back to her. The fact that she wrote with such candour and competence under the circumstances remains a miracle. Yet her poems cannot be made any better than they are.

Set her beside Margaret Cavendish, the eccentric Duchess of Newcastle (1623–1673) and they both come into clearer focus. 'The crazy duchess' was childless, was not Puritan, was probably less deeply but more broadly read than Anne Bradstreet, but enjoyed the society of cultured men, including her poet husband. With him she endured exile in poverty during the Commonwealth, returning with the Restoration. Her wily couplets share the selfish energies of Rochester and Sedley; they have a social tone. Her attempt to bring Metaphysical style into the second half of the seventeenth century is brave and not altogether unsuccessful. In Bradstreet we admire the poet's enormous pertinacity, but the value of the poems depends upon our knowledge of a self-denying life. The Duchess's verse contributes to the better verse of her age, and by being slightly antiquated it has – paradoxically – an air of originality in its conceits. She does not somehow *seem* serious, but when we read 'A Woman drest by Age' from *Phantasm's Masque* (311) and others of her conventionally spiritual poems, we realise how serious she is, though her verse does not run deep.

AN END OF DELICACY

... the Cause[5] was too good to have been fought for ... For men may spare their pains when Nature is at work, and the world will not go the faster for our driving.

Andrew Marvell

Milton marks a beginning more than an end, gathering the energies of the Elizabethan age, reconfiguring the poetic, political and religious trends in ways which close off the past. After Milton, certain forms and styles are out of bounds. But poets grew alongside him on whom his shadow did not fall. Old-fashioned Anglican survivors, they wrote what they had to write regardless of him.

Richard Lovelace, 'the most amiable and beautiful person that ever eye beheld', 'a most beautifull Gentleman', 'loved Adonis', inherited substantial estates in Kent, went from Oxford to Court, served in the wars, was imprisoned for supporting the King and wrote the poem 'Stone walls do not a prison make'. He rejoined the King in 1645. Reported dead, his beloved Lucy Sacheverell, the Lucasta of his verse – 'So you but with a touch of your fair hand / Turn all to saraband' – married elsewhere. His return from the dead was a mistake; in 1648 he was back in prison, preparing his book of poems *Lucasta* for publication. He invested his entire fortune in the Royalist cause, then disappointed and consumptive, became a threadbare object of charity. 'Obiit in a Cellar in Long Acre, a little before the Restauration of his Majestie.' This pell-mell life epitomises the heroic and tragic careering of a young Cavalier, final heir of Wyatt, Surrey and Sidney, exemplary and anachronistic. It is like a cautionary tale from the *Mirror for Magistrates* which no one much read any more. Even the verse is, at first glance, something of an anachronism.

Andrew Marvell's poem commending *Lucasta* (1649) abounds in insect images. It predicts a harsh reception for the thirty-one-year-old Cavalier's first book.

The barbèd censurers begin to look
Like the grim consistory on thy book;

[5] Parliamentarians'

And on each line cast a reforming eye,
Severer than the young Presbytery.

Lovelace's situation was already vexed. Parliament had sequestered his remaining fortune while he was in prison. Marvell looks back to happier days. The poems were composed by a royal favourite, loved by the Court and by the wits. Now, 'Our Civil Wars have lost the civic crown. / He highest builds who with most art destroys.' *Lucasta* appeared in the year of the King's execution and belongs to the fallen order. Marvell's prediction was not far off the mark.

Lucasta achieved small success. Lovelace is now remembered chiefly for 'To Althea, from Prison' ('Stone walls ...') (**295**) and 'To Lucasta, Going to the Wars' ('I could not love thee, dear, so much, / Loved I not honour more') (**296**). But there is more to him than a couple of anthology pieces. His misfortune was to appear in print in the very year his cause was lost. His style was out of fashion, demanding as it does intellectual and prosodic control, conscious devising. Some poems are marred by a preciosity which in Herrick appears charming, but in Lovelace indicates a failure of tact. Formal lapses, gaps in argument, and an occasional lack of prosodic energy, weaken his poems. But the best, perhaps thirty, are accomplished works.

Lovelace, eldest son of a Kentish gentleman, was born either in Holland or in Kent in 1618. His creature poems reflect rural roots where, for example, 'The Grasshopper' (**298**) invites the elder Charles Cotton to carouse:

Up with the day, the sun thou welcom'st then,
    Sport'st in the gilt-plats of his beams,
And all these merry days mak'st merry men,
    Thyself, and melancholy streams.

But ah, the sickle! Golden ears are cropped;
    Ceres and Bacchus bid good night;
Sharp frosty fingers all your flowers have topped,
    And what scythes spared, winds shave off quite.

Poor verdant fool! And now green ice; thy joys
    Large and as lasting, as thy perch of grass,
Bid us lay in 'gainst winter, rain, and poise
    Their floods with an o'erflowing glass.

The moral is rural-courtly, the creature emblematic. 'The Ant' ('Thou, thine own horse and cart, under this plant / Thy spacious tent') (**297**) and

'The Snail' ('Compendious snail! Thou seem'st to me, / Large Euclid's strict epitome') (**299**) are emblematic too, but are more tied in to specific social occasions than 'The Grasshopper'. A happy confluence of Aesop and Tusser? The pastoral of Spenser with the unattenuated voice of Gascoigne? The wit of Donne with the formal tact of Herbert? Or simply an individual figuring of rural realities that body forth the larger social and political realities of the day? These poems, and 'Amarantha' with which *Lucasta* concludes, are Lovelace's chief legacy. 'Amarantha' introduced Marvell to the notion of the political pastoral in tetrameter couplets, 'in which the local landscape comes to represent the whole of England, its flora and fauna emerging as types of the factions which fought out the civil war, and which is presided over by a heroine who gradually develops from a vision of Arcadian innocence into a complex figure of national and personal salvation'.

Lovelace's father was not only a gentleman but a soldier, killed at the siege of Groll when his son was nine. Lovelace became his mother's ward. In 1629 he was admitted to Charterhouse School, possibly on the King's nomination, at the same time as Richard Crashaw, son of an anti-Catholic pamphleteer and Puritan preacher, who was to become a notable recusant poet. Crashaw went to Cambridge and eventually (in every sense) to Rome, Lovelace to Oxford, each to a separate destiny.

In 1631 the King made Lovelace Gentleman Waiter Extraordinary. His adolescent comedy *The Scholars* was played 'with applause'. His accomplishments seem a shadow of Sidney's. Charles Cotton wrote in his memorial verses:

> Thy youth, an abstract of the world's best parts,
> Enured to arms, and exercised in arts;
> Which with the vigour of a man became
> Thine, and thy country's pyramids of flame;
> Two glorious lights to guide our hopeful youth
> Into the paths of honour, and of truth.

Among his other deeds, he was the first literal translator of Catullus into English. In 1636, at Gloucester Hall, Oxford, he was made an honorary MA on the occasion of a visit by the King and Queen. The next year he received a Cambridge MA and went to Court.

When Charles I's serious troubles began, Lovelace served him, first as an ensign in the Bishops' Wars (1639–40), along with the equally ill-fated poets and fellow Cavaliers Sir John Suckling and Thomas Carew. During 1640 he wrote *The Soldier*, a tragedy now lost. He was arrested and committed to the Gatehouse at Westminster for leading the men of Kent in presenting to Parliament the Kentish petition, seeking the retention of

Bishops and the Book of Common Prayer, and supporting the King's authority. (In what a different cause the men of Essex and Kent marched behind Wat Tyler.) He was released on condition that he cease actively supporting the royalist cause, a condition he did not meet. From that point on he began his lavish spending on the King's campaign.

He was with Charles in Oxford in 1645, then travelled abroad and was arrested on his return. The execution of his King changed everything: he had no future in Cromwell's England. For eight years he survived, writing with a different tone and purpose. In 1656 he composed 'The Triumph of Philamore and Amoret' for the marriage of Charles Cotton the younger, the poet who memorialised him. It was his last outstanding poem. It is thought that he died in 1657. *Lucasta, Postume Poems* was assembled and published – unprofitably – in 1659 by his youngest brother.

Donne and Jonson were the Cavalier poets' chief models. Carew (254–259) leaned more to Jonson, which leaves him often stiff and wooden. Lovelace followed Donne, and the flaws in his work might have been remedied had he attended more to Jonson. But he preferred brilliance and surprise to clarity. Thus in 'Ellinda's Glove' he wrote:

> Thou snowy farm with thy five tenements!
>> Tell thy white mistress here was one
>> That called to pay his daily rents;
> But she a-gathering flowers and hearts is gone …

It is pure conceit, carried to extremes: the opening surprises and charms, but surprise passes and deliberate charm outstays its welcome.

Donne is echoed in several poems, notably 'The Scrutiny' and 'Night'. This is not the spirit in which Vaughan echoes Herbert, whom he took spiritually to heart, but something less subtle, for Lovelace is Metaphysical by design, not by nature. 'Gratiana Dancing and Singing' is wildly implausible: when she ceases dancing, 'The floor lay paved with broken hearts'. We hear in Lovelace Continental echoes, too, of writers who were to be important to the Restoration poets, and Rochester in particular.

Just over a hundred poems by Lovelace survive. Even in so small a body of work, the formal variety is enormous. There are poems connected with war and prison; complaints and love and anti-love conceits; poems about creatures; poems on painting (for Lovelace, a friend of Peter Lely, was learned in the art); occasional poems including elegies, epithalamia and anniversary celebrations; pastorals, such as 'Amarantha' and 'Amyntor's Grove'; a formal satire; meditations; dialogues … The range is wider than Herrick's though the final achievement is not so great. Lovelace's trajectory illuminates the trends in English poetry at the time. His early verse is intimate, even private in its concerns, written for a friend or circle of friends, wits and courtiers. When that world crumbled his address became more public: the favoured courtier became an outcast and fugitive.

John Suckling's poetry (277–280) is wryly cynical on the surface, with an embittered wit. In Lovelace, cynicism is thematic, irony is not a technical device but a thematic verity. He is not so obviously accomplished as Carew, but he is more memorable, his development more interesting in its typicality. He survived a great loss and endured the aftermath.

> I would love a Parliament
> As a main prop from heaven sent;
> But ah! who's he that would be wedded
> To th' fairest body that's beheaded?

It is an ungainly stanza; the awkwardness proceeds from and mirrors feeling.

The best Restoration poets resemble Lovelace. Yet even a casual reading shows the coarseness of their work compared to his, and how ready most of them are to be satisfied with mere effect. History has started again and in its new, or renewed, light shadows are shorter and less opaque. Their view of poetry is at once more precise – they have come home from France, after all – and narrower. Though many are courtiers, they are not Cavaliers. Ideals of devotion and service are a thing of the past. Charles I's was the last courtly Court. Lovelace embodies older virtues: an *uomo universale*, courtier, scholar, soldier, lover, musician, connoisseur of painting, latter-day Sidney, devoted to king, mistress and art. 'To Althea, from Prison' is the quintessential Cavalier statement, passionate, *lived*. He was the last of the knight-poets; his death in poverty rather than in service proved that the age of Wyatt, Surrey, Ralegh, Sidney and others of their stamp was over.

The transition was not abrupt: a line cannot be drawn. A poet like Andrew Marvell spans three ages like a delicate but serviceable bridge. The first length spans Charles I's reign and fall, the second spans the Commonwealth, the third the Restoration. 'He was of middling stature, pretty strong sett, roundish faced, cherry cheek't, hazell eie, browne haire. He was in conversation very modest, and of very few words: and though he loved wine he would never drinke hard in company, and was wont to say that, he would not play the goodfellow in any man's company in whose hand he would not trust his life. He had not a generall acquaintance.' Marvell is a poet whose political readjustments in times of turmoil have not told against him. There is something honest-seeming about everything he does, and running through his actions a constant thread of humane concern. The King loved him even when he leaned towards the Puritan cause; at a perilous time he wrote verses commending both

Lovelace and – the only other time he wrote commendatory verse –
Milton's *Paradise Lost*. Even when he celebrated Cromwell in verse, his
praise was temperate. He possesses transparency of conscience to an
unusual degree. Poetry is a delight in language, image and truth. Through
poetry balance is restored even when the world is off its axis.

> And now to the abyss I pass
> Of that unfathomable grass,
> Where men like grasshoppers appear,
> But grasshoppers are giants there:
> They, in their squeaking laugh, contemn
> Us, as we walk more low than them;
> And, from the precipices tall
> Of the green spires, to us do call.

His grasshopper shares much with Lovelace's. Marvell's origins, however,
were less distinguished. His father was a low-church clergyman, 'facetious,
yet Calvinistical'. Marvell was born in Hull in 1621. The town boasted a
good grammar school, which he attended. Then he went to Trinity College,
Cambridge, at the age of twelve, during the poetic ascendancy of Cowley
and Crashaw. He received his BA in 1638–9 and was briefly a convert to
Roman Catholicism. He left the University in 1641 without taking a further
degree. Well-trained in languages, he composed his earliest verses in Greek
and Latin on the death of Princess Anne. Aubrey declares, 'For Latin verses
there was no man could come into competition with him.'

When the Civil War came he was noncommittal. He went abroad for
four of the seven years 1642–9, spending two in Rome. He may have travelled as a tutor in preparation for his later posts. By 1649 he was keeping
royalist company. As well as contributing to *Lucasta*, he wrote verses on
the death of Lord Hastings:

> Go, stand betwixt the morning and the flowers;
> And, ere they fall, arrest the early showers.
> Hastings is dead ...

Already the garden is there. In a poem full of Donne and generalisation,
the mature Marvell stirs.

His Royalist sympathies, though attenuated, had not entirely faded in
1650 when he composed his 'Horatian Ode upon Cromwell's Return from
Ireland' (**305**). It is the most complex and the best directly political poem
in the language. It retains a radical balance in the terms of its celebration
and commendation. Here is how Charles dies on his 'tragic scaffold'. He

… nothing common did or mean
Upon that memorable scene:
   But with his keener eye
   The axe's edge did try:
Nor called the gods with vulgar spite
To vindicate his helpless right,
   But bowed his comely head
   Down as upon a bed.
This was the memorable hour
That first assured the forcèd power.

Like the great historian Edward Hyde, Earl of Clarendon, Marvell cannot quite bring himself to watch as the axe descends. Cromwell, the 'forcèd power', is, by contrast with the ceremonious King, all movement, agitation. He has an 'active star', seeks glory and adventure – in more senses than one. The poem lives because of Marvell's sense of loss – and gain, and because of the pivotal vision of 'A bleeding head', from which the eventual blessing of a strong government flows. Charles embodies right. Marvell, it is recorded, declared that 'men should have trusted the King'. He respects Charles, he admires Cromwell. Cromwell's forced victory was 'To ruin the great work of time':

Though justice against fate complain
And plead the ancient rights in vain:
   But those do hold or break
   As men are strong or weak.   (305)

Might has prevailed. Marvell, never cured of his royalism, at one moment looked forward to a dynasty of Cromwells, but it was not to be.

He found favour with the moderate elements of Cromwell's party and became tutor to Mary, daughter of Lord Fairfax, a distinguished retired general in the Parliamentary cause who had wished – but not quite dared – to save the life of the King, and to whom Milton dedicated a fine sonnet. Marvell spent two years in Fairfax's household at Nunappleton, Yorkshire. Poetically it was a fruitful time. He wrote to praise and please his patron, celebrating Appleton House and the park and creating those poems whose charms are as real as they are hard to define.

In 1653 Milton recommended Marvell for the post of assistant Latin Secretary. Four years later it was awarded him. Meanwhile, residing at Eton, he tutored a ward of Cromwell's and became more firmly a supporter of the Commonwealth. He was intent to serve his country and the de facto government and to make progress himself. In 1655 he published anonymously 'The First Anniversary of the Government under O.C.'.

He was elected MP for Hull in 1660 and held the seat until his death. He supported the Restoration and seems to have been accepted as a man whose loyalty (unlike Milton's) was not in question. In any event, he helped secure Milton's safety and release. He served the Crown in embassies abroad, campaigned for religious toleration and became a satirist against the Court party. He died in 1678 in London. His *Miscellaneous Poems*, including much of his best work, was published in 1681, though the 'Ode' was cancelled from all but one copy and was not reprinted until 1776.

Marvell was not a professional writer. Most of his poems are in one way or another 'flawed'. The tetrameter couplets he favoured prove wearying: the form can dictate rather than receive the poetry. The excessive use of 'do' and 'did' auxiliaries to plump out the metre mars many lines. Some of the conceits are absurd. Many of the poems, even 'Bermudas' (302), fail to establish a consistent perspective: it is not always easy to visualise his visionary world. Other poems are static; an idea is stated and reiterated in various terms, but not developed. This is the case even in 'The Definition of Love' (301), which says memorably in eight ways that his love is impossible, but does not specify why or how, and does not supply the 'occasion'; or in 'A Dialogue between the Resolved Soul and Created Pleasure', which despite its form is not dialogue: instead, voices bump against each other. Intellectual development is often, as in Donne, by sleight of hand, pseudo-logic, false syllogism. There are thematic inconsistencies. In 'Upon Appleton House' he suggests the natural order is superior to artificial order, but describes nature in terms of artifice. He condemns Palladian architecture in stanza six, but fifty-eight stanzas later he evokes the woods, approvingly, in Palladian images. Moral value is sometimes assigned to, rather than discovered in, his images. And Marvell is not usually dramatic in presentation, unlike Donne or Herbert.

Yet because of some spell he casts, he is a poet whose faults we not only forgive but relish. Beneath an inadequate logic the poetry follows its own habits of association and combination. Two modes of discourse are at work; a conscious one, and something unwilled yet compelling. We cannot decide which of a poem's effects are deliberate, and which casual or accidental. They seem products of a not altogether untroubled leisure at Nunappleton. T.S. Eliot contrasts Marvell with Donne. Donne would have been 'an individual at any time and place'; Marvell is 'the product of European, that is to say Latin, culture'. The difference is in the use of the 'I'. Donne's 'I' demands attention, Marvell's directs it. In Marvell the flaws do not disappear beneath gesture; inconsistency and uncertainty are aspects of a mind concerned with subject. The subject is not self. However distinctively he appropriates a landscape or scene, it never becomes a *paysage intérieur*. The macrocosm is never displaced by the microcosm.

In 'To his Coy Mistress' (304) the poet begins with a cool, reasonable proposition. From the temperate beginning the poem gathers speed, rushing to a cruel resolution. Image follows image with precise brevity, each extends and enriches the idea. The imaginative centre holds together a varied development. Marvell does not always discriminate between the fresh and startling and the merely odd, yet what is odd is often delivered with such effective phrasing that it disarms us even in its absurdity, for instance the salmon fishers who 'like Antipodes in shoes / Have shod their heads in their canoes'.

Marvell's verse delivers sharp surprises in part because of its quietness. Surprises emerge, they are not insisted on. He seems always to be *recognising* significance in what he sees. His whole mind is engaged, along with his senses. His intensity is *awareness*; even as he speaks he is aware of things he *might* have said. The Classics shaped his poems, but scripture is never far away. He does not discharge his poems but launches them quietly. They run less smoothly than Herrick's but they run further and deeper. If drama is generated, as in 'To his Coy Mistress', it is by control of pace and imagery, not by situation. His verse is urbane, detached, with recurrent motifs and words and a recognisable tone that distinguishes it from the work of other Metaphysicals. He has his own themes, too. Wise passivity marks some poems, which leads to closeness with the natural world as his imagination relaxes and receives. Other poems strive for contact through passion or activity, a kind of contact in which individuality is lost in the teeming variety of the world. Underlying these themes is the knowledge that in love or action time cannot be arrested or permanence achieved. A sanctioned social order can be ended with an axe, love is finite, we grow old. Political reality drove the theme deep in him. We feel it obliquely in 'The Nymph Complaining for the Death of her Fawn' (303). For an intelligence such as his the lived experience of a crucial historical event was more powerful than any accident of private biography. Perhaps he is naturally a poet of aftermath. Like Herrick, he came late in his 'literary period' and was overlooked by those who might have profited from reading him. Contrasting Marvell with Edmund Waller (his contemporary but more a man of what was to come that of what then was) we can feel the difference. Except in his best poems Waller delivers us finished ideas; Marvell happens upon ideas. He has no settled opinions, except the fundamental ones. His poems balance particulars of which he is certain with conflicting generalities of which he is unsure, as in the line 'courteous briars nail me through', which dissolves the word 'courteous' on the cruel verb and brings into its ambience 'Court' and crucifixion. Such lines, quietly delivered, lead us not to admire his wit but to apprehend his subject. It was already the age of Dryden, and Dryden took wit in a different direction. The age of Dryden was one in which writers took up the pen to set down what they knew, not in order to explore the unfamiliar; it was an age of communication rather than of discovery.

Devotional poets resisted the force of Dryden's example longest. Aubrey was a cousin of Henry Vaughan (1622–1695) and his twin brother Thomas. Aubrey settles an old score on his account. 'Their grandmother was an Aubrey: their father, a coxscombe and no honester than he should be – he cosened me of 50s. once.' The sons, unlike their father, were not temporal schemers. Their eyes were generally fixed on higher things. Henry provides 'authentic tidings of invisible things'. His chief collection of poems, *Silex Scintillans* (*Sparks from the Flint*, 1650, enlarged 1655), was the mature work of a man led to passionate faith by bereavement, illness and the poems of George Herbert. The book's title he explains: 'Certain divine rays break out of the soul in adversity, like sparks of fire out of the afflicted flint.' His hermetic imagination is rarefied compared with Herbert's, and comparison with Herbert is inevitable: as Henry declared, Herbert's 'holy life and verse gained many pious converts (of whom I am the least)'. He frequently echoes in phrase, syntax and development specific poems by Herbert. Edmund Blunden sets them side by side in his poem 'The Age of Herbert and Vaughan':

> In close and pregnant symbol
>   Each primrosed morning showed
> The triune God patrol
>   On every country road,
> In bushy den and dimble.

Blunden is truer to Vaughan than Herbert. Herbert knows an immanent God; Vaughan's God is less immediately present. The poet approaches him through symbol but cannot readily perceive him in natural imagery:

> Some love a rose
> In hand, some in the skin;
>   But cross to those,
> I would have mine within.

Marvell is the poet of green, a 'green thought in a green shade', his eye on a fruitful garden, Vaughan is the poet of white in its implications of moral and spiritual purity, skyscape, cloudscape: 'a white, Celestial thought', the white light of stars, or in his translation of Boethius's, 'that first white age'. The most rapt English devotional poet, the most spiritually attentive, he lived in a spectrum between the pure white of infancy and a recovered whiteness of eternity:

I saw eternity the other night
Like a great ring of pure and endless light,
   All calm as it was bright,
And round beneath it, time in hours, days, years
     Driven by the spheres
Like a vast shadow moved … (310)

'The World' does not sustain intensity throughout, dwindling to deliberate allegory. It examines the shadow, 'The fearful miser on a heap of rust', a vivid moment. The poem has the virtue of describing Vaughan's chosen territory for discovery: areas beyond the senses, accessible only to intuition. 'Invisible things', things he evokes in 'Faith' ('Bright, and blest beam!') (309), 'The Passion' ('O my chief good!'), 'Peace' ('My soul, there is a country') (306) and elsewhere. His achievement is to bring the transcendent almost within reach of the senses.

There's not a wind can stir,
    Or beam pass by,
But straight I think (though far),
    Thy hand is nigh;
    Come, come!
  Strike these lips dumb:
  This restless breath
  That soils thy name,
  Will ne'r be tame
  Until in death.

Such obliquity does not obscure the material world, it illuminates what exists beyond it. Through human love it ascends to the divine, with the light of faith. Images of darkness belong to the world. Images of light – starlight, pure light – belong to the fields of heaven and eternity.

'My brother and I,' Henry wrote, 'were born at Newton in the parish of St Brigets in the year 1621.' Vaughan's father was a second son of a family in the old Anglo-Welsh gentry. Henry's twin became a hermetic philosopher ('Eugenius Philalethes', lover of forgetfulness) whose works were familiar in the next century even to a sceptical Jonathan Swift. A priest, Thomas was ejected from living at Llansantffraed after the Royalist defeat in the Civil War. He died of mercury poisoning in an alchemical experiment in 1666.

More certain knowledge survives about Thomas than about Henry. Henry called himself 'Silurist' to acknowledge his roots and his landscape, because his native Breconshire was once inhibited by the Silures. It is supposed that he went to Jesus College, Oxford, around 1638, took no degree, and turned up in London to study law in 1640. He became, we do not know by what steps, a medical doctor, and spent his later years practising in his Welsh neighbourhood. In the Civil War he probably served with Royalist forces and tasted their defeat, which coincided with personal bereavements. His first book, *Poems, with the Tenth Satire of Juvenal Englished* (1646), was not very distinguished. The conventional 'Amoret' has more literature than flesh on her bones. His second book, *Olor Iscanus* (*Swan of the Usk*, 1651), revealed deepening seriousness. It begins in Wales, his true territory. London, its styles and concerns, are less than an echo. Almost best in the book are his translations of some of the verses from Boethius's *Consolation of Philosophy*, especially 'Metrum 5' with its rhythmic and thematic foretaste of two of his great poems, 'The Retreat' and 'Childhood':

> Happy that first white age! When we
> Lived by the earth's mere charity,
> No soft luxurious diet then
> Had effeminated men...

More than translation, this is a committed Royalist looking to a lost, irrecoverable age. He turns his attention elsewhere and suddenly finds 'a country / Far beyond the stars'. The choice of the word 'country' is significant. His imagination naturally turns to allegory; he is among the last Boethians, seeing into a spiritual future through a lens that most of his contemporaries found clouded and archaic. Remote from London and the hub of fashion, he was free to take bearings with his own instruments.

Silex Scintillans contains his best poetry. The debt to Herbert is great, but when an experience is sufficiently intense Vaughan's own idiom, rhythm and themes make their own space in Herbert territory. His style is thick with Biblical echo and allusion: for Christians steeped in scripture each poem has an immediate sense of familiarity, a resonance as intense as any in Herbert's poems. Vaughan prefaces many pieces with Biblical epigraphs, to underline their source and allegiance. His faith is fresh, the product of an abrupt spiritual conversion and notably lacking in doubt. The dramatic openings and developments, whether simple allegory, allegorical journey or emblem, relate it to and distinguish it from other Metaphysical work. His revelation is certain. At times he experiences a triumphant sense of election, demanding no proof beyond his own certainty. The conversion came from reading Herbert. Vaughan was surprised by grace.

After 1655 he composed little durable verse. *Thalia Rediviva* (1678) revisits the secular world of his first books and adds little to his credit. What happened to his assured genius? Faith may have cooled, conscience (endlessly pining over past sins and excesses) may have smothered the holy Muse. Perhaps work as a doctor overtaxed him, or his brother's death destroyed a crucial stability, or physical frailty undermined his imaginative resolve. Later in life he suffered litigation within the family and squabbles over property. The claims of a secular world clouded the spiritual sky. It was not to be a quiet old age. When he died in 1695, he had written no verse of moment for forty years. His interesting if derivative prose book, *The Mount of Olives*, dates from 1652. His memorable prose and verse belong, at most, to a decade in a life of seventy-odd years. Even that work, by an obscure Welsh doctor buried near the river Usk, was forgotten until the nineteenth century. First for his piety and then for his poetry he was taken off the shelf and re-edited. Since then his reputation has grown.

Silex Scintillans, C.H. Sisson says, is most profitably read as a whole book. The best poems are set in the context of the uneven imagination which produced them. Private experience is communicated in the language of Anglican Christianity. Along with images of light come those of water – baptism, cleansing, rejuvenation. If light is far and starry, water is close, physical and metaphysical or mystical. Vaughan brings us 'authentic tidings of invisible things' but also skilfully presents a created world in which he participated and lived a difficult life. It is not surprising that one of Sisson's finest poems, 'The Usk', is rooted in the landscapes and concerns of Henry – and Thomas – Vaughan.

Vaughan died on the brink of the eighteenth century, the very last voice contained entirely within what many regard as the great century of English poetry, the crucial period of English history in which the age-old order was finally violated, and the Restoration, rather than re-establishing continuities, produced a different kind of dawn.

NEW PILOTS

… Such artless beauty lies in *Shakespeare's* wit,
'Twas well in spite of whim what e'er he writ.
His Excellencies came and were not sought,
His words like casual Atoms made a thought:
Drew up themselves in Rank and File, and writ,
He wond'ring how the devil it was such wit.
Thus like the drunken Tinker, in his Play,
He grew a Prince, and never knew which way.

John Dryden, 'Prologue' to Julius Caesar

In the new dawn the great eagle of English poetry is fit, sleek and well-fed, but its wings have been clipped – tastefully and painlessly, of course – so that the bird finds flight difficult. It will never again convey in its talons a plump and struggling poet like Geoffrey Chaucer to the House of Fame. Next time a poet flies in the flesh, it will not be on 'viewless wings of poesy' but in a machine.

It is hard for a reader arriving at his work in the sequence of English poets not to think ungenerously of John Dryden. He appears to condescend to Chaucer and to Shakespeare. He opens verse to a popular readership – to what in a more cynical age we call a market. His books sold well. Jacob Tonson – who bought *Paradise Lost* for £8 from Milton's widow – says as much; he was willing to pay real money to keep Dryden on his list. Tonson published Addison, and Rowe's edition of Shakespeare, and an edition of Beaumont and Fletcher (he understood how money could be wrung from drama). Between 1684 and 1708 he published *Miscellanies*, which Dryden edited until his death in 1700, and which included work by Pope, Swift and Ambrose Philips. He was the secretary of the immortal Kit-Cat Club, which brought together writers and others of a Whig persuasion – Steele, Congreve, Addison, Vanbrugh among them – to meet at the house of the distinguished pastry-cook Mr Christopher Katt, in Shire Lane (off Temple Bar), whose mutton pies were called kit-cats. Later meetings were held *chez* Tonson at Barn Elms. Godfrey Kneller painted the club members at less than half-length because the low ceiling of Jacob's dining room would not accommodate half-size portraits. The portraits are now in the National Portrait Gallery, where they look sociable but a little stunted. It was clever of Tonson to draw writers around him in a more or less intimate way. He could control them and pick off works as they were completed, without danger of losing them to competitors. It is also not impossible that, though he was a publisher, he *enjoyed* the company of writers, and they his.

Dryden was generally a professional and not a troublesome author. He was hugely accomplished, one of the most radical and resourceful poets in the language. Still, he fills the modern reader with misgivings. Something is missing, something that even a minor poet of the earlier age, and some of his minor contemporaries, possess. That impalpable something is palpably lacking in Dryden. We find him more than a symptom of change: he is also a cause.

He held court at Will's coffee house, as Ben Jonson had done at the Apollo Room; he was sought out by poets and poetasters who wanted to be legitimised. Dryden was more like the despotic French composer Rameau than Jonson. Jonson taught a various discipline, Dryden taught rules by example and precept. 'From his contemporaries,' Doctor Johnson remarked, Dryden 'was in no danger. Standing therefore in the highest place, he had no care to rise by contending with himself; but while there was no name above his own, was willing to enjoy fame on the easiest terms.'

As the century turned, 'a delicate precocious boy' – the young Alexander Pope – was taken to Will's and introduced to Dryden. Inspired by Dryden's clear eminence, Pope wanted it for himself. The quest was for recognised correctness which led to power in a tinpot literary world. Poets were now in competition with one another; there was a pecking order, with rewards according to perceived eminence. There were 'objective' yardsticks of propriety, decorum and form. How gentle by contrast the rule of Jonson: a bibulous, cantankerous but generally benign enabler, he had inspired younger poets and encouraged their verse, while Dryden, by contrast, was a severe, mannerly, powdered, snuff-snorting and cosmopolitan poetic pontiff. The characters of both Jonson and Dryden are over-simplified in summary, but there is undeniably a new tone.

Does something happen to the English imagination in the latter part of the seventeenth century, something radical and irreversible? T.S. Eliot thinks so and calls it a 'dissociation of sensibility'. It is plausible to locate it in the complex historical events that led to the Commonwealth and the Restoration: a break with cultural and spiritual continuities and political certainties; a wave of influence from the Continent, especially France, from where a king returned; a new spirit of scepticism, new codes of decorum and politeness, that Enlightment which cast such murky darkness on the world of instinct, intuition and spontaneity. Something happens to the English mind to create the wide gap between Donne and

Pope, between poets who feel thought and poets who think. For Donne a thought had a context and an occasion, it modified him, it magnetised other thoughts, it was volatile and in process. For Dryden, by contrast, a thought was something to be tidied up and refined for presentation. Poetry's function as a *synthesiser* of experience is first attenuated, then virtually banished in the age Dryden in his maturity inaugurates.

Robert Graves pays him an ambiguous tribute. 'He earned the doubtful glory of having found English poetry brick and left it marble – native brick, imported marble.' He recalls Doctor Johnson's comments on Dryden's *need* to flatter: 'The inevitable consequence of poverty is dependence. Dryden had probably no recourse in his exigencies but to his bookseller.' It is true: Dryden was compelled to get money from Tonson, his bookseller, and to supplement it from those to whom he dedicated his poems and their relations. His bookseller/publisher had his own fish to fry. A writer could expect a limited income from the printing of his work; but like modern poets, he earned real bread from flattery:

Th' unhappy man, who once has trailed a pen,
Lives not to please himself but other men:
Is always drudging, wastes his life and blood,
Yet only eats and drinks what you think good ...

A rule evolved that poets were not to write 'low' any longer. A low style is unsuitable for serious subjects, as for serious patrons. Poets could not write English in the way Chaucer, Skelton, Shakespeare and Jonson had. An unofficial but pervasive censorship developed. It was called Decorum.

In his Preface to *Fables Ancient and Modern*, Dryden reflects on the permanence of Chaucer's characters: 'Mankind is ever the same, and nothing lost out of nature, though every thing is altered.' A confident Augustan sentiment, learned from Lucretius, characterises the father of the eighteenth century, the man Eliot sees as dividing with Milton the heritage of seventeenth-century poetry into two narrower channels. 'In Dryden, wit becomes almost fun, and thereby loses some contact with reality.' Dryden's mature language is prodigiously efficient. It lacks subtlety, intimacy, doubt and fear. It is a language for discourse and definition, not physical evocation or personal statement. Ford is harsh about his legacy: 'It is really to Dryden, writing wholly within the seventeenth century, that the eighteenth owes the peculiar fadedness of all its adjectived nouns and latinised cliché phrases.'

Readers describe his qualities in other than poetic terms. For Johnson he is the 'father of English criticism' and speaks in a 'tone of adamantine confidence'. Arnold calls him 'a classic of our prose'. Through Dryden later ages define priorities. There are many things he is *not*, many things he does not and cannot do. But there are also things he does incomparably well: his place in English poetry, visited grudgingly by new readers but gradually increasing in charm and attraction as they revisit, is a place of lucidity, analysis, critical insight, general 'truth'. Coleridge says, 'Dryden's genius was of that sort which catches fire by its own motion; his chariot wheels *get* hot by driving fast.' The best way to read him, especially the dramatic poems and translations, is not at a student's dogged pace but headlong. Gerard Manley Hopkins called his nature 'masculine': 'his style and his rhythms lay the strongest stress of all our literature on the naked thew and sinew of the English language.' Wyndham Lewis pairs him with Daniel Defoe as a 'tongue that naked goes'.

John Dryden was born at the vicarage of Aldwinkle, Northamptonshire, of Puritan antecedents, in 1631. Educated at Westminster School under Richard Busby ('the flogging schoolmaster' as he came to be known, who included John Locke and Matthew Prior among his pupils) Dryden wrote and published at eighteen his first notable poem, 'Upon the Death of Lord Hastings' (312). It is flawed, combining memorable lines with strained – not to say mixed – metaphors and ill-judged effects: the small-pox spots on the diseased lord are compared with

> rosebuds, stuck i' the lily skin about.
> Each little pimple had a tear in it,
> To wail the fault its rising did commit ...

The work is full of promise; it is a suggestive confusion. A metaphysical impulse runs through it, as does a courtly instinct. Most effective are the moral conclusions, tightly drawn in efficient couplets.

He went to Trinity College, Cambridge, where he did not distinguish himself but took his BA in 1654. He attached himself to his rich cousin Sir Gilbert Pickering, chamberlain to Cromwell, and in 1658 wrote his elegy on Cromwell's death. The metaphors are used decoratively, turned on and off like bulbs to give local illumination, and the matter is uncontrolled in its emotional flow, so that Johnson could declare that Dryden had 'a mind better formed to reason than to feel'. With the Restoration, reason told him to get in the front row of flatterers. In 'Astrea Redux' he praises the King and Sir Robert Howard, whose daughter he later married. Charles II made him Poet Laureate in 1668. An active dramatist from 1663 onward, he pilloried the King's foes in plays and satires.

He was made Historiographer Royal in 1670, a reward for service and for his impressive but over-meticulous poem *Annus Mirabilis* ('The Year of Wonders') of 1666. He prided himself on accuracy in his descriptions of naval encounters and of the Great Fire of London. This is the first poem in which he displays the full authority of his mature style:

Our dreaded Admiral from far they threat,
    Whose batter'd rigging their whole war receives.
All bare, like some old oak which tempests beat,
    He stands, and sees below his scatter'd leaves.

The move from conventionality to the effectively Homeric simile is masterly: the serene remove of the 'old oak' (which is still the ship's oak mast), in its forest, surrounded by bereaving autumn, is philosophically poised and affecting. His patriotism is of a novel, imperial stamp, and Shakespeare has touched his language:

Yet, like an English gen'ral will I die,
    And all the ocean make my spacious grave.
Women and cowards on the land may lie,
    The sea's a tomb that's proper for the brave.

One of the distinctive qualities of Dryden, who seems at times to belong to the following century, is that he is so different in kind from Milton. His English roots are in Chaucer and Shakespeare rather than Spenser.

In 1681 *Absalom and Achitophel* (313) appeared. The first of our great political satires, it attacked Shaftesbury and the party opposed to the Court. A bald, less oblique assault on Shaftesbury, *The Medal*, followed in 1682. It was Dryden's most fruitful period. In the same year he published the Anglican *Religio Laici (A Layman's Faith)* (321). The allegorical *The Hind and the Panther* (314) attempts to vindicate his later (1687) turn to Roman Catholicism.

Much has been made of Dryden's apparently opportunistic shifts of religious and political allegiance. Doctor Johnson justifies the poet's religious sincerity as a Catholic by pointing to the letters and the life. Dryden's sons were all unquestionably devout Roman Catholics, two of whom served the Church. As to his political opportunism, Ford Madox Ford makes the case for him: 'It is difficult to see what other course a man writing on public matters could have taken if he set the peace of a sufficiently tormented country above all other matters.' When James II was dethroned, Dryden was fifty-seven. He had found his faith, remained a Catholic, and lost both his royal appointments under William III. In bitter poems he satirised new time-servers, famously Thomas Shadwell in *MacFlecknoe*.

He published two *Poetical Miscellanies* in 1684 and 1685 which include important poems. Johnson called 'On the Death of Mrs Killigrew' 'the noblest ode that our language has ever produced'. It is masterly, but must strike a modern reader as a coldly deliberate tribute:

Art she had none, yet wanted none:
For Nature did that want supply,
So rich in treasures of her own,
She might our boasted stores defy:
Such noble vigour did her verse adorn,
That it seem'd borrow'd, where 'twas only born.

Convention is refined but not animated. Dryden makes play with the language of virtue; the poem celebrates his subtlety more than it celebrates the unfortunate Mrs Killigrew.

Pope spent his early years in translation, an apprenticeship. Dryden turned seriously to translation only later in life. With collaborators he rendered Ovid's *Epistles*. He was the kind of poet who could maintain an *atelier* because it was in the nature of his poetic language that it was *imitable*, a social mode of discourse. In 1692 his outstanding *Satires of Juvenal and Persius* appeared. Three years before his death in 1700, *The Works of Virgil* was published. Some regard this as Dryden's masterpiece. Pope calls it 'the most noble and spirited translation I know in any language'. His last major work, published in 1700, was *Fables Ancient and Modern*, an anthology of translations from Ovid, Boccaccio and Chaucer, which included one of his most celebrated prose prefaces. Tonson ordered verse by the yard, originally asking for 10,000 lines, and received more than he bargained for, partly because Dryden wrote for money. He was an occasional poet in an even more literal sense than Jonson.

Even the plethora of his critical detractors would agree, Dryden is one of those rare writers, like Spenser, Milton, Wordsworth and Eliot, who by example and critical writing redirect the current of English poetry. Without an understanding of his techniques and concerns, it is hard to make sense of the eighteenth century, on the eve of which he died. Its achievements and *longueurs*, its stylisations, its manners and mannerisms, are figured or prefigured in his writing. He was the architect of that Augustan mansion in English literature which demands more effort from the modern reader than any other. We must adjust to well-proportioned rooms in which familiar things are rendered unnaturally real in definition and made typical; or to satires in which a familiar world is mercilessly turned topsy-turvy. If we judge Dryden by the effect he had, he is great. If we judge the work itself, we cannot deny him greatness, unless on grounds of limited tonal range (and on such grounds Milton himself would fail). Dryden's technical and formal assurance have few parallels. He is a civic, public, social poet. Our age has a distaste for such work and its values, but if we dismiss Dryden, we dismiss the clearest English poet, and the most accomplished of public poets.

Unlike John Wilmot, Earl of Rochester, who went a certain way with reason, then discarded it in favour of instinct because reason led to a dark *cul-de-sac*, Dryden stuck with reason as a sufficient means of exploration and discourse, leading to the portal of Faith. 'A man is to be cheated into passion, but reasoned into truth,' he writes in the Preface to *The Hind and the Panther* (314). Reason has limits, and beyond it faith opens out the way. He evokes the process in one of the most resonant passages of *Religio Laici*: 'Dim, as the borrowed beams of moon and stars / To lonely, weary, wand'ring travellers, / Is Reason to the soul.' Reason in the civic sphere reveals the need for order and authority. It is worth remembering that his three important early poems praised or celebrated figures of authority and power: Hastings, Cromwell, Charles II.

Reason is the root of his aesthetic, its formality audible even when the tone is informal. He is seldom grandiloquent or assertive; a vein of wit runs through even his most sober work. He concurs with Hobbes about the place of fancy and judgement in the creative process. 'Time and education beget experience; experience begets memory; memory begets judgement and fancy, judgement begets the strength and structure, and fancy begets the ornaments of a poem.' Wit is in the interplay of judgement and fancy. Fancy perceives similitude in things dissimilar, judgement perceives distinctions in things similar. Rhyme, he argues, helps to keep fancy under control.

Such a concept of poetry compels a poet to be exact in his use of image and metaphor in order to illuminate and instruct. The truth of a figure – either literal, allegorical or satiric – must be maintained. Implied too is a propensity to work towards general truths. This produces an impersonal tone, so that one can hold Dryden responsible for the whole argument of a poem without always being certain of his personal attitude to particulars.

The gap between Donne and Dryden could not be wider. Descartes and the new philosophy – and Hobbes – come between them. So does Cromwell and then the Restoration, with French habits acquired in exile. Poetry as a serious exercise was called in question. Three modes principally appeal to Dryden, all of them deliberate, public, and in one way or another 'useful'. First are prologues and epilogues to the plays, comical, critical, expository or hortatory. Dryden's comic epilogues are among his best. Mrs Ellen, 'when she was to be carried off dead by the bearers' at the end of *Tyrannick Love* (1670), exclaims, 'Hark, are you mad? You damn'd confounded dog, / I am to rise, and speak the Epilogue.' She addresses the audience courteously as the ghost of the character she has played, and berates the poet:

O Poet, damned dull Poet, who could prove
So senseless! To make Nelly die for Love,
Nay, what's yet worse, to kill me in the prime

> Of Easter-term, in tart and cheese-cake time!
> I'll fit the fop; for I'll not one word say
> T' excuse his godly out of fashion play.
> A play which if you dare but twice sit out,
> You'll all be slander'd, and be thought devout.

Presumably, having delivered her epilogue, she is carted off stage to general applause.

The second acceptable mode of verse is the consciously decorative, rhetorical poem, usually occasional and celebratory. The 'Song for St Cecilia's Day' and 'Alexander's Feast' display the virtuosity of the poet honouring an occasion. Third comes the heroic or religious epic, on a large scale, with ceremonious action, contemporary reference, and didactic intent. The observe of this is the satire which Dryden develops with a metrical virtuosity and clarity of diction unlike Donne's, rejecting *asprezza* and harsher tones. In *Absalom and Achitophel* satire is cruel and direct, but the prosody is impeccable: Achitophel's human deformity is not spared, but it does not distort the surface of the verse:

> A daring pilot in extremity,
> Pleased with the danger, when the waves went high,
> He sought the storms; but, for a calm unfit,
> Would steer too nigh the sands, to boast his wit.
> Great wits are sure to madness near allied,
> And thin partitions do their bounds divide;
> Else, why should he, with wealth and honour blest,
> Refuse his age the needful hours of rest?
> Punish a body which he could not please;
> Bankrupt of life, yet prodigal of ease? (313)

Figurative language is not Dryden's forte. Often it is not integrated with the argument but runs alongside, decorating and heightening but not collaborating with it at a deeper level. Milton exemplifies another mode. In 'lik'ning spiritual to corporeal forms' he begins with figure and metaphor and attempts a realisation which itself carries moral significance; Dryden teases prose meanings into metaphor. In each case a partial process is enacted. Pope, by contrast, thinks in shapes and forms, exploits reversals, contains his meanings in the figures themselves but works as it were with atomised forms and metaphors, divorced from the expected context and releasing new meanings in an original context. His poetry tends to fragment into brilliant shards. Milton's procedure comes closest to the 'organic' concept of poetic form enunciated by Coleridge and exploited by the Romantics. Dryden's procedure is remote from this. He distrusts antithesis, paradox and disjunction and is wary of placing excessive confidence in plain narrative, at least for didactic purposes.

His satires are conceived in a different spirit from Pope's. For Pope the ideal order is no longer tangibly embodied, there is no 'right' party and no legitimate order: his satiric exaggerations do not always suggest a norm, his distortions contain more malice than instructive justness. Dryden accepts the *status quo* as the norm, accepts necessary authority, and places facts rather than values first. This 'philosophical actualism' he learned from Hobbes. Fact, however subversive, has more authority than traditional sanction, in politics as in literature: a king's authority is a formal, not a sacred one; to be of value a poem must be of use. His tendency to stylise material in order to draw its morals, the way attitudes replace passions and figures replace characters, is due in part to Charles II's own taste. From his French exile he brought back a preference for rhymed, formalised dramas. The King was patron: though he did not call the tune, no doubt he tapped out a rhythm with his foot. Dryden obliged his King and his publisher. Flattery is his worst vice, yet he is so assured that he retains, or regains, his integrity.

Doctor Johnson's assessment of Dryden is still the most concise and judicious. Dryden rather than Sidney is 'the father of English criticism', especially on the strength of his *Essay on Dramatic Poesy* (1668). Johnson criticises the inconsistent approach in Dryden's essays, the occasional marring casualness and partiality. But these faults do not imperil a broader achievement which (unlike Milton's or Cowley's) is at root not scholarly but critical. His art is to express clearly what he thinks with vigour. Before Dryden there was 'no poetical diction, no system of words at once refined from the grossness of domestic use, and free from the harshness of terms appropriated to particular arts'.

The advent of 'diction' was a mixed blessing. Dryden intended refined diction to make language transparent, unobtrusive, capable of succinct general statements of truth without obscurity or vulgarity: hence the excellence of his theory and practice of translation. But for some of his followers diction came to mean refinement of manner and affectation. When Johnson claims that he refined the sentiments of poetry, he wishes to praise the public manner and the absence of individual quirkiness. Yet it is the element of individual tone, of apprehensible character or 'voice', that we miss in Dryden. It is overstatement to say that he 'tuned the numbers' of English poetry. He refined the heroic couplet and handed it as a vital instrument to his successors. His prosodic virtuosity in the songs from the plays, in odes and elegies, is not in doubt: but he had equals among his predecessors, not least Jonson. When Dryden 'refined' language, he rid it of dross, but also of much expressive power. He retuned his instrument to certain harmonies but it was incapable of rendering some older and deeper strains. It could only condescend to Shakespeare. The loss is felt not so much in his own work as in the work of his heirs.

Efficiency, his chief virtue, he perfected from his stage writing. What Homer was for Pope, theatre was for Dryden. It gave him a public: there he discovered and perfected a 'popular' style. He was not 'much inclined' by genius to write for the stage, but necessity took him there and instructed him. The many plays contain little of his best writing. One of them, *All for Love*, based on Shakespeare's *Antony and Cleopatra*, retains some theatrical appeal today. But the stage was his pacing-ground. Without that experience it is doubtful that he could have sustained *Absalom and Achitophel*, the best political satire in the language. The satires, full of the political and literary life of the time, retain a wider reference. The prologues and epilogues are not remote from common speech. The allegories, too, reflect his age's intellectual and spiritual concerns. Eliot's tribute to Dryden is partial and paradoxical: 'Dryden appeared to cleanse the language of verse and once more bring it back to prose order. For this reason he is a great poet.' It would be better to say that Dryden suggests an order for poetic language different from his predecessors'. What is prosaic in Dryden is his ideas, not his language. When Eliot suggests that he 'once more' brings the language of poetry back to prose order, we are inclined to ask: when in the history of English poetry up to Dryden's time had the language of poetry followed prose order? Dryden did not take English poetry back but inexorably forward to a new phase. His verse rejects as much as – perhaps more than – it discovers: he discovered what could usefully be discarded.

Dryden had virulent enemies in his time. His satires and the King's favour enraged the Earl of Rochester, who legend says had him mugged one night in a dark passageway off Garrick Street, near Covent Garden. Did the aristocratic Rochester see Dryden as an upstart? Was he troubled by his religion? Did he fear that Dryden might persuade the King out of his patient affection for his troublesome courtier? Or was he simply jealous of the skills and dogged industry of the greatest poet of his age? We are back to *competition* between poets. 'Mr Andrew Marvell (who was a good Judge of Witt) was wont to say that he [Rochester] was the best English Satyrist and had the right veine. 'Twas pitty Death tooke him off so soon.' Marvell was not alone in speaking up for Rochester, a man by turns in and out of favour at Court and volatile, brilliant and unpredictable. At his best, he was also philosophical:

> Nothing, thou elder brother even to shade:
> Thou had'st a being ere the world was made,
> And (well fixed) art alone of ending not afraid. (353)

During his poetic apprenticeship two generations later, Alexander Pope wrote 'Upon Silence' in imitation of Rochester's 'Upon Nothing': 'Silence! Coeval with Eternity; / Thou wert ere future's self began to be.' His piece is a respectful exercise, while Rochester's is one of the few necessary master-pieces the poet wrote. The young Pope took Rochester to heart as a master. Rochester attempted to think in verse, to think even the darkest thoughts, a feat he performed with appalling lucidity in 'Upon Nothing'. He lays bare the philosophical basis for his notorious libertinism. What had seemed vice becomes an expression of something more fashionable in our time, an accepting nihilism.

The poem explains what many see as the saddest squandering of authentic genius in English poetry. When Pope, forty years after his imita-tion of Rochester, came to sleep in the same bed Rochester had graced at Adderbury, he was 'With no poetic ardours fir'd'. No wonder; Rochester left but a small oeuvre to suggest what he might have been capable of. The work is formally conservative and eccentric in theme and subject. Pope came to see him and other poets of Charles II's Court, including Charles Sackville, Earl of Dorset, the beguilingly cheerful and erotic Sir Charles Sedley, Sir George Etherege, William Wycherley and Henry Savile, as a 'mob of gentlemen who wrote verses'. Marvell, more amused and forgiv-ing, called his wry and waggish contemporaries a 'merry gang'. Merry in company they must have been: Samuel Pepys, on 30 May 1668, joined them: 'And so to supper in an arbour: but, Lord! Their mad bawdy talk did make my heart ache! And here I first understood by their talk the meaning of the company that lately were called Ballers: Harris telling how it was by a meeting of some young blades, where he was among them, and my Lady Bennet and her ladies; and their there dancing naked, and all the roguish things of the world. But, Lord! what loose, cursed company was this, that I was in tonight, though full of wit; and worth a man's being in for once, to know the nature of it, and their manner of talk, and lives.'

Charles II's Court was hospitable to wit and culture of an aristocratic and Frenchified kind. It was the Indian summer of 'Court culture'. F.R. Leavis finds the poets lacking in 'positive fineness' and 'implicit subtlety'. The country house was supplanted by the coffee house, the 'fine old order' gone. But something was gained in the way of forthrightness, certain social tones which had not been heard before in 'polite' circles irrupted into the verse, though they were soon to be snuffed out by strict precep-tors for whom purity and propriety of diction were an unbreachable rule.

The Restoration Court frolicked in the austere shadows cast by the Commonwealth: a continuity had been broken, an old order perished. Court writers and politicians experienced an ambivalent euphoria; the stability which empowers poet or statesman to take, as a matter of course, a long view or undertake a long work, would not return for decades. Idealism of a powerful, defeated sort – the moral high ground – seemed to be occupied by the other party. Divine sanction gone, there was less a sense of right than of success in the air. Hobbes, not Filmer or Hooker, was the philosopher of the day. Hobbes affected Rochester (as he did Dryden) deeply. As a courtier, the poet's chief allegiance was to 'pleasure' conceived in a narrow range, and nihilistic atheism.

Charles II's Court continued its connections with France. The circumstances of his restoration contributed alien elements to his reign. Court writers were inevitably self-absorbed in ways it had never occurred to their predecessors to be. The decline in civic courtesy and the frail imperatives of duty and service, and the apparent liberality of the Court milieu attracted the great French philosopher Voltaire. And Voltaire found Rochester's work congenial. In *Lettres philosophiques* he says, 'all the world knows Lord Rochester's reputation'; he will introduce the other Rochester, not just a libertine but a man of genius, '*le grand poète*', with his 'ardent' imagination. Voltaire celebrates the satires which, whether the ideas expressed are true or false, possess real energy. Boileau – and Cowley – were among the Earl's favourite authors. His satire belonged to a contemporary European tradition.

Rochester experimented on his life as his contemporaries experimented in science. It is fashionable to see him as 'essentially serious', a 'radical critic' of his time, even a moral visionary. On the evidence of the verse, apart from 'A Satire Against Mankind', he is neither socially radical nor penetratingly serious. His seriousness of theme emerges in only a few poems and there more as statement than considered argument. Hostile to reason, he denied himself the main avenue of philosophical exploration. Yet this hostility is itself a theme, as in 'Tunbridge Wells':

> Ourselves with noise of reason we do please
> In vain; humanity's our worst disease.
> Thrice happy beasts are, who, because they be
> Of reason void, are so of foppery.

Given this view – and despite his power as a rhetorician – Rochester cannot get far beyond satire. Indeed, within satire he goes only a certain distance. He denies himself the scope of the long poem and works within the confines of received forms. His temperament and antecedents make it hard to imagine what other strategy he could have devised.

He was born in Ditchley, Oxfordshire, in 1647. His father, a Royalist general, led an abortive rising in Yorkshire in 1655 and died in exile two or three years later. Rochester's mother was of a family with Puritan connections. At the age of twelve he went up to Wadham College, Oxford, which was then a centre of the new scientific and intellectual developments that led to the foundation of the Royal Academy. In 1661 the precocious young nobleman was made an MA by the incomparable historian Lord Clarendon himself. The restored King granted him a pension in 1660, in recognition of his father's service. Under such favourable stars, Rochester toured France and Italy and returned to England in 1664, where he made himself visible at Court. His feelings for Charles II were ambiguous, almost those of a young man for a forceful stepfather. Some of his scathing satires are directed against the monarch. In 1665 Rochester was confined to the Tower for attempting to abduct a Somerset heiress, whom he married more conventionally two years later ('I'll hold you six to four I love you with all my heart', he wrote to her later, during one of his infidelities). Thanks to the plague, he was released from the Tower, joined the fleet, and gave intrepid service, though there is evidence that he was less stalwart ashore.

Always in and out of favour, he became a Gentleman of the King's Bedchamber in 1666, which was an honour more than a duty. The remaining fourteen years of his life passed in a series of unsettled and rash acts with periods of study and work. If he wrote the notorious play *Sodom*, it would have been around 1670, and in all likelihood a collaborative effort. Between 1673 and 1676 his best satires and 'Upon Nothing' were composed. In 1675 he was appointed Keeper of Woodstock Park. Later in life he claimed to have been drunk for a five year stretch – country life cannot have been too agreeable. He died, after a dubious conversion exhaustively chronicled by his spiritual monitor, the egregious Gilbert Burnet, in 1680.

We can choose between two versions of Rochester. Sir George Etherege in his play *The Man of Mode* presents him as the charming, inconstant and self-involved Dorimant. We can embellish this image with the story of the smashing of the sundials in the Priory Gardens and the 'murderous affray' at Epsom. On the other hand we have the scholar (on the evidence of Anthony à Wood and of the fragments of his translation of Lucretius). Burnet, who negotiated his reconciliation with God and was at best a Whig rascal, wrote of his good looks, his civility, his intelligence: 'He loved to talk and write of speculative matters, and did so with so fine a thread, that even those who hated the subjects' were charmed by his treatment of them. But, Burnet adds, physical led to intellectual dissipation, 'which made him think nothing diverting which was not extravagant'.

The real Rochester is closer to Etherege's than Burnet's version. Samuel Johnson praises the 'vigour of his colloquial wit'; but the 'glare of his general character diffused itself upon his writings'. The very shortness of his pieces reflects the shortness of his periods of sobriety and study. Nevertheless, the dots of brilliance in the writing, taken together, add up to a reckonable star.

He works in four 'kinds': extended satire, libel or squib, racy anecdote, and love poem. Some of the love poems are spoken by women ('I could love thee till I die' and 'To her Ancient Lover' are among the best). Love is of a resolutely carnal nature: 'Leave this gaudy, gilded Stage' (350), ''Tis not that I am weary grown' (352), 'Absent from thee I languish still' (351) and 'The Mistress' rank high in English love poetry. They are forthright, with an air of sincerity. The anecdote poems, too, have a forceful, grotesque bawdiness and can be erotic and startling. 'Fair Chloris in a pigsty lay' (356) is the best-known. We might consider them down-market eclogues. The squibs and libels marry wit and malice and do some damage to their subjects, notably the King.

In imitating Ovid ('O Love! how cold and slow' and 'The Imperfect Enjoyment' (355)) he moves towards satire. It is useful to compare his imitations with Marlowe's (*Elegia* II, ix and III, vi). Less than a century separates them. Marlowe's versions are *visualised* and governed by vivid metaphor undeflected by wit. Rochester argues rather than evokes; idea is developed at the expense of metaphor. His language is more conventional and polite than Marlowe's. In Marlowe there is a sultry, ambiguous sexuality, in Rochester forthrightness without undertones – what Eliot, writing of Dryden, called 'lack of suggestiveness'. Compare Marlowe's:

> Dost joy to have thy hookèd arrows shakèd
> In naked bone? Love hath my bones left naked.
> So many men and maidens without love!
> Hence with great laud thou may'st a triumph move.

with Rochester's:

> On men disarmed how can you gallant prove?
> And I was long ago disarmed by love.
> Millions of dull men live, and scornful maids:
> We'll own love valiant when he these invades.

Rochester is the more correct; Marlowe, despite, or because of, his awkwardness, the more satisfying. The second line focuses the different genius of each writer, the third epitomises the radical change in sensibility that has occurred.

Age, 'beauty's incurable disease', is the key apprehension of Rochester's harsh vision. He satirises affectation and the social forms which lead to a squandering of possible or actual pleasure; and he satirises excesses which themselves foreshorten pleasure and in which he, as much as the King, indulged. He cannot stop attacking reason, that '*ignis fatuus*', a contrived and distracting sixth sense: 'Huddled in dirt the reasoning engine lies, / Who was so proud, so witty, and so wise.' This sense of mortality is unredeemed by religious certitude. The one virtue Rochester celebrates is love. In 'A Letter from Artemiza in the Town to Chloe in the Country' (357) he writes,

> Love, the most generous passion of the mind,
> The softest refuge innocence can find,
> The safe director of unguided youth ...

It is 'That cordial drop heaven in our cup has thrown / To make the nauseous draught of life go down.'

Love a 'passion of the mind'? Marlowe would not have understood that. Rochester's satire seeks to free the impulse of love from inhibition and convention. He is the apologist for 'sex' rather than courtly or romantic love. Yet underlying even this theme is the pervasive truth presented in 'Upon Nothing':

> Great Negative, how vainly would the wise
> Enquire, define, distinguish, teach, devise,
> Did'st Thou not stand to point their blind philosophies. (353)

His satire is directed at Court and society at large, in the manner of Juvenal, but the objective of his satire is not social. Unlike Dryden's, Rochester's satire is informed by metaphysical despair, not social optimism. The best way of dealing with despair is to laugh, and some of his wicked poems, like those of Sir Charles Sedley, provide a salacious delight not to be found elsewhere in English.

Aubrey chronicles the death of Lord Rochester, with which Burnet filled many sanctimonious pages, in three rapid, telling sentences. 'In his last sickness he was exceedingly penitent and wrote a letter of his repentance to Dr Burnet, which is printed. He sent for all his servants, even the piggard-boy, to come and hear his palinode. He died at Woodstock Park, 26 July 1680; and buried at Spilsbury in the same county, Aug 9 following.'

Among the female poets of their age, Dryden favoured 'the Matchless Orinda', Katherine Philips (1632–64) (322–325), wife of James who, at Cardigan Priory, their Welsh home, set up a kind of intellectual circle called the Society of Friendship and entertained the intelligentsia. 'Orinda', a celebrated translator of Corneille's plays, wrote her poems to other women, in particular Anne Owen, the Viscountess of Dungannon, with whom she maintained an intense and, it is assumed, platonic friendship. She can be simperingly sentimental; she also rises to satire, though she lacks the vigour of the Duchess of Newcastle. She died of smallpox at thirty-two and became a mildly tragic legendary figure.

Aphra Behn (1640–89) (340–342) is more Rochester's kind of poet. She was feisty and self-reliant, the first English woman to become a professional writer. He was her friend and patron, but as irregular in patronage as in everything else. Her colourful life – starting at the age of sixteen with an eight-year trip to Surinam and beyond with her father, the appointed lieutenant governor, who died *en route*; her experience of the new world, of a slave rebellion and other adventures which may or may not be true – gives her exotic appeal. She returned to England in 1664, married a merchant and was bereaved, probably in the plague of 1665. She became a spy in Antwerp, did her work well but was never properly paid. She saw the inside of a debtor's prison in 1668 and resolved never to return. So she became a writer. The theatre was her main market and she wrote fourteen plays. When this market dried up she started writing fiction, or 'faction', including *Oroonoko* (1688), with its not altogether believable basis in her early experiences. She died the next year, poor again, and in considerable pain, and, like earlier female writers, was forgotten.

Some of her poems are songs uprooted from her plays. Some are lascivious entertainments which pull no punches and are as erotic – in a different key – as Sedley's. Indeed some of her poems share lines with his. It would be wrong to claim technical originality for Aphra Behn as a poet. But, as a woman poet, and as a woman writer, she clears an important space; she breaks as many taboos as Mary Wroth (**219–221**) did, and possesses more substantial gifts. Against polite Dryden, impolite Rochester; against proper 'Orinda', we can set the matchless Aphra Behn.

Anne Finch, Countess of Winchilsea (1661–1720) sourly pondered 'the situation of the woman writer'. Her imagination was shaped by the seventeenth century, though it was in the eighteenth that her voice was finally heard. Alexander Pope, who rather liked her, also derided her (with his friends Gay and Arbuthnot) in a play, *Three Hours after Marriage*, in which she appears as Phoebe Clinket, the loopy lady poet. (Sylvia Plath played the part of Phoebe at a Cambridge University production of the play a couple of centuries later.) Many of Finch's contemporaries shared Pope's ambivalence. The only book she published in her lifetime appeared anonymously when she was fifty-two. She had 'the skill to write, the modesty to hide'. Wordsworth prepared a selection of her verse and since that time she has never sunk entirely from sight. He liked her poem 'A Nocturnal Reverie' (**360**) which, he said, contained in its descriptions of groves and meadows at night the only new images of 'external nature' between the poetry of Milton and Thomson.

> When darkened groves their softest shadows wear,
> And falling waters we distinctly hear;
> When through the gloom more venerable shows
> Some ancient fabric, awful in repose,

While sunburnt hills their swarthy looks conceal,
And swelling haycocks thicken up the vale;
When the loosed horse now, as his pasture leads,
Comes slowly grazing through th' adjoining meads,
Whose stealing pace and lengthened shade we fear,
Till torn up forage in his teeth we hear ...

It is a vision closer to nature than Pope's aestheticising in 'Windsor Forest' – a series of observations, not of epithets and qualities. Finch is read today for her poems on the friendship of women and on the situation of women, and for the poems of conjugal contentment, but it is also striking that no other woman poet of the time so bitterly reflects upon the circumstances which inhibited women from expressing themselves in print.

Another strange voice, new and yet with old and tested tonalities, is Edward Taylor (343–349). He was born around 1642 of prosperous Puritan yeoman stock in Leicestershire during the Civil War. Unable to subscribe to the Act of Uniformity after the Restoration, cast out of his job as a schoolmaster, forbidden to go to Oxford or Cambridge, to preach or worship, he emigrated to Boston when he was twenty-six. He was already a firm admirer of Francis Quarles (232–234) and of the Metaphysical poets – not only of Donne and Herbert (whom he echoes) but Vaughan, Traherne (326–330) and Crashaw (285–291) as well. And Du Bartas. Like Anne Bradstreet's, his literary culture suffered a kind of positive arrest on his departure. He attended Harvard College and became a pastor (and physician) in the frontier hamlet of Westfield, a hundred miles west of Boston, retiring in 1725, the father of numerous offspring by two wives and in possession of a library, remarkable for its time, of some two hundred books.

On his death he left a 400 page manuscript of religious poems, composed as part of his spiritual preparation for administering the Lord's Supper, and including two substantial sequences. In 1937 they were discovered in a library and America had another substantial early poet who, a Puritan nourished on the great Anglican Metaphysicals, began to carve out his own kind of poetry on a physical and spiritual frontier. His non-existence in American poetry for the two centuries after his death makes it hard to set him in the American frame: his work is sadly without issue until the twentieth century when poets such as Robert Lowell take apprentice bearings from him. To English readers he seems at first an anachronism, his conceits at times outlandish and mechanical. ('Shall Spirits thus my mammularies suck?' or 'Be thou my Lily, make thou me thy knot: / Be thou my Flowers, I'll be thy flower pot.') Yet he is a figurative thinker, he has a deep sense of evil and of man's fallen nature.

He uses verse as an instrument of redemption, not – as Milton does – of instruction. He can surprise us into a sudden vision of the divine order, a sense of how we might attain unity with God through the created world. 'Shall I not smell thy sweet, oh! Sharon's Rose?' Or, 'Lord, blow the coal: thy love enflame in me.' It is as though his Anglican mentors have leavened his spirit, made him not less severe but more humane, accepting of the forms of grace which pass through the human senses. He is one of those rare Puritans who will risk saying 'yes' to right pleasure.

> How sweet a Lord is mine? If any should
>   Guarded, engardened'd, nay, imbosomed be
> In reeks of odours, gales of spices, folds
>   Of aromatics, Oh! how sweet was he?
>   He would be sweet, and yet his sweetest wave
>   Compar'd to thee my Lord, no sweet would have.

In Taylor, who with Bradstreet stands (long neglected and still little understood) at the start of what was to become a tradition, there is something like the new energy of John Skelton, two hundred years before. There is too, as with Skelton and Donne, a rawness which is the function of a passionate intelligence that refuses to conform to prescriptive rules of form or taste. Taylor's individualism, remote from the aristocratic tenor of the Tudor and Elizabethan poets, expressed in phrasing, imagery and the unfolding form of the poem as argument, is precisely what the decorous strictures of the eighteenth century, already manifest in Dryden, would come to guard poetry and public taste against. The next chapter of English poetry is wonderful, but its wonders are wholly accountable. Many of the best writers of previous generations vanish from circulation. Neglect or incomprehension reward original poets emerging into the Augustan age.

When we consider the enormous competence of Sedley, Sackville and Behn and the warped genius of Rochester, we might conclude that one consequence of the savage disruptions of the English Revolution, and then of the hardly glorious Restoration, was a narrowing of the thematic and spiritual territory in which poets felt empowered to function. Rochester is so much better than his poems: if only he could have possessed Dryden's positive belief and got beyond 'Upon Nothing'! But the apparently effortless and natural depth of the Metaphysicals, the titanic energies of Milton, Dryden's intellectual grappling with the world of the spirit and its institutions, lost imaginative reality. When poetry recovered spiritual ground in the latter half of the eighteenth century, belief had become more a matter of effortful invention than accommodation with faith. The consequences are remarkable. But something unprecedented had happened over the two centuries of poetry represented in this volume. The story of poets and readers and their world, and the story of poetry itself, become progressively a single story here.

Edward Taylor's emigration to the New World is part of that single story, the story that informed Marvell's 'Bermudas' and Shakespeare's *The Tempest*, that colours the imagery of Donne and the imagination of Ralegh. Taylor was wholly alive in the spirit, as men and women uniquely were in the middle of his century. His spirit inhabited a body whose senses remained alert to sensation and wary of temptation. When he writes most exuberantly, then history, poetry and the Christian sacrament achieve a homely harmony, fanciful, unpretentious, and deeply moving. 'Enough! Enough! oh! let me eat my Word': this is as close to the Christian God and to Christ as poetry can come.

And then that sense of a single story, of a common banquet and a communion is over; history and individual lives and art begin to go their separate ways.

Anthology

PREFACE

The poetry of the sixteenth century is far easier to enjoy than that of the fifteenth. The language has pretty much settled down. There are enormous poems, to be sure, but the characteristic voices of the Tudor and Elizabethan courts are elegiac and lyric. The middle-length poems – epyllia for the most part – that are still readable are narratives and the narrative is lively in some of the ways that lyric poetry is. Paradoxically, only Edmund Spenser, a deliberate innovator, seems to belong in spirit to the previous century with his more or less systematic allegory and, in *The Faerie Queene*, his apparent ability to tease his matter out to the end of doom. Doom met him half way and his great poem is only half finished.

The texts of the poems do present problems. Not many original manuscripts survive and the carelessness of early copyists and printers means that there is no authoritative version of many of the poems. Conventions of spelling, punctuation, lineation and indentation varied from one copy or printed version to the next. Where ample manuscripts do exist, for example in the case of Traherne, the bulk of whose work was discovered centuries after his death, the scholar can construct a faithful 'copy', but what merit can there be in such a version for the general reader when the texts of all the surrounding poetry are either unstable or have been modernised? To present Traherne *as he wrote down his poems* is fascinating to the scholar. The reader who seeks to understand him in the context of Herbert, Vaughan and others will be less grateful.

Much modern criticism, starting with Robert Graves's and Laura Riding's influential *A Survey of Modernist Poetry* (1927) and its close reading of Shakespeare's Sonnet 129 (a reading which affected I.A. Richards and helped catalyse William Empson into writing *Seven Types of Ambiguity*, and through him affected the history of a certain kind of criticism and poetry) contrasts early texts with later emendations and modernisations. It shows how some editors forfeit certain elements of language in the interests of heightening others, answering – as it were – to the prejudices of the editor or the age rather than to the essential nature of the poem in question. (These critics insist that each poem has an *essential nature*.) The approaches of Riding and Graves, Empson and then Davie and Ricks, do much to revive interest in the darker corners of the seventeenth century and the neglected core of the eighteenth, with which the next volume in this series opens.

My purpose here is to make the poets presented and excerpted as transparently available to the modern reader as possible. This has entailed a standardisation of spelling (which I extend, aware of the perils, even to Milton) and a simplification of punctuation. It has also involved preferring certain formats to others, so that a poem may appear in an unfamiliar layout, though one which one or another earlier version sanctions. Riding and Graves, Geoffrey Hill and many another poet-critic with a coherently purist perspective, would object to my standardisations, and I understand their objections: often the words I print not only look but may sound different from the words the poets wrote; my punctuation may blur or erase some nuance that a less, or differently, structured punctuation would sanction. But this anthology is introductory in two senses: it represents and it advocates. The attentive reader is directed beyond it, to the wider world of each individual poet. Like all anthologies, this book is approximate.

Even though lyric and elegy were in the ascendant, it is imperative to provide a sampling of the great long poems in the tradition, and I have given substantial extracts, as for example of Marlowe and Milton. The sixteenth and seventeenth centuries were the second and third great ages of translation, and I have not been able to do justice to this area of our poetry. Chapman and Arthur Golding – whose Ovid Ezra Pound endorsed – and Dryden and Pope are among the defining translators of their time.

Even more important were the translators of the Bible, the book which, directly and indirectly, shapes so much of the tradition, and whose radical force remains, in later centuries, enabling and liberating throughout the English-speaking world. In the first part of the sixteenth century William Tyndale translated the scriptures not from the Latin, as the Wycliffites had done in the fourteenth, or from the Greek, as in his very earliest translations, but directly from the Hebrew, referring to the Latin Vulgate, to the work of Erasmus and of Luther. Miles Coverdale was named as the translator of the complete Bible published in 1535 – worked up from Luther's German Bible, the Vulgate, and Tyndale's work. The Psalms used in worship that appear in the Book of Common Prayer, which was largely agreed in 1549 and whose definitive version was published in 1662, are from the Coverdale Bible. The 1611 Authorised Version, the King James Bible, develops Tyndale's texts, with reference to Wycliffe's and others.

This volume cannot adequately represent the Bible (162–177) whose narratives, imagery, techniques and cadences are at the heart of so much religious and secular writing. To do the Bible poetry even the beginning of justice would entail printing from the Old Testament most of Genesis and

Exodus, Ruth, Job and the Psalms, Ecclesiastes, the Song of Songs, Isaiah and Jeremiah; and from the New the Gospel of St John, the first books of Luke, and the entire text of Revelation.

The anthology is intended to be used with the excerpts in the introduction. I have tried generally to avoid duplication. In compiling and modernising texts, I have had recourse to various editions. Many of these are listed in the bibliography. I have tried not to take the liberties I allowed myself in the first volume, where in particular the ballad texts lend themselves, perhaps too readily, to creative editorial engagement.

I represent certain poets – Lord Vaux, Queen Elizabeth, Gascoigne, de Vere, Ralegh, Chapman, Herrick, Carew, Taylor – at greater length than they are generally allowed. In my view their ample restoration is necessary: there is a canonical justice in their restoration to something like a proper place. The relative neglect of some of these writers is baffling.

The anthology begins with the rumbustious mature work of that most unpriestly of priests, John Skelton; it ends not with the vertiginous 'Nothing' of Rochester and his reputed final conversion – after excesses far more extreme than Skelton's – to religious faith, nor the intensely personal faith of Edward Taylor, but with an unresolved voice, that of Anne Finch. Serious, accomplished, polite, her poetry has moved perilously near the strategies of good prose. The coolness and calculation with regard to her readers, the wit and the sentiment, all point in the direction of the social and sociable drawing rooms of the eighteenth century, with their nice inclusions and exclusions of people and of diction, in which excess was bottled up until, in certain notable cases, the bottle burst.

John Skelton (1460?–1529)

1. 'Woefully arrayed'

Woefully arrayed,
  My blood, man,
  For thee ran,
It may not be nayed;°   *denied*
  My body blo° and wan,   *livid*
Woefully arrayed.

Behold me, I pray thee, with all thy whole reason,
  And be not so hard hearted, and for this enchason,°   *cause*
  Sith° I for thy soul sake was slain in good season,   *Since*
Beguiled and betrayed by Judas' false treason;   10
    Unkindly° entreated,   *Unnaturally*
      With sharp cord sore fretted,
      The Jews me threated,
    They mowed,° they grinned, they scornèd me,   *grimaced*
    Condemned to death, as thou must see,
        Woefully arrayed.

Thus naked am I nailed, O man, for thy sake!
I love thee, then love me; why sleep'st thou? awake!
Remember my tender heart-root for thee brake,
With pains my veins constrainèd to crake;°   *crack* 20
    Thus tugged to and fro,
    Thus wrapped all in woe,
    Whereas never man was so,
  Entreated thus in most cruel wise,
  Was like a lamb offered in sacrifice,
       Woefully arrayed.

Of sharp thorn I have worn a crown on my head,
So painèd, so strainèd, so rueful, so red;
Thus bobbed, thus robbed, thus for thy love dead,
Unfeignèd not deignèd my blood for to shed;   30
    My feet and hands sore
    The sturdy nails bore;

What might I suffer more
Than I have done, O man, for thee?
Come when thou list,° welcome to me,   *wishest*
    Woefully arrayed.

Of record thy good Lord I have been and shall be;
I am thine, thou art mine, my brother I call thee;
Thee love I entirely – see what is befall me!
Sore beating, sore threating, to make thee, man, all free: 40
    Why art thou unkind?
    Why hast not me in mind?
    Come yet, and thou shalt find
    Mine endless mercy and grace;
See how a spear my heart did race,°   *pierce*
    Woefully arrayed.

Dear brother, no other thing I of thee desire
But give me thine heart free to reward mine hire:
I wrought thee, I bought thee from eternal fire;
I pray thee array thee toward my high empire,   50
    Above the orient,
    Whereof I am regent,
    Lord God omnipotent,
    With me to reign in endless wealth;
Remember, man, thy soul's health.

Woefully arrayed,
    My blood, man,
    For thee ran,
It may not be nayed;
    My body blo and wan,   60
Woefully arrayed.

2. from *Speak Parrot*

My name is Parrot, a bird of Paradise,
By nature devised of a wondrous kind,
Daintily dieted with diverse delicate spice,
Till Euphrates, that flood, driveth me into Ind;
Where men of that country by fortune me find,
And send me to great ladies of estate;
Then Parrot must have an almond or a date:

A cage curiously carven, with silver pin,
Properly painted, to be my coverture;
A mirror of glass, that I may toot therein;   10
These maidens full merrily with many a diverse flower
Freshly they dress and make sweet my bower,
With, 'Speak, Parrot, I pray you,' full courteously they say;
'Parrot is a goodly bird and a pretty poppinjay.'

With my beak bent, my little wanton eye,
My feathers fresh as is the emerald green,
About my neck a circlet like the rich ruby,
My little legs, my feet both feat° and clean,   *neat*
I am a minion to wait upon a queen;
'My proper Parrot, my little pretty fool' –   20
With ladies I learn, and go with them to school.

'He, ha, ha, Parrot, ye can laugh prettily!'
Parrot hath not dined of all this long day.
Like our puss cat, Parrot can mewte° and cry   *mew*
In Latin, in Hebrew, Araby, and Chaldy;
In Greek tongue Parrot can both speak and say,
As Persius, that poet, doth report of me,
Quis expedivit psittaco suum chaire?[1]

Douce° French of Paris Parrot can learn,   *Sweet*
Pronouncing my purpose after my property,   30
With, *parlez bien*, Parrot, *ou parlez rien*;[2]
With Dutch, with Spanish, my tongue can agree,
In English to God Parrot can supplea,
'Christ save King Henry the Eighth, our royal king,
The red rose in honour to flourish and spring!

With Catherine incomparable, our royal queen also,
That peerless pomegranate, Christ save her noble grace!'
Parrot, *saves habler Castiliano*,[3]
With *fidasso de cosso*[4] in Turkey and in Thrace;
Vis consilii expers, as teacheth me Horace,   40
Mole ruit sua,[5] whose dictes° are pregnant,   *sayings*
Soventez foys, Parrot, *en souvenaunte*.[6]

[1] 'Who helped parrot to say Hello [in Greek]?'
[2] 'Speak well, Parrot, or speak not at all'
[3] 'You know how to speak Spanish [Castilian]'
[4] 'Trust in thyself'

My lady mistress, Dame Philology,
Gave me a gift in my nest when I lay,
To learn all language, and it to speak aptly:
Now *pandez mory*, wax frantic, some men say,
Phroneses for phrenesis may not hold her way.⁷
An almond now for Parrot, delicately drest;
In *Salve festa dies, toto*⁸ is the best.

Moderata juvant,⁹ but *toto* doth excede;   50
Discretion is mother of noble virtues all;
*Myden agen*¹⁰ in Greek tongue we read;
But reason and wit wanteth their provincial
When wilfulness is vicar general.
Haec res acu tangitur,¹¹ Parrot, *par ma foy*:
Ticez-vous, Parrot, *tenez-vous coye*.¹²

Busy, busy, busy, and busyness again!
Que pensez-vous,¹³ Parrot? what meaneth this busyness?
*Vitulus*¹⁴ in Oreb troubled Aron's brain,
Melchizedeck merciful made Moloch merciless;   60
Too wise is no virtue, too meddling, too restless;
In measure is treasure, *cum sensu maturato*;
Ne tropo sanno, ne tropo mato.¹⁵

Aram was fired with Chaldee's fire called Ur;
Jobab was brought up in the land of Hus;
The lineage of Lot took support of Assur;
Jereboseth is Hebrew, who list° the cause discuss.   *wishes*
'Peace, Parrot, ye prate, as ye were *ebrius*:'°   *drunk*
Howst thee, *lyuer god vun hemrik, ic seg*!¹⁶
In Popering grew pears, when Parrot was an egg.   70

---

⁵ 'Strength without wisdom falls in on itself'
⁶ 'Many times … in memory'
⁷ Because of madness (phrenesis), understanding (phronesis) cannot prosper
⁸ 'On feast days *everything* is best'
⁹ 'Moderation delights'
¹⁰ 'Nothing in excess'
¹¹ 'This is spot on'
¹² 'Keep mum … be silent'
¹³ 'What are you thinking?'
¹⁴ The golden calf, a reference to Cardinal Wolsey, reputed to be the son of a butcher
¹⁵ 'With a matured sensibility, neither excessively sane nor excessively mad'
¹⁶ 'Hush thee, dear God of heaven, I say'

'What is this to purpose?' Over in a whinnymeg![17]
Hop Lobin of Lowdeon would have a bit of bread;
The gibbet of Baldock was made for Jack Leg;
An arrow unfeathered and without an head,
A bagpipe without blowing standeth in no stead:
Some run too far before, some run too far behind,
Some be too churlish, and some be too kynde.

Ic dien[18] serveth for the ostrich feather,
Ic dien is the language of the land of Beme;
In Afric tongue *byrsa* is a thong of leather;   80
In Palestina there is Jerusalem.
Colostrum° now for Parrot, white bred and sweet cream!   *Finest milk*
Our Thomasen she doth trip, our Jennet she doth shayle:°   *blunder*
Parrot hath a black beard and a fair green tail.

'Morish mine own shelfe,' the costermonger° sayeth;   *apple-seller*
Fatè, fatè, fatè,[19] ye Irish waterlag;
In flattering fables men find but little faith:
But *moveatur terra*, let the world wag;
Let Sir Wrig-wrag wrestle with Sir Dallyrag;
Every man after his manner of ways,   90
Pawbe une arver,[20] so the Welsh man says.

Such shreds of sentence, strewed in the shop
Of ancient Aristippus and such other mo,°   *more*
I gather together and close in my crop,
Of my wanton conceit, *unde depromo*
Dilemmata docta in pædagogio
Sacro vatum,[21] whereof to you I break:
I pray you, let Parrot have liberty to speak ...

---

[17] The stanza employs Scottish ballad allusions to alert the court to Wolsey's foreign policies.
[18] 'I serve' (the royal motto)
[19] The Parrot imitates the Irish way of pronouncing 'Water'.
[20] 'Every one his own way'
[21] 'From where I produce learned arguments, in the holy school of the soothsayers'

3. To Mistress Margery Wentworth

With marjoram gentle,
The flower of goodlihead,
Embroidered the mantle
Is of your maidenhead.
   Plainly I can not glose;°   *gloss*
Ye be, as I divine,
The pretty primrose,
The goodly columbine.
   With marjoram gentle,
The flower of goodlihead,   10
Embroidered the mantle
Is of your maidenhead.
   Benign, courteous, and meek,
With words well devised;
In you, who list° to seek,   *wishes*
Be virtues well comprised.
   With marjoram gentle,
The flower of goodlihead,
Embroidered the mantle
Is of your maidenhead.   20

4. To Mistress Isabel Pennell

By saint Mary, my lady,
Your mammy and your daddy
Brought forth a goodly baby!
   My maiden Isabel,
Reflaring rosabel,
The flagrant camomel;°   *camomile*
   The ruddy rosary,
The sovereign rosemary,
The pretty strawberry;
   The columbine, the nept,°   *catmint* 10
The gillyvor° well set,   *wall flower*
The proper violet;
   Ennewèd° your colour   *Revived*
Is like the daisy flower
After the April shower;
      Star of the morrow grey,

The blossom on the spray,
The freshest flower of May;
   Maidenly demure,
Of womanhood the lure;   20
Wherefore I make you sure,
   It were an heavenly health,
It were an endless wealth,
A life for God himself,
   To hear this nightingale,
Among the birdès small,
Warbling in the vale,
Dug, dug,
Jug, jug,
Good year and good luck,   30
With chuck, chuck, chuck, chuck!

5. To Mistress Margaret Hussey

   Merry Margaret,
As midsummer flower,
Gentil° as falcon   *Noble*
Or hawk of the tower;
   With solace and gladness,
Much mirth and no madness,
All good and no badness,
So joyously,
So maidenly,
So womanly   10
Her demeaning°   *deportment*
In every thing,
Far, far passing
That I can endite,°   *set down*
Or suffice to write
Of merry Margaret,
As midsummer flower,
Gentil as falcon
Or hawk of the tower;
   As patient and as still   20
And as full of good will
As fair Isaphill;°   *Hypsipyle*
Coriander,

Sweet pomander,
Good Cassander;
Steadfast of thought,
Well made, well wrought;
Far may be sought
Erst° that ye can find   *Before*
So courteous, so kind   30
As merry Margaret,
This midsummer flower,
Gentil as falcon
Or hawk of the tower.

6. 'With lullay, lullay, like a child'

With lullay, lullay, like a child,
Thou sleep'st too long, thou art beguiled.

'My darling dear, my daisy flower,
Let me,' quoth he, 'lie in your lap.'
'Lie still,' quoth she, 'my paramour,
Lie still hardely, and take a nap.'
His head was heavy, such was his hap,
All drowsy, dreaming, drowned in sleep.
That of his love he took no keep,
    With hey, lullay, lullay, like a child,
    Thou sleep'st too long, thou art beguiled.   10

With 'ba, ba, ba,' and 'bas, bas, bas,'
She cherished him both cheek and chin,
That he wist never where he was;
He had forgotten all deadly sin.
He wanted wit her love to win:
He trusted her payment, and lost all his pay:
She left him sleeping, and stole away.
    With hey, lullay, lullay, like a child,
    Thou sleep'st too long, thou art beguiled.   20

The rivers rowth,° the waters wan,*   *rough; dark*
She sparèd not to wet her feet.
She waded over, she found a man
That halsed° her heartily and kissed her sweet: *embraced*

Thus after her cold she caught a heat.
'My lefe,'° she said, 'rowteth* in his bed;   *sweetheart; snores*
Ywis° he hath an heavy head,   *Indeed*
    With hey, lullay, lullay, like a child,
    Thou sleep'st too long, thou art beguiled.

What dream'st thou, drunkard, drowsy pate?   30
Thy lust and liking is from thee gone;
Thou blinkered blowboll, thou wak'st too late,
Behold, thou liest, luggard, alone!
Well may thou sigh, well may thou groan,
To deal with her so cowardly:
Ywis, pole-hatchet,° she bleared thine eye!*   *hatchet-face (?); deceived you*

7. from *The Book of Philip Sparrow*

Pla ce bo,[22]
    Who is there, who?
Di le xi,[23]
    Dame Margery;
Fa, re, my, my,
    Wherefore and why, why?
    For the soul of Philip Sparrow,
That was late slain at Carrow,[24]
Among the Nuns Black,
For that sweet soul's sake,   10
And for all sparrows' souls,
Set in our bead-rolls,°   *rosary prayers*
Pater noster qui,[25]
With an *Ave Mari,*[26]
And with the corner of a Creed,
The more shall be your meed.

    When I remember again
How my Philip was slain,

[22] The beginning of the Vespers of the Roman Catholic Office of the Dead, with allusions throughout to the service and the Psalms (from the Vulgate) appropriate to the occasion
[23] Opening of Psalm 116
[24] Benedictine priory near Norwich, where Jane Scrope, who speaks this part of the poem, lived
[25] 'Our Father, which art'
[26] 'Hail Mary'

Never half the pain
Was between you twain,
Pyramus and Thisbe,   20
As then befell to me.
I wept and I wailed,
The tears down hailed,
But nothing it availed
To call Philip again,
Whom Gib our cat hath slain.
     Gib, I say, our cat,
Worrowed her° on that   *Choked herself*
Which I loved best: 30
It cannot be expressed,
My sorrowful heaviness,
But all without redress;
For within that stound,°   *moment*
Half slumbering, in a swoond
I fell down to the ground.
     Unneth° I cast mine eyes   *Vainly*
Toward the cloudy skies:
But when I did behold
My sparrow dead and cold,   40
No creature but that would
Have ruèd upon me,
To behold and see
What heaviness did me pang;
Wherewith my hands I wrang,
That my sinews cracked,
As though I had been racked,
So pained and so strained,
That no life wellnigh remained.
     I sighed and I sobbed,   50
For that I was robbed
Of my sparrow's life.
O maiden, widow, and wife,
Of what estate ye be,
Of high or low degree,
Great sorrow then ye might see,
And learn to weep at me!
Such pains did me fret,
That mine heart did beat,
My visage pale and dead,   60
Wan, and blue as lead;

The pangs of hateful death
Well nigh had stopped my breath.

    Heu, heu, me,°   *Alas*
That I am woe for thee!
Ad Dominum, cum tribularer, clamavi:[27]
Of God nothing else crave I
But Philip's soul to keep
From the marees° deepe   *marshes*
Of Acherontè's well,   70
That is a flood of hell;
And from the great Plutò,
The prince of endless woe;
And from foul Alecto,
With visage blacke and blo;°   *blue*
And from Medusa that mare°   *female figure*
That like a fiend doth stare;
And from Megaera's adders,
For ruffling of Philip's feathers,
And from her fiery sparklings,   80
For burning of his wings;
And from the smokes sour
Of Proserpina's bower;
And from the dens dark,
Where Cerberus doth bark,
Whom Theseus did affray,°   *frighten*
Whom Hercules did outray,°   *defeat*
As famous poets say;
From that hell-hound,
That lieth in chains bound,   90
With ghastly heads three,
To Jupiter pray we
That Philip preserved may be!
Amen, say ye with me!
    Do mi nus,[28]
      Help now, sweet Jesus!
    Levavi oculos meos in montes:[29]
      Would God I had Zenophontes,
    Or Socrates the wise
To show me their device,   100

[27] In tribulation I cried out to my lord
[28] God (broken into syllables, as if in plain song or prayer)
[29] 'I raised up mine eyes to the hills'

Moderately to take
This sorrow that I make
For Philip Sparrow's sake!
So fervently I shake,
I feel my body quake;
So urgently I am brought
Into careful thought.
Like Andromach, Hector's wife,
Was weary of her life,
When she had lost her joy,   110
Noble Hector of Troy;
In like manner also
Increaseth my deadly woe,
For my sparrow is go.°   *gone*
   It was so pretty a fool,°   *little creature*
It would sit on a stool,
And learned after my school
For to keep his cut,
With, 'Philip, keep your cut!'
   It had a velvet cap,   120
And would sit upon my lap,
And seek after small worms,
And sometime white bread crumbs;
And many times and oft
Between my breastès soft
It would lie and rest;
It was proper and prest.
   Sometimes he would gasp
When he saw a wasp;
A fly or a gnat,   130
He would fly at that;
And prettily he would pant
When he saw an ant.
Lord, how he would pry
After the butterfly!
Lord, how he would hop
After the grassop!°   *grasshopper*
And when I said, 'Phip! Phip!'
Then he would leap and skip,
And take me by the lip.   140
Alas, it will me slo,°   *slay*
That Philip is gone me fro!°...   *from*

Sir Thomas Wyatt (1503?–1542)

8. 'The enemy of life, decayer of all kind'

The enemy of life, decayer of all kind,
That with his cold withers away the green,
This other night me in my bed did find,
And offered me to rid my fever clean;
And I did grant, so did despair me blind.
He drew his bow with arrow sharp and keen,
And strake° the place where love had hit before,   *struck*
And drave° the first dart deeper more and more.   *drove*

9. 'Whoso list to hunt, I know where is an hind'

Whoso list to hunt, I know where is an hind;
But as for me, alas, I may no more;
The vain travail hath wearied me so sore,
I am of them that farthest cometh behind;
Yet may I by no means my wearied mind
Draw from the Deer: but as she fleeth afore,°   *before*
Fainting I follow. I leave off therefore
Since in a net I seek to hold the wind.
Who list her hunt I put him out of doubt,
As well as I may spend his time in vain: 10
And graven with diamonds in letters plain
There is written her fair neck round about:
'*Noli me tangere*[30] for Caesar's I am,
And wild for to hold though I seem tame.'

10. 'My galley chargèd with forgetfulness'

My galley chargèd with forgetfulness
Through sharp seas in winter nights doth pass

---

[30] 'Touch me not' (Christ's words to the woman in the Garden after he had risen from the dead)

'Tween rock and rock; and eke mine enemy, alas,
That is my lord, steereth with cruelness;
And every oar a thought in readiness,
As though that death were light in such a case;
An endless wind doth tear the sail apace
Of forcèd sighs and trusty fearfulness.
A rain of tears, a cloud of dark disdain
Hath done the wearied cords great hindrance,   10
Wreathed with error and eke with ignorance.
The stars be hid that led me to this pain;
Drownèd is reason that should me comfort,
And I remain despairing of the port.

11. 'They flee from me that sometime did me seek'

They flee from me that sometime did me seek
With naked foot stalking in my chamber.
I have seen them gentle, tame and meek
That now are wild and do not remember
That sometime they put themself in danger
To take bread at my hand; and now they range
Busily seeking with a continual change.

Thankèd be fortune, it hath been otherwise
Twenty times better; but once in special,
In thin array after a pleasant guise,   10
When her loose gown from her shoulders did fall
And she me caught in her arms long and small,
Therewithal sweetly did me kiss,
And softly said, 'Dear heart, how like you this?'

It was no dream: I lay broad waking.
But all is turnèd through my gentleness
Into a strange fashion of forsaking;
And I have leave to go of her goodness,
And she also to use newfangleness.
But since that I so kindly am served,   20
I would fain know what she hath deserved.

12. 'What no, pardy, ye may be sure!'

What no, pardy, ye may be sure!
Think not to make me to your lure
With words and cheer so contraring,
Sweet and sour counterweighing;
Too much it were still to endure.
Truth is trayed° where craft is in ure;*   *betrayed; use*
But though ye have had my heart's cure,
Trow° ye I dote without ending?   *Believe*
    What no, pardy!

Though that with pain I do procure   10
For to forget what once was pure
Within my heart, shall still that thing,
Unstable, unsure and wavering,
Be in my mind without recure?
    What no, pardy!

13. 'Ah Robin'

    Ah Robin,
    Jolly Robin,
  Tell me how thy leman° doth   *lover*
And thou shall know of mine.

'My lady is unkind, pardy!'
  'Alack, why is she so?'
'She loveth another better than me,
  And yet she will say no.'

I find no such doubleness,
  I find women true.   10
My lady loveth me doubtless,
  And will change for no new.

'Thou art happy while that doth last,
  But I say as I find:
That women's love is but a blast
  And turneth like the wind.'

If that be true yet, as thou say'st,
   That women turn their heart,
Then speak better of them thou may'st
   In hope to have thy part.   20

'Such folks shall take no harm by love
   That can abide their turn,
But I alas can no way prove
   In love but lack and mourn.'

But if thou wilt avoid thy harm
   Learn this lesson of me:
At others' fires thy self to warm
   And let them warm with thee.

14. 'Once, as me thought, fortune me kissed'

Once, as me thought, Fortune me kissed
And bade me ask what I thought best,
And I should have it as me list
Therewith to set my heart in rest.

I askèd naught but my dear heart
To have for evermore mine own;
Then at an end were all my smart,
Then should I need no more to moan.

Yet for all that, a stormy blast
Had overturned this goodly day   10
And Fortune seemèd at the last
That to her promise she said nay.

But like as one out of despair
To sudden hope revived I;
Now Fortune showeth herself so fair
That I content me wonderly.

My most desire my hand may reach,
My will is alway at my hand;
Me need not long for to beseech
Her that hath power me to command.   20

What earthly thing more can I crave?
What would I wish more at my will?
No thing on earth more would I have,
Save, what I have, to have it still.

For Fortune hath kept her promise
In granting me my most desire:
Of my sufferance I have redress,
And I content me with my hire.

15. 'My lute, awake! perform the last'

My lute, awake! perform the last
Labour that thou and I shall waste
And end that I have now begun;
For when this song is sung and past,
My lute be still, for I have done.

As to be heard where ear is none,
As lead to grave in marble stone,
My song may pierce her heart as soon;
Should we then sigh or sing or moan?
No, no, my lute, for I have done.   10

The rocks do not so cruelly
Repulse the waves continually
As she my suit and affection,
So that I am past remedy,
Whereby my lute and I have done.

Proud of the spoil that thou hast got
Of simple hearts thorough Love's shot
By whom, unkind, thou hast them won,
Think not he hath his bow forgot,
Although my lute and I have done.   20

Vengeance shall fall on thy disdain
That makest but game on earnest pain;
Think not alone under the sun
Unquit° to cause thy lovers plain,   *Unrequited*
Although my lute and I have done.

May chance thee lie withered and old,
The winter nights that are so cold,
Plaining in vain unto the moon;
Thy wishes then dare not be told;
Care then who list, for I have done.　　　　　　　　　　30

And then may chance thee to repent
The time that thou hast lost and spent
To cause thy lovers sigh and swoon;
Then shalt thou know beauty but lent
And wish and want as I have done.

Now cease, my lute; this is the last
Labour that thou and I shall waste,
And ended is that we begun;
Now is this song both sung and past;
My lute, be still, for I have done.

16. 'If in the world there be more woe'

If in the world there be more woe
　　Than I have in my heart,
Where so it is it doth come fro
And in my breast there doth it grow
　　For to increase my smart.
Alas, I am receipt of every care
And of my life each sorrow claims his part.
　　Who list to live in quietness
　　By me let him beware,
　　For I by high disdain　　　　　　　　　　10
　　Am mad without redress;
And unkindness, alas, hath slain
My poor true heart all comfortless.

17. 'Mine own John Poyntz, since ye delight to know'

Mine own John Poyntz, since ye delight to know
　　The cause why that homeward I me draw,
　　And flee the press of courts whereso they go,

Rather than to live thrall, under the awe
   Of lordly looks, wrapped within my cloak,
   To will and lust learning to set a law,
It is not because I scorn or mock
   The power of them to whom Fortune hath lent
   Charge over us, of right, to strike the stroke;
But true it is that I have always meant   10
   Less to esteem them than the common sort
   Of outward things that judge in their intent
Without regard what doth inward resort.
   I grant sometime that of glory the fire
   Doth touch my heart: me list not to report
Blame by honour and honour to desire;
   But how may I this honour now attain
   That cannot dye the colour black a liar?
My Poyntz, I cannot frame my tongue to feign,
   To cloak the truth for praise, without desert,   20
   Of them that list all vice for to retain.
I cannot honour them that sets their part
   With Venus and Bacchus all their life long,
   Nor hold my peace of them although I smart.
I cannot crouch nor kneel, nor do so great a wrong
   To worship them like God on earth alone,
   That are as wolves these silly° lambs among.   *innocent*
I cannot with my words complain and moan
   And suffer naught, nor smart without complaint,
   Nor turn the word that from my mouth is gone.   30
I cannot speak and look like a saint,
   Use wiles for wit and make deceit a pleasure,
   And call craft counsel, for profit still to paint.
I cannot wrest the law to fill the coffer,
   With innocent blood to feed my self fat,
   And do most hurt where most help I offer.
I am not he that can allow the state
   Of high Caesar and damn Cato to die,
   That with his death did 'scape out of the gate
From Caesar's hands, if Livy do not lie,   40
   And would not live where liberty was lost:
   So did his heart the common wealth apply.
I am not he such eloquence to boast
   To make the crow singing as the swan,
   Nor call the lion of coward beasts the most
That cannot take a mouse as the cat can;

And he that dieth for hunger of the gold,
　　Call him Alexander, and say that Pan
Passeth Apollo in music many fold;
　　Praise Sir Thopas for a noble tale　　　　　　　　　　50
　　And scorn the story that the knight told;
Praise him for counsel that is drunk of ale;
　　Grin when he laugheth, that beareth all the sway,
　　Frown when he frowneth and groan when he is pale;
On other's lust to hang both night and day.
　　None of these points would ever frame in me.
　　My wit is naught, I cannot learn the way.
And much the less of things that greater be,
　　That asken help of colours of device
　　To join the mean with each extremity,　　　　　　　　60
With the nearest virtue to cloak alway the vice;
　　And as to purpose likewise it shall fall
　　To press the virtue that it may not rise.
As drunkenness good fellowship to call,
　　The friendly foe with his double face
　　Say he is gentle and courteous therewithal;
And say that Favel° hath a goodly grace　　　　　　　　*Fraud*
　　In eloquence, and cruelty to name
　　Zeal of Justice and change in time and place;
And he that suffereth offence without blame　　　　　　70
　　Call him pitiful, and him true and plain
　　That raileth reckless to every man's shame.
Say he is rude that cannot lie and feign,
　　The lecher a lover, and tyranny
　　To be the right of a prince's reign.
I cannot, I; no, no, it will not be!
　　This is the cause that I could never yet
　　Hang on their sleeves that weigh, as thou mayest see,
A chip of chance more than a pound of wit.
　　This maketh me at home to hunt and to hawk　　　　80
　　And in foul weather at my book to sit;
In frost and snow then with my bow to stalk.
　　No man doth mark whereso I ride or go;
　　In lusty leas in liberty I walk,
And of these news I feel nor weal nor woe,
　　Save that a clog doth hang yet at my heel:
　　No force for that, for it is ordered so
That I may leap both hedge and ditch full well.
　　I am not now in France to judge the wine,

With savoury sauce the delicates to feel;   90
Nor yet in Spain, where one must him incline,
   Rather than to be, outwardly to seem.
   I meddle not with wits that be so fine.
Nor Flander's cheer letteth not my sight to deem
   Of black and white nor taketh my wit away
   With beastliness, they, beasts, do so esteem;
Nor I am not where Christ is given in prey
   For money, poison and treason at Rome,
   A common practice usèd night and day:
But here I am in Kent and Christendom   100
   Among the Muses where I read and rhyme,
   Where if thou list, my Poyntz, for to come,
Thou shalt be judge how I do spend my time.

18. 'And wilt thou leave me thus?'

And wilt thou leave me thus?
Say nay, say nay, for shame,
To save thee from the blame
Of all my grief and grame;°   *sorrow*
And wilt thou leave me thus?
   Say nay, say nay!

And wilt thou leave me thus,
That hath loved thee so long
In wealth and woe among?
And is thy heart so strong   10
As for to leave me thus?
   Say nay, say nay!

And wilt thou leave me thus
That hath given thee my heart,
Never for to depart,
Neither for pain nor smart;
And wilt thou leave me thus?
   Say nay, say nay!

And wilt thou leave me thus

And have no more pity
Of him that loveth thee?
Alas, thy cruelty!
And wilt thou leave me thus?
    Say nay, say nay!

20

19. 'What should I say'

What should I say
Since faith is dead
And truth away
From you is fled?
Should I be led
With doubleness?
Nay, nay, mistress!

I promised you.
You promised me
To be as true
As I would be.
But since I see
Your double heart
Farewell, my part.

10

Thought for to take
It is not my mind
But to forsake
One so unkind
And as I find
So will I trust.
Farewell, unjust!

20

Can ye say nay
But that you said
That I alway
Should be obeyed?
And thus betrayed
Ere that I wist!
Farewell, unkissed!

20. 'I abide and abide and better abide'

I abide and abide and better abide,
And after the old proverb, the happy day;
And ever my lady to me doth say
'Let me alone and I will provide.'
I abide and abide and tarry the tide°   *time*
And with abiding speed well ye may;
Thus do I abide I wot alway,
Neither obtaining nor yet denied.
Aye me! this long abiding
Seemeth to me as who sayeth   10
A prolonging of a dying death
Or a refusing of a desirèd thing:
Much were it better for to be plain
Than to say 'abide' and yet shall not obtain.

Thomas, Lord Vaux (1510–1556)

21. He Desireth Exchange of Life

The day delayed, of that I most do wish,
Wherewith I feed and starve in one degree:
With wish and want still servèd in one dish,
Alive as dead, by proof as you may see.
    To whom of old this proverb well it serves:
    While grass doth grow, the silly horse he starves.

'Tween these extremes, thus do I run the race
Of my poor life, this certainly I know:
'Tween would and want, unwarely that do pass,
More swift then shot out of the Archer's bow.   10
    As Spider draws her line all day,
    I watch the net, and others have the prey.

And as by proof the greedy dog doth gnaw
The barèd bone, all only for the taste:
So to and fro this loathesome life I draw,
With fancies forced, and fed with vain repast.
    Narcissus brought unto the water brink,
    So aye thirst I, the more that I do drink.

Lo thus I die, and yet I seem not sick,   20
With smart unseen my self, my self I wear:
With prone desire and power that is not quick,
With hope aloft, now drenchèd in despair.
    Trained in trust, for no reward assigned,
    The more I haste, the more I come behind.

With hurt to heal, in frozen ice to fry,
With loss, to laugh, this is a wondrous case:
Fast fettered here, is forced away to fly,
As hunted hare that hound hath in the chase.
    With wings and spurs, for all the haste I make,
    As like to lose, as for to draw the stake.   30

The days be long that hang upon desert,
The life is irk° of joys that be delayed: *weary*
The time is short for to requite the smart,
That doth proceed of promise long unpaid.
    That to the last of this my fainting breath,
    I wish exchange of life for happy death.

22. A Lover Disdained, Complaineth

If ever man had love too dearly bought,
Lo I am he that plays within her maze:
And finds no way, to get the same I sought,
But as the deer are driven unto the gaze.
And to augment the grief of my desire,
    My self to burn, I blow the fire:
        But shall I come nigh you?
        Of force I must fly you.

What death, alas, may be compared to this,
I pray within the maze of my sweet foe: 10

And when I would of her but crave a kiss,
Disdain enforceth her awhile to go.
Myself I check: yet do I twist the twine,
   The pleasure hers, the pain is mine,
     But shall I come nigh you?
     Of force I must fly you.

You courtly wights, that wants your pleasant choice,
Lend me a flood of tears, to wail my chance:
Happy are they in love that can rejoice,
To their great pains, where Fortune doth advance.   20
But sith° my suit, alas, cannot prevail,   *since*
   Full fraught with care, in grief still will I wail:
     Sith you will needs fly me,
     I may not come nigh you.

23. He Renounceth All the Effects of Love

   Like as the hart that lifteth up his ears,
To hear the hounds, that hath him in the chase:
Doth cast the wind, in dangers and in fears,
With flying foot, to pass away apace:
   So must I fly of love, the vain pursuit,
   Whereof the gain is lesser than the fruit.

   And I also must loathe those leering looks,
Where love doth lurk still with his subtle slate,
With painted mocks, and inward hidden hooks,
To trap by trust, that lieth not in wait.   10
   The end whereof, assay it who so shall,
   As sugared smart, and inward bitter gall.

   And I must fly such Circean songs,
Wherewith that Circe, Ulysses did enchant:
Those wily wits I mean, with filèd tongues,
That hearts of steel, have power to daunt.
   Whoso as hawk that stoopeth to their call,
   For most desert, receiveth least of all.

   But woe to me that first beheld those eyes,

The trap wherein I say, that I was tane:°   *taken* 20
An outward salve, which inward me destroys,
Whereto I run, as rat unto her bane.
 As to the fish, sometime it doth befall,
 That with the bait, doth swallow hook and all.

 Within my breast, wherewith I daily fed,
The vain repast of amorous hot desire:
With loitering lust, so long that hath me said,
Till he hath brought me to the flaming fire.
 In time, as Phoenix ends her care and carks,
 I make the fire, and burn myself with sparks.   30

24. Bethinking Himself of his End, Writeth Thus

When I behold the bier, my last and posting horse,
That bare shall to the grave, my vile and carrion corse,°   *corpse*
Then say I, 'Silly wretch, why dost thou put thy trust
In things eith° made of clay, that soon will turn to dust.   *each*

'Dost thou not see the young, the hardy and the fair,
That now are past and gone, as though they never were:
Dost thou not see thy self draw hourly to thy last,
As shafts the which are shot at birds that flieth past.

'Dost thou not see how Death through-smiteth with his lance,
Some by war, some by plague, and some with worldly chance: 10
What thing is there on earth, for pleasure that was made,
But goeth more swift away, than doth the summer shade.

'See here the summer flower, that sprung this other day,
But winter weareth as fast, and bloweth clean away:
Even so shalt thou consume, from youth to loathesome age,
For death he doth not spare, the prince more than the page.

'Thy house shall be of clay, a clod under thy head,
Until the latter day, the grave shall be thy bed:
Until the blowing trump, doth say to all and some,
"Rise up out of your grave, for now the Judge is come."'   20

25. The Image of Death

I loathe that I did love,
In youth that I thought sweet:
As time requireth for my behove,°   *use*
Me thinks they are not meet:
My lusts they do me leave,
My fancies all be fled,
And tract of time begins to weave
Grey hairs upon my head.
For age with stealing steps
Hath clawed me with his crutch,   10
And lusty youth away he leaps,
As there had been none such.
My muse doth not delight
Me as she did before;
My hand and pen are not in plight
As they have been of yore.
For reason me denies
All youthly idle rhyme,
And day by day on me he cries,
'Leave off these toys betime!'   20
The wrinkles in my brow,
My furrows in my face,
Say limping Age will hedge him now
Where youth must give him place.
The harbinger of death,
To me I see him ride:
The cough, the cold, the gasping breath
Doth bid me to provide.
A pickaxe and a spade
And eke a shrouding sheet,   30
A house of clay for to be made,
For such a guest most meet.
Methinks I hear the clerk
That knolls the careful knell,
And bids me leave my weary work,
Ere nature me compel.
My keepers knit the knot
That youth doth laugh to scorn:
Of me, that shall be clean forgot
As I had not been born.   40
Thus must I life give up,

Whose badge I long did wear:
To them I yield the wanton cup
That better may it bear.
    Lo, here the bare head skull,
By whose bald sign I know
That stooping age away shall pull
Which youthful years did sow.
    For beauty with her band,
These crooked cares hath wrought,   50
And shipped me into the land,
From whence I first was brought.
    And ye that bide behind,
Have ye none other trust?
As ye of clay were cast by kind,
So shall ye waste to dust.

26. Of a Contented Spirit

When all is done and said, in the end thus shall you find
He most of all doth bathe in bliss, that hath a quiet mind:
And, clear from worldly cares, to dream can be content,
    The sweetest time in all this life, in thinking to be spent.

The body subject is to fickle fortune's power,
And to a million of mishaps is casual every hour;
And death in time doth change it to a clod of clay,
    Whenas the mind, which is divine, runs never to decay.

Companion none is like unto the mind alone;
For many have been harmed by speech; through thinking, few or
    none.   10
Fear oftentimes restraineth words, but makes not thoughts to cease,
    And he speaks best that hath the skill, when for to hold his peace.

Our wealth leaves us at death; our kinsmen at the grave;
But virtues of the mind unto the heavens with us we have:
Wherefore for Virtue's sake, I can be well content
    The sweetest time of all my life, to deem in thinking spent.

Henry Howard, Earl of Surrey (1517?–1547)

27. from Virgil's *Aeneid* Book II

… Ye Trojan ashes, and last flames of mine,
I call in witness, that at your last fall
I fled no stroke of any Greekish sword,
And if the fates would I had fallen in fight,
That with my hand I did deserve it well.
With this from thence I was recuiled° back   *welcomed*
With Iphytus and Pelias alone;   560
Iphytus weak, and feeble all for age,
Pelias lamed by Ulysses' hand.
To Priam's palace cry did call us then.
Here was the fight right hideous to behold,
As though there had no battle been but there,
Or slaughter made elsewhere throughout the town.
A fight of rage and fury there we saw.
The Greeks toward the palace rushèd fast
And, covered with engines, the gates beset,
And reared up ladders against the walls;   570
Under the windows scaling by their steps,
Fenced with shields in their left hands, whereon
They did receive the darts; while their right hands
Gripped for hold the embattle° of the wall.   *battlement*
The Trojans on the other part rend down
The turrets high and eke the palace roof;
With such weapons they shope° them to defend,   *prepared*
Seeing all lost, now at the point of death.
The gilt spars and the beams then threw they down,
Of old fathers the proud and royal works.   580
And with drawn swords some did beset the gates,
Which they did watch, and keep in routs full thick.
Our spirits restored to rescue the king's house,
To help them, and to give the vanquished strength.
  A postern with a blind wicket there was,
A common trade to pass through Priam's house,
On the back side wherof waste houses stood;
Which way eftsiths,° while that our kingdom 'dured,*   *oftentimes; lasted*

The unfortunate Andromache alone
Resorted to the parents of her make,°   *partner (Hector)* 590
With young Astyanax, his grandsire to see.
Here passed I up to the highest tower,
From whence the wretched Trojans did throw down
Darts, spent in waste. Unto a turret then
We stepped, the which stood in a place aloft,
The top wherof did reach well near the stars,
Where we were wont all Troyè to behold,
The Greekish navy, and their tents also.
With instruments of iron gan° we pick,   *began*
To seek where we might find the joining shrunk   600
From that high seat; which we razed, and threw down;
Which falling, gave forthwith a rushing sound,
And large in breadth on Greekish routs it lit.
But soon another sort stepped in their stead;
No stone unthrown, nor yet no dart uncast.
     Before the gate stood Pyrrhus in the porch
Rejoicing in his darts, with glittering arms;
Like to the adder with venomous herbs fed,
Whom cold winter all boln° hid under ground,   *thin*
And shining bright, when she her slough had slung,   610
Her slipper° back doth roll, with forkèd tongue   *slippery*
And raisèd breast lift up against the sun.
With that together came great Periphas;
Automedon eke,° that guided had sometime   *also*
Achilles' horse, now Pyrrhus' armour bare;
And eke with him the warlike Scyrian youth
Assailed the house, and threw flame to the top.
And he an axe before the foremost raught,°   *reached*
Wherewith he gan the strong gates hew and break.
From whence he beat the staples out of brass,   620
He brake the bars, and through the timber pierced
So large a hole, whereby they might discern
The house, the court, the secret chambers eke
Of Priamus and ancient kings of Troy,
And armed foes in the entry of the gate.
     But the palace within confounded was
With wailing, and with rueful shrieks and cries;
The hollow halls did howl of women's plaint;
The clamour strake up to the golden stars.
The 'fraid mothers, wandering through the wide house,   630
Embracing pillars, did them hold and kiss.

Pyrrhus assaileth with his father's might,
Whom nor closures nor keepers might hold out.
With often pushèd ram the gate did shake;
The posts beat down, removèd from their hooks;
By force they made the way, and the entry brake.
And now the Greeks let in, the foremost slew,
And the large palace with soldiers gan to fill.
Not so fiercely doth overflow the fields
The foaming flood, that breaks out of his banks,   640
Whose rage of waters bears away what heaps
Stand in his way, the cotes, and eke the herds,
As in the entry of slaughter furious
I saw Pyrrhus and either° Atrides.   *both*
    There Hecuba I saw, with a hundred more
Of her sons' wives, and Priam at the altar,
Sprinkling with blood his flame of sacrifice.
Fifty bedchambers of his children's wives,
With loss of so great hope of his offspring,
The pillars eke proudly beset with gold   650
And with the spoils of other nations,
Fell to the ground; and whatso that with flame
Untouchèd was, the Greeks did all possess.
    Percase° you would ask what was Priam's fate?   *Maybe*
When of his taken town he saw the chance,°   *fate*
And the gates of his palace beaten down,
His foes amid his secret chambers eke,
The old man in vain did on his shoulders then,
Trembling for age, his cuirass° long disused,   *armour*
His bootless° sword he girded him about,   *useless* 660
And ran amid his foes, ready to die.
    Amid the court, under the heaven, all bare,
A great altar there stood, by which there grew
An old laurel tree, bowing thereunto,
Which with his shadow did embrace the gods.
Here Hecuba, with her young daughters all,
About the altar swarmèd were in vain,
Like doves that flock together in the storm;
The statues of the gods embracing fast.
But when she saw Priam had taken there   670
His armour, like as though he had been young,
'What furious thought, my wretched spouse,' quoth she,
'Did move thee now such weapons for to wield?
Why hastest thou? This time doth not require

Such succour, nor yet such defenders now;
No, though Hector my son were here again.
Come hither; this altar shall save us all,
Or we shall die together.' Thus she said.
Wherewith she drew him back to her, and set
The agèd man down in the holy seat.   680

But lo! Polites, one of Priam's sons,
Escapèd from the slaughter of Pyrrhus,
Comes fleeing through the weapons of his foes,
Searching, all wounded, the long galleries
And the void courts; whom Pyrrhus, all in rage,
Followed fast to reach a mortal wound;
And now in hand, well near strikes with his spear.
Who fleeing forth till he came now in sight
Of his parents, before their face fell down
Yielding the ghost, with flowing streams of blood.   690
Priamus then, although he were half dead,
Might not keep in his wrath, nor yet his words,
But crieth out: 'For this thy wicked work,
And boldness eke such thing to enterprise,
If in the heavens any justice be
That of such things takes any care or keep,
According thanks the gods may yield to thee
And send thee eke thy just deservèd hire,
That made me see the slaughter of my child,
And with his blood defile the father's face.   700
But he, by whom thou feign'st thyself begot,
Achilles, was to Priam not so stern.
For lo! he, tendering my most humble suit
The right and faith, my Hector's bloodless corpse
Rendred, for to be laid in sepulture,
And sent me to my kingdom home again.'
Thus said the aged man, and therewithal
Forceless he cast his weak unwieldy dart,
Which, repulsed from the brass where it gave dint,
Without sound hung vainly in the shield's boss.   710
Quoth Pyrrhus: 'Then thou shalt this thing report:
On message to Pelide my father go,
Show unto him my cruel deeds, and how
Neoptolem° is swervèd out of kind.   *Neoptolemus*
Now shalt thou die,' quoth he. And with that word,
At the altar him trembling gan he draw,

Wallowing through the bloodshed of his son;
And his left hand all claspèd in his hair,
With his right arm drew forth his shining sword,
Which in his side he thrust up to the hilts.   720
Of Priamus this was the fatal fine,°   *end*
The woeful end that was allotted him.
When he had seen his palace all on flame,
With ruin of his Trojan turrets eke.
That royal prince of Asia, which of late
Reigned over so many peoples and realms,
Like a great stock now lieth on the shore;
His head and shoulders parted been in twain,
A body now without renown and fame.
   Then first in me entered the grisly fear;   730
Dismayed I was. Wherewith came to my mind
The image eke of my dear father, when
I thus beheld the king of equal age
Yield up the sprite° with wounds so cruelly.   *soul*
Then thought I of Creusa left alone,
And of my house in danger of the spoil,
And the estate of young Julus eke.
I lookèd back to seek what number then
I might discern about me of my feres,°   *comrades*
But wearied they had left me all alone.   740
Some to the ground were lopen° from above,   *cut down*
Some in the flame their irkèd° bodies cast.   *wearied*
   There was no more but I left of them all,
When that I saw in Vesta's temple sit
Dame Helen, lurking in a secret place, –
Such light the flame did give as I went by,
While here and there I cast mine eyes about.
For she in dread lest that the Trojans should
Revenge on her the ruin of their walls;
And of the Greeks the cruel wreaks also,   750
The fury eke of her forsaken make;°   *partner*
The common bane of Troy and eke of Greece,
Hateful she sat beside the altars hid.
Then boiled my breast with flame and burning wrath
To revenge my town, unto such ruin brought;
With worthy pains on her to work my will.
Thought I: 'Shall she pass to the land of Spart°   *Sparta*
All safe and see Mycene her native land,
And like a queen return with victory

Home to her spouse, her parents, and children, 760
Followed with a train of Trojan maids,
And served with a band of Phrygian slaves;
And Priam eke with iron murdered thus,
And Troy town consumèd all with flame,
Whose shore hath been so oft forebathed in blood?
No! no! For though on women the revenge
Unseemly is, such conquest hath no fame,
To give an end unto such mischief yet
My just revenge shall merit worthy praise;
And quiet eke my mind for to be wroke°   *enforced* 770
On her which was the causer of this flame,
And satisfy the cinder of my fears.'...

28. 'Set me whereas the sun doth parch the green'

Set me whereas the sun doth parch the green,
Or where his beams may not dissolve the ice,
In temperate heat, where he is felt and seen;
With proud people, in presence sad° and wise;   *serious*
Set me in base, or yet in high degree;
In the long night, or in the shortest day;
In clear weather, or where mists thickest be;
In lost youth, or when my hairs be grey;
Set me in earth, in heaven, or yet in hell;
In hill, in dale, or in the foaming flood;   10
Thrall, or at large, alive whereso I dwell;
Sick, or in health; in ill fame, or in good;
Yours will I be, and with that only thought
Comfort myself when that my hap is naught.

29. A Tribute to Thomas Clere

Norfolk sprang thee, Lambeth holds thee dead,
Clere, of the County of Cleremont, though hight;
Within the womb of Ormonde's race thou bred,
And sawest thy cousin crownèd in thy sight.

Shelton for love, Surrey for lord, thou chase; –°   *chose*
Ay me! While life did last that league was tender.
Tracing whose steps thou sawest Kelsall blaze,
Laundersey burnt, and battered Bullen render.
At Muttrell gates, hopeless of all recure,
Thine Earl, half dead, gave in thy hand his will;   10
Which cause did thee this pining death procure,
Ere summers four times seven thou could'st fulfil.
Ah, Clere! if love had booted,° care, or cost,   *been of any use*
Heaven had not won, nor earth so timely lost.

30. The Ages of Man

　　Laid in my quiet bed, in study as I were,
I saw within my troubled head a heap of thoughts appear;
　　And every thought did show so lively in mine eyes,
That now I sighed, and then I smiled, as cause of thought did rise.
　　I saw the little boy, in thought how oft that he
Did wish of God to scape the rod, a tall young man to be;
　　The young man, eke, that feels his bones with pains oppressed,
How he would be a rich old man, to live and lie at rest;
　　The rich old man, that sees his end draw on so sore,
How he would be a boy again, to live so much the more.   10
　　Whereat, full oft I smiled, to see how all these three,
From boy to man, from man to boy, would chop and change degree;
　　And musing thus, I think the case is very strange,
That man from wealth, to live in woe, doth ever seek to change.
　　Thus thoughtful as I lay, I saw my withered skin
How it doth show my dented jaws, the flesh was worn so thin,
　　And eke my toothless chaps, the gates of my right way,
That opes and shuts as I do speak, do thus unto me say;
　　'Thy white and hoarish hairs, the messengers of age,
That show like lines of true belief that this life doth assuage,   20
　　Bids thee lay hand, and feel them hanging on thy chin,
The which do write two ages past, the third now coming in.
　　Hang up, therefore, the bit of thy young wanton time,
And thou that therein beaten art, the happiest life define.'
　　Whereat I sighed and said, 'Farewell! my wonted joy;
Truss up thy pack, and trudge from me to every little boy,
　　And tell them thus from me, their time most happy is,
If to their time, they reason had to know the truth of this.'

31. The Poet's Lament

So cruel prison! How could betide, alas!
As proud Windsor, where I, in lust and joy,
With a King's son my childish years did pass,
In greater feast then Priam's sons of Troy;

Where each sweet place returns a taste full sour,
The large green courts, where we were wont to hove,°   *linger*
With eyes cast up unto the maiden's tower,
And easy sighs, such as folk draw in love.

The stately sales:° the ladies bright of hue;   *halls*
The dances short; long tales of great delight;   10
With words and looks that tigers could but rue,
Where each of us did plead the other's right.

The palm play, where, dispoilèd for the game,
With dazèd eyes oft we by gleams of love
Have missed the ball, and got sight of our dame,
To bait her eyes which kept the leads above.

The gravelled ground: with sleeves tied on the helm,
On foaming horse, with swords and friendly hearts,
With cheer, as though the one should overwhelm,
Where we have fought and chasèd oft with darts.   20

With silver drops the meads° yet spread for ruth,   *meadows*
In active games of nimbleness and strength
Where we did strain, trailed by swarms of youth,
Our tender limbs, that yet shot up in length.

The secret groves, which oft we made resound
Of pleasant plaint and of our ladies' praise,
Recording soft, what grace each one had found,
What hope of speed, what dread of long delays.

The wild forest, the clothèd holt with green,
With reins availed and swift ybreathèd horse,   30
With cry of hounds and merry blasts between,
Where we did chase the fearful hart a force.

The void walls eke, that harboured us each night;

Wherewith, alas, revive within my breast
The sweet accord, such sleeps as yet delight,
The pleasant dreams, the quiet bed of rest,

The secret thoughts imparted with such trust,
The wanton talk, the diverse change of play,
The friendship sworn, each promise kept so just,
Wherewith we passed the winter nights away.   40

And with this thought the blood forsakes my face,
The tears berain my cheek of deadly hue;
The which, as soon as sobbing sighs, alas!
Upsuppèd have, thus I my plaint renew:

'O place of bliss! Renewer of my woes!
Give me accompt° where is my noble fere,   *account*
Whom in thy walls thou did'st each night enclose,
To other lief, but unto me most dear.'

Echo, alas! that doth my sorrow rue,
Returns thereto a hollow sound of plaint.   50
Thus I, alone, where all my freedom grew,
In prison pine with bondage and restraint,

And with remembrance of the greater grief,
To banish the less, I find my chief relief.

32. 'When Windsor walls sustained my wearied arm'

When Windsor walls sustained my wearied arm,
My hand my chin, to ease my restless head,
Each pleasant plot revested green with warm,
The blossomed boughs, with lusty ver° yspread,   *spring*
The flowered meads, the wedded birds so late,
Mine eyes discovered. Then did to mind resort
The jolly woes, the hateless short debate,
The rakehell° life, that longs* to love's disport.   *madcap; belongs*
Wherewith, alas! mine heavy charge of care,
Heaped in my breast, brake forth against my will;   10
And smoky sighs, that overcast the air;
My vapoured eyes such dreary tears distil,

The tender spring to quicken where they fall,
And I half bent° to throw me down withal.   *inclined*

33. 'Wrapped in my careless cloak'

   Wrapped in my careless cloak, as I walk to and fro,
I see how love can show what force there reigneth in his bow;
   And how he shooteth eke, a hardy hart to wound;
And where he glanceth by again, that little hurt is found.
   For seldom is it seen he woundeth hearts alike:
The one may rage, when t'other's love is often far to seek.
   All this I see, with more, and wonder thinketh me
How he can strike the one so sore, and leave the other free.
   I see that wounded wight, that suffreth all this wrong,
How he is fed with yeas and nays, and liveth all too long.   10
   In silence though I keep such secrets to myself,
Yet do I see how she sometime doth yield a look by stealth,
   As though it seemed, 'Ywis,° I will not lose thee so,' –   *Indeed*
When in her heart so sweet a thought did never truly grow.
   Then say I thus: 'Alas, that man is far from bliss
That doth receive for his relief none other gain but this.
   And she, that feeds him so, – I feel, and find it plain –
Is but to glory in her power, that over such can reign.
   Nor are such graces spent but when she thinks that he,
A wearied man, is fully bent such fancies to let free;   20
   Then to retain him still she wrasteth° new her grace,   *changes artificially*
And smileth, lo, as though she would forthwith the man embrace.
   But when the proof is made to try such looks withal,
He findeth then the place all void, and freighted full of gall.
   Lord, what abuse is this! who can such women praise,
That for their glory do devise to use such crafty ways!
   I, that among the rest do sit and mark the row,
Find that in her is greater craft then is in twenty mo.
   When tender years, alas! with wiles so well are sped,
What will she do when hoary hairs are powdered in her head!'   30

34. 'The soote season'

The soote° season, that bud and bloom forth brings,   *sweet*
With green hath clad the hill and eke the vale;

The nightingale with feathers new she sings;
The turtle° to her make hath told her tale.   *turtledove*
Summer is come, for every spray now springs;
The hart hath hung his old head on the pale;
The buck in brake his winter coat he flings;
The fishes float with new repairèd scale;
The adder all her slough away she slings;
The swift swallow pursueth the flies small;   10
The busy bee her honey now she mings.°   *mixes*
Winter is worn, that was the flowers' bale.
And thus I see among these pleasant things
Each care decays, and yet my sorrow springs.

35. A Game of Chess

Although I had a check,
To give the mate is hard,
For I have found a knack
To keep my men on guard.
And you that hardy are
To give so great assay
Unto a man of war –
To drive his men away –,

I rede° you take good heed   *advise*
And mark this foolish verse,   10
For I will so provide
That I will have your ferse.°   *queen*
And when your ferse is had
And all your war is done,
Then shall your self be glad
To end that you begun.

For if by chance I win
Your person in the field,
Too late then come you in
Yourself to me to yield.   20
For I will use my power,
As captain full of might,
And such I will devour
As use° to show me spite.   *customarily*

And for because you gave
Me check in such degree,
This vantage, lo, I have;
Now check, and guard to thee.
Defend it, if thou may;
Stand stiff in thine estate;   30
For sure I will assay,
If I can give thee mate.

36. 'Alas so all things now do hold their peace'

Alas so all things now do hold their peace:
Heaven and earth disturbèd in no thing;
The beasts, the air, the birds their song do cease;
The night's char° the stars about doth bring.   *chariot*
Calm is the sea, the waves work less and less;
So am not I, whom love, alas! doth wring,
Bringing before my face the great increase
Of my desires, whereat I weep and sing
In joy and woe, as in a doubtful ease:
For my sweet thoughts sometime do pleasure bring,   10
But, by and by, the cause of my disease
Gives me a pang that inwardly doth sting,
When that I think what grief it is again
To live and lack the thing should rid my pain.

Nicholas Grimald (1519–1562)

37. The Garden

The issue of great Jove, draw near you, Muses nine:
Help us to praise the blissful plot of garden ground so fine.
The garden gives good food, and aid for leeches' cure:

The garden, full of great delight, his master doth allure.
Sweet sallet° herbs be here, and herbs of every kind: *salad*
The ruddy grapes, the seemly fruits be here at hand to find.
Here pleasance wanteth not, to make a man full fain:
Here marvellous the mixture is of solace, and of gain.
To water sundry seeds, the sorrow by the way
A running river, trilling down with liquor, can convey.   10
Behold, with lively hue, fair flowers that shine so bright:
With riches, like the orient gems, they paint the mold in sight.
Bees, humming with soft sound (their murmur is so small),
Of blooms and blossoms suck the tops, on dewed leaves they fall.
The creeping vine holds down her own bewedded elms
And, wandering out with branches thick, reeds folded overwhelms.
Trees spread their coverts wide, with shadows fresh and gay:
Full well their branchèd boughs defend the fervent sun away.
Birds chatter, and some chirp, and some sweet tunes do yield:
All mirthful, with their songs so blithe, they make both air, and field.   20
The garden, it allures, it feeds, it glads the sprite:°   *spirit*
From heavy hearts all doleful dumps the garden chaseth quite.
Strength it restores to limbs, draws, and fulfils the sight:
With cheer revives the senses all, and maketh labour light.
O, what delights to us the garden ground doth bring!
Seed, leaf, flower, fruit, herb, bee, and tree, and more, than I may sing.

Thomas Tusser (1524?–1580)

38. from *Five Hundred Points of Good Husbandry*

38a. *from Chapter 5*

What lookest thou herein to have?
Fine verses thy fancy to please?
Of many my betters *that* crave,
Look nothing but rudeness in these.

What other thing lookest thou then?
Grave sentences many to find?
Such, poets have twenty and ten,
Yea thousands contenting the mind.

What look ye, I pray you, show what?
Terms painted with rhetoric fine?   10
Good husbandry seeketh not that,
Nor is it any meaning of mine.

What lookest thou, speak at the last?
Good lessons for thee and thy wife?
Then keep them in memory fast,
To help as a comfort to life.

What look ye for more in my book?
Points needful and meet to be known?
Then daily be sure to look,
To save to be sure thine own.   20

38b. *from Chapter 10*

… Make money thy drudge, for to follow thy work,
    make wisdom controller, good order thy clerk:
Provision cater, and skill to be cook,
    make steward of all, pen, ink, and thy book.

Make hunger thy sauce, as a med'cine for health,
    make thirst to be butler, as physic for wealth:
Make eye to be usher, good usage to have,
    make bolt to be porter, to keep out a knave.

Make husbandry baily,° abroad to provide,   *bailiff*
    make housewifery daily, at home for to guide: 30
Make coffer fast locked, thy treasure to keep,
    make house to be sure, the safer to sleep.

Make bandog thy scoutwatch, to bark at a thief,
    make courage for life, to be captain chief:
Make trapdoor thy bulwark, make bell to begin,
    make gunstone and arrow, show who is within.

… Be pinched by lending, for kith nor for kin,
    nor also by spending, by such as come in:
Nor put to thy hand betwixt bark and the tree,
    lest through thy own folly, so pinched thou be.   40

As lending to neighbour, in time of his need,
    wins love of thy neighbour, and credit doth breed:
So never to crave, but to live of thine own,
    brings comforts a thousand, to many unknown.

Who living but lends, and be lent to they must,
    else buying and selling, might lie in the dust:
But shameless and crafty, that desperate are,
    make many full honest, the worser to fare.

At some time to borrow, account it no shame,
    if justly thou keepest, thy touch for the same: 50
Who quick be to borrow, and slow be to pay,
    their credit is naught, go they never so gay.

By shifting and borrowing, who so as lives,
    not well to be thought on, occasion gives:
Then lay to live warily, and wisely to spend,
    for prodigal livers, have seldom good end.

Some spareth too late, and a number with him,
    the fool at the bottom, the wise, at the brim:
Who careth, nor spareth, till spent he hath all,
    of bobbing, not robbing, be fearful he shall.   60

Where wealthiness floweth, no friendship can lack,
    whom poverty pincheth, hath friendship as slack:
Then happy is he, by example that can,
    take heed by the fall, of a mischievèd man.

Who breaketh his credit, or cracketh it twice,
    trust such with a surety, if ye be wise:
Or if he be angry, for asking thy due,
    Once even, to him afterward, lend not anew.

Account it well sold, that is justly well paid,
    and count it well bought, that is never denied: 70

But yet here is t'one, here is t'other doth best,
    for buyer and seller, for quiet and rest.

Leave Princes' affairs undescanted on,
    and tend to such doings as stands thee upon:
Fear God, and offend not the Prince nor his laws,
    and keep thyself out, of the Magistrate's claws.

As interest or usury, playeth the devil,
    so hillback and fillbelly, biteth as evil:
Put dicing among them, and docking the dell,
    and by and by after, of beggary smell.   80

Once weekly remember, thy charges to cast,
    once monthly see how, thy expenses may last:
If quarter declareth, too much to be spent,
    for fear of ill year, take advice of thy rent.

Who orderly entreth, his payment in book,
    may orderly find them again (if he look)
And he that intendeth, but once for to pay,
    shall find this in doing, the quietest way.

In dealing uprightly, this counsel I teach,
    first reckon, then write, ere to purse ye do reach: 90
Then pay and dispatch him, as soon as ye can,
    for ling'ring is hindrance to many a man ...

... The stone that is rolling, can gather no moss,
    who often removeth, is sure of loss:
The rich it compelleth, to pay for his pride,
    the poor, it undoeth on every side.

The eye of the master, enricheth the hutch,
    the eye of the mistress, availeth as much:
Which eye, if it govern, with reason and skill,
    hath servant and service, at pleasure and will.   100

Who seeketh revengement of every wrong,
    in quiet nor safety, continueth long:
So he that of wilfulness trieth the law,
    shall strive for a coxcomb, and thrive as a daw.

To hunters and hawkers, take heed what ye say,
   mild answer with courtesy, drives them away:
So, where a man's better, will open a gap,
   resist not with rudeness for fear of mishap.

A man in this world, for a churl that is known,
   shall hardly in quiet, keep that is his own: 110
Where lowly and such, as of courtesy smells,
   finds favour and friendship, where ever he dwells.

Keep truly thy Sabbath, the better to speed,
   keep servant from gadding, but when it is need:
Keep fishday and fasting day, as they do fall,
   what custom thou keepest, let others keep all.

Though some in their tithing, be slack or too bold,
   be thou unto Godward, not that way too cold:
Evil conscience grudgeth, and yet we do see,
   ill tithers, ill thrivers, most commonly be.   120

Pay weekly thy workman, his household to feed,
   pay quarterly servants, to buy as they need:
Give garment to such, as deserve and no mo,°   *more*
   lest thou and thy wife, without garment do go.

Beware raskabilia,° slothful to work,   *lowborn rabble*
   purloiners and filchers, that loveth to lurk:
Away with such lubbers, so loth to take pain,
   that rules in expenses, but never no gain.

Good wife, and good children, are worthy to eat,
   good servant, good labourer, earneth their meat: 130
Good friend, and good neighbour, that fellowly guest,
   with heartily welcome, should have of the best.

Depart not with all that thou hast to thy child,
   much less unto other, for being beguiled:
Lest, if thou would'st gladly possess it again,
   look, for to come by it, thou wottest° not when.   *knowest*

The greatest preferment, that child we can give,
   is learning and nurture, to train him to live:
Which who so it wanteth, though left as a squire,
   consumeth to nothing, as block in the fire.   140

When God hath so blest thee, as able to live,
   and thou hast to rest thee, and able to give:
Lament thy offences, serve God for amends,
   make soul to be ready, when God for it sends.

Send fruits of thy faith, to heaven aforehand,
   for mercy here doing, God blesseth thy land:
He maketh thy store, with his blessing to swim,
   and after, thy soul to be blessed with him.

Some lay to get riches, by sea and by land,
   and ventureth his life, in his enemy's hand: 150
And setteth his soul upon six or on seven,
   not fearing nor caring, for hell nor for heaven.

Some pincheth and spareth, and pineth his life,
   to coffer up bags, for to leave to his wife:
And she (when he dieth) sets open the chest,
   for such as can soothe her, and all away wrest.

Good husband preventing the frailness of some,
   takes part of God's benefits, as they do come:
And leaveth to wife, and his children the rest,
   each one his own part, as he thinketh it best.   160

These lessons approved, if wisely ye note,
   may save and advantage ye, many a grote:°   *small coin*
Which if ye can follow, occasion found,
   then every lesson, may save ye a pound.

Elizabeth I, Queen of England (1533–1603)

39. An English Hexameter

Persius a crab-staff, bawdy Martial, Ovid a fine wag.

40. Four Knights of Nottinghamshire

Gervase the gentle, Stanhope the stout,
Markham the lion, and Sutton the lout.

41. 'Christ was the Word that spake it'

Christ was the Word that spake it,
He took the bread and brake it,
And what the Word did make it,
That I believe and take it.

42. Written in her French Psalter

No crookèd leg, no blearèd eye,
    No part deformèd out of kind,
Nor yet so ugly half can be
    As is the inward suspicious mind.

43. On Monsieur's Departure

I grieve and dare not show my discontent,
I love and yet am forced to seem to hate,
I do, yet dare not say I ever meant,
I seem stark mute but inwardly do prate.
I am and not, I freeze and yet am burned,
Since from myself another self I turned.

My care is like my shadow in the sun,
Follows me flying, flies when I pursue it,
Stands and lies by me, doth what I have done.
His too familiar care doth make me rue it.   10
No means I find to rid him from my breast,
Till by the end of things it be supprest.

Some gentler passion slide into my mind,
For I am soft and made of melting snow;

Or be more cruel, love, and so be kind.
Let me or float or sink, be high or low.
Or let me live with some more sweet content,
Or die and so forget what love ere meant.

44. 'The doubt of future foes'

The doubt of future foes exiles my present joy,
And wit me warns to shun such snares as threaten mine annoy;
For falsehood now doth flow, and subjects' faith doth ebb,
Which should not be if reason ruled or wisdom weaved the web.
But clouds of joys untried do cloak aspiring minds,
Which turn to rain of late repent by changed course of winds.
The top of hope supposed the root upreared shall be,
And fruitless all their grafted guile, as shortly ye shall see.
The dazzled eyes with pride, which great ambition blinds,
Shall be unsealed by worthy wights whose foresight falsehood finds.   10
The daughter of debate that discord aye doth sow
Shall reap no gain where former rule still peace hath taught to know.
No foreign banished wight shall anchor in this port;
Our realm brooks not seditious sects, let them elsewhere resort.
My rusty sword through rest shall first his edge employ
To poll their tops that seek such change or gape for future joy.

45. 'When I was fair and young'

When I was fair and young, then favour graced me.
Of many was I sought their mistress for to be,
But I did scorn them all and answered them therefore:
Go, go, go, seek some other where, importune me no more.

How many weeping eyes I made to pine in woe,
How many sighing hearts I have not skill to show,
But I the prouder grew and still this spake therefore:
Go, go, go, seek some other where, importune me no more.

Then spake fair Venus' son, that brave victorious boy,
Saying: You dainty dame, for that you be so coy,   10
I will so pluck your plumes as you shall say no more:

Go, go, go, seek some other where, importune me no more.

As soon as he had said, such change grew in my breast
That neither night nor day I could take any rest.
Wherefore I did repent that I had said before:
Go, go, go, seek some other where, importune me no more.

Thomas Sackville, Earl of Dorset (1536–1608)

46. from *A Mirror for Magistrates,* 'Induction'

The wrathful winter 'proaching on apace,
   With blustering blasts had all ybared° the treen,*   *stripped bare; trees*
And old Saturnus with his frosty face
   With chilling cold had pierced the tender green:
   The mantels rent, wherein enwrappèd been
      The gladsome groves that now lie overthrowen,
      The tappets torn, and every bloom down blowen.

The soil that erst so seemly was to seen
   Was all despoilèd of her beauty's hue;
And soot° fresh flowers (wherewith the summer's queen   *sweet* 10
   Had clad the earth) now Boreas' blasts down blew.
And small fowls flocking, in their song did rue
      The winter's wrath, wherewith each thing defaced
      In woeful wise bewailed the summer past.

Hawthorn had lost his motley livery,
   The naked twigs were shivering all for cold:
And dropping down the tears abundantly,
   Each thing (me thought) with weeping eye me told
The cruel season, bidding me withhold
      My self within, for I was gotten out   20
      Into the fields whereas I walked about.

When lo, the night with misty mantels spread

Gan dark the day, and dim the azure skies,
And Venus in her message Hermes sped
  To bloody Mars, to will him not to rise,
While she her self approached in speedy wise:
    And Virgo hiding her disdainful breast
    With Thetis now had laid her down to rest;

Whiles Scorpio dreading Sagittarius' dart,
  Whose bow pressed bent in sight, the string had slipped,   30
Down slid into the Ocean flood apart,
  The Bear that in the Irish seas had dipped
His grisly feet, with speed from thence he whipped:
    For Thetis hasting from the Virgin's bed,
    Pursued the Bear, that e'er° she came was fled;   *before*

And Phaeton now near reaching to his race
  With glistering beams, gold streaming where they bent,
Was pressed to enter in his resting place.
  Erythius that in the cart first went
Had even now attained his journey's stent.°   *destination* 40
    And fast declining hid away his head,
    While Titan couched him in his purple bed;

And pale Cynthia with her borrowed light
  Beginning to supply her brother's place,
Was past the noon's tide six degrees in sight
  When sparkling stars amid the heaven's face
With twinkling light shone on the earth apace,
    That while they brought about the night's chare,°   *chariot*
    The dark had dimmed the day e'er I was ware.

And sorrowing I to see the summer flowers,   50
  The lively green, the lusty leas forlorn,
The sturdy trees so shattered with the showers,
  The fields so fade that flourished so beforne,
It taught me well all earthly things be born
    To die the death, for naught long time may last.
    The summer's beauty yields to winter's blast.

Then looking upward to the heaven's leams°   *rays*
  With night's stars thick powdered everywhere,
Which erst so glistened with the golden streams
  That cheerful Phoebus spread down from his sphere,   60

Beholding dark oppressing day so near:
    The sudden sight reducèd to my mind,
    The sundry changes that in earth we find.

Thus musing on this worldly wealth in thought,
   Which comes and goes more faster than we see
The flickering flame that with the fire is wrought,
   My busy mind presented unto me
Such fall of peers as in this realm had be:
    That oft I wished some would their woes describe,
    To warn the rest whom fortune left alive.   70

And straight forth stalking with redoubled pace
   For that I saw the night drew on so fast,
In black all clad there fell before my face
   A piteous wight, whom woe had all forwast,°   *wasted away*
Forth from her eyen the crystal tears outbrast,
    And sighing sore her hands she wrung and fold,
    Tore all her hair that ruth was to behold ...

... Not worthy Hector worthiest of them all,
   Her hope, her joy, his force is now for naught.   450
O Troy, Troy, Troy, there is no boot but bale,
   The hugy horse within thy walls is brought;
Thy turrets fall, thy knights that whilom fought
    In arms amid the field, are slain in bed,
    Thy gods defiled, and all thy honour dead.

The flames upspring, and cruelly they creep
   From wall to roof, till all to cinders waste,
Some fire the houses where the wretches sleep,
   Some rush in here, some run in there as fast.
In everywhere or sword or fire they taste.   460
    The walls are torn, the towers whirled to the ground,
    There is no mischief but may there be found.

Cassandra yet there saw I how they haled°   *hauled*
   From Pallas' house, with sparkled tress undone,
Her wrists fast bound, and with Greeks rout empaled:
   And Priam eke in vain how he did run
To arms, whom Pyrrhus with despite hath done
    To cruel death, and bathed him in the bane
    Of his son's blood before the altar slain ...

George Gascoigne (1542?–1577)

47. 'And if I did what then?'

And if I did what then?
Are you aggrieved therefore?
The sea hath fish for every man,
And what would you have more?

Thus did my mistress once
Amaze my mind with doubt:
And popped a question for the nonce,
To beat my brains about.

Whereto I thus replied,
Each fisherman can wish,   10
That all the seas at every tide,
Were his alone to fish.

And so did I (in vain),
But since it may not be:
Let such fish there as find the gain,
And leave the loss for me.

And with such luck and loss,
I will content my self:
Till tides of turning time may toss,
Such fishers on the shelf.   20

And when they stick on sands,
That every man may see:
Then will I laugh and clap my hands,
As they do now at me.

48. The Lullaby of a Lover

Sing Lullaby, as women do,

Wherewith they bring their babes to rest,
And Lullaby can I sing too,
As womanly as can the best.
With Lullaby they still the child,
And if I be not much beguiled,
Full many wanton babes have I,
Which must be stilled with Lullaby.

First Lullaby my youthful years,
It is now time to go to bed,   10
For crooked age and hoary hairs
Have won the haven within my head:
With Lullaby then youth be still,
With Lullaby content thy will,
Since courage quails, and comes behind,
Go sleep, and so beguile thy mind.

Next Lullaby my gazing eyes,
Which wonted° were to glance apace.   *accustomed*
For every glass may now suffice,
To show the furrows in my face: 20
With Lullaby then wink awhile,
With Lullaby your looks beguile:
Let no fair face, nor beauty bright,
Entice you eft° with vain delight.   *again*

And Lullaby my wanton will,
Let reason's rule now reign thy thought,
Since all too late I find by skill,
How dear I have thy fancies bought:
With Lullaby now take thine ease,
With Lullaby thy doubts appease: 30
For trust to this, if thou be still,
My body shall obey thy will.

Eke Lullaby my loving boy,
My little Robin take thy rest,
Since age is cold, and nothing coy,
Keep close thy coin, for so is best:
With Lullaby be thou content,
With Lullaby thy lusts relent,
Let others pay which hath mo° pence,   *more*
Thou art too poor for such expense.   40

Thus Lullaby my youth, mine eyes,
My will, my ware, and all that was,
I can no mo delays devise,
But welcome pain, let pleasure pass:
With Lullaby now take your leave,
With Lullaby your dreams deceive,
And when you rise with waking eye,
Remember then this Lullaby.

49. Gascoigne's Good Morrow

You that have spent the silent night
In sleep and quiet rest,
And joy to see the cheerful light
That riseth in the East:
Now clear your voice, now cheer your heart,
Come help me now to sing:
Each willing wight come bear a part,
To praise the heavenly King.

And you whom care in prison keeps,
Or sickness doth suppress,   10
Or secret sorrow breaks your sleeps,
Or dolours do distress;
Yet bear a part in doleful wise,
Yea think it good accord,
And acceptable sacrifice,
Each sprite to praise the Lord.

The dreadful night with darksomeness
Had overspread the light,
And sluggish sleep with drowsiness,
Had over pressed our might: 20
A glass wherein you may behold
Each storm that stops our breath,
Our bed the grave, our clothes like mold,
And sleep like dreadful death.

Yet as this deadly night did last
But for a little space,
And heavenly day now night is past,

Doth show his pleasant face:
So must we hope to see God's face,
At last in heaven on high,
When we have chang'd this mortal place,
For Immortality.

And of such haps and heavenly joys,
As then we hope to hold,
All earthly sights and worldly toys,
Are tokens to behold.
The day is like the day of doom,
The sun, the Son of man,
The skies the heavens, the earth the tomb
Wherein we rest till then.

The Rainbow bending in the sky,
Bedecked with sundry hues,
Is like the seat of God on high,
And seems to tell these news;
That as thereby he promisèd,
To drown the world no more,
So by the blood which Christ hath shed,
He will our health restore.

The misty clouds that fall sometime,
And overcast the skies,
Are like to troubles of our time,
Which do but dim our eyes:
But as such dews are dried up quite,
When Phoebus shows his face,
So are such fancies put to flight,
Where God doth guide by grace.

The carrion crow, that loathsome beast,
Which cries against the rain,
Both for her hue and for the rest,
The Devil resembleth plain:
And as with guns we kill the crow,
For spoiling our relief,
The Devil so must we overthrow,
With gunshot of belief.

The little birds which sing so sweet,

Are like the angels' voice,
Which render God his praises meet,
And teach us to rejoice:
And as they more esteem that mirth,
Than dread the night's annoy,   70
So must we deem our days on earth,
But hell to heavenly joy.

Unto which Joys for to attain
God grant us all his grace,
And send us after worldly pain,
In heaven to have a place.
Where we may still enjoy that light,
Which never shall decay:
Lord for thy mercy lend us might
To see that joyful day.   80

50. Gascoigne's Woodmanship[31]

My worthy Lord, I pray you wonder not
To see your woodman shoot so oft awry,
Nor that he stands amazèd like a sot,
And lets the harmless deer, unhurt, go by.
Or if he strike a Doe which is but carrion,
Laugh not good Lord, but favour such a fault,
Take will in worth, he would fain hit the barren,
But though his heart be good, his hap is not:
And therefore now I crave your Lordship's leave,
To tell you plain what is the cause of this: 10
First if it please your honour to perceive,
What makes your woodman shoot so oft amiss,
Believe me L. the case is nothing strange,
He shoots awry almost at every mark,
His eyes have been so usèd for to range,
That now God knows they be both dim and dark.

[31] Original footnote: 'Written to the L. Grey of Wilton upon this occasion: the said L. Grey delighting (amongst many other good qualities) in choosing of his winter deer, and killing the same with his bow, did furnish the Author with a crossbow *cum pertinenciis* and vouchsafed to use his company in the said exercise, calling him one of his woodmen. Now the Author shooting very often, could never hit any deer, yea and oftentimes he let the herd pass by as though he had not seen them. Whereat when this noble Lord took some pastime, and had often put him in remembrance of his good skill in choosing, and readiness in killing of a winter deer, he thought good thus to excuse it in verse.'

For proof he bears the note of folly now,
Who shot sometime to hit Philosophy,
And ask you why? forsooth I make avow,
Because his wanton wits went all awry.   20
Next that, he shot to be a man of law,
And spent some time with learned Littleton,
Yet in the end, he provèd but a daw,
For law was dark and he had quickly done.
Then could he with FitzHerbert such a brain,
As Tully° had, to write the law by art,   *Cicero*
So that with pleasure, or with little pain,
He might perhaps, have caught a truant's part.
But all too late, he most misliked the thing,
Which most might help to guide his arrow straight: 30
He winkèd wrong, and so let slip the string,
Which cast him wide, for all his quaint conceit.
From thence he shot to catch a courtly grace,
And thought even there to wield the world at will,
But out alas he much mistook the place,
And shot awry at every rover still.
The blazing baits which draw the gazing eye,
Unfeathered there his first affection,
No wonder then although he shot awry,
Wanting the feathers of discretion.   40
Yet more than them, the marks of dignity,
He much mistook and shot the wronger way,
Thinking the purse of prodigality,
Had been best mean to purchase such a prey.
He thought the flattering face which fleareth° still,   *grimaced*
Had been full fraught with all fidelity,
And that such words as courtiers use at will,
Could not have varied from the verity.
But when his bonnet buttonèd with gold,
His comely cape begarded all with gay,   50
His bombast° hose, with linings manifold,   *padded*
His knit silk stocks and all his quaint array,
Had picked his purse of all the Peter pence,
Which might have paid for his promotion,
Then (all too late) he found that light expense,
Had quite quenched out the court's devotion.
So that since then the taste of misery,
Hath been always full bitter in his bit,
And why? forsooth because he shot awry,

Mistaking still the marks which others hit.   60
But now behold what mark the man doth find,
He shoots to be a soldier in his age,
Mistrusting all the virtues of the mind,
He trusts the power of his personage.
As though long limbs led by a lusty heart,
Might yet suffice to make him rich again,
But Flushing frays have taught him such a part,
That now he thinks the wars yield no such gain.
And sure I fear, unless your lordship deign,
To train him yet into some better trade,   70
It will be long before he hit the vein,
Whereby he may a richer man be made.
He cannot climb as other catchers can.
To lead a charge before himself be led,
He cannot spoil the simple sakeless man,
Which is content to feed him with his bread.
He cannot pinch the painful soldier's pay,
And share him out his share in ragged sheets,
He cannot stoop to take a greedy prey
Upon his fellows grovelling in the streets.   80
He cannot pull the spoil from such as pill,
And seem full angry at such foul offence,
Although the gain content his greedy will,
Under the cloak of contrary pretence:
And nowadays, the man that shoots not so,
May shoot amiss, even as your Woodman doth:
But then you marvel why I let them go,
And never shoot, but say 'Farewell forsooth':
Alas my Lord, while I do muse hereon,
And call to mind my youthful years misspent,   90
They give me such a bone to gnaw upon,
That all my senses are in silence pent.
My mind is rapt in contemplation,
Wherein my dazzled eyes only behold,
The black hour of my constellation,
Which framèd me so luckless on the mold:
Yet therewithal I cannot but confess,
That vain presumption makes my heart to swell,
For thus I think, not all the world (I guess)
Shoots bet° than I, nay some shoots not so well.   *better* 100
In Aristotle somewhat did I learn,
To guide my manners all by comeliness,

And Tully taught me somewhat to discern
Between sweet speech and barbarous rudeness.
Old Parkins, Rastall, and Dan Bracten's books,
Did lend me somewhat of the lawless Law,
The crafty Courtiers with their guileful looks,
Must needs put some experience in my maw:
Yet can not these with many mysteries mo,
Make me shoot straight at any gainful prick,   110
Where some that never handled such a bow,
Can hit the white, or touch it near the quick,
Who can nor speak, nor write in pleasant wise,
Nor lead their life by Aristotle's rule,
Nor argue well on questions that arise,
Nor plead a case more than my Lord Mair's mule,
Yet can they hit the marks that I do miss,
And win the mean which may the man maintain.
Now when my mind doth mumble upon this,
No wonder then although I pine for pain: 120
And whiles mine eyes behold this mirror thus,
The herd goeth by, and farewell gentle does:
So that your Lordship quickly may discuss
What blinds mine eyes so oft (as I suppose.)
But since my Muse can to my Lord rehearse
What makes me miss, and why I do not shoot,
Let me imagine in this worthless verse,
If right before me, at my standing's foot
There stood a doe, and I should strike her dead,
And then she prove a carrion carcass too,   130
What figure might I find within my head,
To excuse the rage which ruled me so to do?
Some might interpret by plain paraphrase,
That lack of skill or fortune led the chance,
But I must otherwise expound the case,
I say Jehovah did this doe advance,
And made her bold to stand before me so,
Till I had thrust mine arrow to her heart,
That by the sudden of her overthrow,
I might endeavour to amend my part,   140
And turn mine eyes that they no more behold,
Such guileful marks as seem more than they be:
And though they glister outwardly like gold,
Are inwardly but brass, as men may see:
And when I see the milk hang in her teat,

Methinks it sayeth, old babe now learn to suck,
Who in thy youth could'st never learn the feat
To hit the whites which live with all good luck.
Thus have I told my Lord, (God grant in season)
A tedious tale in rhyme, but little reason.   150

51. The Green Knight's Farewell to Fancy

Fancy (quoth he) farewell, whose badge I long did bear,
And in my hat full harebrainedly, thy flowers did I wear:
Too late I find (at last), thy fruits are nothing worth,
Thy blossoms fall and fade full fast, though bravery bring thee forth.
By thee I hoped always, in deep delights to dwell,
But since I find thy fickleness, *Fancy* (quoth he) *farewell.*

Thou mad'st me live in love, which wisdom bids me hate,
Thou bleard'st mine eyes and mad'st me think, that faith was mine by
     fate:
By thee those bitter sweets, did please my taste alway,
By thee I thought that love was light, and pain was but a play: 10
I thought that beauty's blaze, was meet to bear the bell,
And since I find my self deceived, *Fancy* (quoth he) *farewell.*

The gloss of gorgeous courts, by thee did please mine eye,
A stately sight me thought it was, to see the brave go by:
To see their feathers flaunt, to mark their strange device,
To lie along in ladies' laps, to lisp and make it nice:
To fawn and flatter both, I likèd sometime well,
But since I see how vain it is, *Fancy* (quoth he) *farewell.*

When court had cast me off, I toilèd at the plough.
My fancy stood in strange conceits, to thrive I wot° not how: *knew* 20
By mills, by making malt, by sheep and eke by swine,
By duck and drake, by pig and goose, by calves and keeping kine:
By feeding bullocks fat, when price at markets fell,
But since my swains eat up my gains, *Fancy* (quoth he) *farewell.*

In hunting of the deer, my fancy took delight,
All forests knew, my folly still, the moonshine was my light:
In frosts I felt no cold, a sunburnt hue was best,
I sweat and was in temper still, my watching seemèd rest:
What dangers deep I passed, it folly were to tell,
And since I sigh to think thereon, *Fancy* (quoth he) *farewell.*   30

A fancy fed me once, to write in verse and rhyme,
To wray my grief, to crave reward, to cover still my crime:
To frame a long discourse, on stirring of a straw,
To rumble rhyme in raff and ruff, yet all not worth a haw:
To hear it said *There goeth, the man that writes so well,*
But since I see what poets be, *Fancy* (quoth he) *farewell.*

At music's sacred sound, my fancies eft be gone,
In concords, discords, notes and clefs, in tunes of unison:
In hierarchies and strains, in rests, in rule and space,
In monachords and moving moods, in burdens under base: 40
In descants and in chants, I strainèd many a yell,
But since musicians be so mad, *Fancy* (quoth he) *farewell.*

To plant strange country fruits, to sow such seeds likewise,
To dig and delve for new found roots, where old might well suffice;
To prune the water boughs, to pick the mossy trees,
(Oh how it pleased my fancy once!) to kneel upon my knees,
To graft a pippin stock, when sap begins to swell:
But since the gains scarce quite° the cost, *Fancy* (quoth he) *farewell.* requite

Fancy (quoth he) *farewell,* which made me follow drums,
Where powdered bullets serves for sauce, to every dish that comes: 50
Where treason lurks in trust, where hope all hearts beguiles,
Where mischief lieth still in wait, when fortune friendly smiles:
Where one day's prison proves, that all such heavens are hell,
And such I feel the fruits thereof, *Fancy* (quoth he) *farewell.*

If reason rule my thoughts, and God vouchsafe me grace
Then comfort of Philosophy, shall make me change my race:
And fond I shall it find, that Fancy sets to show,
For weakly stands that building still, which lacketh grace by low:
But since I must accept, my fortunes as they fell,
I say God send me better speed, and *Fancy now farewell.*   60

Edward de Vere, Earl of Oxford (1550–1604)

52. Grief of Mind

What plague is greater than the grief of mind,
The grief of mind that eats in every vein,
In every vein that leaves such clods behind,
Such clods behind as breed such bitter pain,
    So bitter pain that none shall ever find,
    What plague is greater than the grief of mind.

53. Desire

The lively lark stretched forth her wing,
The messenger of morning bright,
And with her cheerful voice did sing
The day's approach, discharging night,
    When that Aurora, blushing red,
    Descried the guilt of Thetis' bed.

I went abroad to take the air
And in the meads I met a knight,
Clad in carnation colour fair.
I did salute this gentle wight: 10
    Of him I did his name inquire
    He sighed and said it was, Desire.

Desire I did desire to stay,
And while with him I cravèd talk
The courteous knight said me no nay,
But hand in hand with me did walk:
    Then of Desire I asked again
    What thing did please and what did pain?

He smiled, and thus he answered then:
'Desire can have no greater pain   20

Than for to see another man
The thing desirèd to obtain:
    Nor greater joy can be than this,
    That to enjoy that others miss.'

54. Love Questions

What is Desire: which doth approve to set on fire each gentle heart?
A fancy strange or god of love, whose pining sweet delight doth smart:
    In gentle winds his dwelling is.

Is he god of peace or war? what be his arms? what is his might?
His war is peace, his peace is war, each grief of his is but delight:
    His bitter ball is sugared bliss.

What be his gifts? how doth he pay? when is he seen? or how conceived?
Sweet dreams in sleep, new thoughts in day, beholding eyes in mind
    received:
    A god that rules and yet obeys.

Why is he naked painted? blind? his sides with shafts? his back with
    brands?   10
Plain without guile, by hap to find pursuing with fair words that
    withstands,
    And when he craves he takes no nays.

What were his parents? gods or no? though living long he is yet a child:
A god's son? who thinks not so? a god begot beguiled:
    Venus his mother, Mars his sire.

What labours doth this god allow? what fruits have lovers for their pains?
Sit still and muse to make a vow their ladies if they true remain,
    A good reward for true desire.

55. Fancy and Desire

    Come hither, shepherd's swain!
    'Sir, what do you require?'

I pray thee show to me thy name!
   'My name is Fond Desire.'

   When wert thou borne, Desire?
   'In pride and pomp of May.'
By whom, sweet boy, wert thou begot?
   'By self-conceit men say.'

   Tell me, who was thy nurse?
   'Fresh youth, in sugared joy.'   10
What was thy meat and daily food?
   'Sad sighs and great annoy.'

   What had'st thou then to drink?
   'Unfeignèd lovers' tears.'
What cradle wert thou rockèd in?
   'In hope devoid of tears.'

   What lulled thee to thy sleep?
   'Sweet thoughts which liked one best.'
And where is now thy dwelling place?
   'In gentle hearts I rest.'   20

   Doth company displease?
   'It doth in many one.'
Where would Desire then choose to be?
   'He loves to muse alone.'

   What feedeth most thy sight?
   'To gaze on beauty still.'
Whom findest thou most thy foe?
   'Disdain of my good will.'

   Will ever age or death,
   Bring thee unto decay?   30
'No, no, Desire both lives and dies
   A thousand times a day.'

   Then, fond Desire, farewell,
   Thou art no mate for me;
I should be loath, methinks, to dwell
   With such a one as thee.

56. Vision of a Fair Maid, with Echo Verses

Sitting alone upon my thought, in melancholy mood
In sight of sea, and at my back an ancient hoary wood,
I saw a fair young lady come, her secret fears to wail,
Clad all in colour of a Nun and covered with a veil:
Yet (for the day was calm and clear) I might discern her face.
As one might see a damask rose hid under crystal glass:
Three times with her soft hand full hard on her left side she knocks
And sighed so sore as might have moved some pity in the rocks:
From sighs, and shedding amber tears, into sweet song she brake
When thus the Echo answered her to every word she spake: 10

O heavens, who was the first that bred in me this fever? Vere,
Who was the first it gave the wound, whose fear I wear for ever? Vere
What tyrant, Cupid, to my harm usurps thy golden quiver? Vere
What wight first caught this heart, and can from bondage it deliver? Vere.
Yet who doth most adore this wight, oh hollow caves tell true? you.
What nymph deserves his liking best, yet doth in sorrow rue? you.
What makes him not reward good will with some reward or ruth? youth.
What makes him show besides his birth, such pride and such untruth?
     youth.
May I his favour match with love; if he my love will try? Aye.
May I requite his birth with faith? then faithful will I die? Aye.   20

And I that knew this lady well, said
     Lord how great a miracle
To her how echo told the truth
     As true as Phoebus' oracle.

57. 'Love is a discord and a strange divorce'

Love is a discord and a strange divorce
Betwixt our sense and rest, by whose power,
As mad with reason, we admit that force,
Which wit or labour never may divorce.
     It is a will that brooketh no consent,
     It would refuse, yet never may repent.

Love's a desire, which for to wair a time,
Doth lose an age of years, and so doth pass,

As doth the shadow severed from his prime,
Seeming as though it were, yet never was.
    Leaving behind, nought but repentant thoughts,
    Of days ill spent, of that which profits noughts.

It's now a peace, and then a sudden war,
A hope, consumed before it is conceived;
At hand it fears, and menaceth afar,
And he that gains, is most of all deceived.
    Love whets the dullest wits, his plagues be such,
    But make the wise by pleasing, dote as much.

Edmund Spenser (1552?–1599)

58. from *The Shepheardes Calender*: October[32]

Piers. Cuddie, for shame hold up thy heavy head,
And let us cast with what delight to chase:
And weary this long lingering Phoebus' race.
Whilom° thou wont* the shepherds' lads to lead,   *Once; were accustomed*
In rhymes, in riddles, and in bidding base:
Now they in thee, and thou in sleep art dead.

Cuddie. Piers, I have pipèd erst so long with pain,
That all mine oaten reeds been rent and wore:
And my poor Muse hath spent her sparèd store,
Yet little good hath got, and much less gain.   10
Such pleasance makes the grasshopper so poor,
And ligg° so late, when Winter doth her strain.   *lie*

---

[32] '*Argument: In Cuddie is set out the perfect pattern of a poet, which finding no maintenance of his state and studies, complaineth of the contempt of poetry, and the causes thereof: Specially having been in all ages, and even amongst the most barbarous always of singular account and honour, and being indeed so worthy and commendable an art: or rather no art, but a divine gift and heavenly instinct not to be gotten by labour and learning, but adorned with both: and poured into the wit by a certain enthusiasmos, and celestial inspiration, as the author hereof elsewhere at large discourseth, in his book called the English Poet, which book being lately come to my hands, I mind also by God's grace upon further advisement to publish.*'

The dapper ditties, that I wont devise,
To feed youth's fancy, and the flocking fry,
Delighten much: what I the bet° for-thy?   *better*
They han the pleasure, I a slender prize.
I beat the bush, the birds to them do fly:
What good thereof to Cuddie can arise?

Piers. Cuddie, the praise is better then the price,
The glory eke much greater than the gain: 20
O what an honour is it, to restrain
The lust of lawless youth with good advice:
Or prick them forth with pleasance of thy vein,
Whereto thou list their trainèd wills entice.

Soon as thou gin'st° to set thy notes in frame,   *begin*
O how the rural routs° to thee do cleave: *troops*
Seemeth thou dost their soul of sense bereave,
All as the shepherd, that did fetch his dame
From Pluto's baleful bower withouten leave:
His music's might the hellish hound did tame.   30

Cuddie. So praisen babes the peacock's spotted train,
And wondren at bright Argus' blazing eye:
But who rewards him e'er the more for-thy,
Or feeds him once the fuller by a grain?
Sike° praise is smoke, that sheddeth in the sky,   *such*
Sike words been wind, and wasten soon in vain.

Piers. Abandon then the base and viler clown,
Lift up thy self out of the lowly dust:
And sing of bloody Mars, of wars, of jousts,
Turn thee to those, that wield the awful crown.   40
To doubted° knights, whose woundless armour rusts,   *doughty*
And helms unbruisèd waxen daily brown.

There may thy Muse display her fluttering wing,
And stretch herself at large from East to West:
Whether thou list in fair Elisa rest,
Or, if thee please in bigger notes to sing,
Advance the worthy whom she loveth best,
That first the white bear to the stake did bring.

And when the stubborn stroke of stronger stounds,°   *troubles*
Has somewhat slacked the tenor of thy string: 50
Of love and lustihood then mayst thou sing,
And carol loud, and lead the miller's round,
All were° Elisa one of thilk same ring.   *so long as*
So mought° our Cuddie's name to heaven sound.   *might*

Cuddie. Indeed the Romish Tityrus,° I hear,   *Virgil*
Through his Mæcenas left his oaten reed:
Whereon he erst had taught his flocks to feed,
And laboured lands to yield the timely ear,
And eft did sing of wars and deadly dread,
So as the heavens did quake his verse to hear.   60

But, ah! Mæcenas is yclad in clay,
And great Augustus long ago is dead:
And all the worthies liggen wrapped in lead,
That matter made for Poets on to play:
For ever, who in derring do were dread,
The lofty verse of them was lovèd aye.

But after virtue gan for age to stoop,
And mighty manhood brought a bed of ease:
The vaunting Poets found naught worth a pea,
To put in press among the learnèd troop.   70
Tho 'gan the streams of flowing wits to cease,
And sunbright honour penned in shameful coop.

And if that any buds of Poesy,
Yet of the old stock gan to shoot again:
Or if men's follies mote be forced to feign,
And roll with rest in rhymes of ribaldry.
Or as it sprung, it wither must again:
Tom Piper makes us better melody.

Piers. O peerless Poesy, where is then thy place?
If nor in prince's palace thou do sit: 80
(And yet is prince's palace the most fit)
Ne breast of baser birth doth thee embrace?
Then make thee wings of thine aspiring wit,
And, whence thou camest, fly back to heaven apace.

Cuddie. Ah, Percy, it is all too weak and wan,
So high to soar, and make so large a flight:
Her piecèd pinions been not so in plight,
For Colin fits such famous flight to scan:
He, were he not with love so ill bedight,
Would mount as high, and sing as soot° as swan.   *sweet* 90

Piers. Ah, fon,° for love does teach him climb so high,   *fool*
And lifts him up out of the loathsome mire:
Such immortal mirror, as he doth admire,
Would raise one's mind above the starry sky,
And cause a caitiff courage to aspire,
For lofty love doth loathe a lowly eye.

Cuddie. All otherwise the state of poet stands,
For lordly love is such a tyrant fell:
That where he rules, all power he doth expel.
The vaunted verse a vacant head demands,   100
Ne wont with crabbèd care the Muses dwell:
Unwisely weaves, that takes two webs in hand.

Who ever casts to compass weighty prize,
And thinks to throw out thundering words of threat,
Let pour in lavish cups and thrifty bits of meat,
For Bacchus' fruit is friend to Phoebus wise.
And when with wine the brain begins to sweat,
The numbers flow as fast as spring doth rise.

Thou kenn'st not, Percy, how the rhyme should rage.
O, if my temples were distained with wine,   110
And girt in garlands of wild ivy twine,
How I could rear the Muse on stately stage,
And teach her tread aloft in buskin fine,
With quaint Bellona in her equipage.

But ah, my courage cools ere it be warm,
Forthy,° content us in this humble shade: *Therefore*
Where no such troublous tides han us assayed;
Here we our slender pipes may safely charm.
Piers. And when my goats shall han° their bellies laid,   *have*
Cuddie shall have a kid to store his farm.   120

from *Amoretti*

59. 'Long-while I sought to what I might compare'

Long-while I sought to what I might compare
    Those powerful eyes, which lighten my dark sprite,
    Yet find I naught on earth to which I dare
    Resemble the image of their goodly light.
Not to the Sun: for they do shine by night;
    Nor to the moon: for they are changèd never;
    Nor to the stars: for they have purer sight;
    Nor to the fire: for they consume not ever;
Nor to the lightning: for they still persever;
    Nor to the diamond: for they are more tender;   10
    Nor unto crystal: for naught may them sever;
    Nor unto glass: such baseness mought offend her;
Then to the Maker's self they likest be,
    Whose light doth lighten all that here we see.

60. 'The rolling wheel that runneth often round'

The rolling wheel that runneth often round,
    The hardest steel in tract of time doth tear:
    And drizzling drops that often do redound,
    The firmest flint doth in continuance wear.
Yet cannot I with many a dropping tear,
    And long entreaty soften her hard heart:
    That she will once vouchsafe my plaint to hear,
    Or look with pity on my painful smart.
But when I plead, she bids me play my part,
    And when I weep, she says tears are but water: 10
    And when I sigh, she says I know the art,
    And when I wail she turns her self to laughter.
So do I weep, and wail, and plead in vain,
    Whiles she as steel and flint doth still remain.

61. 'Was it the work of nature or of art'

Was it the work of nature or of art

Which tempered so the feature of her face:
    That pride and meekness mixed by equal part,
    Do both appear to adorn her beauty's grace?
For with mild pleasance, which doth pride displace,
    She to her love doth lookers' eyes allure:
    And with stern countenance back again doth chase
    Their looser looks that stir up lusts impure,
With such strange terms her eyes she doth inure,
    That with one look she doth my life dismay,   10
    And with another doth it straight recure,
    Her smile me draws, her frown me drives away.
Thus doth she train and teach me with her looks.
    Such art of eyes I never read in books.

62. 'Sweet is the rose, but grows upon a briar'

Sweet is the rose, but grows upon a briar;
    Sweet is the juniper, but sharp his bough;
    Sweet is the eglantine, but pricketh near;
    Sweet is the firbloom, but his branch is rough
Sweet is the cypress, but his rind is tough,
    Sweet is the nut, but bitter is his pill;
    Sweet is the broom-flower, but yet sour enough;
    And sweet is moly, but his root is ill.
So every sweet with sour is tempered still,
    That maketh it be coveted the more: 10
    For easy things that may be got at will,
    Most sorts of men do set but little store.
Why then should I account of little pain,
    That endless pleasure shall unto me gain.

63. 'My love is like to ice, and I to fire'

My love is like to ice, and I to fire;
    How comes it then that this her cold so great
    Is not dissolved through my so hot desire,
    But harder grows the more I her entreat?
Or how comes it that my exceeding heat
    Is not delayed by her heart frozen cold:

But that I burn much more in boiling sweat,
   And feel my flames augmented manifold?
What more miraculous thing may be told
   That fire which all things melts, should harden ice: 10
   And ice which is congealed with senseless cold,
   Should kindle fire by wonderful device.
Such is the power of love in gentle mind,
   That it can alter all the course of kind.

64. 'The Panther knowing that his spotted hide'

The Panther knowing that his spotted hide
   Doth please all beasts but that his looks them fray:
   Within a bush his dreadful head doth hide,
   To let them gaze whilst he on them may prey.
Right so my cruel fair with me doth play,
   For with the goodly semblant of her hue
   She doth allure me to mine own decay,
   And then no mercy will unto me show.
Great shame it is, thing so divine in view,
   Made for to be the world's most ornament,   10
   To make the bait her gazers to embrew,
   Good shames to be so ill an instrument.
But mercy doth with beauty best agree,
   As in their maker ye them best may see.

65. 'One day I wrote her name upon the strand'

One day I wrote her name upon the strand,
   But came the waves and washèd it away:
   Again I wrote it with a second hand,
   But came the tide, and made my pains his prey.
Vain man, said she, that dost in vain assay
   A mortal thing so to immortalise.
   For I myself shall like to this decay,
   And eke my name be wipèd out likewise.
Not so, quod I, let baser things devise,
   To die in dust, but you shall live by fame: 10
   My verse your virtues rare shall eternise,

And in the heavens write your glorious name.
Where whenas death shall all the world subdue,
  Our love shall live, and later life renew.

66. *Prothalamion*

Calm was the day, and through the trembling air,
Sweet breathing Zephyrus did softly play
A gentle spirit, that lightly did delay
Hot Titan's beams, which then did glister fair:
When I whom sullen care,
Through discontent of my long fruitless stay
In prince's court, and expectation vain
Of idle hopes, which still do fly away,
Like empty shadows, did afflict my brain,
Walked forth to ease my pain   10
Along the shore of silver streaming Thames,
Whose rutty bank, the which his river hems,
Was painted all with variable flowers,
And all the meads adorned with dainty gems,
Fit to deck maidens' bowers,
And crown their paramours,
Against the bridal day, which is not long:
  Sweet Thames, run softly, till I end my song.

There, in a meadow, by the river's side,
A flock of nymphs I chancèd to espy,   20
All lovely daughters of the flood thereby,
With goodly greenish locks all loose untied,
As each had been a bride,
And each one had a little wicker basket,
Made of fine twigs entrailèd curiously,
In which they gathered flowers to fill their flasket:
And with fine fingers, cropped full feateously
The tender stalks on high.
Of every sort, which in that meadow grew,
They gathered some; the violet pallid blue,   30
The little daisy, that at evening closes,
The virgin lily, and the primrose true,
With store of vermeil roses,
To deck their bridegrooms' posies,

Against the bridal day, which was not long:
    Sweet Thames, run softly, till I end my song.

With that I saw two swans of goodly hue,
Come softly swimming down along the Lee;
Two fairer birds I yet did never see:
The snow which doth the top of Pindus strew,   40
Did never whiter show,
Nor Jove himself when he a swan would be
For love of Leda, whiter did appear:
Yet Leda was they say as white as he,
Yet not so white as these, nor nothing near;
So purely white they were,
That even the gentle stream, the which them bare,
Seem'd foul to them, and bad his billows spare
To wet their silken feathers, lest they might
Soil their fair plumes with water not so fair,   50
And mar their beauties bright,
That shone as heaven's light,
Against their bridal day, which was not long:
    Sweet Thames, run softly, till I end my song.

Eftsoons the nymphs, which now had flowers their fill,
Ran all in haste, to see that silver brood,
As they came floating on the crystal flood:
Whom when they saw, they stood amazèd still,
Their wondering eyes to fill:
Them seem'd they never saw a sight so fair,   60
Of fowls so lovely, that they sure did deem
Them heavenly born, or to be that same pair
Which through the sky draw Venus' silver team:
For sure they did not seem
To be begot of any earthly seed,
But rather angels or of angels' breed:
Yet were they bred of Summer's-heat° they say,   *Somerset*
In sweetest season, when each flower and weed
The earth did fresh array:
So fresh they seemed as day,   70
Even as their bridal day, which was not long:
    Sweet Thames, run softly, till I end my song.

Then forth they all out of their baskets drew
Great store of flowers, the honour of the field,

That to the sense did fragrant odours yield,
All which upon those goodly birds they threw,
And all the waves did strew,
That like old Peneus' waters they did seem,
When down along by pleasant Tempe's shore
Scattered with flowers, through Thessaly they stream,   80
That they appear through lilies' plenteous store,
Like a bride's chamber floor:
Two of those nymphs, meanwhile, two garlands bound,
Of freshest flowers which in that mead they found,
The which presenting all in trim array,
Their snowy foreheads therewithal they crowned,
Whilst one did sing this lay,
Prepared against that day,
Against their bridal day, which was not long:
   Sweet Thames, run softly, till I end my song.   90

'Ye gentle birds, the world's fair ornament,
And heaven's glories, whom this happy hour
Doth lead unto your lovers' blissful bower,
Joy may you have and gentle hearts' content
Of your love's couplement:
And let fair Venus, that is queen of love,
With her heart-quelling son upon you smile,
Whose smile, they say, hath virtue to remove
All love's dislike, and friendship's faulty guile
For ever to assoil.   100
Let endless peace your steadfast hearts accord,
And blessed plenty wait upon your board,
And let your bed with pleasures chaste abound,
That fruitful issue may to you afford:
Which may your foes confound,
And make your joys redound,
Upon your bridal day, which is not long:
   Sweet Thames, run softly, till I end my song.'

So ended she; and all the rest around
To her redoubled that her undersong,   110
Which said, their bridal day should not be long.
And gentle echo from the neighbour ground,
Their accents did resound.
So forth, those joyous birds did pass along,
Adown the lee, that to them murmured low,

As he would speak, but that he lacked a tongue,
Yet did by signs his glad affection show,
Making his stream run slow.
And all the fowl which in his flood did dwell
Gan flock about these twain, that did excel   120
The rest, so far, as Cynthia doth shend°   *shame*
The lesser stars. So they, enrangèd well,
Did on those two attend,
And their best service lend,
Against their wedding day, which was not long:
  Sweet Thames, run softly, till I end my song.

At length they all to merry London came,
To merry London, my most kindly nurse,
That to me gave this life's first native source,
Though from another place I take my name,   130
An house of ancient fame.
There when they came, whereas those bricky towers,
The which on Thames broad agèd back do ride,
Where now the studious lawyers have their bowers
There whilom wont the Templar Knights to bide,
Till they decayed through pride:
Next whereunto there stands a stately place,
Where oft I gainèd gifts and goodly grace
Of that great Lord, which therein wont to dwell,
Whose want too well now feels my friendless case: 140
But ah, here fits not well
Old woes, but joys to tell
Against the bridal day, which is not long:
  Sweet Thames, run softly, till I end my song.

Yet therein now doth lodge a noble peer,
Great England's glory and the world's wide wonder,
Whose dreadful name late through all Spain did thunder.
And Hercules' two pillars standing near,
Did make to quake and fear:
Fair branch of honour, flower of chivalry,   150
That fillest England with thy triumph's fame,
Joy have thou of thy noble victory,
And endless happiness of thine own name
That promiseth the same:
That through thy prowess and victorious arms,
Thy country may be freed from foreign harms:

And great Elisa's glorious name may ring
Through all the world, filled with thy wide alarms,
Which some brave muse may sing
To ages following,   160
Upon the bridal day, which is not long:
   Sweet Thames, run softly, till I end my song.

From those high towers, this noble lord issuing,
Like radiant Hesper when his golden hair
In the Ocean billows he hath bathèd fair,
Descended to the river's open viewing,
With a great train ensuing.
Above the rest were goodly to be seen
Two gentle knights of lovely face and feature,
Beseeming well the bower of any queen,   170
With gifts of wit and ornaments of nature,
Fit for so goodly stature:
That like the twins of Jove they seem'd in sight,
Which deck the baldric of the heavens bright:
They two forth pacing to the river's side,
Received those two fair birds, their love's delight,
Which at th' appointed tide,
Each one did make his bride,
Against their bridal day, which is not long:
   Sweet Thames, run softly, till I end my Song.   180

67 from *The Faerie Queene*: Book I

Containing the Legend of the Knight of the Red Cross, or of Holiness

Lo I the man, whose Muse whilom did mask,
As time her taught, in lowly shepherd's weeds,
Am now enforced a far unfitter task,
For trumpets stern to change mine oaten reeds,
And sing of knights' and ladies' gentle deeds;
Whose praises having slept in silence long,
Me, all too mean, the sacred Muse areeds
To blazon broad amongst her learnèd throng:
Fierce wars and faithful loves shall moralise my song.

Help then, oh holy Virgin, chief of nine,   10
Thy weaker novice to perform thy will,
Lay forth out of thine everlasting scryne
The antique rolls, which there lie hidden still,
Of faerie knights and fairest Tanaquill,
Whom that most noble Briton prince so long
Sought through the world, and suffered so much ill,
That I must rue his undeservèd wrong:
O help thou my weak wit, and sharpen my dull tongue.

And thou most dreaded imp of highest Jove,
Fair Venus' son, that with thy cruel dart   20
At that good knight so cunningly did'st rove,
That glorious fire it kindled in his heart,
Lay now thy deadly heben° bow apart,   *ebony*
And with thy mother mild come to mine aid:
Come both, and with you bring triumphant Mart,°   *Mars*
In loves and gentle jollities arrayed,
After his murderous spoils and bloody rage allayed.

And with them eke, O Goddess heavenly bright,
Mirror of grace and majesty divine,
Great lady of the greatest isle, whose light   30
Like Phoebus' lamp throughout the world doth shine,
Shed thy fair beams into my feeble eyne,°   *eyes*
And raise my thoughts, too humble and too vile,
To think of that true glorious type of thine,
The argument of mine afflicted style:
The which to hear, vouchsafe, oh dearest dread, awhile.

Canto I

> *The patrons of true Holiness,*
> *Foul Error doth defeat:*
> *Hypocrisy him to entrap*
> *Doth to his home entreat.*   40

A gentle knight was pricking on the plain,
Yclad° in mighty arms and silver shield,   *clothed*
Wherein old dints of deep wounds did remain,
The cruel marks of many a bloody field;
Yet arms till that time did he never wield:
His angry steed did chide his foaming bit,

As much disdaining to the curb to yield:
Full jolly knight he seemed, and fair did sit,
As one for knightly jousts and fierce encounters fit.

But on his breast a bloody cross he bore,   50
The dear remembrance of his dying Lord,
For whose sweet sake that glorious badge he wore,
And dead as living ever him adored.
Upon his shield the like was also scored,
For sovereign hope, which in his help he had:
Right faithful true he was in deed and word,
But of his cheer did seem too solemn sad;
Yet nothing did he dread, but ever was ydrad.°   *feared by others*

Upon a great adventure he was bound,
That greatest Gloriana to him gave,   60
That greatest glorious queen of faerie land,
To win him worship, and her grace to have,
Which of all earthly things he most did crave;
And ever as he rode, his heart did yearn
To prove his puissance° in battle brave   *power*
Upon his foe, and his new force to learn;
Upon his foe, a dragon horrible and stern.

A lovely lady rode him fair beside,
Upon a lowly ass more white than snow,
Yet she much whiter, but the same did hide   70
Under a veil, that wimpled was full low,
And over all a black stole she did throw,
As one that inly mourned: so was she sad,
And heavy sat upon her palfrey slow:
Seemed in heart some hidden care she had,
And by her in a line a milk white lamb she lad.°   *led*

So pure and innocent as that same lamb
She was in life and every virtuous lore,
And by descent from royal lineage came
Of ancient kings and queens, that had of yore   80
Their sceptres stretched from east to western shore,
And all the world in their subjection held;
Till that infernal fiend with foul uproar
Forwasted all their land, and them expelled:
Whom to avenge, she had this knight from far compelled.

Behind her far away a dwarf did lag,
That lazy seemed in being ever last,
Or wearièd with bearing of her bag
Of needments at his back. Thus as they passed,
The day with clouds was sudden overcast,   90
And angry Jove an hideous storm of rain
Did pour into his leman's° lap so fast,   *lover's*
That every wight to shroud° it did constrain,   *cover*
And this fair couple eke to shroud themselves were fain.

Enforced to seek some covert nigh at hand,
A shady grove not far away they spied,
That promised aid the tempest to withstand,
Whose lofty trees, yclad with summer's pride,
Did spread so broad, that heaven's light did hide,
Not pierceable with power of any star: 100
And all within were paths and alleys wide,
With footing worn, and leading inward far:
Fair harbour that them seems; so in they entered are.

And forth they pass, with pleasure forward led,
Joying to hear the birds' sweet harmony,
Which therein, shrouded from the tempest dread,
Seemed in their song to scorn the cruel sky.
Much can they praise the trees so straight and high,
The sailing pine, the cedar proud and tall,
The vine-prop elm, the poplar never dry,   110
The builder oak, sole king of forests all,
The aspen good for staves, the cypress funeral.

The laurel, meed of mighty conquerors
And poets sage, the fir that weepeth still,
The willow worn of forlorn paramours,
The yew obedient to the bender's will,
The birch for shafts,° the sallow* for the mill,   *arrows; shrub willow*
The myrrh sweet bleeding in the bitter wound,
The warlike beech, the ash for nothing ill,
The fruitful olive, and the platane round,   120
The carver holm, the maple seldom inward sound.

Led with delight, they thus beguile the way,
Until the blustering storm is overblown;
When weening to return, whence they did stray,

They cannot find that path, which first was shown,
But wander to and fro in ways unknown,
Furthest from end then, when they nearest ween,°   *think themselves*
That makes them doubt, their wits be not their own:
So many paths, so many turnings seen,
That which of them to take, in diverse doubt they been.   130

At last resolving forward still to fare,
Till that some end they find or in or out,
That path they take, that beaten seemed most bare,
And like to lead the labyrinth about;
Which when by tract they hunted had throughout,
At length it brought them to a hollow cave,
Amid the thickest woods. The champion stout
Eftsoons° dismounted from his courser brave,   *Immediately*
And to the dwarf a while his needless spear he gave.

'Be well aware,' quoth then that Lady mild,   140
'Lest sudden mischief ye too rash provoke:
The danger hid, the place unknown and wild,
Breeds dreadful doubts: oft fire is without smoke,
And peril without show: therefore your stroke,
Sir Knight, with-hold, till further trial made.'
'Ah, Lady,' said he, 'shame were to revoke
The forward footing for an hidden shade:
Virtue gives herself light, through darkness for to wade.'

'Yea, but,' quoth she, 'the peril of this place
I better wot than you, though now too late   150
To wish you back return with foul disgrace;
Yet wisdom warns, whilst foot is in the gate,
To stay the step, ere forcèd to retreat.
This is the wandering wood, this error's den,
A monster vile, whom God and man does hate:
Therefore I rede° beware.' 'Fly, fly,' quoth then   *counsel*
The fearful dwarf: 'this is no place for living men.'

But full of fire and greedy hardiment,
The youthful knight could not for aught be stayed,
But forth unto the darksome hole he went,   160
And lookèd in: his glistering armour made
A little glooming light, much like a shade,
By which he saw the ugly monster plain,

Half like a serpent horribly displayed,
But the other half did woman's shape retain,
Most loathsome, filthy, foul, and full of vile disdain.

And as she lay upon the dirty ground,
Her huge long tail her den all overspread,
Yet was in knots and many boughts° upwound,   *coils*
Pointed with mortal sting. Of her there bred   170
A thousand young ones, which she daily fed,
Sucking upon her poisonous dugs, each one
Of sundry shapes, yet all ill favourèd:
Soon as that uncouth light upon them shone,
Into her mouth they crept, and sudden all were gone.

Their dam upstart, out of her den effraid,°   *frightened*
And rushèd forth, hurling her hideous tail
About her cursèd head, whose folds displayed
Were stretched now forth at length without entrail.°   *twist*
She looked about, and seeing one in mail   180
Armed to point, sought back to turn again;
For light she hated as the deadly bale,°   *affliction*
Aye wont in desert darkness to remain,
Where plain none might her see, nor she see any plain.

Which when the valiant elf perceiv'd, he leapt
As lion fierce upon the flying prey,
And with his trenchant blade her boldly kept
From turning back, and forcèd her to stay:
Therewith enraged she loudly gan to bray,
And turning fierce, her speckled tail advanced,   190
Threatening her angry sting, him to dismay:
Who naught aghast, his mighty hand enhanced:
The stroke down from her head unto her shoulder glanced.

Much daunted with that dint, her sense was dazed,
Yet kindling rage, her self she gathered round,
And all at once her beastly body raised
With doubled forces high above the ground:
Tho wrapping up her wreathèd stern around,
Leapt fierce upon his shield, and her huge train
All suddenly about his body wound,   200
That hand or foot to stir he strove in vain:
God help the man so wrapped in error's endless train!

His lady sad to see his sore constraint,
Cried out, 'Now, now, Sir Knight, show what ye be,
Add faith unto your force, and be not faint:
Strangle her, else she sure will strangle thee.'
That when he heard, in great perplexity,
His gall did grate for grief and high disdain,
And knitting all his force got one hand free,
Wherewith he gripped her gorge with so great pain,   210
That soon to loose her wicked bands did her constrain.

Therewith she spewed out of her filthy maw
A flood of poison horrible and black,
Full of great lumps of flesh and gobbets raw,
Which stunk so vilely, that it first him slack
His grasping hold, and from her turn him back:
Her vomit full of books and papers was,
With loathly frogs and toads, which eyes did lack,
And creeping sought way in the weedy grass:
Her filthy parbreak° all the place defilèd has.   *vomit* 220

As when old father Nilus gins to swell
With timely pride above the Egyptian vale,
His fatty waves do fertile slime outwell,
And overflow each plain and lowly dale:
But when his later spring gins to avail,
Huge heaps of mud he leaves, wherein there breed
Ten thousand kinds of creatures, partly male
And partly female of his fruitful seed;
Such ugly monstrous shapes elsewhere may no man reed.°   *deem*

The same so sore annoyèd has the knight,   230
That wellnigh chokèd with the deadly stink,
His forces fail, ne can no longer fight.
Whose courage when the fiend perceiv'd to shrink,
She pourèd forth out of her hellish sink
Her fruitful cursèd spawn of serpents small,
Deformed monsters, foul, and black as ink,
Which swarming all about his legs did crawl,
And him encumbered sore, but could not hurt at all.

As gentle shepherd in sweet eventide,
When ruddy Phoebus gins to welk° in west,   *wane* 240
High on an hill, his flock to viewen wide,

Marks which do bite their hasty supper best;
A cloud of cumbrous gnats do him molest,
All striving to infix their feeble stings,
That from their noyance he no where can rest,
But with his clownish hands their tender wings
He brusheth oft, and oft doth mar their murmurings,

Thus ill bestead, and fearful more of shame,
Than of the certain peril he stood in,
Half furious unto his foe he came,   250
Resolved in mind all suddenly to win,
Or soon to lose, before he once would lin;°   *desist*
And struck at her with more than manly force,
That from her body full of filthy sin
He raft° her hateful head without remorse;   *bereft*
A stream of coal black blood forth gushèd from her corse.°   *corpse*

Her scattered brood, soon as their parent dear
They saw so rudely falling to the ground,
Groaning full deadly, all with troublous fear,
Gathered themselves about her body round,   260
Weening their wonted entrance to have found
At her wide mouth: but being there withstood
They flockèd all about her bleeding wound,
And suckèd up their dying mother's blood,
Making her death their life, and eke her hurt their good.

That detestable sight him much amazed,
To see th' unkindly° imps of heaven accursed,   *unnatural*
Devour their dam; on whom while so he gazed,
Having all satisfied their bloody thirst,
Their bellies swollen he saw with fulness burst,   270
And bowels gushing forth: well worthy end
Of such as drunk her life, the which them nursed;
Now needeth him no longer labour spend,
His foes have slain themselves, with whom he should contend.

His lady seeing all, that chanced, from far
Approached in haste to greet his victory,
And said, 'Fair Knight, born under happy star,
Who see your vanquished foes before you lie:
Well worthy be you of that Armoury,
Wherein ye have great glory won this day,   280

And proved your strength on a strong enemy,
Your first adventure: many such I pray,
And henceforth ever wish, that like succeed it may.'

Then mounted he upon his steed again,
And with the lady backward sought to wend;
That path he kept, which beaten was most plain,
Ne ever would to any by-way bend,
But still did follow one unto the end,
The which at last out of the wood them brought.
So forward on his way (with God to friend)   290
He passèd forth, and new adventure sought;
Long way he travellèd, before he heard of ought.

At length they chanced to meet upon the way
An agèd sire, in long black weeds yclad,°   *clothed*
His feet all bare, his beard all hoary grey,
And by his belt his book he hanging had;
Sober he seemed, and very sagely sad,
And to the ground his eyes were lowly bent,
Simple in show, and void of malice bad,
And all the way he prayèd, as he went,   300
And often knocked his breast, as one that did repent.

He fair the knight saluted, louting° low,   *bowing*
Who fair him quited, as that courteous was;
And after askèd him, if he did know
Of strange adventures, which abroad did pass.
'Ah, my dear son,' quoth he, 'how should, alas,
Silly old man, that lives in hidden cell,
Bidding his beads all day for his trespass,
Tidings of war and worldly trouble tell?
With holy father sits not with such things to mell.   310

'But if of danger which hereby doth dwell,
And homebred evil ye desire to hear,
Of a strange man I can you tidings tell,
That wasteth all this country far and near.'
'Of such,' said he, 'I chiefly do inquire,
And shall you well reward to show the place,
In which that wicked wight his days doth wear:
For to all knighthood it is foul disgrace,
That such a cursed creature lives so long a space.'

'Far hence,' quoth he, 'in wasteful wilderness 320
His dwelling is, by which no living wight
May ever pass, but thorough great distress.'
'Now,' said the lady, 'draweth toward night,
And well I wot,° that of your later fight *know*
Ye all forwearied be: for what so strong,
But wanting rest will also want of might?
The sun that measures heaven all day long,
At night doth bate° his steeds the ocean waves among. *abate*

'Then with the sun take, Sir, your timely rest,
And with new day new work at once begin: 330
Untroubled night they say gives counsel best.'
'Right well, Sir Knight, ye have advisèd been,'
Quoth then that aged man; 'the way to win
Is wisely to advise; now day is spent;
Therefore with me ye may take up your inn
For this same night.' The knight was well content:
So with that godly father to his home they went.

A little lowly hermitage it was,
Down in a dale, hard by a forest's side,
Far from resort of people, that did pass 340
In travel to and fro: a little wide
There was an holy chapel edified,
Wherein the hermit duly wont to say
His holy things each morn and eventide:
Thereby a crystal stream did gently play,
Which from a sacred fountain welled forth alway.

Arrivèd there, the little house they fill,
Ne look for entertainment, where none was:
Rest is their feast, and all things at their will;
The noblest mind the best contentment has. 350
With fair discourse the evening so they pass:
For that old man of pleasing words had store,
And well could file his tongue as smooth as glass;
He told of saints and popes, and evermore
He strewed an Ave-Mary° after and before. *Hail Mary*

The drooping night thus creepeth on them fast,
And the sad° humour loading their eyelids, *serious*
As messenger of Morpheus on them cast

Sweet slumbring dew, the which to sleep them bids.
Unto their lodgings then his guests he rids: 360
Where when all drowned in deadly sleep he finds,
He to his study goes, and there amids
His magic books and arts of sundry kinds,
He seeks out mighty charms, to trouble sleepy minds.

Then choosing out few words most horrible,
(Let none them read) thereof did verses frame,
With which and other spells like terrible,
He bad awake black Pluto's grisly dame,
And cursèd heaven, and spake reproachful shame
Of highest God, the Lord of life and light;   370
A bold bad man, that dared to call by name
Great Gorgon, prince of darkness and dead night,
At which Cocytus quakes, and Styx is put to flight.

And forth he called out of deep darkness dread
Legions of sprites, the which like little flies
Fluttering about his ever damnèd head,
Await whereto their service he applies,
To aid his friends, or fray his enemies:
Of those he chose out two, the falsest two,
And fittest for to forge true-seeming lies;   380
The one of them he gave a message to,
The other by him self stayed other work to do.

He making speedy way through spersèd° air,   *scattered*
And through the world of waters wide and deep,
To Morpheus' house doth hastily repair.
Amid the bowels of the earth full steep,
And low, where dawning day doth never peep,
His dwelling is; there Tethys his wet bed
Doth ever wash, and Cynthia still doth steep
In silver dew his ever-drooping head,   390
While sad night over him her mantle black doth spread.

Whose double gates he findeth lockèd fast,
The one fair framed of burnished ivory,
The other all with silver overcast;
And wakeful dogs before them far do lie,
Watching to banish care their enemy,
Who oft is wont to trouble gentle sleep.

By them the sprite doth pass in quietly,
And unto Morpheus comes, whom drowned deep
In drowsy fit he finds: of nothing he takes keep.   400

And more, to lull him in his slumber soft,
A trickling stream from high rock tumbling down
And ever-drizzling rain upon the loft,
Mixed with a murmuring wind, much like the sown°   *sound*
Of swarming bees, did cast him in a swoon:
No other noise, nor people's troublous cries,
As still are wont to annoy the wallèd town,
Might there be heard: but careless quiet lies,
Wrapped in eternal silence far from enemies.

The messenger approaching to him spake,   410
But his waste words returned to him in vain:
So sound he slept, that naught might him awake.
Then rudely he him thrust, and pushed with pain,
Whereat he gun° to stretch: but he again   *begun*
Shook him so hard, that forcèd him to speak.
As one then in a dream, whose drier brain
Is tossed with troubled sights and fancies weak,
He mumbled soft, but would not all his silence break.

The sprite then gun more boldly him to wake,
And threatened unto him the dreaded name   420
Of Hecate: whereat he gun to quake,
And lifting up his lumpish head, with blame
Half angry askèd him, for what he came.
'Hither,' quoth he, 'me Archimago sent,
He that the stubborn sprites can wisely tame,
He bids thee to him send for his intent
A fit false dream, that can delude the sleepers sent.'

The God obeyed, and calling forth straight way
A diverse dream out of his prison dark,
Delivered it to him, and down did lay   430
His heavy head, devoid of careful cark,°   *sorrow*
Whose senses all were straight benumbed and stark.
He back returning by the Ivory door
Remounted up as light as cheerful lark,
And on his little wings the dream he bore
In haste unto his lord, where he him left afore.

Who all this while with charms and hidden arts,
Had made a lady of that other sprite,
And framed of liquid air her tender parts
So lively, and so like in all men's sight,   440
That weaker sense it could have ravished quite:
The maker self for all his wondrous wit,
Was nigh beguilèd with so goodly sight:
Her all in white he clad, and over it
Cast a black stole, most like to seem for Una fit.

Now when that idle dream was to him brought,
Unto that elfin knight he bad him fly,
Where he slept soundly void of evil thought,
And with false shows abuse his fantasy,
In sort as he him schoolèd privily: 450
And that new creature born without her due,
Full of the maker's guile, with usage sly
He taught to imitate that Lady true,
Whose semblance she did carry under feignèd hue.

Thus well instructed, to their work they haste,
And coming where the knight in slumber lay,
The one upon his hardy head him placed,
And made him dream of loves and lustful play,
That nigh his manly heart did melt away,
Bathèd in wanton bliss and wicked joy: 460
Then seemèd him his lady by him lay,
And to him plained, how that false wingèd boy,
Her chaste heart had subdued, to learn dame pleasure's toy.

And she herself of beauty sovereign queen,
Fair Venus seemed unto his bed to bring
Her, whom he waking evermore did ween,°   *suppose*
To be the chastest flower, that aye did spring
On earthly branch, the daughter of a king,
Now a loose leman° to vile service bound: *lover*
And eke the Graces seemèd all to sing,   470
'Hymen Io Hymen,' dancing all around,
Whilst freshest Flora her with ivy garland crowned.

In this great passion of unwonted lust,
Or wonted fear of doing aught amiss,
He started up, as seeming to mistrust,

Some secret ill, or hidden foe of his:
Lo there before his face his lady is,
Under black stole hiding her baited hook,
And as half blushing offered him to kiss,
With gentle blandishment and lovely look,   480
Most like that virgin true, which for her knight him took.

All clean dismayed to see so uncouth sight,
And half enragèd at her shameless guise,
He thought have slain her in his fierce despite:
But hasty heat tempering with sufferance wise,
He stayed his hand, and gan himself advise
To prove his sense, and tempt her feignèd truth.
Wringing her hands in women's piteous wise,
Tho gan she weep, to stir up gentle ruth,
Both for her noble blood, and for her tender youth.   490

And said, 'Ah, Sir, my liege lord and my love,
Shall I accuse the hidden cruel fate,
And mighty causes wrought in heaven above,
Or the blind god, that doth me thus amate,°   *subdue*
For hoped love to win me certain hate?
Yet thus perforce he bids me do, or die.
Die is my due: yet rue my wretched state
You, whom my hard avenging destiny
Hath made judge of my life or death indifferently.

'Your own dear sake forced me at first to leave   500
My father's kingdom, –' There she stopped with tears;
Her swollen heart her speech seemed to bereave,
And then again begun, 'My weaker years
Captived to fortune and frail worldly fears,
Fly to your faith for succour and sure aid:
Let me not die in languor and long tears.'
'Why Dame,' quoth he, 'what hath ye thus dismayed?
What frays ye, that were wont to comfort me afraid?'

'Love of your self,' she said, 'and dear constraint
Lets me not sleep, but waste the weary night   510
In secret anguish and unpitied plaint,
Whiles you in careless sleep are drownèd quite.'
Her doubtful words made that redoubted knight
Suspect her truth; yet since no untruth he knew,

Her fawning love with foul disdainful spite
He would not shend,° but said, 'Dear dame I rue,   *reproach*
That for my sake unknown such grief unto you grew.

'Assure your self, it fell not all to ground;
For all so dear as life is to my heart,
I deem your love, and hold me to you bound;   520
Ne let vain fears procure your needless smart,
Where cause is none, but to your rest depart.'
Not all content, yet seemed she to appease
Her mournful plaints, beguilèd of her art,
And fed with words, that could not choose but please;
So sliding softly forth, she turned as to her ease.

Long after lay he musing at her mood,
Much grieved to think that gentle dame so light,
For whose defence he was to shed his blood.
At last dull weariness of former fight   530
Having yrocked asleep his irksome sprite,
That troublous dream gan freshly toss his brain,
With bowers, and beds, and ladies' dear delight:
But when he saw his labour all was vain,
With that misformèd sprite he back returned again.

Sir Walter Ralegh (1552?–1618)

68. Reply to Marlowe[33]

If all the world and love were young
And truth in every shepherd's tongue
These pretty pleasures might me move
To live with thee and be thy love.

But time drives flocks from field to fold
When rivers rage and rocks grow cold;

---

[33] See page 342.

And Philomel becometh dumb;
The rest complains of cares to come.

The flowers do fade, and wanton fields
To wayward winter reckoning yields: 10
A honey tongue, a heart of gall,
Is fancy's spring, but sorrow's fall.

Thy gowns, thy shoes, thy beds of roses,
Thy cap, thy kirtle and thy posies
Soon break, soon wither, soon forgotten,
In folly ripe, in reason rotten.

Thy belt of straw and ivy buds,
Thy coral clasps and amber studs,
All those in me no means can move
To come to thee and be thy love.   20

But could youth last and love still breed,
Had joys no date nor age no need,
Then those delights my mind might move
To live with thee and be thy love.

69. In the Grace of Wit, of Tongue, and Face

Her face, her tongue, her wit, so fair, so sweet, so sharp,
First bent, then drew, now hit, mine eye, mine ear, my heart:
Mine eye, mine ear, my heart, to like, to learn, to love,

Her face, her tongue, her wit, doth lead, doth teach, doth move:
Her face, her tongue, her wit, with beams, with sound, with art,
Doth blind, doth charm, doth rule, mine eye, mine ear, my heart.

Mine eye, mine ear, my heart, with life, with hope, with skill,
Her face, her tongue, her wit, doth feed, doth feast, doth fill.
O face, O tongue, O wit, with frowns, with cheeks, with smart,

Wring not, vex not, wound not, mine eye, mine ear, my heart.   10
This eye, this ear, this heart, shall joy, shall bind, shall swear,
Your face, your tongue, your wit, to serve, to love, to fear.

70. To his Son

Three things there be that prosper all apace
    And flourish while they are asunder far.
But on a day they meet all in a place
    And when they meet they one another mar.

And they be these: the Wood, the Weed, the Wag.
    The Wood is that that makes the gallows tree.
The Weed is that that strings the hangman's bag.
    The Wag, my pretty knave, betokens thee.

Now mark, dear boy, while these assemble not
    Green springs the tree, hemp grows, the wag is wild,   10
But when they meet it makes the timber rot,
    It frets the halter and it chokes the child.

71. The Lie

Go Soul, the body's guest,
    Upon a thankless arrant.°   *errand*
Fear not to touch the best,
    The truth shall be thy warrant.
Go, since I needs must die,
And give the world the lie.

Say to the court, it glows
    And shines like rotten wood;
Say to the church, it shows
    What's good, and doth no good.   10
If church and court reply
Then give them both the lie.

Tell potentates, they live
    Acting by others' action;
Not loved unless they give,
    Not strong but by a faction.
If potentates reply
Give potentates the lie.

Tell men of high condition

    That manage the estate   20
Their purpose is ambition,
    Their practice only hate.
And if they once reply
Then give them all the lie.

Tell them that brave it most
    They beg for more by spending,
Who in their greatest cost
    Seek nothing but commending.
And if they make reply
Then give them all the lie.   30

Tell zeal it wants devotion,
    Tell love it is but lust,
Tell time it is but motion,
    Tell flesh it is but dust.
And wish them not reply
For thou must give the lie.

Tell age it daily wasteth,
    Tell honour how it alters,
Tell beauty how she blasteth,
    Tell favour how it falters.   40
And as they shall reply
Give every one the lie.

Tell wit how much it wrangles
    In tickle points of niceness,
Tell wisdom she entangles
    Herself in over-wiseness.
And when they do reply
Straight give them both the lie.

Tell physic of her boldness,
    Tell skill it is pretension,   50
Tell charity of coldness,
    Tell law it is contention.
And as they do reply
So give them still the lie.

Tell fortune of her blindness,
    Tell nature of decay,

Tell friendship of unkindness,
    Tell justice of delay.
And if they will reply
Then give them all the lie.   60

Tell arts they have no soundness
    But vary by esteeming,
Tell schools they want profoundness
    And stand too much on seeming.
If arts and schools reply
Give arts and schools the lie.

Tell faith it's fled the city,
    Tell how the country erreth,
Tell manhood shakes off pity,
    Tell virtue least preferreth.   70
And if they do reply
Spare not to give the lie.

So when thou hast as I
    Commanded thee done blabbing,
Although to give the lie
    Deserves no less than stabbing,
Stab at thee he that will,
No stab the soul can kill.

72. The Passionate Man's Pilgrimage

Give me my scallop shell of quiet,
    My staff of faith to walk upon,
My scrip of joy, immortal diet,
    My bottle of salvation,
My gown of glory, hope's true gage,
And thus I'll take my pilgrimage.

Blood must be my body's balmer,
    No other balm will there be given,
Whilst my soul, like quiet palmer,
    Travelleth towards the land of heaven,   10
Over the silver mountains

Where spring the nectar fountains.
      There will I kiss
      The bowl of bliss
And drink mine everlasting fill
On every milken hill.
My soul will be a-dry before,
But after, it will thirst no more.

Then by that happy blissful way
    More peaceful pilgrims I shall see   20
That have cast off their rags of clay,
    And walk apparelled fresh like me.
      I'll take them first
      To quench their thirst
    And taste of nectar suckets
      At those clear wells
      Where sweetness dwells
    Drawn up by saints in crystal buckets.

And when our bottles and all we
Are filled with immortality   30
Then the blessed paths we'll travel
Strewed with rubies thick as gravel,
Ceilings of diamonds, sapphire floors,
High walls of coral and pearly bowers.

From thence to heaven's bribeless hall
Where no corrupted voices brawl,
No conscience molten into gold,
No forged accuser bought or sold,
No cause deferred, no vain-spent journey,
For there Christ is the king's attorney,   40
Who pleads for all without degrees
And He hath angels, but no fees.

And when the grand twelve-million jury
Of our sins with direful fury
Against our souls black verdicts give
Christ pleads His death, and then we live.

Be Thou my speaker, taintless pleader,
Unblotted lawyer, true proceeder.
Thou giv'st salvation even for alms
Not with a bribèd lawyer's palms.   50

And this is mine eternal plea
To Him that made heaven, earth, and sea:
That since my flesh must die so soon
And want a head to dine next noon,
Just at the stroke, when my veins start and spread,
Set on my soul an everlasting head.
Then am I ready, like a palmer fit,
To tread those blest paths which before I writ.

Of death and judgement, heaven and hell,
Who oft doth think, must needs die well.   60

73. 'What is our life?'

What is our life? A play of passion.
Our mirth? The music of division.
Our mothers' wombs the tiring-houses° be   *attiring-houses*
Where we are dressed for life's short comedy.
The earth the stage, Heaven the spectator is
Who sits and views whosoe'er doth act amiss.
The graves which hide us from the scorching sun
Are like drawn curtains when the play is done.
Thus playing post we to our latest rest
And then we die in earnest, that's no jest.   10

74. 'As you came from the holy land'

As you came from the holy land
    Of Walsinghame
Met you not with my true love
    By the way as you came?

How shall I know your true love
    That have met many one
As I went to the holy land
    That have come, that have gone?

She is neither white nor brown
    But as the heavens fair.   10
There is none hath a form so divine
    In the earth or the air.

Such a one did I meet, good sir,
    Such an angelic face,
Who like a queen, like a nymph, did appear
    By her gait, by her grace.

She hath left me here all alone,
    All alone, as unknown,
Who sometimes did me lead with herself
    And me loved as her own.   20

What's the cause that she leaves you alone
    And a new way doth take,
Who loved you once as her own
    And her joy did you make?

I have loved her all my youth
    But now old, as you see.
Love likes not the falling fruit
    From the withered tree.

Know that love is a careless child
    And forgets promise past.   30
He is blind, he is deaf when he list
    And in faith never fast.

His desire is a dureless content
    And a trustless joy.
He is won with a world of despair
    And is lost with a toy.

Of womenkind such indeed is the love
    Or the word love abused
Under which many childish desires
    And conceits are excused.   40

But true love is a durable fire
    In the mind ever burning,
Never sick, never old, never dead,
    From itself never turning.

75. from *The 21st (and last) Book of the Ocean*[34]

Out of that mass of miracles, my muse
   Gathered those flowers, to her pure sense pleasing;
Out of her eyes, the store of joys, did choose
   Equal delights, my sorrow's counterpoising.

Her regal looks my vigorous sighs suppressed;
   Small drops of joys sweetened great worlds of woes;
One gladsome day a thousand cares redressed; –
   Whom love defends, what fortune overthrows?

When she did well, what did there else amiss?
   When she did ill, what empires would have pleased?   10
No other power effecting woe or bliss,
   She gave, she took, she wounded, she appeased.

The honour of her love love still devising,
   Wounding my mind with contrary conceit,
Transferred itself sometime to her aspiring,
   Sometime the trumpet of her thought's retreat.

To seek new worlds for gold, for praise, for glory,
   To try desire, to try love severed far,
When I was gone, she sent her memory,
   More strong than were ten thousand ships of war,   20

To call me back, to leave great honour's thought,
   To leave my friends, my fortune, my attempt;
To leave the purpose I so long had sought,
   And hold both cares and comforts in contempt.

Such heat in ice, such fire in frost remained,
   Such trust in doubt, such comfort in despair,
Which, like the gentle lamb, though lately weaned,
   Plays with the dug, though finds no comfort there.

*

But as a body, violently slain,
   Retaineth warmth although the spirit be gone,   30
And by a power in nature moves again
   Till it be laid below the fatal stone;

[34] What follows is a truncated version.

Or as the earth, even in cold winter days,
  Left for a time by her life-giving sun,
Doth by the power remaining of his rays
  Produce some green, though not as it hath done;

Or as a wheel, forced by the falling stream,
  Although the course be turned some other way,
Doth for a time go round upon the beam,
  Till, wanting strength to move, it stands at stay;   40

So my forsaken heart, my withered mind,
  Widow of all the joys it once possessed,
My hopes clean out of sight with forcèd wind,
  To kingdoms strange, to lands far-off addressed,

Alone, forsaken, friendless, on the shore
  With many wounds, with death's cold pangs embraced,
Writes in the dust, as one that could no more,
  Whom love, and time, and fortune, had defaced;

Of things so great, so long, so manifold,
  With means so weak, the soul even then departing   50
The weal, the woe, the passages of old,
  And worlds of thoughts described by one last sighing.

As if, when after Phoebus is descended,
  And leaves a light much like the past day's dawning,
And, every toil and labour wholly ended,
  Each living creature draweth to his resting,

                        *

We should begin by such a parting light
  To write the story of all ages past,
And end the same before the approaching night.

Such is again the labour of my mind,   60
  Whose shroud, by sorrow woven now to end,
Hath seen that ever shining sun declined,
  So many years that so could not descend,

But that the eyes of my mind held her beams
  In every part transferred by love's swift thought;

Far off or near, in waking or in dreams,
    Imagination strong their lustre brought.

Such force her angelic appearance had
    To master distance, time, or cruelty;
Such art to grieve, and after to make glad;   70
    Such fear in love, such love in majesty.

My weary limbs her memory embalmed;
    My darkest ways her eyes make clear as day.
What storms so great but Cynthia's beams appeased?
    What rage so fierce, that love could not allay?

Twelve years entire I wasted in this war;
    Twelve years of my most happy younger days;
But I in them, and they, now wasted are:
    'Of all which past, the sorrow only stays –'

So wrote I once, and my mishap foretold,   80
    My mind still feeling sorrowful success;
Even as before a storm the marble cold
    Doth by moist tears tempestuous times express,

So felt my heavy mind my harms at hand,
    Which my vain thought in vain sought to recure:
At middle day my sun seemed under land,
    When any little cloud did it obscure.

*

Those streams seem standing puddles, which before
    We saw our beauties in, so were they clear;
Belphoebe's course is now observed no more;   90

That fair resemblance weareth out of date;
    Our ocean seas are but tempestuous waves,
And all things base, that blessed were of late …

And as a field, wherein the stubble stands
    Of harvest past, the ploughman's eye offends;
He tills again, or tears them up with hands,
    And throws to fire as foiled and fruitless ends,

And takes delight another seed to sow;
   So doth the mind root up all wonted thought,
And scorns the care of our remaining woe;   100
   The sorrows, which themselves for us have wrought,

Are burnt to cinders by new kindled fires;
   The ashes are dispersed into the air;
The sighs, the groans of all our past desires
   Are clean outworn, as things that never were.

With youth is dead the hope of love's return,
   Who looks not back to hear our after-cries:
Where he is not, he laughs at those that mourn;
   Whence he is gone, he scorns the mind that dies.

When he is absent, he believes no words;   110
   When reason speaks, he, careless, stops his ears;
Whom he hath left, he never grace affords,
   But bathes his wings in our lamenting tears.

Unlasting passion, soon outworn conceit,
   Whereon I built, and on so dureless trust!
My mind had wounds, I dare not say deceit,
   Were I resolved her promise was not just.

Sorrow was my revenge and woe my hate;
   I powerless was to alter my desire;
My love is not of time or bound to date;   120
   My heart's internal heat and living fire

Would not, or could, be quenched with sudden showers;
   My bound respect was not confined to days;
My vowed faith not set to ended hours;
   I love the bearing and not bearing sprays

Which now to others do their sweetness send;
   The incarnate, snow-driven white, and purest azure,
Who from high heaven doth on their fields descend,
   Filling their barns with grain, and towers with treasure.

Erring or never erring, such is love   130
   As, while it lasteth, scorns the account of those

Seeking but self-contentment to improve,
   And hides, if any be, his inward woes,

And will not know, while he knows his own passion,
   The often and unjust perseverance
In deeds of love and state, and every action
   From that first day and year of their joy's entrance.

But I, unblessed and ill-born creature,
   That did embrace the dust her body bearing,
That loved her, both by fancy and by nature,   140
   That drew, even with the milk in my first sucking,

Affection from the parent's breast that bare me,
   Have found her as a stranger so severe,
Improving my mishap in each degree;
   But love was gone: so would I my life were!

A queen she was to me, no more Belphoebe;
   A lion then, no more a milk-white dove;
A prisoner in her breast I could not be;
   She did untie the gentle chains of love.

*

The idea remaining of those golden ages,   150
   That beauty, braving heavens and earth embalming,
Which after worthless worlds but play on stages,
   Such didst thou her long since describe, yet sighing

That thy unable spirit could not find aught,
   In heaven's beauties or in earth's delight,
For likeness fit to satisfy thy thought:
   But what hath it availed thee so to write?

She cares not for thy praise, who knows not theirs;
   It's now an idle labour, and a tale
Told out of time, that dulls the hearer's ears;   160
   A merchandise whereof there is no sale.

Leave them, or lay them up with thy despairs.
   She hath resolved, and judged thee long ago.
Thy lines are now a murmuring to her ears,
   Like to a falling stream, which, passing slow,

Is wont to nourish sleep and quietness;
    So shall thy painful labours be perused,
And draw on rest, which sometime had regard;
    But those her cares thy errors have excused.

Thy days fordone have had their day's reward;   170
    So her hard heart, so her estrangèd mind,
In which above the heavens I once reposed;
    So to thy error have her ears inclined,

And have forgotten all thy past deserving,
    Holding in mind but only thine offence;
And only now affecteth thy depraving,
    And thinks all vain that pleadeth thy defence.

                              *

... But what of those or these? or what of aught
    Of that which was, or that which is, to treat?
What I possess is but the same I sought: 180
    My love was false, my labours were deceit.

Nor less than such they are esteemed to be;
    A fraud bought at the price of many woes;
A guile, whereof the profits unto me:
    Could it be thought premeditate for those?

Witness those withered leaves left on the tree,
    The sorrow-worren face, the pensive mind;
The external shews what may the internal be:
    Cold care hath bitten both the root and rind.

But stay, my thoughts, make end: give fortune way: 190
    Harsh is the voice of woe and sorrow's sound:
Complaints cure not, and tears do but allay
    Griefs for a time, which after more abound.

To seek for moisture in the Arabian sand
    Is but a loss of labour and of rest:
The links which time did break of hearty bands

Words cannot knit, or wailings make anew.
    Seek not the sun in clouds when it is set ...

On highest mountains, where those cedars grew,
    Against whose banks the troubled ocean beat,   200

And were the marks to find thy hopèd port,
    Into a soil far off themselves remove.
On Sestus' shore, Leander's late resort,
    Hero hath left no lamp to guide her love.

Thou look'st for light in vain, and storms arise;
    She sleeps thy death, that erst thy danger sighed;
Strive then no more; bow down thy weary eyes –
    Eyes which to all these woes thy heart have guided.

She is gone, she is lost, she is found, she is ever fair:
    Sorrow draws weakly, where love draws not too: 210
Woe's cries sound nothing, but only in love's ear.
    Do then by dying what life cannot do.

Unfold thy flocks and leave them to the fields,
    To feed on hills, or dales, where likes them best,
Of what the summer or the spring-time yields,
    For love and time hath given thee leave to rest.

Thy heart which was their fold, now in decay
    By often storms and winter's many blast,
All torn and rent becomes misfortune's prey;
    False hope my shepherd's staff, now age hath brast   220

My pipe, which love's own hand gave my desire
    To sing her praises and my woe upon,
Despair hath often threatened to the fire,
    As vain to keep now all the rest are gone.

Thus home I draw, as death's long night draws on;
    Yet, every foot, old thoughts turn back mine eyes:
Constraint me guides, as old age draws a stone
    Against the hill, which over-weighty lies

For feeble arms or wasted strength to move:
    My steps are backward, gazing on my loss,   230
My mind's affection and my soul's sole love,
    Not mixed with fancy's chaff or fortune's dross.

*

My days' delights, my spring-time joys fordone,
Which in the dawn and rising sun of youth
   Had their creation, and were first begun,

   Do in the evening and the winter sad
Present my mind, which takes my time's account,
   The grief remaining of the joy it had.

   My times that then ran o'er themselves in these,
And now run out in others' happiness,   240
   Bring unto those new joys and new-born days.

So could she not if she were not the sun,
   Which sees the birth and burial of all else,
And holds that power with which she first begun,

   Leaving each withered body to be torn
By fortune, and by times tempestuous,
   Which, by her virtue, once fair fruit have borne;

   Knowing she can renew, and can create
Green from the ground, and flowers even out of stone,
   By virtue lasting over time and date,   250

   Leaving us only woe, which, like the moss,
Having compassion of unburied bones,
   Cleaves to mischance, and unrepairèd loss.

For tender stalks –

Sir Philip Sidney (1554–1586)

76. 'My sheep are thoughts, which I both guide and serve'

My sheep are thoughts, which I both guide and serve:
Their pasture is fair hills of fruitless love:

On barren sweets they feed, and feeding starve:
I wail their lot, but will not other prove.

My sheephook is wan hope, which all upholds:
My weeds, desire, cut out in endless folds.
    What wool my sheep shall bear, whiles thus they live,
    In you it is, you must the judgement give.

from *Astrophel and Stella*

77. 'Loving in truth, and fain my love in verse to show'

Loving in truth, and fain my love in verse to show,
That the dear She, might take some pleasure of my pain,
Pleasure might cause her read, reading might make her know,
Knowledge might pity win, and pity grace obtain,
    I sought fit words, to paint the blackest face of woe,
Studying inventions fine, her wits to entertain,
Oft turning others' leaves, to see if thence would flow,
Some fresh and fruitful shower, upon my sunburnt brain.
    But words came halting out, wanting invention's stay,
Invention nature's child, fled stepdame's study's blows: 10
And others' feet, still seemed but strangers in my way,
Thus great with child to speak, and helpless in my throes,
        Biting my tongue and pen, beating my self for spite:
        'Fool,' said my muse to me, 'look in thy heart and write.'

78. 'It is most true, what we call Cupid's dart'

It is most true, what we call Cupid's dart
An image is, which for ourselves we carve
And, fools, adore, in temple of our heart,
Till that good God make church and church-men starve.
    It is most true, that eyes are bound to serve
The inward part, and that the heavenly part
Ought to be king, from whose rules who doth swerve,
Rebels to nature, strive for their own smart.
    True that true beauty virtue is indeed,

Whereof this beauty can but be a shade: 10
Which elements with mortal mixture breed,
True that on earth we are but pilgrims made
     And should in soul, up to our country move:
     True and most true, that I must Stella love.

79. 'You that with allegory's curious frame'

You that with allegory's curious frame
Of others' children changelings use to make,
With me those pains for God-sake do not take,
I list not dig so deep for brazen fame.
When I say Stella, I do mean the same
     Princess of beauty, for whose only sake,
     The reins of love I love, though never slake;
And joy therein, though nations count it shame:
I beg no subject to use eloquence,
Nor hidden ways to guide philosophy,   10
Look at my hands for no such quintessence,
But know that I in pure simplicity,
     Breathe out the flames which burn within my heart,
     Love only leading me into this art.

80. 'With how sad steps, oh Moon, thou climb'st the skies'

With how sad steps, oh Moon, thou climb'st the skies,
How silently, and with how wan a face,
What may it be, that even in heavenly place,
That busy archer his sharp arrows tries?
Sure if that long with love acquainted eyes
     Can judge of love, thou feel'st of Lovers' case,
     I read within thy looks thy languished grace.
To me that feel the like, my state descries.
Then even of fellowship, oh Moon, tell me,
Is constant love deemed there but want of wit?
Are beauties there, as proud as here there be?
Do they above, love to be loved, and yet
     Those lovers scorn, whom that love doth possess?
     Do they call virtue there ungratefulness?

81. 'Come Sleep, oh Sleep, the certain knot of peace'

Come Sleep, oh Sleep, the certain knot of peace,
The bathing place of wits, the balm of woe,
The poor man's wealth, the prisoner's release,
The indifferent judge between the high and low,
With shield of proof, shield me from out the press
    Of these fierce darts, despair at me doth throw;
    O make in me those civil wars to cease:
I will good tribute pay if thou do so.
Take thou of me smooth pillows, sweetest bed,
A chamber deaf of noise, and blind of light,   10
A rosy garland, and a weary head.
And if these things (as being thine in right)
    Move not thy heavy grace, thou shalt in me,
    (Livelier than else) rare Stella's image see.

82. 'As good to write, as for to lie and groan'

As good to write, as for to lie and groan,
O Stella dear, how much thy power hath wrought,
That hast my mind now of the basest brought,
My still kept course while others sleep to moan;
Alas, if thou, the height of virtue's throne,
    Can'st but vouchsafe the influence of a thought,
    Upon a wretch which long thy grace hath sought.
Why then by thee how I am overthrown;
And then think thus, although thy beauty be
Made manifest, by such a victory,   10
Yet noblest Conquerors do wreaks avoid;
    Since then thou hast so far subduèd me,
    That in my heart I offer still to thee,
O do not let thy temple be destroyed.

83. 'What, have I thus betrayed my liberty'

What, have I thus betrayed my liberty,
Can those black beams, such burning marks, engrave
In my free side, or am I borne a slave,

Whose neck becomes such yoke of tyranny?
Or want I sense to feel my misery,
   Or spirit, disdain of such disdain to have,
   Who for long faith some gentle pity crave,
Yet get no alms, but scorn of beggary.
Virtue awake, beauty but beauty is;
I may, I must, I can, I will, I do   10
Leave following that which it is gain to miss,
Let her go: soft, but there she comes, go to,
   Unkind I love you, not, (woe me) that I
   Must make my heart thus give my tongue the lie.

84. 'Oft with true sighs, oft with uncallèd tears'

Oft with true sighs, oft with uncallèd tears,
Now with slow words, now with dumb eloquence,
I Stella's eyes assailed, I closed her ears,
But this at last is her sweetest defence;
That who indeed a sound affection bears,
   So captives to his saint both soul and mind,
That wholly hers, all selfness he forbears.
Thence his desire he learns, his life's course thence,
   Now since this chaste love, hates this love in me;
   With chastened mind I needs must show, that she   10
Shall quickly me from what she hates remove.
   O doctor Cupid, thou for me reply:
   Driven else to grant by angel sophistry,
That I love not, without I leave to love.

85. 'I never drank of Aganippe well'

I never drank of Aganippe well,
Nor never did in shade of Tempe sit:
And Muses scorn with vulgar brains to dwell,
Poor lay-man I, for sacred rites unfit.
   Some do I hear of poets' fury tell,
But God wot, wot not what they mean by it:
And this I swear by blackest brook of hell,
I am no pickpurse of another's wit.

How falls it then, that with so smooth an ease
My thoughts I speak? And what I speak I show   10
In verse; and that my verse best wits doth please,
Guess we the cause. What is it this? Fie, no.
    Or so? Much less. How then? Sure thus it is;
    My lips are sure inspired with Stella's kiss.

86. 'Good brother Philip I have forborne you long'

Good brother Philip I have forborne you long,
I was content you should in favour creep,
While craftily you seemed your cut to keep,
As though that fair soft hand did you great wrong:
I bear with envy, yet I hear your song,
When in her neck you did love ditties peep,
Nay, (more fool I) oft suffered you to sleep,
    In lilies' nest where love's self lies along,
    What? Doth high place ambitious thoughts augment?
Is sauciness reward of courtesy?   10
Cannot such grace your silly self content,
But you must needs with those lips billing be
    And through those lips drink nectar from that tongue?
    Leave that, Sir Philip, lest your neck be wrung.

87. 'Be your words made (good sir) of Indian ware'

Be your words made (good sir) of Indian ware,
That you allow them me by so small rate,
Or do you the Caconians imitate,
Or do you mean my tender ears to spare,
That to my questions you so total are?
When I demand of Phoenix Stella's state,
    You say (forsooth) you left her well too late.
    O God, think you that satisfies my care?
I would know whether she did sit or walk:
How clothed: how waited on: sighed she or smiled: 10
Whereof: with whom: how often did she talk:

With what pastimes, time's journeys she beguiled?
    If her lips deign to sweeten my poor name?
    Say all: and all well said: say still the same.

88. 'My true love hath my heart, and I have his'

My true love hath my heart, and I have his,
    By just exchange one for the other given,
I hold his dear, and mine he can not miss,
    There never was a better bargain driven.
His heart in me keeps me and him in one,
    My heart in him his thoughts and senses guides,
He loves my heart, for once it was his own,
    I cherish his, because in me it bides.

His heart his wound receivèd from my sight,
    My heart was wounded with his wounded heart,   10
For, as from me on him his hurt did light,
    So still methought in me his hurt did smart:
    Both equal hurt in this change sought our bliss:
    My true love hath my heart and I have his.

89. 'Reason, tell me thy mind, if here be reason'

Reason, tell me thy mind, if here be reason
In this strange violence, to make resistance.
Where sweet graces erect the stately banner
Of virtue's regiment, shining in harness
Of fortune's diadems, by beauty mustered.
Say then Reason, I say, what is thy counsel?

Her loose hair be the shot, the breast the pikes be,
Scouts each motion is, the hands be horsemen,
Her lips are the riches the wars to maintain,
Where well couched abides a coffer of pearl,   10
Her legs' carriage is of all the sweet camp:
Say then Reason, I say, what is thy counsel?

Her cannons be her eyes, mine eyes the walls be,

Which at first volley gave too open entry,
Nor rampart did abide; my brain was up blown,
Undermined with a speech the piercer of thoughts.
Thus weakened by my self, no help remaineth.
Say then Reason, I say, what is thy counsel?

And now fame the herald of her true honour,
Doth proclaim with a sound made all by men's mouths   20
That nature sovereign of earthly dwellers,
Commands all creatures, to yield obeisance
Under this, this her own, her only dearling.
Say then Reason, I say, what is thy counsel?

Reason sighs but in end he thus doth answer.
'Naught can reason avail in heavenly matters.'
Thus nature's diamond receives thy conquest,
Thus pure pearl, I do yield, my senses and soul.
Thus sweet pain, I do yield, what ere I can yield,
Reason look to thy self, I serve a goddess.   30

90. 'Up, up Philisides, let sorrows go'

Geron
Up, up Philisides, let sorrows go,
Who yields to woe, doth but increase his smart.
Do not thy heart, to plaintful custom bring,
But let us sing, sweet tunes do passions ease,
An old man hear, who would thy fancies raise.
    Philisides
Who minds to please the mind drowned in annoys
With outward joys, which inly cannot sink,
As well may think with oil to cool the fire:
Or with desire to make such foe a friend,
Who doth his soul to endless malice bend.   10
    Geron
Yet sure an end, to each thing time doth give,
Though woes now live, at length thy woes must die.
Then virtue try, if she can work in thee
That which we see in many time hath wrought,
And weakest hearts to constant temper brought.
    Philisides

Who ever taught a skilless man to teach,
Or stop a breach, that never Cannon saw?
Sweet virtue's law bars not a causeful moan.
Time shall in one my life and sorrows end,
And me perchance your constant temper lend.   20
    Geron
What can amend where physic is refused?
The wits abused with will no counsel take.
Yet for my sake discover us thy grief
Oft comes relief when most we seem in trap.
The stars thy state, fortune may change thy hap.
    Philisides
If fortune's lap became my dwelling place,
And all the stars conspirèd to my good,
Still were I one, this still should be my case,
Ruin's relic, care's web, and sorrow's food:
Since she fair fierce to such a state me calls,   30
Whose wit the stars, whose fortune fortune thralls.
    Geron
Alas what falls are fallen unto thy mind?
That there where thou confessed thy mischief lies
Thy wit dost use still still more harms to find.
Whom wit makes vain, or blinded with his eyes,
What counsel can prevail, or light give light?
Since all his force against himself he tries.
Then each conceit that enters in his sight,
Is made, forsooth, a jurate° of his woes,   *juror*
Earth, sea, air, fire, heaven, hell, and ghastly sprite.   40
Then cries to senseless things, which neither knows
What aileth thee, and if they knew thy mind
Would scorn in man (their king) such feeble shows.
Rebel, rebel, in golden fetters bind
This tyrant Love; or rather do suppress
Those rebel thoughts which are thy slaves by kind.°   *nature*
Let not a glittering name thy fancy dress
In painted clothes, because they call it love.
There is no hate that can thee more oppress.
Begin (and half the work is done) to prove   50
By rising up, upon thyself to stand,
And think she is a she, that doth thee move.
He water plows, and soweth in the sand,
And hopes the flickering wind with net to hold
Who hath his hopes laid up in woman's hand.

What man is he that hath his freedom sold?
Is he a manlike man, that doth not know man
Hath power that Sex with bridle to withhold?
A fickle Sex, and true in trust to no man,
A servant Sex, soon proud if they be coyed, 60
And to conclude thy mistress is a woman.
    Philisides
O gods, how long this old fool hath annoyed
My wearied ears! O gods yet grant me this,
That soon the world of his false tongue be void.
O noble age who place their only bliss
In being heard until the hearer die
Uttering a serpent's mind with serpent's hiss.
Then who will hear a well authorised lie,
(And patience hath) let him go learn of him
What swarms of virtues did in his youth fly 70
Such hearts of brass, wise heads, and garments trim
Were in his days: which heard, one nothing hears,
If from his words the falsehood he do skim.
And herein most their folly vain appears
That since they still allege, *When they were young:*
It shows they fetch their wit from youthful years
Like beast for sacrifice, where, save the tongue
And belly, naught is left, such sure is he,
This live-deadman in this old dungeon flung.
Old houses are thrown down for new we see: 80
The oldest rams are cullèd from the flock:
No man doth wish his horse should agèd be.
The ancient oak well makes a firèd block:
Old men themselves, do love young wives to choose:
Only fond youth admires a rotten stock.
Who once a white long beard, well handle does,
(As his beard him, not he his beard did bear)
Though cradle-witted, must not honour lose.
Oh when will men leave off to judge by hair,
And think them old, that have the oldest mind, 90
With virtue fraught and full of holy fear!
    Geron
If that thy face were hid, or I were blind,
I yet should know a young man speaketh now,
Such wandering reasons in thy speech I find.
He is a beast, that beasts use will allow
For proof of man, who sprung of heavenly fire

Hath strongest soul, when most his reins do bow.
But fondlings fond, know not your own desire
Loath to die young, and then you must be old,
Fondly blame that to which your selves aspire. 100
But this light choller° that doth make you bold, *anger*
Rather to wrong than unto just defence,
Is past with me, my blood is waxen° cold. *grown*
Thy words, though full of malapert° offence, *ill-mannered*
I weigh them not, but still will thee advise
How thou from foolish love may'st purge thy sense.
First think they err, that think them gaily wise,
Who well can set a passion out to show:
Such sight have they that see with goggling eyes.
Passion bears high when puffing wind doth blow, 110
But is indeed a toy, if not a toy,
True cause of evils, and cause of causeless woe.
If once thou may'st that fancy gloss destroy
Within thy self, thou soon wilt be ashamed
To be a player of thine own annoy.
Then let thy mind with better books be tamed,
Seek to espy her faults as well as praise,
And let thine eyes to other sports be framed.
In hunting fearful beasts, do spend some days,
Or catch the birds with pitfalls, or with lime, 120
Or train the fox that trains so crafty lays.
Lie but to sleep, and in the early prime
Seek skill of herbs in hills, haunt brooks near night,
And try with bait how fish will bite sometime.
Go graft again, and seek to graft them right,
Those pleasant plants, those sweet and fruitful trees,
Which both the palate, and the eyes delight.
Cherish the hives of wisely painful bees:
Let special care upon thy flock be stayed,
Such active mind but seldom passion sees. 130

    Philisides
Hath any man heard what this old man said?
Truly not I, who did my thoughts engage,
Where all my pains one look of her hath paid.

Sir Fulke Greville (1554–1628)

91. Epitaph on Sir Philip Sidney

Silence augmenteth grief, writing increaseth rage,
Staled are my thoughts, which loved and lost the wonder of our age,
Yet quickened° now with fire, though dead with frost ere now,   *enlivened*
Enraged I write I know not what, dead, quick,° I know not how.   *alive*

Hard-hearted minds relent and rigour's tears abound,
And envy strangely rues his end, in whom no fault she found.
Knowledge her light hath lost; valour hath slain her knight.
Sidney is dead; dead is my friend; dead is the world's delight.

Place, pensive, wails his fall whose presence was her pride.
Time crieth out, 'My ebb is come; his life was my spring tide.'   10
Fame mourns in that she lost the ground of her reports.
Each living wight laments his lack, and all his sundry sorts.

He was (woe worth that word) to each well-thinking mind
A spotless friend, a matchless man, whose virtue ever shined,
Declaring in his thoughts, his life, and that he writ,
Highest conceits, longest foresights, and deepest works of wit.

He, only like himself, was second unto none,
Whose death (though life) we rue, and wrong, and all in vain do moan.
Their loss, not him, wail they, that fill the world with cries,
Death slew not him, but he made death his ladder to the skies.   20

Now sick of sorrow I, who live, the more the wrong,
Who wishing death, whom death denies, whose thread is all too long,
Who tied to wretched life, who looks for no relief,
Must spend my ever dying days in never ending grief.

Heart's ease and only I, like parallels, run on,
Whose equal length keep equal breadth, and never meet in one.
Yet for not wronging him, my thoughts, my sorrow's cell,
Shall not run out, though leak they will, for liking him so well.

Farewell to you, my hopes, my wonted waking dreams,
Farewell, sometimes enjoyèd joy; eclipsèd are thy beams.   30
Farewell self-pleasing thoughts, which quietness brings forth,
And farewell, friendship's sacred league, uniting minds of worth.

And farewell, merry heart, the gift of guiltless minds,
And all sports which for life's restore variety assigns.
Let all that sweet is void; in me no mirth may dwell.
Philip, the cause of all this woe, my life's content, farewell.

Now rhyme, the son of rage, which art no kin to skill,
And endless grief, which deads my life, yet knows not how to kill,
Go, seek the hapless tomb, which if ye hap to find,
Salute the stones, that keep the limbs, that held so good a mind.   40

92. 'Fair dog, which so my heart dost tear asunder'

Fair dog, which so my heart dost tear asunder,
That my life's blood, my bowels overfloweth,
Alas, what wicked rage conceal'st thou under
These sweet enticing joys, thy forehead showeth?

Me, whom the light-winged god of long hath chased,
Thou hast attained, thou gav'st that fatal wound,
Which my soul's peaceful innocence hath 'rased,°   *erased*
And reason to her servant humour bound.

Kill therefore in the end, and end my anguish,
Give me my death, methinks, 'Even time upbraideth   10
A fullness of the woes, wherein I languish':
Or if thou wilt I live, then pity pleadeth
    Help out of thee, since nature hath revealed,
    That with thy tongue thy bitings may be healed.

93. 'Who ever sails near to Bermuda coast'

Who ever sails near to Bermuda coast,

Goes hard aboard the monarchy of fear,
Where all desires (but life's desire) are lost,
For wealth and fame put off their glories there.

Yet this isle poison-like, by mischief known,
Weans not desire from her sweet nurse, the sea;
But unseen shows us where our hopes be sown,
With woeful signs declaring joyful way.
   For who will seek the wealth of western sun,
   Oft by Bermuda's miseries must run.   10

Who seeks the God of love, in beauty's sky,
Must pass the empire of confusèd passion,
Where our desires to all but horrors die,
Before that joy and peace can take their fashion.

Yet this fair heaven that yields this soul-despair,
Weans not the heart from his sweet god, *affection*;
But rather shows us what sweet joys are there,
Where constancy is servant to perfection.
      Who Cælica's chaste heart then seeks to move,
      Must joy to suffer all the woes of Love.   20

94. 'Farewell sweet boy, complain not of my truth'

Farewell sweet boy, complain not of my truth;
Thy mother loved thee not with more devotion;
For to thy boy's play I gave all my youth,
Young master, I did hope for your promotion.

While some sought honours, princes' thoughts observing,
Many wooed fame, the child of pain and anguish,
Others judged inward good a chief deserving,
I in thy wanton visions joyed to languish.

I bowed not to thy image for succession,
Nor bound thy bow to shoot reformèd kindness,   10
Thy plays of hope and fear were my confession,
The spectacles to my life was thy blindness;
      But now farewell, I will go play me
      With thoughts that please me less, and less betray me.

Chidiock Tichborne (1558?–1586)

95. 'My prime of youth is but a frost of cares'

My prime of youth is but a frost of cares,
My feast of joy is but a dish of pain,
My crop of corn is but a field of tares,
And all my good is but vain hope of gain.
The day is gone and yet I saw no sun,
And now I live, and now my life is done.

The spring is past, and yet it hath not sprung,
The fruit is dead, and yet the leaves are green,
My youth is gone, and yet I am but young,
I saw the world, and yet I was not seen,   10
My thread is cut, and yet it was not spun,
And now I live, and now my life is done.

I sought my death and found it in my womb,
I looked for life and saw it was a shade,
I trod the earth and knew it was my tomb,
And now I die, and now I am but made.
The glass is full, and now the glass is run,
And now I live, and now my life is done.

George Chapman (1559?–1634?)

96. from *Ovid's Banquet of Sense: A Coronet for his Mistress, Philosophy*

Muses that sing love's sensual empery,
And lovers kindling your enragèd fires

At Cupid's bonfires burning in the eye,
Blown with the empty breath of vain desires;
You that prefer the painted cabinet
Before the wealthy jewels it doth store ye,
That all your joys in dying figures set,
And stain the living substance of your glory;
Abjure those joys, abhor their memory,
And let my love the honoured subject be   10
Of love, and honour's complete history.
Your eyes were never yet let in to see
    The majesty and riches of the mind,
    But dwell in darkness; for your god is blind.

97. from *Hero and Leander:* end of the Third Sestiad

Love is a golden bubble full of dreams,
   That waking breaks, and fills us with extremes.
She mused how she could look upon her sire,
And not show that without, that was entire.
For as a glass is an inanimate eye,
And outward forms embraceth inwardly:
So is the eye an animate glass that shows   230
In-forms without us. And as *Phoebus* throws
His beams abroad, though he in clouds be closed,
Still glancing by them till he find opposed,
A loose and rorid° vapour that is fit   *dewy*
To event his searching beams, and useth it
To form a tender twenty-coloured eye,
Cast in a circle round about the sky.
So when our fiery soul, our body's star,
(That ever is in motion circular)
Conceives a form, in seeking to display it   240
Through all our cloudy parts, it doth convey it
Forth at the eye, as the most pregnant place,
And that reflects it round about the face.
And this event uncourtly Hero thought,
Her inward guilt would in her looks have wrought:
For yet the world's stale cunning she resisted
To bear foul thoughts, yet forge what looks she listed,
And held it for a very silly sleight,
To make a perfect metal counterfeit:

Glad to disclaim her self; proud of an art,   250
That makes the face a Pandar to the heart.
Those be the painted moons, whose lights profane
Beauty's true heaven, at full still in their wane.
Those be the lapwing faces that still cry,
Here 'tis, when that they vow is nothing nigh.
Base fools, when every moorish fowl can teach
That which men think the height of human reach.
But custom that the apoplexy is
Of beddred nature, and lives led amiss,
And takes away all feeling of offence,   260
Yet brazed not Hero's brow with impudence;
And this she thought most hard to bring to pass,
To seem in countenance other than she was.
As if she had two souls; one for the face,
One for the heart, and that they shifted place
As either list to utter, or conceal
What they conceived: or as one soul did deal
With both affairs at once, keeps and ejects
Both at an instant contrary effects:
Retention and ejection in her powers   270
Being acts alike: for this one vice of ours,
That forms the thought, and sways the countenance,
Rules both our motion and our utterance.
    These and more grave conceits toiled Hero's spirits:
For though the light of her discursive wits,
Perhaps might find some little hole to pass
Through all these worldly cinctures; yet (alas)
There was a heavenly flame encompassed her;
Her Goddess, in whose phane° she did prefer   *sanctum*
Her virgin vows; from whose impulsive sight   280
She knew the black shield of the darkest night
Could not defend her, nor wit's subtlest art:
This was the point pierced *Hero* to the heart.
Who heavy to the death, with a deep sigh
And hand that languished, took a robe was nigh,
Exceeding large, and of black Cyprus made,
In which she sate, hid from the day in shade,
Even over head and face down to her feet;
Her left hand made it at her bosom meet;
Her right hand leaned on her heart-bowing knee,   290
Wrapt in unshapeful folds: 'twas death to see
Her knee stayed that, and that her falling face

Each limb helped other to put on disgrace.
No form was seen, where form held all her sight:
But like an embrion° that saw never light: *embryo*
Or like a scorchèd statue made a coal
With three-winged lightning: or a wretched soul
Muffled with endless darkness, she did sit:
The night had never such a heavy spirit.
Yet might an imitating eye well see,   300
How fast her clear tears melted on her knee
Through her black veil, and turned as black as it,
Mourning to be her tears: then wrought her wit
With her broke vow, her Goddess's wrath, her fame,
All tools that ingenious despair could frame:
Which made her strew the floor with her torn hair,
And spread her mantle piecemeal in the air.
Like Jove's son's club, strong passion struck her down,
And with a piteous shriek enforced her swoon:
Her shriek, made with another shriek ascend   310
The frighted matron that on her did tend:
And as with her own cry her sense was slain,
So with the other it was called again.
She rose and to her bed made forced way,
And laid her down even where Leander lay:
And all this while the red sea of her blood
Ebbed with Leander: but now turned the flood,
And all her fleet of sprites came swelling in
With child of sail, and did hot fight begin
With those severe conceits, she too much marked,   320
And here Leander's beauties were embarked.
He came in swimming painted all with joys,
Such as might sweeten hell: his thought destroys
All her destroying thoughts: she thought she felt
His heart in hers: with her contentions melt,
And chid her soul that it could so much err,
To check the true joys he deserved in her.
Her fresh heart blood cast figures in her eyes,
And she supposed she saw in Neptune's skies
How her star wandered, washed in smarting brine   330
For her love's sake, that with immortal wine
Should be embathed, and swim in more heart's ease,
Than there was water in the Sestian seas.
Then said her Cupid-prompted spirit, 'Shall I
Sing moans to such delightsome harmony?

Shall slick-tongued fame patched up with voices rude,
The drunken bastard of the multitude,
(Begot when father judgement is away,
And gossip-like, says because others say,
Takes news as if it were too hot to eat, 340
And spits it slavering forth for dog-fees meat)
Make me for forging a fantastic vow,
Presume to bear what makes grave matrons bow?
Good vows are never broken with good deeds,
For then good deeds were bad: vows are but seeds,
And good deeds fruits; even those good deeds that grow
From other stocks, than from the observèd vow.
That is a good deed that prevents a bad:
Had I not yielded, slain my self I had.
Hero Leander is, Leander Hero: 350
Such virtue love hath to make one of two.
If then Leander did my maidenhead get,
Leander being my self I still retain it.
We break chaste vows when we live loosely ever:
But bound as we are, we live loosely never.
Two constant lovers being joined in one,
Yielding to one another, yield to none.
We know not how to vow, till love unblind us,
And vows made ignorantly never bind us.
Too true it is that when 'tis gone men hate 360
The joys as vain they took in love's estate:
But that's, since they have lost, the heavenly light
Should show them way to judge of all things right.
When life is gone death must implant his terror,
As death is foe to life, so love to error.
Before we love how range we through this sphere,
Searching the sundry fancies hunted here:
Now with desire of wealth transported quite
Beyond our free humanity's delight:
Now with ambition climbing falling towers, 370
Whose hope to scale, our fear to fall devours:
Now rapt with pastimes, pomp, all joys impure;
In things without us no delight is sure.
But love with all joys crowned, within doth sit;
O Goddess pity love and pardon it.'
This spake she weeping: but her Goddess' ear
Burned with too stern a heat, and would not hear.
Aye me, hath heaven's straight fingers no more graces,

For such as Hero, than for homeliest faces?
Yet she hoped well, and in her sweet conceit 380
Weighing her arguments, she thought them weight:
And that the logic of Leander's beauty,
And them together would bring proofs of duty.
And if her soul, that was a skilful glance
Of heaven's great essence, found such imperance
In her love's beauties; she had confidence
Jove loved him too, and pardoned her offence.
  Beauty in heaven and earth this grace doth win,
    It supples rigour, and it lessens sin.
Thus, her sharp wit, her love, her secrecy, 390
Trouping together, made her wonder why
She should not leave her bed, and to the temple?
Her health said she must live; her sex dissemble.
She viewed Leander's place, and wished he were
Turned to his place, so his place were Leander.
'Aye me,' said she, 'that love's sweet life and sense
Should do it harm! my love had not gone hence,
Had he been like his place. O blessèd place,
Image of constancy. Thus my love's grace
Parts nowhere but it leaves some thing behind 400
Worth observation: he renowns his kind.
His motion is like heaven's orbicular:
For where he once is, he is ever there.
This place was mine: Leander now 'tis thine;
Thou being my self, then it is double mine:
Mine, and Leander's mine, Leander's mine.
O see what wealth it yields me, nay yields him:
For I am in it, he for me doth swim.
Rich, fruitful love, that doubling self estates
Elixir-like contracts, though separates. 410
Dear place I kiss thee, and do welcome thee,
As from Leander ever sent to me.'

98. from *The Shadow of Night* [35]

... Ye living spirits then, if any live,
Whom like extremes, do like affections give,

---

[35] Extracts from *Hymnus in Noctem* (ll. 288 to the end)

Shun, shun this cruel light, and end your thrall,   290
In these soft shades of sable funeral:
From whence with ghosts, who vengeance holds fro° rest,   *from*
Dog-fiends and monsters haunting the distressed,
As men whose parents tyranny hath slain,
Whose sisters rape, and bondage do sustain.
But you that ne'er had birth, nor ever proved,
How dear a blessing 'tis to be beloved,
Whose friends' idolatrous desire of gold,
To scorn, and ruin have your freedom sold:
Whose virtues feel all this, and show your eyes,   300
Men made of Tartar, and of villainies.
Aspire th' extraction, and the quintessence
Of all the joys in earth's circumference:
With ghosts, fiends, monsters: as men robbed and racked,
Murdered in life: from shades with shadows blacked:
Thunder your wrongs, your miseries and hells,
And with the dismal accents of your knells,
Revive the dead, and make the living die
In ruth, and terror of your tortury:
Still all the power of art into your groans,   310
Scorning your trivial and remissive moans,
Compact of fiction, and hyperboles,
(Like wanton mourners, cloyed with too much ease)
Should leave the glasses of the hearers' eyes
Unbroken, counting all but vanities.
But paint, or else create in serious truth,
A body figured to your virtue's ruth,
That to the sense may show what damnèd sin,
For your extremes this Chaos tumbles in.
But woe is wretched me, without a name: 320
Virtue feeds scorn, and noblest honour, shame:
Pride bathes in tears of poor submission,
And makes his soul, the purple he puts on.
    Kneel then with me, fall worm-like on the ground,
And from th' infectious dunghill of this round,
From men's brass wits, and golden foolery,
Weep, weep your souls, into felicity:
Come to this house of mourning, serve the night,
To whom pale day (with whoredom soakèd quite)
Is but a drudge, selling her beauty's use   330
To rapes, adulteries, and to all abuse.
Her labours feast imperial night with sports,

Where loves are Christmassed, with all pleasures' sorts:
And whom her fugitive, and far-shot rays
Disjoin, and drive into ten thousand ways,
Night's glorious mantle wraps in safe abodes,
And frees their necks from servile labour's loads:
Her trusty shadows succour men dismayed,
Whom day's deceitful malice hath betrayed:
From the silk vapours of her ivory port,   340
Sweet Protean dreams she sends of every sort:
Some taking forms of princes, to persuade
Of men deject, we are their equals made;
Some clad in habit of deceasèd friends,
For whom we mourned, and now have wished amends;
And some (dear favour) lady-like attired,
With pride of beauty's full meridian fired:
Who 'spite our contempts, revive our hearts:
For wisest ladies love the inward parts.

    If these be dreams, even so are all things else,   350
That walk this round by heavenly sentinels:
But from night's port of horn she greets our eyes
With graver dreams inspired with prophesies,
Which oft presage to us succeeding chances,
We proving that awake, they show in trances.
If these seem likewise vain, or nothing are
Vain things, or nothing come to virtue's share:
For nothing more than dreams, with us she finds:
Then since all pleasures vanish like the winds,
And that most serious actions not respecting   360
The second light, are worth but the neglecting,
Since day, or light, in any quality,
For earthly uses do but serve the eye.
And since the eyes most quick and dangerous use,
Inflames the heart, and learns the soul abuse,
Since mournings are preferred to banquetings,
And they reach heaven, bred under sorrow's wings.
Since night brings terror to our frailties still,
And shameless day, doth marble us in ill.

    All you possessed with indepressed spirits,   370
Indued with nimble, and aspiring wits,
Come consecrate with me, to sacred night
Your whole endeavours, and detest the light.
Sweet peace's richest crown is made of stars,
Most certain guides of honoured mariners,

No pen can any thing eternal write,
That is not steeped in humour of the night.
　　Hence beasts, and birds to caves and bushes then,
And welcome night, ye noblest heirs of men,
Hence Phoebus to thy glassy strumpet's bed,　　　　　　　380
And never more let Themis' daughters spread
Thy golden harness on thy rosy horse,
But in close thickets run thy oblique course.
　　See now ascends, the glorious bride of brides,
Nuptials, and triumphs, glittering by her sides,
Juno and Hymen do her train adorn,
Ten thousand torches round about them borne:
Dumb silence mounted on the Cyprian star,
With becks, rebukes the winds before his car,
Where she advanced; beats down with cloudy mace,　　　390
The feeble light to black Saturnius palace:
Behind her, with a brace of silver hinds,
In ivory chariot, swifter than the winds,
Is great Hyperion's hornèd daughter drawn
Enchantress-like, decked in disparent lawn,
Circled with charms, and incantations,
That ride huge spirits, and outrageous passions:
Music, and mood, she loves, but love she hates,
(As curious Ladies do, their public cates)
This train, with meteors, comets, lightnings,　　　　　　400
The dreadful presence of our empress sings:
Which grant for ever (oh eternal night)
Till virtue flourish in the light of light.

99. from *Homer's Iliad*: Book XXII

　　　　　… and now Achilles comes; now near
His Mars-like presence terribly came brandishing his spear;
His right arm shook it; his bright arms like day came glittering on,
Like fire-light, or the light of heaven shot from the rising sun.
This sight outwrought discourse; cold fear shook Hector from his stand;
No more stay now; all ports were left; he fled in fear the hand　　120
Of that fear-master, who hawklike, air's swiftest passenger,
That holds a timorous dove in chase; and with command doth bear
His fiery onset: the dove hastes; the hawk comes whizzing on;
This way and that he turns and winds and cuffs the pigeon;

And till he truss it his great spirit lays hot charge on his wing:
So urged Achilles Hector's flight; so still fear's point did sting
His troubled spirit; his knees wrought hard; along the wall he flew;
In that fair chariot way that runs beneath the tower of view,
And Troy's wild fig-tree; till they reached where those two mother springs
Of deep Scamander poured abroad their silver murmurings.   130
One warm, and casts out fumes, as fire; the other, cold as snow
Or hail dissolved. And when the sun made ardent summer glow,
There water's concrete crystal shined, near which were cisterns made,
All paved and clear; where Trojan wives and their fair daughters had
Laundry for their fine linen weeds, in times of cleanly peace,
Before the Grecians brought their siege. These captains noted these;
One flying; th' other in pursuit; a strong man flew before;
A stronger followed him by far and close up to him bore.
Both did their best; for neither now ran for a sacrifice;
Or for the sacrificer's hide, (our runners' usual prize).   140
These ran for tame-horse Hector's soul. And as two running steeds,
Backed in some set race for a game, that tries their swiftest speeds
(A tripod, or a woman given, for some man's funerals):
Such speed made these men; and on foot, ran thrice about the walls.
   The gods beheld them, all much moved; and Jove said: 'Oh, ill sight!
A man I love much I see forced in most unworthy flight
About great Ilion; my heart grieves; he paid so many vows,
With thighs of sacrificèd beefs, both on the lofty brows
Of Ida, and in Ilion's height. Consult we; shall we free
His life from death, or give it now, to Achilles victory?'   150
   Minerva answered: 'Alter Fate? One long since marked for death
Now take from death? Do thou; but know, he still shall run beneath
Our other censures.' 'Be it then,' replied the Thunderer,
'My loved Tritonia, at thy will; in this I will prefer
Thy free intention; work it all.' Then stooped she from the sky,
To this great combat. Peleus' son pursued incessantly
Still-flying Hector. As a hound, that having roused a hart,
Although he tappish° ne'er so oft and every shrubby part   *seek cover*
Attempts for strength and trembles in; the hound doth still pursue
So close, that not a foot he fails, but hunts it still at view: 160
So plied Achilles Hector's steps; as oft as he assayed
The Dardan ports and towers for strength (to fetch from thence some aid,
With winged shafts), so oft forced he amends of pace, and stepped
Twixt him and all his hopes; and still upon the field he kept
His utmost turnings to the town. And yet, as in a dream,
One thinks he gives another chase; when such a feigned extreme
Possesseth both that he in chase the chaser cannot fly;

Nor can the chaser get to hand his flying enemy:
So nor Achilles' chase could reach the flight of Hector's pace;
Nor Hector's flight enlarge itself of swift Achilles' chase.   170
    But how chanced this? How, all this time, could Hector bear the knees
Of fierce Achilles with his own, and keep off destinies,
If Phoebus (for his last and best) through all that course had failed
To add his succours to his nerves, and (as his foe assailed)
Near and within him fed his 'scape? Achilles yet well knew,
His knees would fetch him; and gave signs to some friends (making show
Of shooting at him) to forbear, lest they detracted so
From his full glory in first wounds, and in the overthrow
Make his hand last. But when they reached the fourth time the two founts,
Then Jove his golden scales weighed up, and took the last accounts   180
Of Fate for Hector; putting in for him and Peleus' son,
Two fates of bitter death; of which high heaven received the one,
The other hell: so low declined the light of Hector's life.
Then Phoebus left him, when war's Queen came to resolve the strife
In the other's knowledge. 'Now,' said she, 'Jove-loved Æacides,
I hope at last to make renown perform a brave access
To all the Grecians; we shall now lay low this champion's height,
Though never so insatiate was his great heart of fight.
Nor must he 'scape our pursuit still; though at the feet of Jove
Apollo bows into a sphere, soliciting more love   190
To his most favoured. Breathe thee then, stand firm; myself will haste,
And hearten Hector to change blows.' She went, and he stood fast,
Leaned on his lance, and much was joyed, that single strokes should try
This fadging° conflict. Then came close the changèd deity   *wearying*
To Hector, like Deiphobus in shape and voice; and said:
    'O brother, thou art too much urged, to be thus combated
About our own walls; let us stand and force to a retreat
The insulting chaser.' Hector joyed at this so kind deceit,
And said: 'O good Deiphobus, thy love was most before
(Of all my brothers) dear to me; but now exceeding more   200
It costs me honour, that, thus urged, thou comest to part the charge
Of my last fortunes; other friends keep town and leave at large
My racked endeavours.' She replied, 'Good brother, 'tis most true;
One after other, King and Queen and all our friends did sue
(Even on their knees) to stay me there, such tremblings shake them all
With this man's terror: but my mind so grieved to see our wall
Girt with thy chases that to death I longed to urge thy stay.
Come, fight we, thirsty of his blood; no more let's fear to lay
Cost on our lances; but approve, if bloodied with our spoils,
He can bear glory to their fleet, or shut up all their toils   210

In his one sufferance on thy lance.' With this deceit, she led,
And (both come near) thus Hector spake: 'Thrice I have compassèd
This great town, Peleus' son, in flight, with aversation,
That out of fate put off my steps; but now all flight is flown,
The short course set up: death or life. Our resolutions yet
Must shun all rudeness; and the gods before our valour set
For use of victory; and they being worthiest witnesses
Of all vows; since they keep vows best, before their deities
Let vows of fit respect pass both; when conquest hath bestowed
Her wreath on either. Here I vow no fury shall be showed   220
That is not manly on thy corpse, but, having spoiled thy arms,
Resign thy person; which swear thou.' These fair and temperate terms,
Far fled Achilles; his brows bent, and out flew this reply.
     'Hector, thou only pestilence in all mortality
To my sere spirits, never set the point twixt thee and me
Any conditions; but as far as men and lions fly
All terms of covenant, lambs and wolves in so far opposite state
(Impossible for love t' atone) stand we, till our souls satiate
The god of soldiers; do not dream that our disjunction can
Endure condition. Therefore now all worth that fits a man   230
Call to thee; all particular parts that fit a soldier;
And they all this include (besides the skill and spirit of war)
Hunger for slaughter, and a hate that eats thy heart to eat
Thy foe's heart. This stirs; this supplies in death the killing heat;
And all this need'st thou. No more flight. Pallas Athena
Will quickly cast thee to my lance; now, now together draw
All griefs for vengeance, both in me and all my friends late dead
That bled thee, raging with thy lance.' This said, he brandishèd
His long lance; and away it sung: which Hector, giving view,
Stooped low, stood firm (foreseeing it best) and quite it overflew,   240
Fastening on earth. Athena drew it and gave her friend,
Unseen of Hector. Hector then thus spake: 'Thou wantest thy end,
God-like Achilles; now I see thou hast not learned my fate
Of Jove at all, as thy high words would bravely intimate;
Much tongue affects thee; cunning words well serve thee to prepare
Thy blows with threats, that mine might faint with want of spirit to dare;
But my back never turns with breath; it was not born to bear
Burdens of wounds; strike home before; drive at my breast thy spear
As mine at thine shall; and try then if heavens will favour thee
With scape of my lance. O would Jove would take it after me,   250
And make thy bosom take it all, an easy end would crown
Our difficult wars were thy soul fled; thou most bane of our town.'
     Thus flew his dart, touched at the midst of his vast shield, and flew

A huge way from it; but his heart wrath entered with the view
Of that hard scape; and heavy thoughts strook through him when he spied
His brother vanished; and no lance beside left. Out he cried,
'Deiphobus! another lance!' Lance nor Deiphobus
Stood near his call. And then his mind saw all things ominous,
And thus suggested: 'Woe is me; the gods have called, and I
Must meet Death here. Deiphobus I well hoped had been by   260
With his white shield; but our strong walls shield him, and this deceit
Flows from Minerva. Now, oh now, ill death comes; no more flight,
No more recovery. O Jove, this hath been otherwise;
Thy bright son and thy self have set the Greeks a greater prize
Of Hector's blood than now; of which (even jealous) you had care.
But Fate now conquers; I am hers. And yet not she shall share
In my renown; that life is left to every noble spirit,
And that some great deed shall beget that all lives shall inherit.'
     Thus forth his sword flew, sharp and broad, and bore a deadly weight,
With which he rushed in. And look how an eagle from her height,   270
Stoops to the rapture of a lamb, or cuffs a timorous hare:
So fell in Hector, and at him Achilles; his mind's fare
Was fierce and mighty: his shield cast a Sun-like radiance,
Helm nodded, and his four plumes shook; and when he raised his lance,
Up Hesperus rose 'mongst the evening stars. His bright and sparkling eyes
Looked through the body of his foe, and sought through all that prize
The next way to his thirsted life. Of all ways only one
Appeared to him; and that was where the unequal winding bone
That joins the shoulders and the neck had place; and where there lay
The speeding way to death; and there his quick eye could display   280
The place it sought, even through those arms his friend Patroclus wore,
When Hector slew him. There he aimed, and there his javelin tore
Stern passage quite through Hector's neck; yet missed it so his throat,
It gave him power to change some words; but down to earth it got
His fainting body. Then triumphed divine Æacides:
'Hector,' said he, 'thy heart supposed that in my friend's decease
Thy life was safe, my absent arm not cared for: Fool! he left
One at the fleet that bettered him, and he it is that reft
Thy strong knees thus. And now the dogs and fowls in foulest use
Shall tear thee up; thy corpse exposed to all the Greeks' abuse.   290
     He, fainting, said: 'Let me implore, even by thy knees and soul
And thy great parents: do not see a cruelty so foul
Inflicted on me. Brass and gold receive at any rate
And quit my person, that the peers and ladies of our state
May tomb it, and to sacred fire turn thy profane decrees.'
     'Dog,' he replied, 'urge not my ruth by parents, soul, nor knees;

I would to God that any rage would let me eat thee raw,
Sliced into pieces; so beyond the right of any law
I taste thy merits; and believe it flies the force of man
To rescue thy head from the dogs. Give all the gold they can,   300
If ten or twenty times so much as friends would rate thy price
Were tendered here, with vows of more, to buy the cruelties
I here have vowed, and after that, thy father with his gold
Would free thy self; all that should fail to let thy mother hold
Solemnities of death with thee, and do thee such a grace,
To mourn thy whole corpse on a bed; which piecemeal I'll deface
With fowls and dogs.' He (dying) said: 'I (knowing thee well) foresaw
Thy now tried tyranny, nor hoped for any other law,
Of nature, or of nations: and that fear forced much more
Than death my flight, which never touched at Hector's foot before.   310
A soul of iron informs thee; mark, what vengeance the equal fates
Will give me of thee for this rage, when in the Scæan gates
Phoebus and Paris meet with thee.' Thus death's hand closed his eyes;
His soul flying his fair limbs to hell, mourning his destinies
To part so with his youth and strength. Thus dead, thus Thetis' son,
His prophecy answered: 'Die thou now; when my short thread is spun,
I'll bear it as the will of Jove.' This said, his brazen spear
He drew, and stuck by: then his arms (that all embrewed were)
He spoiled his shoulders off. Then all the Greeks ran in to him
To see his person, and admired his terror-stirring limb.   320
Yet none stood by that gave no wound to his so goodly form;
When each to other said: 'O Jove, he is not in the storm
He came to fleet in with his fire; he handles now more soft.'
    'O friends,' said stern Æacides, 'now that the gods have brought
This man thus down, I'll freely say, he brought more bane to Greece
Then all his aiders. Try we then (thus armed at every piece,
And girding all Troy with our host) if now their hearts will leave
Their city clear, her clear stay slain, and all their lives receive,
Or hold yet, Hector being no more. But why use I a word
Of any act but what concerns my friend? Dead, undeplored,   330
Unsepulchred, he lies at fleet, unthought on; never hour
Shall make his dead state while the quick enjoys me and this power
To move these movers. Though in hell men say that such as die
Oblivion seizeth, yet in hell in me shall memory
Hold all her forms still of my friend. Now, youths of Greece, to fleet
Bear we this body. Pæans sing, and all our navy greet
With endless honour; we have slain Hector, the period
Of all Troy's glory, to whose worth all vowed as to a god.
    This said, a work not worthy him he set to: of both feet

He bored the nerves through, from the heel to th' ankle, and then knit   340
Both to his chariot with a thong of whitleather, his head
Trailing the centre. Up he got to chariot, where he laid
The arms repurchased, and scourged° on his horse, that freely   *whipped*
   flew.
A whirlwind made of startled dust drave with them, as they drew;
With which were all his black-brown curls knotted in heaps and filed.
And there lay Troy's late gracious, by Jupiter exiled
To all disgrace, in his own land, and by his parents seen ...

Mary Sidney (1561–1621)

100. Deus noster refugium[36]

God gives us strength, and keeps us sound,
   A present help when dangers call;
Then fear not we, let quake the ground,
   And into seas let mountains fall,
   Yea so let seas withal,
In watery hills arise,
   As may the earthly hills appal,
With dread and dashing cries.

For lo, a river streaming joy,
   With purling murmur safely slides,   10
That city washing from annoy,
   In holy shrine where God resides.
   God in her centre bides:
What can this city shake?
   God early aids and ever guides,
Who can this city take?

When nations go against her bent
   And kings with siege her walls enround:

[36] 'God is our refuge', Psalm 46

The void of air his voice doth rent,
    Earth fails their feet with melting ground.   20
    To strength and keep us sound
The God of armies arms:
    Our rock on Jacob's God we found
Above the reach of harms.

O come with me, O come and view
    The trophies of Jehovah's hand:
What wracks from him our foes pursue,
    How clearly he hath purged our land.
    By him wars silent stand:
He brake the archer's bow,   30
    Made chariot's wheel a fiery brand,
And spear to shivers go.

Be still saith he; know, God am I:
    Know I will be with conquest crowned,
Above all nations raisèd high,
    High raised above this earthy round.
    To strength and keep us sound
The God of armies arms:
    Our rock on Jacob's God we found,
Above the reach of harms.   40

101. Miserere mei, Deus[37]

Fountain of pity now with pity flow:
These monsters on me daily gaping go,
    Daily me devour these spies,
    Swarms of foes against me rise,
O God that art more high than I am low.

Still when I fear, yet will I trust in thee:
Thy word, O God, my boast shall ever be;
    God shall be my hopeful stay,
    Fear shall not that hope dismay
For what can feeble flesh do unto me?   10

---

[37] 'Have mercy upon me, O Lord', Psalm 56

I as I can, think, speak, and do the best:
They to the worst my thoughts, words, doings wrest.
    All their hearts with one consent
    Are to work my ruin bent,
From plotting which, they give their heads no rest.

To that intent they secret meetings make,
They press me near my soul in snare to take,
    Thinking slight shall keep them safe.
    But thou, Lord, in wrathful chafe,
Their league so surely linked, in sunder shake.   20

Thou did'st, O Lord, with careful counting, look
On every journey I, poor exile, took:
    Every tear from my sad eyes
    Savèd in thy bottle lies,
These matters are all entered in thy book.

Then when so ever my distressèd sprite
Crying to thee, brings these unto thy sight,
    What remaineth for my foes?
    Blames, and shames, and overthrows,
For God himself I know for me will fight.   30

God's never-falsèd word my boast shall be,
My boast shall be his word to set me free,
    God shall be my hopeful stay;
    Fear shall not that hope dismay,
For what can mortal men do unto me?

For this, to thee, how deeply stand I bound,
Lord, that my soul dost save, my foes confound?
    Ah, I can no payment make,
    But if thou for payment take
The vows I pay, thy praises I resound: 40

Thy praises who from death hast set me free
Whither my feet did, headlong, carry me;
    Making me, of thy free grace,
    There again to take my place,
Where light of life, with living men, I see.

102. **Miserere mei, Deus**[38]

Thy mercy Lord, Lord now thy mercy show,
  On thee I lie,°   *rely*
  To thee I fly,
 Hide me, hive me as thine own
 Till these blasts be overblown,
Which now do fiercely blow.

To highest God I will erect my cry,
  Who quickly shall
  Dispatch this all.
 He shall down from Heaven send   10
 From disgrace me to defend,
His love and verity.

My soul encagèd lies with lions' brood,
  Villains whose hands
  Are fiery brands,
 Teeth more sharp than shaft or spear,
 Tongues far better edge do bear
Than swords to shed my blood.

As high as highest heaven can give thee place,
  O Lord ascend   20
  And thence extend
 With most bright, most glorious show,
 Over all the earth below
The sunbeams of thy face.

Me to entangle every way I go
  Their trap and net
  Is ready set.
 Holes they dig, but their own holes
 Pitfalls make for their own souls:
So, Lord, O serve them so.   30

My heart prepared, preparèd is my heart
  To spread thy praise
  With tunèd lays:
 Wake my tongue, my lute awake,

---

[38] 'Have mercy upon me, O Lord', Psalm 57

Thou my harp the consort make,
Myself will bear a part.

Myself when first the morning shall appear,
  With voice and string
  So will thee sing:
 That this earthly globe, and all   40
 Treading on this earthly ball,
My praising notes shall hear.

For God, my only God, thy gracious love
  Is mounted far
  Above each star,
 Thy unchanged verity
 Heavenly wings do lift as high
As clouds have room to move.

As high as highest heaven can give thee place,
  O Lord ascend   50
  And thence extend
 With most bright, most glorious show
 Over all the earth below
The sunbeams of thy face.

103. Ecce nunc[39]

You that Jehovah's servants are,
Whose careful watch, whose watchful care
 Within his house are spent,
 Say thus with one assent:
 Jehovah's name be praised.
 Then let your hands be raised
  To holiest place,
  Where holiest grace
   Doth aye
    Remain: 10
   And say
    Again,
 Jehovah's name be praised.

[39] 'Lo, now', Psalm 134

Say last unto the company,
    Who tarrying make
    Their leave to take,
All blessings you accompany,
From him in plenty showered,
Whom Sion holds embowered,
    Who heaven and earth of naught hath raised.   20

104. Super flumina[40]

Nigh seated where the river flows,
    That watereth Babel's thankful plain,
Which then our tears in pearlèd rows
    Did help to water with their rain,
The thought of Sion bred such woes,
    That though our harps we did retain,
Yet useless, and untouchèd there
On willows only hanged they were.

Now while our harps were hangèd so,
    The men whose captives then we lay   10
Did on our griefs insulting go,
    And more to grieve us, thus did say:
'You that of music make such show,
    Come sing us now a Sion lay.'
'O no, we have nor voice, nor hand
For such a song, in such a land.'

Though far I lie, sweet Sion hill,
    In foreign soil exiled from thee,
Yet let my hand forget his skill,
    If ever thou forgotten be: 20
And let my tongue fast gluèd still
    Unto my roof lie mute in me:
If thy neglect within me spring,
Or ought I do, but Salem sing.

But thou, O Lord, shalt not forget
    To quit the pains of Edom's race,

[40] 'By the waters of', Psalm 137

Who causelessly, yet hotly set
   Thy holy city to deface,
Did thus the bloody victors whet
   What time they entered first the place: 30
Down, down with it at any hand
Make all flat plain, let nothing stand.

And Babylon, that did'st us waste,
   Thy self shalt one day wasted be:
And happy he, who what thou hast
   Unto us done, shall do to thee,
Like bitterness shall make thee taste,
   Like woeful objects cause thee see:
Yea happy who thy little ones
Shall take and dash against the stones.   40

105. Laudate Dominum[41]

O laud the Lord, the God of hosts commend,
   Exalt his power, advance his holiness:
   With all your might lift his almightiness:
Your greatest praise upon his greatness spend.
Make trumpets' noise in shrillest notes ascend:
   Make lute and lyre his lovèd fame express:
   Him let the pipe, him let the tabret° bless,   *little drum*
Him organs breath, that winds or waters lend.

Let tinging timbrels so his honour sound,
   Let sounding cymbals so his glory ring,   10
That in their tunes such melody be found,
   As fits the pomp of most triumphant king.
Conclude: by all that air, or life enfold,
Let high Jehovah highly be extolled.

---

[41] 'Praise ye the Lord', Psalm 150

Michael Drayton (1563–1631)

106. 'My heart, imprisoned in a hopeless isle'

My heart, imprisoned in a hopeless isle,
Peopled with armies of pale jealous eyes,
The shores beset with thousand secret spies,
Must pass by air, or else die in exile.
He framed him wings with feathers of his thought,
Which by their nature learned to mount the sky;
And with the same he practisèd to fly,
Till he himself this eagle's art had taught.

Thus soaring still, not looking once below,
So near thine eyes' celestial sun aspired,   10
That with the rays his wafting pinions fired;
Thus was the wanton cause of his own woe.
Down fell he, in thy beauty's ocean drenched;
And there he burns in fire that's never quenched.

107. 'Since there's no help, come let us kiss and part'

Since there's no help, come let us kiss and part.
Nay, I have done, you get no more of me;
And I am glad, yea glad with all my heart,
That thus so cleanly I myself can free.
Shake hands for ever, cancel all our vows,
And when we meet at any time again,
Be it not seen in either of our brows
That we one jot of former love retain.

Now at the last gasp of love's latest breath,
When, his pulse failing, passion speechless lies;   10
When faith is kneeling by his bed of death,
And innocence is closing up his eyes –
Now, if thou would'st, when all have given him over,
From death to life thou might'st him yet recover.

108. Ode to the Cambro-Britons and their Harp: His Ballad of Agincourt

Fair stood the wind for France,
When we our sails advance;
Nor now to prove our chance
    Longer will tarry;
But putting to the main,
At Caux, the mouth of Seine,
With all his martial train
    Landed King Harry.

And taking many a fort,
Furnished in warlike sort,   10
Marcheth towards Agincourt
    In happy hour;
Skirmishing day by day
With those that stopped his way,
Where the French general lay
    With all his power.

Which, in his height of pride,
King Henry to deride,
His ransom to provide
    To the King sending;   20
Which he neglects the while,
As from a nation vile
Yet with an angry smile
    Their fall portending.

And turning to his men
Quoth our brave Henry then:
'Though they to one be ten
    Be not amazèd.
Yet have we well begun:
Battles so bravely won   30
Have ever to the sun
    By Fame been raisèd!

'And for myself,' quoth he,
'This my full rest shall be:
England ne'er mourn for me,
    Nor more esteem me;

Victor I will remain,
Or on this earth lie slain;
Never shall she sustain
    Loss to redeem me!   40

'Poitiers and Cressy tell
When most their pride did swell
Under our swords they fell;
    No less our skill is
Than when our grandsire great,
Claiming the regal seat,
By many a warlike feat
    Lopp'd the French lilies.'

The Duke of York so dread
The eager vanguard led;   50
With the main Henry sped
    Amongst his henchmen:
Excester had the rear,
A braver man not there
O Lord, how hot they were
    On the false Frenchmen!

They now to fight are gone;
Armour on armour shone;
Drum now to drum did groan:
    To hear, was wonder;   60
That, with cries they make,
The very earth did shake;
Trumpet to trumpet spake,
    Thunder to thunder.

Well it thine age became,
O noble Erpingham,
Which did'st the signal aim
    To our hid forces;
When, from a meadow by,
Like a storm suddenly,   70
The English archery
    Stuck the French horses

With Spanish yew so strong,
Arrows a cloth-yard long,

That like to serpents stung,
   Piercing the weather.
None from his fellow starts,
But playing manly parts,
And like true English hearts
   Stuck close together.   80

When down their bows they threw,
And forth their bilboes drew,
And on the French they flew,
   Not one was tardy;
Arms were from shoulders sent,
Scalps to the teeth were rent,
Down the French peasants went:
   Our men were hardy.

This while our noble King,
His broad sword brandishing,   90
Down the French host did ding,
   As to o'erwhelm it.
And many a deep wound lent,
His arms with blood besprent,
And many a cruel dent
   Bruisèd his helmet.

Gloucester, that duke so good,
Next of the royal blood,
For famous England stood
   With his brave brother.   100
Clarence, in steel so bright,
Though but a maiden knight,
Yet in that furious fight
   Scarce such another!

Warwick in blood did wade,
Oxford the foe invade,
And cruel slaughter made,
   Still as they ran up.
Suffolk his axe did ply;
Beaumont and Willoughby   110
Bare them right doughtily;
   Ferrers and Fanhope.

Upon Saint Crispin's Day
Fought was this noble fray,
Which fame did not delay
  To England to carry.
O when shall English men
With such acts fill a pen,
Or England breed again
  Such a King Harry?   120

Christopher Marlowe (1564–1593)

109. The Passionate Shepherd to his Love

Come live with me and be my love
And we will all the pleasures prove
That Valleys, groves, hills and fields,
Woods, or steepy mountain yields.

And we will sit upon the Rocks
Seeing the Shepherds feed their flocks,
By shallow Rivers, to whose falls
Melodious birds sings Madrigals.

And I will make thee beds of Roses
And a thousand fragrant posies,   10
A cap of flowers, and a kirtle
Embroidered all with leaves of Myrtle.

A gown made of the finest wool
Which from our pretty Lambs we pull,
Fair lined slippers for the cold:
With buckles of the purest gold.

A belt of straw and Ivy buds
With Coral clasps and Amber studs,
And if these pleasures may thee move,

Come live with me and be my love.   20

The Shepherd Swains shall dance and sing
For thy delight each May-morning.
If these delights thy mind may move,
Then live with me and be my love.

110. from *Hero and Leander*

110a. First Sestiad

On Hellespont, guilty of true love's blood,
In view and opposite two cities stood,
Sea-borderers, disjoined by Neptune's might:
The one Abydos, the other Sestos hight.°   *was called*
At Sestos, Hero dwelt: Hero the fair,
Whom young Apollo courted for her hair,
And offered as a dower his burning throne,
Where she should sit for men to gaze upon.
The outside of her garments were of lawn,
The lining purple silk, with gilt stars drawn,   10
Her wide sleeves green, and bordered with a grove,
Where Venus in her naked glory strove
To please the careless and disdainful eyes
Of proud Adonis that before her lies.
Her kirtle blue, whereon was many a stain,
Made with the blood of wretched lovers slain.
Upon her head she wore a myrtle wreath
From whence her veil reached to the ground beneath.
Her veil was artificial flowers and leaves
Whose workmanship both man and beast deceives.   20
Many would praise the sweet smell as she passed
When 'twas the odour which her breath forth cast.
And there, for honey, bees have sought in vain
And beat from thence, have lighted there again.
About her neck hung chains of pebble stone,
Which, lightened by her neck, like Diamonds shone.
She wore no gloves, for neither sun nor wind
Would burn or parch her hands, but to her mind,
Or warm or cool them, for they took delight
To play upon those hands, they were so white.   30
Buskins of shells all silvered uséd she,

And branched with blushing coral to the knee,
Where sparrows perched, of hollow pearl and gold,
Such as the world would wonder to behold:
Those with sweet water oft her handmaid fills,
Which as she went would chirrup through the bills.
Some say for her the fairest Cupid pined
And looking in her face, was stricken blind.
But this is true, so like was one the other,
As he imagined Hero was his mother;   40
And oftentimes into her bosom flew,
About her naked neck his bare arms threw,
And laid his childish head upon her breast,
And with still panting rocked, there took his rest.
So lovely fair was Hero, Venus' nun,
As nature wept, thinking she was undone;
Because she took more from her than she left
And of such wondrous beauty her bereft:
Therefore, in sign her treasure suffered wrack,
Since Hero's time hath half the world been black.   50
Amorous Leander, beautiful and young,
(Whose tragedy divine Musaeus sung)
Dwelt at Abydos; since him dwelt there none
For whom succeeding times make greater moan.
His dangling tresses that were never shorn
Had they been cut, and unto Colchos borne,
Would have allured the venturous youth of Greece
To hazard more than for the golden Fleece.
Fair Cynthia wished his arms might be her sphere.
Grief makes her pale, because she moves not there.   60
His body was as straight as Circe's wand;
Jove might have sipped out Nectar from his hand.
Even as delicious meat is to the taste,
So was his neck in touching, and surpassed
The white of Pelop's shoulder. I could tell ye
How smooth his breast was, and how white his belly,
And whose immortal fingers did imprint
That heavenly path, with many a curious dint,
That runs along his back, but my rude pen
Can hardly blazon forth the loves of men,   70
Much less of powerful gods. Let it suffice
That my slack muse sings of Leander's eyes,
Those orient cheeks and lips, exceeding his
That leapt into the water for a kiss

Of his own shadow, and despising many,
Died ere he could enjoy the love of any.
Had wild Hippolytus Leander seen,
Enamoured of his beauty had he been.
His presence made the rudest peasant melt,
That in the vast uplandish country dwelt,   80
The barbarous Thracian soldier, moved with naught,
Was moved with him, and for his favour sought.
Some swore he was a maid in man's attire
For in his looks were all that men desire,
A pleasant smiling cheek, a speaking eye,
A brow for love to banquet royally,
And such as knew he was a man would say,
'Leander, thou art made for amorous play:
Why art thou not in love, and loved of all?
Though thou be fair, yet be not thine own thrall.'   90

The men of wealthy Sestos, every year,
(For his sake whom their goddess held so dear,
Rose-cheeked Adonis) kept a solemn feast,
Thither resorted many a wandering guest,
To meet their loves; such as had none at all
Came lovers home from this great festival.
For every street like to a firmament
Glistered with breathing stars, who where they went
Frighted the melancholy earth, which deemed
Eternal heaven to burn, for so it seemed,   100
As if another Phaeton had got
The guidance of the sun's rich chariot.
But far above, the loveliest Hero shined
And stole away th' inchanted gazer's mind,
For like Sea-nymphs inveigling harmony,
So was her beauty to the standers by.
Nor that night-wandering pale and watery star
(When yawning dragons draw her thirling° car,   *whirling*
From Latmus' mount up to the gloomy sky,
Where crowned with blazing light and majesty   110
She proudly sits) more over-rules the flood
Than she the hearts of those that near her stood.
Even as, when gaudy nymphs pursue the chase,
Wretched Ixion's shaggy-footed race,
Incensed with savage heat, gallop amain,
From steep pine-bearing mountains to the plain:

So ran the people forth to gaze upon her,
And all that viewed her were enamoured on her.
And as in fury of a dreadful fight,
Their fellows being slain or put to flight,   120
Poor soldiers stand with fear of death dead strooken,
So at her presence all surprised and tooken,
Await the sentence of her scornful eyes:
He whom she favours lives, the other dies.
There might you see one sigh, another rage,
And some (their violent passions to assuage)
Compile sharp satires, but alas too late,
For faithful love will never turn to hate.
And many seeing great princes were denied,
Pined as they went, and thinking on her died.   130
On this feast day, O cursèd day and hour,
Went Hero thorough Sestos, from her tower
To Venus' temple, where unhappily,
As after chanced, they did each other spy.
So fair a Church as this, had Venus none:
The walls were of discoloured jasper stone,
Wherein was Proteus carved, and overhead
A lively vine of green sea agate spread;
Where by one hand light headed Bacchus hung,
And with the other, wine from grapes out wrung.   140
Of crystal shining fair the pavement was,
The town of Sestos called it Venus' glass.
There might you see the gods in sundry shapes
Committing heady riots, incest, rapes:
For know, that underneath this radiant floor,
Was Danae's statue in a brazen tower,
Jove slyly stealing from his sister's bed
To dally with Idalian Ganymede;
And for his love Europa bellowing loud,
And tumbling with the Rainbow in a cloud,   150
Blood-quaffing Mars, heaving the iron net,
Which limping Vulcan and his cyclops set;
Love kindling fire, to burn such towns as Troy,
Sylvanus weeping for the lovely boy
That now is turned into a cypress tree,
Under whose shade the wood-gods love to be,
And in the midst a silver altar stood;
There Hero, sacrificing turtles' blood,
Vailed° to the ground, veiling her eyelids close,   *Bowed*

And modestly they opened as she rose;   160
Thence flew love's arrow with the golden head,
And thus Leander was enamourèd.
Stone still he stood, and evermore he gazed,
Till with the fire that from his countenance blazed,
Relenting Hero's gentle heart was strook,
Such force and virtue hath an amorous look.

It lies not in our power to love or hate,
For will in us is over-ruled by fate.
When two are stripped, long ere the course begin
We wish that one should lose, the other win.   170
And one especially do we affect,
Of two gold ingots like in each respect,
The reason no man knows, let it suffice,
What we behold is censured by our eyes.
Where both deliberate, the love is slight;
Who ever loved, that loved not at first sight?

He kneeled, but unto her devoutly prayed;
Chaste Hero to herself thus softly said:
'Were I the saint he worships, I would hear him,'
And as she spake those words, came somewhat near him.   180
He started up, she blushed as one ashamed;
Wherewith Leander much more was inflamed.
He touched her hand, in touching it she trembled,
Love deeply grounded hardly is dissembled.
These lovers parleyed by the touch of hands;
True love is mute, and oft amazèd stands.
Thus while dumb signs their yielding hearts entangled,
The air with sparks of living fire was spangled,
And night, deep drenched in misty Acheron,
Heaved up her head, and half the world upon   190
Breathed darkness forth (dark night is Cupid's day),
And now begins Leander to display
Love's holy fire, with words, with sighs and tears,
Which like sweet music entered Hero's ears,
And yet at every word she turned aside,
And always cut him off as he replied.
At last, like to a bold sharp sophister,
With cheerful hope thus he accosted her.

'Fair creature, let me speak without offence,

I would my rude words had the influence 200
To lead thy thoughts, as thy fair looks do mine,
Then should'st thou be his prisoner, who is thine.
Be not unkind and fair; misshapen stuff
Are of behaviour boisterous and rough.
O shun me not, but hear me ere you go,
God knows I cannot force love, as you do.
My words shall be as spotless as my youth,
Full of simplicity and naked truth.
This sacrifice (whose sweet perfume descending
From Venus' altar to your footsteps bending) 210
Doth testify that you exceed her far,
To whom you offer, and whose Nun you are.
Why should you worship her? Her you surpass,
As much as sparkling diamonds flaring glass.
A diamond set in lead his worth retains;
A heavenly Nymph, beloved of human swains,
Receives no blemish, but oft-times more grace,
Which makes me hope, although I am but base,
Base in respect of thee, divine and pure,
Dutiful service may thy love procure, 220
And I in duty will excel all other,
As thou in beauty dost exceed love's mother.
Nor heaven, nor thou, were made to gaze upon;
As heaven preserves all things, so save thou one.
A stately builded ship, well rigged and tall,
The ocean maketh more majestical:
Why vowest thou then to live in Sestos here,
Who on love's seas more glorious would'st appear?
Like untuned golden strings all women are,
Which long time lie untouched will harshly jar. 230
Vessels of brass oft handled brightly shine;
What difference betwixt the richest mine
And basest mould but use? For both, not used,
Are of like worth. Then treasure is abused
When misers keep it; being put to loan,
In time it will return us two for one.
Rich robes themselves and others do adorn;
Neither themselves nor others, if not worn.
Who builds a palace and rams up the gate
Shall see it ruinous and desolate. 240
Ah, simple Hero, learn thy self to cherish;
Lone women like to empty houses perish.

Less sins the poor rich man that starves himself
In heaping up a mass of drossy pelf,
Than such as you: his golden earth remains,
Which, after his decease, some other gains;
But this fair gem, sweet in the loss alone,
When you fleet hence can be bequeathed to none.
Or if it could, down from th' enamelled sky
All heaven would come to claim this legacy, 250
And with intestine broils the world destroy,
And quite confound nature's sweet harmony.
Well therefore by the gods decreed it is,
We human creatures should enjoy that bliss.
One is no number, maids are nothing then,
Without the sweet society of men.
Wilt thou live single still? One shalt thou be,
Though never-singling Hymen couple thee.
Wild savages, that drink of running springs,
Think water far excels all earthly things: 260
But they that daily taste neat wine, despise it.
Virginity, albeit some highly prize it,
Compared with marriage, had you tried them both,
Differs as much as wine and water doth.
Base bullion for the stamp's sake we allow,
Even so for men's impression do we you.
By which alone, our reverend fathers say,
Women receive perfection every way.
This idol which you term virginity
Is neither essence subject to the eye, 270
No, nor to any one exterior sense,
Nor hath it any place of residence,
Nor is 't of earth or mould celestial,
Or capable of any form at all.
Of that which hath no being do not boast:
Things that are not at all, are never lost.
Men foolishly do call it virtuous:
What virtue is it that is born with us?
Much less can honour be ascribed thereto,
Honour is purchased by the deeds we do. 280
Believe me, Hero, honour is not won
Until some honourable deed be done.
Seek you for chastity, immortal fame,
And know that some have wronged Diana's name?
Whose name is it, if she be false or not,

So she be fair, but some vile tongues will blot?
But you are fair (aye me) so wondrous fair,
So young, so gentle, and so debonair,
As Greece will think, if thus you live alone,
Some one or other keeps you as his own.   290
Then, Hero, hate me not, nor from me fly,
To follow swiftly blasting infamy.
Perhaps, thy sacred priesthood makes thee loth,
Tell me, to whom mad'st thou that heedless oath?'

'To Venus,' answered she, and as she spake,
Forth from those two tralucent cisterns brake
A stream of liquid pearl, which down her face
Made milk-white paths, whereon the gods might trace
To Jove's high court. He thus replied: 'The rites
In which love's beauteous empress most delights,   300
Are banquets, Doric music, midnight-revel,
Plays, masks, and all that stern age counteth evil.
Thee as a holy idiot doth she scorn,
For thou in vowing chastity hast sworn
To rob her name and honour, and thereby
Commit'st a sin far worse than perjury,
Even sacrilege against her deity,
Through regular and formal purity.
To expiate which sin, kiss and shake hands,
Such sacrifice as this Venus demands.'   310

Thereat she smiled, and did deny him so,
As put thereby, yet might he hope for mo,°   *more*
Which makes him quickly reinforce his speech,
And her in humble manner thus beseech.

'Though neither gods nor men may thee deserve,
Yet for her sake whom you have vowed to serve,
Abandon fruitless cold virginity,
The gentle queen of love's sole enemy.
Then shall you most resemble Venus' nun,
When Venus' sweet rites are performed and done.   320
Flint-breasted Pallas joys in single life,
But Pallas and your mistress are at strife.
Love, Hero, then, and be not tyrannous,
But heal the heart that thou hast wounded thus,
Nor stain thy youthful years with avarice;

Fair fools delight to be accounted nice.
The richest corn dies, if it be not reaped;
Beauty alone is lost, too warily kept.'
These arguments he used, and many more,
Wherewith she yielded, that was won before.   330
Hero's looks yielded, but her words made war;
Women are won when they begin to jar.
Thus having swallowed Cupid's golden hook,
The more she strived the deeper was she strook.
Yet evilly feigning anger, strove she still,
And would be thought to grant against her will.
So having paused a while, at last she said:
'Who taught thee rhetoric to deceive a maid?
Aye me, such words as these should I abhor,
And yet I like them for the orator.'   340

With that Leander stooped, to have embraced her,
But from his spreading arms away she cast her,
And thus bespake him. 'Gentle youth, forbear
To touch the sacred garments which I wear.
Upon a rock, and underneath a hill,
Far from the town (where all is whist and still,
Save that the sea, playing on yellow sand,
Sends forth a rattling murmur to the land,
Whose sound allures the golden Morpheus,
In silence of the night to visit us)   350
My turret stands, and there God knows I play
With Venus' swans and sparrows all the day.
A dwarfish beldam bears me company,
That hops about the chamber where I lie,
And spends the night (that might be better spent)
In vain discourse, and apish merriment.
Come thither.' As she spake this, her tongue tripped,
For unawares 'Come thither' from her slipped,
And suddenly her former colour changed,
And here and there her eyes through anger ranged.   360
And like a planet, moving several ways
At one self instant, she, poor soul, assays,
Loving, not to love at all, and every part
Strove to resist the motions of her heart.
And hands so pure, so innocent, nay such,
As might have made heaven stoop to have a touch,
Did she uphold to Venus and again

Vowed spotless chastity, but all in vain.
Cupid beats down her prayers with his wings,
Her vows above the empty air he flings; 370
All deep enraged, his sinewy bow he bent,
And shot a shaft that burning from him went,
Wherewith she, strooken, looked so dolefully
As made Love sigh, to see his tyranny.
And as she wept, her tears to pearl he turned,
And wound them on his arm, and for her mourned.
Then towards the palace of the destinies,
Laden with languishment and grief he flies,
And to those stern nymphs humbly made request
Both might enjoy each other, and be blest. 380
But with a ghastly dreadful countenance,
Threatening a thousand deaths at every glance,
They answered Love, nor would vouchsafe so much
As one poor word, their hate to him was such.
Hearken a while, and I will tell you why.

Heaven's wingèd herald, Jove-born Mercury,
The self-same day that he asleep had laid
Enchanted Argus, spied a country maid
Whose careless hair, in stead of pearl t' adorn it,
Glistered with dew, as one that seemed to scorn it. 390
Her breath as fragrant as the morning rose,
Her mind pure, and her tongue untaught to glose.
Yet proud she was (for lofty pride that dwells
In towered courts is oft in shepherds' cells),
And too too well the fair vermilion knew,
And silver tincture of her cheeks, that drew
The love of every swain. On her this god
Enamoured was, and with his snaky rod
Did charm her nimble feet and made her stay,
The while upon a hillock down he lay, 400
And sweetly on his pipe began to play,
And with smooth speech her fancy to assay,
Till in his twining arms he locked her fast,
And then he wooed with kisses, and at last,
As shepherds do, her on the ground he laid,
And tumbling in the grass, he often strayed
Beyond the bounds of shame, in being bold
To eye those parts which no eye should behold.
And like an insolent commanding lover,

Boasting his parentage, would needs discover   410
The way to new Elysium; but she,
Whose only dower was her chastity,
Having striven in vain, was now about to cry,
And crave the help of shepherds that were nigh.
Herewith he staid his fury, and began
To give her leave to rise; away she ran,
After went Mercury, who used such cunning,
As she, to hear his tale, left off her running.
Maids are not won by brutish force and might,
But speeches full of pleasures and delight.   420
And knowing Hermes courted her, was glad
That she such loveliness and beauty had
As could provoke his liking, yet was mute,
And neither would deny nor grant his suit.
Still vowed he love, she, wanting no excuse
To feed him with delays, as women use,
Or thirsting after immortality
(All women are ambitious naturally),
Imposed upon her lover such a task
As he ought not perform, nor yet she ask.   430
A draught of flowing Nectar she requested,
Wherewith the king of gods and men is feasted.
He ready to accomplish what she willed,
Stole some from Hebe (Hebe Jove's cup filled)
And gave it to his simple rustic love,
Which being known (as what is hid from Jove?)
He inly stormed, and waxed more furious,
Than for the fire filched by Prometheus,
And thrusts him down from heaven; he wandering here
In mournful terms, with sad and heavy cheer,   440
Complained to Cupid. Cupid for his sake,
To be revenged on Jove, did undertake,
And those on whom heaven, earth, and hell relies,
I mean the adamantine destinies,
He wounds with love, and forced them equally
To dote upon deceitful Mercury.
They offered him the deadly fatal knife
That shears the slender threads of human life;
At his fair feathered feet the engines laid
Which th' earth from ugly Chaos' den up-weighed;   450
These he regarded not, but did entreat
That Jove, usurper of his father's seat,

Might presently be banished into hell,
And aged Saturn in Olympus dwell.
They granted what he craved, and once again
Saturn and Ops began their golden reign.
Murder, rape, war, lust and treachery
Were with Jove closed in Stygian empery.
But long this blessed time continued not:
As soon as he his wished purpose got   460
He reckless of his promise did despise
The love of th' everlasting destinies.
They seeing it, both Love and him abhorred,
And Jupiter unto his place restored.
And but that learning, in despite of fate,
Will mount aloft, and enter heaven gate,
And to the seat of Jove itself advance,
Hermes had slept in hell with ignorance.
Yet as a punishment they added this,
That he and poverty should always kiss.   470
And to this day is every scholar poor;
Gross gold from them runs headlong to the boor.
Likewise the angry sisters, thus deluded,
To venge themselves on Hermes, have concluded
That Midas' brood shall sit in honour's chair,
To which the Muses' sons are only heir:
And fruitful wits that inaspiring are
Shall discontent run into regions far;
And few great lords in virtuous deeds shall joy,
But be surprised with every garish toy,   480
And still enrich the lofty servile clown,
Who with encroaching guile, keeps learning down.
Then muse not Cupid's suit no better sped,
Seeing in their loves the Fates were injured.

110b. Second Sestiad

... 'O Hero, Hero!' thus he cried full oft,
And then he got him to a rock aloft
Where, having spied her tower, long stared he on 't,
And prayed the narrow toiling Hellespont   150
To part in twain, that he might come and go,
But still the rising billows answered, 'No.'
With that he stripped him to the ivory skin,
And crying, 'Love, I come!' leapt lively in.

Whereat the sapphire-visaged god grew proud
And made his capering Triton sound aloud,
Imagining that Ganymede, displeased,
Had left the heavens; therefore on him he seized.
Leander strived, the waves about him wound,
And pulled him to the bottom, where the ground   160
Was strewed with pearl, and in low coral groves
Sweet-singing Mermaids sported with their loves
On heaps of heavy gold, and took great pleasure
To spurn in careless sort the shipwrack treasure.
For here the stately azure palace stood
Where kingly Neptune and his train abode.
The lusty god embraced him, called him love,
And swore he never should return to Jove.
But when he knew it was not Ganymede,
For under water he was almost dead,   170
He heaved him up, and looking on his face,
Beat down the bold waves with his triple mace,
Which mounted up, intending to have kissed him,
And fell in drops like tears because they missed him.
Leander, being up, began to swim
And, looking back, saw Neptune follow him.
Whereat aghast, the poor soul 'gan to cry,
'O let me visit Hero ere I die.'
The god put Helle's bracelet on his arm
And swore the sea should never do him harm.   180
He clapped his plump cheeks, with his tresses played,
And smiling wantonly, his love bewrayed.
He watched his arms, and as they opened wide,
At every stroke, betwixt them would he slide,
And steal a kiss, and then run out and dance,
And as he turned, cast many a lustful glance,
And threw him gaudy toys to please his eye,
And dive into the water, and there pry
Upon his breast, his thighs, and every limb,
And up again, and close beside him swim.   190
And talk of love. Leander made reply,
'You are deceived, I am no woman I.'
Thereat smiled Neptune, and then told a tale,
How that a shepherd sitting in a vale
Playèd with a boy so fair and kind,
As for his love, both earth and heaven pined;
That of the cooling river durst not drink,

Lest water-nymphs should pull him from the brink.
And when he sported in the fragrant lawns,
Goat-footed Satyrs and up-staring fauns   200
Would steal him thence. Ere half this tale was done,
'Aye me,' Leander cried, 'th' enamoured sun,
That now should shine on Thetis' glassy bower,
Descends upon my radiant Hero's tower.
O that these tardy arms of mine were wings.'
And as he spake, upon the waves he springs.
Neptune was angry that he gave no ear,
And in his heart revenging malice bare:
He flung at him his mace, but as it went,
He called it in, for love made him repent.   210
The mace returning back, his own hand hit,
As meaning to be venged for darting it.
When this fresh-bleeding wound Leander viewed,
His colour went and came, as if he rued
The grief which Neptune felt. In gentle breasts,
Relenting thoughts, remorse and pity rests.
And who have hard hearts and obdurate minds,
But vicious, harebrained, and illiterate hinds?
The god, seeing him with pity to be moved,
Thereon concluded that he was beloved.   220
(Love is too full of faith, too credulous,
With folly and false hope deluding us.)
Wherefore Leander's fancy to surprise,
To the rich ocean for gifts he flies.
'Tis wisdom to give much, a gift prevails,
When deep persuading oratory fails.

By this Leander, being near the land,
Cast down his weary feet, and felt the sand.
Breathless albeit he were, he rested not,
Till to the solitary tower he got.   230
And knocked and called, at which celestial noise
The longing heart of Hero much more joys
Than nymphs and shepherds when the timbrel rings,
Or crooked Dolphin when the sailor sings.
She stayed not for her robes, but straight arose,
And drunk with gladness to the door she goes,
Where seeing a naked man, she screeched for fear
(Such sights as this to tender maids are rare)
And ran into the dark her self to hide.
Rich jewels in the dark are soonest spied: 240

Unto her was he led, or rather drawn,
By those white limbs, which sparkled through the lawn.
The nearer that he came, the more she fled,
And seeking refuge, slipped into her bed.
Whereon Leander sitting thus began,
Though numbing cold, all feeble, faint and wan ...

111. from *Ovid's Elegies*: Book I, Elegy V

In summer's heat and mid-time of the day,
To rest my limbs upon a bed I lay.
One window shut, the other open stood,
Which gave such light as twinkles in a wood,
Like twilight glimpse at setting of the sun,
Or night being past, and yet not day begun.
Such light to shamefaced maidens must be shown,
Where they may sport and seem to be unknown.
Then came Corinna in a long loose gown,
Her white neck hid with tresses hanging down,   10
Resembling fair Semiramis going to bed,
Or Laïs of a thousand wooers sped.
I snatched her gown; being thin, the harm was small,
Yet strived she to be covered therewithal,
And striving thus as one that would be cast,
Betrayed her self, and yielded at the last.
Stark naked as she stood before mine eye,
Not one wen in her body could I spy.
What arms and shoulders did I touch and see,
How apt her breasts were to be pressed by me!   20
How smooth a belly under her waist saw I,
How large a leg, and what a lusty thigh!
To leave the rest, all liked me passing well;
I clinged her naked body, down she fell.
Judge you the rest: being tired she bade me kiss;
Jove send me more such afternoons as this.

112. from *Ovid's Elegies*: Book II, Elegy VI

The parrot from East-India to me sent
Is dead; all fowls her exequies frequent!

Go, goodly birds, striking your breasts bewail,
And with rough claws your tender cheeks assail.
For woeful hairs let piece-torn plumes abound,
For long shrilled trumpets let your notes resound.
Why, Philomel, dost Tereus' lewdness mourn?
All wasting years have that complaint outworn.
Thy tunes let this rare bird's sad funeral borrow,
It is as great, but ancient cause of sorrow.   10
All you whose pinions in the clear air soar,
But most, thou friendly turtle-dove, deplore.
Full concord all your lives was you betwixt,
And to the end your constant faith stood fixed.
What Pylades did to Orestes prove,
Such to the parrot was the turtle-dove.
But what availed this faith? her rarest hue?
Or voice that how to change the wild notes knew?
What helps it thou wert given to please my wench,
Birds' hapless glory, death thy life doth quench.   20
Thou with thy quills might'st make green emeralds dark,
And pass our scarlet of red saffron's mark.
No such voice-feigning bird was on the ground,
Thou spokest thy words so well with stammering sound.
Envy hath rapt thee, no fierce wars thou moved'st,
Vain babbling speech, and pleasant peace thou loved'st.
Behold how quails among their battles live,
Which do perchance old age unto them give.
A little filled thee, and for love of talk,
Thy mouth to taste of many meats did balk.   30
Nuts were thy food, and poppy caused thee sleep,
Pure water's moisture thirst away did keep.
The ravenous vulture lives, the puttock° hovers   *kite*
Around the air, the cadess° rain discovers,   *jackdaw*
And crow survives arms-bearing Pallas' hate,
Whose life nine ages scarce bring out of date.
Dead is that speaking image of man's voice,
The Parrot given me, the far world's best choice.
The greedy spirits take the best things first,
Supplying their void places with the worst.   40
Thersites did Protesilaus survive,
And Hector died, his brothers yet alive.
My wench's vows for thee what should I show,
Which stormy south winds into sea did blow?
The seventh day came, none following might'st thou see,

And the fate's distaff empty stood to thee:
Yet words in thy benumbèd palate rung,
'Farewell, Corinna,' cried thy dying tongue.
Elysium hath a wood of holm-trees black,
Whose earth doth not perpetual green-grass lack;   50
There good birds rest (if we believe things hidden)
Whence unclean fowls are said to be forbidden;
There harmless swans feed all abroad the river,
There lives the phoenix one alone bird ever.
There Juno's bird displays his gorgeous feather,
And loving doves kiss eagerly together.
The parrot into wood received with these,
Turns all the goodly birds to what she please.
A grave her bones hides, on her corpse's great grave,
The little stones these little verses have: 60
'This tomb approves, I pleased my mistress well,
My mouth in speaking did all birds excel.'

113. from *Ovid's Elegies*: Book III, Elegy III

What, are there gods? Herself she hath forswore,
And yet remains the face she had before.
How long her locks were ere her oath she took:
So long they be, since she her faith forsook.
Fair white with rose red was before commixed:
Now shine her looks pure white and red betwixt.
Her foot was small: her foot's form is most fit;
Comely tall was she, comely tall she's yet.
Sharp eyes she had: radiant like stars they be,
By which she perjured oft hath lied by me.   10
In sooth th' eternal powers grant maids society
Falsely to swear, their beauty hath some deity.
By her eyes I remember late she swore,
And by mine eyes, and mine were painèd sore.
Say, gods: if she unpunished you deceive,
For other's faults why do I loss receive?
But did you not so envy Cepheus' daughter,
For her ill-beauteous mother judged to slaughter?
'Tis not enough she shakes your record off
And, unrevenged, mocked Gods with me doth scoff   20
But by my pain to purge her perjuries,

Cozened, I am the cozener's sacrifice.
God is a name, no substance, feared in vain,
And doth the world in fond belief detain,
Or if there be a God, he loves fine wenches,
And all things too much in their sole power drenches.
Mars girts his deadly sword on for my harm,
Pallas' lance strikes me with unconquered arm.
At me Apollo bends his pliant bow,
At me Jove's right-hand lightning hath to throw.   30
The wrongèd gods dread fair ones to offend,
And fear those that to fear them least intend.
Who now will care the altars to perfume?
Tut, men should not their courage so consume.
Jove throws down woods and castles with his fire,
But bids his darts from perjured girls retire.
Poor Semele among so many burned,
Her own request to her own torment turned;
But when her lover came, had she drawn back,
The father's thigh should unborn Bacchus lack.   40
Why grieve I? And of heaven reproaches pen?
The gods have eyes and breasts as well as men.
Were I a god, I should give women leave,
With lying lips my godhead to deceive.
Myself would swear the wenches true did swear,
And I would be none of the gods severe,
But yet their gift more moderately use,
Or in mine eyes, good wench, no pain transfuse,

114. from *Ovid's Elegies*: Book III, Elegy VI

Either she was foul, or her attire was bad,
Or she was not the wench I wish t' have had.
Idly I lay with her, as if I loved not,
And like a burden grieved the bed that moved not.
Though both of us performed our true intent,
Yet could I not cast anchor where I meant.
She on my neck her ivory arms did throw,
Her arms far whiter than the Scythian snow.
And eagerly she kissed me with her tongue,
And under mine her wanton thigh she flung.   10
Yea, and she soothed me up, and called me 'Sir',

And used all speech that might provoke and stir.
Yet like as if cold hemlock I had drunk,
It mockèd me, hung down the head and sunk.
Like a dull cipher or rude block I lay,
Or shade or body was I? Who can say?
What will my age do, age I cannot shun,
When in my prime my force is spent and done?
I blush, that being youthful, hot and lusty,
I prove neither youth nor man, but old and rusty.   20
Pure rose she, like a nun to sacrifice,
Or one that with her tender brother lies.
Yet boarded I the golden Chie twice,
And Libas, and the white cheeked Pitho thrice.
Corinna craved it in a summer's night
And nine sweet bouts we had before daylight.
What, waste my limbs through some Thessalian charms?
May spells and drugs do silly souls such harms?
With virgin wax hath some imbaste my joints
And pierced my liver with sharp needles' points?   30
Charms change corn to grass and make it die;
By charms are running springs and fountains dry.
By charms mast drops from oaks, from vines grapes fall,
And fruit from trees when there's no wind at all.
Why might not then my sinews be enchanted
And I grow faint as with some spirit haunted?
To this add shame: shame to perform it quailed me,
And was the second cause why vigour failed me.
My idle thoughts delighted her no more
Than did the robe or garment which she wore.   40
Yet might her touch make youthful Pylius fire,
And Tython livelier then his years require.
Even her I had, and she had me in vain,
What might I crave more, if I ask again?
I think the great gods grieved they had bestowed
The benefit which lewdly I forslowed.
I wished to be received in, in I get me;
To kiss, I kiss: to lie with her she let me.
Why was I blest? why made king to refuse it?
Chuff-like had I not gold and could not use it?   50
So in a spring thrives he that told so much
And looks upon the fruits he cannot touch.
Hath any rose so from a fresh young maid,
As she might straight have gone to church and prayed?

Well, I believe she kissed not as she should,
Nor used the sleight and cunning which she could.
Huge oaks, hard adamants might she have moved,
And with sweet words cause deaf rocks to have loved,
Worthy she was to move both gods and men,
But neither was I man nor livèd then.   60
Can deaf ear take delight when Phæmius sings?
Or Thamiris in curious painted things?
What sweet thought is there but I had the same?
And one gave place still as another came.
Yet notwithstanding, like one dead I lay,
Drooping more like a rose pulled yesterday.
Now, when he should not jet, he bolts upright,
And craves his task, and seeks to be at fight.
Lie down with shame, and see thou stir no more,
Seeing thou would'st deceive me as before.   70
Thou cozenest me: by thee surprised am I,
And bide sore loss with endless infamy.
Nay more, the wench did not disdain a whit,
To take it in her hand, and play with it.
But when she saw it would by no means stand,
But still drooped down, regarding not her hand,
'Why mock'st thou me,' she cried, 'or being ill,
Who bade thee lie down here against thy will?
Either th' art witched° with blood of frogs new dead,   *bewitched*
Or jaded cam'st thou from some other's bed.'   80
With that, her loose gown on, from me she cast her;
In skipping out her naked feet much graced her.
And lest her maid should know of this disgrace,
To cover it, spilt water in the place.

William Shakespeare (1564–1616)

115. The Phoenix and the Turtle

Let the bird of loudest lay,°   *singing*
   On the sole Arabian tree,

Herald sad and trumpet be,
To whose sound chaste wings obey.

But thou shrieking harbinger,°   *[the screech owl]*
    Foul precurrer° of the fiend,   *forerunner*
    Augur of the fever's end,
To this troop come thou not near!

From this session interdict
    Every fowl of tyrant wing,°   *[bird of prey]* 10
    Save the eagle, feathered king:
Keep the obsequy so strict.

Let the priest in surplice white,
    That defunctive° music can,*   *funereal; knows*
    Be the death-divining swan,
Lest the requiem lack his rite.

And thou treble-dated° crow,   *long-living*
    That thy sable gender mak'st
    With the breath thou giv'st and tak'st,
'Mongst our mourners shalt thou go.   20

Here the anthem doth commence:
    Love and constancy is dead;
    Phoenix and the turtle fled
In a mutual flame from hence.

So they loved, as love in twain
    Had the essence but in one;
    Two distincts, division none:
Number there in love was slain.

Hearts remote, yet not asunder;
    Distance, and no space was seen   30
    'Twixt the turtle and his queen:
But in them it were a wonder.

So between them love did shine,
    That the turtle saw his right
    Flaming in the phoenix's sight;
Either was the other's mine.

Property was thus appalled,
   That the self was not the same;
   Single nature's double name
Neither two nor one was called.   40

Reason in itself confounded
   Saw division grow together,
   To themselves yet either neither,
Simple were so well compounded,

That it cried, 'How true a twain
   Seemeth this concordant one!
   Love hath reason, reason none,
If what parts can so remain.'

Whereupon it made this threne
   To the phoenix and the dove,
   Co-supremes and stars of love,   50
As chorus to their tragic scene.

   Threnos
Beauty, truth, and rarity,
Grace in all simplicity,
Here enclosed, in cinders lie.

Death is now the phoenix's nest;
And the turtle's loyal breast
To eternity doth rest.

Leaving no posterity,
'Twas not their infirmity,   60
It was married chastity.

Truth may seem, but cannot be;
Beauty brag, but 'tis not she;
Truth and beauty buried be.

To this urn let those repair
That are either true or fair;
For these dead birds sigh a prayer.

116. from *The Rape of Lucrece*

With this, they all at once began to say,
Her body's stain her mind untainted clears;   1710
While with a joyless smile she turns away
The face, that map which deep impression bears
Of hard misfortune, carved in it with tears.
  'No, no,' quoth she, 'no dame hereafter living
  By my excuse shall claim excuse's giving.'

Here with a sigh, as if her heart would break,
She throws forth Tarquin's name: 'He, he,' she says,
But more than 'he' her poor tongue could not speak,
Till after many accents and delays,
Untimely breathings, sick and short assays,   1720
  She utters this: 'He, he, fair lords, 'tis he,
  That guides this hand to give this wound to me.'

Even here, she sheathèd in her harmless breast
A harmful knife, that thence her soul unsheathed;
That blow did bail° it from the deep unrest   *release*
Of that polluted prison where it breathed.
Her contrite sighs unto the clouds bequeathed
  Her wingèd sprite and through her wounds doth fly
  Life's lasting date from cancelled destiny.

Stone-still, astonished with this deadly deed   1730
Stood Collatine and all his lordly crew;
Till Lucrece's father, that beholds her bleed,
Himself on her self-slaughtered body threw;
And from the purple fountain Brutus drew
  The murderous knife, and, as it left the place,
  Her blood, in poor revenge, held it in chase;

And bubbling from her breast, it doth divide
In two slow rivers, that the crimson blood
Circles her body in on every side,
Who like a late-sacked island vastly stood   1740
Bare and unpeopled in this fearful flood.
  Some of her blood still pure and red remained,
  And some looked black, and that false Tarquin stained.

About the mourning and congealèd face
Of that black blood a watery rigol goes,

Which seems to weep upon the tainted place;
And ever since, as° pitying Lucrece's woes,   *as if*
Corrupted blood some watery token shows;
    And blood untainted still doth red abide,
    Blushing at that which is so putrefied.   1750

'Daughter, dear daughter,' old Lucretius cries,
'That life was mine which thou hast here deprived.
If in the child the father's image lies,
Where shall I live now Lucrece is unlived?
Thou wast not to this end from me derived.
    If children predecease progenitors,
    We are their offspring, and they none of ours.

'Poor broken glass, I often did behold
In thy sweet semblance my old age new born;
But now that fair fresh mirror, dim and old,   1760
Shows me a bare-boned death by time outworn;
O, from thy cheeks my image thou hast torn,
    And shivered° all the beauty of my glass,   *shattered*
    That I no more can see what once I was.

'O time, cease thou thy course and last no longer,
If they surcease to be that should survive.
Shall rotten death make conquest of the stronger,
And leave the faltering feeble souls alive?
The old bees die, the young possess their hive.
    Then live, sweet Lucrece, live again, and see   1770
    Thy father die, and not thy father thee.'

By this starts Collatine as from a dream,
And bids Lucretius give his sorrow place;
And then in key-cold Lucrece's bleeding stream
He falls, and bathes the pale fear in his face,
And counterfeits to die with her a space;
    Till manly shame bids him possess his breath
    And live to be revengèd on her death.

The deep vexation of his inward soul
Hath served a dumb arrest upon his tongue;   1780
Who, mad that sorrow should his use control
Or keep him from heart-easing words so long,

Begins to talk; but through his lips do throng
    Weak words, so thick come in his poor heart's aid
    That no man could distinguish what he said.

Yet sometime 'Tarquin' was pronouncèd plain,
But through his teeth, as if the name he tore.
This windy tempest, till it blow up rain,
Held back his sorrow's tide, to make it more.
At last it rains, and busy winds give o'er;   1790
    Then son and father weep with equal strife
    Who should weep most, for daughter or for wife.

The one doth call her his, the other his,
Yet neither may possess the claim they lay.
The father says 'She's mine'. 'O, mine she is,'
Replies her husband: 'do not take away
My sorrow's interest; let no mourner say
    He weeps for her, for she was only mine,
    And only must be wailed by Collatine.'

'O,' quoth Lucretius, 'I did give that life   1800
Which she too early and too late hath spilled.'
'Woe, woe,' quoth Collatine, 'she was my wife;
I owed° her, and 'tis mine that she hath killed.'   *owned*
'My daughter' and 'my wife' with clamours filled
    The dispersed air, who, holding Lucrece's life,
    Answered their cries, 'my daughter' and 'my wife'.

Brutus, who plucked the knife from Lucrece's side,
Seeing such emulation in their woe,
Began to clothe his wit in state and pride,
Burying in Lucrece's wound his folly's show.   1810
He with the Romans was esteemèd so
    As silly jeering idiots are with kings,
    For sportive words and uttering foolish things.

But now he throws that shallow habit by
Wherein deep policy did him disguise,
And armed his long-hid wits advisedly
To check the tears in Collatinus' eyes.
'Thou wrongèd lord of Rome,' quoth he, 'arise;
    Let my unsounded self, supposed a fool,
    Now set thy long-experienced wit to school.   1820

'Why, Collatine, is woe the cure for woe?
Do wounds help wounds, or grief help grievous deeds?
Is it revenge to give thyself a blow
For his foul act by whom thy fair wife bleeds?
Such childish humour from weak minds proceeds.
   Thy wretched wife mistook the matter so
   To slay herself, that should have slain her foe.

'Courageous Roman, do not steep thy heart
In such relenting dew of lamentations,
But kneel with me and help to bear thy part   1830
To rouse our Roman gods with invocations
That they will suffer these abominations
   (Since Rome herself in them doth stand disgraced),
   By our strong arms from forth her fair streets chased.

'Now by the Capitol that we adore,
And by this chaste blood so unjustly stained,
By heaven's fair sun that breeds the fat earth's store,
By all our country rights in Rome maintained,
And by chaste Lucrece's soul that late complained
   Her wrongs to us, and by this bloody knife,   1840
   We will revenge the death of this true wife.'

This said, he struck his hand upon his breast,
And kissed the fatal knife to end his vow,
And to his protestation urged the rest,
Who, wondering at him, did his words allow;
Then jointly to the ground their knees they bow,
   And that deep vow which Brutus made before
   He doth again repeat, and that they swore.

When they had sworn to this advisèd doom,
They did conclude to bear dead Lucrece thence,   1850
To show her bleeding body thorough Rome,
And so to publish Tarquin's foul offence;
Which being done with speedy diligence,
   The Romans plausibly did give consent
   To Tarquin's everlasting banishment.

from *The Sonnets*

117. 'When I do count the clock that tells the time'

When I do count the clock that tells the time,
And see the brave day sunk in hideous night,
When I behold the violet past prime,
And sable curls all silvered o'er with white:
When lofty trees I see barren of leaves,
Which erst from heat did canopy the herd
And summer's green all girded up in sheaves
Borne on the bier with white and bristly beard:
Then of thy beauty do I question make
That thou among the wastes of time must go,   10
Since sweets and beauties do themselves forsake,
And die as fast as they see others grow,
    And nothing 'gainst time's scythe can make defence
    Save breed to brave him, when he takes thee hence.

118. 'O that you were your self, but, love, you are'

O that you were your self, but, love, you are
No longer yours, than you your self here live,
Against this coming end you should prepare,
And your sweet semblance to some other give.
So should that beauty which you hold in lease
Find no determination, then you were
Your self again after your self's decease,
When your sweet issue your sweet form should bear.
Who lets so fair a house fall to decay,
Which husbandry in honour might uphold,   10
Against the stormy gusts of winter's day
And barren rage of death's eternal cold?
    O none but unthrifts, dear my love, you know,
    You had a father, let your son say so.

119. 'When I consider every thing that grows'

When I consider every thing that grows
Holds in perfection but a little moment,

That this huge stage presenteth naught but shows
Whereon the stars in secret influence comment;
When I perceive that men as plants increase,
Cheered and checked even by the self-same sky,
Vaunt in their youthful sap, at height decrease,
And wear their brave state out of memory;
Then the conceit of this inconstant stay
Sets you most rich in youth before my sight,   10
Where wasteful time debateth with decay
To change your day of youth to sullied night,
    And all in war with time for love of you,
    As he takes from you, I engraft you new.

120. 'Shall I compare thee to a summer's day'

Shall I compare thee to a summer's day?
Thou art more lovely and more temperate.
Rough winds do shake the darling buds of May
And summer's lease hath all too short a date.
Sometime too hot the eye of heaven shines,
And often is his gold complexion dimmed,
And every fair from fair sometime declines
By chance, or nature's changing course untrimmed.
But thy eternal summer shall not fade
Nor lose possession of that fair thou owest,   10
Nor shall death brag thou wand'rest in his shade
When in eternal lines to time thou growest.
    So long as men can breathe or eyes can see,
    So long lives this, and this gives life to thee.

121. 'Devouring time, blunt thou the lion's paws'

Devouring time, blunt thou the lion's paws,
And make the earth devour her own sweet brood;
Pluck the keen teeth from the fierce tiger's jaws
And burn the long-lived phoenix in her blood.
Make glad and sorry seasons as thou fleet'st,
And do whate'er thou wilt, swift-footed time,
To the wide world and all her fading sweets;

But I forbid thee one most heinous crime:
O carve not with thy hours my love's fair brow,
Nor draw no lines there with thine antique pen,   10
Him in thy course untainted do allow
For beauty's pattern to succeeding men.
    Yet do thy worst old time: despite thy wrong
    My love shall in my verse ever live young.

122. 'A woman's face with nature's own hand painted'

A woman's face with nature's own hand painted
Hast thou, the master mistress of my passion;
A woman's gentle heart, but not acquainted
With shifting change as is false women's fashion;
An eye more bright than theirs, less false in rolling,
Gilding the object whereupon it gazeth;
A man in hue all hues in his controlling,
Which steals men's eyes and women's souls amazeth.
And for a woman wert thou first created,
Till nature as she wrought thee fell a-doting,   10
And by addition me of thee defeated
By adding one thing to my purpose nothing.
    But since she pricked thee out for women's pleasure,
    Mine be thy love, and thy love's use their treasure.

123. 'So is it not with me as with that muse'

So is it not with me as with that muse
Stirred by a painted beauty to his verse,
Who heaven itself for ornament doth use,
And every fair with his fair doth rehearse,
Making a couplement of proud compare
With sun and moon, with earth and sea's rich gems,
With April's first-born flowers and all things rare,
That heaven's air in this huge rondure hems.
O, let me true in love but truly write,
And then believe me, my love is as fair   10
As any mother's child, though not so bright

As those gold candles fixed in heaven's air:
 Let them say more that like of hearsay well:
 I will not praise that purpose not to sell.

124. 'My glass shall not persuade me I am old'

My glass shall not persuade me I am old,
So long as youth and thou are of one date;
But when in thee time's furrows I behold,
Then look I death my days should expiate.
For all that beauty that doth cover thee
Is but the seemly raiment of my heart,
Which in thy breast doth live, as thine in me.
How can I then be elder than thou art?
O therefore love be of thyself so wary
As I not for myself, but for thee will,   10
Bearing thy heart which I will keep so chary
As tender nurse her babe from faring ill.
 Presume not on thy heart when mine is slain;
 Thou gav'st me thine not to give back again.

125. 'Weary with toil, I haste me to my bed'

Weary with toil, I haste me to my bed,
The dear repose for limbs with travel tired,
But then begins a journey in my head
To work my mind, when body's work's expired;
For then my thoughts, from far where I abide,
Intend a zealous pilgrimage to thee,
And keep my drooping eyelids open wide,
Looking on darkness which the blind do see.
Save that my soul's imaginary sight
Presents thy shadow to my sightless view,   10
Which like a jewel hung in ghastly night
Makes black night beauteous and her old face new.
 Lo, thus, by day my limbs, by night my mind,
 For thee, and for myself; no quiet find.

126. 'When in disgrace with Fortune and men's eyes'

When in disgrace with Fortune and men's eyes
I all alone beweep my outcast state,
And trouble deaf heaven with my bootless cries,
And look upon myself and curse my fate,
Wishing me like to one more rich in hope,
Featured like him, like him with friends possessed,
Desiring this man's art, and that man's scope,
With what I most enjoy contented least;
Yet in these thoughts myself almost despising,
Haply I think on thee, and then my state,   10
Like to the lark at break of day arising
From sullen earth, sings hymns at heaven's gate;
    For thy sweet love remembered such wealth brings,
    That then I scorn to change my state with kings.

127. 'When to the sessions of sweet silent thought'

When to the sessions of sweet silent thought
I summon up remembrance of things past,
I sigh the lack of many a thing I sought
And with old woes new wail my dear time's waste.
Then can I drown an eye, unused to flow,
For precious friends hid in death's dateless night,
And weep afresh love's long since cancelled woe,
And moan th' expense of many a vanished sight.
Then can I grieve at grievances foregone,
And heavily from woe to woe tell o'er   10
The sad account of fore-bemoanèd moan,
Which I new pay as if not paid before.
    But if the while I think on thee, dear friend,
    All losses are restored, and sorrows end.

128. 'Take all my loves, my love, yea take them all'

Take all my loves, my love, yea take them all:
What hast thou then more than thou had'st before?
No love, my love, that thou may'st true love call,

All mine was thine, before thou had'st this more:
Then if for my love, thou my love receivest,
I cannot blame thee, for my love thou usest,
But yet be blamed, if thou thy self deceivest
By wilful taste of what thy self refusest.
I do forgive thy robbery, gentle thief,
Although thou steal thee all my poverty: 10
And yet love knows it is a greater grief
To bear love's wrong than hate's known injury.
    Lascivious grace, in whom all ill well shows,
    Kill me with spites, yet we must not be foes.

129. 'So am I as the rich whose blessèd key'

So am I as the rich whose blessèd key
Can bring him to his sweet up-lockèd treasure,
The which he will not every hour survey,
For blunting the fine point of seldom pleasure.
Therefore are feasts so solemn and so rare,
Since, seldom coming, in that long year set,
Like stones of worth they thinly placèd are,
Or captain jewels in the carcanet.
So is the time that keeps you as my chest,
Or as the wardrobe which the robe doth hide,   10
To make some special instant special blest,
By new unfolding his imprisoned pride.
    Blessèd are you whose worthiness gives scope,
    Being had, to triumph, being lacked, to hope.

130. 'What is your substance, whereof are you made'

What is your substance, whereof are you made,
That millions of strange shadows on you tend?
Since every one hath, every one, one shade,
And you but one, can every shadow lend.
Describe Adonis and the counterfeit
Is poorly imitated after you;
On Helen's cheek all art of beauty set,
And you in Grecian tires° are painted new.   *attires*

Speak of the spring and foison° of the year: *harvest*
The one doth shadow of your beauty show,   10
The other as your bounty doth appear,
And you in every blessèd shape we know.
   In all external grace you have some part,
   But you like none, none you, for constant heart.

131. 'Not marble, nor the gilded monuments'

Not marble, nor the gilded monuments
Of princes shall outlive this powerful rhyme,
But you shall shine more bright in these contents
Than unswept stone, besmeared with sluttish time.
When wasteful war shall statues overturn
And broils root out the work of masonry,
Nor Mars his sword, nor war's quick fire shall burn
The living record of your memory.
'Gainst death, and all oblivious enmity
Shall you pace forth, your praise shall still find room   10
Even in the eyes of all posterity
That wear this world out to the ending doom.
   So, till the judgement that yourself arise,
   You live in this, and dwell in lovers' eyes.

132. 'Being your slave what should I do but tend'

Being your slave what should I do but tend
Upon the hours and times of your desire?
I have no precious time at all to spend,
Nor services to do till you require.
Nor dare I chide the world-without-end hour
Whilst I, my sovereign, watch the clock for you,
Nor think the bitterness of absence sour
When you have bid your servant once adieu.
Nor dare I question with my jealous thought
Where you may be, or your affairs suppose,   10
But, like a sad slave, stay and think of naught

Save where you are how happy you make those.
   So true a fool is love that in your will,
   Though you do any thing, he thinks no ill.

133. 'Like as the waves make towards the pebbled shore'

Like as the waves make towards the pebbled shore,
So do our minutes hasten to their end,
Each changing place with that which goes before,
In sequent toil all forwards do contend.
Nativity, once in the main of light,
Crawls to maturity, wherewith being crowned,
Crooked eclipses 'gainst his glory fight,
And time that gave doth now his gift confound.
Time doth transfix the flourish set on youth
And delves the parallels in beauty's brow,   10
Feeds on the rarities of nature's truth
And nothing stands but for his scythe to mow.
   And yet to times in hope my verse shall stand
   Praising thy worth, despite his cruel hand.

134. 'Is it thy will, thy image should keep open'

Is it thy will, thy image should keep open
My heavy eyelids to the weary night?
Dost thou desire my slumbers should be broken
While shadows like to thee do mock my sight?
Is it thy spirit that thou send'st from thee
So far from home into my deeds to pry,
To find out shames and idle hours in me,
The scope and tenure of thy jealousy?
O no, thy love, though much, is not so great.
It is my love that keeps mine eye awake,   10
Mine own true love that doth my rest defeat,
To play the watchman ever for thy sake.
   For thee watch I, whilst thou dost wake elsewhere,
   From me far off; with others all too near.

135. 'When I have seen by time's fell hand defaced'

When I have seen by time's fell hand defaced
The rich proud cost of outworn buried age,
When sometime lofty towers I see down-rased,
And brass eternal slave to mortal rage;
When I have seen the hungry ocean gain
Advantage on the kingdom of the shore,
And the firm soil win of the watery main,
Increasing store with loss, and loss with store;
When I have seen such interchange of state,
Or state itself confounded to decay,   10
Ruin hath taught me thus to ruminate:
That time will come and take my love away.
    This thought is as a death which cannot choose
    But weep to have that which it fears to lose.

136. 'Since brass, nor stone, nor earth, nor boundless sea'

Since brass, nor stone, nor earth, nor boundless sea,
But sad mortality o'ersways their power,
How with this rage shall beauty hold a plea
Whose action is no stronger than a flower?
O how shall summer's honey breath hold out
Against the wrackful siege of battering days,
When rocks impregnable are not so stout,
Nor gates of steel so strong, but time decays?
O fearful meditation: where, alack,
Shall time's best jewel from time's chest lie hid?   10
Or what strong hand can hold his swift foot back,
Or who his spoil of beauty can forbid?
    O none, unless this miracle have might:
    That in black ink my love may still shine bright.

137. 'Tired with all these, for restful death I cry'

Tired with all these, for restful death I cry:
As to behold desert a beggar born,
And needy nothing trimmed in jollity,

And purest faith unhappily forsworn,
And gilded honour shamefully misplaced,
And maiden virtue rudely strumpeted,
And right perfection wrongfully disgraced,
And strength by limping sway disablèd,
And art made tongue-tied by authority,
And folly, doctor-like, controlling skill,   10
And simple truth miscalled simplicity,
And captive good attending captain ill.
    Tired with all these, from these would I be gone,
    Save that to die, I leave my love alone.

138. 'No longer mourn for me when I am dead'

No longer mourn for me when I am dead
Than you shall hear the surly sullen bell
Give warning to the world that I am fled
From this vile world with vilest worms to dwell.
Nay, if you read this line, remember not
The hand that writ it, for I love you so
That I in your sweet thoughts would be forgot,
If thinking on me then should make you woe.
O, if, I say, you look upon this verse,
When I, perhaps, compounded am with clay,   10
Do not so much as my poor name rehearse,
But let your love even with my life decay,
    Lest the wise world should look into your moan
    And mock you with me after I am gone.

139. 'That time of year thou may'st in me behold'

That time of year thou may'st in me behold
When yellow leaves, or none, or few do hang
Upon those boughs which shake against the cold,
Bare ruined choirs, where late the sweet birds sang.
In me thou see'st the twilight of such day
As after sunset fadeth in the west,
Which by and by black night doth take away,
Death's second self that seals up all in rest.

In me thou see'st the glowing of such fire
That on the ashes of his youth doth lie,   10
As the death-bed, whereon it must expire,
Consumed with that which it was nourished by.
    This thou perceiv'st, which makes thy love more strong,
    To love that well, which thou must leave ere long.

140. 'Was it the proud full sail of his great verse'

Was it the proud full sail of his great verse
Bound for the prize of all too precious you
That did my ripe thoughts in my brain inhearse,
Making their tomb the womb wherein they grew?
Was it his spirit, by spirits taught to write
Above a mortal pitch, that struck me dead?
No, neither he, nor his compeers by night
Giving him aid, my verse astonishèd.
He, nor that affable familiar ghost
Which nightly gulls him with intelligence,   10
As victors of my silence cannot boast:
I was not sick of any fear from thence.
    But when your countenance filled up his line,
    Then lacked I matter, that enfeebled mine.

141. 'Farewell! thou art too dear for my possessing'

Farewell! thou art too dear for my possessing,
And like enough thou know'st thy estimate,
The charter of thy worth gives thee releasing;
My bonds in thee are all determinate.°   *expired*
For how do I hold thee but by thy granting,
And for that riches where is my deserving?
The cause of this fair gift in me is wanting,
And so my patent back again is swerving.
Thy self thou gav'st, thy own worth then not knowing,
Or me, to whom thou gav'st it, else mistaking,   10
So thy great gift upon misprision° growing,   *error*

Comes home again, on better judgement making.
  Thus have I had thee as a dream doth flatter,
  In sleep a king, but waking no such matter.

142. 'Say that thou did'st forsake me for some fault'

Say that thou did'st forsake me for some fault,
And I will comment upon that offence,
Speak of my lameness, and I straight will halt,°   *limp*
Against thy reasons making no defence.
Thou can'st not, love, disgrace me half so ill,
To set a form upon desirèd change,
As I'll myself disgrace, knowing thy will.
I will acquaintance strangle and look strange:
Be absent from thy walks and in my tongue
Thy sweet beloved name no more shall dwell,   10
Lest I, too much profane, should do it wrong
And haply of our old acquaintance tell.
    For thee, against my self I'll vow debate,
    For I must ne'er love him whom thou dost hate.

143. 'They that have power to hurt and will do none'

They that have power to hurt and will do none,
That do not do the thing they most do show,
Who moving others are themselves as stone,
Unmovèd, cold, and to temptation slow;
They rightly do inherit heaven's graces
And husband nature's riches from expense;
They are the lords and owners of their faces,
Others, but stewards of their excellence.
The summer's flower is to the summer sweet,
Though to itself it only live and die;   10
But if that flower with base infection meet,
The basest weed outbraves his dignity;
    For sweetest things turn sourest by their deeds:
    Lilies that fester smell far worse than weeds.

144. 'How like a winter hath my absence been'

How like a winter hath my absence been
From thee, the pleasure of the fleeting year!
What freezings have I felt, what dark days seen!
What old December's bareness everywhere!
And yet this time removed was summer's time,
The teeming autumn big with rich increase,
Bearing the wanton burden of the prime,
Like widowed wombs after their lords' decease.
Yet this abundant issue seemed to me
But hope of orphans, and unfathered fruit,　　　　　　　　10
For summer and his pleasures wait on thee,
And thou away, the very birds are mute,
　　Or if they sing, 'tis with so dull a cheer
　　That leaves look pale, dreading the winter's near.

145. 'From you have I been absent in the spring'

From you have I been absent in the spring,
When proud-pied April, dressed in all his trim,
Hath put a spirit of youth in every thing,
That heavy Saturn laughed and leaped with him,
Yet, nor the lays of birds, nor the sweet smell
Of different flowers in odour and in hue
Could make me any summer's story tell,
Or from their proud lap pluck them where they grew:
Nor did I wonder at the lily's white,
Nor praise the deep vermilion in the rose;　　　　　　　　10
They were but sweet, but figures of delight,
Drawn after you, you pattern of all those.
　　Yet seemed it winter still and, you away,
　　As with your shadow I with these did play.

146. 'To me, fair friend, you never can be old'

To me, fair friend, you never can be old,
For as you were when first your eye I eyed,
Such seems your beauty still. Three winters cold

Have from the forests shook three summers' pride,
Three beauteous springs to yellow autumn turned
In process of the seasons have I seen,
Three April perfumes in three hot Junes burned,
Since first I saw you fresh, which yet are green.
Ah, yet doth beauty like a dial hand
Steal from his figure, and no pace perceived,   10
So your sweet hue, which methinks still doth stand,
Hath motion, and mine eye may be deceived,
   For fear of which, hear this, thou age unbred,
   Ere you were born was beauty's summer dead.

147. 'When in the chronicle of wasted time'

When in the chronicle of wasted time
I see descriptions of the fairest wights,
And beauty making beautiful old rhyme
In praise of ladies dead and lovely knights;
Then in the blazon of sweet beauty's best,
Of hand, of foot, of lip, of eye, of brow,
I see their antique pen would have expressed
Even such a beauty as you master now.
So all their praises are but prophecies
Of this our time, all you prefiguring,   10
And, for they looked but with divining eyes,
They had not skill enough your worth to sing:
   For we which now behold these present days
   Have eyes to wonder, but lack tongues to praise.

148. 'Not mine own fears, nor the prophetic soul'

Not mine own fears, nor the prophetic soul
Of the wide world, dreaming on things to come,
Can yet the lease of my true love control,
Supposed as forfeit to a confined doom.
The mortal moon hath her eclipse endured,
And the sad augurs mock their own presage,
Incertainties now crown themselves assured,
And peace proclaims olives of endless age.

Now with the drops of this most balmy time
My love looks fresh, and death to me subscribes,   10
Since, spite of him, I'll live in this poor rhyme,
While he insults o'er dull and speechless tribes.
    And thou in this shalt find thy monument
    When tyrants' crests and tombs of brass are spent.

149. 'Alas, 'tis true, I have gone here and there'

Alas, 'tis true, I have gone here and there
And made myself a motley to the view,
Gored mine own thoughts, sold cheap what is most dear,
Made old offences of affections new.
Most true it is, that I have looked on truth
Askance and strangely; but by all above,
These blenches gave my heart another youth,
And worse essays proved thee my best of love.
Now all is done, have what shall have no end.
Mine appetite I never more will grind   10
On newer proof; to try an older friend,
A god in love, to whom I am confined.
    Then give me welcome, next my heaven the best,
    Even to thy pure and most most loving breast.

150. 'Let me not to the marriage of true minds'

Let me not to the marriage of true minds
Admit impediments; love is not love
Which alters when it alteration finds
Or bends with the remover to remove.
O, no, it is an ever-fixèd mark
That looks on tempests and is never shaken;
It is the star to every wand'ring barque,
Whose worth's unknown, although his height be taken.
Love's not time's fool, though rosy lips and cheeks
Within his bending sickle's compass come.   10
Love alters not with his brief hours and weeks,

But bears it out even to the edge of doom.
   If this be error and upon me proved,
   I never writ, nor no man ever loved.

151. 'O thou, my lovely boy, who in thy power'

O thou, my lovely boy, who in thy power
Dost hold time's fickle glass his fickle hour,
Who hast by waning grown, and therein show'st
Thy lovers withering, as thy sweet self grow'st;
If Nature, sovereign mistress over wrack,
As thou goest onwards, still will pluck thee back,
She keeps thee to this purpose, that her skill
May time disgrace, and wretched minutes kill.
Yet fear her, O thou minion of her pleasure;
She may detain, but not still keep her treasure.   10
   Her audit, though delayed, answered must be,
   And her quietus is to render thee.

152. 'Th' expense of spirit in a waste of shame'

Th' expense of spirit in a waste of shame
Is lust in action, and, till action, lust
Is perjured, murderous, bloody, full of blame,
Savage, extreme, rude, cruel, not to trust;
Enjoyed no sooner but despisèd straight;
Past reason hunted, and no sooner had,
Past reason hated as a swallowed bait,
On purpose laid to make the taker mad;
Mad in pursuit, and in possession so,
Had, having, and in quest to have, extreme;   10
A bliss in proof; and proved, a very woe,
Before, a joy proposed; behind, a dream.
   All this the world well knows, yet none knows well,
   To shun the heaven that leads men to this hell.

153. 'My mistress' eyes are nothing like the sun'

My mistress' eyes are nothing like the sun:
Coral is far more red than her lips' red;
If snow be white, why then her breasts are dun;
If hairs be wires, black wires grow on her head.
I have seen roses damasked, red and white,
But no such roses see I in her cheeks,
And in some perfumes is there more delight,
Than in the breath that from my mistress reeks.
I love to hear her speak, yet well I know
That music hath a far more pleasing sound.   10
I grant I never saw a goddess go:
My mistress when she walks treads on the ground.
    And yet by heaven I think my love as rare,
    As any she belied with false compare.

154. 'When my love swears that she is made of truth'

When my love swears that she is made of truth,
I do believe her, though I know she lies,
That she might think me some untutored youth,
Unlearnèd in the world's false subtleties.
Thus vainly thinking that she thinks me young,
Although she knows my days are past the best,
Simply I credit her false-speaking tongue:
On both sides thus is simple truth suppressed:
But wherefore says she not she is unjust?
And wherefore say not I that I am old?   10
O, love's best habit is in seeming trust,
And age, in love, loves not to have years told.
    Therefore I lie with her, and she with me,
    And in our faults by lies we flattered be.

155. 'In faith, I do not love thee with mine eyes'

In faith, I do not love thee with mine eyes,
For they in thee a thousand errors note;
But 'tis my heart that loves what they despise,

Who, in despite of view, is pleased to dote;
Nor are mine ears with thy tongue's tune delighted;
Nor tender feeling, to base touches prone,
Nor taste, nor smell, desire to be invited
To any sensual feast with thee alone:
But my five wits nor my five senses can
Dissuade one foolish heart from serving thee,   10
Who leaves unswayed the likeness of a man,
Thy proud heart's slave and vassal wretch to be:
    Only my plague thus far I count my gain,
    That she that makes me sin awards me pain.

156. 'Two loves I have, of comfort and despair'

Two loves I have, of comfort and despair,
Which like two spirits do suggest me still;
The better angel is a man right fair,
The worser spirit a woman coloured ill.
To win me soon to hell my female evil
Tempteth my better angel from my side,
And would corrupt my saint to be a devil,
Wooing his purity with her foul pride.
And whether that my angel be turned fiend,
Suspect I may, yet not directly tell,   10
But being both from me, both to each friend,
I guess one angel in another's hell.
    Yet this shall I ne'er know, but live in doubt,
    Till my bad angel fire my good one out.

157. 'Poor soul, the centre of my sinful earth'

Poor soul, the centre of my sinful earth,
Rebuke these rebel powers that thee array,
Why dost thou pine within and suffer dearth
Painting thy outward walls so costly gay?
Why so large cost, having so short a lease,
Dost thou upon thy fading mansion spend?
Shall worms, inheritors of this excess,
Eat up thy charge? Is this thy body's end?

Then, soul, live thou upon thy servant's loss,
And let that pine to aggravate thy store;   10
Buy terms divine in selling hours of dross;
Within be fed, without be rich no more,
    So shalt thou feed on death, that feeds on men,
    And death once dead, there's no more dying then.

Isabella Whitney (fl. 1566–1573)

158. from *An Order Prescribed by I.W. to two of her Younger Sisters Serving in London*

… In mornings when you rise,
    forget not to commend   10
Your selves to God, beseeching him
    from dangers to defend.
Your souls and bodies both,
    your parents and your friends,
Your teachers and your governors
    so pray you that your ends
May be in such a sort
    as God may pleasèd be;
To live to die, to die to live,
    with him eternally.   20

Then justly do such deeds
    as are to you assigned.
All wanton toys, good sisters, now
    exile out of your mind.
I hope you give no cause
    whereby I should suspect;
But this I know too many live
    that would you soon infect,
If God do not prevent,
    or with his grace expel;   30

I cannot speak or write too much
    because I love you well.

Your business soon dispatch
    and listen to no lies,
Nor credit every feignèd tale
    that many will devise.
For words they are but wind.
    yet words may hurt you so
As you shall never brook the same
    if that you have a foe.   40
God shield you from all such
    as would by word or bill
Procure your shame or never cease
    till they have wrought you ill.

See that you secrets seal,
    tread trifles under ground;
If to rehearsal oft you come,
    it will your quiet wound.
Of laughter be not much,
    nor over solemn seem,   50
For then be sure they'll compt° you light   *account*
    or proud will you esteem.
Be modest in a mean,
    be gentle unto all,
Though cause they give of contrary
    yet be to wrath no thrall.
Refer you all to him
    that sits above the skies.
Vengeance is his, he will revenge,
    you need it not devise.   60

And sith that virtue guides
    where both of you do dwell,
Give thanks to God, and painful be
    to please your rulers well.
For fleeting is a foe,
    experience hath me taught:
The rolling stone doth get no moss
    yourselves have heard full oft.
Your business being done,
    and this my scroll perused,   70

The day will end, and that the night
    by you be not abused
I some thing needs must write,
    take pains to read the same.
Henceforth my life as well as pen
    shall your examples frame.

Your masters gone to bed,
    your mistresses at rest,
Their daughters all with haste about
    to get themselves undressed.   80
See that their plate be safe
    and that no spoon do lack,
See doors and windows bolted fast
    for fear of any wrack.
Then help if need there be
    to do some household thing.
If not to bed, referring you
    unto the heavenly King.
Forgetting not to pray
    as I before you taught,   90
And giving thanks for all that he
    hath ever for you wrought.
Good sisters, when you pray
    let me remembered be;
So will I you, and thus I cease,
    till I yourselves do see.

159. from *The manner of her Will, and what she left to London: and
    to all those in it: at her departing*

I, whole in body and in mind,
    but very weak in purse,
Do make, and write my testament
    for fear it will be worse.
And first I wholly do commend,
    my soul and body eke:
To God the Father and the Son,
    so long as I can speak.
And after speech: my soul to him,
    and body to the grave,   10

Till time that all shall rise again
    their Judgement for to have.
And then I hope they both shall meet.
    to dwell for aye in joy,
Whereas° I trust to see my Friends   *When*
    released from all annoy.
Thus have you heard touching my soul,
    and body what I mean;
I trust you all will witness bear,
    I have a steadfast brain.   20
And now let me dispose such things
    as I shall leave behind,
That those which shall receive the same
    may know my willing mind.

I first of all to London leave,
    because I there was bred,
Brave buildings rare, of Churches store,
    and Paul's unto the head.
Between the same, fair streets there be
    and people goodly store;   30
Because their keeping craveth cost
    I yet will leave them more.
First for their food, I butchers leave,
    that every day shall kill:
By Thames you shall have brewers store
    and bakers at your will.
And such as orders do observe
    and eat fish thrice a week,
I leave two streets full fraught therewith,
    they need not far to seek.   40
Wattling Street and Canwick Street
    I full of woollen leave:
And linen store in Friday Street,
    if they me not deceive.
And those which are of calling such,
    that costlier they require,
I mercers leave, with silk so rich
    as any would desire.
In Cheap, of them they store shall find,
    and likewise in that street   50
I goldsmiths leave, with jewels such
    as are for ladies meet.

And plate to furnish cupboards with
   full brave there shall you find,
With purl of silver and of gold
   to satisfy your mind;
With hoods, bongraces,° hats or caps   *bonnet-brim sunshades*
   such store are in that street
As if on t'one side you should miss,
   the t'other serves you feat.   60
For nets of every kind of sort
   I leave within the pawn,
French ruffs, high puns, gorgets and sleeves
   of any kind of lawn.
For purse or knives, for comb or glass
   or any needful knack
I by the stocks have left a boy,
   will ask you what you lack.
I hose do leave in Birchin Lane,
   of any kind of size: 70
For women stitched, for men both trunks
   and those of Gascon guise.
Boots, shoes or pantables° good store,   *slippers*
   Saint Martin's hath for you;
In Cornwall, there I leave you beds,
   and all that longs thereto.
For women shall you tailors have,
   by Bow, the chiefest dwell.
In every lane you some shall find
   can do indifferent well.   80
And for the men, few streets or lanes
   but bodymakers° be: *tailors*
And such as make the sweeping cloaks
   with guards beneath the knee.
Artillery at Temple Bar,
   and dags° at Tower Hill: *chunky pistols*
Swords and bucklers of the best
   are nigh the Fleet until.°   *unto*
Now when thy folk are fed and clad
   with such as I have named,   90
For dainty mouths, and stomachs weak
   some junkets must be framed.
Wherefore I pothecaries leave
   with banquettes in their shop:
Physicians also for the sick

diseases for to stop.
Some roisters° still, must bide in thee   *loudmouths*
   and such as cut it out:°   *show-offs*
That with the guiltless quarrel will
   to let their blood about.   100
For them I cunning surgeons leave,
   some plasters to apply,
That ruffians may not still be hanged
   nor quiet persons die.
For salt, oatmeal, candles, soap,
   or what you else do want,
In many places, shops are full:
   I leave you nothing scant.
If they that keep what I you leave
   ask money when they sell it,   110
At Mint there is such store it is
   unpossible to tell° it.   *count*
At Steelyard store of wines there be
   your dulled minds to glad,
And handsome men that must not wed
   except they leave their trade.
They oft shall seek for proper girls,
   and some perhaps shall find
That need compels, or lucre lures
   to satisfy their mind.   120
And near the same, I houses leave
   for people to repair,
To bathe themselves, so to prevent
   infection of the air.
On Saturdays I wish that those
   which all the week do drug:°   *drudge*
Shall thither trudge, to trim them up
   on Sundays to look smug.
If any other thing be lacked
   in thee, I wish them look;   130
For there it is: I little brought
   but no thing from thee took.
Now, for the people in thee left,
   I have done as I may
And that the poor, when I am gone,
   have cause for me to pray.
I will to prisons portions leave
   what though but very small,

Yet that they may remember me
    occasion be it shall.   140
And first the Counter they shall have
    least they should go to wrack,
Some codgers and some honest men,
    that sergeants draw aback.
And such as friends will not them bail,
    whose coin is very thin,
For them I leave a certain hole
    and little ease within.
The Newgate once a month shall have
    a sessions for its share,   150
Lest being heaped, infection might
    procure a further care.
And at those sessions some shall 'scape
    with burning near the thumb,
And afterward to beg their fees
    till they have got the sum.
And such whose deeds deserveth death
    and twelve have found the same,
They shall be drawn up Hothorn Hill
    to come to further shame.   160
Well, yet to such I leave a nag
    shall soon their sorrows cease,
For he shall either break their necks
    or gallop from the preace.°   *press (crowd)*
The Fleet not in their circuit is,
    yet if I give him naught
It might procure his curse, ere I
    unto the ground be brought...

Thomas Nashe (1567–1601)

160. Spring

Spring, the sweet Spring, is the year's pleasant king,
Then blooms each thing, then maids dance in a ring,

Cold doth not sting, the pretty birds do sing,
   Cuckoo, jug-jug, pu-we, to-witta-woo!

The palm and may make country houses gay,
Lambs frisk and play, the shepherds pipe all day,
And we hear aye birds tune this merry lay,
   Cuckoo, jug-jug, pu-we, to-witta-woo!

The fields breathe sweet, the daisies kiss our feet,
Young lovers meet, old wives a-sunning sit,   10
In every street these tunes our ears do greet,
   Cuckoo, jug-jug, pu-we, to-witta-woo!
      Spring! the sweet Spring!

161. 'Adieu, farewell earth's bliss'

Adieu, farewell earth's bliss,
This world uncertain is.
Fond are life's lustful joys,
Death proves them all but toys.
None from his darts can fly.
I am sick, I must die.
Lord, have mercy on us!

Rich men, trust not in wealth,
Gold cannot buy you health;
Physic himself must fade;   10
All things to end are made.
The plague full swift goes by.
I am sick, I must die.
Lord, have mercy on us!

Beauty is but a flower
Which wrinkles will devour;
Brightness falls from the air,
Queens have died young and fair,
Dust hath closed Helen's eye.
I am sick, I must die.   20
Lord, have mercy on us!

Strength stoops unto the grave,
Worms feed on Hector brave,
Swords may not fight with fate,
Earth still holds ope her gate.
Come, come, the bells do cry.
I am sick, I must die.
Lord, have mercy on us!

Wit with his wantonness
Tasteth death's bitterness.   30
Hell's executioner
Hath no ears for to hear
What vain art can reply:
I am sick, I must die.
Lord, have mercy on us!

Haste, therefore, each degree
To welcome destiny.
Heaven is our heritage,
Earth but a player's stage.
Mount we unto the sky.   40
I am sick, I must die.
Lord, have mercy on us!

The Authorised Version of the Bible (1611)

162. Genesis 1

1 In the beginning God created the heaven and the earth.
2 And the earth was without form, and void; and darkness was upon the
face of the deep. And the Spirit of God moved upon the face of the
waters.
3 And God said, Let there be light: and there was light.
4 And God saw the light, that it was good: and God divided the light
from the darkness.
5 And God called the light Day, and the darkness he called Night. And

the evening and the morning were the first day.

6 And God said, Let there be a firmament in the midst of the waters, and let it divide the waters from the waters.

7. And God made the firmament, and divided the waters which were under the firmament from the waters which were above the firmament: and it was so.

8 And God called the firmament Heaven. And there was evening and there was morning, second day.

9 And God said, Let the waters under the heaven be gathered together unto one place, and let the dry land appear: and it was so.

10 And God called the dry land Earth; and the gathering together of the waters called he Seas: and God saw that it was good.

11 And God said, Let the earth bring forth grass, the herb yielding seed, and the fruit tree yielding fruit after his kind, whose seed is in itself; upon the earth: and it was so.

12 And the earth brought forth grass, and herb yielding seed after his kind, and the tree yielding fruit, whose seed was in itself, after his kind: and God saw that it was good.

13 And the evening and the morning were the third day.

14 And God said, Let there be lights in the firmament of the heaven to divide the day from the night; and let them be for signs, and for seasons, and for days, and years:

15 And let them be for lights in the firmament of the heaven to give light upon the earth: and it was so.

16 And God made two great lights; the greater light to rule the day, and the lesser light to rule the night: he made the stars also.

17 And God set them in the firmament of the heaven to give light upon the earth,

18 And to rule over the day and over the night, and to divide the light from the darkness: and God saw that it was good.

19 And the evening and the morning were the fourth day.

20 And God said, Let the waters bring forth abundantly the moving creature that hath life, and fowl that may fly above the earth in the open firmament of heaven.

21 And God created great whales, and every living creature that moveth, which the waters brought forth abundantly, after their kind, and every winged fowl after his kind: and God saw that it was good.

22 And God blessed them, saying, Be fruitful, and multiply, and fill the waters in the seas, and let fowl multiply in the earth.

23 And the evening and the morning were the fifth day.

24 And God said, Let the earth bring forth the living creature after his kind, cattle, and creeping thing, and beast of the earth after his kind: and it was so.

25 And God made the beast of the earth after his kind, and cattle after their kind, and every thing that creepeth upon the earth after his kind: and God saw that it was good.

26 And God said, Let us make man in our image, after our likeness: and let them have dominion over the fish of the sea, and over the fowl of the air, and over the cattle, and over all the earth, and over every creeping thing that creepeth upon the earth.

27 So God created man in his own image, in the image of God created he him; male and female created he them.

28 And God blessed them, and God said unto them, Be fruitful, and multiply, and replenish the earth, and subdue it: and have dominion over the fish of the sea, and over the fowl of the air, and over every living thing that moveth upon the earth.

29 And God said, Behold, I have given you every herb bearing seed, which is upon the face of all the earth, and every tree, in the which is the fruit of a tree yielding seed; to you it shall be for meat.

30 And to every beast of the earth, and to every fowl of the air, and to every thing that creepeth upon the earth, wherein there is life, I have given every green herb for meat: and it was so.

31 And God saw every thing that he had made, and, behold, it was very good. And the evening and the morning were the sixth day.

163. Genesis 2

1 Thus the heavens and the earth were finished, and all the host of them.

2 And on the seventh day God ended his work which he had made; and he rested on the seventh day from all his work which he had made.

3 And God blessed the seventh day, and sanctified it: because that in it he had rested from all his work which God created and made.

4 These are the generations of the heavens and of the earth when they were created, in the day that the Lord God made the earth and the heavens,

5 And every plant of the field before it was in the earth, and every herb of the field before it grew: for the Lord God had not caused it to rain upon the earth, and there was not a man to till the ground.

6 But there went up a mist from the earth, and watered the whole face of the ground.

7 And the Lord God formed man of the dust of the ground, and breathed into his nostrils the breath of life; and man became a living soul.

8 And the Lord God planted a garden eastward in Eden; and there he put the man whom he had formed.

9 And out of the ground made the Lord God to grow every tree that is pleasant to the sight, and good for food; the tree of life also in the midst of the garden, and the tree of knowledge of good and evil.

10 And a river went out of Eden to water the garden; and from thence it was parted, and became into four heads.

11 The name of the first is Pison: that is it which compasseth the whole land of Havilah, where there is gold;

12 And the gold of that land is good: there is bdellium and the onyx stone.

13 And the name of the second river is Gihon: the same is it that compasseth the whole land of Ethiopia.

14 And the name of the third river is Hiddekel: that is it which goeth toward the east of Assyria. And the fourth river is Euphrates.

15 And the Lord God took the man, and put him into the garden of Eden to dress it and to keep it.

16 And the Lord God commanded the man, saying, Of every tree of the garden thou mayest freely eat:

17 But of the tree of the knowledge of good and evil, thou shalt not eat of it: for in the day that thou eatest thereof thou shalt surely die.

18 And the Lord God said, It is not good that the man should be alone; I will make him an help meet for him.

19 And out of the ground the Lord God formed every beast of the field, and every fowl of the air; and brought them unto Adam to see what he would call them: and whatsoever Adam called every living creature, that was the name thereof.

20 And Adam gave names to all cattle, and to the fowl of the air, and to every beast of the field; but for Adam there was not found an help meet for him.

21 And the Lord God caused a deep sleep to fall upon Adam, and he slept: and he took one of his ribs, and closed up the flesh instead thereof;

22 And the rib, which the Lord God had taken from man, made he a woman, and brought her unto the man.

23 And Adam said, This is now bone of my bones, and flesh of my flesh: she shall be called Woman, because she was taken out of Man.

24 Therefore shall a man leave his father and his mother, and shall cleave unto his wife: and they shall be one flesh.

25 And they were both naked, the man and his wife, and were not ashamed.

164. Genesis 3

1 Now the serpent was more subtle than any beast of the field which the Lord God had made. And he said unto the woman, Yea, hath God said,

Ye shall not eat of every tree of the garden?

2 And the woman said unto the serpent, We may eat of the fruit of the trees of the garden:

3 But of the fruit of the tree which is in the midst of the garden, God hath said, Ye shall not eat of it, neither shall ye touch it, lest ye die.

4 And the serpent said unto the woman, Ye shall not surely die:

5 For God doth know that in the day ye eat thereof, then your eyes shall be opened, and ye shall be as gods, knowing good and evil.

6 And when the woman saw that the tree was good for food, and that it was pleasant to the eyes, and a tree to be desired to make one wise, she took of the fruit thereof, and did eat, and gave also unto her husband with her; and he did eat.

7 And the eyes of them both were opened, and they knew that they were naked; and they sewed fig leaves together, and made themselves aprons.

8 And they heard the voice of the Lord God walking in the garden in the cool of the day: and Adam and his wife hid themselves from the presence of the Lord God amongst the trees of the garden.

9 And the Lord God called unto Adam, and said unto him, Where art thou?

10 And he said, I heard thy voice in the garden, and I was afraid, because I was naked; and I hid myself.

11 And he said, Who told thee that thou wast naked? Hast thou eaten of the tree, whereof I commanded thee that thou shouldest not eat?

12 And the man said, The woman whom thou gavest to be with me, she gave me of the tree, and I did eat.

13 And the Lord God said unto the woman, What is this that thou hast done? And the woman said, The serpent beguiled me, and I did eat.

14 And the Lord God said unto the serpent, Because thou hast done this, thou art cursed above all cattle, and above every beast of the field; upon thy belly shalt thou go, and dust shalt thou eat all the days of thy life:

15 And I will put enmity between thee and the woman, and between thy seed and her seed; it shall bruise thy head, and thou shalt bruise his heel.

16 Unto the woman he said, I will greatly multiply thy sorrow and thy conception; in sorrow thou shalt bring forth children; and thy desire shall be to thy husband, and he shall rule over thee.

17 And unto Adam he said, Because thou hast hearkened unto the voice of thy wife, and hast eaten of the tree, of which I commanded thee, saying, Thou shalt not eat of it: cursed is the ground for thy sake; in sorrow shalt thou eat of it all the days of thy life;

18 Thorns also and thistles shall it bring forth to thee; and thou shalt eat the herb of the field;

19 In the sweat of thy face shalt thou eat bread, till thou return unto the ground; for out of it wast thou taken: for dust thou art, and unto dust shalt thou return.

20 And Adam called his wife's name Eve; because she was the mother of all living.

21 Unto Adam also and to his wife did the Lord God make coats of skins, and clothed them.

22 And the Lord God said, Behold, the man is become as one of us, to know good and evil: and now, lest he put forth his hand, and take also of the tree of life, and eat, and live for ever:

23 Therefore the Lord God sent him forth from the garden of Eden, to till the ground from whence he was taken.

24 So he drove out the man; and he placed at the east of the garden of Eden Cherubims, and a flaming sword which turned every way, to keep the way of the tree of life.

165. Exodus 15

1 Then sang Moses and the children of Israel this song unto the Lord, and spake, saying, I will sing unto the Lord, for he hath triumphed gloriously: the horse and his rider hath he thrown into the sea.

2 The Lord is my strength and song, and he is become my salvation: he is my God, and I will prepare him an habitation; my father's God, and I will exalt him.

3 The Lord is a man of war: the Lord is his name.

4 Pharaoh's chariots and his host hath he cast into the sea: his chosen captains also are drowned in the Red sea.

5 The depths have covered them: they sank into the bottom as a stone.

6 Thy right hand, O Lord, is become glorious in power: thy right hand, O Lord, hath dashed in pieces the enemy.

7 And in the greatness of thine excellency thou hast overthrown them that rose up against thee: thou sentest forth thy wrath, which consumed them as stubble.

8 And with the blast of thy nostrils the waters were gathered together, the floods stood upright as an heap, and the depths were congealed in the heart of the sea.

9 The enemy said, I will pursue, I will overtake, I will divide the spoil; my lust shall be satisfied upon them; I will draw my sword, my hand shall destroy them.

10 Thou didst blow with thy wind, the sea covered them: they sank as lead in the mighty waters.

11 Who is like unto thee, O Lord, among the gods? who is like thee, glorious in holiness, fearful in praises, doing wonders?

12 Thou stretchedst out thy right hand, the earth swallowed them.

13 Thou in thy mercy hast led forth the people which thou hast redeemed: thou hast guided them in thy strength unto thy holy habitation.

14 The people shall hear, and be afraid: sorrow shall take hold on the inhabitants of Palestina.

15 Then the dukes of Edom shall be amazed; the mighty men of Moab, trembling shall take hold upon them; all the inhabitants of Canaan shall melt away.

16 Fear and dread shall fall upon them; by the greatness of thine arm they shall be as still as a stone; till thy people pass over, O Lord, till the people pass over, which thou hast purchased.

17 Thou shalt bring them in, and plant them in the mountain of thine inheritance, in the place, O Lord, which thou hast made for thee to dwell in, in the Sanctuary, O Lord, which thy hands have established.

18 The Lord shall reign for ever and ever.

19 For the horse of Pharaoh went in with his chariots and with his horsemen into the sea, and the Lord brought again the waters of the sea upon them; but the children of Israel went on dry land in the midst of the sea.

20 And Miriam the prophetess, the sister of Aaron, took a timbrel in her hand; and all the women went out after her with timbrels and with dances.

21 And Miriam answered them, Sing ye to the Lord, for he hath triumphed gloriously; the horse and his rider hath he thrown into the sea.

22 So Moses brought Israel from the Red sea, and they went out into the wilderness of Shur; and they went three days in the wilderness, and found no water.

23 And when they came to Marah, they could not drink of the waters of Marah, for they were bitter: therefore the name of it was called Marah.

24 And the people murmured against Moses, saying, What shall we drink?

25 And he cried unto the Lord; and the Lord shewed him a tree, which when he had cast into the waters, the waters were made sweet: there he made for them a statute and an ordinance, and there he proved them,

26 And said, If thou wilt diligently hearken to the voice of the Lord thy God, and wilt do that which is right in his sight, and wilt give ear to his commandments, and keep all his statutes, I will put none of these diseases upon thee, which I have brought upon the Egyptians: for I am the Lord that healeth thee.

27 And they came to Elim, where were twelve wells of water, and threescore and ten palm trees: and they encamped there by the waters.

166. Deuteronomy 32

1 Give ear, O ye heavens, and I will speak; and hear, O earth, the words of my mouth.

2 My doctrine shall drop as the rain, my speech shall distil as the dew, as the small rain upon the tender herb, and as the showers upon the grass:

3 Because I will publish the name of the Lord: ascribe ye greatness unto our God.

4 He is the Rock, his work is perfect: for all his ways are judgement: a God of truth and without iniquity, just and right is he.

5 They have corrupted themselves, their spot is not the spot of his children: they are a perverse and crooked generation.

6 Do ye thus requite the Lord, O foolish people and unwise? is not he thy father that hath bought thee? hath he not made thee, and established thee?

7 Remember the days of old, consider the years of many generations: ask thy father, and he will shew thee; thy elders, and they will tell thee.

8 When the Most High divided to the nations their inheritance, when he separated the sons of Adam, he set the bounds of the people according to the number of the children of Israel.

9 For the Lord's portion is his people; Jacob is the lot of his inheritance.

10 He found him in a desert land, and in the waste howling wilderness; he led him about, he instructed him, he kept him as the apple of his eye.

11 As an eagle stirreth up her nest, fluttereth over her young, spreadeth abroad her wings, taketh them, beareth them on her wings:

12 So the Lord alone did lead him, and there was no strange god with him.

13 He made him ride on the high places of the earth, that he might eat the increase of the fields; and he made him to suck honey out of the rock, and oil out of the flinty rock;

14 Butter of kine, and milk of sheep, with fat of lambs, and rams of the breed of Bashan, and goats, with the fat of kidneys of wheat; and thou didst drink the pure blood of the grape.

15 But Jeshurun waxed fat, and kicked: thou art waxen fat, thou art grown thick, thou art covered with fatness; then he forsook God which made him, and lightly esteemed the Rock of his salvation.

16 They provoked him to jealousy with strange gods, with abominations provoked they him to anger.

17 They sacrificed unto devils, not to God; to gods whom they knew not, to new gods that came newly up, whom your fathers feared not.

18 Of the Rock that begat thee thou art unmindful, and hast forgotten God that formed thee.

19 And when the Lord saw it, he abhorred them, because of the provoking of his sons, and of his daughters.

20 And he said, I will hide my face from them, I will see what their end
shall be: for they are a very froward generation, children in whom is no
faith.

21 They have moved me to jealousy with that which is not God; they
have provoked me to anger with their vanities: and I will move them to
jealousy with those which are not a people; I will provoke them to anger
with a foolish nation.

22 For a fire is kindled in mine anger, and shall burn unto the lowest hell,
and shall consume the earth with her increase, and set on fire the
foundations of the mountains.

23 I will heap mischiefs upon them; I will spend mine arrows upon them.

24 They shall be burnt with hunger, and devoured with burning heat,
and with bitter destruction: I will also send the teeth of beasts upon them,
with the poison of serpents of the dust.

25 The sword without, and terror within, shall destroy both the young
man and the virgin, the suckling also with the man of grey hairs.

26 I said, I would scatter them into corners, I would make the
remembrance of them to cease from among men:

27 Were it not that I feared the wrath of the enemy, lest their adversaries
should behave themselves strangely, and lest they should say, Our hand is
high, and the Lord hath not done all this.

28 For they are a nation void of counsel, neither is there any
understanding in them.

29 O that they were wise, that they understood this, that they would
consider their latter end!

30 How should one chase a thousand, and two put ten thousand to
flight, except their Rock had sold them, and the Lord had shut them up?

31 For their rock is not as our Rock, even our enemies themselves being
judges.

32 For their vine is of the vine of Sodom, and of the fields of Gomorrah:
their grapes are grapes of gall, their clusters are bitter:

33 Their wine is the poison of dragons, and the cruel venom of asps.

34 Is not this laid up in store with me, and sealed up among my
treasures?

35 To me belongeth vengeance and recompense; their foot shall slide in
due time: for the day of their calamity is at hand, and the things that shall
come upon them make haste.

36 For the Lord shall judge his people, and repent himself for his
servants, when he seeth that their power is gone, and there is none shut
up, or left.

37 And he shall say, Where are their gods, their rock in whom they
trusted,

38 Which did eat the fat of their sacrifices, and drank the wine of their

drink offerings? let them rise up and help you, and be your protection.

39 See now that I, even I, am he, and there is no god with me: I kill, and I make alive; I wound, and I heal: neither is there any that can deliver out of my hand.

40 For I lift up my hand to heaven, and say, I live for ever.

41 If I whet my glittering sword, and mine hand take hold on judgement; I will render vengeance to mine enemies, and will reward them that hate me.

42 I will make mine arrows drunk with blood, and my sword shall devour flesh; and that with the blood of the slain and of the captives, from the beginning of revenges upon the enemy.

43 Rejoice, O ye nations, with his people: for he will avenge the blood of his servants, and will render vengeance to his adversaries, and will be merciful unto his land, and to his people.

44 And Moses came and spake all the words of this song in the ears of the people, he, and Hoshea the son of Nun.

45 And Moses made an end of speaking all these words to all Israel:

46 And he said unto them, Set your hearts unto all the words which I testify among you this day, which ye shall command your children to observe to do, all the words of this law.

47 For it is not a vain thing for you; because it is your life: and through this thing ye shall prolong your days in the land, whither ye go over Jordan to possess it.

48 And the Lord spake unto Moses that selfsame day, saying,

49 Get thee up into this mountain Abarim, unto mount Nebo, which is in the land of Moab, that is over against Jericho; and behold the land of Canaan, which I give unto the children of Israel for a possession:

50 And die in the mount whither thou goest up, and be gathered unto thy people; as Aaron thy brother died in mount Hor, and was gathered unto his people:

51 Because ye trespassed against me among the children of Israel at the waters of MeribahKadesh, in the wilderness of Zin; because ye sanctified me not in the midst of the children of Israel.

52 Yet thou shalt see the land before thee; but thou shalt not go thither unto the land which I give the children of Israel.

167. 2 Samuel 22

1 And David spake unto the Lord the words of this song in the day that the Lord had delivered him out of the hand of all his enemies, and out of the hand of Saul:

2 And he said, The Lord is my rock, and my fortress, and my deliverer;

3 The God of my rock; in him will I trust: he is my shield, and the horn of my salvation, my high tower, and my refuge, my saviour; thou savest me from violence.

4 I will call on the Lord, who is worthy to be praised: so shall I be saved from mine enemies.

5 When the waves of death compassed me, the floods of ungodly men made me afraid;

6 The sorrows of hell compassed me about; the snares of death prevented me;

7 In my distress I called upon the Lord, and cried to my God: and he did hear my voice out of his temple, and my cry did enter into his ears.

8 Then the earth shook and trembled; the foundations of heaven moved and shook, because he was wroth.

9 There went up a smoke out of his nostrils, and fire out of his mouth devoured: coals were kindled by it.

10 He bowed the heavens also, and came down; and darkness was under his feet.

11 And he rode upon a cherub, and did fly: and he was seen upon the wings of the wind.

12 And he made darkness pavilions round about him, dark waters, and thick clouds of the skies.

13 Through the brightness before him were coals of fire kindled.

14 The Lord thundered from heaven, and the most High uttered his voice.

15 And he sent out arrows, and scattered them; lightning, and discomfited them.

16 And the channels of the sea appeared, the foundations of the world were discovered, at the rebuking of the Lord, at the blast of the breath of his nostrils.

17 He sent from above, he took me; he drew me out of many waters;

18 He delivered me from my strong enemy, and from them that hated me: for they were too strong for me.

19 They prevented me in the day of my calamity: but the Lord was my stay.

20 He brought me forth also into a large place: he delivered me, because he delighted in me.

21 The Lord rewarded me according to my righteousness: according to the cleanness of my hands hath he recompensed me.

22 For I have kept the ways of the Lord, and have not wickedly departed from my God.

23 For all his judgements were before me: and as for his statutes, I did not depart from them.

24 I was also upright before him, and have kept myself from mine iniquity.

25 Therefore the Lord hath recompensed me according to my righteousness; according to my cleanness in his eye sight.

26 With the merciful thou wilt shew thyself merciful, and with the upright man thou wilt shew thyself upright.

27 With the pure thou wilt shew thyself pure; and with the froward thou wilt shew thyself unsavoury

28 And the afflicted people thou wilt save: but thine eyes are upon the haughty, that thou mayest bring them down.

29 For thou art my lamp, O Lord: and the Lord will lighten my darkness.

30 For by thee I have run through a troop: by my God have I leaped over a wall.

31 As for God, his way is perfect; the word of the Lord is tried: he is a buckler to all them that trust in him.

32 For who is God, save the Lord? and who is a rock, save our God?

33 God is my strength and power: and he maketh my way perfect.

34 He maketh my feet like hinds' feet: and setteth me upon my high places.

35 He teacheth my hands to war; so that a bow of steel is broken by mine arms.

36 Thou hast also given me the shield of thy salvation: and thy gentleness hath made me great.

37 Thou hast enlarged my steps under me; so that my feet did not slip.

38 I have pursued mine enemies, and destroyed them; and turned not again until I had consumed them.

39 And I have consumed them, and wounded them, that they could not arise: yea, they are fallen under my feet.

40 For thou hast girded me with strength to battle: them that rose up against me hast thou subdued under me.

41 Thou hast also given me the necks of mine enemies, that I might destroy them that hate me.

42 They looked, but there was none to save; even unto the Lord, but he answered them not.

43 Then did I beat them as small as the dust of the earth, I did stamp them as the mire of the street, and did spread them abroad.

44 Thou also hast delivered me from the strivings of my people, thou hast kept me to be head of the heathen: a people which I knew not shall serve me.

45 Strangers shall submit themselves unto me: as soon as they hear, they shall be obedient unto me.

46 Strangers shall fade away, and they shall be afraid out of their close places.

47 The Lord liveth; and blessed be my rock; and exalted be the God of the rock of my salvation.

48 It is God that avengeth me, and that bringeth down the people under me.

49 And that bringeth me forth from mine enemies: thou also hast lifted me up on high above them that rose up against me: thou hast delivered me from the violent man.

50 Therefore I will give thanks unto thee, O Lord, among the heathen, and I will sing praises unto thy name.

51 He is the tower of salvation for his king: and sheweth mercy to his anointed, unto David, and to his seed for evermore.

168. Ecclesiastes 12

1 Remember now thy Creator in the days of thy youth, while the evil days come not, nor the years draw nigh, when thou shalt say, I have no pleasure in them;

2 While the sun, or the light, or the moon, or the stars, be not darkened, nor the clouds return after the rain:

3 In the day when the keepers of the house shall tremble, and the strong men shall bow themselves, and the grinders cease because they are few, and those that look out of the windows be darkened,

4 And the doors shall be shut in the streets, when the sound of the grinding is low, and he shall rise up at the voice of the bird, and all the daughters of music shall be brought low;

5 Also when they shall be afraid of that which is high, and fears shall be in the way, and the almond tree shall flourish, and the grasshopper shall be a burden, and desire shall fail: because man goeth to his long home, and the mourners go about the streets:

6 Or ever the silver cord be loosed, or the golden bowl be broken, or the pitcher be broken at the fountain, or the wheel broken at the cistern.

7 Then shall the dust return to the earth as it was: and the spirit shall return unto God who gave it.

8 Vanity of vanities, saith the preacher; all is vanity.

9 And moreover, because the preacher was wise, he still taught the people knowledge; yea, he gave good heed, and sought out, and set in order many proverbs.

10 The preacher sought to find out acceptable words: and that which was written was upright, even words of truth.

11 The words of the wise are as goads, and as nails fastened by the masters of assemblies, which are given from one shepherd.

12 And further, by these, my son, be admonished: of making many books there is no end; and much study is a weariness of the flesh.

13 Let us hear the conclusion of the whole matter: Fear God, and keep his commandments: for this is the whole duty of man.

14 For God shall bring every work into judgement, with every secret thing, whether it be good, or whether it be evil.

169. Song of Songs 1

1 The song of songs, which is Solomon's.

2 Let him kiss me with the kisses of his mouth: for thy love is better than wine.

3 Because of the savour of thy good ointments thy name is as ointment poured forth, therefore do the virgins love thee.

4 Draw me, we will run after thee: the king hath brought me into his chambers: we will be glad and rejoice in thee, we will remember thy love more than wine: the upright love thee.

5 I am black, but comely, O ye daughters of Jerusalem, as the tents of Kedar, as the curtains of Solomon.

6 Look not upon me, because I am black, because the sun hath looked upon me: my mother's children were angry with me; they made me the keeper of the vineyards; but mine own vineyard have I not kept.

7 Tell me, O thou whom my soul loveth, where thou feedest, where thou makest thy flock to rest at noon: for why should I be as one that turneth aside by the flocks of thy companions?

8 If thou know not, O thou fairest among women, go thy way forth by the footsteps of the flock, and feed thy kids beside the shepherds' tents.

9 I have compared thee, O my love, to a company of horses in Pharaoh's chariots.

10 Thy cheeks are comely with rows of jewels, thy neck with chains of gold.

11 We will make thee borders of gold with studs of silver.

12 While the king sitteth at his table, my spikenard sendeth forth the smell thereof.

13 A bundle of myrrh is my well-beloved unto me; he shall lie all night betwixt my breasts.

14 My beloved is unto me as a cluster of camphire in the vineyards of Engedi.

15 Behold, thou art fair, my love; behold, thou art fair; thou hast doves' eyes.

16 Behold, thou art fair, my beloved, yea, pleasant: also our bed is green.

17 The beams of our house are cedar, and our rafters of fir.

170. Isaiah 6

1 In the year that king Uzziah died I saw also the Lord sitting upon a throne, high and lifted up, and his train filled the temple.

2 Above it stood the seraphims: each one had six wings; with twain he covered his face, and with twain he covered his feet, and with twain he did fly.

3 And one cried unto another, and said, Holy, holy, holy, is the Lord of hosts: the whole earth is full of his glory.

4 And the posts of the door moved at the voice of him that cried, and the house was filled with smoke.

5 Then said I, Woe is me! for I am undone; because I am a man of unclean lips, and I dwell in the midst of a people of unclean lips: for mine eyes have seen the King, the Lord of hosts.

6 Then flew one of the seraphims unto me, having a live coal in his hand, which he had taken with the tongs from off the altar:

7 And he laid it upon my mouth, and said, Lo, this hath touched thy lips; and thine iniquity is taken away, and thy sin purged.

8 Also I heard the voice of the Lord, saying, Whom shall I send, and who will go for us? Then said I, Here am I; send me.

9 And he said, Go, and tell this people, Hear ye indeed, but understand not; and see ye indeed, but perceive not.

10 Make the heart of this people fat, and make their ears heavy, and shut their eyes; lest they see with their eyes, and hear with their ears, and understand with their heart, and convert, and be healed.

11 Then said I, Lord, how long? And he answered, Until the cities be wasted without inhabitant, and the houses without man, and the land be utterly desolate,

12 And the Lord have removed men far away, and there be a great forsaking in the midst of the land.

13 But yet in it shall be a tenth, and it shall return, and shall be eaten: as a teil tree, and as an oak, whose substance is in them, when they cast their leaves: so the holy seed shall be the substance thereof.

171. Jeremiah 5

1 Run ye to and fro through the streets of Jerusalem, and see now, and know, and seek in the broad places thereof; if ye can find a man, if there be any that executeth judgement, that seeketh the truth; and I will pardon it.

2 And though they say, The Lord liveth; surely they swear falsely.

3 O Lord, are not thine eyes upon the truth? thou hast stricken them, but they have not grieved; thou hast consumed them, but they have refused to receive correction: they have made their faces harder than a rock; they have refused to return.

4 Therefore I said, Surely these are poor; they are foolish: for they know not the way of the Lord, nor the judgement of their God.

5 I will get me unto the great men, and will speak unto them; for they have known the way of the Lord, and the judgement of their God: but these have altogether broken the yoke, and burst the bonds.

6 Wherefore a lion out of the forest shall slay them, and a wolf of the evenings shall spoil them, a leopard shall watch over their cities: every one that goeth out thence shall be torn in pieces: because their transgressions are many, and their backslidings are increased.

7 How shall I pardon thee for this? thy children have forsaken me, and sworn by them that are no gods: when I had fed them to the full, they then committed adultery, and assembled themselves by troops in the harlots' houses.

8 They were as fed horses in the morning: every one neighed after his neighbour's wife.

9 Shall I not visit for these things? saith the Lord: and shall not my soul be avenged on such a nation as this?

10 Go ye up upon her walls, and destroy; but make not a full end: take away her battlements; for they are not the Lord's.

11 For the house of Israel and the house of Judah have dealt very treacherously against me, saith the Lord.

12 They have belied the Lord, and said, It is not he; neither shall evil come upon us; neither shall we see sword nor famine:

13 And the prophets shall become wind, and the word is not in them: thus shall it be done unto them.

14 Wherefore thus saith the Lord God of hosts, Because ye speak this word, behold, I will make my words in thy mouth fire, and this people wood, and it shall devour them.

15 Lo, I will bring a nation upon you from far, O house of Israel, saith the Lord: it is a mighty nation, it is an ancient nation, a nation whose language thou knowest not, neither understandest what they say.

16 Their quiver is as an open sepulchre, they are all mighty men.

17 And they shall eat up thine harvest, and thy bread, which thy sons and thy daughters should eat: they shall eat up thy flocks and thine herds: they shall eat up thy vines and thy fig trees: they shall impoverish thy fenced cities, wherein thou trustedst, with the sword.

18 Nevertheless in those days, saith the Lord, I will not make a full end with you.

19 And it shall come to pass, when ye shall say, Wherefore doeth the

Lord our God all these things unto us? then shalt thou answer them, Like as ye have forsaken me, and served strange gods in your land, so shall ye serve strangers in a land that is not yours.

20 Declare this in the house of Jacob, and publish it in Judah, saying,

21 Hear now this, O foolish people, and without understanding; which have eyes, and see not; which have ears, and hear not:

22 Fear ye not me? saith the Lord: will ye not tremble at my presence, which have placed the sand for the bound of the sea by a perpetual decree, that it cannot pass it: and though the waves thereof toss themselves, yet can they not prevail; though they roar, yet can they not pass over it?

23 But this people hath a revolting and a rebellious heart; they are revolted and gone.

24 Neither say they in their heart, Let us now fear the Lord our God, that giveth rain, both the former and the latter, in his season: he reserveth unto us the appointed weeks of the harvest.

25 Your iniquities have turned away these things, and your sins have withholden good things from you.

26 For among my people are found wicked men: they lay wait, as he that setteth snares; they set a trap, they catch men.

27 As a cage is full of birds, so are their houses full of deceit: therefore they are become great, and waxen rich.

28 They are waxen fat, they shine: yea, they overpass the deeds of the wicked: they judge not the cause, the cause of the fatherless, yet they prosper; and the right of the needy do they not judge.

29 Shall I not visit for these things? saith the Lord: shall not my soul be avenged on such a nation as this?

30 A wonderful and horrible thing is committed in the land;

31 The prophets prophesy falsely, and the priests bear rule by their means; and my people love to have it so: and what will ye do in the end thereof?

172. from Luke 1

1 Forasmuch as many have taken in hand to set forth in order a declaration of those things which are most surely believed among us,

2 Even as they delivered them unto us, which from the beginning were eyewitnesses, and ministers of the word;

3 It seemed good to me also, having had perfect understanding of all things from the very first, to write unto thee in order, most excellent Theophilus,

4 That thou mightest know the certainty of those things, wherein thou hast been instructed.

5 THERE was in the days of Herod, the king of Judaea, a certain priest named Zacharias, of the course of Abia: and his wife was of the daughters of Aaron, and her name was Elisabeth.

6 And they were both righteous before God, walking in all the commandments and ordinances of the Lord blameless.

7 And they had no child, because that Elisabeth was barren, and they both were now well stricken in years.

8 And it came to pass, that while he executed the priest's office before God in the order of his course,

9 According to the custom of the priest's office, his lot was to burn incense when he went into the temple of the Lord.

10 And the whole multitude of the people were praying without at the time of incense.

11 And there appeared unto him an angel of the Lord standing on the right side of the altar of incense.

12 And when Zacharias saw him, he was troubled, and fear fell upon him.

13 But the angel said unto him, Fear not, Zacharias: for thy prayer is heard; and thy wife Elisabeth shall bear thee a son, and thou shalt call his name John.

14 And thou shalt have joy and gladness; and many shall rejoice at his birth.

15 For he shall be great in the sight of the Lord, and shall drink neither wine nor strong drink; and he shall be filled with the Holy Ghost, even from his mother's womb.

16 And many of the children of Israel shall he turn to the Lord their God.

17 And he shall go before him in the spirit and power of Elias, to turn the hearts of the fathers to the children, and the disobedient to the wisdom of the just; to make ready a people prepared for the Lord.

18 And Zacharias said unto the angel, Whereby shall I know this? for I am an old man, and my wife well stricken in years.

19 And the angel answering said unto him, I am Gabriel, that stand in the presence of God; and am sent to speak unto thee, and to shew thee these glad tidings.

20 And, behold, thou shalt be dumb, and not able to speak, until the day that these things shall be performed, because thou believest not my words, which shall be fulfilled in their season.

21 And the people waited for Zacharias, and marvelled that he tarried so long in the temple.

22 And when he came out, he could not speak unto them: and they perceived that he had seen a vision in the temple: for he beckoned unto them, and remained speechless.

23 And it came to pass, that, as soon as the days of his ministration were accomplished, he departed to his own house.

24 And after those days his wife Elisabeth conceived, and hid herself five months, saying,

25 Thus hath the Lord dealt with me in the days wherein he looked on me, to take away my reproach among men.

26 And in the sixth month the angel Gabriel was sent from God unto a city of Galilee, named Nazareth,

27 To a virgin espoused to a man whose name was Joseph, of the house of David; and the virgin's name was Mary.

28 And the angel came in unto her, and said, Hail, thou that art highly favoured, the Lord is with thee: blessed art thou among women.

29 And when she saw him, she was troubled at his saying, and cast in her mind what manner of salutation this should be.

30 And the angel said unto her, Fear not, Mary: for thou hast found favour with God.

31 And, behold, thou shalt conceive in thy womb, and bring forth a son, and shalt call his name Jesus.

32 He shall be great, and shall be called the Son of the Highest: and the Lord God shall give unto him the throne of his father David:

33 And he shall reign over the house of Jacob for ever; and of his kingdom there shall be no end.

34 Then said Mary unto the angel, How shall this be, seeing I know not a man?

35 And the angel answered and said unto her, The Holy Ghost shall come upon thee, and the power of the Highest shall overshadow thee: therefore also that holy thing which shall be born of thee shall be called the Son of God.

36 And, behold, thy cousin Elisabeth, she hath also conceived a son in her old age: and this is the sixth month with her, who was called barren.

37 For with God nothing shall be impossible.

38 And Mary said, Behold the handmaid of the Lord; be it unto me according to thy word. And the angel departed from her.

39 And Mary arose in those days, and went into the hill country with haste, into a city of Juda;

40 And entered into the house of Zacharias, and saluted Elisabeth.

41 And it came to pass, that, when Elisabeth heard the salutation of Mary, the babe leaped in her womb; and Elisabeth was filled with the Holy Ghost:

42 And she spake out with a loud voice, and said, Blessed art thou among women, and blessed is the fruit of thy womb.

43 And whence is this to me, that the mother of my Lord should come to me?

44 For, lo, as soon as the voice of thy salutation sounded in mine ears, the babe leaped in my womb for joy.

45 And blessed is she that believed: for there shall be a performance of those things which were told her from the Lord.

46 And Mary said, My soul doth magnify the Lord,

47 And my spirit hath rejoiced in God my Saviour.

48 For he hath regarded the low estate of his handmaiden: for, behold, from henceforth all generations shall call me blessed.

49 For he that is mighty hath done to me great things; and holy is his name.

50 And his mercy is on them that fear him from generation to generation.

51 He hath shewed strength with his arm; he hath scattered the proud in the imagination of their hearts.

52 He hath put down the mighty from their seats, and exalted them of low degree.

53 He hath filled the hungry with good things; and the rich he hath sent empty away.

54 He hath holpen his servant Israel, in remembrance of his mercy;

55 As he spake to our fathers, to Abraham, and to his seed for ever.

56 And Mary abode with her about three months, and returned to her own house.

173. John 1

1 In the beginning was the Word, and the Word was with God, and the Word was God.

2 The same was in the beginning with God.

3 All things were made by him; and without him was not any thing made that was made.

4 In him was life; and the life was the light of men.

5 And the light shineth in darkness; and the darkness comprehended it not.

6 There was a man sent from God, whose name was John.

7 The same came for a witness, to bear witness of the Light, that all men through him might believe.

8 He was not that Light, but was sent to bear witness of that Light.

9 That was the true Light, which lighteth every man that cometh into the world.

10 He was in the world, and the world was made by him, and the world knew him not.

11 He came unto his own, and his own received him not.

12 But as many as received him, to them gave he power to become the sons of God, even to them that believe on his name:

13 Which were born, not of blood, nor of the will of the flesh, nor of the will of man, but of God.

14 And the Word was made flesh, and dwelt among us, (and we beheld his glory, the glory as of the only begotten of the Father,) full of grace and truth.

15 John bare witness of him, and cried, saying, This was he of whom I spake, He that cometh after me is preferred before me: for he was before me.

16 And of his fulness have all we received, and grace for grace.

17 For the law was given by Moses, but grace and truth came by Jesus Christ.

18 No man hath seen God at any time, the only begotten Son, which is in the bosom of the Father, he hath declared him.

19 And this is the record of John, when the Jews sent priests and Levites from Jerusalem to ask him, Who art thou?

20 And he confessed, and denied not; but confessed, I am not the Christ.

21 And they asked him, What then? Art thou Elias? And he saith, I am not. Art thou that prophet? And he answered, No.

22 Then said they unto him, Who art thou? that we may give an answer to them that sent us. What sayest thou of thyself?

23 He said, I am the voice of one crying in the wilderness, Make straight the way of the Lord, as said the prophet Esaias.

24 And they which were sent were of the Pharisees.

25 And they asked him, and said unto him, Why baptizest thou then, if thou be not that Christ, nor Elias, neither that prophet?

26 John answered them, saying, I baptize with water: but there standeth one among you, whom ye know not;

27 He it is, who coming after me is preferred before me, whose shoe's latchet I am not worthy to unloose.

28 These things were done in Bethabara beyond Jordan, where John was baptizing.

29 The next day John seeth Jesus coming unto him, and saith, Behold the Lamb of God, which taketh away the sin of the world.

30 This is he of whom I said, After me cometh a man which is preferred before me: for he was before me.

31 And I knew him not: but that he should be made manifest to Israel, therefore am I come baptizing with water.

32 And John bare record, saying, I saw the Spirit descending from heaven like a dove, and it abode upon him.

33 And I knew him not: but he that sent me to baptize with water, the same said unto me, Upon whom thou shalt see the Spirit descending, and

remaining on him, the same is he which baptizeth with the Holy Ghost.

34 And I saw, and bare record that this is the Son of God.

35 Again the next day after John stood, and two of his disciples;

36 And looking upon Jesus as he walked, he saith, Behold the Lamb of God!

37 And the two disciples heard him speak, and they followed Jesus.

38 Then Jesus turned, and saw them following, and saith unto them, What seek ye? They said unto him, Rabbi, (which is to say, being interpreted, Master,) where dwellest thou?

39 He saith unto them, Come and see. They came and saw where he dwelt, and abode with him that day: for it was about the tenth hour.

40 One of the two which heard John speak, and followed him, was Andrew, Simon Peter's brother.

41 He first findeth his own brother Simon, and saith unto him, We have found the Messias, which is, being interpreted, the Christ.

42 And he brought him to Jesus. And when Jesus beheld him, he said, Thou art Simon the son of Jona: thou shalt be called Cephas, which is by interpretation, A stone.

43 The day following Jesus would go forth into Galilee, and findeth Philip, and saith unto him, Follow me.

44 Now Philip was of Bethsaida, the city of Andrew and Peter.

45 Philip findeth Nathanael, and saith unto him, We have found him, of whom Moses in the law, and the prophets, did write, Jesus of Nazareth, the son of Joseph.

46 And Nathanael said unto him, Can there any good thing come out of Nazareth? Philip saith unto him, Come and see.

47 Jesus saw Nathanael coming to him, and saith of him, Behold an Israelite indeed, in whom is no guile!

48 Nathanael saith unto him, Whence knowest thou me? Jesus answered and said unto him, Before that Philip called thee, when thou wast under the fig tree, I saw thee.

49 Nathanael answered and saith unto him, Rabbi, thou art the Son of God; thou art the King of Israel.

50 Jesus answered and said unto him, Because I said unto thee, I saw thee under the fig tree, believest thou? thou shalt see greater things than these.

51 And he saith unto him, Verily, verily, I say unto you, Hereafter ye shall see heaven open, and the angels of God ascending and descending upon the Son of man.

174. John 14

1 Let not your heart be troubled: ye believe in God, believe also in me.

2 In my Father's house are many mansions: if it were not so, I would have told you. I go to prepare a place for you.

3 And if I go and prepare a place for you, I will come again, and receive you unto myself; that where I am, there ye may be also.

4 And whither I go ye know, and the way ye know.

5 Thomas saith unto him, Lord, we know not whither thou goest; and how can we know the way?

6 Jesus saith unto him, I am the way, the truth, and the life: no man cometh unto the Father, but by me.

7 If ye had known me, ye should have known my Father also: and from henceforth ye know him, and have seen him.

8 Philip saith unto him, Lord, shew us the Father, and it sufficeth us.

9 Jesus saith unto him, Have I been so long time with you, and yet hast thou not known me, Philip? he that hath seen me hath seen the Father; and how sayest thou then, Shew us the Father?

10 Believest thou not that I am in the Father, and the Father in me? the words that I speak unto you I speak not of myself: but the Father that dwelleth in me, he doeth the works.

11 Believe me that I am in the Father, and the Father in me: or else believe me for the very works' sake.

12 Verily, verily, I say unto you, He that believeth on me, the works that I do shall he do also; and greater works than these shall he do; because I go unto my Father.

13 And whatsoever ye shall ask in my name, that will I do, that the Father may be glorified in the Son.

14 If ye shall ask any thing in my name, I will do it.

15 If ye love me, keep my commandments.

16 And I will pray the Father, and he shall give you another Comforter, that he may abide with you for ever;

17 Even the Spirit of truth; whom the world cannot receive, because it seeth him not, neither knoweth him: but ye know him; for he dwelleth with you, and shall be in you.

18 I will not leave you comfortless: I will come to you.

19 Yet a little while, and the world seeth me no more; but ye see me: because I live, ye shall live also.

20 At that day ye shall know that I am in my Father, and ye in me, and I in you.

21 He that hath my commandments, and keepeth them, he it is that loveth me: and he that loveth me shall be loved of my Father, and I will love him, and will manifest myself to him.

22 Judas saith unto him, not Iscariot, Lord, how is it that thou wilt manifest thyself unto us, and not unto the world?

23 Jesus answered and said unto him, If a man love me, he will keep my words: and my Father will love him, and we will come unto him, and make our abode with him.

24 He that loveth me not keepeth not my sayings: and the word which ye hear is not mine, but the Father's which sent me.

25 These things have I spoken unto you, being yet present with you.

26 But the Comforter, which is the Holy Ghost, whom the Father will send in my name, he shall teach you all things, and bring all things to your remembrance, whatsoever I have said unto you.

27 Peace I leave with you, my peace I give unto you: not as the world giveth, give I unto you. Let not your heart be troubled, neither let it be afraid.

28 Ye have heard how I said unto you, I go away, and come again unto you. If ye loved me, ye would rejoice, because I said, I go unto the Father: for my Father is greater than I.

29 And now I have told you before it come to pass, that, when it is come to pass, ye might believe.

30 Hereafter I will not talk much with you: for the prince of this world cometh, and hath nothing in me.

31 But that the world may know that I love the Father; and as the Father gave me commandment, even so I do. Arise, let us go hence.

175. John 15

1 I am the true vine, and my Father is the husbandman.

2 Every branch in me that beareth not fruit he taketh away: and every branch that beareth fruit, he purgeth it, that it may bring forth more fruit.

3 Now ye are clean through the word which I have spoken unto you.

4 Abide in me, and I in you. As the branch cannot bear fruit of itself; except it abide in the vine; no more can ye, except ye abide in me.

5 I am the vine, ye are the branches: He that abideth in me, and I in him, the same bringeth forth much fruit: for without me ye can do nothing.

6 If a man abide not in me, he is cast forth as a branch, and is withered; and men gather them, and cast them into the fire, and they are burned.

7 If ye abide in me, and my words abide in you, ye shall ask what ye will, and it shall be done unto you.

8 Herein is my Father glorified, that ye bear much fruit; so shall ye be my disciples.

9 As the Father hath loved me, so have I loved you: continue ye in my love.

10 If ye keep my commandments, ye shall abide in my love; even as I have kept my Father's commandments, and abide in his love.

11 These things have I spoken unto you, that my joy might remain in you, and that your joy might be full.

12 This is my commandment, That ye love one another, as I have loved you.

13 Greater love hath no man than this, that a man lay down his life for his friends.

14 Ye are my friends, if ye do whatsoever I command you.

15 Henceforth I call you not servants; for the servant knoweth not what his lord doeth: but I have called you friends; for all things that I have heard of my Father I have made known unto you.

16 Ye have not chosen me, but I have chosen you, and ordained you, that ye should go and bring forth fruit, and that your fruit should remain: that whatsoever ye shall ask of the Father in my name, he may give it you.

17 These things I command you, that ye love one another.

18 If the world hate you, ye know that it hated me before it hated you.

19 If ye were of the world, the world would love his own: but because ye are not of the world, but I have chosen you out of the world, therefore the world hateth you.

20 Remember the word that I said unto you, The servant is not greater than his lord. If they have persecuted me, they will also persecute you; if they have kept my saying, they will keep yours also.

21 But all these things will they do unto you for my name's sake, because they know not him that sent me.

22 If I had not come and spoken unto them, they had not had sin: but now they have no cloak for their sin.

23 He that hateth me hateth my Father also.

24 If I had not done among them the works which none other man did, they had not had sin: but now have they both seen and hated both me and my Father.

25 But this cometh to pass, that the word might be fulfilled that is written in their law, They hated me without a cause.

26 But when the Comforter is come, whom I will send unto you from the Father, even the Spirit of truth, which proceedeth from the Father, he shall testify of me:

27 And ye also shall bear witness, because ye have been with me from the beginning.

176. John 16

1 These things have I spoken unto you, that ye should not be offended.
2 They shall put you out of the synagogues: yea, the time cometh, that whosoever killeth you will think that he doeth God service.
3 And these things will they do unto you, because they have not known the Father, nor me.
4 But these things have I told you, that when the time shall come, ye may remember that I told you of them. And these things I said not unto you at the beginning, because I was with you.
5 But now I go my way to him that sent me; and none of you asketh me, Whither goest thou?
6 But because I have said these things unto you, sorrow hath filled your heart.
7 Nevertheless I tell you the truth; It is expedient for you that I go away: for if I go not away, the Comforter will not come unto you; but if I depart, I will send him unto you.
8 And when he is come, he will reprove the world of sin, and of righteousness, and of judgement:
9 Of sin, because they believe not on me;
10 Of righteousness, because I go to my Father, and ye see me no more;
11 Of judgement, because the prince of this world is judged.
12 I have yet many things to say unto you, but ye cannot bear them now.
13 Howbeit when he, the Spirit of truth, is come, he will guide you into all truth: for he shall not speak of himself; but whatsoever he shall hear, that shall he speak: and he will shew you things to come.
14 He shall glorify me: for he shall receive of mine, and shall shew it unto you.
15 All things that the Father hath are mine: therefore said I, that he shall take of mine, and shall shew it unto you.
16 A little while, and ye shall not see me: and again, a little while, and ye shall see me, because I go to the Father.
17 Then said some of his disciples among themselves, What is this that he saith unto us, A little while, and ye shall not see me: and again, a little while, and ye shall see me: and, Because I go to the Father?
18 They said therefore, What is this that he saith, A little while? we cannot tell what he saith.
19 Now Jesus knew that they were desirous to ask him, and said unto them, Do ye enquire among yourselves of that I said, A little while, and ye shall not see me: and again, a little while, and ye shall see me?
20 Verily, verily, I say unto you, That ye shall weep and lament, but the world shall rejoice: and ye shall be sorrowful, but your sorrow shall be turned into joy.

21 A woman when she is in travail hath sorrow, because her hour is come: but as soon as she is delivered of the child, she remembereth no more the anguish, for joy that a man is born into the world.

22 And ye now therefore have sorrow: but I will see you again, and your heart shall rejoice, and your joy no man taketh from you.

23 And in that day ye shall ask me nothing. Verily, verily, I say unto you, Whatsoever ye shall ask the Father in my name, he will give it you.

24 Hitherto have ye asked nothing in my name: ask, and ye shall receive, that your joy may be full.

25 These things have I spoken unto you in proverbs: but the time cometh, when I shall no more speak unto you in proverbs, but I shall shew you plainly of the Father.

26 At that day ye shall ask in my name: and I say not unto you, that I will pray the Father for you:

27 For the Father himself loveth you, because ye have loved me, and have believed that I came out from God.

28 I came forth from the Father, and am come into the world: again, I leave the world, and go to the Father.

29 His disciples said unto him, Lo, now speakest thou plainly, and speakest no proverb.

30 Now are we sure that thou knowest all things, and needest not that any man should ask thee: by this we believe that thou camest forth from God.

31 Jesus answered them, Do ye now believe?

32 Behold, the hour cometh, yea, is now come, that ye shall be scattered, every man to his own, and shall leave me alone: and yet I am not alone, because the Father is with me.

33 These things I have spoken unto you, that in me ye might have peace. In the world ye shall have tribulation: but be of good cheer; I have overcome the world.

177. Revelation 22

1 And he shewed me a pure river of water of life, clear as crystal, proceeding out of the throne of God and of the Lamb.

2 In the midst of the street of it, and on either side of the river, was there the tree of life, which bare twelve manner of fruits, and yielded her fruit every month: and the leaves of the tree were for the healing of the nations.

3 And there shall be no more curse: but the throne of God and of the Lamb shall be in it; and his servants shall serve him:

4 And they shall see his face; and his name shall be in their foreheads.

5 And there shall be no night there; and they need no candle, neither light of the sun; for the Lord God giveth them light: and they shall reign for ever and ever.

6 And he said unto me, These sayings are faithful and true: and the Lord God of the holy prophets sent his angel to shew unto his servants the things which must shortly be done.

7 Behold, I come quickly: blessed is he that keepeth the sayings of the prophecy of this book.

8 And I John saw these things, and heard them. And when I had heard and seen, I fell down to worship before the feet of the angel which shewed me these things.

9 Then saith he unto me, See thou do it not: for I am thy fellowservant, and of thy brethren the prophets, and of them which keep the sayings of this book: worship God.

10 And he saith unto me, Seal not the sayings of the prophecy of this book: for the time is at hand.

11 He that is unjust, let him be unjust still: and he which is filthy, let him be filthy still: and he that is righteous, let him be righteous still: and he that is holy, let him be holy still.

12 And, behold, I come quickly; and my reward is with me, to give every man according as his work shall be.

13 I am Alpha and Omega, the beginning and the end, the first and the last.

14 Blessed are they that do his commandments, that they may have right to the tree of life, and may enter in through the gates into the city.

15 For without are dogs, and sorcerers, and whoremongers, and murderers, and idolaters, and whosoever loveth and maketh a lie.

16 I Jesus have sent mine angel to testify unto you these things in the churches. I am the root and the offspring of David, and the bright and morning star.

17 And the Spirit and the bride say, Come. And let him that heareth say, Come. And let him that is athirst come. And whosoever will, let him take the water of life freely.

18 For I testify unto every man that heareth the words of the prophecy of this book, If any man shall add unto these things, God shall add unto him the plagues that are written in this book:

19 And if any man shall take away from the words of the book of this prophecy, God shall take away his part out of the book of life, and out of the holy city, and from the things which are written in this book.

20 He which testifieth these things saith, Surely I come quickly. Amen. Even so, come, Lord Jesus.

21 The grace of our Lord Jesus Christ be with you all. Amen.

Thomas Campion (1567–1620)

178. 'The peaceful western wind'

The peaceful western wind
The winter storms hath tamed,
And nature in each kind
The kind heat hath inflamed.
The forward buds so sweetly breathe
  Out of their earthy bowers,
That heaven, which views their pomp beneath,
  Would fain be decked with flowers.

See how the morning smiles
On her bright eastern hill,
And with soft steps beguiles
Them that lie slumbering still.
The music-loving birds are come
  From cliffs and rocks unknown,
To see the trees and briars bloom
  That late were overflown.

What Saturn did destroy,
Love's queen revives again;
And now her naked boy
Doth in the fields remain:
Where he such pleasing change doth view
  In every living thing,
As if the world were born anew
  To gratify the Spring.

If all things life present,
Why die my comforts then?
Why suffers my content?
Am I the worst of men?
O beauty, be not thou accused
  Too justly in this case:
Unkindly if true love be used,
  'Twill yield thee little grace.

179. 'Now winter nights enlarge'

Now winter nights enlarge
   The number of their hours,
And clouds their storms discharge
   Upon the airy towers;
Let now the chimneys blaze
   And cups o'erflow with wine,
Let well-tuned words amaze
   With harmony divine.
Now yellow waxen lights
   Shall wait on honey Love,   10
While youthful revels, masques, and courtly sights,
   Sleep's leaden spell remove.

This time doth well dispense
   With lovers' long discourse;
Much speech hath some defence,
   Though beauty no remorse.
All do not all things well:
   Some measures comely tread,
Some knotted riddles tell,
   Some poems smoothly read.   20
The Summer hath his joys,
   And Winter his delights;
Though love and all his pleasures are but toys,
   They shorten tedious nights.

180. 'When to her lute Corinna sings'

When to her lute Corrina sings,
Her voice revives the leaden strings,
And doth in highest notes appear
As any challenged echo clear;
But when she doth of mourning speak,
Even with her sighs the strings do break.

And, as her lute doth live or die,
Led by her passion, so must I:
For when of pleasure she doth sing,

My thoughts enjoy a sudden spring;   10
But if she doth of sorrow speak,
Even from my heart the strings do break.

181. 'Follow thy fair sun'

Follow thy fair sun, unhappy shadow:
Though thou be black as night,
And she made all of light,
Yet follow thy fair sun, unhappy shadow.

Follow her whose light thy light depriveth:
Though here thou livest disgraced,
And she in heaven is placed,
Yet follow her whose light the world reviveth.

Follow those pure beams whose beauty burneth,
That so have scorchèd thee,   10
As thou still black must be,
Till her kind beams thy black to brightness turneth.

Follow her while yet her glory shineth:
There comes a luckless night,
That will dim all her light;
And this the black unhappy shade divineth.

Follow still since so thy fates ordained:
The Sun must have his shade,
Till both at once do fade,
The Sun still proved, the shadow still disdained.   20

182. 'The man of life upright'

The man of life upright,
   Whose guiltless heart is free
From all dishonest deeds,
   Or thought of vanity,

The man whose silent days
   In harmless joys are spent,
Whom hopes cannot delude,
   Nor sorrow discontent,

That man needs neither towers
   Nor armour for defence,   10
Nor vaults his guilt to shroud
   From thunder's violence.

He only can behold
   With unaffrighted eyes
The horrors of the deep,
   And terrors of the skies.

Thus, scorning all the cares
   That fate, or fortune brings,
He makes the heaven his book,
   His wisdom heavenly things,   20

Good thoughts his only friends,
   His wealth a well-spent age,
The earth his sober Inn,
   And quiet Pilgrimage.

183. 'To music bent is my retirèd mind'

To music bent is my retirèd mind,
And fain would I some song of pleasure sing:
But in vain joys no comfort now I find:
From heavenly thoughts all true delight doth spring.
Thy power, O God, thy mercies to record
Will sweeten every note, and every word.

All earthly pomp or beauty to express,
Is but to carve in snow, on waves to write.
Celestial things, though men conceive them less,
Yet fullest are they in themselves of light: 10
Such beams they yield as know no means to die:
Such heat they cast as lifts the spirit high.

184. 'Fire, fire, fire, fire!'

Fire, fire, fire, fire!
Lo here I burn in such desire
That all the tears that I can strain
Out of mine idle empty brain
Cannot allay my scorching pain.
    Come Trent, and Humber, and fair Thames,
    Dread Ocean, haste with all thy streams:
    And, if you cannot quench my fire,
    O drown both me and my desire.

Fire, fire, fire, fire!   10
There is no hell to my desire:
See, all the Rivers backward fly,
And th' Ocean doth his waves deny,
For fear my heat should drink them dry.
    Come, heavenly showers, then, pouring down;
    Come, you that once the world did drown:
    Some then you spared, but now save all,
    That else must burn, and with me fall.

185. 'There is a garden in her face'

There is a garden in her face,
Where roses and white lilies grow;
    A heavenly paradise is that place,
Wherein all pleasant fruits do flow.
    There cherries grow, which none may buy
    Till 'Cherry ripe' themselves do cry.

Those cherries fairly do enclose
Of orient pearl a double row,
    Which when her lovely laughter shows,
They look like rose-buds filled with snow.   10
    Yet them nor peer nor prince can buy,
    Till 'Cherry ripe' themselves do cry.

Her eyes like angels watch them still;
Her brows like bended bows do stand,
    Threatening with piercing frowns to kill

All that attempt with eye or hand
   Those sacred cherries to come nigh,
   Till 'Cherry ripe' themselves do cry.

Emilia Lanyer (1569–1645)

186. The Description of Cookham

Farewell, sweet Cookham, where I first obtained
Grace from that Grace where perfect Grace remained;
And where the muses gave their full consent,
I should have power the virtuous to content:
Where princely palace willed me to indite,
The sacred story of the soul's delight,
Farewell, sweet place, where virtue then did rest,
And all delights did harbour in her breast:
Never shall my sad eyes again behold
Those pleasures which my thoughts did then unfold.   10
Yet you, great lady, mistress of that place,
From whose desires did spring this work of grace,
Vouchsafe to think upon those pleasures past
As fleeting worldly joys that could not last,
Or as dim shadows of celestial pleasures
Which are desired above all earthly treasures.
Oh how, me thought, against you thither came,
Each part did seem some new delight to frame!
The house received all ornaments to grace it,
And would endure no foulness to deface it.   20
The walks put on their summer liveries,
And all things else did hold like similes.
The trees with leaves, with fruits, with flowers clad,
Embraced each other, seeming to be glad,
Turning themselves to beauteous canopies,
To shade the bright sun from your brighter eyes:
The crystal streams with silver spangles graced,
While by the glorious sun they were embraced.

The little birds in chirping notes did sing,
To entertain both you and that sweet Spring.   30
And Philomela with her sundry lays,
Both you and that delightful place did praise.
Oh how me thought each plant, each flower, each tree
Set forth their beauties then to welcome thee!
The very hills right humbly did descend
When you to tread upon them did intend,
And as you set your feet, they still did rise,
Glad that they could receive so rich a prize.
The gentle winds did take delight to be
Among those woods that were so graced by thee.   40
And in sad murmur uttered pleasing sound,
That pleasure in that place might more abound:
The swelling banks delivered all their pride,
When such a Phoenix once they had espied.
Each arbor, bank, each seat, each stately tree,
Thought themselves honoured in supporting thee.
The pretty birds would oft come to attend thee,
Yet fly away for fear they should offend thee:
The little creatures in the burrow by
Would come abroad to sport them in your eye;   50
Yet fearful of the bow in your fair hand
Would run away when you did make a stand.
Now let me come unto that stately tree
Wherein such goodly prospects you did see;
That oak that did in height his fellows pass,
As much as lofty trees low growing grass:
Much like a comely cedar straight and tall,
Whose beauteous stature far exceeded all.
How often did you visit this fair tree
Which seeming joyful in receiving thee   60
Would like a palm tree spread his arms abroad,
Desirous that you there should make abode:
Whose fair green leaves much like a comely veil,
Defended Phoebus when he would assail;
Whose pleasing boughs did yield a cool fresh air,
Joying his happiness when you were there.
Where being seated you might plainly see
Hills, vales, and woods, as if on bended knee
They had appeared, your honour to salute,
Or to proffer some strange unlooked for suit,   70
All interlaced with brooks and crystal springs,

A prospect fit to please the eyes of kings.
And thirteen shires appeared all in your sight,
Europe could not afford much more delight.
What was there then but gave you all content,
While you the time in meditation spent
Of their Creator's power, which there you saw,
In all his creatures held a perfect law;
And in their beauties did you plain descry
His beauty, wisdom, grace, love, majesty.   80
In these sweet woods how often did you walk
With Christ and his apostles there to talk,
Placing his holy writ in some fair tree
To meditate what you therein did see;
With Moses you did mount his holy hill
To know his pleasure and perform his will.
With lovely David did you often sing,
His holy hymns to heaven's eternal king.
And in sweet music did your soul delight,
To sound his praises, morning, noon, and night.   90
With blessed Joseph you did often feed
Your pined brethren, when they stood in need.
And that sweet Lady sprung from Clifford's race
Of noble Bedford's blood, fair stem of grace,
To honourable Dorset now espoused,
In whose fair breast true virtue then was housed.
Oh what delight did my weak spirits find
In those pure parts of her well-framèd mind,
And yet it grieves me that I cannot be
Near unto her, whose virtues did agree   100
With those fair ornaments of outward beauty
Which did enforce from all both love and duty.
Unconstant fortune, thou art most to blame,
Who casts us down into so low a frame
Where our great friends we cannot daily see,
So great a difference is there in degree.
Many are placèd in those orbs of state,
Partners in honour, so ordained by fate;
Nearer in show, yet farther off in love,
In which the lowest always are above.   110
But whither am I carried in conceit?
My wit too weak to conster of the great.
Why not? Although we are but born of earth,
We may behold the heavens, despising death;

And loving heaven that is so far above,
May in the end vouchsafe us entire love.
Therefore sweet memory do thou retain
Those pleasures past, which will not turn again;
Remember beauteous Dorset's former sports, 120
So far from being touched by ill reports;
Wherein my self did always bear a part,
While reverend love presented my true heart.
Those recreations let me bear in mind
Which her sweet youth and noble thoughts did find,
Whereof deprived, I evermore must grieve,
Hating blind fortune, careless to relieve.
And you sweet Cookham, whom these ladies leave,
I now must tell the grief you did conceive
At their departure; when they went away,
How every thing retained a sad dismay. 130
Nay long before, when once an inkling came,
Me thought each thing did unto sorrow frame.
The trees that were so glorious in our view
Forsook both flowers and fruit when once they knew
Of your depart, their very leaves did wither,
Changing their colours as they grew together.
But when they saw this had no power to stay you,
They often wept, though speechless, could not pray you,
Letting their tears in your fair bosoms fall,
As if they said, 'Why will ye leave us all?' 140
This being vain, they cast their leaves away,
Hoping that pity would have made you stay.
Their frozen tops, like age's hoary hairs,
Shows their disaster, languishing in fears:
A swarthy riveled rind° all over spread,   *shrivelled bark*
Their dying bodies half alive, half dead.
But your occasions called you so away
That nothing there had power to make you stay.
Yet did I see a noble grateful mind
Requiting each according to their kind, 150
Forgetting not to turn and take your leave
Of these sad creatures, powerless to receive
Your favour, when with grief you did depart,
Placing their former pleasures in your heart;
Giving great charge to noble memory,
There to preserve their love continually:
But specially the love of that fair tree

That first and last you did vouchsafe to see,
In which it pleased you oft to take the air
With noble Dorset, then a virgin fair;   160
Where many a learned book was read and scanned;
To this fair tree, taking me by the hand
You did repeat the pleasures which had past,
Seeming to grieve they could no longer last.
And with a chaste yet loving kiss took leave,
Of which sweet kiss I did it soon bereave,
Scorning a senseless creature should possess
So rare a favour, so great happiness.
No other kiss it could receive from me
For fear to give back what it took of thee.   170
So I ingrateful creature did deceive it
Of that which you vouchsafe in love to leave it.
And though it oft had given me much content,
Yet this great wrong I never could repent,
But of the happiest made it most forlorn,
To show that nothing's free from fortune's scorn,
While all the rest with this most beauteous tree
Made their sad consort sorrow's harmony.
The flowers that on the banks and walks did grow
Crept in the ground, the grass did weep for woe.   180
The winds and waters seemed to chide together
Because you went away they knew not whither;
And those sweet brooks that ran so fair and clear
With grief and trouble wrinkled did appear.
Those pretty birds that wonted were to sing,
Now neither sing, nor chirp, nor use their wing,
But with their tender feet on some bare spray
Warble forth sorrow, and their own dismay.
Fair Philomela leaves her mournful ditty,
Drowned in dead sleep, yet can procure no pity.   190
Each arbour, bank, each seat, each stately tree,
Looks bare and desolate now for want of thee,
Turning green tresses into frosty grey,
While in cold grief they wither all away.
The sun grew weak, his beams no comfort gave,
While all green things did make the earth their grave.
Each briar, each bramble, when you went away
Caught fast your clothes, thinking to make you stay.
Delightful Echo, wonted to reply
To our last words, did now for sorrow die.   200

The house cast off each garment that might grace it,
Putting on Dust and Cobwebs to deface it.
All desolation then there did appear,
When you were going whom they held so dear.
This last farewell to Cookham here I give:
When I am dead thy name in this might live
Wherein I have performed her noble 'hest,
Whose virtues lodge in my unworthy breast,
And ever shall, so long as life remains,
Tying my heart to her by those rich chains.   210

John Donne (1571?–1631)

187. The Canonisation

For God's sake hold your tongue, and let me love,
    Or chide my palsy, or my gout,
My five grey hairs, or ruined fortune flout,
    With wealth your state, your mind with arts improve
        Take you a course, get you a place,
        Observe his honour, or his grace,
    Or the King's real, or his stampèd face
        Contemplate, what you will, approve,
        So you will let me love.

Alas, alas, who's injured by my love?   10
    What merchant's ships have my sighs drowned?
Who says my tears have overflowed his ground?
    When did my colds a forward spring remove?
        When did the heats which my veins fill
        Add one more, to the plaguey Bill?
Soldiers find wars, and lawyers find out still
    Litigious men, which quarrels move,
    Though she and I do love.

Call us what you will, we are made such by love;
    Call her one, me another fly,
We're tapers too, and at our own cost die,
    And we in us find the eagle and the dove,
        The Phoenix riddle hath more wit
        By us, we two being one, are it.
So, to one neutral thing both sexes fit,
    We die and rise the same, and prove
    Mysterious by this love.

We can die by it, if not live by love,
    And if unfit for tombs and hearse
Our legend be, it will be fit for verse;
    And if no piece of chronicle we prove,
        We'll build in sonnets pretty rooms;
        As well a well-wrought urn becomes
The greatest ashes, as half-acre tombs,
    And by these hymns, all shall approve
    Us canonised for Love.

And thus invoke us: 'You whom reverend love
    Made one another's hermitage;
You, to whom love was peace, that now is rage,
    Who did the whole world's soul contract, and drove
        Into the glasses of your eyes
        (So made such mirrors, and such spies,
That they did all to you epitomise),
    Countries, towns, courts: beg from above
    A pattern of our love.'

20

30

40

188. The Flea

Mark but this flea, and mark in this,
How little that which thou deniest me is;
It sucked me first, and now sucks thee,
And in this flea, our two bloods mingled be;
Thou know'st that this cannot be said
A sin, nor shame nor loss of maidenhead,
    Yet this enjoys before it woo,
    And pampered swells with one blood made of two,
    And this, alas, is more than we would do.

Oh stay, three lives in one flea spare,   10
Where we almost, yea more than married are.
This flea is you and I, and this
Our marriage bed, and marriage temple is;
Though parents grudge, and you, w' are met,
And cloistered in these living walls of Jet.
    Though use make you apt to kill me,
      Let not to that, self-murder° added be,   *suicide*
    And sacrilege, three sins in killing three.

Cruel and sudden, hast thou since
Purpled thy nail, in blood of innocence?   20
Wherein could this flea guilty be,
Except in that drop which it sucked from thee?
Yet thou triumph'st, and say'st that thou
Find'st not thy self, nor me the weaker now;
    'Tis true, then learn how false fears be;
      Just so much honour, when thou yield'st to me,
    Will waste, as this flea's death took life from thee.

189. The Sun Rising

    Busy old fool, unruly Sun,
      Why dost thou thus,
Through windows, and through curtains call on us?
Must to thy motions lovers' seasons run?
    Saucy pedantic wretch, go chide
      Late schoolboys, and sour 'prentices,
  Go tell court huntsmen, that the King will ride,
  Call country ants to harvest offices;
Love, all alike, no season knows, nor clime,
Nor hours, days, months, which are the rags of time.   10

    Thy beams, so reverend and strong
      Why should'st thou think?
I could eclipse and cloud them with a wink,
But that I would not lose her sight so long;
    If her eyes have not blinded thine,
      Look, and tomorrow late, tell me
  Whether both th' Indias of spice and Mine
  Be where thou left'st them, or lie here with me.

Ask for those Kings whom thou saw'st yesterday
And thou shalt hear, 'All here in one bed lay.'   20

     She is all states, and all princes, I,
       Nothing else is.
Princes do but play us, compared to this
All honour's mimic; all wealth alchemy;
     Thou sun art half as happy as we,
      In that the world's contracted thus;
   Thine age asks ease, and since thy duties be
   To warm the world, that's done in warming us.
Shine here to us, and thou art everywhere;
This bed thy centre is, these walls, thy sphere.   30

190. The Good-Morrow

I wonder by my troth, what thou, and I
Did, till we loved? Were we not weaned till then?
But sucked on country pleasures, childishly?
Or snorted we in the seven sleepers' den?
'Twas so; but° this, all pleasures fancies be.   *except for*
If ever any beauty I did see
Which I desired, and got, 'twas but a dream of thee.

And now good morrow to our waking souls,
Which watch not one another out of fear;
For love, all love of other sights controls,   10
And makes one little room an everywhere.
Let sea-discoverers to new worlds have gone,
Let maps to other, worlds on worlds have shown,
Let us possess one world, each hath one, and is one.

My face in thine eye, thine in mine appears,
And true plain hearts do in the faces rest;
Where can we find two better hemispheres
Without sharp North, without declining West?
Whatever dies, was not mixed equally;
If our two loves be one, or, thou and I   20
Love so alike, that none do slacken, none can die.

191. 'Go, and catch a falling star'

Go, and catch a falling star,
   Get with child a mandrake root,
Tell me where all past years are,
   Or who cleft the Devil's foot,
Teach me to hear Mermaids singing,
   Or to keep off envy's stinging,
      And find
      What wind
Serves to advance an honest mind.

If thou be'st born to strange sights,   10
   Things invisible to see,
Ride ten thousand days and nights
   Till age snow white hairs on thee,
Thou, when thou return'st, wilt tell me
All strange wonders that befell thee,
      And swear
      No where
Lives a woman true, and fair.

If thou find'st one, let me know;
   Such a Pilgrimage were sweet.   20
Yet do not, I would not go,
   Though at next door we might meet,
Though she were true when you met her,
And last till you write your letter,
      Yet she
      Will be
False, ere I come, to two or three.

192. The Indifferent

'I can love both fair and brown,
Her whom abundance melts, and her whom want betrays,
Her who loves loneness best, and her who masks and plays,
Her whom the country formed, and whom the town,
Her who believes, and her who tries,
Her who still weeps with spongy eyes
And her who is dry cork and never cries;

I can love her, and her, and you and you,
I can love any, so she be not true.

'Will no other vice content you?   10
Will it not serve your turn to do as did your mothers?
Or have you all old vices spent, and now would find out others?
Or doth a fear that men are true torment you?
Oh we are not, be not you so,
Let me, and do you, twenty know.
Rob me, but bind me not, and let me go.
Must I, who came to travail thorough you,
Grow your fixed subject, because you are true?'

Venus heard me sigh this song
And by love's sweetest part, variety, she swore   20
She heard not this till now; and that it should be so no more.
She went, examined, and returned ere long
And said, 'Alas, some two or three
Poor Heretics in love there be,
Which think to 'stablish dangerous constancy.
But I have told them, since you will be true,
You shall be true to them, who are false to you.'

193. A Nocturnal upon Saint Lucy's Day, Being the Shortest Day

'Tis the year's midnight, and it is the day's,
Lucy's, who scarce seven hours herself unmasks.
    The sun is spent, and now his flasks°   *the stars*
     Send forth light squibs, no constant rays;
      The world's whole sap is sunk:
The general balm th' hydroptic° earth hath drunk,   *suffering from dropsy*
Whither as to the bed's-feet life is shrunk,
Dead and interred; yet all these seem to laugh,
Compared with me, who am their epitaph.

Study me then, you who shall lovers be   10
At the next world, that is, at the next Spring,
    For I am every dead thing,
     In whom love wrought new alchemy.
      For his art did express
A quintessence even from nothingness,

From dull privations and lean emptiness
He ruined me, and I am re-begot
Of absence, darkness, death; things which are not.

All others from all things draw all that's good,
Life, soul, form, spirit, whence they being have;   20
    I, by love's limbeck, am the grave
    Of all, that's nothing. Oft a flood
        Have we two wept, and so
Drowned the whole world, us two; oft did we grow
To be two chaoses, when we did show
Care to aught else; and often absences
Withdrew our souls and made us carcasses.

But I am by her death (which word wrongs her)
Of the first nothing the elixir grown;
    Were I a man, that I were one,   30
    I needs must know, I should prefer,
        If I were any beast,
Some ends, some means; yea plants, yea stones detest
And love; all, all some properties invest,
If I an ordinary nothing were,
As shadow, a light, and body must be here.

But I am none; nor will my sun renew.
You lovers for whose sake the lesser sun
    At this time to the goat is run
    To fetch new lust and give it you,   40
        Enjoy your summer all,
Since she enjoys her long night's festival,
Let me prepare towards her, and let me call
This hour her vigil, and her eve, since this
Both the year's and the day's deep midnight is.

194. A Valediction: Forbidding Mourning

As virtuous men pass mildly away
    And whisper to the souls to go,
Whilst some of their sad friends do say,
    'The breath goes now,' and some say, 'no,'

So let us melt, and make no noise,
　　No tear-floods nor sigh-tempests move,
'Twere profanation of our joys
　　To tell the laity our love.

Moving of th' earth brings harms and fears,
　　Men reckon what it did and meant; 10
But trepidation of the spheres,
　　Though greater far, is innocent.

Dull sublunary lovers' love
　　(Whose soul is sense) cannot admit
Absence, because it doth remove
　　Those things which elemented it.

But we by a love so much refined
　　That our selves know not what it is,
Inter-assurèd of the mind,
　　Care less eyes, lips, and hands to miss. 20

Our two souls, therefore, which are one,
　　Though I must go, endure not yet
A breach, but an expansion
　　Like gold to airy thinness beat.

If they be two, they are two so
　　As stiff twin compasses are two,
Thy soul the fixed foot makes no show
　　To move, but doth if the other do.

And though it in the centre sit,
　　Yet when the other far doth roam, 30
It leans and hearkens after it
　　And grows erect as that comes home.

Such wilt thou be to me, who must
　　Like th' other foot, obliquely run.
Thy firmness makes my circle just
　　And makes me end where I begun.

195. The Anniversary

All Kings, and all their favourites,
  All glory of honours, beauties, wits,
The sun itself, which makes times, as they pass,
Is elder by a year now than it was
When thou and I first one another saw:
All other things to their destruction draw;
  Only our love hath no decay;
This, no tomorrow hath, nor yesterday,
Running, it never runs from us away
But truly keeps his first, last, everlasting day.   10

Two graves must hide thine and my corse,°   *corpse*
  If one might, death were no divorce.
Alas, as well as other princes, we
(Who prince enough in one another be)
Must leave at last in death these eyes, and ears,
Oft fed with true oaths and with sweet salt tears;
  But souls where nothing dwells but love
(All other thoughts being inmates) then shall prove
This, or a love increasèd there above,
When bodies to their graves, souls from their graves remove.   20

And then we shall be throughly blest,
  But we no more, than all the rest.
Here upon earth we are Kings, and none but we
Can be such Kings, nor of such subjects be.
Who is so safe as we? where none can do
Treason to us, except one of us two.
  True and false fears let us refrain,
Let us love nobly and live and add again
Years and years unto years, till we attain
To write three score: this is the second of our reign.   30

196. Twickenham Garden

Blasted with sighs and surrounded with tears,
  Hither I come to seek the spring,
  And at mine eyes and at mine ears
Receive such balms, as else cure every thing.

But O, self traitor, I do bring
The spider love, which transubstantiates all,
   And can convert Manna to gall;
And that this place may thoroughly be thought
   True Paradise, I have the serpent brought.

'Twere wholesomer for me that winter did   10
   Benight the glory of this place,
   And that a grave frost did forbid
These trees to laugh and mock me to my face;
   But that I may not this disgrace
Endure, nor yet leave loving, love let me
   Some senseless piece of this place be;
Make me a mandrake, so I may grow here,
   Or a stone fountain weeping out my year.

Hither with crystal vials, lovers come
   And take my tears, which are love's wine,   20
   And try your mistress' tears at home,
For all are false that taste not just like mine;
   Alas, hearts do not in eyes shine,
Nor can you more judge women's thoughts by tears
   Than by her shadow, what she wears.
O perverse sex, where none is true but she
   Who's therefore true, because her truth kills me.

197. The Ecstasy

Where, like a pillow on a bed,
   A pregnant bank swelled up to rest
The violet's reclining head,
   Sat we two, one another's best.
Our hands were firmly cemented
   With a fast balm, which thence did spring,
Our eye-beams twisted, and did thread
   Our eyes, upon one double string;
So to intergraft our hands as yet
   Was all the means to make us one,   10
And pictures in our eyes to get
   Was all our propagation.
As twixt two equal armies, fate

Suspends uncertain victory,
Our souls (which to advance their state
   Were gone out) hung twixt her and me.
And whilst our souls negotiate there,
   We like sepulchral statues lay;
All day, the same our postures were
   And we said nothing all the day.   20
If any, so by love refined
   That he soul's language understood,
And by good love were grown all mind,
   Within convenient distance stood,
He (though he knows not which soul spake,
   Because both meant, both spake the same)
Might thence a new concoction take,
   And part far purer than he came.
This Ecstasy doth unperplex
   (We said) and tell us what we love;   30
We see by this it was not sex
   We see, we saw not what did move,
But as all several souls contain
   Mixture of things, they know not what,
Love these mixed souls doth mix again,
   And makes both one, each this and that.
A single violet transplant,
   The strength, the colour, and the size,
(All which before was poor, and scant)
   Redoubles still, and multiplies.   40
When love with one another so
   Interinanimates two souls,
That abler soul which thence doth flow
   Defects of loneliness controls.
We then who are this new soul know
   Of what we are composed and made,
For th' atomies of which we grow
   Are souls whom no change can invade.
But O alas, so long, so far
   Our bodies why do we forbear?   50
They are ours though not we; we are
   The intelligences, they the spheres.
We owe them thanks because they thus
   Did us to us at first convey,
Yielded their senses' force to us,
   Nor are dross to us, but allay.

On man heaven's influence works not so
    But that it first imprints the air,
For soul into the soul may flow,
    Though it to body first repair.   60
As our blood labours to beget
    Spirits, as like souls as it can,
Because such fingers need to knit
    That subtle knot, which makes us man,
So must pure lovers' souls descend
    To affections and to faculties,
Which sense may reach and apprehend,
    Else a great prince in prison lies.
To our bodies turn we then, that so
    Weak men on love revealed may look;   70
Love's mysteries in souls do grow,
    But yet the body is his book.
And if some lover such as we
    Have heard this dialogue of one,
Let him still mark us, he shall see
    Small change, when we are to bodies gone.

198. The Autumnal

No Spring nor Summer beauty hath such grace
    As I have seen in one autumnal face.
Young beauties force our love, and that's a rape,
    This doth but counsel, yet you cannot 'scape.
If 'twere a shame to love, here 'twere no shame,
    Affections here take reverence's name.
Were her first years the golden age; that's true,
    But now she's gold oft tried, and ever new.
That was her torrid and inflaming time,
    This is her tolerable tropic clime.   10
Fair eyes, who asks more heat, than comes from hence,
    He in a fever wishes pestilence.
Call not these wrinkles graves; if graves they were,
    They were love's graves; for else he is nowhere.
Yet lies not love dead here but here doth sit
    Vowed to this trench, like an anchorite.
And here, till hers which must be his death, come
    He doth not dig a grave, but build a tomb.

Here dwells he, though he sojourn everywhere;
    In Progress, yet his standing house is here.   20
Here, where still evening is, not noon nor night;
    Where no voluptuousness yet all delight.
In all her words unto all hearers fit,
    You may at Revels, you at counsel sit.
This is love's timber, youth his under-wood;
    There he, as wine in June, enrages blood
Which then comes seasonablest when our taste
    And appetite to other things are past.
Xerxes' strange Lydian love, the platane tree
    Was loved for age, none being so large as she,   30
Or else because being young, nature did bless
    Her youth with age's glory, barrenness.
If we love things long sought, age is a thing
    Which we are fifty years in compassing.
If transitory things, which soon decay,
    Age must be loveliest at the latest day.
But name not Winter-faces, whose skin's slack;
    Lank, as an unthrift's purse; but a soul's sack;
Whose eyes seek light within, for all here's shade;
    Whose mouths are holes, rather worn out, than made   40
Whose every tooth to a several place is gone,
    To vex their souls at Resurrection;
Name not these living Death'sheads unto me,
    For these, not Ancient, but Antique be;
I hate extremes; yet I had rather stay
    With Tombs than Cradles to wear out a day.
Since such love's motion natural is, may still
    My love descend, and journey down the hill,
Not panting after growing beauties, so,
    I shall ebb out with them, who homeward go.   50

from *Holy Sonnets*

199. 'Thou hast made me. And shall thy work decay?'

Thou hast made me. And shall thy work decay?
Repair me now, for now mine end doth haste.
I run to death and death meets me as fast
And all my pleasures are like yesterday.

I dare not move my dim eyes any way,
Despair behind, and death before doth cast
Such terror, and my feeble flesh doth waste
By sin in it, which it towards hell doth weigh.
Only thou art above, and when towards thee
By thy leave I can look, I rise again;   10
But our old subtle foe so tempteth me,
That not one hour myself I can sustain.
Thy grace may wing me to prevent his art
And thou like adamant draw mine iron heart.

200. 'I am a little world made cunningly'

I am a little world made cunningly
Of elements, and an angelic sprite;
But black sin hath betrayed to endless night
My world's both parts, and (oh) both parts must die.
You which beyond that heaven which was most high
Have found new spheres, and of new land can write,
Power new seas in mine eyes, that so I might
Drown my world with my weeping earnestly,
Or wash it if it must be drowned no more:
But oh it must be burnt! alas the fire   10
Of lust and envy have burnt it heretofore,
And made it fouler. Let their flames retire,
And burn me, oh Lord, with a fiery zeal
Of thee and thy house, which doth in eating heal.

201. 'This is my play's last scene, here heavens appoint'

This is my play's last scene, here heavens appoint
My pilgrimage's last mile; and my race
Idly yet quickly run, hath this last pace,
My span's last inch, my minute's latest point,
And gluttonous death will instantly unjoint
My body, and soul, and I shall sleep a space,
But my ever-waking part shall see that face
Whose fear already shakes my every joint:
Then as my soul to heaven, her first seat, takes flight

And earth-born body in the earth shall dwell,   10
So fall my sins that all may have their right,
To where they are bred and would press me, to hell.
Impute me righteous, thus purged of evil,
For thus I leave the world, the flesh, the devil.

202. 'At the round earth's imagined corners, blow'

At the round earth's imagined corners, blow
Your trumpets, angels, and arise, arise
From death, you numberless infinities
Of souls, and to your scattered bodies go,
All whom the flood did, and fire shall o'erthrow,
All whom war, death, age, agues, tyrannies,
Despair, law, chance, hath slain, and you whose eyes
Shall behold God and never taste death's woe.
But let them sleep, Lord, and me mourn a space
For, if above all these my sins abound,   10
'Tis late to ask abundance of thy grace,
When we are there; here on this lowly ground,
Teach me how to repent; for that's as good
As if thou hadst sealed my pardon, with thy blood.

203. 'Death be not proud, though some have called thee'

Death be not proud, though some have called thee
Mighty and dreadful, for thou art not so,
For those whom thou think'st thou dost overthrow
Die not, poor death, nor yet can'st thou kill me;
From rest and sleep, which but thy pictures be,
Much pleasure, then from thee, much more must flow,
And soonest our best men with thee do go,
Rest of their bones and souls' delivery.
Thou art slave to fate, chance, kings, and desperate men
And dost with poison, war, and sickness dwell.   10
And poppy or charms can make us sleep as well
And better than thy stroke; why swell'st thou then?
One short sleep past, we wake eternally
And death shall be no more; death thou shalt die.

204. 'What if this present were the world's last night?'

What if this present were the world's last night?
Mark in my heart, O soul, where thou dost dwell,
The picture of Christ crucified and tell
Whether his countenance can thee afright,
Tears in his eyes quench the amazing light,
Blood fills his frowns, which from his pierced head fell.
And can that tongue adjudge thee unto hell,
Which prayed forgiveness for his foes' fierce spite?
No, no; but as in my idolatry
I said to all my profane mistresses,   10
Beauty, of pity, foulness only is
A sign of rigour: so I say to thee,
To wicked spirits are horrid shapes assigned,
This beauteous form assures a piteous mind.

205. 'Batter my heart, three personed God; for you'

Batter my heart, three personed God; for you
As yet but knock, breathe, shine, and seek to mend;
That I may rise and stand, o'erthrow me and bend
Your force, to break, blow, burn and make me new.
I, like an usurped town to another due,
Labour to admit you, but Oh, to no end,
Reason your viceroy in me, me should defend
But is captived and proves weak or untrue.
Yet dearly I love you, and would be loved fain,
But am betrothed unto your enemy;   10
Divorce me, untie, or break that knot again,
Take me to you, imprison me, for I
Except you enthrall me, never shall be free
Nor ever chaste, except you ravish me.

206. A Hymn to God the Father

I

Wilt thou forgive that sin where I begun,
   Which was my sin, though it were done before?

Wilt thou forgive those sins through which I run,
 And do them still, though still I do deplore?
  When thou hast done, thou hast not done,
   For I have more.

II
Wilt thou forgive that sin by which I've won
 Others to sin, and made my sin their door?
Wilt thou forgive that sin which I did shun
 A year or two, but wallowed in, a score?   10
  When thou hast done, thou hast not done,
   For I have more.

III
I have a sin of fear that when I have spun
 My last thread, I shall perish on the shore;
Swear by thyself that at my death thy Sun°   *Sun/Son*
  Shall shine as it shines now, and heretofore;
   And having done that, thou hast done,
    I have no more.

Ben Jonson (1572–1637)

207. Hymn to Diana

Queen and Huntress, chaste and fair,
Now the sun is laid to sleep,
Seated in thy silver chair
State in wonted manner keep:
 Hesperus entreats thy light,
 Goddess excellently bright.

Earth, let not thy envious shade
Dare itself to interpose;
Cynthia's shining orb was made
Heaven to clear when day did close: 10

Bless us then with wishèd sight,
Goddess excellently bright.

Lay thy bow of pearl apart
And thy crystal-shining quiver;
Give unto the flying hart
Space to breathe, how short soever:
    Thou that mak'st a day of night,
    Goddess excellently bright!

208. 'Slow, slow, fresh fount, keep time with my salt tears'

Slow, slow, fresh fount, keep time with my salt tears;
    Yet slower, yet, O faintly, gentle springs:
List to the heavy part the music bears,
    Woe weeps out her division, when she sings.
        Droop herbs, and flowers,
        Fall grief in showers,
        Our beauties are not ours:
           O, I could still,
Like melting snow upon some craggy hill,
    Drop, drop, drop, drop,   10
Since nature's pride is, now, a withered daffodil.

209. To William Camden

Camden, most reverend head, to whom I owe
All that I am in arts, all that I know
(How nothing's that?), to whom my country owes
The great renown and name wherewith she goes.
Than thee the age sees not that thing more grave,
More high, more holy, that she more would crave.
What name, what skill, what faith hast thou in things!
What sight in searching the most antique springs!
What weight, and what authority in thy speech!
Man scarce can make that doubt, but thou can'st teach.   10
Pardon free truth, and let thy modesty,

Which conquers all, be once overcome by thee.
Many of thine this better could, than I,
But for their powers, accept my piety.

210. '"Buzz," quoth the blue-fly'

'Buzz,' quoth the blue-fly,
   'Hum,' quoth the bee;
'Buzz' and 'Hum' they cry,
   And so do we.
In his ear, in his nose,
   Thus, do you see?
He eat the dormouse,
   Else it was he.

211. On My First Daughter

Here lies to each her parents' ruth,
Mary, the daughter of their youth;
Yet all heaven's gifts, being heaven's due,
It makes the father, less, to rue.
At six months' end, she parted hence
With safety of her innocence;
Whose soul heaven's queen (whose name she bears)
In comfort of her mother's tears,
Hath placed amongst her virgin train,
Where, while that severed doth remain,   10
This grave partakes the fleshly birth.
Which cover lightly, gentle earth.

212. On My First Son

Farewell, thou child of my right hand, and joy;
My sin was too much hope of thee, loved boy.
Seven years thou wert lent to me, and I thee pay,
Exacted by thy fate, on the just day.
O, could I lose all father now. For why

Will man lament the state he should envy?
To have so soon 'scaped world's, and flesh's rage,
And if no other misery, yet age?
Rest in soft peace and, asked, say here doth lie
Ben Jonson his best piece of poetry.   10
For whose sake henceforth all his vows be such,
As what he loves may never like too much.

213. To the Memory of my Beloved, the Author, Mr William Shakespeare, and What he hath Left Us

To draw no envy (Shakespeare) on thy name,
Am I thus ample to thy book and fame;
While I confess thy writings to be such
As neither man nor muse can praise too much.
'Tis true, and all men's suffrage. But these ways
Were not the paths I meant unto thy praise;
For seeliest° ignorance on these may light,   *blindest*
Which, when it sounds at best, but echoes right;
Or blind affection, which doth ne'er advance
The truth, but gropes, and urgeth all by chance;   10
Or crafty malice might pretend this praise,
And think to ruin, where it seemed to raise.
These are as° some infamous bawd or whore   *as if*
Should praise a matron. What could hurt her more?
But thou art proof against them, and indeed,
Above th' ill fortune of them, or the need.
I therefore will begin. Soul of the age!
The applause, delight, the wonder of our stage!
My Shakespeare, rise! I will not lodge thee by
Chaucer, or Spenser, or bid Beaumont lie   20
A little further, to make thee a room:
Thou art a monument without a tomb
And art alive still while thy book doth live
And we have wits to read and praise to give.
That I not mix thee so, my brain excuses,
I mean with great, but disproportioned muses;
For if I thought my judgement were of years,
I should commit thee surely with thy peers
And tell how far thou did'st our Lyly outshine,
Or sporting Kyd, or Marlowe's mighty line.   30

And though thou had'st small Latin and less Greek,
From thence to honour thee, I would not seek
For names; but call forth thundering Aeschylus,
Euripides and Sophocles to us,
Pacuvius, Accius, him° of Cordoba dead,   *Seneca*
To life again, to hear thy buskin° tread,   *footwear for tragedy*
And shake a stage; or, when thy socks° were on,   *footwear for comedy*
Leave thee alone for the comparison
Of all that insolent Greece or haughty Rome
Sent forth, or since did from their ashes come.   40
Triumph, my Britain, thou hast one to show
To whom all scenes of Europe homage owe.
He was not of an age but for all time,
And all the muses still were in their prime,
When like Apollo he came forth to warm
Our ears, or like a Mercury to charm!
Nature herself was proud of his designs
And joyed to wear the dressing of his lines
Which were so richly spun, and woven so fit
As, since, she will vouchsafe no other wit.   50
The merry Greek, tart Aristophanes,
Neat Terence, witty Plautus, now not please,
But antiquated and deserted lie,
As they were not of Nature's family.
Yet must I not give Nature all: thy art,
My gentle Shakespeare, must enjoy a part.
For though the poet's matter nature be,
His art doth give the fashion. And that he
Who casts to write a living line must sweat
(Such as thine are) and strike the second heat   60
Upon the muses' anvil: turn the same
(And himself with it) that he thinks to frame;
Or for the laurel he may gain a scorn,
For a good poet's made, as well as born.
And such wert thou. Look how the father's face
Lives in his issue, even so the race
Of Shakespeare's mind and manners brightly shines
In his well-turnèd and true-filèd lines,
In each of which he seems to shake a lance,
As brandished at the eyes of ignorance.   70
Sweet Swan of Avon, what a sight it were
To see thee in our waters yet appear,
And make those flights upon the banks of Thames

That so did take Eliza and our James!
But stay, I see thee in the hemisphere
Advanced, and made a constellation there!
Shine forth, thou star of poets, and with rage
Or influence chide or cheer the drooping stage;
Which, since thy flight from hence, hath mourned like night,
And despairs day, but for thy volume's light.   80

214. To Penshurst

Thou art not, Penshurst, built to envious show
    Of touch, or marble; nor can'st boast a row
Of polished pillars, or a roof of gold:
    Thou hast no lantern, whereof tales are told;
Or stair, or courts; but stand'st an ancient pile,
    And these grudged at, art reverenced the while.
Thou joy'st in better marks, of soil, of air,
    Of wood, of water: therein thou art fair.
Thou hast thy walks for health, as well as sport:
    Thy mount, to which the dryads do resort,   10
Where Pan and Bacchus their high feasts have made
    Beneath the broad beech and the chestnut shade;
That taller tree, which of a nut was set,
    At his° great birth, where all the muses met.   *Sir Philip Sidney's*
There, in the writhèd bark, are cut the names
    Of many a sylvan, taken with his flames
And thence the ruddy satyrs oft provoke
    The lighter fauns to reach thy Lady's Oak.
Thy copse, too, named of Gamage, thou hast there,
    That never fails to serve thee seasoned deer   20
When thou would'st feast, or exercise thy friends.
    The lower land, that to the river bends,
Thy sheep, thy bullocks, kine and calves do feed:
    The middle grounds thy mares, and horses breed.
Each bank doth yield thee coneys; and the tops,
    Fertile of wood, Ashore, and Sidney's copse,
To crown thy open table, doth provide
    The purpled pheasant with the speckled side;
The painted partridge lies in every field
    And, for thy mess, is willing to be killed.   30
And if the high-swollen Medway fail thy dish,

Thou hast thy ponds, that pay thee tribute fish,
Fat, aged carps, that run into thy net,
   And pikes, now weary their own kind to eat,
As loath, the second draught, or cast to stay,
   Officiously, at first, themselves betray;
Bright eels, that emulate them, and leap on land
   Before the fisher, or into his hand.
Then hath thy orchard fruit, thy garden flowers,
   Fresh as the air, and new as are the hours.   40
The early cherry, with the later plum,
   Fig, grape, and quince, each in his time doth come:
The blushing apricot, and woolly peach
   Hang on thy walls, that every child may reach.
And though thy walls be of the country stone,
   They're reared with no man's ruin, no man's groan;
There's none that dwell about them wish them down,
   But all come in, the farmer and the clown,
And no one empty-handed, to salute
   Thy lord and lady, though they have no suit.   50
Some bring a capon, some a rural cake,
   Some nuts, some apples; some that think they make
The better cheeses bring them, or else send
   By their ripe daughters, whom they would commend
This way to husbands; and whose baskets bear
   An emblem of themselves, in plum, or pear.
But what can this (more than express their love)
   Add to thy free provisions, far above
The need of such? whose liberal board doth flow
   With all that hospitality doth know!   60
Where comes no guest but is allowed to eat,
   Without his fear, and of thy lord's own meat;
Where the same beer and bread and self-same wine
   That is his lordship's, shall be also mine.
And I not fain to sit (as some, this day,
   At great men's tables) and yet dine away.
Here no man tells° my cups; nor, standing by,   *counts*
   A waiter doth my gluttony envy:
But gives me what I call and lets me eat;
   He knows below he shall find plenty of meat;   70
Thy tables hoard not up for the next day.
   Nor when I take my lodging need I pray
For fire, or lights, or livery: all is there,
   As if thou then wert mine, or I reigned here:

There's nothing I can wish, for which I stay.
    That found King James when, hunting late, this way,
With his brave son, the prince, they saw thy fires
    Shine bright on every hearth as the desires
Of thy Penates° had been set on flame   *household gods*
    To entertain them; or the country came,   80
With all their zeal, to warm their welcome here.
    What (great, I will not say, but) sudden cheer
Did'st thou then make them! and what praise was heaped
    On thy good lady then! who therein reaped
The just reward of her high housewifery:
    To have her linen, plate, and all things nigh
When she was far: and not a room but dressed
    As if it had expected such a guest!
These, Penshurst, are thy praise, and yet not all.
    Thy lady's noble, fruitful, chaste withal.   90
His children thy great lord may call his own:
    A fortune, in this age, but rarely known.
They are, and have been taught religion: thence
    Their gentler spirits have sucked innocence.
Each morn and even, they are taught to pray
    With the whole household and may, every day,
Read, in their virtuous parents' noble parts,
    The mysteries of manners, arms, and arts.
Now, Penshurst, they that will proportion thee
    With other edifices, when they see   100
Those proud, ambitious heaps, and nothing else,
    May say, their lords have built, but thy lord dwells.

215. To Sir Robert Wroth

How blest art thou, can'st love the country, Wroth,
    Whether by choice, or fate, or both;
And, though so near the city and the court
    Art taken with neither's vice, nor sport:
That at great times art no ambitious guest
    Of sheriff's dinner, or mayor's feast;
Nor com'st to view the better cloth of state;
    The richer hangings, or crown-plate;
Nor throng'st (when masquing is) to have a sight
    Of the short bravery of the night;   10

To view the jewels, stuffs, the pains, the wit
   There wasted, some not paid for yet!
But can'st, at home, in thy securer rest,
   Live, with unbought provision blest;
Free from proud porches or their gilded roofs,
   'Mongst lowing herds, and solid hoofs:
Alongst the curlèd woods and painted meads,
   Through which a serpent river leads
To some cool, courteous shade, which he calls his,
   And makes sleep softer than it is!   20
Or, if thou list the night in watch to break,
   Abed can'st hear the loud stag speak,
In spring, oft rousèd for thy master's sport,
   Who, for it, makes thy house his court;
Or with thy friends the heart of all the year
   Divid'st, upon the lesser deer;
In autumn, at the partridge mak'st a flight,
   And giv'st thy gladder guests the sight;
And, in the Winter, hunt'st the flying hare,
   More for thy exercise, than fare;   30
While all that follow their glad ears apply
   To the full greatness of the cry:
Or hawking at the river or the bush,
   Or shooting at the greedy thrush,
Thou dost with some delight the day outwear,
   Although the coldest of the year!
The whil'st the several seasons thou hast seen
   Of flowery fields, of copses green,
The mowèd meadows with the fleecèd sheep,
   And feasts, that either shearers keep;   40
The ripened ears, yet humble in their height,
   And furrows laden with their weight;
The apple-harvest, that doth longer last;
   The hogs returned home fat from mast;
The trees cut out in log, and those boughs made
   A fire now, that lent a shade!
Thus Pan and Sylvane having had their rites,
   Comus puts in, for new delights;
And fills thy open hall with mirth and cheer,
   As if in Saturn's reign it were;   50
Apollo's harp and Hermes' lyre resound,
   Nor are the muses strangers found:

The rout of rural folk come thronging in
    (Their rudeness then is thought no sin);
Thy noblest house affords them welcome grace;
    And the great heroes of her race
Sit mixed with loss of state or reverence.
    Freedom doth with degree dispense.
The jolly wassail walks the often round,
    And in their cups, their cares are drowned.   60
They think not, then, which side the cause shall lease,
    Nor how to get the lawyer fees.
Such and no other was that age of old,
    Which boasts t' have had the head of gold.
And such, since thou can'st make thine own content,
    Strive, Wroth, to live long innocent.
Let others watch in guilty arms and stand
    The fury of a rash command,
Go enter breaches, meet the cannon's rage,
    That they may sleep with scars in age,   70
And show their feathers shot and colours torn,
    And brag that they were therefore born.
Let this man sweat and wrangle at the bar,
    For every price in every jar,
And change possessions oft'ner with his breath
    Than either money, war, or death:
Let him, than hardest sires, more disinherit,
    And each-where boast it as his merit
To blow up orphans, widows and their states;°   *estates*
    And think his power doth equal fate's.   80
Let that go heap a mass of wretched wealth,
    Purchased by rapine, worse than stealth,
And brooding o'er it sit with broadest eyes,
    Not doing good, scarce when he dies.
Let thousands more go flatter vice and win
    By being organs to great sin;
Get place and honour, and be glad to keep
    The secrets that shall break their sleep;
And, so they ride in purple, eat in plate,
    Though poison, think it a great fate.   90
But thou, my Wroth, if I can truth apply,
    Shalt neither that, nor this envy:
Thy peace is made; and when man's state is well
    'Tis better, if he there can dwell.

God wisheth none should wrack on a strange shelf;
    To him, man's dearer, than t' himself.
And howsoever we may think things sweet,
    He always gives what he knows meet;
Which who can use is happy. Such be thou.
    Thy morning's and thy evening's vow   100
Be thanks to him, and earnest prayer, to find
    A body sound, with sounder mind;
To do thy country service, thyself right;
    That neither want do thee afright,
Nor death; but when thy latest sand is spent,
    Thou may'st think life a thing but lent.

216. Song. To Celia

Come, my Celia, let us prove
While we may the sports of love;
Time will not be ours forever;
He at length our good will sever.
Spend not then his gifts in vain.
Suns that set may rise again:
But if once we lose this light
'Tis with us perpetual night.
Why should we defer our joys?
Fame and rumour are but toys.   10
Cannot we delude the eyes
Of a few poor household spies?
Or his easier ears beguile,
So removèd by our wile?
'Tis no sin love's fruit to steal,
But the sweet theft to reveal:
To be taken, to be seen,
These have crimes accounted been.

217. A Hymn to God the Father

Hear me, O God!
    A broken heart
    Is my best part:

Use still thy rod,
    That I may prove
    Therein thy Love.

If thou had'st not
    Been stern to me,
    But left me free,
I had forgot   10
    My self and thee.

For sin's so sweet
    As minds ill bent
    Rarely repent,
Until they meet
    Their punishment.

Who more can crave
    Than thou hast done:
    That gav'st a Son
To free a slave?   20
    First made of nought;
    Withal since bought.

Sin, death and hell,
    His glorious Name
    Quite overcame,
Yet I rebel
    And slight the same.

But I'll come in,
    Before my loss,
    Me farther toss,   30
As sure to win
    Under his Cross.

218. Ode to Himself upon the Censure of his 'New Inn'

    Come, leave the loathèd stage,
    And the more loathsome age
Where pride and impudence, in faction knit,
    Usurp the chair of wit:

Indicting and arraigning every day
    Something they call a play.
  Let their fastidious, vain
  Commission of the brain
Run on and rage, sweat, censure and condemn:
They were not made for thee, less thou for them.   10

    Say that thou pour'st them wheat,
    And they will acorns eat;
'Twere simple fury still thyself to waste
    On such as have no taste!
To offer them a surfeit of pure bread
    Whose appetites are dead!
  No, give them grains their fill,
  Husks, draff to drink and swill:
If they love lees, and leave the lusty wine,
Envy them not, their palate's with the swine.   20

    No doubt some mouldy tale,
    Like Pericles, and stale
As the shrieve's° crust, and nasty as his fish,   *jailor's*
    Scraps out of every dish
Thrown forth, and raked into the common tub,
    May keep up the play club.
  Broome's° sweepings do as well   *Richard Brome*
  There, as his master's meal;
For who the relish of these guests will fit,
Needs set them but the alms-basket of wit.   30

    And much good do it ye then,
    Brave plush-and-velvet men
Can feed on orts; and safe in your scene° clothes,   *stage*
    Dare quit,° upon your oaths,   *acquit*
The stagers, and the stage-wrights too (your peers)
    Of larding your large ears
  With rage of comic socks,
  Wrought upon twenty blocks;
Which, if they're torn, and turned, and patched enough,
The gamesters share your gilt,° and you their stuff.   *(pun on 'guilt')* 40

    Leave things so prostitute,
    And take the Alcaic lute;
Or thine own Horace, or Anacreon's lyre;
    Warm thee by Pindar's fire:

And though thy nerves be shrunk, and blood be cold,
    Ere years have made thee old,
   Strike that disdainful heat
   Throughout, to their defeat:
As curious fools, and envious of thy strain,
May blushing swear, no palsy's in thy brain.   50

    But when they hear thee sing
    The glories of thy king,
His zeal to God, and his just awe o'er men,
    They may, blood-shaken then,
Feel such a flesh-quake to possess their powers,
    That no tuned harp like ours
   In sound of peace or wars,
   Shall truly hit the stars
When they shall read the acts of Charles his reign,
And see his chariot triumph 'bove his wain.   60

Mary Wroth (1587?–1652?)

219. 'This night the moon eclipsèd was'

This night the moon eclipsèd was
   Alas,
But quickly she did brightlier shine
   Divine,
Prognosticating by sweet rain
That all things should be clear again.

Sweet rain foretells us good to grow,
   And flow,
Cool drops' sweet moisture, flowers bring
   To spring,   10
Which fruit brings forth, and so shall we
Live hopefully all good to see.

But in this time the sun is lost
   And crossed,
Thought in Antipodes not quite bereft
   Nor left,
But in just course shall come again,
And with pure light both shine, and reign.

220. 'Lying upon the beach'

Lying upon the beach,
   Below me on the sands,
I saw within small reach
   A lady lie in bands,
With arms across, and hands
Infolded in those twines,
Whereby a true love shines
And for love's triumph stands.

'Alas,' cried she, 'can love
   Bequeath me no small space   10
Where I may live and love
   But run in ruin's race?
Nor yet to gain death's trace,
You locks of his own hair,
Witness I still you bear
In my heart's dearest place,

'But O false is his heart,
   Yet faithful is his hair,
Dead is his love, a pretty art
   If we these two compare.   20
Hair once cut off hath share
With death, love's life being fled,
To shadow hair is fled,
So are my joys to care.

'Unconstant man, yet dear
   Behold thy hair outlive
Thy faith, thy worth, and clear
   As thine eyes, which did drive

Wrack to my heart, take back
These relics, lay the rack   30
On shrivelled hearts, and cry
Hair outlives Constancy.'

221. from *Pamphilia to Amphilanthus*

21

When last I saw thee, I did not thee see,
It was thine image which in my thoughts lay
So lively figured, as no time's delay
Could suffer me in heart to parted be.
And sleep so favourable is to me,
As not to let thy loved remembrance stray
Lest that I waking might have cause to say,
There was one minute found to forget thee.
Then, since my faith is such, so kind my sleep,
That gladly thee presents into my thought,   10
And still true Lover like thy face doth keep,
So as some pleasure shadow-like is wrought,
Pity my loving, nay of consience give
Reward to me in whom thy self doth live

22

Like to the Indians scorchèd with the sun,
The sun which they do as their God adore,
So am I used by love, for evermore
I worship him, less favours have I won.
Better are they who thus to blackness run,
And so can only whiteness' want deplore:
I who pale and white am with grief's store
Nor can have hope, but to see hopes undone,
Besides their sacrifice received in sight
Of their chose° Saint, mine hid as worthless rite.   *chosen* 10
Grant me to see where I my offerings give,
Then let me wear the mark of Cupid's might
In heart, as they in skin of Phoebus' light,
Not ceasing offerings to love while I live.

23

When every one to pleasing pastime hies
Some hunt, some hawk, some play, while some delight
In sweet discourse, and music shows joy's might,
Yet I my thoughts do far above these prize.
The joy which I take is, that free from eyes
I sit and wonder at this day-like night,
So to dispose themselves as void of right,
And leave true pleasure for poor vanities.
When others hunt, my thoughts I have in chase;
If hawk, my mind at wishèd end doth fly: 10
Discourse, I with my spirit talk and cry;
While others music choose as greatest grace.
'O God,' say I, 'can these fond pleasures move,
Or music be but in sweet thoughts of love?'

Robert Herrick (1591–1674)

222. The Carcanet

Instead of orient pearls, of jet
I sent my love a carcanet.
About her spotless neck she knit
The lace, to honour me, or it.
Then think how rapt was I to see
My jet t' enthral such ivory.

223. To Live Merrily, and to Trust to Good Verses

Now is the time for mirth,
   Nor cheek, or tongue be dumb,

For with the flow'ry earth
    The golden pomp is come.

The golden pomp is come;
    For now each tree does wear
(Made of her pap and gum)
    Rich beads of amber here.

Now reigns the rose, and now
    Th' Arabian dew besmears
My uncontrollèd brow
    And my retorted hairs.

Homer, this health to thee,
    In sack of such a kind
That it would make thee see
    Though thou wert ne'er so blind.

Next, Virgil, I'll call forth
    To pledge this second health
In wine, whose each cup's worth
    An Indian commonwealth.

A goblet next I'll drink
    To Ovid, and suppose,
Made he the pledge, he'd think
    The world had all one nose.°   *[play on Ovid's name Naso]*

Then this immensive cup
    Of aromatic wine,
Catullus, I quaff up
    To that terse muse of thine.

Wild I am now with heat;
    O Bacchus! cool thy rays!
Or frantic I shall eat
    Thy thyrse, and bite the bays.

Round, round, the roof does run;
    And being ravished thus,
Come, I will drink a tun
    To my Propertius.

Now, to Tibullus, next,
    This flood I drink to thee:

10

20

30

But stay; I see a text,
   That this presents to me.   40

Behold, Tibullus lies
   Here burnt, whose small return
Of ashes, scarce suffice
   To fill a little urn.

Trust to good verses then;
   They only will aspire,
When pyramids, as men,
   Are lost, i' th' funeral fire.

And when all bodies meet
   In Lethe to be drowned,   50
Then only numbers sweet,
   With endless life are crowned.

224. The Definition of Beauty

Beauty, no other thing is, than a beam
Flashed out between the middle and extreme.

225. Delight in Disorder

A sweet disorder in the dress
Kindles in clothes a wantonness;
A lawn about the shoulders thrown
Into a fine distraction;
An erring lace, which here and there
Enthrals the crimson stomacher;
A cuff neglectful, and thereby
Ribbons to flow confusedly;
A winning wave (deserving note)
In the tempestuous petticoat;   10
A careless shoestring, in whose tie
I see a wild civility;
Do more bewitch me, than when art
Is too precise in every part.

226. Upon Julia's Clothes

When as in silks my Julia goes,
Then, then (methinks) how sweetly flows
That liquefaction of her clothes.

Next, when I cast mine eyes and see
That brave vibration each way free,
O how that glittering taketh me!

227. Upon Mr Ben. Jonson.

After the rare arch-poet Jonson died,
The sock grew loathsome, and the buskin's pride,
Together with the stage's glory stood
Each like a poor and pitied widowhood.
The cirque profaned was, and all postures racked,
For men did strut, and stride, and stare, not act.
Then temper flew from words; and men did squeak,
Look red, and blow, and bluster, but not speak.
No holy rage, or frantic fires did stir,
Or flash about the spacious theatre.   10
No clap of hands, or shout, or praise's-proof
Did crack the play-house sides, or cleave her roof.
Artless the scene was; and that monstrous sin
Of deep and arrant ignorance came in;
Such ignorance as theirs was, who once hissed
At thy unequalled play, the *Alchemist*.
Oh fie upon 'em! Lastly too, all wit
In utter darkness did, and still will sit
Sleeping the luckless age out, till that she
Her resurrection has again with thee.   20

228. A Panegyric to Sir Lewis Pemberton

Till I shall come again, let this suffice,
    I send my salt, my sacrifice
To thee, thy lady, younglings, and as far

As to thy genius and thy lar;°   *household god*
To the worn threshold, porch, hall, parlour, kitchen,
   The fat-fed smoking temple, which in
The wholesome savour of thy mighty chines
   Invites to supper him who dines,
Where laden spits, wrapped with large ribs of beef;
   Not represent, but give relief   10
To the lank stranger and the sour swain;
   Where both may feed, and come again.
For no black-bearded vigil from thy door
   Beats with a buttoned-staff the poor:
But from thy warm-love-hatching gates each may
   Take friendly morsels, and there stay
To sun his thin-clad members, if he likes,
   For thou no porter keep'st who strikes.
No comer to thy roof his guest-rite wants;
   Or staying there, is scourged with taunts   20
Of some rough groom, who (irked with corns) says, 'Sir,
   Y' ave dipped too long i' th' vinegar;
And with our broth and bread, and bits; Sir, friend,
   Y' ave farced well, pray make an end;
Two days y' ave larded here; a third, ye know,
   Makes guests and fish smell strong; pray go
You to some other chimney, and there take
   Essay of other giblets; make
Merry at another's hearth; y' are here
   Welcome as thunder to our beer: 30
Manners knows distance, and a man unrude
   Would soon recoil, and not intrude
His stomach to a second meal.' No, no,
   Thy house, well fed and taught, can show
No such crabbed vizard: thou hast learnt thy train,
   With heart and hand to entertain:
And by the arms-full (with a breast unhid)
   As the old race of mankind did,
When either's heart, and either's hand did strive
   To be the nearer relative: 40
Thou dost redeem those times; and what was lost
   Of ancient honesty, may boast
It keeps a growth in thee; and so will run
   A course in thy fame's-pledge, thy son.
Thus, like a Roman tribune, thou thy gate
   Early sets ope to feast, and late:

Keeping no currish waiter to affright,
    With blasting eye, the appetite,
Which fain would waste upon thy cates,° but that   *food*
    The trencher-creature marketh what   50
Best and more suppling piece he cuts, and by
    Some private pinch tells danger's nigh
A hand too desperate, or a knife that bites
    Skin deep into the pork, or lights
Upon some part of kid, as if mistook,
    When checked by the butler's look.
No, no, thy bread, thy wine, thy jocund beer
    Is not reserved for Trebius[42] here,
But all who at thy table seated are
    Find equal freedom, equal fare;   60
And thou, like to that hospitable god
    Jove, joy'st when guests make their abode
To eat thy bullock's thighs, thy veals, thy fat
    Wethers, and never grudged at.
The pheasant, partridge, godwit, reeve, ruff, rail,
    The cock, the curlew, and the quail;
These, and thy choicest viands, do extend
    Their taste unto the lower end
Of thy glad table: not a dish more known
    To thee, than unto any one: 70
But as thy meat, so thy immortal wine
    Makes the smirk° face of each to shine,   *pleasant*
And spring fresh rosebuds, while the salt, the wit
    Flows from the wine, and graces it:
While reverence, waiting at the bashful board,
    Honours my lady and my lord.
No scurrile jest, no open scene is laid
    Here, for to make the face afraid;
But temperate mirth dealt forth, and so discreet-
    ly that it makes the meat more sweet;   80
And adds perfumes unto the wine, which thou
    Dost rather pour forth, than allow
By cruse and measure; thus devoting wine,
    As the Canary Isles were thine:
But with that wisdom, and that method, as
    No one that's there his guilty glass
Drinks of distemper, or has cause to cry

[42] A butt of Juvenalian satire

Repentance to his liberty.
No, thou know'st order, ethics, and hast read
   All economics, know'st to lead   90
A house-dance neatly, and can'st truly show
   How far a figure ought to go,
Forward, or backward, side-ward, and what pace
   Can give, and what retract a grace;
What gesture, courtship; comeliness agrees,
   With those thy primitive decrees,
To give subsistence to thy house, and proof
   What genii support thy roof;
Goodness and greatness; not the oaken piles;
   For these, and marbles, have their whiles   100
To last, but not their ever: virtue's hand
   It is, which builds, 'gainst fate to stand.
Such is thy house, whose firm foundation's trust
   Is more in thee, than in her dust,
Or depth. These last may yield, and yearly shrink,
   When what is strongly built, no chink
Or yawning rupture can the same devour,
   But fixed it stands, by her own power,
And well-laid bottom, on the iron and rock,
   Which tries, and counter-stands the shock   110
And ram of time, and by vexation grows
   The stronger: virtue dies when foes
Are wanting to her exercise, but great
   And large she spreads, by dust and sweat.
Safe stand thy walls, and thee, and so both will,
   Since neither's height was raised by th' ill
Of others; since no stud, no stone, no piece,
   Was reared up by the poor-man's fleece:
No widow's tenement was racked to gild
   Or fret thy ceiling, or to build   120
A sweating-closet, to anoint the silk-
   Soft-skin, or bathe in asses' milk:
No orphan's pittance, left him, served to set
   The pillars up of lasting jet,
For which their cries might beat against thine ears,
   Or in the damp jet read their tears.
No plank from hallowed altar does appeal
   To yond Star Chamber, or does seal
A curse to thee, or thine; but all things even
   Make for thy peace, and pace to heaven.   130

Go on directly so, as just men may
   A thousand times, more swear, than say,
This is that princely Pemberton, who can
   Teach man to keep a God in man:
And when wise poets shall search out to see
   Good men, they find them all in thee.

229. To the Virgins, to Make Much of Time

Gather ye rosebuds while ye may,
   Old time is still a-flying;
And this same flower that smiles today,
   Tomorrow will be dying.

The glorious lamp of heaven, the sun,
   The higher he's a-getting;
The sooner will his race be run,
   And nearer he's to setting.

That age is best which is the first,
   When youth and blood are warmer;   10
But being spent, the worse, and worst
   Times, still succeed the former.

Then be not coy, but use your time;
   And while ye may, go marry:
For having lost but once your prime,
   You may for ever tarry.

230. To Daffodils

Fair daffodils, we weep to see
   You haste away so soon:
As yet the early-rising sun
   Has not attained his noon.
        Stay, stay,
     Until the hasting day
        Has run
     But to the evensong;

And, having prayed together, we
    Will go with you along.   10

We have short time to stay, as you,
  We have as short a spring;
As quick a growth to meet decay,
  As you, or any thing.
      We die,
As your hours do, and dry
      Away,
Like to the Summer's rain;
Or as the pearls of morning's dew
    Ne'er to be found again.   20

231. His Request to Julia

Julia, if I chance to die
Ere I print my poetry,
I most humbly thee desire
To commit it to the fire.
Better 'twere my book were dead
Then to live not perfected.

Francis Quarles (1592–1644)

232. 'Man's body's like a house: his greater bones'

Man's body's like a house: his greater bones
Are the main timber, and the lesser ones
Are smaller splints; his ribs are laths, daubed o'er,
Plastered with flesh and blood; his mouth's the door,
His throat's the narrow entries, and his heart
Is the great chamber, full of curious art.
His midriff is a large partition-wall

'Twixt the great chamber and the spacious hall;
His stomach is the kitchen, where the meat
Is often but half sod, for want of heat.   10
His spleen's a vessel nature does allot
To take the scum that rises from the pot;
His lungs are like the bellows, that respire
In every office, quickening every fire;
His nose the chimney is, whereby are vented
Such fumes as with the bellows are augmented.
His bowels are the sink, whose part's to drain
All noisome filth, and keep the kitchen clean.
His eyes are crystal windows, clear and bright,
Let in the object, and let out the sight.   20
And as the timber is or great or small,
Or strong or weak, 'tis apt to stand or fall.
Yet is the likeliest building sometimes known
To fall by obvious chances; overthrown
Oft times by tempests, by the full-mouthed blasts
Of heaven; sometimes by fire; sometimes it wastes
Through unadvised neglect; put case the stuff
Were ruin-proof; by nature strong enough
To conquer time, and age; put case it should
Ne'er know an end, alas our leases would.   30
What hast thou then, proud flesh and blood, to boast?
Thy days are evil at best; but few at most;
But sad at merriest; and but weak at strongest;
Unsure at surest; and but short at longest.

233. 'Why dost thou shade thy lovely face?'

Why dost thou shade thy lovely face? Oh, why
Does that eclipsing hand so long deny
The sunshine of thy soul-enlivening eye?

Without that light, what light remains in me?
Thou art my life, my way, my light; in thee
I live, I move, and by thy beams I see.

Thou art my life; if thou but turn away
My life's a thousand deaths: thou art my way;
Without thee, Lord, I travel not, but stray.

My light thou art; without thy glorious sight   10
Mine eyes are darkened with perpetual night.
My God, thou art my way, my life, my light.

Thou art my way; I wander if thou fly:
Thou art my light; if hid, how blind am I!
Thou art my life; if thou withdraw, I die.

Mine eyes are blind and dark, I cannot see;
To whom or whither should my darkness flee,
But to the light? and who's that light but thee?

My path is lost, my wandering steps do stray;
I cannot safely go, nor safely stay;   20
Whom should I seek but thee, my path, my way?

Oh, I am dead: to whom shall I, poor I,
Repair? to whom shall my sad ashes fly,
But life? and where is life but in thine eye?

And yet thou turn'st away thy face, and fly'st me;
And yet I sue for grace, and thou deny'st me;
Speak, art thou angry, Lord, or only try'st me?

Unscreen those heavenly lamps, or tell me why
Thou shad'st thy face; perhaps thou think'st no eye
Can view those flames, and not drop down and die.   30

If that be all, shine forth, and draw thee nigher;
Let me behold and die, for my desire
Is phoenix-like to perish in that fire.

Death-conquered Laz'rus was redeemed by thee;
If I am dead, Lord, set death's prisoner free;
Am I more spent, or stink I worse than he?

If my puffed life be out, give leave to tine°   *enclose*
My shameless snuff at that bright lamp of thine;
Oh, what's thy light the less for lighting mine?

If I have lost my path, great Shepherd, say,   40
Shall I still wander in a doubtful way?
Lord, shall a lamb of Israel's sheepfold stray?

Thou art the pilgrim's path, the blind man's eye,
The dead man's life; on thee my hopes rely;
If thou remove, I err, I grope, I die.

Disclose thy sunbeams; close thy wings, and stay;
See, see how I am blind, and dead, and stray,
O thou that art my light, my life, my way.

234. Sighs

at the contemporary deaths of those incomparable sisters, The Countess of Cleveland and Mistress Cicily Killigrew

If our
Sad eyes could rain
For every drop, a shower,
Our needless quill might then refrain
This heavy task: but since our tears are pent
Within our straitened eyes, our pen must give them vent.

Blunt quill,
And dost thou think
To glorify thy skill
In sooty characters of ink?   10
Or that thy easy language can proclaim
An accent half so shrill, as the loud trump of fame?

But tell,
O tell me why
Should our sad lines compel
A tear, or force a trickling eye?
We beg it not: what gentle eye embalms
The precious dust of saints, brings offerings, and not alms.

You whom
Victorious passion   20
Hath foiled and overcome
With sighs and tears, not wept for fashion,
Come bear a part: these obsequies do sue
To entertain such guests, such guests alone as you.

Rash fates!
Were you advised
At how extreme great rates
True honour and perfection's prized,
When you in twice two days, surprisèd more,
Than ages can prescribe, than ages can restore.   30

Repose,
O gentle earth,
This sacred dust, kept close,
As relics of our buried mirth:
Let time preserve your holy turfs unstirred:
This age will scarce unlock your gates for such a third.

In this
Cold bed of clay,
Unstained perfection is
Laid down to sleep, till break a day   40
Which, when the early morning trump shall sound,
With joy, with robes, with crowns shall wake, be clothed, be crowned.

Sad tomb!
Had'st thou the might
To understand for whom
Thy marble curtains make this night,
Thou'ld'st vie with Mahomet's (if such there be):
Two stones support but his, two saints are props to thee.

We should
Invoke to aid,   50
And challenge (if we would)
Assistance from the heavenly Maid;
But we forbear. The Spirit of grief infuses
More salt into our quill, than all the sacred Muses.

Provoke
Loud storms to blow;
Or smothering flax to smoke,
Full seas to swell, spring tides to flow;
For us; we need no aid, nor will suborn
The help of foreign art. True grief knows how to mourn.   60

Hard stones,
If hearts should not,
Would cleave and split with groans
Ere so much worth should lie forgot:
At such a loss, should stones forbear to break
Their flinty silence, stones, the very stones would speak.

To speak
Bare truth, would try
A faith that were not weak;
'Twould seem a rank hyperbole,   70
To make but half their excellence appear,
For whom we mourn, for whom we justify this tear.

If not
The height of blood,
Virtue without a spot,
And all those gifts that earth calls good,
May lend some privilege to life, nor add
Some sand to nature's glass, what matter good or bad!

Persuade,
Persuade not me,   80
False earth, to trust thy aid,
Or build my hopes on it, or thee:
Give all thou hast, alas, thou can'st not make
Estates for more than life: thou dost but give, and take.

Stone hearts
Let me bespeak
You all to play your parts.
If you be too too hard to break,
Too stout for drops to pierce, yet come,
You'll serve for stuff; to build their honourable tomb.   90

To break
The peace of saints,
In taking leave to speak
Our real griefs in vain complaints
Is but a trick of earth: why should we thus
Afflict our souls for them, that find no grief; but us?

Attend,
You gentle ears
A while, and we will end
Our sighs, and wipe away your tears;   100
We'll change our scene, and we'll unsad our style;
We'll teach your sighs to sing; we'll teach your tears to smile.

Report.
You blessed peers
Of the eternal court,
Your Hallelujahs mixed with theirs:
Welcome these saints to that celestial choir,
Where griefs do not explore, where joys do not expire.

And you,
O blessed pair,   110
That now have interview
With thrones and seraphims; that share
With powers and angels: O what oratory
Can colour out your joys? What pen can chant your glory?

Shall then
The puddle tears
Of earth begotten men
Wash your white names, or cloy your ears?
No, no, 'tis pity tears should intercept
The peace of your sweet rest, where tears are never wept.   120

Shed tears?
Had they been tied
To serve their weary years
At earth's hard trade, and then denied
A common rest, this had been apt to breed
A thousand, thousand tears: this had been grief indeed!

Enough:
Let this suffice
To show how poor a puff
Is earth, and all that earth can prize: 130
Wealth, honour, beauty, in whose flames we burn,
Give warning in the bed, and leave us at the Urn.

Without
The least surmise
Of unbelief, or doubt,
Our mountain faith doth canonise
These saints; whose dying ashes did confer
To their Redeemer's birth, gifts passing gold and myrrh.

My pen,
Thou hast transgressed;   140
Archangels, and not men
Should sing the story of their rest:
But we have done, we leave them to the trust
Of heaven's eternal tower, and kiss their sacred dust.

George Herbert (1593–1633)

235. The Altar

A broken altar, Lord, thy servant rears,
Made of a heart, and cemented with tears,
Whose parts are as thy hand did frame;
No workman's tool hath touched the same.
A heart alone
Is such a stone
As nothing but
Thy power doth cut.
Wherefore each part
Of my hard heart   10
Meets in this frame
To praise thy name,
That, if I chance to hold my peace,
These stones to praise thee may not cease.
O let thy blessed sacrifice be mine
And sanctify this altar to be thine.

236. Easter Wings

> Lord, who createdst man in wealth and store,
> Though foolishly he lost the same,
> Decaying more and more,
> Till he became
> Most poor.
> With thee
> O let me rise
> As larks, harmoniously,
> And sing this day thy victories:
> Then shall the fall further the flight in me.   10
>
> My tender age in sorrow did begin,
> And still with sicknesses and shame
> Thou didst so punish sin,
> That I became
> Most thin.
> With thee
> Let me combine,
> And feel this day thy victory:
> For, if I imp my wing on thine,
> Affliction shall advance the flight in me.   20

237. Sighs and Groans

O do not use me
After my sins! Look not on my desert
But on thy glory! Then thou wilt reform
And not refuse me: for thou only art
The mighty God, but I a silly worm;
   O do not bruise me!

O do not urge me!
For what account can thy ill steward make?
I have abused thy stock, destroyed thy woods,
Sucked all thy magazines; my head did ache   10
Till it found out how to consume thy goods;
   O do not scourge me!

O do not blind me!
I have deserved that an Egyptian night
Should thicken all my powers; because my lust
Hath still sewed fig-leaves to exclude thy light;
But I am frailty, and already dust;
    O do not grind me!

    O do not fill me
With the turned vial of thy bitter wrath!   20
For thou hast other vessels full of blood,
A part whereof my Saviour emptied hath,
E'en unto death; since he died for my good,
    O do not kill me!

    But O reprieve me!
For thou hast life and death at thy command;
Thou art both judge and saviour, feast and rod,
Cordial and corrosive; put not thy hand
Into the bitter box; but O my God,
    My God, relieve me!   10

238. Church Music

Sweetest of sweets, I thank you: when displeasure
    Did through my body wound my mind,
You took me thence, and in your house of pleasure
    A dainty lodging me assigned.

Now I in you without a body move,
    Rising and falling with your wings;
We both together sweetly live and love,
    Yet say sometimes, *God help poor Kings.*

Comfort, I'll die; for if you post from me,
    Sure shall I do so, and much more;
But if I travel in your company,   10
    You know the way to heaven's door.

239. The Pulley

When God at first made man,
Having a glass of blessings standing by,
'Let us,' said he, 'pour on him all we can;
Let the world's riches, which dispersèd lie,
    Contract into a span.'

    So strength first made a way;
Then beauty flowed, then wisdom, honour, pleasure;
When almost all was out, God made a stay,
Perceiving that alone of all his treasure
    Rest in the bottom lay.   10

    'For if I should,' said he,
'Bestow this jewel also on my creature,
He would adore my gifts instead of me,
And rest in nature, not the God of nature.
    So both should losers be.

    'Yet let him keep the rest,
But keep them with repining restlessness;
Let him be rich and weary, that at least,
If goodness lead him not, yet weariness
    May toss him to my breast.'   20

240. Affliction (I)

When first thou didst entice to thee my heart,
    I thought the service brave:
So many joys I writ down for my part
    Besides what I might have
Out of my stock of natural delights,
Augmented with thy gracious benefits.

I lookèd on thy furniture so fine
    And made it fine to me:
Thy glorious household-stuff did me entwine
    And 'tice me unto thee.   10

Such stars I counted mine; both heaven and earth
Paid me my wages in a world of mirth.

What pleasures could I want, whose King I served,
    Where joys my fellows were?
Thus argued into hopes, my thoughts reserved
    No place for grief or fear.
Therefore my sudden soul caught at the place
And made her youth and fierceness seek thy face.

At first thou gav'st me milk and sweetnesses;
    I had my wish and way;   20
My days were strewed with flowers and happiness;
    There was no month but May.
But with my years sorrow did twist and grow,
And made a party unawares for woe.

My flesh began unto my soul in pain,
    Sicknesses cleave my bones;
Consuming agues dwell in every vein
    And tune my breath to groans.
Sorrow was all my soul; I scarce believed,
Till grief did tell me roundly, that I lived.   30

When I got health, thou took'st away my life,
    And more; for my friends die;
My mirth and edge was lost, a blunted knife
    Was of more use than I.
Thus thin and lean without a fence or friend,
I was blown through with every storm and wind.

Whereas my birth and spirit rather took
    The way that takes the town,
Thou didst betray me to a lingering book
    And wrap me in a gown.   40
I was entangled in the world of strife,
Before I had the power to change my life.

Yet, for I threatened oft the siege to raise,
    Not simpering all mine age,
Thou often didst with academic praise
    Melt and dissolve my rage.

I took thy sweetened pill, till I came where
I could not go away, nor persevere.

Yet lest perchance I should too happy be
    In my unhappiness,   50
Turning my purge to food, thou throwest me
    Into more sicknesses.
Thus doth thy power cross-bias me, not making
Thine own gift good, yet me from my ways taking.

Now I am here, what thou wilt do with me
    None of my books will show;
I read, and sigh, and wish I were a tree,
    For sure then I should grow
To fruit or shade: at least some bird would trust
Her household to me, and I should be just.   60

Yet, though thou troublest me, I must be meek;
    In weakness must be stout.
Well, I will change the service, and go seek
    Some other master out.
Ah my dear God! Though I am clean forgot,
Let me not love thee, if I love thee not.

241. Prayer (I)

Prayer the church's banquet, angels' age,
    God's breath in man returning to his birth,
    The soul in paraphrase, heart in pilgrimage,
The Christian plummet sounding heaven and earth;
Engine against th' Almighty, sinners' tower,
    Reversed thunder, Christ-side-piercing spear,
    The six-days' world-transposing in an hour,
A kind of tune, which all things hear and fear;
Softness, and peace, and joy, and love, and bliss,
    Exalted manna, gladness of the best,   10
    Heaven in ordinary, man well dressed,
The milky way, the bird of paradise,
    Church-bells beyond the stars heard, the soul's blood,
    The land of spices; something understood.

242. The Temper (I)

How should I praise thee, Lord! How should my rhymes
    Gladly engrave thy love in steel,
  If what my soul doth feel sometimes,
    My soul might ever° feel!   *always*

Although there were some forty heavens, or more,
    Sometimes I peer above them all,
  Sometimes I hardly reach a score,
    Sometimes to hell I fall.

O rack me not to such a vast extent;
    Those distances belong to thee: 10
  The world's too little for thy tent,
    A grave too big for me.

Wilt thou meet arms with man, that thou dost stretch
    A crumb of dust from heaven to hell?
  Will great God measure with a wretch?
    Shall he thy stature spell?

O let me, when thy roof my soul hath hid,
    O let me roost and nestle there:
  Then of a sinner thou art rid,
    And I of hope and fear.   20

Yet take thy way; for sure thy way is best;
    Stretch or contract me thy poor debtor;
  This is but tuning of my breast
    To make the music better.

Whether I fly with angels, fall with dust,
    Thy hands made both, and I am there;
  Thy power and love, my love and trust
    Make one place every where.

243. Vanity (I)

  The fleet astronomer can bore
And thread the spheres with his quick piercing mind;

He views their stations, walks from door to door,
   Surveys, as if he had designed
To make a purchase there: he sees their dances,
     And knoweth long before
Both their full-eyed aspects, and secret glances.

   The nimble diver with his side
Cuts through the working waves, that he may fetch
His dearly earnèd pearl, which God did hide   10
     On purpose from the venturous wretch;
That he might save his life, and also hers,
     Who with excessive pride
Her own destruction and his danger wears.

   The subtle chymic can divest
And strip the creature naked, till he find
The callow principles within their nest:
   There he imparts to them his mind,
Admitted to their bed-chamber, before
     They appear trim and dressed   20
To ordinary suitors at the door.

   What hath not man sought out and found,
But his dear God? Who yet his glorious law
Embosoms in us, mellowing the ground
   With showers and frosts, with love and awe,
So that we need not say, 'Where's this command?'
     Poor man, thou searchest round
To find out *death*, but missest *life* at hand.

244.   Jordan (I)

Who says that fictions only and false hair
Become a verse? Is there in truth no beauty?
Is all good structure in a winding stair?
May no lines pass, except they do their duty
   Not to a true, but painted chair?

Is it no verse, except enchanted groves
And sudden arbours shadow coarse-spun lines?
Must purling streams refresh a lover's loves?

Must all be veiled, while he that reads, divines,
    Catching the sense at two removes?   10

Shepherds are honest people; let them sing.
Riddle who list, for me, and pull for prime:
I envy no man's nightingale or spring;
Nor let them punish me with loss of rhyme,
    Who plainly say, *My God, My King.*

245. Church Monuments

While that my soul repairs to her devotion,
Here I intomb my flesh, that it betimes
May take acquaintance of this heap of dust;
To which the blast of death's incessant motion,
Fed with the exhalation of our crimes,
Drives all at last. Therefore I gladly trust

My body to this school, that it may learn
To spell his elements, and find his birth
Written in dusty heraldry and lines,
Which dissolution sure doth best discern,   10
Comparing dust with dust, and earth with earth.
These laugh at jet, and marble put for signs,

To sever the good fellowship of dust,
And spoil the meeting. What shall point out them,
When they shall bow, and kneel, and fall down flat
To kiss those heaps, which now they have in trust?
Dear flesh, while I do pray, learn here thy stem
And true descent; that when thou shalt grow fat,

And wanton in thy cravings, thou mayest know,
That flesh is but the glass, which holds the dust   20
That measures all our time; which also shall
Be crumbled into dust. Mark here below
How tame these ashes are, how free from lust,
That thou may'st fit thyself against thy fall.

246. Virtue

Sweet day, so cool, so calm, so bright,
The bridal of the earth and sky:
The dew shall weep thy fall tonight,
    For thou must die.

Sweet rose, whose hue angry and brave
Bids the rash gazer wipe his eye:
Thy root is ever in its grave,
    And thou must die.

Sweet spring, full of sweet days and roses,
A box where sweets compacted lie;   10
My music shows ye have your closes,
    And all must die.

Only a sweet and virtuous soul,
Like seasoned timber, never gives;
But though the whole world turn to coal,
    Then chiefly lives.

247. Man

    My God, I heard this day,
That none doth build a stately habitation
    But he that means to dwell therein.
    What house more stately hath there been,
Or can be, than is man? to whose creation
    All things are in decay.

    For man is every thing,
And more: he is a tree, yet bears no fruit;
    A beast, yet is, or should be more.
    Reason and speech we only bring.   10
Parrots may thank us, if they are not mute,
    They go upon the score.

    Man is all symmetry,
Full of proportions, one limb to another,
    And all to all the world besides;

Each part may call the farthest, brother,
For head with foot hath private amity,
    And both with moons and tides.

    Nothing hath got so far,
But man hath caught and kept it as his prey.   20
    His eyes dismount the highest star:
    He is in little all the sphere.
Herbs gladly cure our flesh, because that they
    Find their acquaintance there.

    For us the winds do blow,
The earth doth rest, heaven move, and fountains flow.
    Nothing we see, but means our good,
    As our delight, or as our treasure:
The whole is, either our cupboard of food
    Or cabinet of pleasure.   30

    The stars have us to bed;
Night draws the curtain, which the sun withdraws;
    Music and light attend our head.
    All things unto our flesh are kind
In their descent and being; to our mind
    In their ascent and cause.

    Each thing is full of duty:
Waters united are our navigation;
    Distinguished, our habitation;
    Below, our drink; above, our meat;   40
Both are our cleanliness. Hath one such beauty?
    Then how are all things neat?

    More servants wait on man
Than he'll take notice of; in every path
    He treads down that which doth befriend him
    When sickness makes him pale and wan.
Oh mighty love! Man is one world, and hath
    Another to attend him.

    Since then, my God, thou hast
So brave a palace built: O dwell in it,   50
    That it may dwell with thee at last!
    Till then, afford us so much wit

That, as the world serves us, we may serve thee,
    And both thy servants be.

248. Life

I made a posy while the day ran by.
Here will I smell my remnant out, and tie
    My life within this band.
But time did beckon to the flowers, and they
By noon most cunningly did steal away
    And withered in my hand.

My hand was next to them, and then my heart.
I took, without more thinking, in good part
    Time's gentle admonition,
Who did so sweetly death's sad taste convey,   10
Making my mind to smell my fatal day,
    Yet sugaring the suspicion.

Farewell dear flowers, sweetly your time ye spent,
Fit, while ye lived, for smell or ornament,
    And after death for cures.
I follow straight without complaints or grief;
Since if my scent be good, I care not, if
    It be as short as yours.

249. Mortification

How soon doth man decay!
When clothes are taken from a chest of sweets
    To swaddle infants, whose young breath
        Scarce knows the way,
    Those clouts are little winding sheets
Which do consign and send them unto death.

    When boys go first to bed,
They step into their voluntary graves;
    Sleep binds them fast; only their breath
        Makes them not dead;   10

Successive nights, like rolling waves,
Convey them quickly, who are bound for death.

When youth is frank and free
And calls for music, while his veins do swell,
All day exchanging mirth and breath
In company,
That music summons to the knell,
Which shall befriend him at the house of death.

When man grows staid and wise,
Getting a house and home, where he may move   20
Within the circle of his breath,
Schooling his eyes,
That dumb enclosure maketh love
Unto the coffin, that attends his death.

When age grows low and weak,
Marking his grave, and thawing every year,
Till all do melt, and drown his breath
When he would speak;
A chair or litter shows the bier
Which shall convey him to the house of death.   30

Man, ere he is aware,
Hath put together a solemnity,
And dressed his hearse, while he has breath
As yet to spare.
Yet Lord; instruct us so to die,
That all these dyings may be life in death.

250. Death

Death, thou wast once an uncouth hideous thing,
Nothing but bones,
The sad effect of sadder groans:
Thy mouth was open, but thou could'st not sing.

For we considered thee as at some six
Or ten years hence,
After the loss of life and sense,
Flesh being turned to dust, and bones to sticks.

We looked on this side of thee, shooting short;
    Where we did find   10
  The shells of fledge souls left behind,
Dry dust, which sheds no tears, but may extort.

But since our Saviour's death did put some blood
    Into thy face,
  Thou art grown fair and full of grace,
Much in request, much sought for, as a good.

For we do now behold thee gay and glad,
    As at Doomsday,
  When souls shall wear their new array,
And all thy bones with beauty shall be clad.   20

Therefore we can go die as sleep, and trust
    Half that we have
  Unto an honest faithful grave;
Making our pillows either down, or dust.

251. The Collar

  I struck the board, and cried, 'No more,
    I will abroad.
  What? shall I ever sigh and pine?
My lines and life are free; free as the road,
  Loose as the wind, as large as store.
    Shall I be still in suit?
  Have I no harvest but a thorn
  To let me blood, and not restore
What I have lost with cordial fruit?
    Sure there was wine   10
  Before my sighs did dry it: there was corn
  Before my tears did drown it.
  Is the year only lost to me?
    Have I no bays to crown it?
No flowers, no garlands gay? All blasted?
    All wasted?
  Not so, my heart: but there is fruit,
    And thou hast hands.
  Recover all thy sigh-blown age

On double pleasures: leave thy cold dispute   20
Of what is fit, and not. Forsake thy cage,
      Thy rope of sands,
Which petty thoughts have made, and made to thee
  Good cable, to enforce and draw,
      And be thy law,
  While thou did'st wink and would'st not see.
      Away; take heed:
      I will abroad.
Call in thy death's head there: tie up thy fears.
      He that forbears   30
    To suit and serve his need,
      Deserves his load.'
But as I raved and grew more fierce and wild
      At every word,
  Me thoughts I heard one calling, 'Child!':
      And I replied, 'My Lord.'

252. The Flower

  How fresh, O Lord, how sweet and clean
Are thy returns! Even as the flowers in spring;
  To which, besides their own demean,
The late-past frosts tributes of pleasure bring.
    Grief melts away
    Like snow in May,
  As if there were no such cold thing.

  Who would have thought my shrivelled heart
Could have recovered greenness? It was gone
  Quite underground; as flowers depart   10
To see their mother root, when they have blown,
    Where they together
    All the hard weather,
  Dead to the world, keep house unknown.

  These are thy wonders, Lord of power,
Killing and quickening, bringing down to hell
  And up to heaven in an hour;
Making a chiming of a passing-bell;
    We say amiss,

This or that is: 20
  Thy word is all, if we could spell.

  O that I once past changing were,
Fast in thy Paradise, where no flower can wither!
  Many a spring I shoot up fair,
Offering at heaven, growing and groaning thither;
     Nor doth my flower
     Want a spring-shower,
  My sins and I joining together;

  But while I grow in a straight line,
Still upwards bent, as if heaven were mine own,   30
  Thy anger comes, and I decline.
What frost to that? What pole is not the zone,
     Where all things burn
     When thou dost turn,
  And the least frown of thine is shown?

  And now in age I bud again,
After so many deaths I live and write;
  I once more smell the dew and rain
And relish versing. O my only light,
     It cannot be   40
     That I am he
  On whom thy tempests fell all night.

  These are thy wonders, Lord of love,
To make us see we are but flowers that glide,
  Which when we once can find and prove,
Thou hast a garden for us, where to bide.
     Who would be more,
     Swelling through store,
  Forfeit their paradise by their pride.

253. Love (III)

Love bade me welcome, yet my soul drew back,
  Guilty of dust and sin.
But quick-eyed Love, observing me grow slack
  From my first entrance in,

Drew nearer to me, sweetly questioning,
    If I lacked any thing.

'A guest,' I answered, 'worthy to be here.'
    Love said, 'You shall be he.'
'I the unkind, ungrateful? Ah my dear,
    I cannot look on thee.'   10
Love took my hand, and smiling did reply,
    'Who made the eyes but I?'

'Truth, Lord, but I have marred them; let my shame
    Go where it doth deserve.'
'And know you not,' says Love, 'who bore the blame?'
    'My dear, then I will serve.'
'You must sit down,' says Love, 'and taste my meat.'
    So I did sit and eat.

Thomas Carew (1595–1640)

254. A Cruel Mistress

We read of kings and gods that kindly took
A pitcher filled with water from the brook;
But I have daily tendered without thanks
Rivers of tears that overflow their banks.
A slaughtered bull will appease angry Jove
A horse the sun, a lamb the god of love,
But she disdains the spotless sacrifice
Of a pure heart that at her altar lies.
Vesta is not displeased if her chaste urn
Do with repairèd fuel ever burn;   10
But my saint frowns though to her honoured name
I consecrate a never dying flame.
Th' Assyrian king did none i' th' furnace throw,
But those that to his image did not bow;
With bended knees I daily worship her,

Yet she consumes her own idolater.
Of such a goddess no times leave record,
That burnt the temple where she was adored.

255. Mediocrity° in Love Rejected

Temperance

Give me more love, or more disdain;
    The torrid, or the frozen zone,
Bring equal ease unto my pain;
    The temperate affords me none:
Either extreme, of love, or hate,
Is sweeter than a calm estate.

Give me a storm; if it be love,
    Like Danäe in that golden shower
I swim in pleasure; if it prove
    Disdain, that torrent will devour   10
My vulture hopes; and he's possessed
Of heaven, that's but from hell released;
    Then crown my joys, or cure my pain;
    Give me more love, or more disdain.

256. To Saxham

Though frost, and snow, locked from mine eyes
That beauty which without door lies,
Thy gardens, orchards, walks, that so
I might not all thy pleasures know;
Yet, Saxham, thou within thy gate
Art of thy self so delicate,
So full of native sweets that bless
Thy roof with inward happiness,
As neither from, nor to thy store
Winter takes aught, or Spring adds more.   10
The cold and frozen air had sterved°   *killed with cold*
Much poor, if not by thee preserved;
Whose prayers have made thy table blest
With plenty, far above the rest.
The season hardly did afford

Coarse cates unto thy neighbour's board,
Yet thou hadst dainties, as the sky
Had only been thy votary;
Or else the birds, fearing the snow
Might to another deluge grow,   20
The pheasant, partridge, and the lark
Flew to thy house, as to the ark.
The willing ox of himself came
Home to the slaughter, with the lamb,
And every beast did thither bring
Himself, to be an offering.
The scaly herd more pleasure took
Bathed in thy dish, than in the brook.
Water, earth, air did all conspire
To pay their tributes to thy fire,   30
Whose cherishing flames themselves divide
Through every room, where they deride
The night and cold abroad; whilst they
Like suns within, keep endless day.
Those cheerful beams send forth their light
To all that wander in the night,
And seem to beckon from aloof°   *afar*
The weary pilgrim to thy roof;
Where if, refreshed, he will away,
He's fairly welcome, or if stay   40
Far more, which he shall hearty find,
Both from the master and the hind.
The stranger's welcome, each man there
Stamped on his cheerful brow, doth wear;
Nor doth this welcome, or his cheer
Grow less, 'cause he stays longer here.
There's none observes (much less repines)
How often this man sups or dines.
Thou hast no porter at the door
T' examine, or keep back the poor;   50
Nor locks, nor bolts; thy gates have been
Made only to let strangers in:
Untaught to shut, they do not fear
To stand wide open all the year,
Careless who enters, for they know
Thou never didst deserve a foe,
And as for thieves, thy bounty's such,
They cannot steal, thou giv'st so much.

257. Maria Wentworth

Thomæ Comitis Cleveland, filia præmortuæ prima Virginiam animam exhaluit.
An. Dom. Æt. suæ.[43]

And here the precious dust is laid,
Whose purely-tempered clay was made
So fine, that it the guest betrayed.

Else the soul grew so fast within
It broke the outward shell of sin
And so was hatched a cherubin.

In height, it soared to God above;
In depth it did to knowledge move,
And spread in breadth to general love.

Before, a pious duty shined   10
To parents; courtesy behind;
On either side an equal mind.

Good to the poor, to kindred dear,
To servants kind, to friendship clear,
To nothing but herself severe.

So though a virgin, yet a bride
To every grace, she justified
A chaste polygamy, and died.

Learn from hence, Reader, what small trust
We owe this world, where virtue must,   20
Frail as our flesh, crumble to dust.

258. 'Would you know what's soft?'

Would you know what's soft? I dare
Not bring you to the down, or air,

---

[43] '... daughter of Thomas, Earl of Cleveland, having died early, breathed out her virgin spirit in 1632, in her eighteenth year'

Nor to stars to show what's bright,
Nor to snow to teach you white.

Nor if you would music hear,
Call the orbs to take your care,
Nor to please your sense bring forth,
Bruisèd nard or what's more worth,

Or on food were your thoughts placed,
Bring you nectar, for a taste.   10
Would you have all these in one,
Name my mistress, and 'tis done.

259. The Hue and Cry

In love's name you are charged hereby
To make a speedy Hue and Cry,
After a face which t' other day
Stole my wandering heart away.
To direct you these (in brief,)
Are ready marks to know the thief;

Her hair a net of beams would prove,
Strong enough to captive Jove
In his eagle's shape. Her brow
Is a comely field of snow.   10
Her eye so rich, so pure a grey,
Every beam creates a day.
And if she but sleep (not when
The sun seres) 'tis night again.
In her cheeks are to be seen,
Of flowers both the king and queen,
Thither by the graces led,
And freshly laid in nuptial bed.
On whom lips like nymphs do wait,
Who deplore their virgin state,   20
Oft they blush, and blush for this,
That they one another kiss,
But observe besides the rest,
You shall know this felon best,
By her tongue, for if your ear

Once a heavenly music hear,
Such as neither gods nor men,
But from that voice, shall hear again
That that is she. O straight surprise,
And bring her unto love's assize!   30
If you let her go she may,
Antedate the latter day,
Fate and philosophy control,
And leave the world without a soul.

Edmund Waller (1606–1687)

260. Song

   Go, lovely rose,
Tell her that wastes her time and me,
That now she knows,
When I resemble° her to thee,   *compare*
How sweet and fair she seems to be.

   Tell her that's young,
And shuns to have her graces spied,
That had'st thou sprung
In deserts, where no men abide,
Thou must have uncommended died.   10

   Small is the worth
Of beauty from the light retired:
Bid her come forth,
Suffer herself to be desired,
And not blush so to be admired.

   Then die, that she
The common fate of all things rare
May read in thee;
How small a part of time they share
That are so wondrous sweet and fair.   20

261. The Self-Banished

It is not that I love you less
Than when before your feet I lay,
But to prevent the sad increase
Of hopeless love, I keep away.

In vain (alas!) for everything
Which I have known belong to you
Your form does to my fancy bring,
And makes my old wounds bleed anew.

Who in the spring from the new sun
Already has a fever got,   10
Too late begins those shafts to shun,
Which Phoebus through his veins has shot.

Too late he would the pain assuage
And to thick shadows does retire;
About with him he bears the rage
And in his tainted blood the fire.

But vowed I have and never must,
Your banished servant, trouble you;
For if I break, you may distrust
The vow I made to love you, too.   20

262. At Penshurst (II)

While in the park I sing, the listening deer
Attend my passion, and forget to fear.
When to the beeches I report my flame,
They bow their heads, as if they felt the same.
To gods appealing, when I reach their bowers
With loud complaints, they answer me in showers.
'To thee a wild and cruel soul is given,
More deaf than trees, and prouder than the heaven.
Love's foe professed, why dost thou falsely feign
Thyself a Sidney? From which noble strain   10
He sprung, that could so far exalt the name
Of love, and warm our nation with his flame;

EDMUND WALLER · 503

That all we can of love, or high desire,
Seems but the smoke of amorous Sidney's fire.
Nor call her mother, who so well does prove
One breast may hold both chastity and love.
Never can she, that so exceeds the spring
In joy and bounty, be supposed to bring
One so destructive. To no human stock
We owe this fierce unkindness, but the rock,   20
That cloven rock produced thee, by whose side
Nature, to recompense the fatal pride
Of such stern beauty, placed those healing springs,
Which not more help, than that destruction, brings.
Thy heart no ruder than the rugged stone
I might, like Orpheus, with my numerous moan
Melt to compassion; now, my traitorous song
With thee conspires to do the singer wrong,
While thus I suffer not myself to lose
The memory of what augments my woes,   30
But with my own breath still foment the fire,
With flames as high as fancy can aspire.'
    This last complaint the indulgent ears did pierce
Of just Apollo, president of verse;
Highly concernèd that the Muse should bring
Damage to one whom he had taught to sing,
Thus he advised me: 'On yon agèd tree
Hang up thy lute, and hie thee to the sea,
That there with wonders thy diverted mind
Some truce, at least, may with this passion find.'   40
    Ah, cruel nymph! from whom her humble swain
Flies for relief unto the raging main,
And from the winds and tempests doth expect
A milder fate than from her cold neglect!
Yet there he'll pray that the unkind may prove
Blessed in her choice; and vows this endless love
Springs from no hope of what she can confer,
But from those gifts which heaven has heaped on her.

263. Of the Last Verses in the Book

When we for age could neither read nor write,
The subject made us able to indite;

The soul, with nobler resolutions decked,
The body stooping, does herself erect.
No mortal parts are requisite to raise
Her that, unbodied, can her Maker praise.

The seas are quiet when the winds give o'er;
So, calm are we, when passions are no more!
For then we know how vain it was to boast
Of fleeting things, so certain to be lost.   10
Clouds of affection from our younger eyes
Conceal that emptiness which age descries.

The soul's dark cottage, battered and decayed,
Lets in new light through chinks that time has made;
Stronger by weakness, wiser, men become
As they draw near to their eternal home.
Leaving the old, both worlds at once they view,
That stand upon the threshold of the new.

John Milton (1608–1674)

264. To the Lord General Cromwell

On the proposals of certain ministers at the Committee for Propagation of the Gospel.

Cromwell, our chief of men, who through a cloud
    Not of war only, but detractions rude,
    Guided by faith and matchless fortitude
    To peace and truth thy glorious way hast ploughed,
And on the neck of crownèd fortune proud
    Hast reared God's trophies, and his work pursued,
    While Darwen stream with blood of Scots imbrued,
    And Dunbar field resounds thy praises loud,
And Worcester's laureate wreath; yet much remains

To conquer still; peace hath her victories 10
    No less renowned than war, new foes arise
Threatening to bind our souls with secular chains;
    Help us to save free conscience from the paw
    Of hireling wolves whose gospel is their maw.

265. 'How soon hath time, the subtle thief of youth'

How soon hath time, the subtle thief of youth,
    Stolen on his wing my three and twentieth year!
    My hasting days fly on with full career,
    But my late spring no bud or blossom show'th.
Perhaps my semblance might deceive the truth,
    That I to manhood am arrived so near,
    And inward ripeness doth much less appear,
    That some more timely-happy spirits indu'th.
Yet be it less or more, or soon or slow,
    It shall be still in strictest measure even, 10
    To that same lot, however mean, or high,
Toward which time leads me, and the will of heaven;
    All is, if I have grace to use it so,
    As ever in my great Task-Master's eye.

266. On the late Massacre in Piedmont

Avenge, O Lord, thy slaughtered saints, whose bones
    Lie scattered on the Alpine mountains cold,
    Even them who kept thy truth so pure of old
    When all our fathers worshipped stocks and stones,
Forget not: in thy book record their groans
    Who were thy sheep and in their ancient fold
    Slain by the bloody Piedmontese that rolled
    Mother with infant down the rocks. Their moans
The vales redoubled to the hills, and they
    To heaven. Their martyred blood and ashes sow 10
    O'er all th' Italian fields where still doth sway
The triple tyrant; that from these may grow
    A hundred-fold, who having learnt thy way
    Early may fly the Babylonian woe.

267. On his Blindness

When I consider how my light is spent,
    E'er half my days, in this dark world and wide,
    And that one talent which is death to hide,
    Lodged with me useless, though my soul more bent
To serve therewith my Maker, and present
    My true account, lest he returning chide,
    'Doth God exact day-labour, light denied?'
    I fondly° ask. But patience to prevent   *foolishly*
That murmur, soon replies, 'God doth not need
    Either man's work or his own gifts, who best   10
    Bear his mild yoke, they serve him best, his state
Is kingly. Thousands at his bidding speed
    And post o'er land and ocean without rest;
    They also serve who only stand and wait.'

268. 'Methought I saw my late espousèd saint'

Methought I saw my late espousèd saint
    Brought to me like Alcestis from the grave,
    Whom Jove's great son to her glad husband gave,
    Rescued from death by force though pale and faint;
Mine as whom washed from spot of child-bed taint,
    Purification in the old law did save,
    And such, as yet once more I trust to have
    Full sight of her in Heaven without restraint,
Came vested all in white, pure as her mind;
    Her face was veiled, yet to my fancied sight,   10
    Love, sweetness, goodness, in her person shined
So clear, as in no face with more delight.
    But O as to embrace me she inclined,
    I waked, she fled, and day brought back my night.

269. At a Solemn Music

Blest pair of sirens, pledges of heaven's joy,
Sphere-born harmonious sisters, voice, and verse,
Wed your divine sounds, and mixed power employ

Dead things with inbreathed sense able to pierce,
And to our high-raised fantasy present,
That undisturbèd song of pure content,
Aye sung before the sapphire-coloured throne
To him that sits thereon
With saintly shout, and solemn jubilee,
Where the bright seraphim in burning row   10
Their loud uplifted angel trumpets blow,
And the cherubic host in thousand choirs
Touch their immortal harps of golden wires,
With those just spirits that wear victorious palms,
Hymns devout and holy psalms
Singing everlastingly;
That we on Earth with undiscording voice
May rightly answer that melodious noise;
As once we did, till disproportioned sin
Jarred against nature's chime, and with harsh din   20
Broke the fair music that all creatures made
To their great Lord, whose love their motion swayed
In perfect diapason, whilst they stood
In first obedience, and their state of good.
O may we soon again renew that song,
And keep in tune with heaven, till God ere long
To his celestial consort us unite,
To live with him, and sing in endless morn of light.

270. L'Allegro

Hence loathed Melancholy
    Of Cerberus, and blackest midnight born,
In Stygian cave forlorn
    'Mongst horrid shapes, and shrieks, and sights unholy,
Find out some uncouth cell,
    Where brooding darkness spreads his jealous wings,
And the night-raven sings;
    There under ebon shades and low-browed rocks,
As ragged as thy locks,
    In dark Cimmerian desert ever dwell.   10
But come thou goddess fair and free,
In heaven yclept° Euphrosyne,   *called*
And by men, heart-easing Mirth,

Whom lovely Venus at a birth
With two sister graces more
To ivy-crownèd Bacchus bore;
Or whether (as some sager sing)
The frolic wind that breathes the Spring,
Zephyr, with Aurora playing,
As he met her once a-Maying,   20
There on beds of violets blue,
And fresh-blown roses washed in dew,
Filled her with thee, a daughter fair,
So buxom, blithe and debonair.
Haste thee, Nymph, and bring with thee
Jest and youthful jollity,
Quips and cranks, and wanton wiles,
Nods, and becks, and wreathèd smiles,
Such as hang on Hebe's cheek,
And love to live in dimple sleek;   30
Sport that wrinkled care derides,
And laughter holding both his sides.
Come, and trip it as ye go
On the light fantastic toe,
And in thy right hand lead with thee
The mountain nymph, sweet liberty;
And if I give thee honour due,
Mirth, admit me of thy crew
To live with her, and live with thee,
In unreprovèd pleasures free;   40
To hear the lark begin his flight,
And singing startle the dull night,
From his watch-tower in the skies,
Till the dappled dawn doth rise;
Then to come in spite of sorrow,
And at my window bid good morrow,
Through the sweet-briar or the vine,
Or the twisted eglantine;
While the cock with lively din,
Scatters the rear of darkness thin,   50
And to the stack or the barn door
Stoutly struts his dames before,
Oft listening how the hounds and horn
Clearly rouse the slumbering morn
From the side of some hoar hill,
Through the high wood echoing shrill;

Sometime walking, not unseen,
By hedgerow elms, on hillocks green,
Right against the eastern gate,
Where the great sun begins his state,   60
Robed in flames, and amber light,
The clouds in thousand liveries dight.
While the plowman near at hand,
Whistles o'er the furrowed land,
And the milkmaid singeth blithe,
And the mower whets his scythe,
And every shepherd tells his tale
Under the hawthorn in the dale.
Straight mine eye hath caught new pleasures
Whilst the landscape round it measures: 70
Russet lawns and fallows grey
Where the nibbling flocks do stray,
Mountains on whose barren breast
The labouring clouds do often rest;
Meadows trim with daisies pied,
Shallow brooks and rivers wide.
Towers and battlements it sees
Bosomed high in tufted trees,
Where perhaps some beauty lies,
The cynosure of neighbouring eyes.   80
Hard by, a cottage chimney smokes
From betwixt two agèd oaks,
Where Corydon and Thyrsis met
Are at their savoury dinner set
Of herbs and other country messes,
Which the neat-handed Phyllis dresses;
And then in haste her bower she leaves,
With Thestylis to bind the sheaves;
Or if the earlier season lead,
To the tanned haycock in the mead,   90
Sometimes with secure delight
The up-land hamlets will invite,
When the merry bells ring round,
And the jocund rebecks sound
To many a youth and many a maid
Dancing in the chequered shade;
And young and old come forth to play
On a sunshine holiday,
Till the livelong daylight fail,

Then to the spicy nut-brown ale,   100
With stories told of many a feat,
How fairy Mab the junkets eat;
She was pinched and pulled, she said,
And he, by friar's lantern led,
Tells how the drudging goblin sweat
To earn his cream-bowl duly set,
When in one night, ere glimpse of morn,
His shadowy flail hath threshed the corn
That ten day-labourers could not end,
Then lies him down the lubber fiend,   110
And stretched out all the chimney's length,
Basks at the fire his hairy strength;
And crop-full out of doors he flings,
Ere the first cock his matin rings.
Thus done the tales, to bed they creep,
By whispering winds soon lulled asleep.
Towered cities please us then,
And the busy hum of men,
Where throngs of knights and barons bold
In weeds of peace high triumphs hold,   120
With store of ladies, whose bright eyes
Rain influence, and judge the prize
Of wit or arms, while both contend
To win her grace, whom all commend.
There let Hymen oft appear
In saffron robe, with taper clear,
And pomp, and feast, and revelry,
With masque and antique pageantry;
Such sights as youthful poets dream
On summer eves by haunted stream.   130
Then to the well-trod stage anon,
If Jonson's learned sock be on,
Or sweetest Shakespeare, fancy's child,
Warble his native wood-notes wild;
And ever against eating cares,
Lap me in soft Lydian airs,
Married to immortal verse,
Such as the meeting soul may pierce
In notes, with many a winding bout
Of linkèd sweetness long drawn out,   140
With wanton heed and giddy cunning,
The melting voice through mazes running,

Untwisting all the chains that tie
The hidden soul of harmony.
That Orpheus' self may heave his head
From golden slumber on a bed
Of heaped Elysian flowers, and hear
Such strains as would have won the ear
Of Pluto, to have quite set free
His half-regained Eurydice.   150
These delights, if thou can'st give,
Mirth, with thee I mean to live.

271. Il Penseroso

Hence, vain deluding joys,
    The brood of folly without father bred,
How little you bested°   *avail*
    Or fill the fixèd mind with all your toys;
Dwell in some idle brain,
    And fancies fond with gaudy shapes possess,
As thick and numberless
    As the gay motes that people the sunbeams,
Or likest hovering dreams,
    The fickle pensioners of Morpheus' train.   10
But hail, thou goddess sage and holy,
Hail, divinest Melancholy,
Whose saintly visage is too bright
To hit the sense of human sight;
And therefore to our weaker view
O'erlaid with black, staid wisdom's hue;
Black, but such as in esteem,
Prince Memnon's sister might beseem,
Or that starred Ethiope queen that strove
To set her beauty's praise above   20
The sea-nymphs', and their powers offended.
Yet thou art higher far descended:
Thee bright-haired Vesta long of yore
To solitary Saturn bore;
His daughter she (in Saturn's reign,
Such mixture was not held a stain).
Oft in glimmering bowers and glades
He met her, and in secret shades

Of woody Ida's inmost grove,
While yet there was no fear of Jove. 30
Come, pensive Nun, devout and pure,
Sober, steadfast, and demure,
All in a robe of darkest grain,
Flowing with majestic train,
And sable stole of cypress lawn
Over thy decent shoulders drawn.
Come, but keep thy wonted state,
With even step and musing gait,
And looks commercing with the skies,
Thy rapt soul sitting in thine eyes; 40
There held in holy passion still,
Forget thy self to marble, till
With a sad leaden downward cast
Thou fix them on the earth as fast.
And join with thee calm peace and quiet,
Spare fast, that oft with gods doth diet,
And hears the muses in a ring
Aye round about Jove's altar sing;
And add to these retirèd Leisure,
That in trim gardens takes his pleasure; 50
But first, and chiefest, with thee bring
Him that yon soars on golden wing,
Guiding the fiery-wheelèd throne,
The cherub Contemplation,
And the mute Silence hist along,
'Less° Philomel* will deign a song   *in case; nightingale*
In her sweetest, saddest plight,
Smoothing the rugged brow of night,
While Cynthia° checks her dragon yoke   *the moon*
Gently o'er th' accustomed oak; 60
Sweet bird, that shunn'st the noise of folly,
Most musical, most melancholy!
Thee, chauntress, oft the woods among
I woo to hear thy evensong;
And missing thee, I walk unseen
On the dry smooth-shaven green,
To behold the wandering moon
Riding near her highest noon,
Like one that had been led astray
Through the heaven's wide pathless way; 70
And oft, as if her head she bowed,

Stooping through a fleecy cloud.
Oft on a plat of rising ground,
I hear the far-off curfew sound
Over some wide-watered shore,
Swinging slow with sullen roar;
Or if the air will not permit,
Some still removèd place will fit,
Where glowing embers through the room
Teach light to counterfeit a gloom, 80
Far from all resort of mirth,
Save the cricket on the hearth,
Or the bellman's drowsy charm,
To bless the doors from nightly harm.
Or let my lamp at midnight hour
Be seen in some high lonely tower,
Where I may oft out-watch the Bear,
With thrice great Hermes, or unsphere
The spirit of Plato to unfold
What worlds or what vast regions hold 90
The immortal mind that hath forsook
Her mansion in this fleshly nook;
And of those daemons that are found
In fire, air, flood, or under ground,
Whose power hath a true consent
With planet or with element.
Sometime let gorgeous tragedy
In sceptred pall come sweeping by,
Presenting Thebes, or Pelops' line,
Or the tale of Troy divine, 100
Or what (though rare) of later age
Ennobled hath the buskined stage.
But O, sad virgin, that thy power
Might raise Musaeus from his bower,
Or bid the soul of Orpheus sing
Such notes as, warbled to the string,
Drew iron tears down Pluto's cheek
And made Hell grant what love did seek;
Or call up him that left half told
The story of Cambuscan bold,° *Chaucer's unfinished 'Squire's Tale'* 110
Of Camball and of Algarsife,
And who had Canace to wife,
That owned the virtuous ring and glass,
And of the wondrous horse of brass

On which the Tartar king did ride;
And if aught else great bards beside
In sage and solemn tunes have sung,
Of tourneys and of trophies hung,
Of forests, and enchantments drear,
Where more is meant than meets the ear.   120
Thus, night, oft see me in thy pale career,
Till civil-suited morn appear,
Not tricked and frounced as she was wont
With the Attic boy to hunt,
But kerchiefed in a comely cloud,
While rocking winds are piping loud,
Or ushered with a shower still,
When the gust hath blown his fill,
Ending on the rustling leaves,
With minute drops from off the eaves.   130
And when the sun begins to fling
His flaring beams, me, goddess bring
To archèd walks of twilight groves,
And shadows brown that Sylvan loves,
Of pine or monumental oak,
Where the rude axe with heavèd stroke
Was never heard the nymphs to daunt,
Or fright them from their hallowed haunt.
There in close covert by some brook,
Where no profaner eye may look,   140
Hide me from day's garish eye,
While the bee with honeyed thigh,
That at her flowery work doth sing,
And the waters murmuring
With such consort as they keep,
Entice the dewy-feathered sleep;
And let some strange mysterious dream
Wave at his wings in airy stream
Of lively portraiture displayed,
Softly on my eyelids laid.   150
And as I wake, sweet music breathe
Above, about, or underneath,
Sent by some spirit to mortals good,
Or th' unseen genius of the wood.
But let my due feet never fail
To walk the studious cloisters pale,
And love the high embowèd roof,

With antique pillars' massy proof;
And storied windows richly dight,
Casting a dim religious light.   160
There let the pealing organ blow
To the full voicèd choir below,
In service high and anthems clear,
As may with sweetness, through mine ear,
Dissolve me into ecstasies,
And bring all heaven before mine eyes.
And may at last my weary age
Find out the peaceful hermitage,
The hairy gown and mossy cell,
Where I may sit and rightly spell   170
Of every star that heaven doth show,
And every herb that sips the dew;
Till old experience do attain
To something like prophetic strain.
These pleasures melancholy give,
And I with thee will choose to live.

272. Lycidas

In this monody the author bewails a learnèd friend, unfortunately drowned in his
passage from Chester on the Irish Seas, 1637. And by occasion foretells the ruin of our
corrupted clergy then in their height.

Yet once more, O ye laurels, and once more
Ye myrtles brown, with ivy never sere,
I come to pluck your berries harsh and crude,
And with forced fingers rude,
Shatter your leaves before the mellowing year.
Bitter constraint, and sad occasion dear,
Compels me to disturb your season due:
For Lycidas is dead, dead ere his prime,
Young Lycidas, and hath not left his peer.
Who would not sing for Lycidas? He knew   10
Himself to sing, and build the lofty rhyme.
He must not float upon his watery bier
Unwept, and welter to the parching wind,
Without the meed of some melodious tear.
    Begin then, sisters of the sacred well

That from beneath the seat of Jove doth spring,
Begin, and somewhat loudly sweep the string.
Hence with denial vain, and coy excuse;
So may some gentle muse
With lucky words favour my destined urn,   20
And as he passes turn,
And bid fair peace be to my sable shroud.
For we were nursed upon the self-same hill,
Fed the same flock, by fountain, shade, and rill.
   Together both, ere the high lawns appeared
Under the opening eye-lids of the morn,
We drove afield, and both together heard
What time the grey-fly winds her sultry horn,
Battening our flocks with the fresh dews of night,
Oft till the star that rose, at evening, bright   30
Toward heaven's descent had sloped his westering wheel.
Meanwhile the rural ditties were not mute,
Tempered to th' oaten flute;
Rough satyrs danced, and fauns with cloven heel
From the glad sound would not be absent long,
And old Damoetas loved to hear our song.
   But O the heavy change, now thou art gone,
Now thou art gone, and never must return!
Thee, shepherd, thee the woods and desert caves,
With wild thyme and the gadding vine o'ergrown,   40
And all their echoes mourn.
The willows and the hazel copses green,
Shall now no more be seen
Fanning their joyous leaves to thy soft lays.
As killing as the canker to the rose,
Or taint-worm to the weanling herds that graze,
Or frost to flowers, that their gay wardrobe wear,
When first the whitethorn blows;
Such, Lycidas, thy loss to shepherd's ear.
   Where were ye, nymphs, when the remorseless deep   50
Closed o'er the head of your loved Lycidas?
For neither were ye playing on the steep,
Where your old bards, the famous druids lie,
Nor on the shaggy top of Mona high,
Nor yet where Deva spreads her wizard stream.
Aye me, I fondly dream,
Had ye been there! For what could that have done?
What could the muse herself that Orpheus bore,

The muse herself, for her enchanting son
Whom universal nature did lament, 60
When by the rout that made the hideous roar
His gory visage down the stream was sent,
Down the swift Hebrus to the Lesbian shore?
   Alas! What boots it with incessant care
To tend the homely slighted shepherd's trade,
And strictly meditate the thankless muse?
Were it not better done as others use,
To sport with Amaryllis in the shade,
Or with the tangles of Neaera's hair?
Fame is the spur that the clear spirit doth raise 70
(That last infirmity of noble mind)
To scorn delights, and live laborious days;
But the fair guerdon when we hope to find,
And think to burst out into sudden blaze,
Comes the blind fury with th' abhorred shears,
And slits the thin spun life. 'But not the praise,'
Phoebus replied, and touched my trembling ears;
'Fame is no plant that grows on mortal soil,
Nor in the glistering foil
Set off to th' world, nor in broad rumour lies, 80
But lives and spreads aloft by those pure eyes
And perfect witness of all judging Jove;
As he pronounces lastly on each deed,
Of so much fame in heaven expect thy meed.'
   O fountain Arethuse, and thou honoured flood,
Smooth-sliding Mincius, crowned with vocal reeds,
That strain I heard was of a higher mood.
But now my oat proceeds,
And listens to the herald of the sea
That came in Neptune's plea. 90
He asked the waves, and asked the felon winds,
What hard mishap hath doomed this gentle swain?
And questioned every gust of rugged wings
That blows from off each beakèd promontory;
They knew not of his story,
And sage Hippotades their answer brings,
That not a blast was from his dungeon strayed;
The air was calm, and on the level brine
Sleek Panope with all her sisters played.
It was that fatal and perfidious bark 100
Built in th' eclipse, and rigged with curses dark,

That sunk so low that sacred head of thine.
    Next Camus, reverend sire, went footing slow,
His mantle hairy, and his bonnet sedge,
Inwrought with figures dim, and on the edge
Like to that sanguine flower inscribed with woe.
'Ah, who hath reft,' quoth he, 'my dearest pledge?'
Last came, and last did go,
The pilot of the Galilean lake,
Two massy keys he bore of metals twain 110
(The golden opes, the iron shuts amain).
He shook his mitred locks, and stern bespake,
'How well could I have spared for thee, young swain,
Enough of such as for their bellies' sake,
Creep and intrude and climb into the fold!
Of other care they little reck'ning make
Than how to scramble at the shearers' feast,
And shove away the worthy bidden guest.
Blind mouths! that scarce themselves know how to hold
A sheep-hook, or have learned aught else the least 120
That to the faithful herdman's art belongs!
What recks it them? What need they? They are sped;
And when they list, their lean and flashy songs
Grate on their scrannel pipes of wretched straw;
The hungry sheep look up, and are not fed,
But swollen with wind, and the rank mist they draw,
Rot inwardly, and foul contagion spread;
Besides what the grim wolf with privy paw
Daily devours apace, and nothing said;
But that two-handed engine at the door 130
Stands ready to smite once, and smite no more.'
    Return, Alpheus, the dread voice is past,
That shrunk thy streams; return Sicilian muse,
And call the vales, and bid them hither cast
Their bells and flowerets of a thousand hues.
Ye valleys low where the mild whispers use
Of shades and wanton winds and gushing brooks,
On whose fresh lap the swart star sparely° looks, *seldom*
Throw hither all your quaint enamelled eyes,
That on the green turf suck the honeyed showers, 140
And purple all the ground with vernal flowers.
Bring the rathe primrose that forsaken dies.
The tufted crowtoe, and pale jessamine,
The white pink, and the pansy freaked with jet,

The glowing violet,
The musk-rose, and the well attired woodbine.
With cowslips wan that hang the pensive head,
And every flower that sad embroidery wears.
Bid amaranthus all his beauty shed,
And daffadillies fill their cups with tears,   150
To strew the laureate hearse where Lycid lies.
For so to interpose a little ease,
Let our frail thoughts dally with false surmise;
Aye me! Whilst thee the shores and sounding seas
Wash far away, where'er thy bones are hurled,
Whether beyond the stormy Hebrides,
Where thou perhaps under the whelming tide
Visit'st the bottom of the monstrous world;
Or whether thou, to our moist vows denied,
Sleep'st by the fable of Bellerus old,   160
Where the great vision of the guarded mount
Looks toward Namancos and Bayona's hold:
Look homeward, angel, now, and melt with ruth;
And, O ye dolphins, waft the hapless youth.
     Weep no more, woeful shepherds, weep no more,
For Lycidas, your sorrow, is not dead,
Sunk though he be beneath the watery floor;
So sinks the day-star in the ocean bed,
And yet anon repairs his drooping head,
And tricks his beams, and with new spangled ore   170
Flames in the forehead of the morning sky:
So Lycidas sunk low, but mounted high,
Through the dear might of him that walked the waves,
Where, other groves and other streams along,
With nectar pure his oozy locks he laves,
And hears the unexpressive nuptial song
In the blest kingdoms meek of joy and love.
There entertain him all the saints above,
In solemn troops and sweet societies
That sing, and singing in their glory move,   180
And wipe the tears for ever from his eyes.
Now, Lycidas, the shepherds weep no more;
Henceforth thou art the genius of the shore
In thy large recompense, and shalt be good
To all that wander in that perilous flood.
     Thus sang the uncouth swain to th' oaks and rills,
While the still morn went out with sandals grey;

He touched the tender stops of various quills,
With eager thought warbling his Doric lay:
And now the sun had stretched out all the hills,   190
And now was dropped into the western bay;
At last he rose, and twitched his mantle blue:
Tomorrow to fresh woods, and pastures new.

273. from *Paradise Lost*, Book I

Of man's first disobedience, and the fruit
Of that forbidden tree, whose mortal taste
Brought death into the world, and all our woe,
With loss of Eden, till one greater Man
Restore us, and regain the blissful seat,
Sing, heav'nly muse, that on the secret top
Of Oreb, or of Sinai, didst inspire
That shepherd, who first taught the chosen seed,
In the beginning how the heav'ns and earth
Rose out of Chaos; or if Sion hill   10
Delight thee more, and Siloa's brook that flowed
Fast by the oracle of God, I thence
Invoke thy aid to my adventurous song,
That with no middle flight intends to soar
Above th' Aonian Mount, while it pursues
Things unattempted yet in prose or rhyme.
And chiefly thou, O Spirit, that dost prefer
Before all temples th' upright heart and pure,
Instruct me, for thou know'st; thou from the first
Wast present, and with mighty wings outspread   20
Dove-like satst brooding on the vast abyss
And mad'st it pregnant: what in me is dark
Illumine, what is low raise and support;
That to the height of this great argument
I may assert Eternal Providence,
And justify the ways of God to men.

274. from *Paradise Lost*, Book III

Hail, holy light, offspring of heaven first-born,
Or of th' eternal coeternal beam

May I express thee unblamed? Since God is light,
And never but in unapproachèd light
Dwelt from eternity, dwelt then in thee,
Bright effluence of bright essence increate.
Or hear'st thou° rather pure ethereal stream,   *are you known as*
Whose fountain who shall tell? Before the sun,
Before the heavens thou wert, and at the voice
Of God, as with a mantle didst invest   10
The rising world of waters dark and deep,
Won from the void and formless infinite.
Thee I revisit now with bolder wing,
Escaped the Stygian pool, though long detained
In that obscure sojourn, while in my flight
Through utter and through middle darkness borne
With other notes than to th' Orphèan lyre
I sung of Chaos and eternal night,
Taught by the heav'nly Muse to venture down
The dark descent, and up to reascend,   20
Though hard and rare. Thee I revisit safe,
And feel thy sovran vital lamp; but thou
Revisit'st not these eyes, that roll in vain
To find thy piercing ray, and find no dawn;
So thick a drop serene hath quenched their orbs,
Or dim suffusion veiled. Yet not the more
Cease I to wander where the muses haunt
Clear spring, or shady grove, or sunny hill,
Smit with the love of sacred song; but chief
Thee, Sion, and the flowery brooks beneath   30
That wash thy hallowed feet, and warbling flow,
Nightly I visit; nor sometimes forget
Those other two equalled with me in fate,
So were I equalled with them in renown,
Blind Thamyris and blind Maeonides,
And Tiresias and Phineus prophets old.
Then feed on thoughts that voluntary move
Harmonious numbers, as the wakeful bird
Sings darkling, and in shadiest covert hid
Tunes her nocturnal note. Thus with the year   40
Seasons return; but not to me returns
Day, or the sweet approach of ev'n or morn,
Or sight of vernal bloom, or summer's rose,
Or flocks, or herds, or human face divine;

But cloud instead, and ever-during dark
Surrounds me, from the cheerful ways of men
Cut off; and for the book of knowledge fair
Presented with a universal blank
Of Nature's works to me expunged and razed, 50
And wisdom at one entrance quite shut out.
So much the rather thou, celestial Light,
Shine inward, and the mind through all her powers
Irradiate, there plant eyes, all mist from thence
Purge and disperse, that I may see and tell
Of things invisible to mortal sight.

275. from *Paradise Lost,* Book V

Now morn her rosy steps in th' eastern clime
Advancing, sowed the earth with orient pearl,
When Adam waked, so customed, for his sleep
Was airy light, from pure digestion bred,
And temperate vapours bland, which th' only sound
Of leaves and fuming rills, Aurora's fan,
Lightly dispersed, and the shrill matin song
Of birds on every bough; so much the more
His wonder was to find unwakened Eve
With tresses discomposed, and glowing cheek, 10
As through unquiet rest. He on his side
Leaning half-raised, with looks of cordial love
Hung over her enamoured, and beheld
Beauty, which whether waking or asleep,
Shot forth peculiar graces; then with voice
Mild, as when Zephyrus on Flora breathes,
Her hand soft touching, whispered thus: 'Awake
My fairest, my espoused, my latest found,
Heav'n's last best gift, my ever new delight,
Awake, the morning shines, and the fresh field 20
Calls us, we lose the prime, to mark how spring
Our tended plants, how blows the citron grove,
What drops the myrrh, and what the balmy reed,
How nature paints her colours, how the bee
Sits on the bloom extracting liquid sweet.'
    Such whispering waked her…

276. from *Paradise Lost*, Book IX

No more of talk where God or angel guest
With man, as with his friend, familiar used
To sit indulgent, and with him partake
Rural repast, permitting him the while
Venial discourse unblamed. I now must change
Those notes to tragic; foul distrust, and breach
Disloyal on the part of man, revolt
And disobedience; on the part of heav'n,
Now alienated, distance and distaste,
Anger and just rebuke, and judgment giv'n,   10
That brought into this world a world of woe,
Sin and her shadow death, and misery,
Death's harbinger. Sad task, yet argument
Not less but more heroic than the wrath
Of stern Achilles on his foe pursued
Thrice fugitive about Troy wall; or rage
Of Turnus for Lavinia disespoused;
Or Neptune's ire, or Juno's, that so long
Perplexed the Greek and Cytherea's son;
If answerable style I can obtain   20
Of my celestial patroness, who deigns
Her nightly visitation unimplored,
And dictates to me slumb'ring, or inspires
Easy my unpremeditated verse:
Since first this subject for heroic song
Pleased me long choosing, and beginning late,
Not sedulous by nature to indite
Wars, hitherto the only argument
Heroic deemed, chief mastery to dissect
With long and tedious havoc fabled knights   30
In battles feigned (the better fortitude
Of patience and heroic martyrdom
Unsung), or to describe races and games,
Or tilting furniture, emblazoned shields,
Impresses quaint, caparisons and steeds,
Bases and tinsel trappings, gorgeous knights
At joust and tournament; then marshalled feast
Served up in hall with sewers and seneschal;
The skill of artifice or office mean
Not that which justly gives heroic name   40
To person or to poem. Me of these

Nor skilled nor studious, higher argument
Remains, sufficient of itself to raise
That name, unless an age too late, or cold
Climate, or years, damp my intended wing
Depressed; and much they may, if all be mine,
Not hers who brings it nightly to my ear.
 The sun was sunk, and after him the star
Of Hesperus, whose office is to bring
Twilight upon the earth, short arbiter   50
'Twixt day and night, and now from end to end
Night's hemisphere had veiled the horizon round,
When Satan, who late fled before the threats
Of Gabriel out of Eden, now improved
In meditated fraud and malice, bent
On Man's destruction, maugre° what might hap   *despite*
Of heavier on himself; fearless returned.
By night he fled, and at midnight returned
From compassing the earth, cautious of day
Since Uriel, regent of the sun, descried   60
His entrance and forewarned the cherubim
That kept their watch. Thence, full of anguish, driv'n,
The space of seven continued nights he rode
With darkness; thrice the equinoctial line
He circled, four times crossed the car of night
From pole to pole, traversing each colure;
On the eighth returned and, on the coast averse
From entrance or cherubic watch, by stealth
Found unsuspected way. There was a place
(Now not, though sin, not time, first wrought the change) 70
Where Tigris, at the foot of Paradise,
Into a gulf shot underground, till part
Rose up a fountain by the Tree of Life.
In with the river sunk and with it rose
Satan, involved in rising mist; then sought
Where to lie hid; sea he had searched and land
From Eden over Pontus, and the pool
Maeotis, up beyond the river Ob;
Downward as far antarctic; and in length
West from Orontes to the ocean barred   80
At Darien; thence to the land where flows
Ganges and Indus. Thus the orb he roamed
With narrow search, and with inspection deep
Considered every creature, which of all

Most opportune might serve his wiles, and found
The serpent subtlest beast of all the field.
Him after long debate, irresolute
Of thoughts revolved, his final sentence chose
Fit vessel, fittest imp of fraud, in whom
To enter, and his dark suggestions hide   90
From sharpest sight; for in the wily snake,
Whatever sleights, none would suspicious mark,
As from his wit and native subtlety
Proceeding, which, in other beasts observed,
Doubt might beget of diabolic pow'r
Active within beyond the sense of brute.
Thus he resolved, but first from inward grief
His bursting passion into plaints thus poured:
    'O Earth, how like to Heav'n, if not preferred
More justly, seat worthier of gods, as built   100
With second thoughts, reforming what was old!
For what God after better worse would build?
Terrestrial heav'n, danced round by other heav'ns
That shine, yet bear their bright officious lamps,
Light above light, for thee alone, as seems,
In thee concentring all their precious beams
Of sacred influence! As God in heav'n
Is centre, yet extends to all, so thou
Centring receiv'st from all those orbs; in thee,
Not in themselves, all their known virtue appears,   110
Productive in herb, plant, and nobler birth
Of creatures animate with gradual life
Of growth, sense, reason, all summed up in man.
With what delight could I have walked thee round,
If I could joy in aught; sweet interchange
Of hill and valley, rivers, woods, and plains,
Now land, now sea, and shores with forest crowned,
Rocks, dens, and caves! But I in none of these
Find place or refuge; and the more I see
Pleasures about me, so much more I feel   120
Torment within me, as from the hateful siege
Of contraries: all good to me becomes
Bane, and in heav'n much worse would be my state.
But neither here seek I, no, nor in heav'n,
To dwell, unless by mast'ring heav'n's Supreme;
Nor hope to be myself less miserable
By what I seek, but others to make such

As I, though thereby worse to me redound;
For only in destroying I find ease
To my relentless thoughts; and him destroyed,   130
Or won to what may work his utter loss,
For whom all this was made, all this will soon
Follow, as to him linked in weal or woe:
In woe then, that destruction wide may range.
To me shall be the glory sole among
The infernal powers, in one day to have marred
What he, Almighty styled, six nights and days
Continued making, and who knows how long
Before had been contriving? Though perhaps
Not longer than since I in one night freed   140
From servitude inglorious well-nigh half
Th' angelic name, and thinner left the throng
Of his adorers. He, to be avenged,
And to repair his numbers thus impaired;
Whether such virtue, spent of old, now failed
More angels to create (if they at least
Are his created), or to spite us more;
Determined to advance into our room
A creature formed of earth, and him endow,
Exalted from so base original,   150
With heav'nly spoils, our spoils. What he decreed
He effected; man he made, and for him built
Magnificent this world, and earth his seat,
Him lord pronounced and, O indignity!
Subjected to his service angel wings,
And flaming ministers, to watch and tend
Their earthy charge. Of these the vigilance
I dread, and to elude, thus wrapped in mist
Of midnight vapour glide obscure, and pry
In every bush and brake where hap may find   160
The serpent sleeping, in whose mazy folds
To hide me and the dark intent I bring.
O foul descent! that I, who erst contended
With Gods to sit the highest, am now constrained
Into a beast, and, mixed with bestial slime,
This essence to incarnate and imbrute,
That to the height of deity aspired!
But what will not ambition and revenge
Descend to? Who aspires must down as low
As high he soared, obnoxious first or last   170

To basest things. Revenge, at first thought sweet,
Bitter ere long back on itself recoils.
Let it! I reck not, so it light well aimed,
Since higher I fall short, on him who next
Provokes my envy, this new favourite
Of heav'n, this man of clay, son of despite,
Whom us the more to spite, his maker raised
From dust: spite then with spite is best repaid.'
   So saying, through each thicket, dank or dry,
Like a black mist low-creeping, he held on   180
His midnight search, where soonest he might find
The serpent. Him fast sleeping soon he found,
In labyrinth of many a round self-rolled,
His head the midst, well stored with subtle wiles;
Not yet in horrid shade or dismal den,
Nor nocent yet, but on the grassy herb
Fearless, unfeared, he slept. In at his mouth
The Devil entered, and his brutal sense,
In heart or head, possessing soon inspired
With act intelligential, but his sleep   190
Disturbed not, waiting close th' approach of morn.
   Now whenas sacred light began to dawn
In Eden on the humid flow'rs, that breathed
Their morning incense, when all things that breathe
From th' Earth's great altar send up silent praise
To the Creator, and his nostrils fill
With grateful smell, forth came the human pair,
And joined their vocal worship to the choir
Of creatures wanting voice; that done, partake
The season, prime for sweetest scents and airs;   200
Then commune how that day they best may ply
Their growing work; for much their work outgrew
The hands' dispatch of two gard'ning so wide;
And Eve first to her husband thus began:
   'Adam, well may we labour still to dress
This garden, still to tend plant, herb, and flow'r,
Our pleasant task enjoined; but till more hands
Aid us the work under our labour grows,
Luxurious by restraint; what we by day
Lop overgrown, or prune or prop or bind,   210
One night or two with wanton growth derides,
Tending to wild. Thou, therefore, now advise,
Or hear what to my mind first thoughts present:

Let us divide our labours; thou where choice
Leads thee, or where most needs, whether to wind
The woodbine round this arbour, or direct
The clasping ivy where to climb; while I,
In yonder spring of roses intermixed
With myrtle, find what to redress till noon;
For while so near each other thus all day   220
Our task we choose, what wonder if so near
Looks intervene and smiles, or objects new
Casual discourse draw on, which intermits
Our day's work, brought to little though begun
Early, and th' hour of supper comes unearned!'
    To whom mild answer Adam thus returned:
'Sole Eve, associate sole, to me beyond
Compare above all living creatures dear,
Well hast thou motioned, well thy thoughts employed,
How we might best fulfil the work which here   230
God hath assigned us, nor of me shalt pass
Unpraised; for nothing lovelier can be found
In woman than to study household good,
And good works in her husband to promote.
Yet not so strictly hath our Lord imposed
Labour as to debar us when we need
Refreshment, whether food or talk between,
Food of the mind, or this sweet intercourse
Of looks and smiles; for smiles from reason flow,
To brute denied, and are of love the food,   240
Love not the lowest end of human life.
For not to irksome toil, but to delight
He made us, and delight to reason joined.
These paths and bowers doubt not but our joint hands
Will keep from wilderness with ease, as wide
As we need walk, till younger hands ere long
Assist us. But if much converse perhaps
Thee satiate, to short absence I could yield.
For solitude sometimes is best society,
And short retirement urges sweet return.   250
But other doubt possesses me, lest harm
Befall thee, severed from me; for thou know'st
What hath been warned us; what malicious foe,
Envying our happiness, and of his own
Despairing, seeks to work us woe and shame
By sly assault; and somewhere nigh at hand

Watches, no doubt, with greedy hope to find
His wish and best advantage, us asunder,
Hopeless to circumvent us joined, where each
To other speedy aid might lend at need.   260
Whether his first design be to withdraw
Our fealty from God, or to disturb
Conjugal love; than which perhaps no bliss
Enjoyed by us excites his envy more;
Or this or worse, leave not the faithful side
That gave thee being, still shades thee and protects.
The wife, where danger or dishonour lurks,
Safest and seemliest by her husband stays,
Who guards her, or with her the worst endures.'
   To whom the virgin majesty of Eve,   270
As one who loves, and some unkindness meets,
With sweet austere composure thus replied:
'Offspring of heav'n and earth, and all earth's lord!
That such an enemy we have, who seeks
Our ruin, both by thee informed I learn,
And from the parting angel overheard
As in a shady nook I stood behind
Just then returned at shut of evening flow'rs.
But that thou shouldst my firmness therefore doubt
To God or thee, because we have a foe   280
May tempt it, I expected not to hear.
His violence thou fear'st not, being such
As we, not capable of death or pain,
Can either not receive or can repel.
His fraud is then thy fear; which plain infers
Thy equal fear that my firm faith and love
Can by his fraud be shak'n or seduced:
Thoughts, which how found they harbour in thy breast,
Adam, misthought of her to thee so dear!'
   To whom with healing words Adam replied: 290
'Daughter of God and man, immortal Eve!
For such thou art, from sin and blame entire;
Not diffident of thee do I dissuade
Thy absence from my sight, but to avoid
Th' attempt itself; intended by our foe.
For he who tempts, though in vain, at least asperses
The tempted with dishonour foul, supposed
Not incorruptible of faith, not proof
Against temptation. Thou thyself with scorn

And anger would'st resent the offered wrong,   300
Though ineffectual found; misdeem not, then,
If such affront I labour to avert
From thee alone, which on us both at once
The enemy, though bold, will hardly dare,
Or, daring, first on me th' assault shall light.
Nor thou his malice and false guile contemn;
Subtle he needs must be who could seduce
Angels; nor think superfluous other's aid.
I from the influence of thy looks receive
Access in every virtue; in thy sight   310
More wise, more watchful, stronger, if need were
Of outward strength; while shame, thou looking on,
Shame to be overcome or overreached,
Would utmost vigour raise, and raised unite.
Why shouldst not thou like sense within thee feel
When I am present, and thy trial choose
With me, best witness of thy virtue tried?'
    So spake domestic Adam in his care
And matrimonial love; but Eve, who thought
Less attributed to her faith sincere,   320
Thus her reply with accent sweet renewed:
    'If this be our condition, thus to dwell
In narrow circuit strait'ned by a foe,
Subtle or violent, we not endued
Single with like defence, wherever met,
How are we happy, still in fear of harm?
But harm precedes not sin: only our foe
Tempting affronts us with his foul esteem
Of our integrity; his foul esteem
Sticks no dishonour on our front, but turns   330
Foul on himself. Then wherefore shunned or feared
By us? Who rather double honour gain
From his surmise proved false, find peace within,
Favour from Heav'n, our witness, from th' event?
And what is faith, love, virtue, unassayed
Alone, without exterior help sustained?
Let us not then suspect our happy state
Left so imperfect by the Maker wise
As not secure to single or combined.
Frail is our happiness, if this be so,   340
And Eden were no Eden thus exposed.'
    To whom thus Adam fervently replied:

'O woman, best are all things as the will
Of God ordained them; his creating hand
Nothing imperfect or deficient left
Of all that he created, much less man
Or aught that might his happy state secure,
Secure from outward force. Within himself
The danger lies, yet lies within his power:
Against his will he can receive no harm.   350
But God left free the will; for what obeys
Reason is free, and reason he made right,
But bid her well beware and still erect,
Lest by some fair appearing good surprised
She dictate false, and misinform the will
To do what God expressly hath forbid.
Not then mistrust, but tender love enjoins,
That I should mind thee oft, and mind thou me.
Firm we subsist, yet possible to swerve,
Since reason not impossibly may meet   360
Some specious object by the foe suborned
And fall into deception unaware,
Not keeping strictest watch as she was warned.
Seek not temptation, then, which to avoid
Were better; and most likely if from me
Thou sever not; trial will come unsought.
Wouldst thou approve thy constancy, approve
First thy obedience; th' other who can know,
Not seeing thee attempted, who attest?
But if thou think trial unsought may find   370
Us both securer than thus warned thou seem'st,
Go; for thy stay, not free, absents thee more;
Go in thy native innocence; rely
On what thou hast of virtue, summon all,
For God towards thee hath done his part: do thine.'
    So spake the patriarch of mankind; but Eve
Persisted; yet submiss, though last, replied:
    'With thy permission, then, and thus forewarned,
Chiefly by what thy own last reasoning words
Touched only, that our trial when least sought   380
May find us both perhaps far less prepared,
The willinger I go, nor much expect
A foe so proud will first the weaker seek;
So bent, the more shall shame him his repulse.'
    Thus saying, from her husband's hand her hand

Soft she withdrew, and, like a wood-nymph light,
Oread or dryad or of Delia's train,
Betook her to the groves, but Delia's self
In gait surpassed and goddess-like deport,
Though not as she with bow and quiver armed,   390
But with such gard'ning tools as art, yet rude,
Guiltless of fire had formed, or angels brought.
To Pales, or Pomona, thus adorned,
Likest she seemed Pomona when she fled
Vertumnus or to Ceres in her prime,
Yet virgin of Proserpina from Jove.
Her long with ardent look his eye pursued
Delighted, but desiring more her stay;
Oft he to her his charge of quick return
Repeated; she to him as oft engaged   400
To be returned by noon amid the bower,
And all things in best order to invite
Noontide repast or afternoon's repose.
O much deceived, much failing, hapless Eve,
Of thy presumed return, event perverse!
Thou never from that hour in Paradise
Found'st either sweet repast or sound repose:
Such ambush, hid among sweet flowers and shades,
Waited with hellish rancour imminent
To intercept thy way, or send thee back   410
Despoiled of innocence, of faith, of bliss.
    For now, and since first break of dawn, the Fiend,
Mere serpent in appearance, forth was come,
And on his quest where likeliest he might find
The only two of mankind, but in them
The whole included race, his purposed prey.
In bower and field he sought, where any tuft
Of grove or garden-plot more pleasant lay,
Their tendance or plantation for delight;
By fountain or by shady rivulet   420
He sought them both, but wished his hap might find
Eve separate; he wished, but not with hope
Of what so seldom chanced, when to his wish,
Beyond his hope, Eve separate he spies,
Veiled in a cloud of fragrance where she stood
Half-spied, so thick the roses bushing round
About her glowed, oft stooping to support
Each flower of tender stalk whose head, though gay

Carnation, purple, azure, or specked with gold,
Hung drooping unsustained. Them she upstays   430
Gently with myrtle band, mindless the while
Herself; though fairest unsupported flow'r,
From her best prop so far, and storm so nigh.
Nearer he drew, and many a walk traversed
Of stateliest covert, cedar, pine, or palm;
Then voluble and bold, now hid, now seen
Among thick-wov'n arborets and flow'rs
Imbordered on each bank, the hand of Eve:
Spot more delicious than those gardens feigned
Or of revived Adonis or renowned   440
Alcinous, host of old Laertes' son,
Or that, not mystic, where the sapient king
Held dalliance with his fair Egyptian spouse.
Much he the place admired, the person more.
As one who, long in populous city pent,
Where houses thick and sewers annoy the air,
Forth issuing on a summer's morn, to breathe
Among the pleasant villages and farms
Adjoined, from each thing met conceives delight:
The smell of grain, or tedded grass, or kine,   450
Or dairy, each rural sight, each rural sound;
If chance with nymph-like step fair virgin pass,
What pleasing seemed, for her now pleases more,
She most, and in her look sums all delight:
Such pleasure took the Serpent to behold
This flow'ry plat, the sweet recess of Eve
Thus early, thus alone. Her heav'nly form
Angelic, but more soft and feminine,
Her graceful innocence, her every air
Of gesture or least action, overawed   460
His malice, and with rapine sweet bereaved
His fierceness of the fierce intent it brought.
That space the Evil One abstracted stood
From his own evil, and for the time remained
Stupidly good, of enmity disarmed,
Of guile, of hate, of envy, of revenge.
But the hot hell that always in him burns,
Though in mid heav'n, soon ended his delight,
And tortures him now more, the more he sees
Of pleasure not for him ordained. Then soon   470
Fierce hate he recollects, and all his thoughts

Of mischief; gratulating, thus excites:
　　'Thoughts, whither have ye led me, with what sweet
Compulsion thus transported to forget
What hither brought us? Hate, not love, nor hope
Of Paradise for hell, hope here to taste
Of pleasure, but all pleasure to destroy,
Save what is in destroying; other joy
To me is lost. Then let me not let pass
Occasion which now smiles. Behold alone　　　　　　　　　480
The woman, opportune to all attempts,
Her husband, for I view far round, not nigh,
Whose higher intellectual more I shun,
And strength, of courage haughty, and of limb
Heroic built, though of terrestrial mould,
Foe not informidable, exempt from wound,
I not; so much hath Hell debased, and pain
Enfeebled me, to what I was in heav'n.
She fair, divinely fair, fit love for gods,
Not terrible, though terror be in love　　　　　　　　　490
And beauty, not approached by stronger hate,
Hate stronger, under show of love well feigned,
The way which to her ruin now I tend.'
　　So spake the enemy of mankind, enclosed
In serpent, inmate bad, and toward Eve
Addressed his way: not with indented wave
Prone on the ground, as since, but on his rear,
Circular base of rising folds that tow'red
Fold above fold, a surging maze: his head
Crested aloft, and carbuncle his eyes;　　　　　　　　　500
With burnished neck of verdant gold, erect
Amidst his circling spires that on the grass
Floated redundant. Pleasing was his shape,
And lovely, never since of serpent kind
Lovelier; not those that in Illyria changed
Hermione and Cadmus, or the god
In Epidaurus; nor to which transformed
Ammonian Jove, or Capitoline was seen,
He with Olympias, this with her who bore
Scipio, the height of Rome. With tract oblique　　　　　510
At first, as one who sought access but feared
To interrupt, sidelong he works his way.
As when a ship, by skilful steersman wrought
Nigh river's mouth or foreland, where the wind

Veers oft, as oft so steers, and shifts her sail,
So varied he, and of his tortuous train
Curled many a wanton wreath in sight of Eve,
To lure her eye. She, busied, heard the sound
Of rustling leaves, but minded not, as used
To such disport before her through the field   520
From every beast, more duteous at her call
Than at Circean call the herd disguised.
He, bolder now, uncalled before her stood,
But as in gaze admiring. Oft he bowed
His turret crest and sleek enamelled neck,
Fawning, and licked the ground whereon she trod.
His gentle dumb expression turned at length
The eye of Eve to mark his play; he, glad
Of her attention gained, with serpent tongue
Organic, or impulse of vocal air,   530
His fraudulent temptation thus began:
    'Wonder not, sovran mistress (if perhaps
Thou canst who art sole wonder), much less arm
Thy looks, the heav'n of mildness, with disdain,
Displeased that I approach thee thus and gaze
Insatiate, I thus single, nor have feared
Thy awful brow, more awful thus retired.
Fairest resemblance of thy Maker fair,
Thee all things living gaze on, all things thine
By gift, and thy celestial beauty adore,   540
With ravishment beheld, there best beheld
Where universally admired; but here,
In this enclosure wild, these beasts among,
Beholders rude and shallow to discern
Half what in thee is fair, one man except
Who sees thee (and what is one?) who shouldst be seen
A goddess among gods, adored and served
By angels numberless, thy daily train?'
    So glozed the tempter, and his proem tuned;
Into the heart of Eve his words made way,   550
Though at the voice much marvelling; at length,
Not unamazed, she thus in answer spake:
    'What may this mean? Language of man pronounced
By tongue of brute, and human sense expressed?
The first at least of these I thought denied
To beasts, whom God on their creation-day
Created mute to all articulate sound;

The latter I demur, for in their looks
Much reason, and in their actions oft appears.
Thee, Serpent, subtlest beast of all the field   560
I knew, but not with human voice endued;
Redouble then this miracle, and say
How cam'st thou speakable of mute, and how
To me so friendly grown above the rest
Of brutal kind that daily are in sight:
Say, for such wonder claims attention due.'
    To whom the guileful Tempter thus replied:
'Empress of this fair world, resplendent Eve!
Easy to me it is to tell thee all
What thou command'st, and right thou shouldst be obeyed.   570
I was at first as other beasts that graze
The trodden herb, of abject thoughts and low
As was my food, nor aught but food discerned
Or sex, and apprehended nothing high:
Till on a day roving the field, I chanced
A goodly tree far distant to behold,
Loaden with fruit of fairest colours mixed,
Ruddy and gold. I nearer drew to gaze,
When from the boughs a savoury odour blown,
Grateful to appetite, more pleased my sense   580
Than smell of sweetest fennel, or the teats
Of ewe or goat dropping with milk at ev'n,
Unsucked of lamb or kid, that tend their play.
To satisfy the sharp desire I had
Of tasting those fair apples, I resolved
Not to defer; hunger and thirst at once,
Powerful persuaders, quickened at the scent
Of that alluring fruit, urged me so keen.
About the mossy trunk I wound me soon;
For high from ground the branches would require   590
Thy utmost reach or Adam's: round the tree
All other beasts that saw, with like desire
Longing and envying stood, but could not reach.
Amid the tree now got, where plenty hung
Tempting so nigh, to pluck and eat my fill
I spared not; for such pleasure till that hour
At feed or fountain never had I found.
Sated at length, ere long I might perceive
Strange alteration in me, to degree
Of reason in my inward powers, and speech   600

Wanted not long, though to this shape retained.
Thenceforth to speculations high or deep
I turned my thoughts, and with capacious mind
Considered all things visible in heav'n,
Or earth, or middle, all things fair and good.
But all that fair and good in thy divine
Semblance, and in thy beauty's heav'nly ray,
United I beheld; no fair to thine
Equivalent or second; which compelled
Me thus, though importune perhaps, to come   610
And gaze, and worship thee of right declared
Sovran of creatures, universal dame!'
    So talked the spirited sly Snake; and Eve,
Yet more amazed, unwary thus replied:
    'Serpent, thy overpraising leaves in doubt
The virtue of that fruit, in thee first proved.
But say, where grows the tree, from hence how far?
For many are the trees of God that grow
In Paradise, and various, yet unknown
To us; in such abundance lies our choice   620
As leaves a greater store of fruit untouched,
Still hanging incorruptible, till men
Grow up to their provision, and more hands
Help to disburden nature of her bearth.'
    To whom the wily adder, blithe and glad:
'Empress, the way is ready and not long:
Beyond a row of myrtles, on a flat,
Fast by a fountain, one small thicket past
Of blowing myrrh and balm; if thou accept
My conduct, I can bring thee thither soon.'   630
    'Lead, then,' said Eve. He leading swiftly rolled
In tangles, and made intricate seem straight,
To mischief swift. Hope elevates, and joy
Brightens his crest. As when a wand'ring fire,
Compact of unctuous vapour which the night
Condenses, and the cold environs round,
Kindled through agitation to a flame
(Which oft, they say, some evil spirit attends),
Hovering and blazing with delusive light,
Misleads th' amazed night-wanderer from his way   640
To bogs and mires, and oft through pond or pool,
There swallowed up and lost, from succour far:
So glistered the dire Snake, and into fraud

Led Eve our credulous mother, to the tree
Of prohibition, root of all our woe;
Which when she saw, thus to her guide she spake:
   'Serpent, we might have spared our coming hither,
Fruitless to me, though fruit be here to excess,
The credit of whose virtue rest with thee,
Wondrous indeed, if cause of such effects! 650
But of this tree we may not taste nor touch:
God so commanded, and left that command
Sole daughter of his voice; the rest, we live
Law to ourselves: our reason is our law.'
   To whom the tempter guilefully replied:
'Indeed? Hath God then said that of the fruit
Of all these garden trees ye shall not eat,
Yet lords declared of all in earth or air?'
   To whom thus Eve, yet sinless: 'Of the fruit
Of each tree in the garden we may eat; 660
But of the fruit of this fair tree, amidst
The garden, God hath said, "Ye shall not eat
Thereof; nor shall ye touch it, lest ye die."'
   She scarce had said, though brief; when now more bold
The tempter, but with show of zeal and love
To man, and indignation at his wrong,
New part puts on, and as to passion moved,
Fluctuates disturbed, yet comely, and in act
Raised, as of some great matter to begin.
As when of old some orator renowned 670
In Athens or free Rome, where eloquence
Flourished, since mute, to some great cause addressed,
Stood in himself collected, while each part,
Motion, each act, won audience ere the tongue
Sometimes in height began, as no delay
Of preface brooking through his zeal of right;
So standing, moving, or to height upgrown,
The tempter, all impassioned, thus began:
   'O sacred, wise, and wisdom-giving plant,
Mother of science! now I feel thy power 680
Within me clear, not only to discern
Things in their causes, but to trace the ways
Of highest agents, deemed however wise.
Queen of this universe, do not believe
Those rigid threats of death; ye shall not die:
How should ye? By the fruit? it gives you life

To knowledge. By the Threat'ner? Look on me,
Me who have touched and tasted, yet both live
And life more perfect have attained than fate
Meant me, by vent'ring higher than my lot. 690
Shall that be shut to man which to the beast
Is open? or will God incense his ire
For such a petty trespass, and not praise
Rather your dauntless virtue, whom the pain
Of death denounced, whatever thing death be,
Deterred not from achieving what might lead
To happier life, knowledge of good and evil?
Of good, how just? of evil (if what is evil
Be real), why not known, since easier shunned?
God therefore cannot hurt ye, and be just; 700
Not just, not God; not feared then, nor obeyed:
Your fear itself of death removes the fear.
Why then was this forbid? Why but to awe,
Why but to keep ye low and ignorant,
His worshippers? He knows that in the day
Ye eat thereof, your eyes, that seem so clear,
Yet are but dim, shall perfectly be then
Opened and cleared, and ye shall be as gods,
Knowing both good and evil as they know.
That ye should be as gods, since I as man, 710
Internal man, is but proportion meet,
I of brute human; ye of human gods.
So ye shall die perhaps, by putting off
Human, to put on gods; death to be wished,
Though threat'ned, which no worse than this can bring.
And what are gods that man may not become
As they, participating godlike food?
The gods are first, and that advantage use
On our belief; that all from them proceeds.
I question it; for this fair earth I see, 720
Warmed by the sun, producing every kind,
Them nothing. If they all things, who enclosed
Knowledge of good and evil in this tree,
That whoso eats thereof forthwith attains
Wisdom without their leave? And wherein lies
Th' offence, that man should thus attain to know?
What can your knowledge hurt him, or this tree
Impart against his will, if all be his?
Or is it envy, and can envy dwell

In heav'nly breasts? These, these and many more   730
Causes import your need of this fair fruit.
Goddess humane, reach then, and freely taste!'
   He ended; and his words, replete with guile,
Into her heart too easy entrance won.
Fixed on the fruit she gazed, which to behold
Might tempt alone; and in her ears the sound
Yet rung of his persuasive words, impregned
With reason, to her seeming, and with truth;
Meanwhile the hour of noon drew on and waked
An eager appetite, raised by the smell   740
So savoury of that fruit, which with desire,
Inclinable now grown to touch or taste,
Solicited her longing eye; yet first
Pausing a while, thus to herself she mused:
   'Great are thy virtues, doubtless, best of fruits,
Though kept from man, and worthy to be admired,
Whose taste, too long forborne, at first assay
Gave elocution to the mute, and taught
The tongue not made for speech to speak thy praise.
Thy praise he also who forbids thy use   750
Conceals not from us, naming thee the Tree
Of Knowledge, knowledge both of good and evil;
Forbids us then to taste, but his forbidding
Commends thee more, while it infers the good
By thee communicated, and our want;
For good unknown sure is not had, or had
And yet unknown, is as not had at all.
In plain then, what forbids he but to know,
Forbids us good, forbids us to be wise?
Such prohibitions bind not. But if death   760
Bind us with after-bands, what profits then
Our inward freedom? In the day we eat
Of this fair fruit, our doom is we shall die.
How dies the serpent? He hath eat'n, and lives
And knows and speaks and reasons and discerns,
Irrational till then. For us alone
Was death invented? Or to us denied
This intellectual food, for beasts reserved?
For beasts it seems; yet that one beast which first
Hath tasted envies not, but brings with joy   770
The good befall'n him, author unsuspect,
Friendly to man, far from deceit or guile.

What fear I then? rather, what know to fear
Under this ignorance of good and evil,
Of God or death, of law or penalty?
Here grows the cure of all: this fruit divine,
Fair to the eye, inviting to the taste,
Of virtue to make wise. What hinders then
To reach and feed at once both body and mind?'
    So saying, her rash hand in evil hour 780
Forth-reaching to the fruit, she plucked, she eat.
Earth felt the wound, and nature from her seat,
Sighing through all her works, gave signs of woe
That all was lost. Back to the thicket slunk
The guilty serpent, and well might; for Eve,
Intent now wholly on her taste, naught else
Regarded: such delight till then, as seemed,
In fruit she never tasted, whether true
Or fancied so through expectation high
Of knowledge, nor was Godhead from her thought. 790
Greedily she engorged without restraint,
And knew not eating death. Satiate at length,
And height'ned as with wine, jocund and boon,
Thus to herself she pleasingly began:
    'O sovran, virtuous, precious of all trees
In Paradise! of operation blest
To sapience, hitherto obscured, infamed,
And thy fair fruit let hang, as to no end
Created; but henceforth my early care,
Not without song, each morning, and due praise, 800
Shall tend thee, and the fertile burden ease
Of thy full branches, offered free to all;
Till dieted by thee I grow mature
In knowledge, as the gods who all things know;
Though others envy what they cannot give;
For had the gift been theirs, it had not here
Thus grown. Experience, next to thee I owe,
Best guide: not following thee, I had remained
In ignorance; thou open'st wisdom's way
And giv'st access, though secret she retire. 810
And I perhaps am secret: heav'n is high;
High and remote to see from thence distinct
Each thing on earth; and other care perhaps
May have diverted from continual watch
Our great Forbidder, safe with all his spies

About him. But to Adam in what sort
Shall I appear? Shall I to him make known
As yet my change, and give him to partake
Full happiness with me, or rather not,
But keep the odds of knowledge in my power   820
Without copartner? So to add what wants
In female sex, the more to draw his love,
And render me more equal, and perhaps;
A thing not undesirable, sometime
Superior; for, inferior, who is free?
This may be well. But what if God have seen,
And death ensue? Then I shall be no more,
And Adam, wedded to another Eve
Shall live with her enjoying, I extinct;
A death to think. Confirmed then I resolve: 830
Adam shall share with me in bliss or woe.
So dear I love him that with him all deaths
I could endure, without him live no life.'
    So saying, from the tree her step she turned,
But first, low reverence done as to the power
That dwelt within, whose presence had infused
Into the plant sciential sap, derived
From nectar, drink of gods. Adam the while,
Waiting desirous her return, had wove
Of choicest flow'rs a garland, to adorn   840
Her tresses and her rural labours crown,
As reapers oft are wont their harvest-queen.
Great joy he promised to his thoughts, and new
Solace in her return, so long delayed;
Yet oft his heart, divine of something ill,
Misgave him; he the falt'ring measure felt,
And forth to meet her went, the way she took
That morn when first they parted. By the Tree
Of Knowledge he must pass; there he her met,
Scarce from the tree returning; in her hand   850
A bough of fairest fruit that downy smiled,
New gathered, and ambrosial smell diffused.
To him she hasted; in her face excuse
Came prologue, and apology to prompt,
Which with bland words at will she thus addressed:
    'Hast thou not wondered, Adam, at my stay?
Thee I have missed, and thought it long, deprived
Thy presence, agony of love till now

Not felt, nor shall be twice, for never more
Mean I to try, what rash untried I sought, 860
The pain of absence from thy sight. But strange
Hath been the cause, and wonderful to hear:
This tree is not, as we are told, a tree
Of danger tasted, nor to evil unknown
Op'ning the way, but of divine effect
To open eyes and make them gods who taste;
And hath been tasted such. The serpent wise,
Or not restrained as we, or not obeying,
Hath eat'n of the fruit, and is become
Not dead, as we are threat'ned, but thenceforth 870
Endued with human voice and human sense,
Reasoning to admiration, and with me
Persuasively hath so prevailed that I
Have also tasted, and have also found
Th' effects to correspond: opener mine eyes,
Dim erst, dilated spirits, ampler heart,
And growing up to Godhead, which for thee
Chiefly I sought, without thee can despise;
For bliss, as thou hast part, to me is bliss;
Tedious, unshared with thee, and odious soon. 880
Thou, therefore, also taste, that equal lot
May join us, equal joy, as equal love;
Lest thou not tasting, different degree
Disjoin us, and I then too late renounce
Deity for thee, when fate will not permit.'
 Thus Eve with count'nance blithe her story told;
But in her cheek distemper flushing glowed.
On th' other side, Adam, soon as he heard
The fatal trespass done by Eve, amazed,
Astonied stood and blank, while horror chill 890
Ran through his veins and all his joints relaxed.
From his slack hand the garland wreathed for Eve
Down dropped, and all the faded roses shed.
Speechless he stood and pale, till thus at length
First to himself he inward silence broke:
 'O fairest of creation, last and best
Of all God's works, creature in whom excelled
Whatever can to sight or thought be formed
Holy, divine, good, amiable, or sweet!
How art thou lost, how on a sudden lost, 900
Defaced, deflow'red, and now to death devote!

Rather, how hast thou yielded to transgress
The strict forbiddance, how to violate
The sacred fruit forbidd'n? Some cursèd fraud
Of enemy hath beguiled thee, yet unknown,
And me with thee hath ruined, for with thee
Certain my resolution is to die.
How can I live without thee, how forgo
Thy sweet converse, and love so dearly joined,
To live again in these wild woods forlorn?   910
Should God create another Eve, and I
Another rib afford, yet loss of thee
Would never from my heart; no, no! I feel
The link of nature draw me: flesh of flesh,
Bone of my bone thou art, and from thy state
Mine never shall be parted, bliss or woe.'
    So having said, as one from sad dismay
Recomforted and, after thoughts disturbed
Submitting to what seemed remediless,
Thus in calm mood his words to Eve he turned: 920
    'Bold deed thou hast presumed, advent'rous Eve,
And peril great provoked, who thus hast dared
Had it been only coveting to eye
That sacred fruit, sacred to abstinence;
Much more to taste it, under ban to touch.
But past who can recall, or done undo?
Not God omnipotent, nor fate. Yet so
Perhaps thou shalt not die; perhaps the fact
Is not so heinous now, foretasted fruit,
Profaned first by the Serpent, by him first   930
Made common and unhallowed ere your taste;
Nor yet on him found deadly; he yet lives,
Lives, as thou saidst, and gains to live as man,
Higher degree of life: inducement strong
To us, as likely tasting to attain
Proportional ascent; which cannot be
But to be gods or angels, demi-gods.
Nor can I think that God, Creator wise,
Though threat'ning, will in earnest so destroy
Us his prime creatures, dignified so high,   940
Set over all his works, which in our fall,
For us created, needs with us must fail,
Dependent made; so God shall uncreate,
Be frustrate, do, undo, and labour lose,

Not well conceived of God, who, though his power
Creation could repeat, yet would be loth
Us to abolish, lest the Adversary
Triumph and say: "Fickle their state whom God
Most favours; who can please him long? Me first
He ruined, now mankind; whom will he next?" 950
Matter of scorn not to be given the Foe;
However, I with thee have fixed my lot,
Certain to undergo like doom; if death
Consort with thee, death is to me as life:
So forcible within my heart I feel
The bond of nature draw me to my own,
My own in thee, for what thou art is mine;
Our state cannot be severed, we are one,
One flesh; to lose thee were to lose myself.'
    So Adam; and thus Eve to him replied: 960
'O glorious trial of exceeding love,
Illustrious evidence, example high!
Engaging me to emulate, but, short
Of thy perfection, how shall I attain,
Adam? From whose dear side I boast me sprung,
And gladly of our union hear thee speak,
One heart, one soul in both; whereof good proof
This day affords, declaring thee resolved,
Rather than death, or aught than death more dread
Shall separate us, linked in love so dear, 970
To undergo with me one guilt, one crime,
If any be, of tasting this fair fruit,
Whose virtue (for of good still good proceeds,
Direct, or by occasion) hath presented
This happy trial of thy love, which else
So eminently never had been known.
Were it I thought death menaced would ensue
This my attempt, I would sustain alone
The worst, and not persuade thee, rather die
Deserted than oblige thee with a fact 980
Pernicious to thy peace, chiefly assured
Remarkably so late of thy so true,
So faithful love unequalled. But I feel
Far otherwise th' event, not death, but life
Augmented, opened eyes, new hopes, new joys,
Taste so divine, that what of sweet before
Hath touched my sense, flat seems to this and harsh.

On my experience, Adam, freely taste,
And fear of death deliver to the winds!'
    So saying, she embraced him, and for joy   990
Tenderly wept, much won that he his love
Had so ennobled, as of choice to incur
Divine displeasure for her sake, or death.
In recompense (for such compliance bad
Such recompense best merits), from the bough
She gave him of that fair enticing fruit
With liberal hand. He scrupled not to eat
Against his better knowledge, not deceived,
But fondly overcome with female charm.
Earth trembled from her entrails, as again   1000
In pangs, and nature gave a second groan;
Sky loured and, muttering thunder, some sad drops
Wept at completing of the mortal sin
Original; while Adam took no thought,
Eating his fill, nor Eve to iterate
Her former trespass feared, the more to soothe
Him with her loved society, that now,
As with new wine intoxicated both,
They swim in mirth, and fancy that they feel
Divinity within them breeding wings   1010
Wherewith to scorn the earth. But that false fruit
Far other operation first displayed,
Carnal desire inflaming. He on Eve
Began to cast lascivious eyes; she him
As wantonly repaid; in lust they burn,
Till Adam thus 'gan Eve to dalliance move:
    'Eve, now I see thou art exact of taste
And elegant, of sapience no small part,
Since to each meaning "savour" we apply,
And palate call "judicious". I the praise   1020
Yield thee, so well this day thou hast purveyed.
Much pleasure we have lost, while we abstained
From this delightful fruit, nor known till now
True relish, tasting. If such pleasure be
In things to us forbidden, it might be wished
For this one tree had been forbidden ten.
But come; so well refreshed, now let us play,
As meet is after such delicious fare;
For never did thy beauty, since the day
I saw thee first and wedded thee, adorned   1030

With all perfections, so inflame my sense
With ardour to enjoy thee, fairer now
Than ever, bounty of this virtuous tree!'
    So said he, and forbore not glance or toy
Of amorous intent, well understood
Of Eve, whose eye darted contagious fire.
Her hand he seized, and to a shady bank,
Thick overhead with verdant roof embow'red,
He led her, nothing loth; flow'rs were the couch,
Pansies and violets and asphodel   1040
And hyacinth, earth's freshest, softest lap.
There they their fill of love and love's disport
Took largely, of their mutual guilt the seal,
The solace of their sin, till dewy sleep
Oppressed them, wearied with their amorous play.
    Soon as the force of that fallacious fruit,
That with exhilarating vapour bland
About their spirits had played, and inmost powers
Made err, was now exhaled, and grosser sleep
Bred of unkindly fumes, with conscious dreams   1050
Encumbered, now had left them, up they rose
As from unrest, and each the other viewing,
Soon found their eyes how opened, and their minds
How darkened; innocence, that as a veil
Had shadowed them from knowing ill, was gone;
Just confidence and native righteousness
And honour, from about them, naked left
To guilty shame; he covered, but his robe
Uncovered more. So rose the Danite strong,
Herculean Samson, from the harlot-lap   1060
Of Philistèan Dalilah, and waked
Shorn of his strength, they destitute and bare
Of all their virtue. Silent, and in face
Confounded, long they sat, as strucken mute;
Till Adam, though not less than Eve abashed,
At length gave utterance to these words constrained:
    'O Eve, in evil hour thou didst give ear
To that false worm, of whomsoever taught
To counterfeit man's voice; true in our fall,
False in our promised rising; since our eyes   1070
Opened we find indeed, and find we know
Both good and evil, good lost and evil got,
Bad fruit of knowledge, if this be to know,

Which leaves us naked thus, of honour void,
Of innocence, of faith, of purity,
Our wonted ornaments now soiled and stained,
And in our faces evident the signs
Of foul concupiscence; whence evil store,
Even shame, the last of evils; of the first
Be sure then. How shall I behold the face   1080
Henceforth of God or angel, erst with joy
And rapture so oft beheld? Those heav'nly shapes
Will dazzle now this earthly, with their blaze
Insufferably bright. O might I here
In solitude live savage, in some glade
Obscured, where highest woods impenetrable
To star or sunlight spread their umbrage broad
And brown as evening! Cover me, ye pines,
Ye cedars, with innumerable boughs
Hide me, where I may never see them more.   1090
But let us now, as in bad plight, devise
What best may for the present serve to hide
The parts of each from other that seem most
To shame obnoxious, and unseemliest seen;
Some tree, whose broad smooth leaves, together sewed,
And girded on our loins, may cover round
Those middle parts, that this newcomer, shame,
There sit not, and reproach us as unclean.'
   So counselled he, and both together went
Into the thickest wood; there soon they chose   1100
The fig-tree; not that kind for fruit renowned,
But such as at this day to Indians known
In Malabar or Deccan spreads her arms
Branching so broad and long, that in the ground
The bended twigs take root, and daughters grow
About the mother tree, a pillared shade
High overarched, and echoing walks between;
There oft the Indian herdsman shunning heat
Shelters in cool, and tends his pasturing herds
At loop-holes cut through thickest shade. Those leaves   1110
They gathered, broad as Amazonian targe,
And with what skill they had, together sewed,
To gird their waist; vain covering if to hide
Their guilt and dreaded shame. O how unlike
To that first naked glory! Such of late
Columbus found th' American so girt

With feathered cincture, naked else and wild
Among the trees on isles and woody shores.
Thus fenced and, as they thought, their shame in part
Covered, but not at rest or ease of mind,   1120
They sat them down to weep; nor only tears
Rained at their eyes, but high winds worse within
Began to rise, high passions, anger, hate,
Mistrust, suspicion, discord, and shook sore
Their inward state of mind, calm region once
And full of peace, now tossed and turbulent;
For understanding ruled not, and the will
Heard not her lore, both in subjection now
To sensual appetite, who, from beneath
Usurping over sovran reason, claimed   1130
Superior sway. From thus distempered breast
Adam, estranged in look and altered style,
Speech intermitted, thus to Eve renewed:
    'Would thou hadst hearkened to my words, and stayed
With me, as I besought thee, when that strange
Desire of wand'ring, this unhappy morn,
I know not whence possessed thee; we had then
Remained still happy; not, as now, despoiled
Of all our good, shamed, naked, miserable!
Let none henceforth seek needless cause to approve   1140
The faith they owe; when earnestly they seek
Such proof, conclude they then begin to fail.'
    To whom, soon moved with touch of blame, thus Eve:
'What words have passed thy lips, Adam severe!
Imput'st thou that to my default, or will
Of wandering, as thou call'st it, which who knows
But might as ill have happened thou being by,
Or to thyself perhaps? Hadst thou been there,
Or here th' attempt, thou couldst not have discerned
Fraud in the Serpent, speaking as he spake;   1150
No ground of enmity between us known
Why he should mean me ill or seek to harm.
Was I to have never parted from thy side?
As good have grown there still a lifeless rib.
Being as I am, why didst not thou, the head,
Command me absolutely not to go,
Going into such danger, as thou saidst?
Too facile then, thou didst not much gainsay,
Nay, didst permit, approve, and fair dismiss.

Hadst thou been firm and fixed in thy dissent,   1160
Neither had I transgressed, nor thou with me.'
    To whom, then first incensed, Adam replied:
'Is this the love, is this the recompense
Of mine to thee, ingrateful Eve, expressed
Immutable when thou wert lost, not I,
Who might have lived and joyed immortal bliss,
Yet willingly chose rather death with thee?
And am I now upbraided as the cause
Of thy transgressing? Not enough severe,
It seems, in thy restraint! What could I more?   1170
I warned thee, I admonished thee, foretold
The danger, and the lurking enemy
That lay in wait; beyond this had been force,
And force upon free will hath here no place.
But confidence then bore thee on, secure
Either to meet no danger, or to find
Matter of glorious trial; and perhaps
I also erred in overmuch admiring
What seemed in thee so perfect that I thought
No evil durst attempt thee, but I rue   1180
That error now, which is become my crime,
And thou th' accuser. Thus it shall befall
Him who to worth in women overtrusting
Lets her will rule; restraint she will not brook,
And, left to herself, if evil thence ensue,
She first his weak indulgence will accuse.'
    Thus they in mutual accusation spent
The fruitless hours, but neither self-condemning,
And of their vain contest appeared no end.

Sir John Suckling (1609–1642)

227. 'Why so pale and wan, fond lover?'

Why so pale and wan, fond lover?
    Prithee why so pale?

Will, when looking well can't move her,
   Looking ill prevail?
   Prithee why so pale?

Why so dull and mute, young sinner?
   Prithee why so mute?
Will, when speaking well can't win her,
   Saying nothing do it?
   Prithee why so mute?   10

Quit, quit for shame, this will not move,
   This cannot take her;
If of herself she will not love,
   Nothing can make her:
   The devil take her.

278. 'No, no, fair heretic, it needs must be'

No, no, fair heretic, it needs must be
   But an ill love in me,
   And worse for thee.

For were it in my power
To love thee now this hour,
   More than I did the last;

I would then so fall,
   I might not love at all;

Love that can flow, and can admit increase,
Admits as well an ebb, and may grow less.   10

True love is still the same; the torrid zones
   And those more frigid ones
   It must not know:

For love grown cold or hot
   Is lust, or friendship, not
   The thing we have;
For that's a flame would die,
Held down, or up too high:

Then think I love more than I can express,
And would love more, could I but love thee less.   20

279. 'Of thee (kind boy) I ask no red and white'

Of thee (kind boy) I ask no red and white
    To make up my delight,
    No odd becoming graces,
Black eyes, or little know-not-whats, in faces;
Make me but mad enough, give me good store
Of love, for her I court,
    I ask no more,
'Tis love in love that makes the sport.

There's no such thing as that we beauty call,
    It is mere cosenage all;   10
    For though some long ago
Liked certain colours mingled so and so,
That doth not tie me now from choosing new,
If I a fancy take
    To black and blue,
That fancy doth it beauty make.

'Tis not the meat, but 'tis the appetite
    Makes eating a delight,
    And if I like one dish
More than another, that a pheasant is;   20
What in our watches, that in us is found,
So to the height and nick
    We up be wound,
No matter by what hand or trick.

280. Against Fruition

Stay here fond youth and ask no more, be wise,
Knowing too much long since lost Paradise;
The virtuous joys thou hast, thou would'st should still
Last in their pride; and would'st not take it ill

If rudely from sweet dreams (and for a toy)
Thou wert waked? He wakes himself that does enjoy.

Fruition adds no new wealth, but destroys,
And while it pleaseth much the palate, cloys;
Who thinks he shall be happier for that,
As reasonably might hope he might grow fat   10
By eating to a surfeit; this once past,
What relishes? Even kisses lose their taste.

Urge not 'tis necessary, alas! We know
The homeliest thing which mankind does is so;
The world is of a vast extent we see,
And must be peopled; children there must be;
So must bread too; but since there are enough
Born to the drudgery, what need we plough?

Women enjoyed (what e'er before t' have been)
Are like romances read, or sights once seen: 20
Fruition's dull, and spoils the play much more
Than if one read or knew the plot before;
'Tis expectation makes a blessing dear,
Heaven were not heaven, if we knew what it were.

And as in prospects we are there pleased most
Where something keeps the eye from being lost,
And leaves us room to guess, so here restraint
Holds up delight, that with excess would faint.
They who know all the wealth they have, are poor;
He's only rich that cannot tell his store.   30

Anne Bradstreet (1612–1672)

281. An Apology

To finish what's begun was my intent,
My thoughts and my endeavours thereto bent;

Essays I many made but still gave out,
The more I mused, the more I was in doubt:
The subject large, my mind and body weak,
With many more discouragements did speak.
All thoughts of further progress laid aside,
Though oft persuaded, I as oft denied,
At length resolved, when many years had passed,
To prosecute my story to the last;   10
And for the same, I hours not few did spend,
And weary lines (though lank) I many penned:
But 'fore I could accomplish my desire,
My papers fell a prey to th' raging fire.
And thus my pains (with better things) I lost,
Which none had cause to wail, nor I to boast.
No more I'll do sith I have suffered wrack,
Although my monarchies their legs do lack:
Nor matter is 't this last, the world now sees,
Hath many Ages been upon his knees.   20

282. Upon the Burning of our House[44]

In silent night when rest I took,
For sorrow near I did not look,
I wakened was with thundering noise
And piteous shrieks of dreadful voice.
That fearful sound of 'Fire!' and 'Fire!'
Let no man know is my desire.

I, starting up, the light did spy,
And to my God my heart did cry
To strengthen me in my distress
And not to leave me succourless.   10
Then coming out beheld a space,
The flame consume my dwelling place.

And, when I could no longer look,
I blest His name that gave and took,
That laid my goods now in the dust:

[44] 'Here follows some verses upon the burning of our house, July 10th, 1666. Copied out of a loose paper.'

Yea so it was, and so 'twas just.
It was His own: it was not mine;
Far be it that I should repine.

He might of all justly bereft,
But yet sufficient for us left.   20
When by the ruins oft I passed,
My sorrowing eyes aside did cast,
And here and there the places spy
Where oft I sate, and long did lie.

Here stood that trunk, and there that chest;
There lay that store I counted best;
My pleasant things in ashes lie,
And them behold no more shall I.
Under thy roof no guest shall sit,
Nor at thy table eat a bit.   30

No pleasant tale shall e'er be told,
Nor things recounted done of old.
No candle e'er shall shine in thee,
Nor bridegroom's voice e'er heard shall be.
In silence ever shalt thou lie;
Adieu, Adieu; All's vanity.

Then straight I gin my heart to chide,
'And did thy wealth on earth abide?
Did'st fix thy hope on mouldering dust,
The arm of flesh did'st make thy trust?   40
Raise up thy thoughts above the sky
That dunghill mists away may fly.

'Thou hast an house on high erect,
Framed by that mighty Architect,
With glory richly furnishèd,
Stands permanent though this be fled.
It's purchasèd, and paid for too
By Him who hath enough to do.

'A price so vast as is unknown,
Yet, by His gift, is made thine own.'   50
There's wealth enough, I need no more;
Farewell my pelf, farewell my store.

The world no longer let me love,
My hope and treasure lies above.

283. In Reference to her Children

I had eight birds hatched in one nest,
Four cocks there were, and hens the rest,
I nursed them up with pain and care,
Nor cost, nor labour did I spare,
Till at the last they felt their wing,
Mounted the trees, and learned to sing.
Chief of the brood then took his flight,
To regions far, and left me quite;
My mournful chirps I after send,
Till he return, or I do end: 10
'Leave not thy nest, thy dam and sire,
Fly back and sing amidst this choir.'
My second bird did take her flight,
And with her mate flew out of sight;
Southward they both their course did bend,
And seasons twain they there did spend:
Till after blown by southern gales,
They norward steered with fillèd sails.
A prettier bird was nowhere seen,
Along the beach among the treen.°   *trees* 20
I have a third of colour white,
On whom I placed no small delight;
Coupled with mate loving and true,
Hath also bid her dam adieu,
And where Aurora first appears,
She now hath perched, to spend her years.
One to the academy flew
To chat among that learned crew:
Ambition moves still in his breast
That he might chant above the rest,   30
Striving for more than to do well,
That nightingales he might excel.
My fifth, whose down is yet scarce gone,
Is 'mongst the shrubs and bushes flown,
And as his wings increase in strength,
On higher boughs he'll perch at length.

My other three still with me nest,
Until they're grown, then as the rest,
Or here or there, they'll take their flight,
As is ordained, so shall they light.   40
If birds could weep, then would my tears
Let others know what are my fears
Lest this my brood some harm should catch,
And be surprised for want of watch,
Whilst pecking corn, and void of care
They fall un'wares in fowler's snare:
Or whilst on trees they sit and sing,
Some untoward boy at them do fling;
Or whilst allured with bell and glass,
The net be spread, and caught, alas.   50
Or lest by lime-twigs they be foiled,
Or by some greedy hawks be spoiled.
O would my young, ye saw my breast,
And knew what thoughts there sadly rest,
Great was my pain when I you bred,
Great was my care when I you fed,
Long did I keep you soft and warm,
And with my wings kept off all harm.
My cares are more, and fears, than ever,
My throbs such now, as 'fore were never: 60
Alas my birds, you wisdom want,
Of perils you are ignorant,
Oft times in grass, on trees, in flight,
Sore accidents on you may light.
O to your safety have an eye,
So happy may you live and die:
Meanwhile my days in tunes I'll spend,
Till my weak lays with me shall end.
In shady woods I'll sit and sing,
And things that past, to mind I'll bring.   70
Once young and pleasant, as are you,
But former toys (no joys) adieu.
My age I will not once lament,
But sing, my time so near is spent.
And from the top bough take my flight
Into a country beyond sight
Where old ones instantly grow young,
And there with seraphims set song;
No seasons cold, nor storms they see,

But spring lasts to eternity.   80
When each of you shall in your nest
Among your young ones take your rest,
In chirping language oft them tell
You had a Dam that loved you well,
That did what could be done for young,
And nursed you up till you were strong,
And 'fore she once would let you fly,
She showed you joy and misery;
Taught what was good, and what was ill,
What would save life, and what would kill.   90
Thus gone, amongst you I may live,
And dead, yet speak and counsel give.
Farewell, my birds, farewell, adieu,
I happy am, if well with you.

284. A Dialogue between Old England and New

Concerning their present Troubles, Anno 1642

   New England
Alas dear mother, fairest queen and best,
With honour, wealth, and peace, happy and blest;
What ails thee, hang thy head, and cross thine arms?
And sit i' th' dust, to sigh these sad alarms?
What deluge of new woes thus overwhelm
The glories of thy ever famous realm?
What means this wailing tone, this mournful guise?
Ah, tell thy daughter, she may sympathise.
   Old England
Art ignorant indeed of these my woes?
Or must my forcèd tongue these griefs disclose?   10
And must myself dissect my tattered state,
Which 'mazèd Christendom stands wondering at?
And thou a child, a limb, and dost not feel
My fainting weakened body now to reel?
This physic purging potion, I have taken,
Will bring consumption, or an ague quaking,
Unless some cordial thou fetch from high,
Which present help may ease my malady.
If I decease, dost think thou shalt survive?

Or by my wasting state dost think to thrive? 20
Then weigh our case, if 't be not justly sad;
Let me lament alone, while thou art glad.
   New England
And thus (alas) your state you much deplore
In general terms, but will not say wherefore.
What medicine shall I seek to cure this woe,
If th' wound so dangerous I may not know.
But you perhaps would have me guess it out:
What hath some Hengist like that Saxon stout
By fraud or force usurped thy flowering crown,
Or by tempestuous wars thy fields trod down? 30
Or hath Canutus, that brave valiant Dane
The regal peaceful sceptre from thee ta'en?
Or is't a Norman, whose victorious hand
With English blood bedews thy conquered land?
Or is't intestine wars that thus offend?
Do Maud and Stephen for the crown contend?
Do barons rise and side against their king,
And call in foreign aid to help the thing?
Must Edward be deposed? or is 't the hour
That second Richard must be clapped i' th' tower? 40
Or is 't the fatal jar again begun
That from the red white pricking roses sprung?
Must Richmond's aid, the nobles now implore?
To come and break the tushes of the Boar,
If none of these, dear mother, what's your woe?
Pray do you fear Spain's bragging Armado?
Doth your ally, fair France, conspire your wrack,
Or do the Scots play false, behind your back?
Doth Holland quit you ill for all your love?
Whence is the storm, from earth or heaven above? 50
Is 't drought, is 't famine, or is 't pestilence?
Dost feel the smart, or fear the consequence?
Your humble child entreats you, show your grief,
Though arms, nor purse she hath for your relief,
Such is her poverty; yet shall be found
A suppliant for your help, as she is bound.
   Old England
I must confess some of those sores you name,
My beauteous body at this present maim;
But foreign foe, nor feignèd friend I fear,
For they have work enough (thou know'st) elsewhere 60

Nor is it Alcie's son, nor Henry's daughter;
Whose proud contention cause this slaughter,
Nor nobles siding, to make John no king,
French Jews unjustly to the crown to bring;
No Edward, Richard, to lose rule and life,
Nor no Lancastrians to renew old strife:
No Duke of York, nor Earl of March to soil
Their hands in kindred's blood whom they did foil
No crafty tyrant now usurps the seat,
Who nephews slew that so he might be great;   70
No need of Tudor, roses to unite,
None knows which is the red, or which the white;
Spain's braving Fleet, a second time is sunk,
France knows how oft my fury she hath drunk;
By Edward third, and Henry fifth of fame,
Her lilies in mine Arms avouch the same.
My sister Scotland hurts me now no more,
Though she hath been injurious heretofore;
What Holland is I am in some suspense,
But trust not much unto his excellence.   80
For wants, sure some I feel, but more I fear,
And for the Pestilence, who knows how near;
Famine and Plague, two Sisters of the Sword,
Destruction to a Land, doth soon afford:
They're for my punishment ordained on high,
Unless our tears prevent it speedily.
But yet I answer not what you demand,
To show the grievance of my troubled land.
Before I tell th' effect, I'll show the cause
Which are my sins, the breach of sacred laws,   90
Idolatry supplanter of a nation,
With foolish superstitious adoration,
Are liked and countenanced by men of might,
The Gospel trodden down and hath no right;
Church offices were sold and bought for gain,
That Pope had hope to find Rome here again,
For oaths and blasphemies, did ever ear
From Beelzebub himself such language hear;
What scorning of the saints of the most high?
What injuries did daily on them lie?   100
What false reports, what nick-names did they take
Not for their own, but for their master's sake?
And thou, poor soul, wert jeered among the rest,

Thy flying for the truth was made a jest.
For Sabbath-breaking, and for drunkenness,
Did ever land profaneness more express?
From crying blood yet cleansèd am not I,
Martyrs and others, dying causelessly.
How many princely heads on blocks laid down
For naught but title to a fading crown?   110
'Mongst all the cruelties by great ones done
Of Edward's youths, and Clarence's hapless son,
O Jane why did'st thou die in flowering prime?
Because of royal stem, that was thy crime.
For bribery, adultery and lies,
Where is the nation I can't paralyse.
With usury, extortion and oppression,
These be the Hydras of my stout transgression.
These be the bitter fountains, heads and roots,
Whence flowed the source, the sprigs, the boughs and fruits   120
Of more than thou can'st hear or I relate,
That with high hand I still did perpetrate.
For these were threatenèd the woeful day,
I mocked the preachers, put it far away;
The Sermons yet upon record do stand
That cried destruction to my wicked land.
I then believed not, now I feel and see,
The plague of stubborn incredulity.
Some lost their livings, some in prison pent,
Some fined, from house and friends to exile went.   130
Their silent tongues to heaven did vengeance cry,
Who saw their wrongs, and hath judged righteously
And will repay it seven-fold in my lap.
This is fore-runner of my afterclap.
Nor took I warning by my neighbours' falls,
I saw sad Germany's dismantled walls,
I saw her people famished, nobles slain,
Her fruitful land, a barren heath remain.
I saw unmoved, her armies foiled and fled,
Wives forced, babes tossed, her houses calcinèd.   140
I saw strong Rochel yielded to her foe,
Thousands of starvèd Christians there also.
I saw poor Ireland bleeding out her last,
Such cruelties as all reports have past;
Mine heart obdurate stood not yet aghast.
Now sip I of that cup, and just 't may be

The bottom dregs reservèd are for me.
   New England
To all you've said, sad mother, I assent,
Your fearful sins great cause there's to lament,
My guilty hands in part hold up with you,   150
A sharer in your punishment's my due.
But all you say amounts to this effect,
Not what you feel, but what you do expect,
Pray in plain terms, what is your present grief?
Then let's join heads and hearts for your relief.
   Old England
Well, to the matter then, there's grown of late
'Twixt king and peers a question of state:
Which is the chief, the law, or else the king?
One said, it's he, the other no such thing.
'Tis said, my better part in parliament   160
To ease my groaning land, showed their intent,
To crush the proud, and right to each man deal,
To help the church, and stay the commonweal.
So many obstacles came in their way,
As puts me to a stand what I should say;
Old customs, new prerogatives stood on,
Had they not held law fast, all had been gone:
Which by their prudence stood them in such stead
They took high Strafford lower by the head.
And to their laud be 't spoke, they held i' th' tower   170
All England's metropolitan that hour;
This done, an act they would have passèd fain,
No prelate should his bishopric retain;
Here tugged they hard (indeed), for all men saw
This must be done by Gospel, not by law.
Next the militia they urgèd sore,
This was denied, (I need not say wherefore)
The king displeased at York, himself absents,
They humbly beg return, show their intents;
The writing, printing, posting to and fro,   180
Shows all was done, I'll therefore let it go.
But now I come to speak of my disaster,
Contention grown, 'twixt subjects and their master;
They worded it so long, they fell to blows,
That thousands lay on heaps, here bleeds my woes,
I that no wars so many years have known,
Am now destroyed and slaughtered by mine own;

But could the field alone this strife decide,
One battle, two or three, I might abide;
But these may be beginnings of more woe. 190
Who knows, but this may be my overthrow.
Oh pity me in this sad perturbation,
My plundered towns, my houses' devastation,
My weeping virgins and my young men slain;
My wealthy trading fallen, my dearth of grain,
The seed-times come, but ploughman hath no hope
Because he knows not who shall inn his crop;
The poor they want their pay, their children bread,
Their woeful mothers' tears unpitièd.
If any pity in thy heart remain, 200
Or any child-like love thou dost retain,
For my relief, do what there lies in thee,
And recompense that good I've done to thee.
   New England
Dear Mother, cease complaints and wipe your eyes,
Shake off your dust, cheer up, and now arise.
You are my mother nurse, and I your flesh,
Your sunken bowels gladly would refresh,
Your griefs I pity, but soon hope to see
Out of your troubles much good fruit to be;
To see those latter days of hoped for good, 210
Though now beclouded all with tears and blood:
After dark Popery the day did clear,
But now the sun in's brightness shall appear.
Blest be the nobles of thy noble land,
With ventured lives for truth's defence that stand.
Blest be thy commons, who for common good,
And thy infringèd laws have boldly stood.
Blest be thy counties, who did aid thee still,
With hearts and states to testify their will.
Blest be thy preachers, who do cheer thee on, 220
O cry the sword of God, and Gideon;
And shall I not on them wish Mero's curse,
That help thee not with prayers, arms and purse?
And for myself let miseries abound,
If mindless of thy state I e'er be found.
These are the days the church's foes to crush,
To root out Popelings head, tail, branch and rush;
Let's bring Baal's vestments forth to make a fire,
Their mitres, surplices, and all their tire,

Copes, rotchets, crosiers and such empty trash,   230
And let their names consume, but let the flash
Light Christendom, and all the world to see
We hate Rome's whore, with all her trumpery.
Go on brave Essex with a loyal heart,
Not false to King, nor to the better part;
But those that hurt his people and his crown,
As duty binds, expel and tread them down.
And ye brave nobles chase away all fear,
And to this hopeful cause closely adhere;
O mother, can you weep, and have such peers,   240
When they are gone, then drown yourself in tears,
If now you weep so much, that then no more
The briny ocean will o'erflow your shore.
These, these are they I trust, with Charles our King,
Out of all mists such glorious days shall bring;
That dazzled eyes beholding much shall wonder
At that thy settled peace, thy wealth and splendour.
Thy church and weal established in such manner,
That all shall joy, that thou displayed'st thy banner;
And discipline erected so I trust,   250
That nursing kings shall come and lick thy dust:
Then justice shall in all thy courts take place,
Without respect of person, or of case;
Then bribes shall cease, and suits shall not stick long
Patience and purse of clients oft to wrong:
Then high commissions shall fall to decay,
And pursuivants and catchpoles want their pay.
So shall thy happy nation ever flourish,
When truth and righteousness they thus shall nourish
When thus in peace, thine armies brave send out, 260
To sack proud Rome, and all her vassals rout;
There let thy name, thy fame, and glory shine,
As did thine ancestors' in Palestine:
And let her spoils full pay, with interest be,
Of what unjustly once she polled from thee.
Of all the woes thou can'st, let her be sped,
And on her pour the vengeance threatenèd;
Bring forth the beast that ruled the world with 's beck,
And tear his flesh, and set your feet on 's neck;
And make his filthy den so desolate,   270
To th' 'stonishment of all that knew his state:
This done with brandished swords to Turkey go,

For then what is 't, but English blades dare do,
And lay her waste for so's the sacred doom,
And do to Gog as thou hast done to Rome.
Oh Abraham's seed lift up your heads on high,
For sure the day of your redemption's nigh;
The scales shall fall from your long blinded eyes,
And him you shall adore who now despise,
Then fullness of the nations in shall flow,   280
And Jew and Gentile to one worship go;
Then follows days of happiness and rest:
Whose lot doth fall to live therein is blest.
No Canaanite shall then be found i' th' Land,
And holiness on horses' bells shall stand.
If this make way thereto, then sigh no more,
But if at all, thou did'st not see 't before.
Farewell, dear mother, rightest cause prevail,
And in a while you'll tell another tale.

Richard Crashaw (1613?–1649)

285. Upon the Holy Sepulchre

Here where our Lord once laid his head,
Now the grave lies burièd.

286. Upon the Crown of Thorns Taken Down from the Head of our Blessed Lord, all Bloody

Know'st thou this, Soldier? 'Tis a much-changed plant which yet
    Thy self did'st set.

O who so hard a Husbandman did ever find;
    A soil so kind?

Is not the soil a kind one, which returns
   Roses for Thorns?

287. Upon our Saviour's Tomb Wherein Never Man was Laid

How life and death in thee
   Agree!
Thou had'st a virgin womb,
   And tomb,
A Joseph did betroth
   Them both.

288. On Mr George Herbert's Book entitled *The Temple* of Sacred Poems, Sent to a Gentlewoman

Know you, fair, on what you look?
Divinest love lies in this book,
Expecting fire from your eyes
To kindle this his sacrifice.
When your hands untie these strings
Think you have an angel by the wings,
One that gladly will be nigh
To wait upon each morning sigh,
To flutter in the balmy air
Of your well-perfumèd prayer.   10
These white plumes of his heel lend you,
Which every day to heaven will send you,
To take acquaintance of the sphere,
And all the smooth-faced kindred there.
   And though Herbert's name do owe
   These devotions, fairest, know
   That while I lay them on the shrine
   Of your white hand, they are mine.

289. Upon a Gnat Burnt in a Candle

Little – buzzing – wanton elf,
Perish there, and thank thy self.

Thou deserv'st thy life to lose
For distracting such a Muse.
Was it thy ambitious aim
By thy death to purchase fame?
Did'st thou hope he would in pity
Have bestowed a funeral ditty
On thy ghost? And thou in that
To have outlived Virgil's gnat? 10
No, the treason thou hast wrought
Might forbid thee such a thought.
If that night's work do miscarry,
Or a syllable but vary,
A greater foe thou shalt me find,
The destruction of thy kind.
Phoebus, to revenge thy fault,
In a fiery trap thee caught,
That thy wingèd mates might know it
And not dare disturb a Poet. 20
Dear and wretched was thy sport
Since thyself was crushèd for 't.
Scarcely had that life a breath,
Yet it found a double death:
Playing in the golden flames,
Thou fell'st into an inky Thames,
Scorched and drowned. That petty sun
A pretty Icarus hath undone.

290. 'Lord, when the sense of thy sweet grace'

I
Lord, when the sense of thy sweet grace
Sends up my soul to seek thy face.
Thy blessed eyes breed such desire,
I die in love's delicious fire.

O love, I am thy sacrifice.
Be still triumphant, blessed eyes.
Still shine on me, fair suns, that I
Still may behold, though still I die.

II
Though still I die, I live again;
Still longing so to be still slain,   10
So gainful is such loss of breath.
I die even in desire of death.

Still live in me this loving strife
Of living death and dying life.
For while thou sweetly slayest me
Dead to my self, I live in Thee.

291. An Apology for the Foregoing Hymn

as having been writ when the author was yet among the Protestants

Thus have I back again to thy bright name
(Fair flood of holy fires!) transfused the flame
I took from reading thee, 'tis to thy wrong
I know, that in my weak and worthless song
Thou here art set to shine where thy full day
Scarce dawns. O pardon if I dare to say
Thine own dear books are guilty. For from thence
I learned to know that love is eloquence.
That hopeful maxim gave me heart to try
If, what to other tongues is tuned so high,   10
Thy praise might not speak English too; forbid
(By all thy mysteries that here lie hid)
Forbid it, mighty Love! let no fond hate
Of names and words, so far prejudicate.
Souls are not Spaniards too, one friendly flood
Of baptism blends them all into a blood.
Christ's faith makes but one body of all souls
And love's that body's soul, no law controls
Our free traffic for heaven we may maintain
Peace, sure, with piety, though it come from Spain.   20
What soul so e'er, in any language, can
Speak heaven like hers is my soul's countryman.
O 'tis not Spanish, but 'tis heaven she speaks!
'Tis heaven that lies in ambush there, and breaks
From thence into the wondering reader's breast;
Who feels his warm heart into a nest

Of little eagles and young loves, whose high
Flights scorn the lazy dust, and things that die.

There are now, whose draughts (as deep as hell)
Drink up all Spain in sack. Let my soul swell   30
With thee, strong wine of love! let others swim
In puddles; we will pledge this seraphim
Bowls full of richer blood than blush of grape
Was ever guilty of, change we too our shape
(My soul). Some drink from men to beasts, o then
Drink we till we prove more, not less, than men,
And turn not beasts, but angels. Let the king
Me ever into these his cellars bring
Where flows such wine as we can have of none
But Him who trod the wine-press all alone.   40
Wine of youth, life, and the sweet deaths of love;
Wine of immortal mixture; which can prove
Its tincture from the rosy nectar; wine
That can exalt weak earth, and so refine
Our dust, that at one draught, mortality
May drink itself up, and forget to die.

Abraham Cowley (1618–1667)

292. The Given Heart

I wonder what those lovers mean, who say
    They have given their hearts away.
    Some good kind lover tell me how;
For mine is but a torment to me now.

If so it be one place both hearts contain,
    For what do they complain?
    What courtesy can Love do more,
Than to join hearts that parted were before?

Woe to her stubborn heart, if once mine come
    Into the self-same room;   10
     'Twill tear and blow up all within,
Like a granado shot into a magazine.

Then shall love keep the ashes, and torn parts,
    Of both our broken hearts;
     Shall out of both one new one make,
From hers, the alloy; from mine, the metal take.

For of her heart he from the flames will find
    But little left behind;
     Mine only will remain entire;
No dross was there, to perish in the fire.   20

293. The Wish

Well then; I now do plainly see
    This busy world and I shall ne'er agree.
    The very honey of all earthly joy
    Does of all meats the soonest cloy;
And they (methinks) deserve my pity
     Who for it can endure the stings,
     The crowd, and buzz, and murmurings
Of this great hive, the city.

Ah, yet, ere I descend to th' grave
May I a small house and large garden have!   10
And a few friends, and many books, both true,
Both wise, and both delightful too!
    And since love ne'er will from me flee,
A mistress moderately fair,
And good as guardian angels are,
    Only beloved, and loving me.

    O fountains! when in you shall I
Myself eased of unpeaceful thoughts espy?
O fields! O woods! when shall I be made
The happy tenant of your shade?   20
    Here's the spring-head of pleasure's flood:
Here's wealthy nature's treasury,

Where all the riches lie that she
   Has coined and stamped for good.

   Pride and ambition here
Only in far-fetched metaphors appear;
Here nought but winds can hurtful murmurs scatter,
And nought but Echo flatter.
   The gods, when they descended hither
From heaven, did always choose their way   30
And therefore we may boldly say
   That 'tis the way to thither.

   How happy here should I
And one dear she live, and embracing die!
She who is all the world, and can exclude
In deserts solitude.
   I should have then this only fear:
Lest men, when they my pleasures see,
Should hither throng to live like me,
   And so make a city here.   40

Richard Lovelace (1618–1657)

293. La Bella Bona-Roba[45]

I cannot tell who loves the skeleton
Of a poor marmoset, nought but bone, bone;
Give me a nakedness with her clothes on.

Such whose white-satin upper coat of skin,
Cut upon velvet rich incarnadine,
Has yet a body (and of flesh) within.

Sure it is meant good husbandry in men,

[45] The Beautiful Courtesan

Who do incorporate with airy lean,
T' repair their sides, and get their rib again.

Hard hap unto that huntsman that decrees   10
Fat joys for all his sweat, when as he sees,
After his 'say,° nought but his keeper's fees.   *attempt*

Then, love, I beg, when next thou tak'st thy bow,
Thy angry shafts, and dost heart-chasing go,
Pass rascal deer, strike me the largest doe.

295. To Althea, from Prison

When love with unconfinèd wings
    Hovers within my gates,
And my divine Althea brings
    To whisper at the grates:
When I lie tangled in her hair,
    And fettered to her eye,
The gods that wanton in the air,
    Know no such liberty.

When flowing cups run swiftly round
    With no allaying Thames,   10
Our careless heads with roses bound,
    Our hearts with loyal flames;
When thirsty grief in wine we steep,
    When healths and draughts go free,
Fishes that tipple in the deep,
    Know no such liberty.

When (like committed linnets) I
    With shriller throat shall sing
The sweetness, mercy, majesty,
    And glories of my King;   20
When I shall voice aloud, how good
    He is, how great should be;
Enlargèd winds that curl the flood,
    Know no such liberty.

Stone walls do not a prison make,

Nor iron bars a cage;
Minds innocent and quiet take
   That for an hermitage;
If I have freedom in my love,
   And in my soul am free;   30
Angels alone that soar above,
   Enjoy such liberty.

296. To Lucasta, Going to the Wars

Tell me not, sweet, I am unkind,
   That from the nunnery
Of thy chaste breast, and quiet mind
   To war and arms I fly.

True; a new mistress now I chase,
   The first foe in the field;
And with a stronger faith embrace
   A sword, a horse, a shield.

Yet this inconstancy is such
   As you too shall adore: 10
I could not love thee, dear, so much,
   Loved I not honour more.

297. The Ant

Forbear thou great good husband, little ant;
   A little respite from thy flood of sweat;
Thou, thine own horse and cart, under this plant
   Thy spacious tent, fan thy prodigious heat;
Down with thy double load of that one grain;
It is a granary for all thy train.

Cease large example of wise thrift, a while,
   (For thy example is become our law),
And teach thy frowns a seasonable smile:
   So Cato sometimes the naked florals saw.   10
And thou, almighty foe, lay by thy sting,
Whilst thy unpaid musicians, crickets, sing.

Lucasta, she that holy makes the day,
   And 'stils new life in fields of feuillèmort:°   *dead leaf colour*
Hath back restored their verdure with one ray,
   And with her eye bid all to play and sport.
Ant, to work still, age will thee truant call;
And to save now, th' art worse than prodigal.

Austere and Cynic! not one hour t' allow,
   To lose with pleasure what thou got'st with pain,   20
But drive on sacred festivals thy plough,
   Tearing highways with thy o'erchargèd wain.
Not all thy lifetime one poor minute live,
And thy o'erlaboured bulk with mirth relieve?

Look up then, miserable Ant, and spy
   Thy fatal foes, for breaking of her law:
Hovering above thee, madam, Margaret Pie,
   And her fierce servant, meagre Sir John Daw:
Thy self and storehouse now they do store up
And thy whole harvest too within their crop.   30

Thus we unthrifty thrive within earth's tomb,
   For some more ravenous and ambitious jaw:
The grain in th' ant's, the ants in the pie's womb,
   The pie in th' hawk's, the hawk's i' th' eagle's maw:
So scattering to hoard 'gainst a long day,
Thinking to save all, we cast all away.

298. The Grasshopper

To my Noble Friend, Mr Charles Cotton: Ode

O thou that swing'st upon the waving hair
   Of some well-fillèd oaten beard,
Drunk every night with a delicious tear
   Dropped thee from heaven, where now th' art reared;

The joys of earth and air are thine entire,
   That with thy feet and wings dost hop and fly;

And when thy poppy works thou dost retire
    To thy carved acorn-bed to lie.

Up with the day, the sun thou welcom'st then,
    Sport'st in the gilt-plats of his beams,   10
And all these merry days mak'st merry men,
    Thyself, and melancholy streams.

But ah the sickle! Golden ears are cropped;
    Ceres and Bacchus bid good night;
Sharp frosty fingers all your flowers have topped,
    And what scythes spared, winds shave off quite.

Poor verdant fool! And now green ice; thy joys
    Large and as lasting, as thy perch of grass,
Bid us lay in 'gainst winter, rain, and poise
    Their floods, with an o'erflowing glass.   20

Thou best of men and friends! We will create
    A genuine summer in each other's breast;
And spite of this cold time and frozen fate
    Thaw us a warm seat to our rest.

Our sacred hearths shall burn eternally
    As vestal flames; the north wind, he
Shall strike his frost-stretched wings, dissolve and fly
    This Ætna in epitome.

Dropping December shall come weeping in,
    Bewail th' usurping of his reign;   30
But when in showers of old Greek we begin,
    Shall cry, he hath his crown again!

Night as clear Hesper shall our tapers whip
    From the light casements where we play,
And the dark hag from her black mantle strip,
    And stick there everlasting day.

Thus richer than untempted kings are we,
    That asking nothing, nothing need:
Though lord of all what seas embrace, yet he
    That wants himself, is poor indeed.   40

299. The Snail

Wise emblem of our politic world,
Sage snail, within thine own self curled;
Instruct me softly to make haste,
Whilst these my feet go slowly fast.
    Compendious snail! Thou seem'st to me,
Large Euclid's strict epitome;
And in each diagram, dost fling
Thee from the point unto the ring.
A figure now triangular,
An oval now, and now a square;   10
And then a serpentine dost crawl
Now a straight line, now crook'd, now all.
    Preventing rival of the day,
Th' art up and openest thy ray,
And ere the morn cradles the moon,
Th' art broke into a beauteous noon.
Then when the sun sups in the deep
Thy silver horns ere Cynthia's peep;
And thou from thine own liquid bed,
New Phoebus, heav'st thy pleasant head.   20
    Who shall a name for thee create,
Deep riddle of mysterious state:
Bold nature, that gives common birth
To all products of seas and earth,
Of thee, as earthquakes, is afraid,
Nor will thy dire delivery aid.
    Thou thine own daughter then, and sire,
That son and mother art entire,
That big still with thy self dost go,
And liv'st an agèd embryo;   30
That like the cubs of India,
Thou from thy self a while dost play:
But frighted with a dog or gun,
In thine own belly thou dost run,
And as thy house was thine own womb,
So thine own womb concludes thy tomb.
    But now I must (analysed king)
Thy economic virtues sing.
Thou great stayed husband, still within,
Thou, thee, that's thine, dost discipline;   40
And when thou art to progress bent,

Thou mov'st thy self and tenement,
As warlike Scythians travelled, you
Remove your men and city too;
Then after a sad dearth and rain,
Thou scatterest thy silver train;
And when the trees grow naked and old,
Thou clothest them with cloth of gold,
Which from thy bowels thou dost spin,
And draw from the rich mines within.   50
    Now hast thou changed thee saint, and made
Thyself a fane that's cupola'd;
And in thy wreathèd cloister thou
Walkest thine own Grey Friar, too;
Strict, and locked up, th' art hood all o'er
And ne'er eliminat'st thy door.
On salads thou dost feed severe,
And 'stead of beads thou drop'st a tear,
And when to rest each calls the bell,
Thou sleep'st within thy marble cell,   60
Where in dark contemplation placed
The sweets of nature thou dost taste;
Who now with time thy days resolve,
And in a jelly thee dissolve
Like a shot star, which doth repair
Upward, and rarefy the air.

Andrew Marvell (1621–1678)

300. The Mower to the Glow-Worms

Ye living lamps, by whose dear light
The nightingale does sit so late,
And studying all the summer night
Her matchless songs does meditate;

Ye country comets, that portend
No war, nor prince's funeral,

Shining unto no higher end
Then to presage the grass's fall;

Ye glow-worms, whose officious flame
To wandering mowers shows the way,
That in the night have lost their aim,
And after foolish fires do stray;

Your courteous lights in vain you waste,
Since Juliana here is come,
For she my mind hath so displaced
That I shall never find my home.

301. The Definition of Love

My love is of a birth as rare
As 'tis for object strange and high:
It was begotten by despair
Upon impossibility.

Magnanimous despair alone
Could show me so divine a thing,
Where feeble hope could ne'er have flown
But vainly flapped its tinsel wing.

And yet I quickly might arrive
Where my extended soul is fixed,   10
But fate does iron wedges drive,
And always crowds itself betwixt.

For fate with jealous eye does see
Two perfect loves; nor lets them close:
Their union would her ruin be,
And her tyrannic power depose.

And therefore her decrees of steel
Us as the distant poles have placed,
(Though love's whole world on us doth wheel)
Not by themselves to be embraced,   20

Unless the giddy heaven fall
And earth some new convulsion tear,
And, us to join, the world should all
Be cramped into a planisphere.

As lines so loves oblique may well
Themselves in every angle greet:
But ours so truly parallel,
Though infinite, can never meet.

Therefore the love which us doth bind,
But fate so enviously debars,   30
Is the conjunction of the mind,
And opposition of the stars.

302. Bermudas

Where the remote Bermudas ride
In th' ocean's bosom unespied,
From a small boat, that rowed along,
The listening winds received this song.
    'What should we do but sing his praise
That led us through the watery maze,
Unto an isle so long unknown,
And yet far kinder than our own?
Where he the huge sea-monsters wracks,
That lift the deep upon their backs.   10
He lands us on a grassy stage;
Safe from the storms, and prelate's rage.
He gave us this eternal spring,
Which here enamels every thing;
And sends the fowls to us in care,
On daily visits through the air.
He hangs in shades the orange bright,
Like golden lamps in a green night;
And does in the pomegranates close,
Jewels more rich than Ormus shows.   20
He makes the figs our mouths to meet;
And throws the melons at our feet;
But apples plants of such a price,
No tree could ever bear them twice.

With cedars, chosen by his hand,
From Lebanon, he stores the land.
And makes the hollow seas, that roar,
Proclaim the ambergris on shore.
He cast (of which we rather boast)
The Gospel's pearl upon our coast.   30
And in these rocks for us did frame
A temple, where to sound his Name.
Oh let our voice His praise exalt,
Till it arrive at heaven's vault:
Which thence (perhaps) rebounding, may
Echo beyond the Mexique bay.'
    Thus sung they, in the English boat,
An holy and a cheerful note,
And all the way, to guide their chime,
With falling oars they kept the time.   40

303. The Nymph Complaining for the Death of her Fawn

The wanton troopers riding by
Have shot my fawn and it will die.
Ungentle men! They cannot thrive
To kill thee. Thou ne'er didst alive
Them any harm: alas nor could
Thy death yet do them any good.
I'm sure I never wished them ill;
Nor do I for all this; nor will:
But if my simple prayers may yet
Prevail with heaven to forget   10
Thy murder, I will join my tears
Rather than fail. But, O my fears!
It cannot die so. Heaven's King
Keeps register of every thing:
And nothing may we use in vain.
Even beasts must be with justice slain;
Else men are made their deodands.
Though they should wash their guilty hands
In this warm life blood, which doth part
From thine, and wound me to the heart,   20
Yet could they not be clean: their stain
Is dyed in such a purple grain.

There is not such another in
The world, to offer for their sin.
　　Unconstant Sylvio, when yet
I had not found him counterfeit,
One morning, I remember well,
Tied in this silver chain and bell,
Gave it to me: nay and I know
What he said then; I'm sure I do.　　　　　　　　　　　　30
Said he, 'Look how your huntsman here
Hath taught a fawn to hunt his dear.'°　　　　　*(pun on 'deer')*
But Sylvio soon had me beguiled.
This waxèd tame, while he grew wild,
And quite regardless of my smart,
Left me his fawn, but took his heart.
　　Thenceforth I set myself to play
My solitary time away,
With this: and very well content,
Could so mine idle life have spent.　　　　　　　　　40
For it was full of sport; and light
Of foot, and heart; and did invite
Me to its game: it seemed to bless
Itself in me. How could I less
Than love it? O I cannot be
Unkind, to a beast that loveth me.
　　Had it lived long, I do not know
Whether it too might have done so
As Sylvio did: his gifts might be
Perhaps as false or more than he.　　　　　　　　　50
But I am sure, for ought that I
Could in so short a time espy,
Thy love was far more better than
The love of false and cruel man.
　　With sweetest milk, and sugar, first
It at mine own fingers nursed.
And as it grew, so every day
It waxed more white and sweet than they.
It had so sweet a breath! And oft
I blushed to see its foot more soft　　　　　　　　　60
And white, shall I say than my hand?
Nay, any lady's of the land.
　　It is a wondrous thing, how fleet
'Twas on those little silver feet.
With what a pretty skipping grace,

It oft would challenge me the race:
And when 't had left me far away,
'Twould stay, and run again, and stay.
For it was nimbler much than hinds;
And trod, as on the four winds.   70
   I have a garden of my own,
But so with roses overgrown,
And lilies, that you would it guess
To be a little wilderness.
And all the springtime of the year
It only lovèd to be there.
Among the beds of lilies, I
Have sought it oft, where it should lie;
Yet could not, till itself would rise,
Find it, although before mine eyes.   80
For, in the flaxen lilies' shade,
It like a bank of lilies laid.
Upon the roses it would feed,
Until its lips even seemed to bleed,
And then to me 'twould boldly trip,
And print those roses on my lip.
But all its chief delight was still
On roses thus itself to fill;
And its pure virgin limbs to fold
In whitest sheets of lilies cold.   90
Had it lived long, it would have been
Lilies without, roses within.
   O help! O help! I see it faint
And die as calmly as a saint.
See how it weeps. The tears do come
Sad, slowly dropping like a gum.
So weeps the wounded balsam; so
The holy frankincense doth flow.
The brotherless Heliades
Melt in such amber tears as these.   100
   I in a golden vial will
Keep these two crystal tears, and fill
It till it do o'erflow with mine;
Then place it in Diana's shrine.
   Now my sweet fawn is vanished to
Whither the swans and turtles go
In fair Elysium to endure,
With milk-white lambs and ermines pure.

O do not run too fast: for I
Will but bespeak thy grave, and die.   110
    First my unhappy statue shall
Be cut in marble; and withal,
Let it be weeping too: but there
The engraver sure his art may spare;
For I so truly thee bemoan,
That I shall weep though I be stone:
Until my tears, still dropping, wear
My breast, themselves engraving there.
There at my feet shalt thou be laid,
Of purest alabaster made: 120
For I would have thine image be
White as I can, though not as thee.

304. To his Coy Mistress

Had we but world enough, and time,
This coyness, Lady, were no crime.
We would sit down, and think which way
To walk, and pass our long love's day.
Thou by the Indian Ganges' side
Should'st rubies find; I by the tide
Of Humber would complain. I would
Love you ten years before the Flood:
And you should if you please refuse
Till the conversion of the Jews.   10
My vegetable love should grow
Vaster then empires, and more slow.
An hundred years should go to praise
Thine eyes, and on thy forehead gaze;
Two hundred to adore each breast,
But thirty thousand to the rest.
An age at least to every part,
And the last age should show your heart.
For, Lady, you deserve this state,
Nor would I love at lower rate.   20

But at my back I always hear
Time's wingèd chariot hurrying near;
And yonder all before us lie

Deserts of vast eternity.
Thy beauty shall no more be found,
Nor, in thy marble vault, shall sound
My echoing song; then worms shall try
That long preserved virginity,
And your quaint honour turn to dust,
And into ashes all my lust.   30
The grave's a fine and private place,
But none I think do there embrace.
   Now therefore, while the youthful hue
Sits on thy skin like morning dew,
And while thy willing soul transpires
At every pore with instant fires,
Now let us sport us while we may;
And now, like amorous birds of prey,
Rather at once our time devour
Than languish in his slow-chapped power.   40
Let us roll all our strength, and all
Our sweetness, up into one ball
And tear our pleasures with rough strife
Thorough° the iron gates of life.   *Through*
Thus, though we cannot make our sun
Stand still, yet we will make him run.

305. An Horatian Ode upon Cromwell's Return from Ireland

The forward youth that would appear
Must now forsake his muses dear,
   Nor in the shadows sing,
   His numbers languishing.
'Tis time to leave the books in dust
And oil the unused armour's rust:
   Removing from the wall
   The corslet of the hall.
So restless Cromwell could not cease
In the inglorious arts of peace,   10
   But through adventurous war
   Urgèd his active star.
And, like the three-forked lightning, first
Breaking the clouds where it was nursed,
   Did through his own side

His fiery way divide.
For 'tis all one to courage high
The emulous or enemy;
    And with such to inclose
    Is more than to oppose.   20
Then burning through the air he went,
And palaces and temples rent:
    And Caesar's head at last
    Did through his laurels blast.
'Tis madness to resist or blame
The force of angry heaven's flame:
    And, if we would speak true,
    Much to the man is due,
Who, from his private gardens, where
He lived reservèd and austere,   30
    As if his highest plot
    To plant the bergamot,
Could by industrious valour climb
To ruin the great work of time,
    And cast the kingdom old
    Into another mould.
Though justice against fate complain
And plead the ancient rights in vain:
    But those do hold or break
    As men are strong or weak.   40
Nature that hateth emptiness
Allows of penetration less;
    And therefore must make room
    Where greater spirits come.
What field of all the Civil Wars,
Where his were not the deepest scars?
    And Hampton shows what part
    He had of wiser art,
Where, twining subtle fears with hope,
He wove a net of such a scope,   50
    That Charles himself might chase
    To Caresbrook's narrow case;
That thence the royal actor born
The tragic scaffold might adorn
    While round the armèd bands
    Did clap their bloody hands.
He nothing common did or mean
Upon that memorable scene:

But with his keener eye
   The axe's edge did try: 60
Nor called the gods with vulgar spite
To vindicate his helpless right,
   But bowed his comely head
   Down as upon a bed.
This was that memorable hour
Which first assured the forcèd power.
   So when they did design
   The Capitol's first line,
A bleeding head where they begun,
Did fright the architects to run;   70
   And yet in that the state
   Foresaw its happy fate.
And now the Irish are ashamed
To see themselves in one year tamed:
   So much one man can do,
   That does both act and know.
They can affirm his praises best,
And have, though overcome, confessed
   How good he is, how just,
   And fit for highest trust: 80
Nor yet grown stiffer with command,
But still in the Republic's hand:
   How fit he is to sway
   That can so well obey.
He to the Commons' feet presents
A kingdom, for his first year's rents:
   And, what he may, forbears
   His fame to make it theirs:
And has his sword and spoils ungirt,
To lay them at the public's skirt.   90
   So when the falcon high
   Falls heavy from the sky,
She, having killed, no more does search,
But on the next green bough to perch;
   Where, when he first does lure,
   The falconer has her sure.
What may not then our isle presume
While victory his crest does plume!
   What may not others fear
   If thus he crown each year!   100
A Caesar he ere long to Gaul,

To Italy an Hannibal,
   And to all states not free
   Shall climacteric be.
The Pict no shelter now shall find
Within his parti-coloured mind;
   But from this valour sad
   Shrink underneath the plaid:
Happy if in the tufted brake
The English hunter him mistake;   110
   Nor lay his hounds in near
   The Caledonian deer.
But thou the wars' and fortune's son
March indefatigably on;
   And for the last effect
   Still keep thy sword erect:
Besides the force it has to fright
The spirits of the shady night,
   The same arts that did gain
   A power must it maintain.   120

Henry Vaughan (1622–1695)

306. Peace

My soul, there is a country
   Far beyond the stars,
Where stands a wingèd sentry
   All skilful in the wars,
There above noise and danger
   Sweet peace sits crowned with smiles,
And one born in a manger
   Commands the beauteous files.
He is thy gracious friend,
   And (O my soul, awake!)   10
Did in pure love descend
   To die here for thy sake.
If thou can'st get but thither,
   There grows the flower of peace,

The rose that cannot wither,
   Thy fortress, and thy ease.
Leave then thy foolish ranges,
   For none can thee secure,
But one, who never changes,
   Thy God, thy life, thy cure.   20

307. The Relapse

My God, how gracious art thou! I had slipped
   Almost to hell,
And on the verge of that dark, dreadful pit
   Did hear them yell,
But O thy love! thy rich, almighty love
   That saved my soul,
And checked their fury, when I saw them move,
   And heard them howl;
O my sole comfort, take no more these ways,
   This hideous path,   10
And I will mend my own without delays.
   Cease thou thy wrath!
I have deserved a thick, Egyptian damp,
   Dark as my deeds,
Should mist within me, and put out that lamp
   Thy spirit feeds;
A darting conscience full of stabs, and fears;
   No shade but yew,
Sullen, and sad eclipses, cloudy spheres,
   These are my due.   20
But he that with his blood (a price too dear)
   My scores did pay,
Bid me, by virtue from him, challenge here
   The brightest day;
Sweet, downy thoughts; soft lily-shades; calm streams,
   Joys full, and true;
Fresh, spicy mornings; and eternal beams
   These are his due.

308. The Retreat

Happy those early days, when I
Shined in my angel-infancy!

Before I understood this place
Appointed for my second race,
Or taught my soul to fancy aught
But a white, celestial thought;
When yet I had not walked above
A mile or two from my first love,
And looking back (at that short space)
Could see a glimpse of his bright face;   10
When on some gilded cloud or flower
My gazing soul would dwell an hour,
And in those weaker glories spy
Some shadows of eternity;
Before I taught my tongue to wound
My conscience with a sinful sound,
Or had the black art to dispense
A several sin to every sense,
But felt through all this fleshly dress
Bright shoots of everlastingness.   20
    O how I long to travel back
And tread again that ancient track!
That I might once more reach that plain
Where first I left my glorious train,
From whence the enlightened spirit sees
That shady city of palm trees;
But (ah) my soul with too much stay
Is drunk, and staggers in the way.
Some men a forward motion love,
But I by backward steps would move,   30
And when this dust falls to the urn
In that state I came, return.

309. Faith

Bright, and blest beam! whose strong projection
    Equal to all,
Reacheth as well things of dejection
    As the high, and tall;
How hath my God by raying thee
    Enlarged his spouse,
And of a private family
    Made open house?

All may be now co-heirs; no noise
   Of bond, or free   10
Can interdict us from those joys
   That wait on thee.
The law and ceremonies made
   A glorious night,
Where stars, and clouds, both light, and shade
   Had equal right;
But, as in nature, when the day
   Breaks, night adjourns,
Stars shut up shop, mists pack away,
   And the moon mourns;   20
So when the sun of righteousness
   Did once appear,
That scene was changed, and a new dress
   Left for us here;
Veils became useless, altars fell,
   Fires smoking die;
And all that sacred pomp and shell
   Of things did fly;
Then did He shine forth, whose sad fall
   And bitter fights   30
Were figured in those mystical
   And cloudy rites;
And as i' th' natural sun, these three,
   Light, motion, heat,
So are now faith, hope, charity
   Through him complete.
Faith spans up bliss; what sin, and death
   Put us quite from,
Lest we should run for 't out of breath,
   Faith brings us home;   40
So that I need no more, but say
   'I do believe,'
And my most loving Lord straightway
   Doth answer, 'Live.'

310. The World

I saw eternity the other night
Like a great ring of pure and endless light,

All calm, as it was bright,
And round beneath it, time in hours, days, years
    Driven by the spheres
Like a vast shadow moved, in which the world
  And all her train were hurled;
The doting lover in his quaintest strain
    Did there complain,
Near him, his lute, his fancy and his flights,   10
    Wits sour delights,
With gloves, and knots the silly snares of pleasure
    Yet his dear treasure
All scattered lay, while he his eyes did pour
    Upon a flower.

The darksome statesman hung with weights and woe
Like a thick midnight fog moved there so slow
  He did not stay, nor go;
Condemning thoughts (like sad eclipses) scowl
    Upon his soul,   20
And clouds of crying witnesses without
  Pursued him with one shout.
Yet digged the mole, and lest his ways be found
    Worked under ground,
Where he did clutch his prey, but one did see
    That policy,
Churches and altars fed him, perjuries
    Were gnats and flies,
It rained about him blood and tears, but he
    Drank them as free.   30

The fearful miser on a heap of rust
Sat pining all his life there, did scarce trust
  His own hands with the dust,
Yet would not place one piece above, but lives
    In fear of thieves.
Thousands there were as frantic as himself
  And hugged each one his pelf,
The down-right epicure placed heaven in sense
    And scorned pretence
While others slipped into a wide excess   40
    Said little less;
The weaker sort slight, trivial wares enslave
    Who think them brave,

And poor, despisèd truth sat counting by
    Their victory.

Yet some, who all this while did weep and sing,
And sing and weep, soared up into the ring,
    But most would use no wing.
'O fools,' said I, 'thus to prefer dark night
    Before true light,   50
To live in grots, and caves, and hate the day
    Because it shows the way,
The way which from this dead and dark abode
    Leads up to God,
A way where you might tread the sun, and be
    More bright than he.'
But as I did their madness so discuss
    One whispered thus,
'This ring the bride-groom did for none provide
    But for his bride.'   60

Margaret Cavendish, Duchess of Newcastle
(1623–1673)

311. from *Phantasm's Masque*[46]

A Lady Dressed by Love
Her hair with lover's hopes curled in long rings,
Her braids hard plaited with his protestings;
But often with her lover's damps of doubt,

---

[46] 'The Scene is Poetry. The Stage is the Brain whereon it is acted. First is presented a dumb show, as a young lady in a ship swimming over the scene in various weather; afterwards this ship comes back again, having a commander of war as its owner; in various weather it being in great distress, Jupiter relieves it. Then appear six masquers in several dresses; as dressed by Love, Valour, Honour, Youth, Age, Vanity. Vanity signifies the world, and Age mortality. Then there are presented in a show the nine muses, who dance a measure in four and twenty figures, and nine musical instruments, made of goose-quills, playing several tunes as they dance. Then the Chorus speaks. The Bride and Bridegroom going to the temple, Fancy speaks the Prologue to Judgement, as king; Vanity speaks an Epilogue to the Thoughts, which are spectators; Honour speaks another.'

And windy fears, these curlèd rings went out;
Strings round her neck of threaded tears she wore,
Which, dropped from the lover's eyes, his image bore;
His sighs, as pendants, did hang at each ear,
Which did much trouble her when they heavy were;
Her gown was made of admiration,
Embroideries of praises placed thereon;   10
Ribbons hung of love-verses here and there,
According as the several fancies were;
With some she tied her looking-glass of pride,
And fan of good opinion by her side;
Sometimes love pleasure took, a veil to place
Of glances, which did cover all her face.

   A Lady Dressed by Youth
Her hair had curls of pleasure and delight,
Through which her skin did cast a glimmering light;
As lace, her bashful eyelids downwards hung,
A modest countenance o'er her face was flung;   20
Blushes, as coral beads she strung, to wear
About her neck, and pendants for each ear;
Her gown was by proportion cut and made,
With veins embroidered, with complexion laid;
Light words with ribbons of chaste thoughts she ties,
And loose behaviour, which through errors flies;
Rich jewels of bright honour she did wear,
By noble actions placèd everywhere:
Thus dressed, to fame's great court straightways she went,
There danced a ball with youth, love, mirth, content.   30

   A Woman Dressed by Age
A milk-white hair-lace wound up all her hairs,
And a deaf coif did cover both her ears;
A sober look about her face she ties,
And a dim sight doth cover half her eyes;
About her neck a kercher of coarse skin,
Which time had crumpled, and worn creases in;
Her gown was turned to melancholy black,
Which loose did hang upon her sides and back;
Her stockings cramps had knit, red worsted gout,
And pains, as garters, tied her legs about;   40
A pair of palsy-gloves her hands did cover,
With weakness stitched, and numbness trimmed all over;

Her shoes were corns, and hard skin sewed together,
Hard skin was soles, and corns the upper leather;
A mantle of diseases laps her round;
And thus she's dressed, till death her lays i' th' ground.

  A Masquer Dressed by Vanity
The perfumed powder in 's long curls of hair,
Were like lime-twigs to catch a maid that's fair;
His glistering suit, whose seams by pride were laced,
Was made a bawd for to corrupt the chaste;   50
A cut-work band, which vanity had wrought,
The price, by which his mistress's love was bought;
Silk-stockings, garters, roses all of gold
Were bribes, by which his mistress's love did hold;
The several coloured ribbons he did wear
Were pages, which to her did letters bear;
Feathers, like sails, did wave with every wind,
Yet by these sails he finds his mistress kind;
His flattering tongue persuades a simple maid
That all is truth, when all is false he said.   60

  A Masquer Dressed by Honour and Time
His hair did white, like silver ribbons show,
Knots of experience were tied into;
His head was covered all with wisdom's hat,
Good management the hatband was round that;
His garments loose yet manly did appear,
Though time had crumpled them, no spots were there;
His cloak made of a free and noble mind,
Within with generosity was lined;
And gloves of bounty, which his hands did cover,
Were stitched with love, with free hearts trimmed all over;   70
A sword of valour hung close by his side,
To cut off all base fears, and haughty pride;
His boots were honesty, to walk or ride,
And spurs of good desires them firmly tied:
And thus both time and honour did their best;
Time gave him wit, honour him finely dressed.

John Dryden (1631–1700)

312. Upon the Death of Lord Hastings

Must noble Hastings immaturely die,
The honour of his ancient family,
Beauty and learning thus together meet,
To bring a winding for a wedding sheet?
Must virtue prove death's harbinger? Must she,
With him expiring, feel mortality?
Is death, sin's wages, grace's now? Shall art
Make us more learnèd, only to depart?
If merit be disease; if virtue, death;
To be good, not to be; who'd then bequeath   10
Himself to discipline? Who'd not esteem
Labour a crime? Study self-murder deem?
Our noble youth now have pretence to be
Dunces securely, ignorant healthfully.
Rare linguist, whose worth speaks itself, whose praise,
Though not his own, all tongues besides do raise;
Than whom great Alexander may seem less,
Who conquered men, but not their languages.
In his mouth nations speak, his tongue might be
Interpreter to Greece, France, Italy.   20
His native soil was the four parts o' the earth,
All Europe was too narrow for his birth.
A young apostle; and (with reverence may
I speak 't) inspired with gift of tongues, as they.
Nature gave him, a child, what men in vain
Oft strive, by art though furthered, to obtain.
His body was an orb, his sublime soul
Did move on virtue's and on learning's pole,
Whose regular motions better to our view,
Than Archimedes' sphere, the heavens did show.   30
Graces and virtues, languages and arts,
Beauty and learning, filled up all the parts.
Heaven's gifts, which do like falling stars appear
Scattered in others, all, as in their sphere,
Were fixed, and conglobate in 's soul, and thence

Shone through his body, with sweet influence,
Letting their glories so on each limb fall,
The whole frame rendered was celestial.
Come, learned Ptolemy, and trial make,
If thou this hero's altitude can'st take; 40
But that transcends thy skill: thrice happy all,
Could we but prove thus astronomical.
Lived Tycho now, struck with this ray which shone
More bright i' the morn, than others beam at noon,
He'd take his astrolabe, and seek out here
What new star 'twas did gild our hemisphere.
Replenished then with such rare gifts as these,
Where was room left for such a foul disease?
The nation's sin hath drawn that veil, which shrouds
Our day-spring in so sad benighting clouds. 50
Heaven would no longer trust its pledge, but thus
Recalled it; rapt its Ganymede from us.
Was there no milder way but the smallpox,
The very filth'ness of Pandora's box?
So many spots, like næves, our Venus soil?
One jewel set off with so many a foil,
Blisters with pride swelled, which through 's flesh did sprout
Like rosebuds, stuck i' the lily-skin about.
Each little pimple had a tear in it,
To wail the fault its rising did commit, 60
Which, rebel-like, with its own lord at strife,
Thus made an insurrection 'gainst his life.
Or were these gems sent to adorn his skin
The cabinet of a richer soul within?
No comet need foretell his change drew on,
Whose corpse might seem a constellation.
Oh had he died of old, how great a strife
Had been, who from his death should draw their life;
Who should, by one rich draught, become whatever
Seneca, Cato, Numa, Cæsar, were: 70
Learned, virtuous, pious, great; and have by this
An universal metempsychosis.
Must all these aged sires in one funeral
Expire? all die in one so young, so small?
Who, had he lived his life out, his great fame
Had swollen 'bove any Greek or Roman name.
But hasty winter, with one blast, hath brought
The hopes of autumn, summer, spring, to nought.

Thus fades th' oak i' the sprig, i' th' blade the corn;
Thus without young, this phoenix dies, newborn.   80
Must then old three-legged greybeards with their gout,
Catarrhs, rheums, aches, live three ages out?
Time's offal, only fit for the hospital,
Or to hang an antiquary's rooms withal!
Must drunkards, lechers, spent with sinning, live
With such helps as broths, possets, physic give?
None live, but such as should die? Shall we meet
With none but ghostly fathers in the street?
Grief makes me rail, sorrow will force its way,
And showers of tears tempestuous sighs best lay.   90
The tongue may fail, but overflowing eyes
Will weep out lasting streams of elegies.

But thou, O virgin-widow, left alone,
Now thy beloved, heaven-ravished spouse is gone,
Whose skilful sire in vain strove to apply
Medicines, when thy balm was no remedy;
With greater than Platonic love, O wed
His soul, though not his body, to thy bed.
Let that make thee a mother, bring thou forth
The ideas of his virtue, knowledge, worth;   100
Transcribe th' original in new copies, give
Hastings o' th' better part: so shall he live
In 's nobler half, and the great grandsire be
Of an heroic divine progeny:
An issue which to eternity shall last,
Yet but the irradiations which he cast.
Erect no mausoleums, for his best
Monument is his spouse's marble breast.

313. from *Absalom and Achitophel*

In pious times, ere priestcraft did begin,
Before polygamy was made a sin;
When man on many multiplied his kind,
Ere one to one was cursèdly confined;
When nature prompted, and no law denied,
Promiscuous use of concubine and bride;
Then Israel's monarch after heaven's own heart

His vigorous warmth did variously impart
To wives and slaves; and, wide as his command,
Scattered his Maker's image through the land.   10
Michal, of royal blood, the crown did wear,
A soil ungrateful to the tiller's care.
Not so the rest; for several mothers bore
To godlike David several sons before.
But since like slaves his bed they did ascend,
No true succession could their seed attend.
Of all the numerous progeny was none
So beautiful, so brave, as Absalon,
Whether inspired by some diviner lust
His father got him with a greater gust,   20
Or that his conscious destiny made way
By manly beauty, to imperial sway.
Early in foreign fields he won renown
With kings and states, allied to Israel's crown;
In peace the thoughts of war he could remove
And seemed as he were only born for love.
Whate'er he did, was done with so much ease,
In him alone 'twas natural to please;
His motions all accompanied with grace
And paradise was opened in his face.   30
With secret joy indulgent David viewed
His youthful image in his son renewed;
To all his wishes nothing he denied
And made the charming Annabel his bride.
What faults he had, – for who from faults is free?
His father could not, or he would not see.
Some warm excesses, which the law forbore,
Were construed youth that purged by boiling o'er;
And Amnon's murder, by a specious name,
Was called a just revenge for injured fame.   40
Thus praised and loved, the noble youth remained,
While David undisturbed in Sion reigned.
But life can never be sincerely blest;
Heaven punishes the bad, and proves the best.
The Jews, a headstrong, moody, murmuring race,
As ever tried the extent and stretch of grace;
God's pampered people, whom, debauched with ease,
No king could govern, nor no God could please;
Gods they had tried of every shape and size
That godsmiths could produce, or priests devise;   50

These Adam-wits, too fortunately free,
Began to dream they wanted liberty:
And when no rule, no precedent was found,
Of men, by laws less circumscribed and bound,
They led their wild desires to woods and caves
And thought that all but savages were slaves.
They who, when Saul was dead, without a blow,
Made foolish Ishbosheth the crown forego;
Who banished David did from Hebron bring,
And with a general shout proclaimed him king;   60
Those very Jews, who at their very best,
Their humour more than loyalty expressed,
Now wondered why so long they had obeyed
An idol monarch, which their hands had made;
Thought they might ruin him they could create,
Or melt him to that golden calf, – a state.
But these were random bolts; no formed design,
Nor interest made the factious crowd to join:
The sober part of Israel, free from stain,
Well knew the value of a peaceful reign;   70
And, looking backward with a wise affright,
Saw seams of wounds, dishonest to the sight;
In contemplation of whose ugly scars
They cursed the memory of civil wars.
The moderate sort of men, thus qualified,
Inclined the balance to the better side;
And David's mildness managed it so well,
The bad found no occasion to rebel.
But when to sin our biassed nature leans,
The careful devil is still at hand with means,   80
And providently pimps for ill desires;
The good old cause, revived, a plot requires.
Plots, true or false, are necessary things,
To raise up commonwealths, and ruin kings.
    The inhabitants of old Jerusalem
Were Jebusites; the town so called from them;
And theirs the native right.
But when the chosen people grew more strong,
The rightful cause at length became the wrong;
And every loss the men of Jebus bore   90
They still were thought God's enemies the more.
Thus worn or weakened, well or ill content,
Submit they must to David's government;

Impoverished and deprived of all command,
Their taxes doubled as they lost their land;
And, what was harder yet to flesh and blood,
Their gods disgraced, and burned like common wood.
This set the heathen priesthood in a flame;
For priests of all religions are the same.
Of whatsoe'er descent their godhead be,   100
Stock, stone, or other homely pedigree,
In his defence his servants are as bold,
As if he had been born of beaten gold.
The Jewish rabbins, though their enemies,
In this conclude them honest men and wise;
For 'twas their duty, all the learned think,
To espouse his cause, by whom they eat and drink.
From hence began that plot, the nation's curse;
Bad in itself; but represented worse;
Raised in extremes, and in extremes decried;   110
With oaths affirmed, with dying vows denied;
Not weighed nor winnowed by the multitude,
But swallowed in the mass, unchewed and crude.
Some truth there was, but dashed and brewed with lies,
To please the fools, and puzzle all the wise.
Succeeding times did equal folly call,
Believing nothing, or believing all.
The Egyptian rites the Jebusites embraced,
Where gods were recommended by their taste.
Such savoury deities must needs be good,   120
As served at once for worship and for food.
By force they could not introduce these gods,
For ten to one in former days was odds,
So fraud was used, the sacrificer's trade;
Fools are more hard to conquer than persuade.
Their busy teachers mingled with the Jews,
And raked for converts even the court and stews;
Which Hebrew priests the more unkindly took
Because the fleece accompanies the flock.
Some thought they God's anointed meant to slay   130
By guns, invented since full many a day;
Our author swears it not; but who can know
How far the devil and Jebusites may go?
This plot, which failed for want of commonsense,
Had yet a deep and dangerous consequence;

For as, when raging fevers boil the blood,
The standing lake soon floats into a flood,
And every hostile humour, which before
Slept quiet in its channels, bubbles o'er;
So several factions, from this first ferment,   140
Work up to foam, and threat the government.
Some by their friends, more by themselves thought wise,
Opposed the power to which they could not rise;
Some had in courts been great, and, thrown from thence,
Like fiends, were hardened in impenitence;
Some by their monarch's fatal mercy grown,
From pardoned rebels kinsmen to the throne
Were raised in power and public office high;
Strong bands, if bands ungrateful men could tie.
    Of these the false Achitophel was first,   150
A name to all succeeding ages cursed,
For close designs, and crooked counsels fit,
Sagacious, bold, and turbulent of wit;
Restless, unfixed in principles and place;
In power unpleased, impatient of disgrace;
A fiery soul, which, working out its way,
Fretted the pigmy-body to decay,
And o'er-informed the tenement of clay.
A daring pilot in extremity,
Pleased with the danger, when the waves went high,   160
He sought the storms; but, for a calm unfit,
Would steer too nigh the sands, to boast his wit.
Great wits are sure to madness near allied,
And thin partitions do their bounds divide;
Else, why should he, with wealth and honour blest,
Refuse his age the needful hours of rest?
Punish a body which he could not please,
Bankrupt of life, yet prodigal of ease?
And all to leave what with his toil he won,
To that unfeathered two-legged thing, a son   170
Got, while his soul did huddled notions try,
And born a shapeless lump, like anarchy.
In friendship false, implacable in hate;
Resolved to ruin, or to rule the state.
To compass this the triple bond he broke;
The pillars of the public safety shook,
And fitted Israel for a foreign yoke;

Then, seized with fear, yet still affecting fame,
Usurped a patriot's all-atoning name.
So easy still it proves in factious times, 180
With public zeal to cancel private crimes.
How safe is treason, and how sacred ill,
Where none can sin against the people's will?
Where crowds can wink, and no offence be known,
Since in another's guilt they find their own?
Yet fame deserved no enemy can grudge;
The statesman we abhor, but praise the judge.
In Israel's courts ne'er sat an Abbethdin
With more discerning eyes, or hands more clean,
Unbribed, unsought, the wretched to redress, 190
Swift of dispatch, and easy of access.
Oh! had he been content to serve the crown,
With virtue only proper to the gown;
Or had the rankness of the soil been freed
From cockle, that oppressed the noble seed;
David for him his tuneful harp had strung,
And heaven had wanted one immortal song.
But wild ambition loves to slide, not stand,
And fortune's ice prefers to virtue's land.
Achitophel, grown weary to possess 200
A lawful fame, and lazy happiness,
Disdained the golden fruit to gather free,
And lent the crowd his arm to shake the tree.
Now, manifest of crimes contrived long since,
He stood at bold defiance with his prince;
Held up the buckler of the people's cause
Against the crown, and skulked behind the laws …

314. from *The Hind and the Panther*

A milk-white Hind, immortal and unchanged,
Fed on the lawns, and in the forest ranged.
Without unspotted, innocent within,
She feared no danger, for she knew no sin.
Yet had she oft been chased with horns and hounds
And Scythian shafts; and many wingèd wounds
Aimed at her heart; was often forced to fly,
And doomed to death, though fated not to die.

Not so her young; for their unequal line
Was hero's make, half human, half divine.　　　　　　　10
Their earthly mould obnoxious was to fate,
Th' immortal part assumed immortal state.
Of these a slaughtered army lay in blood,
Extended o'er the Caledonian wood,
Their native walk; whose vocal blood arose,
And cried for pardon on their perjured foes.
Their fate was fruitful, and the sanguine seed,
Endued with souls, increased the sacred breed.
So captive Israel multiplied in chains,
A numerous exile, and enjoyed her pains.　　　　　　20
With grief and gladness mixed, their mother viewed
Her martyred offspring, and their race renewed;
Their corps to perish, but their kind to last,
So much the deathless plant the dying fruit surpassed.

Panting and pensive now she ranged alone,
And wandered in the kingdoms, once her own.
The common hunt, though from their rage restrained
By sovereign power, her company disdained;
Grinned as they passed, and with a glaring eye
Gave gloomy signs of secret enmity.　　　　　　　　30
'Tis true, she bounded by, and tripped so light,
They had not time to take a steady sight,
For Truth has such a face and such a mien,
As to be loved needs only to be seen.

The bloody Bear, an Independent beast,
Unlicked to form, in groans her hate expressed.
Among the timorous kind the Quaking Hare
Professed neutrality, but would not swear.
Next her the buffoon Ape, as atheists use,
Mimicked all sects, and had his own to choose:　　　40
Still when the Lion looked, his knees he bent,
And paid at church a courtier's compliment.

The bristled Baptist Boar, impure as he,
(But whitened with the foam of sanctity,)
With fat pollutions filled the sacred place,
And mountains levelled in his furious race:
So first rebellion founded was in grace.
But since the mighty ravage which he made
In German forests had his guilt betrayed,
With broken tusks, and with a borrowed name,　　　50

He shunned the vengeance, and concealed the shame;
So lurked in sects unseen. With greater guile
False Reynard fed on consecrated spoil:
The graceless beast by Athanasius first
Was chased from Nice; then, by Socinus nursed,
His impious race their blasphemy renewed,
And nature's King through nature's optics viewed.
Reversed, they viewed him lessened to their eye,
Nor in an infant could a God descry:
New swarming sects to this obliquely tend,   60
Hence they began, and here they all will end.
    What weight of ancient witness can prevail,
If private reason hold the public scale?
But, gracious God, how well dost thou provide
For erring judgements an unerring guide!
Thy throne is darkness in th' abyss of light,
A blaze of glory that forbids the sight.
O teach me to believe Thee thus concealed,
And search no farther than Thyself revealed;
But her alone for my director take,   70
Whom Thou hast promised never to forsake!
My thoughtless youth was winged with vain desires,
My manhood, long misled by wandering fires,
Followed false lights; and when their glimpse was gone,
My pride struck out new sparkles of her own.
Such was I, such by nature still I am,
Be thine the glory, and be mine the shame.
Good life be now my task: my doubts are done:
(What more could fright my faith, than Three in One?)
Can I believe eternal God could lie   80
Disguised in mortal mould and infancy?
That the great Maker of the world could die?
And after that trust my imperfect sense
Which calls in question his omnipotence?
Can I my reason to my faith compel,
And shall my sight, and touch, and taste rebel?
Superior faculties are set aside,
Shall their subservient organs be my guide?
Then let the moon usurp the rule of day,
And winking tapers show the sun his way;   90
For what my senses can themselves perceive,
I need no revelation to believe.

315. 'Can life be a blessing'

Can life be a blessing,
Or worth the possessing,
Can life be a blessing if love were away?
Ah no! though our love all night keep us waking,
And though he torment us with cares all the day,
Yet he sweetens, he sweetens our pains in the taking,
There's an hour at the last, there's an hour to repay.

In every possessing,
The ravishing blessing,
In every possessing the fruit of our pain,   10
Poor lovers forget long ages of anguish,
Whate'er they have suffered and done to obtain;
'Tis a pleasure, a pleasure to sigh and to languish,
When we hope, when we hope to be happy again.

316. An Epilogue

You saw your wife was chaste, yet throughly tried,
And, without doubt, you are hugely edified;
For, like our hero, whom we showed today,
You think no woman true, but in a play.
Love once did make a pretty kind of show;
Esteem and kindness in one breast would grow;
But 'twas heaven knows how many years ago.
Now some small chat, and guinea expectation,
Gets all the pretty creatures in the nation.
In comedy your little selves you meet;   10
'Tis Covent Garden drawn in Bridges Street.
Smile on our author then, if he has shown
A jolly nut-brown bastard of your own.
Ah! happy you, with ease and with delight,
Who act those follies, poets toil to write!
The sweating Muse does almost leave the chase;
She puffs, and hardly keeps your Protean vices pace.
Pinch you but in one vice, away you fly
To some new frisk of contrariety.
You roll like snowballs, gathering as you run,   20
And get seven devils, when dispossessed of one.
Your Venus once was a Platonic queen,

Nothing of love beside the face was seen;
But every inch of her you now uncase,
And clap a vizard-mask upon the face;
For sins like these, the zealous of the land,
With little hair, and little or no band,
Declare how circulating pestilences
Watch, every twenty years, to snap offences.
Saturn, e'en now, takes doctoral degrees;   30
He'll do your work this summer without fees.
Let all the boxes, Phoebus, find thy grace,
And, ah, preserve the eighteen-penny place!
But for the pit confounders, let them go,
And find as little mercy as they show!
The actors thus, and thus thy poets pray;
For every critic saved, thou damn'st a play.

317. Prologue Spoken at the Opening of the New House

A plain-built house, after so long a stay,
Will send you half unsatisfied away;
When, fallen from your expected pomp, you find
A bare convenience only is designed.
You, who each day can theatres behold,
Like Nero's palace, shining all with gold,
Our mean ungilded stage will scorn, we fear,
And, for the homely room, disdain the cheer
Yet now cheap druggets to a mode are grown,
And a plain suit, since we can make but one,   10
Is better than to be by tarnished gawdry known.
They, who are by your favours wealthy made,
With mighty sums may carry on the trade;
We, broken bankers, half destroyed by fire,
With our small stock to humble roofs retire;
Pity our loss, while you their pomp admire.
For fame and honour we no longer strive;
We yield in both, and only beg – to live;
Unable to support their vast expense,
Who build and treat with such magnificence,   20
That, like the ambitious monarchs of the age,
They give the law to our provincial stage.
Great neighbours enviously promote excess,

While they impose their splendour on the less;
But only fools, and they of vast estate,
The extremity of modes will imitate,
The dangling knee-fringe, and the bib-cravat.
Yet if some pride with want may be allowed,
We in our plainness may be justly proud;
Our Royal Master willed it should be so; 30
Whate'er he's pleased to own, can need no show:
That sacred name gives ornament and grace,
And, like his stamp, makes basest metal pass.
'Twere folly now a stately pile to raise,
To build a playhouse while you throw down plays;
While scenes, machines, and empty operas reign,
And for the pencil you the pen disdain;
While troops of famished Frenchmen hither drive,
And laugh at those upon whose alms they live:
Old English authors vanish, and give place 40
To these new conquerors of the Norman race.
More tamely than your fathers you submit;
You're now grown vassals to them in your wit.
Mark, when they play, how our fine fops advance
The mighty merits of their men of France,
Keep time, cry, 'Ben!' and humour the cadence.
Well, please yourselves; but sure 'tis understood,
That French machines have ne'er done England good.
I would not prophesy our house's fate;
But while vain shows and scenes you overrate, 50
'Tis to be feared –
That, as a fire the former house o'erthrew,
Machines and tempests will destroy the new.

318. Prologue to the King and Queen, upon the Union of the Two Companies

Since faction ebbs, and rogues grow out of fashion,
Their penny scribes take care t' inform the nation,
How well men thrive in this or that plantation:

How Pennsylvania's air agrees with Quakers,
And Carolina's with Associators;
Both e'en too good for madmen and for traitors.

Truth is, our land with saints is so run o'er,
And every age produces such a store,
That now there's need of two New Englands more.

What's this, you'll say, to us, and our vocation?   10
Only thus much, that we have left our station,
And made this theatre our new plantation.

The factious natives never could agree;
But aiming, as they called it, to be free,
Those playhouse Whigs set up for property.

Some say, they no obedience paid of late;
But would new fears and jealousies create,
Till topsy-turvy they had turned the state.

Plain sense, without the talent of foretelling,
Might guess 'twould end in downright knocks and quelling;   20
For seldom comes there better of rebelling.

When men will, needlessly, their freedom barter
For lawless power, sometimes they catch a Tartar; –
There's a damned word that rhymes to this, called Charter.

But, since the victory with us remains,
You shall be called to twelve in all our gains,
If you'll not think us saucy for our pains.

Old men shall have good old plays to delight them;
And you, fair ladies and gallants, that slight them,
We'll treat with good new plays, if our new wits can write them.   30

We'll take no blundering verse, no fustian tumour,
No dribbling love, from this or that presumer;
No dull fat fool shammed on the stage for humour:

For, faith, some of them such vile stuff have made,
As none but fools or fairies ever played;
But 'twas, as shopmen say, to force a trade.

We've given you tragedies, all sense defying,
And singing men, in woeful metre dying;
This 'tis when heavy lubbers will be flying.

All these disasters we will hope to weather;   40
We bring you none of our old lumber hither;
Whig poets and Whig sheriffs may hang together.

319. Song for St Cecilia's Day, 1687

From harmony, from heavenly harmony
    This universal frame began:
  When nature underneath a heap
    Of jarring atoms lay
  And could not heave her head,
The tuneful voice was heard from high,
    Arise, ye more than dead!
Then cold and hot and moist and dry
In order to their stations leap,
    And music's power obey.   10
From harmony, from heavenly harmony
    This universal frame began:
    From harmony to harmony
Through all the compass of the notes it ran,
The diapason closing full in man.

What passion cannot music raise and quell?
    When Jubal struck the corded shell
  His listening brethren stood around,
  And, wondering, on their faces fell
  To worship that celestial sound.   20
Less than a god they thought there could not dwell
    Within the hollow of that shell
    That spoke so sweetly and so well.
What passion cannot music raise and quell?

  The trumpet's loud clangour
    Excites us to arms,
  With shrill notes of anger
    And mortal alarms.
  The double double double beat
    Of the thundering drum   30
  Cries 'Hark! the foes come;
Charge, charge, 'tis too late to retreat!'

The soft complaining flute
In dying notes discovers
    The woes of hopeless lovers,
Whose dirge is whispered by the warbling lute.

    Sharp violins proclaim
Their jealous pangs and desperation,
Fury, frantic indignation,
Depth of pains, and height of passion   40
    For the fair, disdainful dame.

But oh! what art can teach,
What human voice can reach
    The sacred organ's praise?
Notes inspiring holy love,
Notes that wing their heavenly ways
    To mend the choirs above.

Orpheus could lead the savage race,
And trees unrooted left their place
    Sequacious of the lyre: 50
But bright Cecilia raised the wonder higher:
When to her organ vocal breath was given
An angel heard, and straight appeared
    Mistaking earth for heaven.

    Grand Chorus
As from the power of sacred lays
    The spheres began to move,
And sung the great Creator's praise
    To all the blest above;
So when the last and dreadful hour
This crumbling pageant shall devour,   60
The trumpet shall be heard on high,
The dead shall live, the living die,
And music shall untune the sky.

320. Alexander's Feast, or, The Power of Music

'Twas at the royal feast for Persia won
    By Philip's warlike son:

Aloft in awful state
The godlike hero sat
On his imperial throne.
His valiant peers were placed around,
Their brows with roses and with myrtles bound
(So should desert in arms be crowned);
The lovely Thais by his side
Sat like a blooming eastern bride,   10
In flower of youth and beauty's pride.
Happy, happy, happy pair!
  None but the brave,
  None but the brave,
None but the brave deserves the fair.

Timotheus placed on high
  Amid the tuneful choir,
  With flying fingers touched the lyre;
The trembling notes ascend the sky
  And heavenly joys inspire.   20
    The song began from Jove,
    Who left his blissful seat above;
(Such is the power of mighty love).
A dragon's fiery form belied the god;
Sublime on radiant spires he rode,
  When he to fair Olympia pressed,
  A while he sought her snowy breast;
Then round her slender waist he curled,
And stamped an image of himself; a sovereign of the world.
The listening crowd admire the lofty sound,
A present deity! they shout around;   30
A present deity! the vaulted roofs rebound:
    With ravished ears
    The monarch hears;
    Assumes the god,
    Affects to nod,
And seems to shake the spheres.

The praise of Bacchus then the sweet musician sung:
Of Bacchus, ever fair and ever young:
  The jolly god in triumph comes;
  Sound the trumpets, beat the drums;   40
    Flushed with a purple grace

He shows his honest face.
Now give the hautboys breath. He comes, he comes!
   Bacchus! Ever fair and young,
     Drinking joys did first ordain;
      Bacchus' blessings are a treasure;
      Drinking is the soldier's pleasure:
        Rich the treasure,
        Sweet the pleasure,
      Sweet is pleasure after pain.   50

Soothed with the sound, the king grew vain,
   Fought all his battles o'er again,
And thrice he routed all his foes, and thrice he slew the slain.
     The master saw the madness rise,
     His glowing cheeks, his ardent eyes;
     And while he heaven and earth defied,
     Changed his hand, and checked his pride.
       He chose a mournful muse,
       Soft pity to infuse;
     He sung Darius, great and good!   60
       By too severe a fate,
    Fallen, fallen, fallen, fallen,
       Fallen from his high estate,
         And weltering in his blood:
   Deserted at his utmost need,
   By those his former bounty fed;
   On the bare earth exposed he lies
   Without a friend to close his eyes.
With downcast looks the joyless victor sat
   Revolving in his altered soul,   70
     The various turns of chance below;
   And now and then a sigh he stole
    And tears began to flow.

The mighty master smiled to see
That love was in the next degree;
'Twas but a kindred sound to move,
For pity melts the mind to love.
Softly sweet, in Lydian measures,
Soon he soothed his soul to pleasures.
War, he sung, is toil and trouble;   80
Honour but an empty bubble;
Never ending, still beginning,

Fighting still, and still destroying;
If the world be worth thy winning,
   Think, O think it worth enjoying!
   Lovely Thais sits beside thee;
   Take the good the gods provide thee.
The many rend the skies with loud applause,
So love was crowned, but music won the cause.
     The prince, unable to conceal his pain,   90
       Gazed on his fair
       Who caused his care,
   And sighed and looked, sighed and looked,
   Sighed and looked, and sighed again.
At length, with love and wine at once oppressed,
The vanquished victor sunk upon her breast.

Now strike the golden lyre again,
A louder yet, and yet a louder strain.
Break his bands of sleep asunder,
And rouse him, like a rattling peal of thunder.   100
       Hark, hark the horrid sound
         Has raised up his head
         As awaked from the dead,
      And amazed he stares around.
Revenge, revenge! Timotheus cries,
      See the furies arise!
   See the snakes that they rear,
   How they hiss in their hair!
And the sparkles that flash from their eyes!
      Behold a ghastly band,   110
      Each a torch in his hand!
Those are Grecian ghosts that in battle were slain.
      And unburied remain
      Inglorious on the plain:
      Give the vengeance due
      To the valiant crew.
Behold how they toss their torches on high,
   How they point to the Persian abodes,
And glittering temples of their hostile gods.
   The princes applaud with a furious joy,   120
And the king seized a flambeau with zeal to destroy;
   Thais led the way,
   To light him to his prey,
And like another Helen, fired another Troy.

Thus long ago,
'Ere heaving bellows learned to blow,
  While organs yet were mute,
Timotheus with his breathing flute,
    And sounding lyre,
Could swell the soul to rage, or kindle soft desire.   130
  But when divine Cecilia came,
  Inventress of the vocal frame,
The sweet enthusiast, from her sacred store,
  Enlarged the former narrow bounds
  And added length to solemn sounds
With nature's mother-wit, and arts unknown before.
  Let old Timotheus yield the prize,
    Or both divide the crown;
  He raised a mortal to the skies,
    She drew an angel down.   140

321. from *Religio Laici,* or, *A Layman's Faith*

Dim, as the borrowed beams of moon and stars
To lonely, weary, wandering travellers,
Is reason to the soul: and as on high
Those rolling fires discover but the sky,
Not light us here; so reason's glimmering ray
Was lent, not to assure our doubtful way,
But guide us upward to a better day.
And as those nightly tapers disappear
When day's bright lord ascends our hemisphere,
So pale grows reason at religion's sight,   10
So dies, and so dissolves in supernatural light.
Some few, whose lamp shone brighter, have been led
From cause to cause, to nature's secret head,
And found that one first principle must be:
But what, or who, that universal He,
Whether some soul encompassing this ball,
Unmade, unmoved, yet making, moving all;
Or various atoms' interfering dance
Leaped into form, the noble work of chance;
Or this great all was from eternity,   20
Not even the Stagyrite himself could see,
And Epicurus guessed as well as he.

As blindly groped they for a future state,
As rashly judged of providence and fate;
But least of all could their endeavours find
What most concerned the good of human kind;
For happiness was never to be found,
But vanished from them like enchanted ground.
One thought content the good to be enjoyed;
This every little accident destroyed;   30
The wiser madmen did for virtue toil,
A thorny or, at best, a barren soil;
In pleasure some their glutton souls would steep,
But found their line too short, the well too deep,
And leaky vessels which no bliss could keep.
Thus anxious thoughts in endless circles roll,
Without a centre where to fix the soul:
In this wild maze their vain endeavours end.
How can the less the greater comprehend?
Or finite reason reach infinity?   40
For what could fathom God, were more than he.
    The Deist thinks he stands on firmer ground;
Cries eureka! the mighty secret's found:
God is that spring of good, supreme and best,
We made to serve, and in that service blest;
If so, some rules of worship must be given,
Distributed alike to all by heaven;
Else God were partial, and to some denied
The means his justice should for all provide.
This general worship is to praise and pray;   50
One part to borrow blessings, one to pay;
And when frail nature slides into offence,
The sacrifice for crimes is penitence.
Yet since the effects of providence, we find,
Are variously dispensed to human kind;
That vice triumphs, and virtue suffers here,
(A brand that sovereign justice cannot bear)
Our reason prompts us to a future state,
The last appeal from fortune and from fate,
Where God's all righteous ways will be declared: 60
The bad meet punishment, the good reward.
    Thus man by his own strength to heaven would soar,
And would not be obliged to God for more.
Vain, wretched creature, how art thou misled,
To think thy wit these god-like notions bred!

These truths are not the product of thy mind
But dropped from heaven, and of a nobler kind.
Revealed religion first informed thy sight,
And reason saw not, till faith sprung the light.
Hence all thy natural worship takes the source;   70
'Tis revelation what thou think'st discourse.
Else how com'st thou to see these truths so clear,
Which so obscure to heathens did appear?
Not Plato these, nor Aristotle found,
Nor he whose wisdom oracles renowned.
Hast thou a wit so deep, or so sublime,
Or can'st thou lower dive, or higher climb?
Can'st thou by reason more of godhead know
Than Plutarch, Seneca, or Cicero?
Those giant wits, in happier ages born,   80
When arms and arts did Greece and Rome adorn,
Knew no such system; no such piles could raise
Of natural worship, built on prayer and praise
To one sole God.
Nor did remorse, to expiate sin, prescribe,
But slew their fellow-creatures for a bribe:
The guiltless victim groaned for their offence,
And cruelty and blood was penitence.
If sheep and oxen could atone for men,
Ah! at how cheap a rate the rich might sin!   90
And great oppressors might heaven's wrath beguile,
By offering his own creatures for a spoil!
    Dar'st thou, poor worm, offend infinity?
And must the terms of peace be given by thee?
Then thou art justice in the last appeal;
Thy easy God instructs thee to rebel;
And, like a king remote and weak, must take
What satisfaction thou art pleased to make ...

Katherine Philips, 'the Matchless Orinda' (1632–1664)

322. Epitaph on her Son H.P. at St Syth's Church, where her Body also Lies Interred

What on earth deserves our trust?
Youth and beauty both are dust.
Long we gathering are with pain,
What one moment calls again.
Seven years childless, marriage past,
A son, a son is born at last:
So exactly limbed and fair,
Full of good spirits, mien, and air,
As a long life promisèd,
Yet, in less than six weeks dead.   10
Too promising, too great a mind
In so small room to be confined:
Therefore, as fit in heaven to dwell,
He quickly broke the prison shell.
So the subtle alchemist,
Can't with Hermes' Seal resist
The powerful spirit's subtler flight,
But 'twill bid him long goodnight.
And so the sun if it arise
Half so glorious as his eyes,   20
Like this infant, takes a shroud,
Buried in a morning cloud.

323. Wiston Vault

And why this vault and tomb? Alike we must
Put off distinction, and put on our dust.
Nor can the stateliest fabric help to save
From the corruptions of a common grave;
Nor for the resurrection more prepare,
Than if the dust were scattered into air.
What then? Th' ambition's just, say some, that we
May thus perpetuate our memory.

Ah, false vain task of art! Ah, poor weak man!
Whose monument does more than 's merit can: 10
Who by his friends best care and love's abused,
And in his very epitaph accused:
For did they not suspect his name would fall,
There would not need an epitaph at all.
But after death too I would be alive,
And shall, if my Lucasia do, survive.
I quit these pomps of death, and am content,
Having her heart to be my monument:
Though ne'er stone to me, 'twill stone for me prove,
By the peculiar miracles of love.   20
There I'll inscription have which no tomb gives,
Not, 'Here Orinda lies,' but, 'Here she lives.'

324. To Mr Henry Lawes

Nature, which is the vast creation's soul,
That steady curious agent in the whole,
The art of heaven, the order of this frame,
Is only number in another name.
For as some king conquering what was his own,
Hath choice of several titles to his crown;
So harmony on this score now, that then,
Yet still is all that takes and governs men.
Beauty is but composure, and we find
Content is but the concord of the mind,   10
Friendship the unison of well-tuned hearts,
Honour the chorus of the noblest parts,
And all the world on which we can reflect
Music to th' ear, or to the intellect.
If then each man a little world must be,
How many worlds are copied out in thee,
Who art so richly formèd, so complete
T' epitomise all that is good and great;
Whose stars this brave advantage did impart,
Thy nature's as harmonious as thy art?   20
Thou dost above the poets' praises live,
Who fetch from thee th' eternity they give.
And as true reason triumphs over sense,
Yet is subjected to intelligence:

So poets on the lower world look down,
But Lawes on them; his height is all his own.
For, like divinity itself, his lyre
Rewards the wit it did at first inspire.
And thus by double right poets allow
His and their laurel should adorn his brow.   30
Live then, great soul of nature, to assuage
The savage dullness of this sullen age.
Charm us to sense; for though experience fail
And reason too, thy numbers may prevail.
Then, like those ancients, strike, and so command
All nature to obey thy generous hand.
None will resist but such who needs will be
More stupid than a stone, a fish, a tree.
Be it thy care our age to new-create:
What built a world may sure repair a state.   40

325. On the Welsh Language

If honour to an ancient name be due,
Or riches challenge it for one that's new,
The British language claims in either sense,
Both for its age, and for its opulence.
But all great things must be from us removed,
To be with higher reverence beloved.
So landscapes which in prospects distant lie,
With greater wonder draw the pleasèd eye.
Is not great Troy to one dark ruin hurled,
Once the famed scene of all the fighting world?   10
Where's Athens now, to whom Rome learning owes,
And the safe laurels that adorned her brows?
A strange reverse of fate she did endure,
Never once greater, than she's now obscure.
E'en Rome herself can but some footsteps show
Of Scipio's times, or those of Cicero.
And as the Roman and the Grecian state,
The British fell, the spoil of time and fate.
But though the language hath the beauty lost,
Yet she has still some great remains to boast   20
For 'twas in that, the sacred bards of old,
In deathless numbers did their thoughts unfold.

In groves, by rivers, and on fertile plains,
They civilised and taught the listening swains;
Whilst with high raptures, and as great success,
Virtue they clothed in music's charming dress.
This Merlin spoke, who in his gloomy cave,
E'en destiny herself seemed to enslave.
For to his sight the future time was known
Much better than to others is their own.   30
And with such state, predictions from him fell,
As if he did decree, and not foretell.
This spoke King Arthur, who, if fame be true,
Could have compelled mankind to speak it too.
In this once Boadicea valour taught,
And spoke more nobly than her soldiers fought:
Tell me what hero could do more than she,
Who fell at once for fame and liberty?
Nor could a greater sacrifice belong,
Or to her children's, or her country's wrong.   40
This spoke Caractacus, who was so brave,
That to the Roman Fortune check he gave:
And when their yoke he could decline no more,
He it so decently and nobly wore,
That Rome herself with blushes did believe,
A Britain would the law of honour give;
And hastily his chains away she threw,
Lest her own captive else should her subdue.

Thomas Traherne (1637–1674)

326. The Recovery

Sin! Wilt thou vanquish me?
And shall I yield the victory?
Shall all my joys be spoiled,
And pleasures soiled
By thee?

      Shall I remain
      As one that's slain
And never more lift up the head?
    Is not my saviour dead?
His blood, thy bane; my balsam, bliss, joy, wine;   10
Shall thee destroy; heal, feed, make me divine.

327. Wonder

How like an angel came I down!
How bright are all things here!
When first among his works I did appear
O how their glory me did crown?
The world resembled his eternity,
In which my soul did walk;
And everything that I did see,
Did with me talk.

The skies in their magnificence,
The lively, lovely air;   10
Oh how divine, how soft, how sweet, how fair!
The stars did entertain my sense,
And all the works of God so bright and pure,
So rich and great did seem,
As if they ever must endure,
In my esteem.

A native health and innocence
Within my bones did grow,
And while my God did all his glories show,
I felt a vigour in my sense   20
That was all spirit. I within did flow
With seas of life, like wine;
I nothing in the world did know,
But 'twas divine.

Harsh ragged objects were concealed,
Oppressions, tears and cries,
Sins, griefs, complaints, dissensions, weeping eyes,
Were hid: and only things revealed,

Which heavenly spirits, and the angels prize.
The state of innocence 30
And bliss, not trades and poverties,
Did fill my sense.

The streets were paved with golden stones,
The boys and girls were mine.
Oh how did all their lovely faces shine!
The sons of men were holy ones.
In joy, and beauty, then appeared to me,
And every thing which here I found,
While like an angel I did see,
Adorned the ground. 40

Rich diamond and pearl and gold
In every place was seen;
Rare splendours, yellow, blue, red, white and green,
Mine eyes did everywhere behold.
Great wonders clothed with glory did appear,
Amazement was my bliss.
That and my wealth was everywhere:
No joy to this!

Cursed and devised proprieties,
With envy, avarice 50
And fraud, those fiends that spoil even paradise,
Fled from the splendour of mine eyes.
And so did hedges, ditches, limits, bounds,
I dreamed not aught of those,
But wandered over all men's grounds,
And found repose.

Properties themselves were mine,
And hedges, ornaments;
Walls, boxes, coffers, and their rich contents
Did not divide my joys, but all combine. 60
Clothes, ribbons, jewels, laces, I esteemed
My joys by others worn;
For me they all to wear them seemed
When I was born.

328. The Preparative

My body being dead, my limbs unknown;
    Before I skilled to prize
    Those living stars mine eyes,
Before my tongue or cheeks were to me shown,
  Before I knew my hands were mine,
Or that my sinews did my members join,
  When neither nostril, foot, nor ear,
As yet was seen, or felt, or did appear;
    I was within
A house I knew not, newly clothed with skin.   10

Then was my soul my only all to me,
    A living endless eye,
    Just bounded with the sky,
Whose power, whose act, whose essence was to see.
  I was an inward sphere of light,
Or an interminable orb of sight,
  An endless and a living day,
A vital sun that round about did ray
    All life, all sense,
A naked simple pure intelligence.   20

I then no thirst nor hunger did perceive,
    No dull necessity,
    No want was known to me;
Without disturbance then I did receive
  The fair ideas of all things,
And had the honey even without the stings.
  A meditating inward eye
Gazing at quiet did within me lie,
    And everything
Delighted me that was their heavenly king.   30

For sight inherits beauty, hearing sounds,
    The nostril sweet perfumes,
    All tastes have hidden rooms
Within the tongue; and feeling feeling wounds
  With pleasure and delight: but I
Forgot the rest, and was all sight, or eye.
  Unbodied and devoid of care,
Just as in heaven the holy angels are.

   For simple sense
Is lord of all created excellence.   40

Being thus prepared for all felicity,
   Not prepossessed with dross,
   Nor stiffly glued to gross
And dull materials that might ruin me,
  Not fettered by an iron fate
With vain affections in my earthy state
  To anything that might seduce
My sense, or else bereave it of its use,
   I was as free
  As if there were nor sin, nor misery.   50

Pure empty powers that did nothing loathe,
   Did like the fairest glass,
   Or spotless polished brass,
Themselves soon in their object's image clothe.
  Divine impressions when they came,
Did quickly enter and my soul inflame.
  'Tis not the object, but the light
That maketh heaven; 'tis a purer sight.
   Felicity
Appears to none but them that purely see. 60

A disentangled and a naked sense,
   A mind that's unpossessed,
   A disengagèd breast,
An empty and a quick intelligence
  Acquainted with the golden mean,
An even spirit pure and serene,
  Is that where beauty, excellence,
And pleasure keep their court of residence.
   My soul retire,
Get free, and so thou shalt even all admire. 70

329. Speed

   The liquid pearl in springs,
   The useful and the precious things
   Are in a moment known.
Their very glory does reveal their worth,

(And that doth set their glory forth);
As soon as I was born, they all were shown.

    True living wealth did flow,
    In crystal streams below
    My feet, and trilling down
In pure, transparent, soft, sweet, melting pleasures,   10
    Like precious and diffusive treasures,
At once my body fed, and soul did crown.

    I was as high and great,
    As kings are in their seat.
    All other things were mine.
The world my house, the creatures were my goods,
    Fields, mountains, valleys, woods,
Men and their arts to make me rich combine.

    Great, lofty, endless, stable,
    Various and innumerable,   20
    Bright, useful, fair, divine,
Immovable and sweet the treasures were,
    The sacred objects did appear
Most rich and beautiful, as well as mine.

    New all! New burnished joys;
    Though now by other toys
    Eclipsed: new all and mine.
Great truth so sacred seemed for this to me,
    Because the things which I did see
Were such, my state I knew to be divine.   30

    Nor did the angels' faces,
    The glories, and the graces,
    The beauty, peace and joy
Of heaven itself, more sweetness yield to me.
    Till filthy sin did all destroy,
These were the offspring of the deity.

330. Love

    O nectar! O delicious stream!
O ravishing and only pleasure! Where

Shall such another theme
Inspire my tongue with joys, or please mine ear!
    Abridgement of delights!
      And queen of sights!
O mine of rarities! O kingdom wide!
O more! O cause of all! O glorious bride!
  O God! O bride of God! O king!
  O soul and crown of everything!   10

  Did not I covet to behold
Some endless monarch, that did always live
    In palaces of gold
Willing all kingdoms, realms and crowns to give
    Unto my soul? Whose love
      A spring might prove
Of endless glories, honours, friendships, pleasures,
Joys, praises, beauties and celestial treasures!
  Lo, now I see there's such a King,
  The fountainhead of everything!   20

  Did my ambition ever dream
Of such a lord, of such a love? Did I
    Expect so sweet a stream
As this at any time? Could any eye
    Believe it? Why all power
      Is usèd here
Joys down from heaven on my head to shower
And Jove beyond the fiction doth appear
  Once more in golden rain to come
  To Danaë's pleasing fruitful womb.   30

  His Ganymede! His life! His joy!
Or he comes down to me, or takes me up
    That I might be his boy,
And fill, and taste, and give, and drink the cup.
    But these (though great) are all
      Too short and small,
Too weak and feeble pictures to express
The true mysterious depths of blessedness.
  I am his image, and his friend.
  His son, bride, glory, temple, end.   40

Charles Sackville, Earl of Dorset (1638–1706)

331. Advice to Lovers

Damon, if thou wilt believe me,
   'Tis not sighing round the plain,
Song nor sonnet can relieve thee;
   Faint attempts in love are vain.

Urge but home the fair occasion,
   And be master of the field;
To a powerful kind invasion
   'Twere a madness not to yield.

Though she swears she'll ne'er permit you,
   Cries you're rude and much to blame,   10
And with tears implores your pity,
   Be not merciful, for shame.

When the fierce assault is over,
   Chloris time enough may find
This, her cruel furious lover,
   Much more gentle, not so kind.

Love gives out a large commission,
   Still indulgent to the brave;
But one sin of base omission
   Never woman yet forgave.   20

But true vigour in performing
   Turns the tragic scene to farce;
And she'll rise appeased next morning,
   With dry eyes and a wet a – .

332. Epitaph on Mrs Lundy

Here lies little Lundy a yard deep or more
That never lay silent or quiet before,

For her brain was still working, her tongue was still prating,
And the pulse of her heart continually beating
To the utmost extremes of loving and hating.
Her reason and humour were always at strife,
But yet she performed all the duties of life,
For she was a true friend and a pretty good wife.
So indulgent a mother that no one could say
Whether Minty or Patty did rule or obey,   10
For the government changed some ten times a day.
At the hour of her birth some lucky star gave her
Wit and beauty enough to have lasted for ever;
But fortune, still froward when nature is kind,
A narrow estate maliciously joined
To a very great genius and a generous mind.
Her body was made of that superfine clay,
Which is apt to be brittle for want of allay;
And when, without show of outward decay,
It began by degrees to moulder away,   20
Her soul, then too busy on some foreign affair,
Of its own pretty dwelling took so little care
That the tenement fell for want of repair.
Far be from hence both the fool and the knave,
But let all who pretend to be witty or brave,
Whether generous friend or amorous slave,
Contribute some tears to water her grave.

333. To Mr Edward Howard, on his Incomparable, Incomprehensible Poem Called 'The British Princes'

Come on, ye critics! Find one fault who dare,
For, read it backward like a witch's prayer,
'Twill do as well; throw not away your jests
On solid nonsense that abides all tests.
Wit, like tierce claret, when 't begins to pall
Neglected lies, and 's of no use at all;
But in its full perfection of decay,
Turns vinegar and comes again in play.
This simile shall stand in thy defence
'Gainst such dull rogues as now and then write sense.   10
He lies, dear Ned, who says thy brain is barren,

Where deep conceits, like vermin, breed in carrion.
Thou hast a brain, such as thou hast, indeed –
On what else should thy worm of fancy feed?
Yet in a filbert I have often known
Maggots survive when all the kernel's gone.
Thy style's the same whatever be the theme,
As some digestions turn all meat to phlegm:
Thy stumbling, foundered jade can trot as high
As any other Pegasus can fly.   20
As skilful divers to the bottom fall
Sooner than those that cannot swim at all,
So in this way of writing without thinking
Thou hast a strange alacrity in sinking:
Thou writ'st below e'en thy own natural parts
And with acquirèd dullness and new arts
Of studied nonsense tak'st kind reader's heart.
So the dull eel moves nimbler in the mud
Than all the swift-finned racers of the flood.
Therefore, dear Ned, at my advice forbear   30
Such loud complaints 'gainst critics to prefer,
Since thou art turned an arrant libeller:
Thou set'st thy name to what thyself dost write;
Did ever libel yet so sharply bite?

334. On the Countess Dowager of Manchester

Courage, dear Moll, and drive away despair.
Mopsa, who in her youth was scarce thought fair,
In spite of age, experience, and decays,
Sets up for charming in her fading days;
Snuffs her dim eyes to give one parting blow,
Have at the heart of every ogling beau!
This goodly goose, all feathered like a jay,
So gravely vain and so demurely gay,
Last night, to grace the Court, did overload
Her bald buff forehead with a high commode;   10
Her steps were managed with such tender art,
As if each board had been a lover's heart.
In all her air, in every glance, was seen
A mixture strange, 'twixt fifty and fifteen.
Crowds of admiring fops about her press;

Hampden himself delivers their address,
Which she, accepting with a nice disdain,
Owns them her subjects and begins to reign.
Fair Queen of Fopland is her royal style:
Fopland, the greatest part of this great isle!   20
Nature did ne'er more equally divide
A female heart, 'twixt piety and pride.
Her watchful maids prevent the peep of day,
And all in order on her toilet lay:
Prayer books and patch box, sermon notes and paint,
At once t' improve the sinner and the saint.
    Farewell, friend Moll: expect no more from me;
    But if you would a full description see,
    You'll find her somewhere in the litany
    With pride, vainglory, and hypocrisy.   30

Sir Charles Sedley (1638–1701)

335. To Nysus

How shall we please this age? If in a song
We put above six lines, they count it long;
If we contract it to an epigram,
As deep the dwarfish poetry they damn;
If we write plays, few see above an act,
And those lewd masks or noisy fops distract:
Let us write satire then, and at our ease
Vex th' ill-natured fools we cannot please.

336. Song

Phyllis, let's shun the common fate,
And let our love ne'er turn to hate;
I'll dote no longer than I can

Without being called a faithless man.
When we begin to want discourse,
And kindness seems to taste of force,
As freely as we met, we'll part,
Each one possessed of their own heart.
Thus whilst rash fools themselves undo,
We'll game, and give off savers too;   10
So equally the match we'll make,
Both shall be glad to draw the stake:
A smile of thine shall make my bliss,
I will enjoy thee in a kiss;
If from this height our kindness fall,
We'll bravely scorn to love at all:
If thy affection first decay,
I will the blame on nature lay.
Alas, what cordial can remove
The hasty fate of dying love?   20
Thus we will all the world excel
In loving, and in parting well.

337. To Celia

As in those nations, where they yet adore
Marble and cedar, and their aid implore,
'Tis not the workman, nor the precious wood,
But 'tis the worshipper that makes the god;
So, cruel fair, though heaven has given you all
We mortals virtue or can beauty call,
'Tis we that give the thunder to your frowns,
Darts to your eyes, and to ourselves the wounds:
Without our love, which proudly you deride,
Vain were your beauty, and more vain your pride; 10
All envied beings that the world can show,
Still to some meaner things their greatness owe,
Subjects make kings, and we (the numerous train
Of humble lovers) constitute thy reign.
This difference only beauty's realm may boast,
Where most it favours, it enslaves the most;
And they to whom it is indulgent found,
Are ever in the surest fetters bound:
What tyrant yet, but thee, was ever known

Cruel to those that served to make him one? 20
Valour's a vice, if not with honour joined,
Beauty a raging plague, if never kind.

338. Song

Hears not my Phyllis, how the birds
    Their feathered mates salute?
They tell their passion in their words;
    Must I alone be mute?
Phyllis, without frown or smile,
Sat and knotted all the while.

The god of love in thy bright eyes
    Does like a tyrant reign;
But in thy heart, a child he lies
    Without his dart or flame. 10
Phyllis, without frown or smile,
Sat and knotted all the while.

So many months in silence past,
    And yet in raging love,
Might well deserve one word at last
    My passion should approve.
Phyllis, without frown or smile,
Sat and knotted all the while.

Must then your faithful swain expire,
    And not one look obtain, 20
Which he, to soothe his fond desire,
    Might pleasingly explain?
Phyllis, without frown or smile,
Sat and knotted all the while.

339. On the Happy Corydon and Phyllis

Young Corydon and Phyllis,
Sat in a lovely grove,
Contriving crowns of lilies,

Repeating toys of love,
    And something else, but what I dare not name.

But as they were a-playing,
She ogled so the swain,
It saved her plainly saying,
'Let's kiss to ease our pain,
    And something else, but what I dare not name.'   10

A thousand times he kissed her,
Laying her on the green;
But as he further pressed her
A pretty leg was seen,
    And something else, but what I dare not name.

So many beauties viewing,
His ardour still increased,
And greater joys pursuing,
He wandered o'er her breast,
    And something else, but what I dare not name.   20

A last effort she trying
His passion to withstand,
Cried, but 'twas faintly crying,
'Pray take away your hand,
    And something else, but what I dare not name.'

Young Corydon, grown bolder,
The minutes would improve,
'This is the time,' he told her
'To show you how I love,
    And something else, but what I dare not name.'   30

The nymph seemed almost dying,
Dissolved in amorous heat,
She kissed, and told him sighing,
'My dear, your love is great,
    And something else, but what I dare not name.'

But Phyllis did recover,
Much sooner than the swain,
She blushing asked her lover,
'Shall we not kiss again,
    And something else, but what I dare not name?'   40

Thus love his revels keeping,
Till nature at a stand,
From talk they fell to sleeping
Holding each other's hand
    And something else, but what I dare not name.

Aphra Behn (1640–1689)

340. The Cabal at Nickey Nackeys

A pox of the statesman that's witty,
Who watches and plots all the sleepless night:
For seditious harangues, to the whigs of the city;
And maliciously turns a traitor in spite.
Let him wear and torment his lean carrion:
    To bring his sham-plots about,
      Till at last king, bishop and baron,
For the public good he have quite rooted out.

    But we that are no politicians,
But rogues that are impudent, barefaced and great,   10
Boldly head the rude rabble in times of sedition,
And bear all down before us, in church and in state.
Your impudence is the best state-trick;
    And he that by law means to rule,
      Let his history with ours be related;
And though we are the knaves, we know who's the fool.

341. Song from *Abdelazar*

Love in fantastic triumph sat
    Whilst bleeding hearts around him flowed,

For whom fresh pains he did create
    And strange tyrannic power he showed.
From thy bright eyes he took his fire
    Which round about in sport he hurled;
But 'twas from mine he took desire
    Enough to undo the amorous world.
From me he took his sighs and tears,
    From thee his pride and cruelty;   10
From me his languishments and fears,
    And every killing dart from thee;
Thus thou and I the god have armed
    And set him up a deity;
But my poor heart alone is harmed,
    Whilst thine the victor is, and free.

342. The Disappointment

One day the amorous Lysander,
By an impatient passion swayed,
Surprised fair Chloris, that loved maid,
Who could defend herself no longer;
All things did with his love conspire,
The gilded planet of the day,
In his gay chariot, drawn by fire,
Was now descending to the sea,
And left no light to guide the world,
But what from Chloris' brighter eyes was hurled.   10

In a lone thicket, made for love,
Silent as yielding maid's consent,
She with a charming languishment
Permits his force, yet gently strove.
Her hands his bosom softly meet,
But not to put him back designed,
Rather to draw him on inclined,
Whilst he lay trembling at her feet;
Resistance 'tis too late to show,
She wants the power to say, 'Ah! what do you do?'   20

Her bright eyes sweet, and yet severe,
Where love and shame confusedly strive,

Fresh vigour to Lysander give:
And whispering softly in his ear,
She cried, 'Cease ... cease ... your vain desire,
Or I'll call out ... What would you do?
My dearer honour, e'en to you,
I cannot ... must not give ...; retire,
Or take that life whose chiefest part
I gave you with the conquest of my heart.'   30

But he as much unused to fear,
As he was capable of love,
The blessèd minutes to improve,
Kisses her lips, her neck, her hair!
Each touch her new desires alarms!
His burning trembling hand he pressed
Upon her melting snowy breast,
While she lay panting in his arms!
All her unguarded beauties lie
The spoils and trophies of the enemy.   40

And now, without respect or fear
He seeks the objects of his vows;
His love no modesty allows:
By swift degrees advancing where
His daring hand that altar seized,
Where gods of love do sacrifice;
That awful throne, that paradise,
Where rage is tamed and anger pleased;
That living fountain, from whose trills
The melted soul in liquid drops distils.   50

Her balmy lips encountering his,
Their bodies as their souls are joined,
Where both in transports were confined,
Extend themselves upon the moss.
Chloris half dead and breathless lay,
Her eyes appeared like humid light,
Such as divides the day and night;
Or falling stars, whose fires decay;
And now no signs of life she shows,
But what in short breath sighs returns and goes.   60

He saw how at her length she lay,

He saw her rising bosom bare,
Her loose thin robes, through which appear
A shape designed for love and play;
Abandoned by her pride and shame,
She does her softest sweets dispense,
Offering her virgin innocence
A victim to love's sacred flame
Whilst th' o'er ravished shepherd lies,
Unable to perform the sacrifice.   70

Ready to taste a thousand joys,
Thee too transported hapless swain,
Found the vast pleasure turned to pain:
Pleasure, which too much love destroys!
The willing garments by he laid,
And heaven all open to his view;
Mad to possess, himself he threw
On the defenceless lovely maid.
But oh! what envious gods conspire
To snatch his power, yet leave him the desire!   80

Nature's support, without whose aid
She can no human being give,
Itself now wants the art to live,
Faintness it slackened nerves invade:
In vain th' enragèd youth assayed
To call his fleeting vigour back,
No motion 'twill from motion take,
Excess of love his love betrayed;
In vain he toils, in vain commands,
Th' insensible fell weeping in his hands.   90

In this so amorous cruel strife,
Where love and fate were too severe,
The poor Lysander in despair,
Renounced his reason with his life.
Now all the brisk and active fire
That should the nobler part inflame,
Unactive frigid, dull became,
And left no spark for new desire;
Not all her naked charms could move,
Or calm that rage that had debauched his love.   100

Chloris returning from the trance
Which love and soft desire had bred,
Her timorous hand she gently laid,
Or guided by design or chance,
Upon that fabulous priapus,
That potent god (as poets feign).
But never did young shepherdess
(Gathering of fern upon the plain)
More nimbly draw her fingers back,
Finding beneath the verdant leaves a snake.   110

Then Chloris her fair hand withdrew,
Finding that god of her desires
Disarmed of all his powerful fires,
And cold as flowers bathed in the morning-dew.
Who can the nymph's confusion guess?
The blood forsook the kinder place,
And strewed with blushes all her face,
Which both disdain and shame express;
And from Lysander's arms she fled,
Leaving him fainting on the gloomy bed.   120

Like lightning through the grove she hies,
Or Daphne from the Delphic god;
No print upon the grassy road
She leaves, t' instruct pursuing eyes.
The wind that wantoned in her hair,
And with her ruffled garments played,
Discovered in the flying maid
All that the gods e'er made of fair.
So Venus, when her love was slain,
With fear and haste flew o'er the fatal plain.   130

The nymph's resentments, none but I
Can well imagine, and condole;
But none can guess Lysander's soul
But those who swayed his destiny:
His silent griefs, swell up to storms,
And not one god, his fury spares,
He cursed his birth, his fate, his stars,
But more the shepherdess's charms;
Whose soft bewitching influence,
Had damned him to the hell of impotence.   140

Edward Taylor (1642?–1729)

343. An Epitaph for the Holy and Reverend Man of God, Mr Samuel Hooker

Pastor of the Church of Christ at Farmington … who slept in Christ … Anno Domini 1697.

A turf of glory, rich celestial dust,
A bit of Christ here in death's cradle hushed.
An orb of heavenly sunshine, a bright star
That never glimmered, ever shining fair,
A paradise bespangled all with grace,
A curious web o'erlaid with holy lace,
A magazine of prudence; golden pot
Of gracious flowers never to be forgot;
Farmington's glory, and its pulpit's grace
Lies here a-crystallising till the trace   10
Of time is at an end and all out run.
Then shall arise and quite outshine the sun.

344. Thy Name is an ointment poured out

My dear, dear Lord, I do thee Saviour call;
    Thou in my very soul art, as I deem,
So high, not high enough; so great, too small;
    So dear, not dear enough in my esteem;
    So noble, yet so base; too low; too tall;
    Thou full, and empty art; nothing, yet all.

A precious pearl, above all price dost 'bide.
    Rubies no rubies are at all to thee.
Blushes of burnished glory sparkling slide
    From every square in various coloured glee,   10
    Nay life itself in sparkling spangles choice.
    A precious pearl thou art above all price.

Oh! that my soul, heaven's workmanship (within
    My wickered cage), that bird of paradise
Inlined with glorious grace up to the brim
    Might be thy cabinet, oh pearl of price.
    Oh! let thy pearl, Lord, cabinet in me.
    Is 't then be rich! nay rich enough for thee.

My heart, oh Lord, for thy pomander gain.
    Be thou thyself my sweet perfume therein.   20
Make it thy box, and let thy precious name
    My precious ointment be emboxed therein.
    If I thy box and thou my ointment be,
    I shall be sweet, nay, sweet enough for thee.

Enough! Enough! Oh! Let me eat my Word.
    For if accounts be balanced any way,
Can my poor eggshell ever be an hoard
    Of excellence enough for thee? Nay, nay.
    Yet may I purse, and thou my money be.
    I have enough. Enough in having thee.   30

345. The Reflection

Lord, art thou at the table head above
    Meat, medicine, sweetness, sparkling beauties to
Enamour souls with flaming flakes of love,
    And not my trencher, nor my cup o'erflow?
    Be n't I a bidden guest? Oh! Sweat mine eye,
    O'erflow with tears: Oh! Draw thy fountains dry.

Shall I not smell thy sweet, oh! Sharon's rose?
    Shall not mine eye salute thy beauty? Why?
Shall thy sweet leaves their beauteous sweets upclose,
    As half ashamed my sight should on them lie?   10
    Woe's me! for this my sighs shall be in grain
    Offered on sorrow's altar for the same.

Had not my soul's thy conduit, pipes stopped been
    With mud, what ravishment would'st thou convey?
Let grace's golden spade dig till the spring
    Of tears arise, and clear this filth away.

Lord, let thy spirit raise my sighings till
These pipes my soul do with thy sweetness fill.

Earth once was paradise of heaven below
    Till inkfaced sin had it with poison stocked   20
And chased this paradise away into
    Heaven's upmost loft, and it in glory locked.
    But thou, sweet Lord, hast with thy golden key
    Unlocked the door, and made a golden day.

Once at thy feast, I saw thee pearl-like stand
    'Tween heaven and earth where heaven's bright glory all
In streams fell on thee, as a floodgate and,
    Like sun beams through thee, on the world to fall.
    Oh! Sugar sweet then! My dear sweet Lord, I see
    Saints' heavens-lost happiness restored by thee.   30

Shall heaven and earth's bright glory all up lie
    Like sunbeams bundled in the sun, in thee?
Dost thou sit rose at table head, where I
    Do sit, and carv'st no morsel sweet for me?
    So much before, so little now! Sprindge,° Lord,   *Snare*
    Thy rosy leaves, and me their glee afford.

Shall not thy rose my garden fresh perfume?
    Shall not thy beauty my dull heart assail?
Shall not thy golden gleams run through this gloom?
    Shall my black velvet mask thy fair face veil?   40
    Pass o'er my faults: shine forth, bright sun; arise,
    Enthrone thy rosy-self within mine eyes.

346. God hath highly exalted him

Look till thy looks look wan, my soul; here's ground.
    The world's bright eyes dashed out, day-light so brave
Bemidnighted; the sparkling sun, paled round
    With flowering rays lies buried in its grave.
    The candle of the world blown out, down fell.
    Life knocked a head by death: heaven by hell.

Alas! This world all filled up to the brim
    With sins, deaths, devils, crowding men to hell.

For whose relief God's milkwhite lamb stepped in
    Whom those cursed imps did worry, flesh, and fell.   10
    Tread under foot, did clap their wings and so
    Like dunghill cocks over their conquered crow.

Brave pious fraud; as if the setting sun
    Dropped like a ball of fire into the seas,
And so went out. But to the east come, run:
    You'll meet the morn shrined with its flowering rays.
    This lamb in laying of these lions dead,
    Drank of the brook, and so lift up his head.

Oh! Sweet, sweet joy! These rampant fiends befooled:
    They made their gall his winding sheet; although   20
They of the heart-ache die must, or be cold
    With inflammation of the lungs, they know.
    He's cancelling the bond, and making pay;
    And balancing accounts: it's reckoning day.

See how he from the counthouse shining went,
    In flashing folds of burnished glory, and
Dashed out all curses from the covenant;
    Hath justice's acquittance in his hand;
    Plucked out death's sting, the serpent's head did maul;
    The bars and gates of hell he brake down all.   30

The curse thus lodged within his flesh, and cloyed,
    Can't run from him to his, so much he gave.
And like a giant he awoke, beside,
    The sun of righteousness rose out of 's grave.
    And setting foot upon its neck I sing,
    'Grave, where's thy victory? Death, where's thy sting?'

347. Of His fulness we all receive: and grace –

When I, Lord, send some bits of glory home
    (For lumps I lack), my messenger, I find,
Bewildered, lose his way being alone
    In my befogged dark fancy, clouded mind.
    Thy bits of glory packed in shreds of praise
    My messenger doth lose, losing his ways.

Lord, clear the coast and let thy sweet sun shine
    That I may better speed a second time.
Oh! fill my pipkin with thy blood red wine:
    I'll drink thy health. To pledge thee is no crime.   10
    Although I but an earthen vessel be,
    Convey some of thy fulness into me.

Thou, thou my Lord, art full, top full of grace,
    The golden sea of grace, whose springs thence come,
And precious drills, boiling in every place.
    Untap thy cask, and let my cup catch some.
Although it's in an earthen vessel's case,
    Let it no empty vessel be of grace.

Let thy choice cask shed, Lord, into my cue
    A drop of juice pressed from thy noble vine.   20
My bowl is but an acorn cup, I sue
    But for a drop: this will not empty thine.
    Although I'm in an earthen vessel's place,
    My vessel make a vessel, Lord, of grace.

My earthen vessel make thy font also,
    And let thy sea my spring of grace in 't raise.
Spring up, oh well. My cup with grace make flow.
    Thy drops will on my vessel ting thy praise.
    I'll sing this song when I these drops embrace.
    My vessel now's a vessel of thy grace.   30

348. The same shall be clothed in white raiment

Nay, may I, Lord, believe it? Shall my skeg
    Be rayed in thy white robes? My thatched old crib
(Immortal purse hung on a mortal peg),
    Wilt thou with fairest array in heaven rig?
    I'm but a jumble of gross elements,
    A snail horn where an evil spirit tents.

A dirt ball dressed in milk white lawn and decked
    In tissue tagged with gold, or ermine's flush,

That mocks the stars and sets them in a fret
    To see themselves outshone thus. Oh, they blush.   10
   Wonders stand gastard° here. But yet, my Lord,   *terrified*
   This is but faint to what thou dost afford.

I'm but a ball of dirt. Wilt thou adorn
   Me with thy web wove in thy loom divine,
The whitest web in glory, that the morn,
   Nay, that all angel glory, doth o'ershine?
   They wear no such. This whitest lawn most fine
   Is only worn, my Lord, by thee and thine.

This says no flurr of wit nor new coined shape
   Of frolic fancy in a rampant brain.   20
It's juice divine, bled from the choicest grape
   That ever Zion's vineyard did maintain.
   Such mortal bits immortalised shall wear
   More glorious robes, than glorious angels bear.

Their web is wealthy, wove of wealthy silk
   Well wrought indeed, it's all branched taffity.
But this thy web more white by far than milk
   Spun on thy wheel twine of thy deity
   Wove in thy web, fulled in thy mill by hand,
   Makes them in all their bravery seem tanned.   30

This web is wrought by best, and noblest art
   That heaven doth afford of twine most choice,
All branched, and richly flowered in every part
   With all the sparkling flowers of paradise
   To be thy ware alone, who hast no peer
   And robes for glorious saints to thee most dear.

Wilt thou, my Lord, dress my poor withered stump
   In this rich web whose whiteness doth excel
The snow, though 'tis most black? And shall my lump
   Of clay wear more than e'er on angels fell?   40
   What, shall my bit of dirt be decked so fine
   That shall angelic glory all outshine?

Shall things run thus? Then Lord, my tumbrel
   Unload of all its dung, and make it clean.
And load it with thy wealthiest grace until

Its wheels do crack, or axletree complain.
I fain would have it cart thy harvest in,
Before it's loosèd from its axlepin.

Then screw my strings up to thy tune that I
   May load thy glory with my songs of praise.   50
Make me thy shalm, thy praise my songs, whereby
   My mean Shoshannim may thy Michtams raise.
   And when my clay ball's in thy white robes dressed
   My tune perfume thy praise shall with the best.

349. The joy of thy Lord

Lord, do away my motes: and mountains great,
   My nut is vitiate. Its kernel rots.
Come, kill the worm that doth its kernel eat
   And strike thy sparks within my tinderbox.
   Drill through my metal heart an hole wherein
   With grace's cotters to thyself it pin.

A lock of steel upon my soul, whose key
   The serpent keeps, I fear, doth lock my door.
O pick 't, and through the key hole make thy way
   And enter in and let thy joys run o'er.   10
   My wards are rusty. Oil them till they trig
   Before thy golden key: thy oil makes glib.

Take out the splinters of the world that stick
   So in my heart. Friends, honours, riches, and
The shivers in 't of hell whose venoms quick
   And fiery make it swollen and rankling stand.
   These wound and kill; those shackle strongly to
   Poor knobs of clay, my heart. Hence sorrows grow.

Cleanse and enlarge my cask: It is too small
   And tartarised with worldly dregs dried in 't.   20
It's bad mouthed too, and though thy joys do call,
   That boundless are, it ever doth them stint.
   Make me thy crystal cask; those wines in 't tun
   That in the rivers of thy joys do run.

Lord make me, though sucked through a straw or quill,
   Taste of the rivers of thy joys, some drop.
'Twill sweeten me: and all my love distil
   Into thy glass, and me for joy make hop.
   'Twill turn my water into wine, and fill
   My harp with songs my master's joys distil.

John Wilmot, Earl of Rochester (1647–1680)

350. 'Leave this gaudy gilded stage'

Leave this gaudy gilded stage
From custom more than use frequented
Where fools of either sex and age
Crowd to see themselves presented.
To love's theatre the bed
Youth and beauty fly together
And act so well, it may be said,
The laurel there was due to either.
'Twixt strifes of love and war the difference lies in this:
When neither overcomes love's triumph greater is.   10

351. 'Absent from thee I languish still'

Absent from thee I languish still,
   Then ask me not, when I return?
The straying fool 'twill plainly kill,
   To wish all day, all night to mourn.

Dear; from thine arms then let me fly,
   That my fantastic mind may prove
The torments it deserves to try,
   That tears my fixed heart from my love.

When wearied with a world of woe
   To thy safe bosom I retire 10
Where love and peace and truth does flow,
   May I contented there expire.

Lest once more wandering from that heaven
   I fall on some base heart unblessed;
Faithless to thee, false, unforgiven,
   And lose my everlasting rest.

352. Upon his Leaving his Mistress

'Tis not that I'm weary grown,
Of being yours, and yours alone;
But with what face can I incline
To damn you to be only mine?
   You whom some kinder power did fashion,
By merit, and by inclination,
The joy at least of one whole nation
Let meaner spirits of your sex
With humbler aims their thoughts perplex
   And boast, if by their arts they can, 10
Contrive to make one happy man;
Whilst moved by an impartial sense,
Favours like nature you dispense,
With universal influence.

See the kind seed-receiving earth,
To every grain affords a birth;
On her no showers unwelcome fall,
Her willing womb retains 'em all,
And shall my Celia be confined?
   No, live up to thy mighty mind, 20
And be the mistress of mankind.

353. Upon Nothing

Nothing, thou elder brother even to shade,
Thou had'st a being ere the world was made

And (well fixed) art alone of ending not afraid.

Ere time and place were, time and place were not,
When primitive Nothing, something straight begot
Then all proceeded from the great united what;

Something, the general attribute of all
Severed from thee its sole original
Into thy boundless self must undistinguished fall.

Yet something did thy mighty power command   10
And from thy fruitful emptiness's hand
Snatched men, beasts, birds, fire, water, air and land.

Matter, the wicked'st offspring of thy race
By form assisted flew from thy embrace
And rebel-light obscured thy reverend dusky face.

With form and matter, time and place did join;
Body thy foe with these did leagues combine
To spoil thy peaceful realm and ruin all thy line.

But turncoat-time assists the foe in vain
And bribed by thee destroys their short lived reign   20
And to thy hungry womb drives back thy slaves again.

Though mysteries are barred from laic eyes
And the divine alone with warrant pries
Into thy bosom, where thy truth in private lies,

Yet this of thee the wise may truly say:
Thou from the virtuous Nothing dost delay
And to be part of thee the wicked wisely pray.

Great Negative, how vainly would the wise
Enquire, define, distinguish, teach, devise,
Did'st Thou not stand to point their blind philosophies.   30

Is or is not, the two great ends of fate
And true or false the subject of debate
That perfect or destroy the vast designs of state –

When they have wracked the politician's breast

Within thy bosom most securely rest
And when reduced to thee are least unsafe and best.

But, Nothing, why does Something still permit
That sacred monarchs should at counsel sit
With persons highly thought, at best for Nothing fit,

Whilst weighty Something modestly abstains
From princes' coffers and from statesmen's brains
And Nothing there like stately Nothing reigns?

Nothing, who dwell'st with fools in grave disguise,
For whom they reverend shapes and forms devise,
Lawn-sleeves and furs and gowns, when they like thee look wise:

French truth, Dutch prowess, British policy,
Hibernian learning, Scotch civility,
Spaniards' dispatch, Danes' wit, are mainly seen in thee;

The great man's gratitude to his best friend
Kings' promises, whores' vows towards thee they bend.
Flow swiftly into thee, and in thee ever end.

354. To her Ancient Lover

Ancient person, for whom I
All the flattering youth defy:
Long be it e'er thou grow old,
Aching, shaking, crazy cold.
But still continue as thou art,
Ancient person of my heart.

On thy withered lips and dry,
Which like barren furrows lie;
Brooding kisses I will pour,
Shall thy youthful heat restore.
Such kind showers in autumn fall,
And a second spring recall:
Nor from thee will ever part,
Ancient person of my heart.

Thy nobler part, which but to name
In our sex would be counted shame,
By age's frozen grasp possessed,
From his ice shall be released,
And soothed by my reviving hand,
In former warmth and vigour stand.   20
All a lover's wish can reach,
For thy joy my love shall teach;
And for thy pleasure shall improve,
All that art can add to love.
Yet still I love thee without art,
Ancient person of my heart.

355. The Imperfect Enjoyment

Naked she lay, clasped in my longing arms,
I filled with love, and she all over charms,
Both equally inspired with eager fire,
Melting through kindness, flaming in desire;
With arms, legs, lips, close clinging to embrace,
She clips me to her breast, and sucks me to her face.
The nimble tongue (love's lesser lightning) played
Within my mouth, and to my thoughts conveyed
Swift orders, that I should prepare to throw
The all-dissolving thunderbolt below.   10
My fluttering soul, sprung with the pointed kiss,
Hangs hovering o'er her balmy brinks of bliss.
But whilst her busy hand would guide that part
Which should convey my soul up to her heart
In liquid raptures, I dissolve all o'er,
Melt into sperm, and spend at every pore.
A touch from any part of her had done 't,
Her hand, her foot, her very look's a cunt.
Smiling, she chides in a kind murmuring noise,
And from her body wipes the clammy joys;   20
When with a thousand kisses, wandering o'er
My panting bosom, 'Is there then no more?'
She cries. All this to love, and rapture's due,
Must we not pay a debt to pleasure too?
But I the most forlorn, lost man alive,
To show my wished obedience vainly strive,

I sigh, 'Alas!' and kiss, but cannot swive.
Eager desires confound my first intent,
Succeeding shame does more success prevent,
And rage, at last, confirms me impotent.   30
Even her fair hand, which might bid heat return
To frozen age, and make cold hermits burn,
Applied to my dead cinder, warms no more,
Than fire to ashes, could past flames restore.
Trembling, confused, despairing, limber, dry,
A wishing, weak, unmoving lump I lie.
This dart of love, whose piercing point oft tried,
With virgin blood, ten thousand maids, has died;
Which nature still directed with such art,
That it through every cunt, reached every heart.   40
Stiffly resolved, 'twould carelessly invade,
Woman or man, nor aught its fury stayed,
Where e'er it pierced, a cunt it found or made.
Now languid lies, in this unhappy hour,
Shrunk up, and sapless, like a withered flower.
Thou treacherous, base deserter of my flame,
False to my passion, fatal to my fame;
Through what mistaken magic dost thou prove
So true to lewdness, so untrue to love?
What oyster, cinder, beggar, common whore   50
Did'st thou e'er fail in all thy life before?
When vice, disease and scandal lead the way,
With what officious haste dost thou obey?
Like a rude roaring hector, in the streets,
That scuffles, cuffs, and ruffles all he meets;
But if his king, or country, claim his aid,
The rakehell villain shrinks, and hides his head:
Even so thy brutal valour is displayed,
Breaks every stew, does each small whore invade,
But when great love, the onset does command,   60
Base recreant, to thy prince, thou dar'st not stand.
Worst part of me, and henceforth hated most,
Through all the town, a common fucking post;
On whom each whore relieves her tingling cunt,
As hogs on gates do rub themselves and grunt.
May'st thou to ravenous cankers be a prey,
Or in consuming weepings waste away.
May strangury, and stone, thy days attend,
May'st thou ne'er piss, who did'st refuse to spend,

When all my joys did on false thee depend.　　　70
And may ten thousand abler pricks agree,
To do the wronged Corinna right for thee.

356. 'Fair Chloris in a pigsty lay'

Fair Chloris in a pigsty lay,
　　Her tender herd lay by her.
She slept; in murmuring gruntlings they
Complaining of the scorching day
　　Her slumbers thus inspire.

She dreamed while she with careful pains
　　Her snowy arms employed
In ivory pails to fill out grains,
One of her love convicted swains
　　Thus hasting to her cried.　　　10

'Fly nymph, oh fly e'er 'tis too late
　　A dear loved life to save
Rescue your bosom pig from fate
Who now expires hung in the gate
　　That leads to Flora's cave.

Myself had tried to set him free
　　Rather than brought the news,
But I am so abhorred by thee
That even thy darling's life from me
　　I know thou would'st refuse.'　　　20

Struck with the news as quick she flies
　　As blushes to her face:
Not the bright lightning from the skies
Nor love shot from her brighter eyes
　　Move half so swift a pace.

This plot it seems the lustful slave
　　Had laid against her honour
Which not one god took care to save
For he pursues her to the cave
　　And throws himself upon her　　　30

Now piercèd is her virgin zone,
   She feels the foe within it.
She hears a broken amorous groan,
The panting lover's fainting moan
   Just in the happy minute.

Frighted she wakes and waking frigs;
   Nature thus kindly eased
In dreams raised by her murmuring pigs
And her own thumb between her legs,
   She's innocent and pleased.   40

357. A Letter from Artemiza in the Town to Chloe in the Country

Chloe, in verse by your command I write;
Shortly you'll bid me ride astride, and fight.
These talents better with our sex agree,
Than lofty flights of dangerous poetry.
Amongst the men (I mean) the men of wit
(At least they passed for such, before they writ)
How many bold adventurers for the bays
(Proudly designing large returns of praise),
Who durst that stormy pathless world explore,
Were soon dashed back, and wrecked on the dull shore,   10
Broke of that little stock, they had before?
How would a woman's tottering barque be tossed,
Where stoutest ships (the men of wit) are lost?
When I reflect on this, I straight grow wise,
And my own self thus gravèly I advise.
Dear Artemiza, poetry's a snare:
Bedlam has many mansions: have a care.
Your muse diverts you, makes the reader sad;
You fancy you're inspired, he thinks you mad.
Consider too, 'twill be discreetly done,   20
To make yourself the fiddle of the town,
To find th' ill-humoured pleasure at their need,
Cursed, if you fail, and scorned, though you succeed.
Thus, like an arrant woman, as I am,
No sooner well convinced, writing's a sham,
That whore is scarce a more reproachful name
Than Poetess –

As men that marry, or as maids that woo,
'Cause 'tis the very worst thing they can do,
Pleased with the contradiction and the sin 30
Methinks I stand on thorns, till I begin.
   You expect at least to hear what loves have passed
In this lewd town since you and I met last.
What change has happened of intrigues, and whether
The old ones last, and who and who's together.
But how, my dearest Chloe, shall I set
My pen to write, what I would fain forget,
Or name that lost thing (love) without a tear
Since so debauched by ill-bred customs here?
Love, the most generous passion of the mind, 40
The softest refuge innocence can find,
The safe director of unguided youth,
Fraught with kind wishes and secured by truth,
That cordial drop heaven in our cup has thrown
To make the nauseous draught of life go down,
On which one only blessing God might raise
In lands of atheists subsidies of praise
(For none did e'er so dull, and stupid prove,
But felt a god, and blest his power in love),
This only joy, for which poor we were made, 50
Is grown like play, to be an arrant trade;
The rooks creep in, and it has got of late
As many little cheats and tricks as that.
But what yet more a woman's heart would vex
'Tis chiefly carried on by our own sex,
Our silly sex, who born like monarchs free,
Turn gypsies for a meaner liberty,
And hate restraint, though but from infamy.
They call whatever is not common, nice,
And deaf to nature's rule, or love's advice, 60
Forsake the pleasure, to pursue the vice.
To an exact perfection they have wrought
The action love, the passion is forgot.
'Tis below wit, they tell you, to admire,
And e'en without approving they desire.
Their private wish obeys the public voice,
'Twixt good and bad whimsy decides, not choice.
Fashions grow up for taste, at forms they strike:
They know, what they would have, not what they like.
Bovey's a beauty, if some few agree, 70

To call him so, the rest to that degree
Affected are, that with their ears they see.
Where I was visiting the other night,
Comes a fine lady with her humble knight
Who had prevailed on her, through her own skill,
At his request, though much against his will,
To come to London.
As the coach stopped, we heard her voice more loud
Than a great bellied woman's in a crowd,
Telling the knight, that her affairs require, 80
He for some hours obsequiously retire.
I think, she was ashamed, to have him seen
(Hard fate of husbands); the gallant had been,
Though a diseased ill-favoured fool, brought in.
'Dispatch,' says she, 'that business you pretend,
Your beastly visit to your drunken friend;
A bottle ever makes you look so fine!
Methinks I long to smell you stink of wine.
Your country drinking breath's enough to kill,
Sour ale corrected with a lemon pill. 90
Prithee farewell, we'll meet again anon.'
The necessary thing bows, and is gone.
She flies upstairs and all the haste does show
That fifty antic postures will allow,
And then bursts out, 'Dear Madam, am not I
The alteredst creature breathing, let me die.
I find myself ridiculously grown
Embarassé with being out of town,
Rude and untaught, like any Indian queen;
My country nakedness is strangely seen. 100
How is love governed? Love, that rules the state,
And, pray, who are the men most worn of late?
When I was married, fools were *à la mode*,
The men of wit were then held *incommode*,
Slow of belief and fickle in desire,
Who, ere they'll be persuaded, must inquire
As if they came to spy, not to admire.
With searching wisdom fatal to their ease
They still find out, why, what may, should not please;
Nay, take themselves for injured if we dare 110
Make 'em think better of us than we are,
And if we hide our frailties from their sights,
Call us deceitful jilts and hypocrites.

They little guess, who at our arts are grieved,
The perfect joy of being well deceived.
Inquisitive as jealous cuckolds grow,
Rather than not be knowing they will know
What being known creates their certain woe.
Women should these of all mankind avoid;
For wonder by clear knowledge is destroyed.   120
Woman, who is an arrant bird of night,
Bold in the dusk, before a fool's dull sight,
Should fly when reason brings the glaring light:
But the kind easy fool, apt to admire
Himself, trusts us; his follies all conspire
To flatter his, and favour our desire.
Vain of his proper merit he with ease
Believes we love him best, who best can please.
On him our gross dull common flatteries pass,
Ever most joyful, when most made an ass.   130
Heavy, to apprehend, though all mankind
Perceive us false, the fop concerned is blind,
Who doting on himself,
Thinks every one, that sees him, of his mind.
These are true women's men.' Here forced to cease
Through want of breath, not will, to hold her peace,
She to the window runs, where she had spied
Her much esteemed dear friend the monkey tied.
With forty smiles, as many antic bows,
As if 't had been the lady of the house,   140
The dirty chattering monster she embraced,
And made it this fine tender speech at last:
'Kiss me, thou curious miniature of man,
How odd thou art, how pretty, how Japan!
Oh, I could live, and die with thee.' Then on
For half an hour in compliment she run.
    I took this time to think what nature meant
When this mixed thing into the world she sent,
So very wise, yet so impertinent;
One who knew everything, who God thought fit   150
Should be an ass through choice, not want of wit;
Whose foppery without the help of sense
Could ne'er have rose to such an excellence.
Nature's as lame, in making a true fop,
As a philosopher; the very top
And dignity of folly we attain

By studious search and labour of the brain,
By observation, counsel and deep thought;
God never made a coxcomb worth a groat.
We owe that name to industry and arts: 160
An eminent fool must be a fool of parts;
And such a one was she, who had turned o'er
As many books as men, loved much, read more,
Had a discerning wit; to her was known
Everyone's fault and merit but her own.
All the good qualities that ever blest
A woman, so distinguished from the rest,
Except discretion only, she possessed.
   And now, 'Mon cher dear Pug,' she cries, 'adieu,'
And the discourse broke off does thus renew.   170
'You smile to see me, whom the world perchance
Mistakes to have some wit, so far advance
The interest of fools, that I approve
Their merit more than men's of wit, in love.
But in our sex too many proofs there are
Of such, whom wits undo, and fools repair.
This in my time was so observed a rule,
Hardly a wench in town, but had her fool.
The meanest common slut, who long was grown
The jest and scorn of every pit-buffoon,   180
Had yet left charms enough, to have subdued
Some fop or other, fond to be thought lewd.
Foster could make an Irish lord a Nokes,
And Betty Morris had her City cokes.
A woman's ne'er so ruined, but she can
Be still revenged on her undoer, man.
How lost so e'er, she'll find some lover more
A lewd abandoned fool, than she's a whore.
That wretched thing Corinna, who had run
Through all the several ways of being undone,   190
Cozened at first by love, and living then
By turning the too-dear-bought trick on men:
Gay were the hours, and winged with joys they flew,
When first the town her early beauties knew,
Courted, admired and loved, with presents fed,
Youth in her looks, and pleasure in her bed,
Till fate, or her ill angel thought it fit,
To make her dote upon a man of wit,
Who found, 'twas dull, to love above a day,

Made his ill-natured jest, and went away.   200
Now scorned by all, forsaken and oppressed,
She's a memento mori to the rest.
Diseased, decayed, to take up half a crown,
Must mortgage her long scarf, and manteau gown.
Poor creature! Who unheard of as a fly,
In some dark hole must all the winter lie,
And want, and dirt endure a whole half year,
That for one month she tawdry may appear.
In Easter term she gets her a new gown,
When my young master's worship comes to town,   210
From pedagogue and mother just set free,
The heir and hopes of a great family,
Who with strong ale and beef the country rules,
And ever since the Conquest have been fools.
And now with careful prospect to maintain
This character, lest crossing of the strain
Should mend the booby-breed, his friends provide
A cousin of his own, to be his bride.
And thus set out
With an estate, no wit, and a young wife   220
(The solid comforts of a coxcomb's life)
Dunghill and pease forsook, he comes to town,
Turns spark, learns to be lewd, and is undone.
Nothing suits worse with vice than want of sense,
Fools are still wicked at their own expense.
This o'ergrown schoolboy lost Corinna wins,
And at first dash to make an ass begins:
Pretends to like a man who has not known
The vanities nor vices of the town.
Fresh in his youth and faithful in his love,   230
Eager of joys, which he does seldom prove,
Healthful and strong, he does no pains endure
But what the fair one he adores can cure.
Grateful for favours does the sex esteem
And libels none for being kind to him.
Then of the lewdness of the times complains,
Rails at the wits and atheists and maintains
'Tis better than good sense, than power, or wealth,
To have a love untainted, youth, and health.
The unbred puppy, who had never seen   240
A creature look so gay, or talk so fine,
Believes, then falls in love, and then in debt,

Mortgages all, e'en to th' ancient seat,
To buy this mistress a new house for life;
To give her plate and jewels, robs his wife;
And when to the height of fondness he is grown,
'Tis time to poison him, and all's her own.
Thus meeting in her common arms his fate,
He leaves her bastard heir to his estate;
And, as the race of such an owl deserves,   250
His own dull lawful progeny he starves.
Nature who never made a thing in vain,
But does each insect to some end ordain,
Wisely contrived kind keeping fools, no doubt,
To patch up vices men of wit wear out.'
Thus she ran on two hours, some grains of sense
Still mixed with volleys of impertinence.
    But now 'tis time, I should some pity show
To Chloe, since I cannot choose but know
Readers must reap the dullness writers sow.   260
By the next post such stories I will tell
As joined with these shall to a volume swell,
As true as heaven, more infamous than hell;
But you are tired, and so am I. Farewell.

Anne Finch, Countess of Winchilsea (1661–1720)

358. from The Petition for an Absolute Retreat

(Inscribed to the Right Honourable Catharine Countess of Thanet, mentioned
in the poem under the name of Arminda)

Give me, O indulgent fate!
Give me yet before I die
A sweet but absolute retreat,
'Mongst paths so lost and trees so high
That the world may ne'er invade
Through such windings and such shade
My unshaken liberty.

No intruders thither come
Who visit but to be from home!
None who their vain moments pass   10
Only studious of their glass;
News, that charm to listening ears,
That false alarm to hopes and fears,
That common theme for every fop
From the statesman to the shop,
In those coverts ne'er be spread,
Of who's deceased, and who's to wed.
Be no tidings thither brought
But silent as a midnight thought
Where the world may ne'er invade   20
Be those windings and that shade!

Courteous fate! afford me there
A table spread, without my care,
With what the neighbouring fields impart,
Whose cleanliness be all its art.
When of old the calf was dressed
(Though to make an angel's feast)
In the plain unstudied sauce
Nor truffle nor morillia was;
Nor could the mighty patriarchs' board   30
One far-fetched ortolan afford.
Courteous fate! then give me there
Only plain and wholesome fare;
Fruits indeed (would heaven bestow)
All that did in Eden grow,
All but the forbidden tree
Would be coveted by me;
Grapes with juice so crowded up
As breaking through the native cup;
Figs yet growing candied o'er   40
By the sun's attracting power;
Cherries, with the downy peach
All within my easy reach;
Whilst creeping near the humble ground
Should the strawberry be found
Springing wheresoe'er I strayed
Through those windings and that shade.
For my garments, let them be
What may with the time agree;

Warm when Phoebus does retire 50
And is ill-supplied by fire:
But when he renews the year
And verdant all the fields appear
Beauty everything resumes,
Birds have dropped their winter plumes,
When the lily full-displayed
Stands in purer white arrayed
Than that vest which heretofore
The luxurious monarch wore,
When from Salem's gates he drove 60
To the soft retreat of love,
Lebanon's all burnished house
And the dear Egyptian spouse.
Clothe me, fate, though not so gay,
Clothe me light and fresh as May!
In the fountains let me view
All my habit cheap and new
Such as, when sweet zephyrs fly,
With their motions may comply,
Gently waving to express 70
Unaffected carelessness.
No perfumes have there a part
Borrowed from the chemist's art,
But such as rise from flowery beds,
Or the falling jasmine sheds!
'Twas the odour of the field
Esau's rural coat did yield
That inspired his father's prayer
For blessings of the earth and air:
Of gums or powders had it smelt, 80
The supplanter, then unfelt,
Easily had been descried
For one that did in tents abide,
For some beauteous handmaid's joy,
And his mother's darling boy.

Let me then no fragrance wear
But what the winds from gardens bear
In such kind surprising gales
As gathered from Fidentia's vales
All the flowers that in them grew; 90
Which intermixing as they flew

In wreathen garlands dropped again
On Lucullus and his men;
Who, cheered by the victorious sight,
Trebled numbers put to flight.
Let me when I must be fine
In such natural colours shine;
Wove and painted by the sun;
Whose resplendent rays to shun
When they do too fiercely beat   100
Let me find some close retreat
Where they have no passage made
Through those windings, and that shade.

359. The Atheist and the Acorn

'Methinks this world is oddly made,
    And everything's amiss,'
A dull presuming atheist said,
As stretched he lay beneath a shade;
    And instancèd in this:

'Behold,' quoth he, 'that mighty thing,
    A pumpkin, large and round,
Is held but by a little string,
Which upwards cannot make it spring,
    Or bear it from the ground.   10

'Whilst on this oak, a fruit so small,
    So disproportioned, grows;
That, who with sense surveys this all,
This universal casual ball,
    Its ill contrivance knows.

'My better judgement would have hung
    That weight upon a tree,
And left this mast, thus slightly strung,
'Mongst things which on the surface sprung,
    And small and feeble be.'   20

No more the caviller could say
    Nor farther faults descry,

For as he upwards gazing lay,
An acorn, loosened from the stay,
   Fell down upon his eye.

Th' offended part with tears ran o'er,
   As punished for the sin:
Fool! had that bough a pumpkin bore,
Thy whimsies must have worked no more,
   Nor skull had kept them in.   30

360. A Nocturnal Reverie

In such a night, when every louder wind
Is to its distant cavern safe confined,
And only gentle Zephyr fans his wings,
And lonely Philomel, still waking, sings;
Or from some tree, framed for the owl's delight,
She, hollowing clear, directs the wanderer right;
In such a night, when passing clouds give place,
Or thinly veil the heaven's mysterious face;
When in some river, overhung with green,
The waving moon and trembling leaves are seen;   10
When freshened grass now bears itself upright,
And makes cool banks to pleasing rest invite,
Whence springs the woodbine and the bramble-rose
And where the sleepy cowslip sheltered grows;
Whilst now a paler hue the foxglove takes,
Yet chequers still with red the dusky brakes:
When scattered glow worms, but in twilight fine,
Show trivial beauties watch their hour to shine;
Whilst Salisbury stands the test of every light,
In perfect charms and perfect virtue bright: 20
When odours, which declined repelling day,
Through temperate air uninterrupted stray;
When darkened groves their softest shadows wear,
And falling waters we distinctly hear;
When through the gloom more venerable shows
Some ancient fabric, awful in repose,
While sunburnt hills their swarthy looks conceal,
And swelling haycocks thicken up the vale:
When the loosed horse now, as his pasture leads,

Comes slowly grazing through th' adjoining meads, 30
Whose stealing pace and lengthened shade we fear,
Till torn up forage in his teeth we hear;
When nibbling sheep at large pursue their food,
And unmolested kine rechew the cud;
When curlews cry beneath the village-walls,
And to her straggling brood the partridge calls;
Their shortlived jubilee the creatures keep,
Which but endures, whilst tyrant-man does sleep:
When a sedate content the spirit feels,
And no fierce light disturbs, whilst it reveals; 40
But silent musings urge the mind to seek
Something, too high for syllables to speak;
Till the free soul, to a composedness charmed,
Finding the elements of rage disarmed,
O'er all below a solemn quiet grown,
Joys in th' inferior world, and thinks it like her own:
In such a night let me abroad remain,
Till morning breaks, and all's confused again;
Our cares, our toils, our clamours are renewed,
Or pleasures, seldom reached, again pursued. 50

361. Mercury and the Elephant: a prefatory fable

As Mercury travelled through a wood,
(Whose errands are more fleet than good)
An elephant before him lay,
That much encumbered had the way:
The messenger, who's still in haste,
Would fain have bowed, and so have passed;
When up arose th' unwieldy brute,
And would repeat a late dispute,
In which (he said) he'd gained the prize
From a wild boar of monstrous size. 10
'But Fame,' quoth he, 'with all her tongues,
Who lawyers, ladies, soldiers wrongs,
Has, to my disadvantage, told
An action throughly bright and bold;
Has said, that I foul play had used,
And with my weight th' opposer bruised;
Had laid my trunk about his brawn,

Before his tushes could be drawn;
Had stunned him with a hideous roar,
And twenty-thousand scandals more: 20
But I defy the talk of men
Or voice of brutes in every den;
Th' impartial skies are all my care,
And how it stands recorded there.
Amongst you gods; pray, what is thought?'
    Quoth Mercury, 'Then have you Fought!'

Solicitous thus should I be
For what's said of my verse and me;
Or should my friends excuses frame,
And beg the critics not to blame   30
(Since from a female hand it came)
Defects in judgement, or in wit;
They'd but reply, 'Then has she Writ!'

Our vanity we more betray
In asking what the world will say
Than if, in trivial things like these,
We wait on the event with ease;
Nor make long prefaces, to show
What men are not concerned to know:
For still untouched how we succeed,   40
'Tis for themselves, not us, they read;
Whilst that proceeding to requite,
We own (who in the muse delight)
'Tis for our selves, not them, we write.
Betrayed by solitude to try
Amusements, which the prosperous fly;
And only to the press repair
To fix our scattered papers there;
Though whilst our labours are preserved,
The printers may, indeed, be starved.   50

ACKNOWLEDGEMENTS

I am indebted to many individuals for support and help with *The Story of Poetry*. Sarah Rigby assisted with preparing the text; Evelyn Schlag commented on much of what I call the informal history as it was written or adapted from *Lives of the Poets*. Colleagues at Carcanet, Pamela Heaton and Joyce Nield in particular, encouraged me. At Manchester Metropolitan University, Professor Janet Beer was cheerfully supportive. At the John Rylands University Library Stella Halkyard provided a reassuring presence. I was also inspired by my friend Adel Asker. Angel García-Gómez endured the writing of this book, as of many earlier ones, with patience.

Some passages in this book draw on material included in my *50 British Poets 1300–1900* (1980) and on essays and reviews I have written over the last thirty years.

OUTLINE BIBLIOGRAPHY

A full bibliography for a composite book of this nature would be as long as the book itself. This is a summary list of editions of poetry and poets' prose I have used, many of them available in libraries, bookshops or on the web. Other editions exist. The dates I give are generally of the volumes I have consulted. I provide a merely preliminary list of secondary works, critical and contextual. I omit most monographs and biographies. Readers will discover that in the cases of some significant poets, critical volumes and biographies are in print while no edition of the work is currently available.

I have a preference for critical writing by practising poets, from Dryden through Jonson, Coleridge, Arnold, Pound, Ford, Eliot, Rickword, Graves, Sisson, Davie, down to the present day.

EDITIONS AND SELECTIONS (VERSE AND PROSE)
Bacon, Sir Francis *Works* (seven volumes, London, 1890)
Behn, Aphra *The Works of Aphra Behn* (London, 1915)
Bradstreet, Anne *The Works of Anne Bradstreet in Verse and Prose* (Chesterton, Mass., 1867)
— *Poems* (New York, 1970)
Campion, Thomas *Works* (London, 1970)
— *Observations on the Art of English Poesie* (London, 1969)
Carew, Thomas *The Poems of Thomas Carew* (Oxford, 1970)
— *Cavalier Poets: selected poems* (ed. Clayton, Oxford, 1978)
Cavendish, Margaret, Duchess of Newcastle *Poems and Fancies* (London, 1653)
— *Natures Pictures* (London, 1656)
Chapman, George *The Poems* (New York, 1962)
— *Chapman's Homer* (Princeton, 1956)
Cowley, Abraham *Poetry and Prose* (London, 1949)
Crashaw, Richard *The Poems, English, Latin and Greek* (London, 1957)
Daniel, Samuel *Poems and a Defence of Ryme* (Cambridge, Mass., 1930)
— *A Selection from the Poetry of Samuel Daniel & Michael Drayton* (London, 1899)
Davenant, Sir William *The Shorter Poems and Songs from the Plays and Masques* (Oxford, 1972)
De Vere, Edward, Earl of Oxford *Poems* (London, 1904)
Donne, John *Poetical Works* (ed. Grierson, Oxford, 1971)

— *Complete English Poems* (Harmondsworth, 1971)
— *Selected Letters* (Manchester, 2002)
Drayton, Michael *Works* (five volumes, Oxford, 1932–3)
— *A Selection from the Poetry of Samuel Daniel & Michael Drayton* (London, 1899)
Drummond of Hawthornden, William *Poems and Prose* (Edinburgh, 1976)
Dryden, John *Poetical Works* (Oxford, 1967)
— *Of Dramatic Poesy and Other Critical Essays* (London, 1971)
Elizabeth I *Poems of Queen Elizabeth I* (Providence, R.I., 1964)
Finch, Anne, Countess of Winchilsea *The Poems of Anne, Countess of Winchilsea* (Chicago, 1903)
Gascoigne, George *Complete Works* (two volumes, London, 1907–1910)
— *The Green Knight: selected poetry and prose* (Manchester, 1982)
Greville, Fulke *Poems and Dramas of Fulke Greville, First Lord Brooke* (London, 1939)
— *The Prose Works of Fulke Greville, Lord Brooke* (Oxford, 1986)
Grimald, Nicholas *The Life and Poems* (North Haven, 1969)
Hawes, Stephen in *English Verse between Chaucer and Surrey* (ed. Hammond, Oxford, 1927)
Herbert, George *Poems* (Oxford, 1961)
Herrick, Robert *Poetical Works* (Oxford, 1956)
— *Cavalier Poets: selected poems* (ed. Clayton, Oxford, 1978)
Jonson, Ben *The Complete Poems* (Harmondsworth, 1975)
Lanyer, Emilia *The Poems of Shakespeare's Dark Lady* (London, 1978)
Lovelace, Richard *Poems* (Oxford, 1930)
— *Cavalier Poets: selected poems* (ed. Clayton, Oxford, 1978)
Marlowe, Christopher *Complete Poems and Translations* (Harmondsworth, 1971)
Marvell, Andrew *Complete Poems* (Harmondsworth, 1972)
Milton, John *Poetical Works* (Oxford, 1966)
— *Poems* (Carey & Fowler, London, 1968)
More, Sir Thomas *The English Works* (volumes one and two, London, 1931)
Thomas Nashe *Selected Writings* (Harvard, 1965)
— *The Unfortunate Traveller and Other Works* (Harmondsowrth, 1989)
Percy, Thomas *Reliques of Ancient English Poetry* (London, 1765)
Philips, Katherine *Poems, By the Most Deservedly Admired Mrs Katherine Philips, The Matchless Orinda* (London, 1667)
Quarles, Francis *The Complete Works* (three volumes, 1880–1)
Ralegh, Sir Walter *Selected Writings* (Manchester, 1984)
Rochester, John Wilmot, Earl of *Complete Works* (Harmondsworth, 1994)
Sackville, Thomas, Earl of Dorset *Poetical works of Surrey and Sackville* (Oxford, 1854)
Sedley, Sir Charles *Poetical and Dramatic Works* (London, 1928)
Shakespeare, William *The Sonnets and Narrative Poems* (New York, 1992)
Sidney, Mary, Countess of Pembroke *The Psalms of Sir Philip Sidney and the Countess of Pembroke* (New York, 1963)
Sidney, Sir Philip *Poems* (Oxford, 1962)
— *Arcadia* (Harmondsworth, 1977)

— *An Apology for Poetry* (Manchester, 1964)

Skelton, John *Poems* (Oxford, 1969)

Spenser, Edmund *Poetical Works* (Oxford, 1970)

Suckling, Sir John *The Works* (Oxford, 1971)

— *Cavalier Poets: selected poems* (ed. Clayton, Oxford, 1978)

Surrey, Henry Howard, Earl of *Poems* (Oxford, 1964)

Taylor, Edward *Poems* (New Haven, 1960)

— *Poetical Works* (Princeton, 1967)

Traherne, Thomas *Selected Poems and Prose* (Harmondsworth, 1991)

Turberville, George *English Poets II* (Oxford, 1810)

Tusser, Thomas *Five Hundred Points of Good Husbandry* (Oxford, 1984)

Vaughan, Henry *Complete Poems* (Harmondsworth, 1976)

Vaux, Thomas, Lord *Songes and Sonettes* ('Tottel's Miscellany', Cambridge, Mass., 1924–37)

Waller, Edmund *The Poems of Edmund Waller* (London, 1893)

Whitney, Isabella *The Copy of a letter, lately written in meeter, by a yonge Gentilwoman: to her unconstant lover* (London, 1567)

— *A sweet nosegay or pleasant posye* (London, 1573)

Wroth, Mary *The Poems of Lady Mary Wroth* (Baton Rouge, 1983)

Wyatt, Sir Thomas *The Complete Poems* (New Haven, 1978)

SOME ANTHOLOGIES

Fifteen Poets from Gower to Arnold (Oxford, 1940)

Allison, A.W. et al. *The Norton Anthology of Poetry* (New York, 1983)

Chambers, E.K. *The Oxford Book of Sixteenth Century Verse* (Oxford, 1966)

Clayton, Thomas *Cavalier Poets: selected poems* (Oxford, 1978)

Davie, Donald *The New Oxford Book of Christian Verse* (Oxford, 1981)

Gilbert, Sandra M. and Susan Gubar *The Norton Anthology of Literature by Women: the traditions in English* (New York, 1996)

Greer, G. et al. *Kissing the Rod: an anthology of seventeenth-century women's verse* (London, 1988)

Hymns Ancient and Modern (London, 1916)

Johnson, Samuel *The Works of the English Poets, with Prefaces, biographical and critical* (seventy-five volumes, London, 1790)

Moore, Geoffrey *American Literature: a representative anthology of American writing from Colonial times to the present* (London, 1964)

Parfitt, George *Silver Poets of the Seventeenth Century* (London, 1974)

Pritchard, R.E. *Poetry by English Women: Elizabethan to Victorian* (Manchester, 1990)

Reese, M.A. *Elizabethan Verse Romances* (London, 1968)

Rennison, Nick and Michael Schmidt *Poets on Poets* (Manchester, 1997)

Tomlinson, Charles *Oxford Book of Verse in English Translation* (1980)

Tottel, Richard *Songes and Sonettes* ('Tottel's Miscellany', Cambridge, Mass., 1924–37)

— *The Paradyse of Daynty Devises* (Cambridge, Mass., 1924–37)

Williams, John *English Renaissance Poetry: a collection of shorter poems from Skelton to Jonson* (Fayetteville, Arkansas, 1990)

Woudhuysen, H.R. *The Penguin Book of Renaissance Verse* (Harmondsworth, 1993)

HISTORY AND SECONDARY

Addison, Joseph *Critical Essays from the Spectator* (Oxford, 1970)
Attridge, Derek *Poetic Rhythm* (Cambridge, 1995)
Aubrey, John *Brief Lives* (London, 1949)
Bate, Walter Jackson *The Burden of the Past and the English Poet* (London, 1971)
Bennett, Joan *Five Metaphysical Poets* (Cambridge, 1966)
Bloom, Harold *The Anxiety of Influence* (Oxford, 1973)
— *Figures of Capable Imagination* (New York, 1976)
— *Ruin the Sacred Truths: poetry and belief from the Bible to the present* (Cambridge, Mass., 1989)
Blunden, Edmund *A Selection of his Poetry and Prose* (London, 1950)
Bradford, Richard *A Linguistic History of English Poetry* (London, 1993)
Brogan, T.V.F. (ed.) *The New Princeton Handbook of Poetic Terms* (Princeton, 1994)
Brooks, Cleanth *The Well Wrought Urn* (London, 1968)
Brooks, Cleanth and Robert Penn Warren *Understanding Poetry* (New York, 1938)
Burrow, Colin *Epic Romance: Homer to Milton* (Oxford, 1993)
Bush, Douglas *English Literature in the Earlier Seventeenth Century 1600–1660* (Oxford, 1946)
Buxton, John *Elizabethan Taste* (London, 1963)
Cambridge History of English Literature (ed. Sir A.W. Ward and A.R. Waller, fifteen volumes, 1907)
Corns, Thomas *Uncloistered Virtue: English Political Literature, 1640–1660* (Oxford, 1992)
Craig, Cairns ed. *History of Scottish Literature* (four volumes, Aberdeen, 1987–89)
Croft, P.J. *Autograph Poetry in the English Language* (two volumes, London, 1973)
Daiches, David ed. *A Critical History of English Literature* (four volumes, London, 1969)
Davie, Donald *Older Masters* (Manchester, 1992)
— *Purity of Diction in English Verse* and *Articulate Energy* (Manchester, 1994)
Edwards, Michael *Towards a Christian Poetics* (London, 1984)
Eliot, Thomas Stearns *The Sacred Wood: essays on poetry and criticism* (London, 1920)
— *Notes Towards the Definition of Culture* (London, 1948)
— *To Criticize the Critic and other writings* (London, 1965)
— *The Letters of T.S. Eliot 1898–1922* (London, 1971)
— *Selected Essays* (London, 1975)
Empson, William *Milton's God* (London, 1961)
— *Some Versions of Pastoral* (Harmondsworth, 1966)
— *Seven Types of Ambiguity* (Harmondsworth, 1973)
Everett, Barbara *Poets in their Time: essays on English poetry from Donne to Larkin* (London, 1986)
Ford, Boris (ed.) *New Pelican Guide to English Literature* (nine volumes, Harmondsworth, 1988)

Ford, Ford Madox *The March of Literature* (London, 1947)

Fowler, Alastair *A History of English Literature: forms and kinds from the Middle Ages to the present* (Oxford, 1987)

Frye, Northrop *The Return of Eden: Five Essays on Milton's Epics* (Toronto, 1965)

Fussell, Paul *Poetic Metre and Poetic Form* (New York, 1979)

Graves, Robert *Collected Writings on Poetry* (Manchester, 1995)

Gunn, Thom *The Occasions of Poetry, Essays in Criticism and Autobiography* (London, 1985)

— *Shelf Life: essays, memoirs and interview* (London, 1993)

Hammond, Gerald *Fleeting Things: English poets and poems, 1616–1660* (Cambridge, Mass., 1990)

Helgerson, Richard *Self-Crowned Laureates: Spenser, Jonson, Milton, and the Literary System* (Berkeley, 1983)

Hill, Christopher *Milton and the English Revolution* (Oxford, 1977)

Hill, Geoffrey *The Lords of Limit* (London, 1984)

Johnson, Samuel *Lives of the English Poets* (London, 1975)

Kermode, Frank (ed.) *The Living Milton: Essays by Various Hands* (London, 1960)

— *The Classic* (London, 1975)

— *Poetry, Narrative, History* (1990)

Leavis, Frank Raymond *The Common Pursuit* (London, 1952)

— *Revaluation: tradition and development in English poetry* (Harmondsworth, 1964)

Lever, J.W. *The Elizabethan Love Sonnet* (London, 1956)

Lewis, Clive Staples *The Allegory of Love: a study in mediaeval tradition* (Oxford, 1936)

— *English Literature in the Sixteenth Century* (Oxford, 1953)

— *The Discarded Image: an introduction to Mediaeval and Renaissance Literature* (Cambridge, 1964)

Lucas, John *England and Englishness: ideas of nationhood in English poetry 1688–1900* (London, 1990)

Nowottny, Winifred *The Language Poets Use* (London, 1962)

Parry, Graham *The Seventeenth Century: The Intellectual and Cultural Context of English Literature, 1603–1700* (London, 1989)

Patrides, C.A. and Raymond Waddington (eds.) *The Age of Milton: Backgrounds to Seventeenth-Century Literature* (Manchester, 1980)

Plant, Marjorie *The English Book Trade: an economic history of the making and sale of books* (London, 1939)

Pound, Ezra *The Literary Essays of Ezra Pound* (London, 1954)

— *Selected Prose 1909–1965* (London, 1973)

— *The ABC of Reading* (London, 1991)

Preminger, Alex and T.V.F. Brogan (eds.) *The New Princeton Encyclopaedia of Poetry and Poetics* (Princeton, 1993)

Prince, Frank Templeton *The Italian Element in Milton's Verse* (Oxford, 1962)

Richards, I.A. *Principles of Literary Criticism* (London, 1967)

Ricks, Christopher *The Force of Poetry* (Oxford, 1984)

— *Milton's Grand Style* (Oxford, 1963)

Rickword, Edgell *Essays and Opinions 1921–1931* (Manchester, 1974)

— *Literature in Society* (Manchester, 1978)

Sisson, Charles Hubert *The Avoidance of Literature: collected essays* (Manchester, 1979)

— *In Two Minds* (Manchester, 1990)

— *English Perspectives* (Manchester, 1992)

Smith, Nigel *Literature and Revolution in England, 1640–1660* (New Haven, 1994)

Spingarn, J.E. *A History of Literary Criticism in the Renaissance* (New York, 1908)

Swinburne, Algernon Charles *George Chapman: a critical essay* (New York, 1977)

Swiss, Margo and David A. Kent (eds.) *Heirs of Fame: Milton and Writers of the English Renaissance* (Lewisburg, 1995)

Tate, Allen *Essays of Four Decades* (London, 1970)

Tillyard, E.M.W. *The Metaphysicals and Milton* (London, 1956)

— *Milton* (London, 1967)

Tuve, Rosemond *Elizabethan and Metaphysical Imagery* (Chicago, 1947)

Warton, Thomas *The History of English Poetry: from the close of the eleventh to the commencement of the eighteenth century* (four volumes, 1924)

Wilding, Michael *Dragon's Teeth: Literature in the English Revolution* (Oxford, 1987)

Willey, Basil *The Seventeenth Century Background* (London, 1934)

GENERAL INDEX

INDEX OF FIRST LINES AND EXTRACTS

O laud the Lord, the God of hosts commend, 337

O nectar! O delicious stream!, 625

O that you were your self, but, love, you are, 369

O thou that swing'st upon the waving hair, 574

O thou, my lovely boy, who in thy power, 384

Of man's first disobedience, and the fruit, 520

Of thee (kind boy) I ask no red and white, 552

Oft with true sighs, oft with uncallèd tears, 307

On Hellespont, guilty of true love's blood, 343

Once, as me thought, fortune me kissed, 213

One day I wrote her name upon the strand, 269

One day the amorous Lysander, 635

Out of that mass of miracles, my muse, 296

Persius a crab-staff, bawdy Martial, Ovid a fine wag, 243

Phyllis, let's shun the common fate, 630

Pla ce bo, 206

Poor soul, the centre of my sinful earth, 386

Prayer the church's banquet, angels' age, 485

Queen and Huntress, chaste and fair, 449

Reason, tell me thy mind, if here be reason, 309

Remember now thy Creator in the days of thy youth, 407

Run ye to and fro through the streets of Jerusalem, 409

Say that thou did'st forsake me for some fault, 380

Set me whereas the sun doth parch the green, 231

Shall I compare thee to a summer's day, 370

Silence augmenteth grief, writing increaseth rage, 314

Sin! Wilt thou vanquish me?, 620

Since brass, nor stone, nor earth, nor boundless sea, 377

Since faction ebbs, and rogues grow out of fashion, 607

Since there's no help, come let us kiss and part, 338

Sing Lullaby, as women do, 249

Sitting alone upon my thought, in melancholy mood, 262

Slow, slow, fresh fount, keep time with my salt tears, 450

So am I as the rich whose blessèd key, 374

So cruel prison! How could betide, alas!, 233–4

So is it not with me as with that muse, 371

Spring, the sweet Spring, is the year's pleasant king, 393

Stay here fond youth and ask no more, be wise, 552

Sweet day, so cool, so calm, so bright, 489

Sweet is the rose, but grows upon a briar, 268

Sweetest of sweets, I thank you: when displeasure, 482

Take all my loves, my love, yea take them all, 373

Tell me not, sweet, I am unkind, 573

Th' expense of spirit in a waste of shame, 384

That time of year thou may'st in me behold, 378

The day delayed, of that I most do wish, 220

The doubt of future foes exiles my present joy, 245

The enemy of life, decayer of all kind, 210

The fleet astronomer can bore, 486

The forward youth that would appear, 584

The issue of great Jove, draw near you, Muses nine, 237

The liquid pearl in springs, 624

The lively lark stretched forth her wing, 259

The man of life upright, 425

The Panther knowing that his spotted hide, 269

The parrot from East-India to me sent, 357

The peaceful western wind, 423

The perfumed odour in 's long curls of hair, 594

The rolling wheel that runneth often round, 267

The song of songs, which is Solomon's, 408

The soote season, that bud and bloom forth brings, 235

The wanton troopers riding by, 580

The wrathful winter 'proaching on apace, 246

Then sang Moses and the children of Israel this sung unto the Lord, 400

There is a garden in her face, 427

These things have I spoken unto you, that ye should not be offended, 420

They flee from me that sometime did me seek, 211

They that have power to hurt and will do none, 380

INDEX OF TITLES